Data Mining with Microsoft® SQL Server® 2008

Data Mining with Microsoft® SQL Server®2008

Jamie MacLennan
ZhaoHui Tang
Bogdan Crivat

WILEY

Wiley Publishing, Inc.

Data Mining with Microsoft®SQL Server®2008

Published by
Wiley Publishing, Inc.
10475 Crosspoint Boulevard
Indianapolis, IN 46256
www.wiley.com

Copyright © 2009 by Wiley Publishing, Inc., Indianapolis, Indiana

Published by Wiley Publishing, Inc., Indianapolis, Indiana

Published simultaneously in Canada

ISBN: 978-0-470-27774-4

Manufactured in the United States of America

10 9 8 7 6 5 4 3 2 1

For general information on our other products and services please contact our Customer Care Department within the U.S. at (800) 762-2974, outside the United States at (317) 572-3993, or fax (317) 572-4002.

Library of Congress Cataloging-in-Publication Data

MacLennan, Jamie.
    Data mining with Microsoft SQL server 2008 / Jamie MacLennan, Bogdan Crivat, ZhaoHui Tang.
        p. cm.
    Includes index.
    ISBN 978-0-470-27774-4 (paper/website)
    1.   SQL server. 2.   Data mining.   I. Crivat, Bogdan. II. Tang, Zhaohui. III. Title.
    QA76.9.D343M335 2008
    005.75'85 — dc22

                                                       2008035467

Wiley also publishes its books in a variety of electronic formats. Some content that appears in print may not be available in electronic books.

To Logan, because he needs it the most.

— Jamie MacLennan

*This book is for Cosmin, with great hope that he will
someday find math (and data mining) to be
fun and interesting.*

— Bogdan Crivat

About the Authors

Jamie MacLennan is the principal development manager of SQL Server Analysis Services at Microsoft. In addition to being responsible for the development and delivery of the Data Mining and OLAP technologies for SQL Server, MacLennan is a proud husband and father of four. He has more than 25 patents and patents pending for his work on SQL Server Data Mining. MacLennan has written extensively on the data mining technology in SQL Server, including many articles in *MSDN Magazine*, *SQL Server Magazine*, and postings on SQLServerDataMining.com and his blog at http://blogs.msdn.com/jamiemac. This is his second edition of *Data Mining with SQL Server*. MacLennan has been a featured and invited speaker at conferences worldwide, including Microsoft TechEd, Microsoft TechEd Europe, SQL PASS, the Knowledge Discovery and Data Mining (KDD) conference, the Americas Conference on Information Systems (AMCIS), and the Data Mining Cup conference.

ZhaoHui Tang is a group program manager at Microsoft adCenter Labs, where he manages a number of research projects related to paid search and content ads. He is the inventor of Microsoft Keyword Services Platform. Prior to adCenter, he spent six years as a lead program manager in the SQL Server Business Intelligence (BI) group, mainly focusing on data mining development. He has written numerous articles for both academic and industrial publications, such as *The VLDB Journal* and *SQL Server Magazine*. He is a frequent speaker at business intelligence conferences. He was also a co-author of the previous edition of this book, *Data Mining with SQL Server 2005*.

Bogdan Crivat is a senior software design engineer in SQL Server Analysis Services at Microsoft, working primarily on the Data Mining platform.

Crivat has written various articles on data mining for *MSDN Magazine* and *Access/VB/SQL Advisor Magazine,* as well as numerous postings on the SQLServerDataMining.com website and on the MSDN Forums. He presented at various Microsoft and data mining professional conferences. Crivat also blogs about SQL Server Data Mining at www.bogdancrivat.net/dm.

Credits

Executive Editor
Robert Elliott

Development Editor
Kevin Shafer

Technical Editors
Raman Iyer; Shuvro Mitra

Production Editor
Dassi Zeidel

Copy Editor
Kathryn Duggan

Editorial Manager
Mary Beth Wakefield

Production Manager
Tim Tate

Vice President and Executive Group Publisher
Richard Swadley

Vice President and Executive Publisher
Joseph B. Wikert

Project Coordinator, Cover
Lynsey Stanford

Proofreader
Publication Services, Inc.

Indexer
Ted Laux

Cover Image
© Darren Greenwood/Design Pics/Corbis

Acknowledgments

First of all we would like to acknowledge the help from our data mining team members and other colleagues in the Microsoft SQL Server Business Intelligence (BI) organization. In addition to creating the best data mining package on the planet, most of them gave up some of their free time to review the text and sample code. Direct thanks go to Shuvro Mitra, Raman Iyer, Dana Cristofor, Jeanine Nelson-Takaki, and Niketan Pansare for helping review our text to ensure that it makes sense and that our samples work. Thanks also to the rest of the data mining team, including Donald Farmer, Tatyana Yakushev, Yimin Wu, Fernando Godinez Delgado, Gang Xiao, Liu Tang, and Bo Simmons for building such a great product. In addition, we would like to thank the SQL BI management of Kamal Hathi and Tom Casey for supporting data mining in SQL Server.

SQL Server 2008 Data Mining (including the Data Mining Add-Ins) is a product jointly developed by the SQL Server Analysis Services team and other teams inside Microsoft. We would like to thank colleagues from Excel —notably Rob Collie, Howie Dickerman, and Dan Battagin, whose valuable input into the design of the Data Mining Add-Ins guaranteed their success. Also thanks to those in the Machine Learning and Applied Statistics (MLAS) Group, headed by Research Manager David Heckerman, who continue to advise us on deep algorithmic issues in our product. We would like to thank David Heckerman, Jesper Lind, Alexei Bocharov, Chris Meek, Bo Thiesson, and Max Chickering for their contributions.

We would like to give special thanks to Kevin Shafer for his close editing of our text, which has greatly improved the quality of this manuscript. Also thanks to Wiley Publications acquisitions editor Bob Elliot for his support and patience.

Special thanks from Jamie to his wife, April, who yet again supported him through the ups and downs of authoring a book, particularly during painful rewrites and recaptures of screen shots, while taking care of our kids and the world around me. Elalu, honey.

Bogdan would like to thank his wife, Irinel, for supporting him, reviewing his chapters, and some really helpful hints for capturing screen shots.

Contents at a Glance

Contents

Foreword

The world is absolutely exploding with digitally born data. Financial transactions, online advertising analytics, consumer preference information, and the results of scientific discovery mean tremendous volumes of data exist in both structured and unstructured stores today. And it is growing faster than ever before, fueled by both technology and a new generation of people adopting and integrating technology into all aspects of their lives.

Business intelligence practitioners struggle to make sense of the data in their charge to help their businesses operate with better understanding of what is influencing results. Trends are evolving and changing more quickly than ever before. It is no longer enough to look at historical data to just determine what happened. Aided by data mining, you can more readily understand why something happened. It can make the difference in whether history — good or bad — repeats itself. Because trends change at such great speed today, automated analysis and sophisticated algorithms for identifying trends, finding outliers, and predicting future courses quickly can be the difference between winning and just competing. Data mining provides the means to make sense of tremendous volumes of data by automating the processes of categorizing and clustering common elements, identifying trends and anomalies in the data, and predicting what will happen given those factors.

I have had the pleasure to work alongside (and learn directly from) Jamie MacLennan and Bogdan Crivat. They are passionate about the difference that technology can make in our lives, and committed to putting the tools necessary to make sense of the expanding world of data into everyone's hands. In this book, they share their passions with you, clearly explaining data mining concepts, and how to apply them in common situations using the very algorithms and tools they authored themselves as part of Microsoft SQL Server. This book provides an opportunity for you to learn straight from the source, too. I am sure you will discover that this text is a valuable resource.

Tom Casey
General Manager, SQL Server Business Intelligence
Microsoft Corporation

Introduction

Microsoft SQL Server 2008 is the third version of SQL Server that ships with included data mining technology. Since it was introduced in SQL Server 2000, data mining has become a key feature of the larger product. Data mining has grown from an isolated part of SQL Server Analysis Services with two algorithms, to an intrinsic part of the SQL Server Business Intelligence (BI) platform that is fully integrated with OLAP, Integration Services, and Reporting Services. Other Microsoft applications (such as Microsoft Dynamix CRM and Microsoft Performance Point Server) seamlessly integrate SQL Server Data Mining to accentuate their functionality with predictive power.

SQL Server Data Mining has become the most widely deployed data mining server in the industry, with many third-party software and consulting companies building on, specializing, and extending the platform. Enterprise, small and medium business, and even academic and scientific users have all adopted or switched to SQL Server Data Mining because of its scalability, availability, extensive functionality, and ease of use.

This book serves as a guide to SQL Server Data Mining, explaining how it works, providing detailed technical and practical discussions of the SQL Server Data Mining technology, and demonstrating why you should deploy and use SQL Server Data Mining for yourself.

How This Book Is Organized

This book is written to provide you with the knowledge necessary to implement successful data mining solutions using SQL Server, by introducing the overall space, familiarizing you with the tools, giving depth and breadth on the

Microsoft data mining algorithms, and then providing details on various ways to implement data mining solutions.

The book starts with introductory chapters that outline the tools, technologies, and ideas you need to leverage SQL Server Data Mining. Then each of the SQL Server data mining algorithms is described in detail in its own chapter. The subsequent chapters describe how you can integrate SQL Server Data Mining into other parts of the SQL Server BI suite. The latter part of the book deals with architecture and programming issues, and gives examples of some data mining implementation scenarios.

Following is a brief description of the chapters:

- **Chapter 1: Introduction to Data Mining** — This chapter introduces not only the book, but also the technology. It contains a detailed definition of what exactly is meant by the term *data mining*, and discusses what kinds of problems are addressed by this technology.

- **Chapter 2: Applied Data Mining Using Office 2007** — This chapter provides an overview of the Table Analysis Tools for Office 2007 add-in, which is a rich set of tools for Excel that are usable by any information worker. This chapter explains how and why you use these tools, and provides guidance on how to get the best results.

- **Chapter 3: Data Mining Concepts and DMX** — This chapter is critical to understanding the SQL Server Data Mining platform. It explains the underlying concepts of how you should think about a data mining problem, as well as providing a learn-by-example framework for Data Mining Extensions (DMX) to SQL.

- **Chapter 4: Using SQL Server Data Mining** — This chapter introduces you to building data mining solutions using Business Intelligence Development Studio (BI Dev Studio). In addition to a basic overview, it provides a wide range of tips and tricks that can make the difference between a successful project and a failed one. This chapter also covers using SQL Server Management Studio to access and secure data mining objects. In addition, it tells you how you can expose your data mining models through SQL Server Reporting Services.

- **Chapter 5: Implementing a Data Mining Process Using Office 2007** — This chapter explores the remaining tools in the Data Mining Add-ins for Office 2007. As described in this chapter, these tools provide more functionality than BI Dev Studio and SQL Server Management Studio alone, but they also have limitations that prevent them from exposing the full functionality of SQL Server Data Mining. In any case, this chapter will allow you to best take advantage of the Microsoft Office tools for data mining.

- **Chapters 6-12: the algorithm chapters** — Each of these chapters is devoted to one or more of the algorithms included with SQL Server Data Mining. In each of the chapters, you will find a basic description of the algorithm, followed by usage scenarios that will help you understand how, when, and where you apply each algorithm. Each chapter describes how you create, train, interpret, and apply models using the specified algorithms. The chapters wrap up with a deeper technical dive into how the algorithms work.

- **Chapter 13: Mining OLAP Cubes** — This chapter provides a brief introduction to Online Analytical Processing (OLAP) and the OLAP functionality of SQL Server Analysis Services. The chapter examines how and when you perform data mining on OLAP cubes. It also includes details on how to implement popular OLAP mining scenarios.

- **Chapter 14: Data Mining with SQL Server Integration Services** — This chapter introduces SQL Server Integration Services (SSIS) and describes its various components. It then details the tasks and transformations that you use to implement data mining solutions in your data integration packages. This chapter also describes how to use the text mining components to prepare unstructured data for data mining scenarios.

- **Chapter 15: SQL Server Data Mining Architecture** — This is the first chapter that moves away from tools and concepts and starts to delve into the programming and administration aspects of SQL Server Data Mining. This chapter discusses the architecture of a server-based data mining system, including the XML for Analysis (XMLA) protocol that underlies all client-server communication. The chapter also describes the administration of a data mining server, including server properties that are important for SQL Server Data Mining and data mining security roles.

- **Chapter 16: Programming SQL Server Data Mining** — This chapter details the programming interfaces for SQL Server Data Mining, and includes several examples of the programmatic creation, training, and application of data mining objects.

- **Chapter 17: Extending SQL Server Data Mining** — This chapter describes how you can extend SQL Server Data Mining with your own functionality. It shows you how to create stored procedures for adding operations to DMX. It also describes how you can implement your own data mining algorithms to plug into SQL Server Data Mining and exploit its features. Additionally, this chapter describes how you can write your own data mining visualizations to display patterns in either the supplied algorithms or your own algorithm implementations, and embed them in BI Dev Studio and SQL Server Management Studio.

- **Chapter 18: Implementing a Web Cross-Selling Application** — This chapter walks you through a common data mining scenario — implementing a recommendation engine and integrating it into a retail website. It includes sample queries and code to get you started.

- **Chapter 19: Conclusion and Additional Resources** — In addition to wrapping up the book, this chapter provides a list of valuable links where you can find additional information and help with your data mining projects. It also includes references to some other reading materials that you can refer to if you want to learn more about data mining.

This book also includes two helpful appendixes:

- **Appendix A: Data Sets** — This appendix contains a brief description of the various data sets used in this book.

- **Appendix B: Supported Functions** — This appendix provides, for your reference, a list of all the supported DMX functions. It also contains lists of all Visual Basic for Applications (VBA) and Excel functions that you can call from DMX. It also describes some supplemental stored procedures provided by the authors to assist with the sample queries presented throughout the text.

Who Should Read This Book

This book is primarily designed for the SQL Server user who is curious about data mining. A working knowledge of SQL will be greatly beneficial in understanding DMX and the DMX queries sprinkled throughout the book. However, non–SQL users can still benefit from the Office 2007 and the algorithm chapters. Readers who are interested in programming SQL Server Data Mining should understand .NET and the C# languages to apply the relevant chapters.

For those of you who have read the previous edition of this book, *Data Mining with SQL Server 2005* (Indianapolis: Wiley, 2005), welcome back! In this text, you will find comprehensive material on the new functionality of Microsoft SQL Server 2008 Data Mining plus new examples for most algorithm and scenarios described in the text.

Conventions

To help you get the most from the text and keep track of what's happening, a number of conventions are used throughout the book.

NOTE Notes and other information that is supplemental to the current discussion are offset and placed in italics like this.

Within the main text, the following conventions are used:

- Important words or terms are *italicized* when they are first introduced in the text.
- Combination keyboard strokes are shown like this: Ctrl+A.
- Filenames, URLs, and code within the text are differentiated from the rest of the text with a special font, as shown in this example: `persistence.properties`
- Blocks (or snippets) of code are shown two different ways:

```
In code examples, new and important code is highlighted with
a gray background.
```

```
The gray highlighting is not used for code that's less important in the
present context, or has been shown before.
```

Tools You Will Need

In order to get the most benefit from this book, you will need access to the SQL Server 2008 Analysis Services software. SQL Server 2008 Analysis Services is included with the Standard, Enterprise, and Developer editions of Microsoft SQL Server 2008. Time-based evaluation versions are available for download at `http://www.microsoft.com/sql`. To follow along with Chapters 2 and 5, you will also need Microsoft Office 2007 and SQL Server 2008 Data Mining Add-Ins for Office 2007. Evaluation versions of Microsoft Office 2007 are available at `www.microsoft.com/office`, and the free download of the Data Mining Add-Ins is available at `www.microsoft.com/sql/dm`.

You'll also want to have the AdventureWorksDW2008 database installed. Instructions for accessing this database can be found in the ReadMe file on this book's website.

What's on the Website

Most chapters in this book have supplemental materials that you can download from `www.wiley.com/go/data_mining_SQL_2008`. As appropriate for the chapter, the site contains SQL Server database backups, SQL Server Analysis Services database backups, project files, DMX query files, and/or source code.

Each chapter directory contains a `readme` file that describes how to use the downloads for that chapter.

This book will launch you into the world of SQL Server Data Mining. After you absorb all the information contained within, you will be well on your way to adding predictive and descriptive analytics to your daily life. With its powerful development environment and APIs, Microsoft SQL Server Data Mining can change how you and every user in your organization view and interact with data. Take the leap and discover the hidden sweets locked away in the data you have been hoarding over the years — one taste and you'll be hooked!

Introduction to Data Mining in SQL Server 2008

It's always necessary to explain exactly what is meant by the term *data mining*. You would hope that any particular technology has a name that is either absolutely clear as to what it means (such as *reporting*) or completely devoid of meaning, but catchy, so the association is unique (such as *Silverlight*). However, this is not the case for data mining. The term *data mining* has been used to mean anything from ad hoc queries, rules-based notifications, or pivot-chart analysis to evil government domestic-spying programs. As it is used in this book, data mining is the process of analyzing data to find hidden patterns using automatic methodologies. This type of data mining is often referred to using other terms such as *machine learning, knowledge discovery in databases (KDD),* or *predictive analytics*. Although each of these terms has a slightly different connotation, they overlap enough to be functionally equivalent with data mining in the sense used here.

By far, the trendiest term today is *predictive analytics*, which many companies ironically are using to differentiate what they do from "data mining." The inherent implication is that data mining is limited to the discovery of patterns, whereas predictive analytics allows the application of the patterns to new data to *impute* (or *predict*) unknown values. The motivation behind using the term *predictive analytics* is precisely this dilution of the meaning of data mining as it has been used in recent years. Predictive analytics, however, is an incomplete term because it ignores the descriptive nature of data mining. Therefore, until a marketing genius comes up with a clever, meaningless name like "Sparky," the term we use will remain *data mining*.

NOTE The authors of this book by no means endorse using the term *Sparky* when referring to SQL Server Data Mining. If you call Microsoft Technical Support about a problem because your Sparky model isn't processing correctly, or because you can't set proper security credentials on your Sparky server, do not expect a rational answer. As with all data mining problems, rational results come from rational inputs.

So, what does data mining do, and why do you need it? Over the past several years, compute power has increased exponentially according to the well-known Moore's law. However, unbeknownst to most, hard-drive capacity has increased at an order of magnitude greater than that of processor power. That is, the capability to store data has greatly outpaced the capability to process it. As a result, large volumes of data have been generated and persisted in databases. Much of this data comes from business software, such as financial applications, enterprise resource planning (ERP) systems, customer relationship management (CRM) systems, and server logs from web servers, or even the database servers hosting the data. The result of this unceasing data collection is that organizations have become data-rich and knowledge-poor. The collections of data are so vast that the practical use of these stores of data becomes limited. The main purpose of data mining is to extract knowledge from the data at hand, increasing its intrinsic value and making the data useful.

For example, Figure 1-1 shows a relational table containing a list of high school seniors. For each student, the table records information such as gender, IQ, parental income, and whether or not students were encouraged by their parents to attend college, along with their actual intention to attend college. Using this data, how can you answer the question, "What drives high school graduates to attend college?"

Using traditional methods, you can write queries or slice the data using Online Analytical Processing (OLAP) tools to find out how many male students attend college versus female students. You could also write a query to see the relationship between parental encouragement and attendance plans. But what about male students who are encouraged by their parents? Or, what about female students who are not encouraged by their parents? You must write dozens of such queries to cover all the possible combinations.

Numerical columns such as ParentIncome or IQ are more difficult to analyze. For example, you would need to arbitrarily choose ranges in these numeric values to determine how an income range of $40,000 to $50,000 impacted a decision to attend college. Even with this fairly simple data set, ad hoc queries and OLAP are not suited to the task. Imagine if there were hundreds of columns in this table. You would quickly end up with an intractable number of possibilities to test in order to answer a basic question about the meaning of your data.

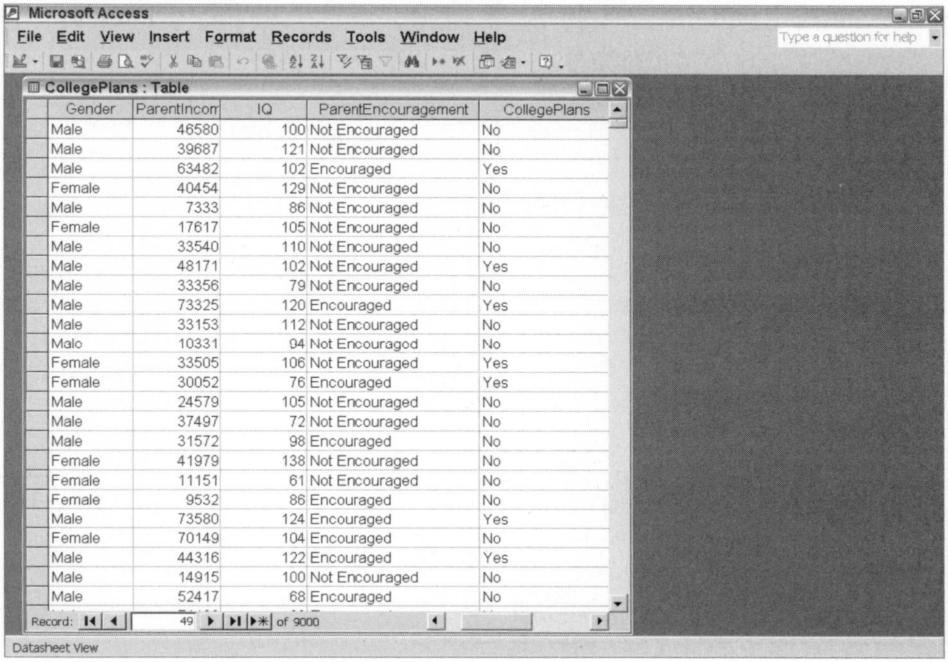

Gender	ParentIncom	IQ	ParentEncouragement	CollegePlans
Male	46580	100	Not Encouraged	No
Male	39687	121	Not Encouraged	No
Male	63482	102	Encouraged	Yes
Female	40454	129	Not Encouraged	No
Male	7333	86	Not Encouraged	No
Female	17617	105	Not Encouraged	No
Male	33540	110	Not Encouraged	No
Male	48171	102	Not Encouraged	Yes
Male	33356	79	Not Encouraged	No
Male	73325	120	Encouraged	Yes
Male	33153	112	Not Encouraged	No
Male	10331	94	Not Encouraged	No
Female	33505	106	Not Encouraged	Yes
Female	30052	76	Encouraged	Yes
Male	24579	105	Not Encouraged	No
Male	37497	72	Not Encouraged	No
Male	31572	98	Encouraged	No
Female	41979	138	Not Encouraged	No
Female	11151	61	Not Encouraged	No
Female	9532	86	Encouraged	No
Male	73580	124	Encouraged	Yes
Female	70149	104	Encouraged	No
Male	44316	122	Encouraged	Yes
Male	14915	100	Not Encouraged	No
Male	52417	68	Encouraged	No

Figure 1-1 Student table

In contrast, the data mining approach for this problem is almost the reverse of the query-and-explore method. Instead of guessing a hypothesis and trying it out in different ways, you ask the question in terms of the data that can support many hypotheses, and allow your data mining system to explore them for you.

In this case, you indicate that the columns `IQ`, `Gender`, `ParentIncome`, and `ParentEncouragement` are to be used as hypotheses in determining `CollegePlans`. As the data mining system passes over the data, it analyzes the influence of each input column on the target column.

Figure 1-2 shows the hypothetical result of a decision tree algorithm operating on this data set. In this case, each path from the root node to the leaf node forms a rule about the data. Looking at this tree, you see that students with IQs greater than 100 and who are encouraged by their parents are highly likely to attend college. In this case, you have extracted knowledge from the data.

As shown here, data mining applies algorithms such as decision trees, clustering, association, time series, and so on to a data set, and then analyzes its contents. This analysis produces patterns, which can be explored for valuable information. Depending on the underlying algorithm, these patterns can be in the form of trees, rules, clusters, or simply a set of mathematical formulas. The information found in the patterns can be used for reporting (to guide marketing strategies, for instance) and for prediction. For example, if you could collect data about undecided students, you could select those who are likely to be interested in continued education and preemptively market to that audience.

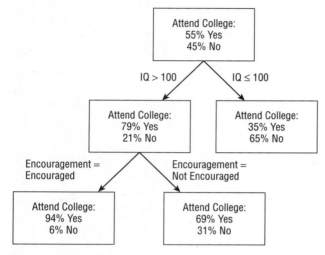

Figure 1-2 Decision tree

Business Problems for Data Mining

Data mining techniques can be used in virtually all business applications, answering various types of businesses questions. In truth, given the software available today, all you need is the motivation and the know-how. In general, data mining can be applied whenever something could be known, but is not. The following examples describe some scenarios:

- **Recommendation generation** — What products or services should you offer to your customers? Generating recommendations is an important business challenge for retailers and service providers. Customers who are provided appropriate and timely recommendations are likely to be more valuable (because they purchase more) and more loyal (because they feel a stronger relationship to the vendor). For example, if you go to online stores such as Amazon.com or Barnesandnoble.com to purchase an item, you are provided with recommendations about other items you may be interested in. These recommendations are derived from using data mining to analyze purchase behavior of all of the retailer's customers, and applying the derived rules to your personal information.

- **Anomaly detection** — How do you know whether your data is "good" or not? Data mining can analyze your data and pick out those items that don't fit with the rest. Credit card companies use data mining–driven anomaly detection to determine if a particular transaction is valid. If the data mining system flags the transaction as anomalous, you get a call to see if it was really you who used your card. Insurance companies also use anomaly detection to determine if claims are fraudulent. Because these companies process thousands of claims a day, it is impossible to investigate each case, and data mining can identify which claims are likely to be false. *Anomaly detection* can even be used to validate *data entry* — checking to see if the data entered is correct at the point of entry.

- **Churn analysis** — Which customers are most likely to switch to a competitor? The telecom, banking, and insurance industries face severe competition. On average, obtaining a single new mobile phone subscriber costs more than $200. Every business would like to retain as many customers as possible. *Churn analysis* can help marketing managers identify the customers who are likely to leave and why, and as a result, they can improve customer relations and retain customers.

- **Risk management** — Should a loan be approved for a particular customer? Since the subprime mortgage meltdown, this is the single most common question in banking. Data mining techniques are used to determine the *risk* of a loan application, helping the loan officer make appropriate decisions on the cost and validity of each application.

- **Customer segmentation** — How do you think of your customers? Are your customers the indescribable masses, or can you learn more about your customers to have a more intimate and appropriate discussion with them. *Customer segmentation* determines the behavioral and descriptive profiles for your customers. These profiles are then used to provide personalized marketing programs and strategies that are appropriate for each group.

- **Targeted ads** — Web retailers or portal sites like to personalize their content for their Web customers. Using navigation or online purchase patterns, these sites can use data mining solutions to display *targeted advertisements* to their Web navigators.

- **Forecasting** — How many cases of wine will you sell next week in this store? What will the inventory level be in one month? Data mining *forecasting techniques* can be used to answer these types of time-related questions.

Data Mining Tasks

For each question that can be asked of a data mining system, there are many tasks that may be applied. In some cases, an answer will become obvious with the application of a single task. In others, you will explore and combine multiple tasks to arrive at a solution. The following sections describe the general data mining tasks.

Classification

Classification is the most common data mining task. Business problems such as churn analysis, risk management, and targeted advertising usually involve classification.

Classification is the act of assigning a category to each case. Each case contains a set of attributes, one of which is the *class* attribute. The task requires finding a model that describes the class attribute as a function of input attributes. In the College Plans data set shown in Figure 1-1, the *class* is the `CollegePlans` attribute with two states: `Yes` and `No`. A classification model will use the other attributes of a case (the *input* attributes) to determine patterns about the class (the *output* attribute). Data mining algorithms that require a target to learn against are considered *supervised* algorithms.

Typical classification algorithms include decision trees, neural network, and Naïve Bayes.

Clustering

Clustering is also called *segmentation*. It is used to identify natural groupings of cases based on a set of attributes. Cases within the same group have more or less similar attribute values.

Figure 1-3 shows a very simple customer data set containing two attributes: `Age` and `Income`. The clustering algorithm groups the data set into three segments based on these two attributes. Cluster 1 contains a younger population with low income. Cluster 2 contains middle age customers with higher income. Cluster 3 is a group of older individuals with a relatively low income.

Clustering is an *unsupervised* data mining task. There is no single attribute used to guide the training process, so all input attributes are treated equally. Most clustering algorithms build the model through a number of iterations, and stop when the model *converges* (that is, the boundaries of these segments are stabilized).

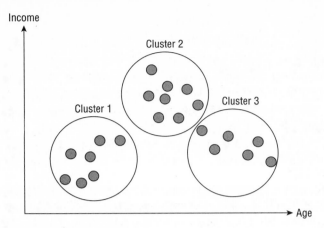

Figure 1-3 Clustering

Association

Association is also called *market basket analysis*. A typical association business problem is to analyze a sales transaction table and identify those products often in the same shopping basket. The common usage of association is to identify common sets of items and rules for the purpose of cross-selling, as shown in Figure 1-4.

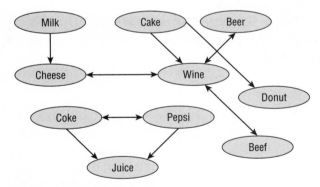

Figure 1-4 Product association

In terms of association, each piece of information is considered an item. The association task has two goals: to find those items that appear together frequently, and from that, to determine rules about the associations.

Regression

The *regression* task is similar to classification, except that instead of looking for patterns that describe a class, the goal is to find patterns to determine a *numerical value*. Simple linear line-fitting techniques are an example of regression, where the result is a function to determine the output based on the values of the inputs. More advanced forms of regression support categorical inputs as well as numerical inputs. The most popular techniques used for regression are linear regression and logistic regression. Other techniques supported by SQL Server Data Mining are regression trees (part of the Microsoft Decision Trees algorithm) and neural networks.

Regression is used to solve many business problems — for example, to predict a coupon redemption rate based on the face value, distribution method, distribution volume, and season, or to predict wind velocities based on temperature, air pressure, and humidity.

Forecasting

Forecasting is yet another important data mining task. What will the stock value of Microsoft Corporation (NASDAQ symbol MSFT) be tomorrow? What will the sales amount of wine be next month? Forecasting can help answer these questions. As input, it takes sequences of numbers indicating a series of values through time, and then it imputes future values of those series using a variety of machine-learning and statistical techniques that deal with seasonality, trending, and noisiness of data.

Figure 1-5 shows two curves. The solid line curve is the actual time-series data on Microsoft stock value, and the dotted curve is a time-series model that predicts values based on past values.

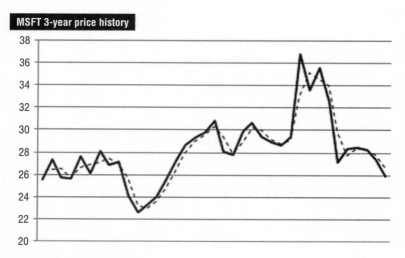

Figure 1-5 Time series

Sequence Analysis

Sequence analysis is used to find patterns in a series of events called a *sequence*. For example, a DNA sequence is a long series composed of four different states: A, G, C, and T. A click sequence on the Web contains a series of URLs. In certain circumstances, you may model customer purchases as a sequence of data. For example, a customer first buys a computer, and then buys speakers, and finally buys a webcam. Both sequence and time-series data are similar in that they contain adjacent observations that are order-dependent. The difference is that where a time series contains numerical data, a sequence series contains discrete states.

Figure 1-6 shows Web click sequences from a news website. Each node is a URL category, and the lines represent transitions between them. Each transition is associated with a weight, representing the probability of the transition between one URL and another.

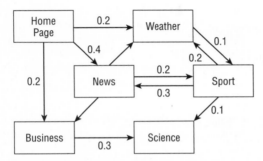

Figure 1-6 Web navigation sequence

Deviation Analysis

Deviation analysis is used to find rare cases that behave very differently from the norm. Deviation analysis is widely applicable, the most common usage being credit card fraud detection. Identifying abnormal cases among millions of transactions is a very challenging task. Other applications include network intrusion detection, manufacture error analysis, and so on.

There is no standard technique for deviation analysis. Usually, analysts apply decision trees, clustering, or neural network algorithms for this task.

Data Mining Project Cycle

From the initial business problem formation through to deployment and sustained management, most data mining projects pass through the same phases.

Business Problem Formation

What are the problems you are trying to solve? What techniques are you going to apply to solve the problem? How do you know if you will be successful? These are important questions to ask before embarking on any project.

You may find that a simple OLAP, reporting, or data integration solution may be sufficient. A predictive or data mining solution involves determining the unknown, relying on a belief that making sense of that unknown will add value. This is a shaky precipice from which to begin any business endeavor. Luckily, successful data mining solutions have been shown to have an average of 150-percent return on investment (ROI), so that makes justification easier.

Data Collection

Business data is stored in many systems across an enterprise. For example, at Microsoft, there are hundreds of online transaction processing (OLTP) databases and more than 70 data warehouses. The first step is to pull the relevant data into a database or a data mart where the data analysis is applied. For example, if you want to analyze your website's click stream, the first step is to download the log data from your web servers.

Sometimes you might be lucky and find that there is already an existing data warehouse on the subject of your analysis. However, in many cases, the data in the data warehouse is not rich enough and must be supplemented with additional data. For example, the log data from the web servers contains only data about web behavior and little (if any) data about the customers. You may need to gather customer information from other company systems or purchase demographic data to build models that meet your business requirements.

Data Cleaning and Transformation

Data cleaning and transformation are the most resource-consuming steps in a data mining project. The purpose of *data cleaning* is to remove noise and irrelevant information from the data set. The purpose of *data transformation* is to modify the source data in ways that make it useful for mining.

Various techniques are applied to clean and transform data, including the following:

- **Numerical transformation** — For continuous data such as income and age, a typical transformation is to bin (or *discretize*) the data into buckets. For example, you may want to bin Age into five predefined age groups. SQL Server Data Mining has automatic discretization methods, but if you have meaningful groupings, they may be more informative both from a business sense and an algorithmic sense. Additionally, continuous data is often *normalized*. Normalization maps all numerical values to a range (such as between 0 and 1) or to have a specific standard deviation (such as 1).

- **Grouping** — Discrete data often has more distinct values than are useful. You can group these values to reduce the model complexity. For example, the column Profession may have many different types of engineers, such as Software Engineer, Telecom Engineer, Mechanical Engineer, and so on. You can group all of these professions to the single value Engineer.

- **Aggregation** — Aggregation is an important transformation to derive additional value from your data. Suppose you want to group customers based on their phone usage. If the call detail record information is too detailed for the model, you must aggregate all the calls into a few derived attributes such as total number of calls and the average call duration. These derived attributes can later be used in the model.

- **Missing value handling** — Most data sets contain missing values. This can be caused by many different things. For example, you may have two customer tables coming from two OLTP databases that, when merged, have missing values because the tables are not aligned. Another example occurs when customers don't supply data values such as age. Another is when you have stock market values with blanks because the markets are closed on weekends and holidays.

  Addressing missing values is important, because it is reflected in the business value of your solution. You may need to retain the missing data (for example, customers who refuse to report their age may have other interesting things in common). You may need to discard the entire record (having too many unknowns could pollute your model). Or, you may simply be able to replace missing values with some other value (such as the previous value for time-series data such as stock market values, or the most popular value). For more advanced cases, you can use data mining to predict the most likely value for each missing case.

- **Removing outliers** — *Outliers* are abnormal data and can be real or (as is often the case) errors. Abnormal data has an effect on the quality of your results. The best way to deal with outliers typically is to simply remove them before beginning the analysis. For example, you could remove 0.5 percent of the customers with highest or lowest income to eliminate any situations of people having negative or extremely unlikely incomes.

SQL Server Integration Services (SSIS), which is included with Microsoft SQL Server, is an excellent tool for performing data cleaning and transformation tasks.

Model Building

Model building is the core of data mining, though it is not as time- and resource-intensive as data transformation. When you understand the shape of the business problem and the type of data mining task, it is relatively easy to pick algorithms that are suitable. Usually, you don't know which algorithm is the best fit for the problem until you have built the model. The accuracy of an algorithm depends on the nature of the data. For example, a decision tree algorithm is usually a very good choice for any classifications. However, if the relationships among attributes are complicated, a neural network may perform better.

A good approach is to build multiple models using different algorithms, and then compare the accuracy of these models. Even with a single algorithm, you can tune the parameter settings to optimize the model accuracy.

Model Assessment

In the model assessment stage, you use tools to determine the accuracy of the models that were created, and you examine the models to determine the meaning of discovered patterns and how they apply to your business. For example, a model may determine that *Relationship = Husband* ⇨ *Gender = Male* with 100-percent confidence. Although the rule is valid, it doesn't contain any business value. It is very important to work with business analysts who have the proper domain knowledge to validate the discoveries.

Sometimes, the model doesn't contain useful patterns. This is generally because the set of variables in the model are not the right ones to solve your business problem. You may need to repeat the data cleaning and transformation steps, or even redefine your problem in order to derive more meaningful variables. Data mining is an exploratory process, and it often takes a few iterations before you find the right model.

Reporting and Prediction

In many organizations, the goal of data miners is to deliver reports to marketing executives. SQL Server Data Mining is integrated with SQL Server Reporting Services to generate reports directly from data mining results. Reports may contain predictions (such as lists of customers with the highest value potential) or the rules found in the data mining analysis.

To provide predictions, you apply the selected model against new cases of data. Consider a banking scenario where you build a model about loan risk prediction. Every day there are thousands of new loan applications. You can use the risk prediction model to predict the potential risk for each of these loan applications.

Application Integration

You can close the analysis loop by embedding data mining directly into business applications. For example, CRM applications may have data mining features that group customers into segments, or allow you to select leads based on their likelihood to convert into paying customers. ERP applications may use data mining features to forecast production and inventory depletion. A manufacturing application can predict product-defect rates and determine the causes for these defects. Online stores can give customers real-time product recommendations. Integrating data mining into applications enables you to create applications that can be updated continuously and are customized to every user or usage scenario.

Model Management

In some situations, the patterns found by data mining are more stable and can simply be left alone. In most cases, however, the patterns vary frequently. For example, in an online store, new products appear almost every day, meaning that new rules about the products are also appearing almost every day. The validity of a mining model can be very short-lived. When the validity of a model has worn out, it must be retrained on new data. Ultimately, updating models should be done in an automated process based on business needs. Such automation can be performed using SSIS.

Similar to data, mining models also must be secured. The patterns discovered by data mining are the summary of sensitive data and can contain the most important facts about your business. Mining models should be treated as first-class citizens in any IT department, where administrators can assign and revoke user access rights as necessary.

Summary

This chapter introduced data mining to prepare you for applying the materials later in the book. At this point, you should have a general idea of the business problems addressed by data mining, the methods available for solving them, and the project cycle you undertake in order to create a solution. The remainder of this book will describe the data mining tools provided with SQL Server 2008 to implement solutions to the problems discussed in this chapter and more. The various data mining methods described in this chapter are tied to specific data mining algorithms in Chapters 6 through 12. Although some data mining projects may not require every step of the data mining process, most do in some way or another.

The Table Analysis Tools for Excel 2007 described in Chapter 2 encapsulates much of the data mining process and, therefore, makes data mining accessible to any Excel user.

Applied Data Mining Using
Microsoft Excel 2007

For many people, Microsoft Excel is the beginning and end of data analysis. It is a great tool for viewing data, performing calculations, and even building advanced financial models. This chapter presents a set of SQL Server Data Mining tools that are intended to bring the power of predictive analytics to the fingertips of Excel users.

The tools are provided as a freely downloadable add-in for Microsoft Excel 2007. At least the Professional edition of Microsoft Excel is required. If you do not have Microsoft Excel 2007, a free evaluation version is available. Just go to www.trymicrosoftoffice.com and select the Office Professional 2007 version.

The tools presented in this chapter were designed with the idea of empowering information workers (people who work with computer data and not necessarily IT specialists) with predictive analytics and do not require a background in data mining or statistics. They encapsulate some common tasks that typically employ data mining techniques but aim to hide the complexity behind an easy-to-use interface.

If this is the first time you've experimented with predictive analytics, these tools will give you a glimpse at the potential data mining offers for analyzing your data. If you are a seasoned analyst, these tools provide a quick way to get insights to your data.

In this chapter, you will learn how to install and set up the Table Analysis Tools for Excel 2007 add-in, how to use each tool, and how to interpret the results. Some details about how each tool works are also included, mainly as references to other chapters in the book. By the time you complete this chapter, you will be able to effectively use data mining to perform the followings tasks on your Excel tables:

- Analyze how values in a data column are influenced by values in all other columns
- Detect groups of rows with similar characteristics
- Automatically populate a column with values based on a few examples you provide
- Perform forecasting on a time series
- Find rows that are unlike most other rows (interesting or anomalous)
- Perform a scenario (goal-seeking or what-if) analysis
- Create a powerful (yet easy-to-use) prediction calculator
- Perform shopping basket analysis and identify cross-sales opportunities

Setting Up the Table Analysis Tools

SQL Server 2008 Data Mining Add-Ins for Microsoft Office 2007 is a freely downloadable package that allows you to unleash the power of SQL Server Data Mining in your Microsoft Office application. To get the add-ins, the simplest way is to use your web browser to navigate to the Data Mining team's web page at www.sqlserverdatamining.com. The SQL Server 2008 Data Mining Add-Ins for Microsoft Office 2007 download link is visibly featured on the home page.

To use the add-ins, you will need an instance of SQL Server Analysis Services installed and running in your network (or on your machine). Analysis Services is included in the Microsoft SQL Server package, so you will probably need to ask your database administrator to point you to an Analysis Services installation. If Analysis Services is not available, you can download a free evaluation copy of Microsoft SQL Server 2008. The download link is also featured on the home page of the sqlserverdatamining.com website.

When you have Analysis Services running (locally or somewhere on the local network), you can install the Data Mining Add-Ins. The package contains three add-ins: Table Analysis Tools (the focus of this chapter), Data Mining Client, and Data Mining Templates for Visio. The package also includes a Server Configuration Utility, a tool that handles the details of configuring the add-ins and the connection to Analysis Services. To continue with this chapter, you are only required to install the Table Analysis Tools and the Server Configuration Utility. However, you should install all components, because the other add-ins will be discussed in detail in Chapter 5.

After installing the add-ins, run the Getting Started application from `Start\All Programs\Microsoft SQL Server 2008 DM Add-ins\Getting Started)`. This application provides you with the following three options:

- Download an evaluation copy of SQL Server 2008 (with Analysis Services)
- Use an instance of Analysis Services that you administer
- Connect to an Analysis Services instance that you do not administer

Configuring Analysis Services with Administrative Privileges

If you have administrative privileges on an Analysis Services instance, then select the second option on the first page of the Getting Started application and click the Next button. The second page allows you to run the Server Configuration Utility included in the add-ins. Click the link in the middle of the page to launch the Server Configuration Utility, a different application that will configure your server for you to use with Table Analysis Tools. This Utility is a step-by-step wizard application. Click Next on the first Utility page to go to the configuration steps.

Follow these steps to configure Analysis Services to be used with Table Analysis Tools:

1. At the first step of the Server Configuration Utility, specify the name of the Analysis Services instance that you want to connect to. The default (`localhost`) assumes that you have Analysis Services installed locally. If this is not the server you are using, type in the correct server name. Then click Next to move to the second step. At this point, an error may occur. The error indicates that either the server name is incorrectly typed, or you do not actually have connection privileges on that server. If you don't have the necessary privileges, refer to the following section, "Using Analysis Services without Administrative Privileges," which discusses setting up everything when you are not an administrator.

2. At the second Server Configuration Utility step, configure the server to allow creation of session mining models, or transient data models that disappear when they are no longer used. You will do this by making sure that the "Allow creating temporary mining models" checkbox is checked. The tool detects whether the setting is already enabled on the server. In this case, the checkbox will be already checked. The server should allow creation of temporary mining models for the Table Analysis Tools to work.

3. At the third Server Configuration Utility step, specify the Analysis Services database that you want to use as a sandbox for data models created

by the add-ins. You can create a new database (if you are an administrator on the Analysis Services instance), or select from a list of existing databases.

4. At the last Server Configuration Utility step, you can grant permissions to other users on the add-ins database. Upon completing this last step, click the Finish button to complete the server configuration task.

The Server Configuration Utility applies your changes to the Analysis Services server and informs you of any errors that may occur. If no error occurs, you can go to the last page of the Getting Started application by clicking the Close button. From the last page, you can launch the sample workbook included in the add-ins. You also have the option to participate anonymously in Microsoft's Customer Experience Improvement Program. A link on that page leads to a detailed presentation of this program, and you should choose to participate.

Configuring Analysis Services without Administrative Privileges

If you *do not* have administrative privileges on an Analysis Services instance, then select the third option on the first page of the Getting Started application and click the Next button. The second page of the Getting Started application allows you to specify the e-mail address and name of the IT administrator who can set up Analysis Services for you and prepares a message for that person with detailed instructions on how to set up the server. You will have a chance to review and modify the message before it is sent.

After the message is sent, you should follow up with your IT department to get the name of the server and database where you have access. When you get this information, you can start using the add-ins. If you cannot get access to an Analysis Services instance, you can still download an evaluation copy of SQL Server 2008 and set it up on your machine. If you choose to do so, review the previous "Configuring Analysis Services with Administrative Privileges" section, because you will likely have administrative privileges on your private installation.

The last page of the Getting Started application provides the option to participate anonymously in Microsoft's Customer Experience Improvement Program. A link on that page leads to a detailed presentation of this program, and you should choose to participate.

NOTE The name of an Analysis Services server has two components: a machine name and an instance name. Multiple instances of Analysis Services may run on the same machine. If your server name contains only a machine name (such as `localhost`), then it is referring the *default* instance. Otherwise, the name looks like `localhost\AS2008`. If your administrator provided a server name that includes an instance, you must type the full machine name plus the instance name in the first page of the Server Configuration Utility.

What the Add-Ins Expect

You can use the Table Analysis Tools only on Excel table objects. An Excel table is a special form of spreadsheet range. Any range can be converted to a table. You will need to select all data in your range, and then click the Format as Table button, as shown in Figure 2-1. If the first row of your range contains the column names, be sure to indicate this in the Format as Table dialog box, so that the column names are preserved in your table.

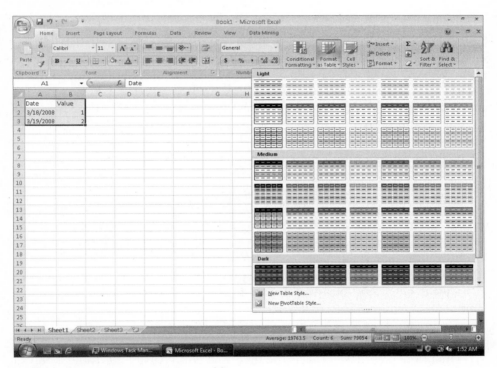

Figure 2-1 Formatting a range as a table

With your range formatted as a table, the Table Analysis Tools should be available whenever you click inside the table. In the Excel ribbon bar, a new ribbon named Analyze appears under the Table Tools collection, as shown in Figure 2-2.

The Analyze ribbon will go away as soon as you click outside the table and show up whenever you click inside a table. If you can see the Analyze ribbon when you click on your table, then everything is in place for using the Table Analysis Tools.

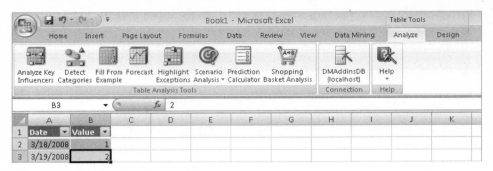

Figure 2-2 Analyze ribbon in the Table Tools collection

The Analyze ribbon contains three chunks of controls. The first chunk includes the Table Analysis Tools, which are discussed in detail later. The second chunk contains the Connection button, which you can use to change the current connection at any time. The Table Analysis Tools add-in maintains a list of connections, and you can select which connection you want to use at any time. The first time you use the Table Analysis Tools, no connection has been configured yet, and the connection button has the <No Connection> label.

The third chunk of the Analyze ribbon, labeled Help, allows you to launch the documentation browser, or to navigate to a Microsoft Internet location where you will find videos and tutorials for using the Table Analysis Tools.

In an Excel table, the Table Analysis Tools expect your data rows to represent entities and the data columns to represent properties of those entities. The values in a column must have the same semantics on the whole table in order for the Table Analysis Tools to be able to use it.

The examples discussed in this chapter use the sample Excel workbook included in the Table Analysis Tools add-in. To load the workbook, choose Start ➪ All Programs ➪ Microsoft SQL Server 2008 DM Add-ins ➪ Sample Excel Data. In the workbook, select the `Table Analysis Tools Sample` spreadsheet, and then click inside the table to ensure that the Analyze ribbon is accessible.

As mentioned earlier, if this is the first time you've used the Table Analysis Tools add-in, the Connection button is labeled <No Connection>. Click the button to create a new connection. The Analysis Services Connection dialog box appears, which usually displays a list of available connections. However, because no connection has been created yet, you need to click the New button. A new dialog box titled Connect to Analysis Services then appears, as shown in Figure 2-3.

In the Connect to Analysis Services dialog box, enter your server name (be sure to include any instance name, if one was indicated by your IT administrator), and then click inside the Catalog Name drop-down box to display a list of all the catalogs that are accessible under your credentials.

Typically, you will see at least two entries in the list: the database you (or your administrator) created for use with the add-ins, and a Default entry. You should select the explicitly named catalog. The Default selection instructs the add-ins to connect to the first database on the server that you can access. If you have access to multiple server catalogs, using this option may result in confusion.

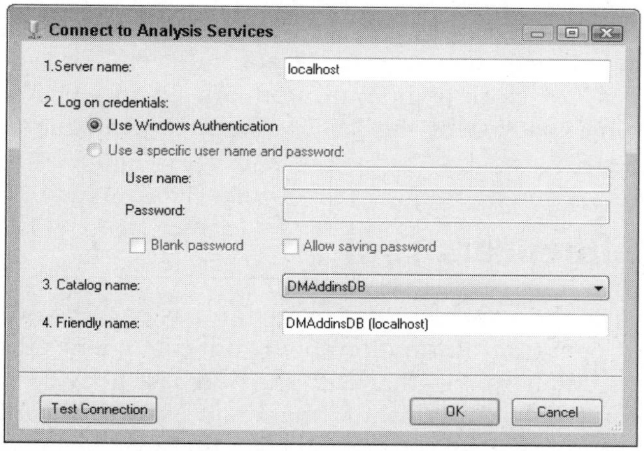

Figure 2-3 Creating a new connection to Analysis Services

By default, the Use Windows Authentication button in the Connect to Analysis Services dialog box is selected as the option for passing credentials (as shown previously in Figure 2-3). That is because Analysis Services supports only Windows-authenticated clients. However, as you may already know if you have used Analysis Services in the past, Analysis Services provides an option of connecting over HTTP. The HTTP endpoint may require basic authentication (with a specific user name and password), and the same endpoint is responsible for using Windows authentication to connect to Analysis Services.

If your connection uses the Analysis Services HTTP endpoint feature, type the URL (starting with the `http://`or `https://` prefix) in the Server Name field of the Connect to Analysis Services dialog box (shown previously in Figure 2-3). If your HTTP connection requires basic authentication, click the Use a Specific Name and Password button, and enter your user name and password in the corresponding fields (which are also shown in Figure 2-3).

After entering all the information in the Connect to Analysis Services dialog box, it is a good idea to use the Test Connection button to ensure that everything works properly. Click OK to close this dialog box, and then close the Analysis Services Connections dialog box as well. You are now ready to use the add-ins.

> **NOTE** If you want to use the add-ins outside your corporate environment, you may do so if your IT department uses the Analysis Services HTTP endpoint solution. Typically, such a deployment would use HTTPS and basic authentication to restrict your access to your enterprise domain. The add-ins allow HTTP or HTTPS connections with basic authentication, using the mechanism described earlier.

What to Do If You Need Help

If the documentation included with the product is not sufficient, or you get an error message that is not clear or helpful, you can always post a question in the "Data Mining" section of the MSDN Forums, available at http://forums.microsoft.com/MSDN.

The Analyze Key Influencers Tool

Imagine the following scenario. You are a store manager and as part of your store activity, you collect demographic information about your customers. This information is preserved in a database, together with the purchase activity of the customers. At some point, you load all this information in Excel and want to find how customer demographics may relate to the fact that the customer bought (or did not buy) a certain product.

The Analyze Key Influencers tool does exactly this. It analyzes the correlation between all columns in your table and a specified target column. The result is a report that identifies the columns having significant influence on the target and explains in detail how this influence manifests itself.

In the Sample Excel Data workbook, select the Table Analysis Tools Sample spreadsheet. Click the first button on the Analyze ribbon, Analyze Key Influencers. This brings up the Analyze Key Influencers dialog box shown in Figure 2-4.

You will need to select your target column. For this example, select the Occupation column. By default, the tool will analyze correlations between all the other columns in the table and your selected target. If you do not want to analyze all columns (and want to leave some columns out of the analysis), select the Choose Columns to Be Used for Analysis link in the dialog box to manually indicate columns for analysis. In general, you want to analyze all the columns, because the tool will only extract the actual influencers. However, if your target column contains values computed as a function of another single column, you may want to remove that influential column from the analysis. For example, if your target column includes the function = LEFT (A2, 3) (the first three characters of the text in column A), you should remove column A from the columns being analyzed, because the strong dependency detected between column A and your target will overshadow the less-evident influences of other columns.

Figure 2-4 Analyze Key Influencers dialog box

After you have selected your target, click the Run button. The task should complete in a few seconds and produce a report similar to the one shown in Figure 2-5, as well as a new dialog box shown in Figure 2-6.

	A	B	C	D	E
1		**Key Influencers Report for 'Occupation'**			
2					
3		**Key Influencers and their impact over the values of 'Occupation'**			
4	Filter by 'Column' or 'Favors' to see how various columns influence 'Occupation'				
5	**Column**	**Value**	**Favors**	**Relative Impact**	
6	Income	39050 - 71062	Skilled Manual		
7	Region	North America	Skilled Manual		
8	Commute Distance	5-10 Miles	Skilled Manual		
9	Cars	2	Skilled Manual		
10	Age	< 37	Skilled Manual		
11	Children	1	Skilled Manual		
12	Education	High School	Skilled Manual		
13	Income	< 39050	Clerical		
14	Region	Europe	Clerical		
15	Commute Distance	0-1 Miles	Clerical		
16	Cars	0	Clerical		
17	Education	Partial College	Clerical		
18	Education	Partial High School	Clerical		
19	Age	>= 65	Clerical		
20	Commute Distance	10+ Miles	Professional		
21	Income	39050 - 71062	Professional		
22	Commute Distance	2-5 Miles	Professional		
23	Cars	4	Professional		
24	Income	71062 - 97111	Professional		
25	Region	North America	Professional		

Introduction   Table Analysis Tools Sample   Influencers for Occupation

Figure 2-5 The main report generated by Analyze Key Influencers

You will learn how to use this dialog box after the main report is discussed in the next section. For now, just use the mouse to move this dialog box into the white area of the spreadsheet. *Do not close it* — it cannot be brought back without running the task again.

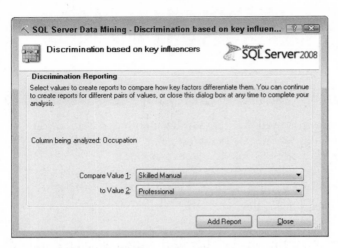

Figure 2-6 The dialog box for discrimination analysis

The Main Influencers Report

The main report consists of a table with four columns: Column, Value, Favors, and Relative Impact. The table contains multiple sections, identified by different colors in the last column and different values in the Value column. Each of the sections represents the key influencers for one distinct value of the target column. For example, the first report section in Figure 2-5 shows which factors in other columns favor a value of Skilled Manual in the target column (Occupation).

The report section on Skilled Manual can be interpreted as this: customers with an Income (the Column column of the report) in the range of 39050 - 71062 (the Value column of the report) are very likely to have the Skilled Manual value in the Occupation column. Therefore, an Income in the range of 39000 - 71062 is the strongest influencer for the Skilled Manual occupation. Then (moving to the next report row for the same Skilled Manual value), the next influencer is the North America region, a slightly less important influencer than the income. (The relative importance of influencers for each target state is described by the bar in the Relative Impact column of the report.) Another influencer (relatively about half as important as Region) is a commute distance of 5 - 10 Miles. The number of Cars, the Age, and the number of Children are also influencers, but to a lesser degree.

The next section of the report explains the influencers for the Clerical value of the Occupation column, and should be interpreted similarly.

When interpreting the report, keep in mind that, although the bar lengths may suggest otherwise, you should not assume that an `Income` of `39000 - 71062` influences a `Skilled Manual` occupation exactly as much as an income of `<39050` influences a `Clerical` occupation. The lengths of the bars are meaningful only within the report subsection that deals with a single target column value.

WHAT IS AN INFLUENCER?

Consider the first influencer reported in Figure 2-5. As mentioned before, you should interpret it as meaning an `Income` in the range of `39050 - 71062` is the strongest influencer for the `Skilled Manual` occupation.

This means that an income in this range appears, proportionally, more often in rows with `Skilled Manual` occupation than in rows with any other value for `Occupation`. This property qualifies this income range as an influencer for the `Skilled Manual` occupation. Also, out of all other influencers, this one appears most often together with a `Skilled Manual` occupation and/or least often together with a different `Occupation` value — which qualifies it as the strongest influencer. All influencers for a specific state are ranked, with the strongest getting a score of `100` and the weakest getting a score of `0`. The length of the bars in the `Relative Impact` column is the ranking score for each influencer.

If a column (either the target column or another column included in analysis) contains many different numeric values, then the tool treats those values as an interval (that is, minimum value to maximum value) rather than distinct states. The interval is partitioned in ranges, or *buckets* (in a process called *discretization*, which is described in detail in Chapter 3). Each range is treated as a distinct value, as illustrated by the `Income` values shown previously in Figure 2-5.

As with most reports generated by the Table Analysis Tools, the main influencers report () is formatted as an Excel table. Therefore, various Excel table features can be applied on top of the reports. Using the filtering of rows based on column values provides some interesting insights into the Key Influencers report.

To apply filtering to the report in Figure 2-5, start by clicking the down arrow button next to the column title. For example, click the down arrow button next to the Value column title, as shown in Figure 2-7. A list with all the values in the first column (the influencers' name) is shown, allowing you to select the values to be displayed. To see only how `Income` influences the values in the `Occupation` column, select the `Income` value (that is, place a check mark next to `Income`, and toggle the check marks so they do not appear next to any other influencer). The result of the filtering operation is a simplified report, as shown in Figure 2-8.

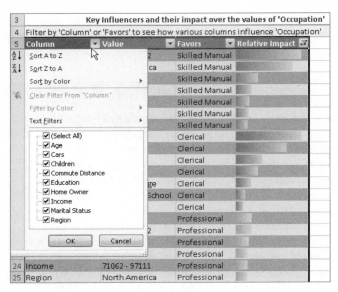

Figure 2-7 Filtering table rows by values in one column

	Column	Value	Favors	Relative Impact
6	Income	39050 - 71062	Skilled Manual	
13	Income	< 39050	Clerical	
21	Income	39050 - 71062	Professional	
24	Income	71062 - 97111	Professional	
30	Income	< 39050	Manual	
39	Income	97111 - 127371	Management	
43	Income	>= 127371	Management	
49	Income	71062 - 97111	Management	
54				
55				

Figure 2-8 A filtered view of the report in Figure 2-5

Filtering can be applied on any column of the report. Therefore, you can drill into the Key Influencers report and see the impact a certain influencer (for example, Income in Figure 2-8) has on all the target column values. Or you can filter by target column and see only those influencers favoring one or more target states.

The Discrimination Report

Notice in Figure 2-5 that an Income in the range of 39000 - 71062 is a strong influencer for both the Skilled Manual and the Professional values of the target `Occupation` column, which suggests that such an income range is more common to these two occupations than to any other occupation. The tool also discriminates between the influencers for any two distinct states of the target column, using the dialog box shown earlier in Figure 2-6. This dialog box (which appears after the Analyze Key Influencers tool is started) completes the main report. It allows the selection of any two states of the target column and can be used to generate a discrimination report for each such pair of target states.

To generate a discrimination report, start by selecting two distinct states of the target column. For example, select `Skilled Manual` as the first value and `Professional` as the second value. Then, in the dialog box shown in Figure 2-6, click the Add Report button. The resulting report is shown in Figure 2-9.

	Column	Value	Favors Skilled Manual	Favors Professional
57	Discrimination between factors leading to 'Skilled Manual' and 'Professional'			
58	Filter by 'Column' to see how different values favor 'Skilled Manual' or 'Professional'			
59	Column	Value	Favors Skilled Manual	Favors Professional
60	Income	< 39050		
61	Commute Distance	10+ Miles		
62	Cars	4		
63	Income	97111 - 127371		
64	Income	>= 127371		
65	Age	< 37		
66	Children	1		
67	Age	55 - 65		
68	Commute Distance	2-5 Miles		
69	Cars	2		
70	Commute Distance	1-2 Miles		
71	Cars	3		
72	Children	5		
73	Income	71062 - 97111		
74	Education	Partial High School		
75	Commute Distance	0-1 Miles		
76	Children	0		

Figure 2-9 Discrimination report between Skilled Manual and Professional

The discrimination report added this way compares influencers for only the two target column values selected in the dialog box. Practically, a discrimination report is the main key influencers report generated only on top of those rows in the original table where `Occupation` is either `Skilled Manual` or `Professional`. Consequently, the discrimination report is useful only when the target column has more than two distinct states.

This report also has four columns: `Column`, `Value`, `Favors Skilled Manual`, and `Favors Professional`. The names of the last two columns are changed to match your selection in the discrimination dialog box (shown previously in Figure 2-6). The first two columns describe the influencers. The last two columns represent the relative impact of each influencer on one or the other of the target states you selected. The influencers are presented in descending order of importance.

The influencers presented in the discrimination report are often very different from those presented in the main report. Some influencers from the main report are not present in the discrimination report. These influencers (such as an `Income` value between `39000 - 71062`) are important when comparing `Skilled Manual` or `Professional` against all other `Occupation` types. But they do not differentiate between these two occupations, and so are not included in the discrimination report. Other influencers (such as an `Income` value < `39050`) do not appear in the main report, or suggest other `Occupation` values than those being compared in Figure 2-9. They show up in the discrimination report because, over the reduced set of data rows having either `Skilled Manual` or `Professional` as an `Occupation` value, they strongly influence one of these states.

After a discrimination report is generated, the dialog box remains on top of the Excel spreadsheet, which enables you to generate subsequent reports for any pair of target column states. However, once the dialog box is closed, you can display it only by running the Analyze Key Influencers tool again.

REMOVING THE KEY INFLUENCERS REPORTS

All the output of the Analyze Key Influencers task is included in the new spreadsheet generated for the main and discrimination reports. Deleting the spreadsheet removes all changes performed by this task.

Summary of the Analyze Key Influencers Task

The Analyze Key Influencers task explains how values in various table columns influence values in a specified target column. The tool can also be used to explore a new dataset, as long as you know (before running it) which column is interesting for your analysis (so that you can pick your target). Numeric columns with many distinct states are discretized, as described in detail in Chapter 3.

The implementation creates a temporary mining model using the Naive Bayes algorithm, described in detail in Chapter 6. The main influencers report is obtained by discriminating between each value of the target column and all other values. A discrimination report is generated by discriminating between two values of the target column.

The Detect Categories Tool

When operating with a large number of data entities, it is convenient to group them into a manageable number of groups so that all the entities belonging to one group are very similar. Rather than dealing with hundreds or thousands of entities, you can now deal with a small number of groups of similar objects. This practice (often called *clustering* or *segmentation*) eases many data analysis tasks or business processes.

The Detect Categories table analysis tool finds natural groups in the data. It analyzes your data, finds the most common combinations of column values, and then defines groups based on these common patterns. It provides a detailed description of the groups it identifies, and it can label each row in the original data with the name of the group to which it belongs.

The tool is a powerful instrument for exploring new datasets. The detailed descriptions generated for each category constitute an intuitive summary of the dataset.

Launching the Tool

In the `Sample Excel Data` workbook, select the `Table Analysis Tools Sample` spreadsheet, and then select the second button on the Analyze ribbon, Detect Categories (shown previously in Figure 2-2). This brings up the Detect Categories dialog box shown in Figure 2-10.

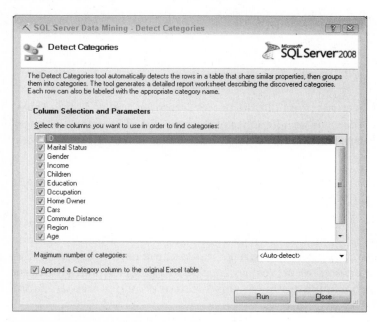

Figure 2-10 Detect Categories dialog box

The Detect Categories dialog box has three sections that may need your input.

The first section is the list of columns to be analyzed. The dialog box contains a list of all the columns in the Excel table, with check boxes allowing you to select for each column whether or not it should be included in the analysis. The Table Analysis Tools use a heuristic to find out which columns are interesting for data analysis, and which can (or should) be ignored.

The ID column is an example of a column that should be ignored. It contains unique identifiers for each row of the table, and likely does not contain any insights about the data. The heuristic detects this, and, as shown in Figure 2-10, it suggests removing this column from analysis. You may want to ignore other columns, either because they are not interesting at all, or because you simply want to direct the analysis to a specific column set.

If you know beforehand how many categories you would like your data to be partitioned into, select that number in the Maximum Number of Categories drop-down box. The list contains numbers from 2 to 10, plus an <Auto-detect> option, but you can type in any integer greater than 1 (in case you want more than 10 categories). The <Auto-detect> option will try to identify the actual number of natural categories in the data.

The Detect Categories dialog box also allows you to specify whether you want a Category column to be added to the original Excel table. Upon exploring the categories detected by the tool, you may want to see the exact category to which each row belongs, so the Append a Category Column to the Original Excel Table option is selected by default.

After you've entered your options, click the Run button to launch the tool execution.

NOTE The same heuristic is used by the Detect Categories tool and other Table Analysis Tools, and the same user interface elements (a list of columns with check boxes) are employed by other tools for column selection, as you will see later in this chapter.

The Categories Report

The tool may take several seconds to complete, and the result is a newly generated spreadsheet report titled Categories Report. The report contains three sections. The first section presents the categories and the number of rows determined to belong to each category. The second section describes the characteristics of each category, and the third section provides a visualization of the data in each category.

Categories and the Number of Rows in Each

Figure 2-11 shows the first section of the report. It consists of two columns: one containing the category name, and the second showing the count of data rows that are included in each category. The Category Name column is editable, and changes in this column will propagate to the rest of the report. The row counts are presented together with a horizontal bar that enables you to compare the category sizes (represented by length), as well as to easily identify each category by color.

5	Category Name	Row Count	
6	Category 1		189
7	Category 2		141
8	Category 3		158
9	Category 4		149
10	Category 5		126
11	Category 6		129
12	Category 7		108

Figure 2-11 Categories and the number of data rows they include

The initial category names are just ordinals. You can meaningfully label all the categories after inspecting the second section of the report.

Characteristics of Each Category

Figure 2-12 shows the second section of the report. It contains the characteristics for each category (listed in the order of their importance) in a table with four columns. The first column is the category name. The next two columns (Column and Value) identify a characteristic attribute of the current category. For example, Category 1 is characterized by very low income, below $39,050. The last column tells how important the current characteristic is in describing the current category. For example, most of the rows in Category 1 contain an Income value lower than $39,050. Just like in the case of Analyze Key Influencers, numeric columns with a large number of distinct values are discretized.

15			Category Characteristics	
16	Filter the table by 'Category' to see the characteristics of different categories.			
17	Category	Column	Value	Relative Importance
18	Category 1	Income	Very Low: < 39050	
19	Category 1	Region	Europe	
20	Category 1	Occupation	Manual	
21	Category 1	Occupation	Clerical	
22	Category 1	Commute Distance	0-1 Miles	
23	Category 1	Cars	0	
24	Category 1	Children	2	
25	Category 1	Children	1	
26	Category 1	Education	Partial High School	
27	Category 1	Education	High School	
28	Category 1	Children	3	

Figure 2-12 Category characteristics

This section of the report uses Excel data filtering to initially show a single category (Category 1). Use the filter icon next to the name of the Category column to choose another category to display, or to display multiple categories at once.

Based on the characteristics for each category, you can derive meaningful category labels. For example, Category 1 can be labeled, based on the characteristics in Figure 2-12, as Very Low Income, Manual and Clerical. Similarly, after applying the filter to display the characteristics for Category 5, you can label it with some more meaningful name, such as Professionals with more than 3 cars. To change the name of a category, go to the first section of the report, click inside the Category name area for that respective category, and type in the new name. The second section of the report updates automatically to the new name.

If you peek at the original data spreadsheet, you will see that a new column containing the category label was added at the end of the table. The values in that column are also updated automatically when you rename categories. Using Excel filtering on the newly added Category column, you can now show only rows belonging to a certain category. For example, you can choose to display only those rows that correspond to the Professionals with more than 3 cars category. You will notice that most of the rows in this category match the category description.

NOTE The last column of the report, Relative Importance, ranks characteristics within one category. For example, an Income lower than $39,050 is the most important characteristic of Category 1. This means that such an Income is most likely to appear for a row in this category, but you should not interpret this importance as a hard rule for all rows. Rows with an Income lower than $39,050 may appear in other categories, and rows in Category 1 may have an Income in a different range, although this does not happen often in the Excel table.

The Category Profiles Chart

The third section of the report is the category profiles chart, shown in Figure 2-13.

The chart presents the distribution (number of data rows) having a certain characteristic across all the detected categories. For clarity, the default rendering of the chart shows only the distribution of the first attribute, which is Age in Figure 2-13. Each vertical bar represents the distribution of a column inside a group of rows (one category or the whole table). Within a vertical bar, each colored segment represents the number of data rows having a specific value of that column. The length of a segment represents the proportion (not the absolute number) of data rows in the current group having a certain property. A legend that maps colors to distinct column states is visible on the right side of the chart. The horizontal axis of the chart shows the column whose

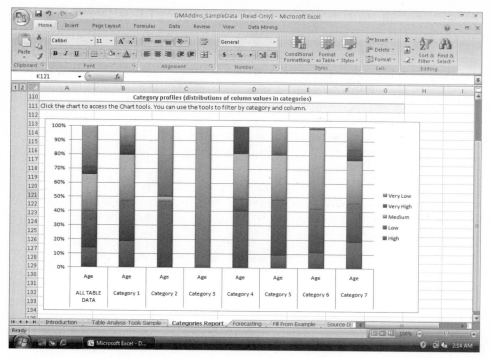

Figure 2-13 Category profiles chart

distribution is analyzed and identifies the group of rows considered for each vertical bar.

This type of chart (called a *PivotChart*) is a very powerful instrument offered by Excel. It allows slicing and dicing of the data by category and characteristics and provides a clear picture of the distribution of values across the detected categories, as well as in the original Excel table. To interact with the chart, you must ensure that the PivotTable Field List control (on the right side of Figure 2-13) is visible in Excel. If you cannot see the Field List, do the following:

1. Click inside the chart to show the specific ribbons.

2. Select the Analyze menu option under the PivotChart Tools collection.

3. Click the Field List button in the ribbon.

The PivotTable Field List control allows you to filter the information displayed inside the chart. The chart is already filtered to show only the first column (which in Figure 2-13 is Age). By clicking the filter icon next to the Column field, you can select to display other columns (individually or together). You can also filter by category to visualize the distribution of data only in certain categories detected by the tool. Figure 2-14 shows the distribution of Occupation in the whole table, and in the two categories renamed in the previous section (Low Income, Manual and Clerical and Professionals with more than 3 cars).

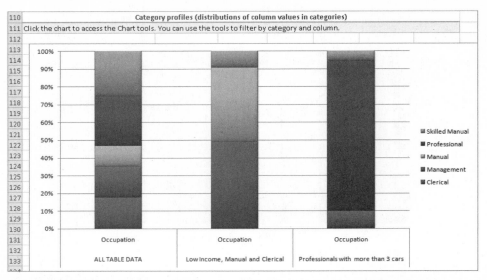

Figure 2-14 A filtered category profiles chart showing the distribution of professions across the whole table and two categories

> **NOTE** The category labels are not refreshed automatically in the category profiles chart. To update the chart to reflect your new category names, right-click on the chart border and select the Refresh Data option.

REMOVING THE CATEGORIES OUTPUT

The output of the Detect Categories tool consists of the newly generated Categories Report spreadsheet and, optionally, of a new column added to the original Excel table — a column that contains the category label for each data row. To completely remove the tool's output, you have to delete the Categories Report spreadsheet, as well as the Category Label column.

Summary of the Detect Categories Tool

The Detect Categories tool finds groups of Excel table rows that share similar characteristics. The characteristics shared in each category are presented in a report. This tool can be used to add more information (category labels) to a well-known dataset, or to explore a new dataset.

The implementation creates a temporary mining model using the Microsoft Clustering algorithm, discussed in Chapter 9.

The Fill From Example Tool

You are probably already familiar with the Excel AutoFill feature. If not, try the following:

1. Type **1**, **2**, and **3** on three consecutive rows in a spreadsheet.
2. Select all three cells.
3. Grab (by pressing the left button of your mouse) the lower corner of the selection.
4. Pull the selection down a few cells, without releasing the button.

   Excel analyzes the cells in the selected area (the ones containing 1, 2, and 3), determines the relationship between the values, and extends that relationship to new cells. The feature is very useful when your selected cells contain complex formulae linking other cells on the same row.

The Fill From Example data mining tool extends the Excel AutoFill feature by taking into consideration more than just the content of the selected cells. It functions only on table columns, by detecting patterns linking other cells on the same row with the target column and extending those patterns to new rows. For instance, the Fill From Example tool can be used to fill in the blanks in a spreadsheet by populating the empty cells with the most probable value. It can also be used in an iterative manner, where an expert partially populates a column with new information, runs the Fill From Example tool, refines the result, and runs the tool again until the result is satisfactory.

You will find the sample data demonstrating this tool in the `Fill From Example` spreadsheet of the sample workbook included with the Excel add-ins. The table in this spreadsheet contains a partially filled column: `High Value Customer`. Assume that a seasoned sales specialist (an expert) assigned flags (`Yes` or `No`) to a few customers in the table, based on the specialist's experience and customer knowledge. The Fill From Example tool learns, based on the flags assigned by the specialist, and automatically fills the rest of the column with `Yes` and `No` flags.

NOTE The more hints you provide the Fill From Example tool, the better the results. A single occurrence of `Yes` (or `No`) in the `High Value Customer` column is hardly enough for the tool to learn meaningful patterns. When using Fill From Example, be sure to provide at least four or five examples for each type of result (that is, four to five examples for `Yes`, and four or five examples for `No`).

Running the Tool and Interpreting the Results

To run the Fill From Example tool, select the third button on the Analyze ribbon, Fill From Example (refer to Figure 2-2). This brings up the Fill From Example dialog box, shown in Figure 2-15.

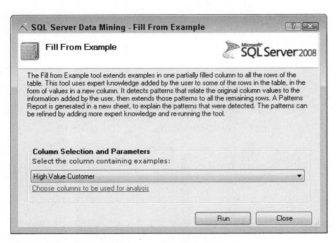

Figure 2-15 Fill From Example dialog box

In the dialog box, you must select the column containing the partial information entered by the specialists (in this case, the `High Value Customer` column). The tool tries to detect the intended target column by sampling some rows and finding the column that contains blanks (that is, the column is partially filled). This heuristic does a good job in this example. However, if it is a different column you want to use, you can select it from the drop-down list in the dialog box.

As part of the same heuristic analysis, the tool tries to detect the columns that may be significant for the analysis. This detection focuses mostly on finding and excluding those columns that seem to contain unique identifiers, which are typically not significant for pattern analysis. In general, you may use the default selection and click the Run button. However, the specialist who partially filled the target column may have ignored certain columns that are, in his or her experience, not significant.

If you click the Choose Columns to Be Used for Analysis link, you launch a new dialog box, shown in Figure 2-16. This dialog box contains a list of all columns in the table, with check boxes. A checked column is considered interesting by the tool's heuristic, whereas an unchecked column was considered not significant. You can use this dialog box to change the column selection based on the specialist's advice, or on advanced knowledge about data.

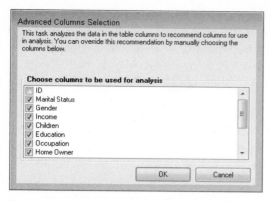

Figure 2-16 Advanced Columns Selection dialog box with the ID column (containing unique identifiers) ignored by the tool's heuristic

When you are satisfied with the column selection, click OK in the Advanced Columns Selection dialog box, and click the Run button for the tool to perform the analysis. After the execution completes, two new elements are added to your workbook. First, a new column is added to your table, containing the auto-fill results produced by the tool. Second, a new spreadsheet is added to your workbook, summarizing the patterns detected by the tool and used for auto-filling. The pattern report shown in Figure 2-17 is very similar to the one generated by the Analyze Key Influencers tool discussed earlier in this chapter. It shows how values in other columns of the table favor values in the column being extended.

	Key Influencers and their impact over the values of 'High Value Customer'			
3				
4	Filter by 'Column' or 'Favors' to see how various columns influence 'High Value Customer'			
5	Column	Value	Favors	Relative Impact
6	Region	Pacific	No	
7	Commute Distance	5-10 Miles	No	
8	Gender	Female	No	
9	Education	Partial High School	No	
10	Education	Bachelors	No	
11	Commute Distance	1-2 Miles	No	
12	Occupation	Professional	No	
13	Commute Distance	2-5 Miles	Yes	
14	Children	5	Yes	
15	Region	Europe	Yes	
16	Home Owner	No	Yes	
17	Education	Partial College	Yes	
18	Children	3	Yes	
19	Cars	2	Yes	
20				

Figure 2-17 The patterns report generated by the Fill From Example tool

The patterns report explains the rules detected by the tool by analyzing the non-empty cells in the original `High Value Customer` column. For example, the report shown in Figure 2-17 shows that European customers with a commute distance of 2 to 5 Miles and 5 children are generally considered high-value customers. Effectively, the tool computes (for each possible value of every column in the Excel table) a Yes-weight (the propensity of that column to indicate a value of Yes in the High Value Customer column) and a No-weight. These weights may be significant (in which case they will appear in the report) or not (such as the No-weight of a value of 5 for the Number of Children column, which is not included in the report).

Back to the original spreadsheet, a new column was added to your Excel table. The column has the name of the original column followed by the _Extended suffix, so in the current example, the column is named High Value Customer_Extended. The new column contains the non-empty values of the original High Value Customer column, plus the values computed by the tool wherever the original contains blanks. The new values are computed individually for each row of the table where the original is empty. The computation combines the Yes-weights and No-weights for all the cells in the row. If the combined Yes-weight exceeds the combined No-weight, the new column contains a Yes value; otherwise, the column contains a No value. More details about this computation are discussed in Chapter 12.

NOTE The target column may have more than two values, leading to separate weights being computed for each possible value. Furthermore, the target column may contain many different numeric values. In this case, the method for combining the individual weights of the other columns' values is slightly different, but the overall behavior is the same.

Refining the Results

If the new values in High Value Customer_Extended are what you expected (and the patterns are reasonable), you are probably done with the Fill From Example tool. However, often this is not the case. The set of hint values in the original High Value Customer may be too small, or the patterns may not reflect your expectations. In either of these cases, the results of the tool may be refined.

For example, based on your experience, assume that the customer with 1 car and a commute distance of less than 1 mile, at row 18 in the spreadsheet, is not a high-value customer, although the tool signaled it as being one. Modify the High Value Customer column in the spreadsheet by replacing the blank with your expert knowledge, as shown in Figure 2-18. Then, run the Fill From Example tool one more time.

The new information is taken into account in the second run. The set of patterns is refreshed in the newly generated spreadsheet and the values of the High Value Customer_Extended column are recomputed based on the new patterns. In general, a few iterations should be enough to get you the expected results. In these iterations, besides providing new hints to the tool, you may consider changing the list of columns used in analysis (in the Advanced Columns Selection dialog box shown previously in Figure 2-16) to get rid of unintended patterns detected by the tool.

Occupation	Home Owner	Cars	Commute Distance	Region	Age	High Value Customer	High Value Customer_Extended
Skilled Manual	Yes	0	0-1 Miles	Europe	42	Yes	Yes
Clerical	Yes	1	0-1 Miles	Europe	43	Yes	Yes
Professional	No	2	2-5 Miles	Europe	60	Yes	Yes
Professional	Yes	1	5-10 Miles	Pacific	41	No	No
Clerical	No	0	0-1 Miles	Europe	36	Yes	Yes
Manual	Yes	0	1-2 Miles	Europe	50	No	No
Management	Yes	4	0-1 Miles	Pacific	33	No	No
Skilled Manual	Yes	0	0-1 Miles	Europe	43	Yes	Yes
Clerical	Yes	2	5-10 Miles	Pacific	58	No	No
Manual	Yes	1	0-1 Miles	Europe	48	Yes	Yes
Skilled Manual	No	2	1-2 Miles	Pacific	54		No
Professional	No	4	10+ Miles	Pacific	36		No
Professional	Yes	4	0-1 Miles	Europe	55		Yes
Clerical	Yes	1	1-2 Miles	Europe	35		Yes
Skilled Manual	No	1	0-1 Miles	Pacific	45	No	Yes
Manual	Yes	1	0-1 Miles	Europe	38		Yes
Clerical	No	2	1-2 Miles	Pacific	59		Yes
Clerical	Yes	0	0-1 Miles	Europe	47		No
Clerical	Yes	1	1-2 Miles	Europe	35		Yes
Clerical	Yes	2	5-10 Miles	Pacific	55		No
Clerical	Yes	0	0-1 Miles	Europe	36		No

Figure 2-18 Refining the results of the Fill From Example tool

REMOVING THE FILL FROM EXAMPLE OUTPUT

The output of the Fill From Example tool consists of the newly generated patterns spreadsheet and the new column added to the original Excel table. To completely remove the tool's output, you have to delete the patterns spreadsheet, as well as the predictions column.

Summary of the Fill From Example Tool

The Fill From Example tool can fill in the blanks in a specific Excel table column. The tool learns from existing data, and the results can be refined with multiple iterations. The implementation creates a temporary mining model using Microsoft Logistic Regression algorithm, as discussed in Chapter 12.

The Forecasting Tool

Once again, imagine you are a retail manager. Your company collects sales data for various products, in various regions. An analysis of this information should provide insights into how the sales are going to evolve in the future. The

Forecasting tool analyzes series of numeric information, detects the patterns that govern the evolution of the series, and extrapolates these patterns to produce forecasts for the future evolution of the series.

The tool analyzes the data for the following categories of patterns:

- **Trends** — Directions of evolution for the series that have durability. For example, a series' values may grow over time (an *ascending trend*) or decrease (a *descending trend*).

- **Periodicities** (also known as seasonality) — Regular intervals when an event occurs. For example, certain sales tend to go up in the holiday season and drop after New Year's Day — such an event has a yearly periodicity. Another example would be if the number of readers for a web page goes up every Monday and drops over the weekends, it has a weekly periodicity.

- **Cross-correlations** — A more complex pattern, showing a dependency between the values of one series and the values of a different series, at the same or a different moment in time. For example, the stock price for an agricultural company in one year may depend on the wheat production in the previous year.

The Forecast tool detects (or allows you to specify) such patterns and employs them in producing the forecast. The tool expects each series to be represented as a column of the Excel table. If your data is organized by rows, select the whole table and use the Copy command, followed by the Paste Special command. In the Paste Special dialog box, select the Transpose option to get your series in columns before using the Forecast tool.

NOTE To enable the Forecast tool to detect cross-correlations between series, you must connect to an Enterprise Edition of SQL Server Analysis Services.

Launching the Tool and Specifying Options

The sample data for this tool is available in the `Forecasting` spreadsheet of the sample workbook. The spreadsheet contains monthly sales amount totals for a bicycle model in three regions of the world, for about three years. One of the columns, `Year/Month`, is a time stamp. You will learn how to use the tool to forecast the evolution of the sales amounts in the three regions for the next six months.

To launch the tool, select the fourth button on the Analyze ribbon, Forecast (shown previously in Figure 2-2). This produces the dialog box shown in Figure 2-19.

This dialog box contains a list of all the numeric columns in the Excel table. The list has a check box for each item, allowing you to select the columns that will be included in the analysis. If a column looks like a unique identifier for each row, it is unchecked in the list (it is likely to be a time stamp). The tool uses a simple heuristic to decide whether a column is checked or not (mostly by looking at the number of distinct values). If the heuristic is wrong in your case, just change the default suggestion by checking or unchecking columns in the list. Keep in mind that an unchecked column is completely excluded from analysis. Therefore, any possible cross-correlations linking it to a checked column will be lost.

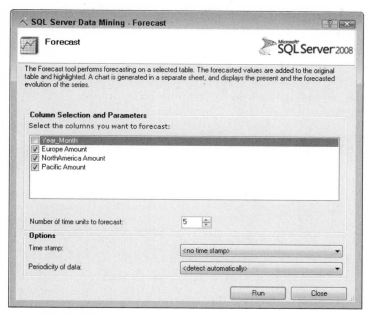

Figure 2-19 Forecast dialog box

> **NOTE** If a series in your table does not appear in the list of columns, it most likely contains at least one value that is not numeric. The tool can handle empty cells, but it will exclude a mostly numeric column if it contains even one non-numeric value (such as N/A). To run the analysis, replace any non-numeric value with either a number or a blank.

After you have ensured that your column selection is correct, pick the number of time units to forecast. The default is set to 5 (so the forecast will contain the next five numbers in each series). For this example, because the sample data contains monthly sales and you want to forecast the next six months, change the number of units to 6.

Optionally, you may pick a time stamp column. The time stamp column is not included in the analysis, but it's used in the report generated after analysis. Select the Year_Month column as a time stamp. Note that the actual name of the column, Year/Month, was changed to Year_Month to make the name compatible with the SQL Server Analysis Services engine that powers the Table Analysis Tools.

The last control on the Forecast dialog box allows you to specify the periodicity of the data (assuming you already know this, and want to direct the tool to use a specific periodicity). If you leave this option in the default state, the tool will try to automatically detect the periodicity. Note that your selection will force the tool to include a certain periodicity, raise the sensitivity threshold for periodicity detection, and might prevent the algorithm from detecting other periodicities.

The following periodicity options are available in the list (together with the actual number of time units to be considered for each option):

- **<detect automatically>** — The tool will scan the data to detect any periodicities.
- **Hourly** — The tool looks for a periodicity of 12.
- **Daily** — The tool looks for periodicities of 5 and 7 (working days and days in a week, respectively).
- **Weekly** — The tool looks for periodicities of 4 and 13 (weeks in a month and in a quarter, respectively).
- **Monthly** — The tool looks for a periodicity of 12 (months in a year).
- **Quarterly** — The tool looks for a periodicity of 4 (quarters in a year).
- **Yearly** — The tool will automatically detect periodicities.

Remember, these are just hints for the tool. Additional automatically detected periodicities will be used (if present in the data). If you are not sure which periodicity option to choose, the default option will usually work well.

After you specify your options, click the Run button to execute the Forecast tool.

Interpreting the Results

The Forecast tool appends the forecasted values at the end of the table, as you can see in Figure 2-20. The newly added values are highlighted. The other columns in the table (not included in the analysis) are also extended to have the same number of rows, but they are not highlighted upon running the tool.

The tool also generates a forecasting report in a new spreadsheet inserted in the workbook right after the sheet containing the data table. The report is a chart built on top of the table data, as shown in Figure 2-21. The chart presents both the historical evolutions of the series being analyzed and the forecasted evolution. The historical evolution is presented with a solid line, and the forecasted values use a dashed line and a slightly paler shade. If you selected a time stamp column in the Forecast dialog box, the values in that column appear as labels of the horizontal axis. The horizontal axis represents the time, and the vertical axis represents the value of the series. Therefore, the chart should be interpreted in the sense that a series evolved historically according to the solid line, from left to right, and will most likely evolve according to the dashed line.

36	200401	138349.4	212389.08	110734.52
37	200402	198344.14	205329.11	108539.53
38	200403	182129.21	214584.07	110859.52
39	200404	182254.21	214609.07	117619.49
40	200405	184774.2	405993.24	103849.55
41	200406	295483.72	297803.71	115249.5
42		184306.0323	289657.7535	85701.6478
43		144563.065	287474.2001	85885.22423
44		127951.9745	246325.1756	85918.73182
45		125262.3327	385199.6905	85834.37076
46		119828.9563	371575.1437	85658.65469
47				

Figure 2-20 Series values forecast by the tool

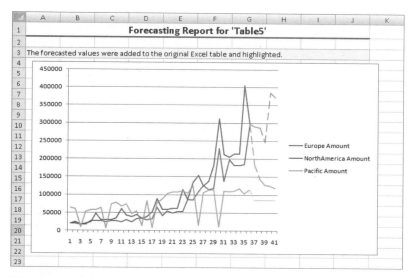

Figure 2-21 forecasting report generated by the tool

In addition to reviewing the raw values (both historical and forecasted), analyzing the forecasting report may provide some interesting insights into the series evolutions. For example, in Figure 2-21, follow the evolution of the North America sales series. You will notice that the series has spikes around the 200112, 200212, and 200312 timestamps (some other spikes are visible as well). These time stamps represent month of December in 2001, 2002, and 2003, respectively, so it is reasonable to assume that the spikes are a result of the yearly holiday season. The forecasted values for these series end in November 2004 (the last historical time stamp is 200405, hence May, and the tool was used to produce the next six values). The series ends on an ascending trend (leading to high sales in December 2004), which suggests that the tool detected the yearly periodicity of 12 and used that in the forecast.

More detailed insights about the series evolution (historical or forecasted) can be gained by using the Microsoft Time Series algorithm and associated viewer, as discussed in Chapter 8.

REMOVING THE FORECAST OUTPUT

To completely remove the output of the Forecast tool, you must delete the spreadsheet containing the forecasting chart, as well as the highlighted rows with forecasted series values. These rows are appended at the end of the original Excel table.

Summary of the Forecast Tool

The Forecast tool evaluates trends, periodicities, and cross-correlations in numeric series to forecast the next data steps for the series. It expects each data series to be a column of the Excel table. The Forecast tool creates a temporary mining model using the Microsoft Time Series algorithm discussed in Chapter 8.

The Highlight Exceptions Tool

The Highlight Exceptions tool is designed to find needles in haystacks. To be more precise, it is designed to find everything that is hiding in a haystack and that is not hay. Its goal is to find those rows in the Excel table that are unlike most other rows. Such rows may result from data-entry errors (such as an incorrect Copy/Paste operation, or an error resulting from the Excel AutoFill mechanism). Some other such rows may be correct (in the sense that the information does actually reflect the reality), but just uncommon, and therefore, interesting.

You can use the tool to find data-entry errors (and correct them). You may also use it to clean up data before further analysis. It may be an interesting first step when you're looking at a completely new dataset, because Highlight Exceptions emphasizes the most interesting data rows.

Using the Tool

For the examples in this discussion, you will use the `Table Analysis Tools Sample` spreadsheet from the sample workbook. Click inside the table (to make the Analyze ribbon visible), and then select the fifth button in the ribbon, Highlight Exceptions (shown previously in Figure 2-2). This launches the tool's dialog box, as shown in Figure 2-22.

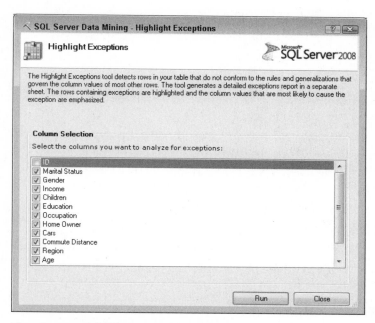

Figure 2-22 Highlight Exceptions dialog box

Just like in the Detect Categories tool, the first thing you should do is ensure that the correct columns are considered for analysis. The list of table columns appears in the dialog box, with a check box for each column. A checked column will be used during analysis, and an unchecked column will be ignored. The tool will not detect any exceptions in unchecked columns.

However, certain column types may negatively affect the result of the analysis. For example, using a column that contains unique row identifiers (a key column) in analysis will lead to many undesirable exceptions being highlighted. Also, columns containing free-form text may lead to the same result. The tool uses a heuristic based on the table data to suggest columns to be used in analysis. Note how the ID column is unchecked by default, because it contains unique identifiers. As mentioned, you can manually change the suggested column selection by checking or unchecking columns in the list.

After you have selected the list of columns to be included in analysis, click the Run button. The execution may take a bit longer than for other table analysis tools. While the tool is running, you will see a progress status dialog box, as shown in Figure 2-23.

Figure 2-23 The progress status dialog box for the Highlight Exception tool

If the system seems unresponsive at any time during this process, you can click the Cancel button, effectively terminating the execution. Note that this progress status dialog box appears in all the Table Analysis Tools.

During execution, the Highlight Exception tool performs the following steps:

1. It analyzes the Excel table data and detects common patterns.

2. It compares all table rows against the patterns and marks certain rows as exceptions (those rows that do not match the common patterns).

3. For each such row, it identifies the column that seems to cause the exception.

4. For each column in the Excel table, it computes a count of exceptions (rows) caused by that column.

When this execution is finished, a new spreadsheet is generated that contains an outlier report, or a summary of the exceptions detected in your Excel table, as shown in Figure 2-24.

The highlight exceptions report presents a list of all the Excel table columns, together with the number of exceptions caused by each column. The report also contains an exception threshold area (near the top). The default threshold value is 75. Changing the threshold value will result in the tool highlighting more or less exceptions. You should think of the threshold as an exception bar. If you lower the bar, you have more exceptions. For example, if you set the exception threshold value to 0, all the rows in the table will be marked as exceptions. On the other hand, raising the bar reduces the number of highlighted exceptions. A bar of 100 will not highlight any exception. The default value (75) provides a reasonable number of exceptions on most datasets. You can change the threshold value by typing in the report cell, or by using the numeric up/down control next to the cell. The values should be in the 0-to-100 range. (Any value smaller than `0` will generate the same effect as `0`, and any value larger than `100` have the same effect as `100`.)

	A	B	C	D	E
1	**Highlight Exceptions Report for Table2**				
2	The outlier cells are highlighted in the original table.				
3					
4	Exception threshold (more or fewer exceptions)	75			
5					
6	**Column**	**Outliers**			
7	Marital Status	0			
8	Gender	0			
9	Income	4			
10	Children	9			
11	Education	1			
12	Occupation	3			
13	Home Owner	0			
14	Cars	7			
15	Commute Distance	4			
16	Region	0			
17	Age	6			
18	Purchased Bike	0			
19	Category	0			
20	Total	34			
21					

Figure 2-24 Exception summary after running Highlight Exceptions

Back in the original spreadsheet, the rows containing exceptions are colored with a shade of brown and for each row, the column that is the most probable exception cause is highlighted with yellow. Figure 2-25 shows an example of the shading.

NOTE The exceptions presented in Figure 2-25 appear close to the end of the table in the sample spreadsheet.

985	15982	Married	Male	110000	5	Partial College	Professional	Yes	4	2-5 Miles	North Ame	46	No
986	28625	Single	Male	40000	2	Partial College	Clerical	No	1	1-2 Miles	North Ame	47	Yes
987	11269	Married	Male	130000	2	Graduate Degree	Management	Yes	2	0-1 Miles	North Ame	41	No
988	25148	Married	Male	60000	2	High School	Professional	No	2	1-2 Miles	North Ame	48	Yes
989	13920	Single	Female	50000	4	Bachelors	Skilled Manua	Yes	2	0-1 Miles	North Ame	42	No
990	23704	Single	Male	40000	5	High School	Professional	Yes	4	10+ Miles	North Ame	60	Yes
991	28972	Single	Female	60000	3	Graduate Degree	Management	Yes	2	10+ Miles	North Ame	66	No
992	22730	Married	Male	70000	5	Bachelors	Management	Yes	2	10+ Miles	North Ame	63	No
993	29134	Married	Male	60000	4	Bachelors	Skilled Manua	No	3	10+ Miles	North Ame	42	No
994	14332	Single	Female	30000	0	High School	Skilled Manua	No	2	5-10 Miles	North Ame	26	No
995	19117	Single	Female	60000	1	Graduate Degree	Professional	Yes	0	2-5 Miles	North Ame	36	Yes
996	22864	Married	Male	90000	2	Partial College	Professional	No	0	5-10 Miles	North Ame	49	Yes
997	11292	Single	Male	150000	1	Partial College	Professional	No	3	0-1 Miles	North Ame	44	Yes
998	13466	Married	Male	80000	5	Partial College	Professional	Yes	3	1-2 Miles	North Ame	46	No

Figure 2-25 Exception rows highlighted in the original Excel table

Understanding exactly the reason for each exception requires a good understanding of the dataset. In this particular example, some exceptions can be easily explained. For example, the last exception in Figure 2-25, for the user at line 996 with an ID (the first column) of 22864, the tool indicates the number of cars (0) as the cause of the exception. You can interpret this as stating the fact that most professionals living within 5 to 10 miles of work have at least one car.

Assume that this is a data-entry error and you know (or can find out) that a particular customer actually has one car. You can try to correct the error by typing **1** in the Cars column. The Highlight Exceptions tool detects the change and reevaluates the whole row with the new data. As a result, the row is no longer marked as an exception. If you revert the change (either by typing **0** or by using the Undo key sequence Ctrl+Z), the tool will again mark the row as an exception.

More Complex Interactions

The features of Excel enable you to interact with the exception highlighting results. You can see in real time how exception threshold changes affect the number of highlighted exceptions by executing the following steps:

1. Select View from the top menu bar.

2. Click the New Window button to open a new Excel window with the same workbook.

3. Click the Arrange All button and choose the Vertical arrangement option.

4. In one of the two vertical windows, select the Table Analysis Tools Sample spreadsheet.

5. In the other vertical window, select the Table2 Outliers spreadsheet

6. Lower the value of the Exception Threshold field by using the mouse or typing in a new value.

When displaying both spreadsheets at the same time (as shown in Figure 2-26), you can see how lowering the threshold leads to more rows being highlighted, whereas raising the threshold reduces the number of rows.

After you select the desired threshold level, finding the actual highlighted exceptions in the original Excel table may be an issue, particularly if the table has a large number of rows. The exceptions may be at the end of the table, or anywhere in the middle, and occasionally you will need to do some serious vertical scrolling to find them.

Luckily, Excel provides a better way to find the exceptions, by allowing you to sort the table rows by color. Notice how, in Figure 2-24 (shown previously), the Children column is the source for most exceptions (9 of the 34 exceptions highlighted by default seem to be caused by this column). In the original spreadsheet, click the drop-down button next to the `Children` column heading, select the Sort by Color option (Figure 2-27), and then pick the yellow shade. The exceptions will now be highlighted.

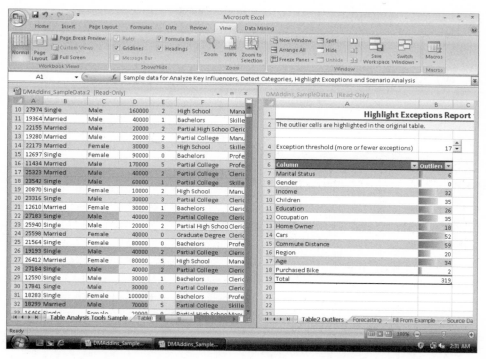

Figure 2-26 Side-by-side view of the source data and the exceptions report

The Sort option under the Data menu bar selection allows you to author complex, multi-level sorting criteria that can be used to display all the exceptions at the beginning of the table. Note that you can also filter columns by color to display only those rows that contain an exception.

Whenever you do an operation that changes data in the Excel table, the affected data rows are reevaluated against the learned patterns to see if the new content is an exception. When you perform an operation that involves rearranging or changing a large number of rows (such as filtering, sorting, or changing calculations that apply to a full column), such reevaluation requests are generated for each affected row. When the number of reevaluation requests exceeds a small threshold, the tool may choose to reevaluate the whole table, because this bulk operation is faster than individually evaluating each row. As a result, you may notice the progress status dialog box showing up after any operations affecting a large number of cells in the table.

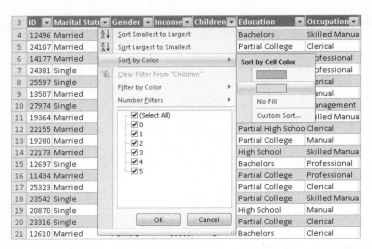

Figure 2-27 Sorting a column by color to display the exceptions near the top of the table

Limitations and Troubleshooting

As you learned earlier in this chapter (and will see in detail in the ''A Technical Overview of the Table Analysis Tools'' section at the end of this chapter), the Table Analysis Tools create and use temporary objects on an Analysis Services server. These temporary objects are not persisted in the spreadsheet and are removed automatically from the server if they are not used for a while (to conserve server resources).

The automatic row reevaluation provided by Highlight Exception relies heavily on interacting with the server objects. Consequently, the reevaluation can be performed only in the same Excel session that the tool was run. After you close the spreadsheet and open it again, reevaluation cannot function. The highlighting remains visible, and the exception threshold still functions. So, you can send a spreadsheet by e-mail to present the exceptions list to a colleague, but the color formatting of the data becomes static, and any changes in the spreadsheet content are ignored. To switch back to interactive mode, you must run the Highlight Exceptions tool again.

While in interactive mode, the Highlight Exceptions tool responds to data changes only in the range that was originally used in training. Therefore, the tool cannot detect (or handle) row additions at the end of the table. These are not checked for exceptions. If you insert a row in the middle of the table, it will be evaluated and highlighted, but the last row of the table will move out of the active area, and data changes in this row no longer trigger reevaluation.

REMOVING THE HIGHLIGHT EXCEPTIONS OUTPUT

The Highlight Exceptions tool generates multiple, complex conditional formatting styles for the data in the table. Also, it uses a hidden spreadsheet that contains scores for each cell in the table. It is rather difficult to clean all these manually. Therefore, the tool has an option to automatically clean the output. To do so, run the tool again on the same table. The second execution over the same table will produce a dialog box like the one shown in this graphic.

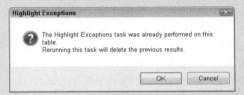

Click the OK button to delete the previous results, and then click Cancel to prevent the tool from actually running again.

Summary of the Highlight Exceptions Tool

The Highlight Exceptions tool detects (in your data) rows that are unlike most other rows. These may be anomalies (such as data-entry errors) or simply interesting, unusual rows. The implementation creates a temporary mining model using the Microsoft Clustering algorithm (discussed in Chapter 9), and measures the distance between each row in the table and all the clusters detected by the model. When a row seems far from all clusters, it is marked as an exception.

The Scenario Analysis Tool

If a car travels at 60 mph for two hours, how much distance will it cover? You find the answer easily, because you know the formula linking speed and time to distance. If speed and time were columns in an Excel spreadsheet, you could easily populate a third column with a formula that multiplies the two quantities to calculate the distance for each car in your spreadsheet. You can also figure out very easily the speed at which the car travels 150 miles in two hours. If your data and your formulas get more complex (or you do not feel like using your math skills), you can use Excel's built-in Scenario Analysis tool (under the Data ribbon, the What-If Analysis menu), which attempts to find a value for one of the terms of a formula that leads to the desired outcome. These kinds of problems are often referred to as *simulation problems*.

Now, assume that you are a high school principal and have demographic information about students and their college plans. For example, you know that John has an IQ of 100, did not receive a scholarship, and plans to attend college. Kevin, with an IQ of 110, also plans to attend college, after securing a scholarship of $10,000 a year. Janet, on the other hand, a really bright student, does not plan to attend college.

You cannot change various demographics such as the hair color or the parent income, but it is in your power to help Janet secure a scholarship. How big of a sum should you offer her so that she is more likely to attend college? Would she plan to attend if you secured a $5,000 scholarship for her? Although these are simulation problems, they are very different from the speed example. The major difference is that there is no simple formula linking the demographics and scholarship information to the fact that a student plans (or does not plan) to attend college.

The Scenario Analysis component of the Table Analysis Tools contains two tools — What-If and Goal-Seek — that are designed to solve exactly these types of problems. Before moving to the details for each tool, you'll learn a few details about how the tools work.

Even though there are two entry points and slightly different interfaces, the two tools are actually the same tool, which first analyzes your data and discovers the patterns linking all the columns in the table to the target column (which in the aforementioned example is the column containing the college plans of the students). By default, both tools perform their tasks on the currently selected row in the Excel table. They can also be applied to all the rows in the table in a single step.

When using the Goal Seek tool, you specify the goal (in Janet's case, the goal is to have a value of `Yes` in the `Plans to attend college` column). Then, you choose the column you want to change (again, assuming that you can change the value of the `Scholarship` column in this example) and let the tool search all the possible values of that column (in this case, `Scholarship`) to find the one that maximizes the likelihood that the goal is reached.

When using What-If, you get to specify a new value for any column in the data table, and see how this hypothetical change affects the outcome column. For example, if you select Janet's row in the Excel table, you can specify a value of `5000` ($5,000) in the `Scholarship` column to see how this is likely to affect Janet's college plans.

Likely and *likelihood* are keywords for the Scenario Analysis component. When you have formulas linking various columns to the outcome column, the solution for a simulation problem is exact (that is, it can be obtained by solving an equation), or a solution does not exist at all. When using Scenario Analysis, no result can be qualified as *exact*. The tool determines how likely an outcome is (or which is the most likely outcome, in the case of What-If analysis), based on the patterns it learned from your data.

> **NOTE** The likelihood characteristic of the Scenario Analysis tools has a consequence — the tools will provide an answer even if the question does not make much sense. If you use the tool to find out what happens to a student's hair color if you change their parents' income, you will get a result. But unless all the students in a certain demographic group in your school decide to dye their hair red, the result is probably meaningless. Therefore, use your domain knowledge when employing the tools to analyze only scenarios that actually make sense.

Different from the other Table Analysis Tools, the Scenario Analysis tools do not generate reports in a new spreadsheet. Most of the interaction happens in the tools' dialog boxes.

For this section, you will once again use the `Table Analysis Tools Sample` spreadsheet from the sample workbook. For the sake of exemplifying the tools, while reading this section, you can assume that it is actually in your power to modify customer attributes such as `Education`, `Occupation`, and `Age`. Therefore, you can also assume that it makes sense to perform a goal-seek type of analysis.

The Goal Seek Tool

As mentioned previously, the Goal Seek tool finds solutions to questions such as, "What is the value in column X so that column Y has a value of Z?" The examples presented in this section use the Goal Seek tool first to find how to change the commute distance for a customer in order to get that customer to purchase a bike, and then how to change the education of a customer to change the customer's income.

To launch the tool, you first select a cell in the Excel table. To get exactly the same results as presented here, select a cell on row 15 of the spreadsheet, which contains a customer with the ID of 12697. As you can see, this customer has a commute distance of more than 10 miles, lives in the Pacific region, and did not purchase a bike.

From the Analyze ribbon (shown previously in Figure 2-2), select the Goal Seek button under Scenario Analysis, which delivers the dialog box shown in Figure 2-28. You will first use the Goal Seek tool to find the commute distance value that will make this customer most likely to buy a bike.

The Goal Seek dialog box consists of three groups with options that you can modify: Goal to Seek, What to Change, and Specify Row or Table. You cannot modify the Results.

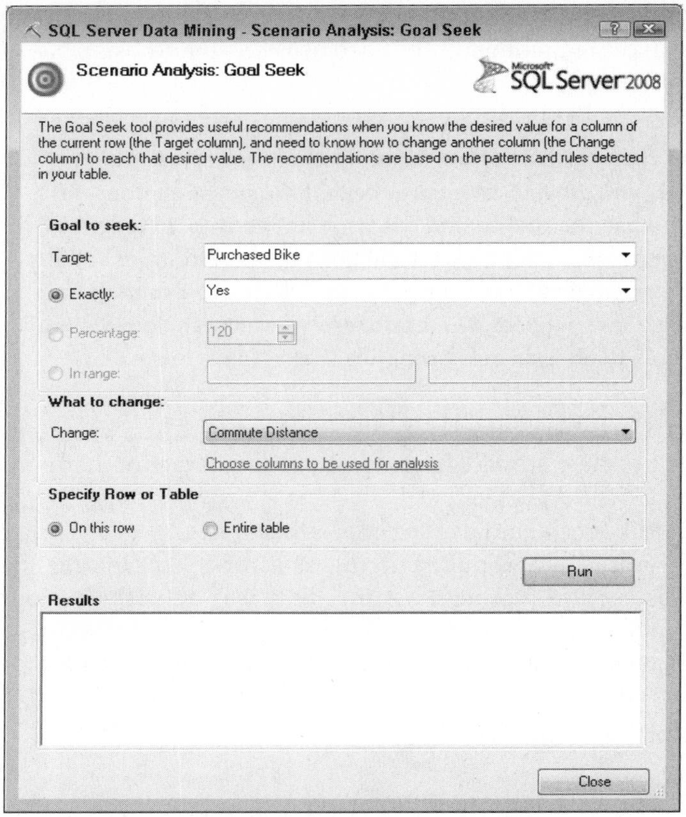

Figure 2-28 Goal Seek dialog box

The first group, Goal to Seek, allows you to specify the goal you want to reach for the currently selected row. The first control in the group is a drop-down list of columns in the table. Click the button next to the drop-down list and select the column that needs to reach the goal. For this example, select the Purchased Bike column.

The next three lines allow you to specify the goal value for the column you selected. Depending on the values in the target column, some of the lines may be disabled. If your target column contains numerical values, then your goal may be a percentage of the old value, or a range. If, on the other hand, the column contains categorical data (such as Yes and No, as is the case for Purchased Bike), then Percentage and Range options do not make sense and are disabled, leaving you with the option to specify exactly one target. Therefore, click the Exactly button and use the drop-down to select (or type in) the value that represents your desired outcome, in this case Yes.

The second group in the dialog, What to Change, is where you specify the column to be changed in order to reach your goal. Use the drop-down list to select the column to change, in this case `Commute Distance`. In the same group, you have the option to select the list of columns to be used in analysis. In addition to the modified column and the target column, other table columns will be used in this analysis, because they may contain interesting patterns that affect the target column. The tool uses a heuristic to select the columns to be used in analysis. You can supersede the heuristic's selection by clicking the Choose Columns to Be Used for Analysis link.

The third group, Specify Row or Table, allows you to choose whether the results should be presented for the current row only, or for the whole table. For now, leave the current selection, On this Row, unchanged.

When you've specified all the inputs, click the Run button to run the analysis and get the result. The result is displayed in the Results box and for this example, looks like Figure 2-29.

Figure 2-29 Successful Goal Seek results

Figure 2-29 shows a typical result for a successful Goal Seek operation. The first element of the result is the status: `Goal Seeking for Purchase Bike has found a solution`. The tool was able to find a value for `Commute Distance` that, together with all other attributes of the currently selected row, makes the customer a very probable bike buyer. The second element of the result is the actual solution: `Commute Distance = 0-1 Miles`. If the customer's commute distance will change to less than 1 mile, then the customer is very likely to buy a bike. The third element of the result tells you how confident you can be in this result. In this case, the confidence is very good.

As you may notice, nothing changes in the Excel table. All the interaction so far is inside the dialog box. Now try to get the same result (a `Purchased Bike` value of `Yes`) for the next row in the table, by changing the `Occupation` column (select `Occupation` in the What to Change drop-down list) and then clicking the Run button to run the tool.

First, you will notice that the second result is produced much faster than the first. The tool already learned the patterns in your data and is now able to reuse them for analysis. The new result is shown in Figure 2-30 and is considerably different from the one in Figure 2-29. First, the status line is different — this time the tool was not able to find a solution. Instead, the tool suggests changing the `Occupation` column to a `Manual` value, which is the change that is most likely to produce the desired outcome (convert the customer to a bike buyer). However, even the `Manual` value is very unlikely to produce the desired outcome.

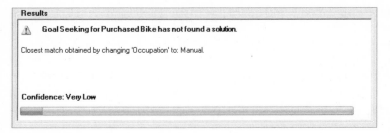

Figure 2-30 Result of an unsuccessful Goal Seek analysis

Using Goal Seek for a Numeric Goal

Whereas you must specify the exact goal (that is, the exact value you want in your target column, such as `Yes` for `Purchase Bike`) for categorical columns, the goals for numeric columns may be expressed as a percentage of the initial value, or as ranges. To simulate such a scenario, select a cell on row 15 of the spreadsheet (which contains a customer with the `ID` of `12697`), and then launch the Goal Seek tool.

This time, choose `Income` as your target. Notice how the Percentage and Range options become available (they are disabled for categorical columns such as `Purchase Bike`). Choose the Percentage option and set the target percentage to `150`. The percentage is applied to the original value in the target (`Income`) column, so the new goal is 150 percent of 90000, or `135000`. If the percentage is greater than `100`, the tool will consider any result that meets or exceeds the percentage as a success. If the percentage is lower than `100`, a successful result must be less than or equal to the percentage. For example, if you choose a percentage of `90`, a resulting `Income` of `81000` or less is considered a success.

In the What to Change section, select the `Education` column, and then run the tool on the current row. A successful result looks the same for a numeric or categorical column (shown previously in Figure 2-29). An unsuccessful result looks like Figure 2-31.

Note that the result of an unsuccessful analysis includes the actual result (as both a value and a percentage) in the output. Using the Goal Seek tool with a Range goal is similar to using the tool with a Percentage goal. Note that the exact goal option (the Exactly button in the Goal to Seek section) typically produces poor results when used for a numeric column.

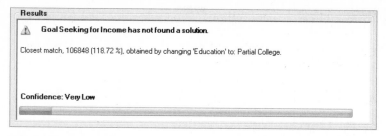

Figure 2-31 Result of an unsuccessful Goal Seek analysis for a numeric target column

Using Goal Seek for the Whole Table

The Goal Seek tool can be applied to all rows in the table. To do that, select the Entire Table option in the Specify Row or Table group. When you run a Goal Seek analysis on the whole table, each row produces a result. The set of results is appended to the original table as two additional columns, as shown in Figure 2-32.

	Occupation	Home Ow	C	Commute Dist	Region	Age	Purchased B	Goal: Purchased Bike=Yes	Recommended Commute Distance
4	Skilled Manua	Yes	0	0-1 Miles	Europe	42	No	✓	2-5 Miles
5	Clerical	Yes	1	0-1 Miles	Europe	43	No	✓	2-5 Miles
6	Professional	No	2	2-5 Miles	Europe	60	No	✗	0-1 Miles
7	Professional	Yes	1	5-10 Miles	Pacific	41	Yes	✓	5-10 Miles
8	Clerical	No	0	0-1 Miles	Europe	36	Yes	✓	0-1 Miles
9	Manual	Yes	0	1-2 Miles	Europe	50	No	✓	0-1 Miles
10	Management	Yes	4	0-1 Miles	Pacific	33	Yes	✓	0-1 Miles
11	Skilled Manua	Yes	0	0-1 Miles	Europe	43	Yes	✓	0-1 Miles
12	Clerical	Yes	2	5-10 Miles	Pacific	58	No	✗	2-5 Miles
13	Manual	Yes	1	0-1 Miles	Europe	48	Yes	✓	0-1 Miles
14	Skilled Manua	No	2	1-2 Miles	Pacific	54	Yes	✓	1-2 Miles
15	Professional	No	4	10+ Miles	Pacific	36	No	✓	0-1 Miles
16	Professional	Yes	4	0-1 Miles	Europe	55	No	✗	2-5 Miles
17	Clerical	Yes	1	1-2 Miles	Europe	35	Yes	✓	1-2 Miles

Figure 2-32 Results for Goal Seek on the whole table

The first column added to the table contains the status of running the Goal Seek operation for each row. The icons represent the success or failure of the operation. An *x* in a red dot represents a failure (Goal Seek was not able to find a solution), and a check mark in a green dot represents a success (Goal Seek did find a solution).

When a solution is found, it is displayed in the second column. When a solution is not found, the second column contains the value that is most likely to produce the desired outcome. If a row already contains the desired outcome, then it is marked as a success, and the suggested change column contains the original data value. In Figure 2-32, for those rows where `Purchase Bike` was already `Yes`, the suggested commute distance is not changed.

Goal Seek can be a time-consuming operation, particularly if you need to change a numeric column (the tool must consider a wide range of possible values before finding the one that is most likely to lead to your goal). Consequently, running the Goal Seek tool on a full table may take some time.

NOTE The Goal Seek tool is based entirely on patterns learned from the table data. Therefore, it functions correctly only if the goal value you seek already appears in the table in some data rows before you run the tool. For example, the Goal Seek will not function correctly if your goal is a value of Maybe for the Purchase Bike column, because that column can contain only Yes or No values. This is easy to detect and correct for categorical columns that have a reduced set of values. It is not so easy to detect for numerical columns.

Assume that the Income column contains values between 10000 and 100000. If you set a percentage goal of 120 percent and run the Goal Seek on the whole table, the goal for at least one of the rows will be 120000, a value out of the range seen in the table. The tool will not find any patterns leading to such a value. Therefore, when running the tool for the whole table with a numeric goal column, you should use a Range goal and make sure the goal range fits within the range of the goal column.

The What-If Tool

The What-If tool estimates the impact that changes in one column have over a different column (the target column) of the table. To get exactly the same results as presented here (as with the previous discussion), select a cell on row 15 of the spreadsheet, which contains a customer with the ID of 12697. Note that the customer is not a bike buyer and has no children. To launch the What-If tool, select the What-If button under Scenario Analysis on the Analyze ribbon (previously shown Figure 2-2). The What-If dialog box appears as shown in Figure 2-33.

The What-If dialog box consists of three groups with options that you can modify: Scenario, What Happens To, and Specify Row or Table. You cannot modify the Results. In this example, you'll use the What-If tool to see if a change in the number of children is likely to make this customer a bike buyer.

The first group, Scenario, allows you to describe the change to simulate. The first control in the group is a drop-down list of columns in the table. Click the button next to the drop-down list and select the column that changes. For this example, select the Children column. The next two lines allow you to specify the change for the column you selected. For all columns, you can specify the new (changed) value in the To Value field. For numeric columns with many different values, you can also specify a percentage change. If the column is not numeric, or it has only a few values (such as the Children column), the

Percentage option is disabled. The currently selected customer has 0 children. For this example, set a new value of 1 in the To Value field.

The second group in the dialog, What Happens To, is where you specify the target column to be estimated in the context of the simulation. Use the drop-down list to select the column, in this case `Purchase Bike`. In the same group, you have the option to select the list of columns to be used in analysis. In addition to the modified column and the target column, other table columns will be used in this analysis, because they may contain interesting patterns that affect the target column. The tool uses a heuristic to select the columns to be used in analysis. You can supersede the heuristic's selection by clicking the Choose Columns to Be Used for Analysis link.

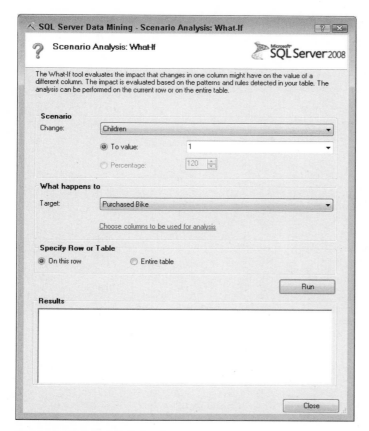

Figure 2-33 What-If dialog box

The third group, Specify Row or Table, allows you to choose whether the results should be presented for the current row only, or for the whole table. For now, leave the current selection, On This Row, unchanged.

When you have specified all inputs, click the Run button to run the analysis and get the result. The result is displayed in the Results box and for this example, looks like Figure 2-34.

Figure 2-34 shows a typical result for a What-If operation. The first element of the result is the status: `What-If Analysis for Purchase Bike has found a solution`. The tool executed successfully, and determined the most likely value for `Purchase Bike` in the context of changing the number of children from `0` to `1`. The second element of the result is the actual result: `'Purchase Bike' = Yes`. Having a child will likely make this customer a bike buyer. The third element of the result tells you how confident you can be in this result. In this case, the confidence is very good.

Figure 2-34 What-If analysis results

Just like Goal Seek, What-If does not change the Excel table when executed on a single row. All the interaction so far is inside the dialog box. By clicking on a different table row, you can evaluate the impact of the same change on that row.

Using What-If for the Whole Table

The What-If tool can be applied to all the rows in the table. To do this, select the Entire Table option in the Specify Row or Table group. When you run a What-If analysis on the whole table, each row produces a result. The set of results is appended to the original table as two additional columns, as shown in Figure 2-35. The results in Figure 2-35 were obtained after evaluating the impact that changing `Education` to `Bachelors` has on `Purchase Bike` for all the table rows.

3	Commute Dista ▼	Region ▼	Age ▼	Purchased E ▼	New Purchased Bike ▼	Confidenc ▼
4	0-1 Miles	Europe	42	No	Yes	
5	0-1 Miles	Europe	43	No	Yes	
6	2-5 Miles	Europe	60	No	No	
7	5-10 Miles	Pacific	41	Yes	Yes	
8	0-1 Miles	Europe	36	Yes	Yes	
9	1-2 Miles	Europe	50	No	Yes	
10	0-1 Miles	Pacific	33	Yes	Yes	
11	0-1 Miles	Europe	43	Yes	Yes	
12	5-10 Miles	Pacific	58	No	No	
13	0-1 Miles	Europe	48	Yes	Yes	
14	1-2 Miles	Pacific	54	Yes	Yes	
15	10+ Miles	Pacific	36	No	Yes	
16	0-1 Miles	Europe	55	No	No	

Figure 2-35 Results for What-If on the whole table

The first column added to the table contains the simulation result, the estimated new `Purchased Bike` value for each table row. The second column, `Confidence`, tells you how much confidence is associated with the simulation result for each row. A high value represents a high confidence.

Although it's relatively time-consuming, running a What-If analysis on a full table is significantly less expensive than running Goal Seek on the entire table.

WHAT CONFIDENCE TELLS YOU

With both Goal Seek and What-If tools, a confidence is associated with the result. This confidence is a number in the 0-to-100 range, with 100 being the maximum possible confidence and 0 the minimum. However, 0 and 100 are theoretical limits — the tools will never produce a result with these levels of confidence.

The confidence gives you an image of how many rows in the original table support the simulation result. Consider this very simple example. Say you have a table with three columns — `Commute Distance`, `Occupation`, and `Purchase Bike` — and you are running a What-If analysis on a customer with a `Commute Distance` of `2 miles` and an `Occupation` of `Professional`. Your goal is to estimate the `Purchase Bike` value if `Occupation` becomes `Management`.

(continued)

WHAT CONFIDENCE TELLS YOU *(continued)*

If most rows with a `Commute Distance` of `2 miles` and an `Occupation` of `Management` have `Yes` in the `Purchase Bike` column, then the What-If analysis returns `Yes` with high confidence. The same applies for a value of `No`. If these rows are split around 50–50 percent, then the confidence is low. The algorithm for computing the confidence is actually more complex — it can handle situations where no other row in the table has the same combination of values.

NOTE The dialog boxes for What-If and Goal Seek do not capture the focus of your mouse or keyboard. As a result, after running one of these tools on one table row, you can click on the Excel spreadsheet and change the current selection. Whenever a Scenario Analysis tool is executed, it uses the row containing the currently selected cell. Therefore, you can execute a scenario analysis on multiple rows without closing the dialog box.

REMOVING THE SCENARIO ANALYSIS OUTPUT

The Scenario Analysis tools do not modify your original data unless they are executed over the entire table. In that case, the result of the execution is a set of columns appended to the right side of the table. Removing these columns (if they are present) restores the original state of the spreadsheet.

Summary of the Scenario Analysis Tool

The Scenario Analysis tool simulates the impact that changes in one column may have on a different column in your table (the target column). You can use this simulation to estimate the most likely new values for the target column by running the What-If tool. The simulation may also be used to determine what change is most likely to generate a desired outcome in the target column by running the Goal Seek tool. The implementation creates temporary mining models using the Microsoft Logistic Regression algorithm, discussed in Chapter 12.

The Prediction Calculator Tool

Imagine you are a salesperson, dealing with many customers and having to select the customers with whom to follow up to close a transaction. Following up comes at a cost: time you need to spend with the customer and marketing materials you will present them. So, you need to carefully pick the follow-ups. On the other hand, too high a bar leads to many lost opportunities.

Now imagine that you are the data analyst in charge of empowering the sales staff with the tools required to do their jobs. By the time you finish this book, you will be able to build complex data mining models that accurately predict if a customer is worth following up on or not. However, the sales staff will likely not be able to use your mining models, because most are working in the field and probably do not even have access to a data mining server.

A simple solution is a scorecard tool, which allows the salesperson to assign a score to each customer based on individual attributes. Table 2-1 shows such a tool.

Table 2-1 Sample Scorecard Tool to Determine Whether to Follow Up with a Customer

CUSTOMER ATTRIBUTE		SCORE
Children at home		
	0	0
	1–3	20
	>3	50
Commute Distance		
	1–5 Miles	30
	5–10 Miles	20
	>10 Miles	0
Number of cars		
	0	50
	1–2	20
	>2	0

With a scorecard such as this, a salesperson can now compute a score for each customer, by adding the individual scores produced by that customer's attributes. For example, a customer with 2 children, a commute distance of 6 miles, and 1 car has a score of 60.

As a data analyst, you must produce such a scorecard and tell the salesperson how to use the score. Typically, you would use a threshold, something like "If the total score is at least 50, then the customer is likely to buy a bike, so go on, follow up!"

The Prediction Calculator tool produces such a scorecard. The tool is an easy-to-use prediction engine that does not require any server connection to make predictions about new data. It also assists you in detecting the optimum threshold for using the scorecard — a threshold that minimizes any costs associated with incorrect predictions and maximizes any profits associated with a correct prediction.

The Prediction Calculator tool can perform only binary predictions. It can be used to predict whether a column will have a certain value or not, but not to select between multiple alternatives. For example, you can predict whether the Hair Color is black or not, or whether the Income is in the range of 70000 to 80000 or not, but you cannot use the tool to predict whether the Hair Color is black, brown, or blonde.

The Prediction Calculator functions, to some extent, similarly to the Analyze Key Influencers tool, by detecting the influence of each value of each attribute on the target value. The Key Influencers tool filters out the weak influencers and presents only the strong ones. The Prediction Calculator assigns a score to each influencer, and you get the prediction result by summing the scores for all attributes.

Running the Tool

The sample data for this tool is available in the Table Analysis Tools Sample spreadsheet of the sample workbook. To launch the tool, click the Prediction Calculator button in the Analyze ribbon (shown previously in Figure 2-2). The Prediction Calculator dialog box appears, as shown in Figure 2-36.

In this example, you will use the Prediction Calculator tool to generate a scorecard that predicts, based on demographics, whether a customer is likely to purchase a bike or not. In the dialog box, select the column that contains the values to predict — in this case, Purchase Bike. Next, specify the target value for the prediction. If your column is numeric with a large number of values (such as Income), you can specify either an exact value or a range of values as your target. Otherwise, the Range option is disabled, and you must specify an exact target value. For this exercise, specify the Yes value for the Purchase Bike column by selecting (or typing) Yes in the Exactly field.

The tool will work by analyzing patterns that link values in all other columns to values in your target column, Purchase Bike. A heuristic is used to select the significant columns and to ignore the columns that seem to contain unique row identifiers. You can specify your own column selection by clicking the Choose Columns to Be Used for Analysis link, just like in other tools discussed in this chapter.

The last step before running the tool is selecting the output options — the set of reports to be generated by the tool. The tool will always generate an operational calculator report, which can be used to perform predictions. Optionally, the tool may generate a prediction report (used to tune the prediction tool) and a printer-ready report. For this exercise, do not change the default selection, which includes the two optional reports.

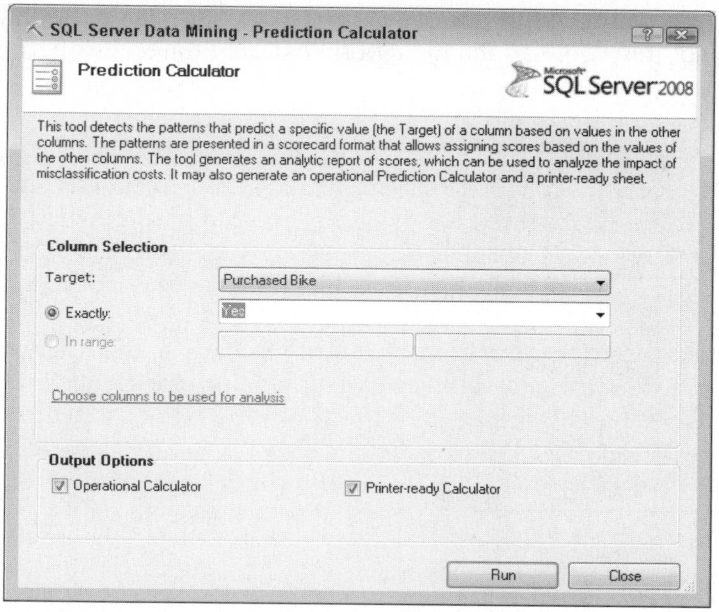

Figure 2-36 Prediction Calculator dialog box

After you've specified all inputs, click the Run button to launch the tool. In a few seconds, the reports are generated (in new spreadsheets of the same workbook). For now, ignore the spreadsheet selected by default, `Prediction Report`, and click on the next spreadsheet, labeled `Prediction Calculator`.

The Prediction Calculator Spreadsheet

Figure 2-37 shows the operational Prediction Calculator report, which can be used interactively to perform predictions.

The report contains a table with one row for each column in the source Excel table, except the target column (`Purchase Bike`). The first column of the report table contains the name of the original table columns associated with each row.

The second column (`Value`) contains values for the respective columns. This column is highlighted with a different color (the default Excel cell style for input values), suggesting that you can modify the values of the cells.

Click a cell in the `Value` column — for example, the cell associated with `Gender`. A drop-down control appears at the right end of the cell, allowing you to select a value for `Gender`. You can either use the drop-down list or type in your value. Note, however, that any typed value must be a valid `Gender` value in the original table. Otherwise, Excel will raise the error message, `The value you entered is not valid`. Numeric columns with a large number of distinct values are partitioned in ranges, or buckets (in a process called discretization, described in detail in Chapter 3). Each range is treated as a distinct value, as you can see in the `Age` column in Figure 2-37. After you run the Prediction Calculator tool, this column contains the most popular value for each column in the original table.

3	Suggested Threshold to maximize profit:		540
4			
5	*Select or type a value in the Value column of the table below to see how it affects the score.*		
6	**Attribute** ▾	**Value** ▾	**Relative Impact** ▾
7	Marital Status	Married	0
8	Gender	Male ▾	0
9	Income	Female / Male	116
10	Children	0	140
11	Education	Bachelors	36
12	Occupation	Professional	77
13	Home Owner	Yes	0
14	Cars	2	20
15	Commute Distance	0-1 Miles	89
16	Region	North America	0
17	Age	< 37	49
18	Total		527
19			
20	Prediction for 'Yes'		FALSE
21			

Figure 2-37 An operational Prediction Calculator report

The third column of the report contains the `Relative Impact` (or score) associated with the value you selected. The score changes as you change the value. In Figure 2-37, a value of `Male` for `Gender` is associated with a score of 0. Changing the `Gender` value to `Female` will change the score. The `Relative Impact` column is also highlighted with a special color to suggest that it should not be modified manually.

The last row of the table contains the total (summed) points for the customer described by your selection in the `Value` column. In Figure 2-37, the total is 519 points.

This total is compared against the threshold at the top of the report (540, in this example). If the total exceeds the threshold, the predicted value for `Purchased Bike` is `Yes`, suggesting that such a customer (as described by the values you entered) is likely a bike buyer. Otherwise, the predicted value is not `Yes` (and the prediction for `Yes` is false). In the particular case when the target column (`Purchased Bike` in this case) has only two states, `Yes` and `No`, a false prediction for `Yes` means `No` (the customer is not likely to buy a bike). However, if your target column contains more than two states, a false prediction for `Yes` cannot be associated with any other specific value.

As an example, try to use the calculator to predict whether a new customer will buy a bike or not. Enter the customer's demographics as shown here:

▪ `Married` for `Marital Status`

▪ `Male` for `Gender`

- 97111-127371 for Income
- 3 for Children
- Graduate Degree for Education
- Professional for Occupation
- Yes for Home Owner
- 2 for Cars
- 0-1 Miles for Commute Distance
- North America for Region
- 46-55 for Age

The total is modified to 603, which exceeds the 558 threshold. Therefore, the prediction is Yes, and the customer is likely to buy a bike.

The scores associated with each column value are normalized to ensure the following:

- The relative importance of the scores is preserved.
- The minimum score that can be generated by the calculator is 0.
- The maximum score that can be generated by the calculator is 1000.

NOTE Later in this chapter, you will learn how the threshold is computed and how you can modify it to improve the results of the calculator.

The second part of the report contains a score breakdown — all scores associated with all possible values of all table columns that were used in analysis (except the target column). The score breakdown table is similar to the Key Influencers report discussed earlier in this chapter. A major difference is that all states of all columns are included (not only those that favor strongly the Yes target value for Purchased Bike). The last column of the score breakdown contains the relative impact that each column value has on the target of the prediction, or the contribution of that column value in the calculator.

The Printable Calculator Spreadsheet

Select the third report generated by the Prediction Calculator tool, the spreadsheet named Printable Calculator. This spreadsheet contains a printer-ready prediction calculator. All columns used in analysis are included in the report, together with their associated score, plus instructions on how to use the printout.

An offline user is supposed to manually check the column values associated with a new customer, and then add the scores for each column and compare the total against the threshold, which is specified at the bottom of the printable report.

Refining the Results

The first report generated by the Prediction Calculator tool is not designed to execute predictions. It is an interactive tool for measuring and tweaking the performance of the prediction calculator. Before moving into details, you will learn a bit about how the tool's performance is assessed.

In the current example, you used the Prediction Calculator to predict, based on demographic information, whether or not a customer will buy a bike. The Prediction Calculator associates a score with each column value. If the sum of these scores for a customer is equal to or exceeds a threshold, then the prediction is positive (the customer will likely buy a bike). If the sum of these scores is less than the threshold, then the prediction is negative.

The predictions can be classified into the following four categories:

- **True negative predictions** — This is another correct prediction, but it's a negative one. The tool predicts that a customer is not a bike buyer and if you ask the customer, you find out that, indeed, the customer is not interested in buying a bike

- **False positive predictions, also known as Type I errors** — This is an incorrect positive prediction. The tool predicts that a customer is a bike buyer but when you ask the customer, you find out that he or she is not interested in buying a bike.

- **False negative predictions, also known as Type II errors** — This is another kind of incorrect prediction, a negative one. The tool predicts that the customer is not a bike buyer, but you find out later that he or she was actually interested in buying a bike.

Your goal in using the calculator is to correctly identify as many bike buyers as possible. In this scenario, consider the following:

- A true positive prediction produces value — the profit margin associated with selling a bike.

- A true negative prediction does not produce value, nor does it produce any loss — it saves you the marketing effort on an uninterested customer.

- A false positive prediction may produce some loss — the marketing cost associated with that customer.

- A false negative prediction does not produce value — it may represent a lost opportunity to sell a bike.

The total profit generated by the tool is the total profit margin associated with true positive predictions, minus the total marketing cost associated with false positive predictions.

Suppose that you are using the scorecard to identify high-risk patients. In this case, a true positive prediction does not bring you any easily measurable profit margin (it is difficult to quantify the value of early detection of a high-risk patient). The profit is also zero for a true negative prediction. A false positive prediction may have some cost associated with extra investigations, whereas a false negative prediction has a very serious cost associated with patient risks — costs of treating a more advanced disease or liability.

From these two examples, you can understand that any revenue from using the Prediction Calculator derives from the value of correct predictions (true positive or true negative), whereas any cost derives from incorrect predictions (false negative or false positive). The profit generated by the Prediction Calculator is the sum of revenues associated with correct predictions (profit, which may be zero), minus the sum of costs associated with incorrect predictions (which, again, may be zero).

Defining these revenues and costs depends on your specific application. After these costs are defined, you can use the Prediction Report spreadsheet to tune your Prediction Calculator to maximize the profit. Figure 2-38 shows the Prediction Report tuning tool.

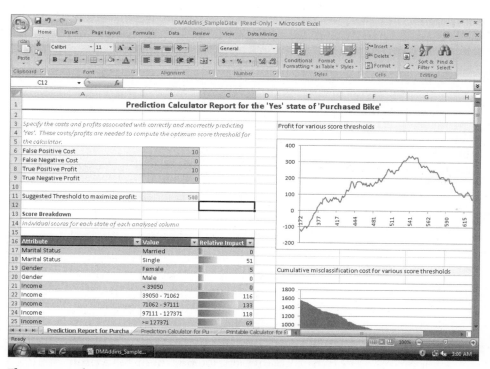

Figure 2-38 The spreadsheet containing the Prediction Report tool

By default, the tool associates a profit of $10 with a true positive prediction and a cost of $10 with a false positive prediction. These defaults represent a direct marketing scenario, where a true positive leads to revenue and a false positive leads to losses related to direct marketing costs.

The first part of the Prediction Report tool contains a breakdown of profits and costs associated with each type of prediction, as shown in Figure 2-39.

6	False Positive Cost	10
7	False Negative Cost	0
8	True Positive Profit	10
9	True Negative Profit	0
10		
11	Suggested Threshold to maximize profit:	540

Figure 2-39 The profits and costs section of the Prediction Report tool

Use this section of the tool to specify your own costs and profits, depending on the business scenario for which you are building the calculator.

During execution, the tool creates a set of randomly selected table rows for testing purposes. The Prediction Calculator is used for each of these rows in order to compute the row scores. By comparing the scores of the test rows against the actual value of the target column for the same rows, the tool computes the optimum threshold for the Prediction Calculator as the threshold that maximizes the profit (revenue from correct predictions, minus costs from incorrect predictions) over the test set.

Take a simple example, which considers only Commute Distance and Children. Assume that the test set contains five rows, as shown in Table 2-2. (The scores are hypothetical, and not those generated for the whole table.)

Table 2-2 Test Rows for Prediction Calculator

ID	COMMUTE DISTANCE	CHILDREN	PURCHASE BIKE	SCORE
1	0–1 Miles	0	Yes	524
2	2–5 Miles	5	Yes	723
3	1–2 Miles	2	Yes	615
4	2–5 Miles	5	No	723
5	10+ Miles	0	No	220

Also assume that the following things are true:

- A correct prediction (true positive or true negative) has a profit of $10.
- An incorrect prediction (false positive or false negative) has a cost of $10.

The test table contains four possible scores: 220, 524, 615, and 723 (which appears twice). If the threshold is set to 524, then any score greater than or equal to 524 generates a positive prediction (correct or incorrect), and any score below 524 generates a negative prediction (correct or incorrect). For a threshold of 524, the test table produces the following:

- Three true positive predictions (rows with IDs 1, 2, and 3), resulting in a total revenue of $30.

- One true negative prediction (row 5), resulting in a total revenue of $10.

- Zero false negative predictions.

- One false positive predictions (row 4), resulting in a total cost of $10.

Therefore, the total profit associated with a score threshold of 524 is $30.

If you repeat this experiment for all distinct score values in the test set, as well as for 0 and 1000 (the minimum and maximum possible scores), the total profit follows the values shown in Table 2-3

Table 2-3 Total Profit for Various Thresholds

THRESHOLD	TRUE POSITIVES	TRUE NEGATIVES	FALSE POSITIVES	FALSE NEGATIVES	TOTAL PROFIT
0	3 *(1, 2, 3)*	0	2 *(4, 5)*	0	$10
220	3 *(1, 2, 3)*	0	2 *(4, 5)*	0	$10
(221–523)	3 *(1, 2, 3)*	1 *(5)*	1 *(4)*	0	$30
524	3 *(1, 2, 3)*	1 *(5)*	1 *(4)*	0	$30
(525–614)	2 *(2, 3)*	1 *(5)*	1 *(4)*	1 *(1)*	$10
615	2 *(2, 3)*	1 *(5)*	1 *(4)*	1 *(2)*	$10
(616–722)	1 *(2)*	1 *(5)*	1 *(4)*	2 *(1, 3)*	−$10
723	1 *(2)*	1 *(5)*	1 *(4)*	2 *(1, 3)*	−$10
(724–999)	0	2 *(4, 5)*	0	3 *(1, 2, 3)*	−$10
1000	0	2 *(4, 5)*	0	3 *(1, 2, 3)*	−$10

As a result, the total profit provided by the tool is $30, and it is maximized when the threshold is in the range of 221 to 524. Actually, the test set granularity does not permit comparing values in this range, so the tool will recommend a threshold of 221 (the first in the range) as the optimum threshold.

All these computations are performed automatically as you change the profits and costs section shown previously in Figure 2-39.

NOTE If your table has very few rows (less than 100), then all of the table rows are used for testing, not just a selected sample.

A diagram presenting the evolution of the profit for various thresholds is included in the Prediction Report spreadsheet, as shown in Figure 2-40. Another diagram, presenting only the cumulative costs associated with incorrect predictions, is also included in the spreadsheet, as shown in Figure 2-41. The diagrams in Figure 2-40 and Figure 2-41 use a profit of $10 for any correct prediction (true positive or true negative), and a cost of $10 for any incorrect (false positive or false negative) prediction.

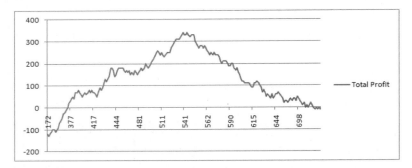

Figure 2-40 The evolution of total profit for various score thresholds

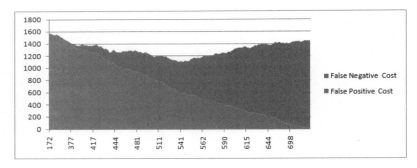

Figure 2-41 The costs of misclassification for various score thresholds

If you interpret the diagram in Figure 2-40 in the context of the direct marketing scenario of the example (the Prediction Calculator is used to identify likely bike buyers in order to send them direct marketing materials), you see how the profit starts very low, for a low threshold. In this case, the number of false positives is very large, so lots of marketing material is wasted without producing any profit. As the score threshold grows, the number of false positives is reduced, and the costs associated with marketing material produce revenue (from selling bikes). As the score threshold grows even further, the number of false negatives (customers ignored because their score does not meet the bar) takes a toll on the total profit.

The diagrams change as you modify the profits and costs associated with correct and incorrect predictions. Also, the optimum threshold is computed automatically as explained earlier. The new threshold is propagated to the operational calculator and the printer-ready calculator spreadsheets.

Using the Results

The first spreadsheet generated by the Prediction Calculator is the Prediction Report, which is intended to allow you to determine the optimal threshold for optimizing the profits and costs derived by using the tool.

After determining the optimal threshold, you can use and share your actual Prediction Calculator report (the second spreadsheet generated by the tool) with other Excel users. Simply share the workbook containing this spreadsheet with other Excel users to make the Prediction Calculator tool available to them. If your environment contains a deployment of SharePoint Excel Services, you can publish the spreadsheet and make it available offline for predictions.

If you must accommodate users who do not have access to a computer, then the third spreadsheet, the Printable Calculator, will meet your needs. Just print that spreadsheet and share the printouts, along with instructions on how to use the tool.

REMOVING THE PREDICTION CALCULATOR OUTPUT

The Prediction Calculator tool does not modify your original data. The result of the execution is a set of new spreadsheets added to your workbook. Removing these spreadsheets restores the original state of the workbook.

Summary of the Prediction Calculator Tool

The Prediction Calculator tool generates a scorecard calculator that can be used to make predictions without requiring a server connection. The tool's output can be tuned to minimize costs or maximize profits. The generated scorecard can be shared as an Excel spreadsheet, published in SharePoint Excel Services, or printed out to be used offline.

The implementation creates temporary mining models using the Microsoft Logistic Regression algorithm, discussed in Chapter 12.

The Shopping Basket Analysis Tool

The Shopping Basket Analysis tool works on transaction tables structured as shown in Table 2-4. In a transaction table, each data row represents an item that participates in a transaction. Because one transaction will likely include more than one item, multiple rows in a transaction table are associated with the same transaction. Each row in a transaction table contains at least two columns. One of these columns identifies the transaction that includes the current row, and the other column identifies the actual item.

Table 2-4 Transaction Table

TRANSACTION ID	ITEMS IN TRANSACTION
T1	Beer
T1	Chips
T2	Milk
T2	Chips
T2	Beer
T3	Milk
T4	Chips

For example, a transaction identifier may be the name of a customer. In this case, the items are the products that were purchased by the customer. Given the fact that each customer has purchased one or more items, there is a one-to-many relationship between the customers and the products in the transaction table.

Although this tool's name, Shopping Basket Analysis, suggests a retail application, you can use it for any one-to-many relationship. For example, you could use this tool to analyze web logs and detect keywords that appear together in query strings, or web pages that are visited frequently in the same browsing session, or even gene combinations that are often associated with a certain condition.

During analysis, the tool first identifies bundles of items that appear often together in transactions (for example, products that sell together). The second part of the analysis builds a set of recommendations. A recommendation is a statement of the form, "Transactions that contain Beer will likely contain Chips" This statement is based on the frequent occurrence of Chips in the transactions that include Beer. Note that these recommendations are not symmetric. Even if all transactions that contain Beer also include Chips (hence a recommendation such as the earlier one), there could be many transactions in the system that include Chips and no Beer. Therefore, the reciprocal recommendation (implying Beer in transactions containing Chips) may not be valid.

NOTE The Shopping Basket Analysis tool requires your data table to be sorted in ascending order by the transaction identifier column.

Using the Tool

The sample data for the Shopping Basket Analysis tool is available in the last spreadsheet of the sample workbook, named Associate. The table in the spreadsheet contains a transaction table with multiple columns. Each row in the table represents one product that was sold as part of a transaction. The first column (Order Number) is a transaction identifier. The second column (Category) contains a higher-level description of the product, and the third column (Product) is the actual product name. The last column (Product Price) represents the sale price of each product.

In general, the sale price for a product need not be constant across the transaction table. Often, promotions reduce the price of one product when it is purchased together with a different product, or in large quantities.

To run the tool, select the Shopping Basket Analysis button in the Analyze ribbon (shown previously in Figure 2-2). This launches a dialog box such as the one shown in Figure 2-42.

The dialog box requires that you specify the transaction identifier column of the table (in the Transaction ID field) and the column containing the item (in the Item field). The tool uses a heuristic to find the most likely transaction identifier column and the column containing the product. As you can see in Figure 2-42, it suggests Order Number as the transaction identifier.

You can run the tool to find groups of products that often appear together in transactions. If this is your goal, select the Product column in the Item field. Or you can run the analysis at the Category level to find categories of products that sell together. For this, select the Category column in the Item field. The rest of the example looks for products that sell together. Therefore, select the Product column in the Item field in order to get the same results.

If your table contains a value column associated with each item being analyzed, specify that column in the Item Value field. Note that the value need not be a price. It can be a profit margin, a tax amount, or any quantity that can be aggregated and is valuable for your analysis. For this example, leave the default selection (the Product Price column) as the Item Value. (For now, ignore the Advanced option in the dialog box — you'll learn about it later.)

Click the Run button to perform the Shopping Basket Analysis operation.

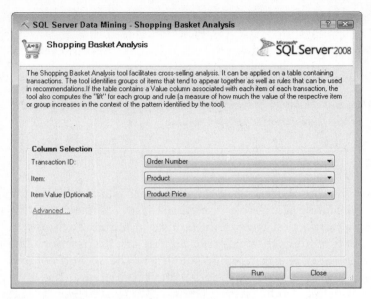

Figure 2-42 Shopping Basket Analysis dialog box

The Bundled Item Report

The first report generated by the Shopping Basket Analysis tool describes the bundles of items that frequently appear together in the transactions. As you can see in the example shown in Figure 2-43, the Bundled Item report contains one row for each group of products that frequently appear together in transactions.

	Bundle of items	Bundle size	Number of sales	Average Value Per Sale	Overall value of Bundle
5	Fender Set - Mountain, Mountain-200	2	438	2341.97	1025782.86
6	Mountain Bottle Cage, Mountain-200	2	430	2329.98	1001891.4
7	Mountain-200, Sport-100	2	407	2373.98	966209.86
8	Touring-1000, Sport-100	2	344	2438.06	838692.64
9	Mountain Bottle Cage, Mountain-200, Water Bottle	3	344	2334.97	803229.68
10	Mountain-200, Water Bottle	2	344	2324.98	799793.12
11	HL Mountain Tire, Mountain-200	2	314	2354.99	739466.86
12	Mountain-200, Patch kit	2	209	2884.98	602960.82
13	Touring-1000, Road Bottle Cage	2	216	2393.06	516900.96

Figure 2-43 Bundled Item report for products and their prices

The first column of the report (`Bundle of items`) contains the products in the group, separated with a comma. The second column (`Bundle size`) contains the number of products in the group (the size of the bundle). The third column (`Number of sales`) tells you how many transactions contain all of the products in the bundle.

The fourth column (`Average Value Per Sale`) and the fifth column (`Overall value of Bundle`) describe the value of the bundles, based on the selection you chose for the Item Value option in the initial dialog box shown previously in Figure 2-42 (the price of the products in transactions). The `Average Value Per Sale` column contains the average value of the bundle in all transactions that contain all items in the bundle. To obtain this value, the tool does the following:

- Traverses all transactions that contain all items in the bundle
- Sums the value of each product in the bundle
- Divides the resulting sum by the number of transactions containing the bundle

The `Overall value of Bundle` column is obtained in much the same way as the average value, without the last step that computes the average. By default, the Bundled Item report is sorted in descending order of the overall bundle value.

If you did not make a selection for the Item Value option in the tool dialog box (shown previously in Figure 2-42), certain properties of the bundles cannot be computed. In this case, the tool generates a simplified report, such as the one shown in Figure 2-44. Note how the value-related columns (`Average Value Per Sale` and `Overall value of Bundle`) are not included in the simplified report. The Bundled Item report is sorted in descending order of the `Number of Sales` column.

	Bundle of items	Bundle size	Number of sales
5	Mountain Bottle Cage, Water Bottle	2	998
6	Road Bottle Cage, Water Bottle	2	897
7	Mountain Tire Tube, Sport-100	2	749
8	Water Bottle, Sport-100	2	651
9	HL Mountain Tire, Mountain Tire Tube	2	552
10	Road Tire Tube, Sport-100	2	519
11	Touring Tire, Touring Tire Tube	2	507
12	Mountain Tire Tube, Patch kit	2	447
13	Fender Set - Mountain, Mountain-200	2	438
14	ML Mountain Tire, Mountain Tire Tube	2	435
15	Mountain Bottle Cage, Mountain-200	2	430

Figure 2-44 Bundled Item report for products without an Item Value column

The Recommendations Report

Whereas the Bundled Item report provides a descriptive view of the frequent buying patterns of your customers, the second report generated by the Shopping Basket Analysis tool, Recommendations, provides actionable items for the person performing the analysis.

The recommendations on this report are based on products that were purchased together by many customers, and can be used for direct marketing such as the familiar phrase, "People who bought the items in your shopping basket also liked these other items," for up-sell opportunities. Also, you can use the recommendations for product placements (inside a store or on a web page) to facilitate cross-sales.

Figure 2-45 shows the Recommendations report. The first two columns of the report contain the recommendations. The first column (Selected Item) contains the products that trigger a recommendation. The second column (Recommendation) shows the actual recommendation (the product that is frequently bought together with the selected item).

	Selected Item	Recommendation	Sales of Selected Item	Linked Sales	% of linked sa	Average value of reco	Overall value of linked s
5	Mountain Tire Tube	Sport-100	1782	749	42.03%	22.69276655	40438.51
6	All-Purpose Bike Stand	Patch kit	130	54	41.54%	234.6881538	30509.46
7	Half-Finger Gloves	Sport-100	849	352	41.46%	22.38454653	19004.48
8	Touring-1000	Sport-100	811	344	42.42%	22.90081381	18572.56
9	Touring Tire Tube	Touring Tire	897	507	56.52%	16.38565217	14697.93
10	Road-550-W	Sport-100	618	264	42.72%	23.06368932	14253.36
11	Mountain Bottle Cage	Water Bottle	1201	998	83.10%	4.146561199	4980.02
12	Touring-2000	Sport-100	211	86	40.76%	22.00540284	4643.14
13	Road Bottle Cage	Water Bottle	1005	897	89.25%	4.453761194	4476.03
14	ML Road Tire	Road Tire Tube	533	363	68.11%	6.122645403	3263.37

Figure 2-45 Recommendations report for products and their prices

The first recommendation in Figure 2-45 should be interpreted as, "The people who purchased the Mountain Tire Tube frequently also purchase the Sport-100 helmet"

The rest of the columns in the report provide details for each recommendation. The third column (Sales of Selected Items) tells you how many transactions contain the selected item. In the first recommendation, 1782 transactions include the Mountain Tire Tube. The fourth column (Linked Sales) tells how many of these transactions also contain the recommended item, the Sport-100 helmet. You can see that 749 transactions contain both the Mountain Tire Tube and the Sport-100 helmet. The fifth column (% of linked sales) expresses the same number as a percentage of Mountain Tire Tube transactions.

The last two columns of the report appear only if you made a selection for the Item Value option in the Shopping Basket Analysis dialog box. These columns quantify the value of the recommendation in terms of the value of the item being recommended.

The Overall value of Linked Sales column contains the total value of the recommended products. In the example being used here, this value contains the sum of the price for the Sport-100 helmet in all the 749 transactions that contain both the recommended product (the helmet) and the recommending product (the Mountain Tire Tube). By default, the Recommendations report is sorted in descending order of this Overall value of linked sales column.

The Average value of recommendation column shows the overall value of linked sales divided by the number of transactions that contain the recommending item (the Mountain Tire Tube). This number is the average value you will gain by recommending a Sport-100 helmet to all Mountain Tire Tube buyers.

The report looks slightly different if you did not make a selection for the Item Value option in the Shopping Basket dialog box. In this case, the value columns of the report cannot be computed, and they are replaced by an `Importance` column with a score for each recommendation, as shown in Figure 2-46.

4	Selected Item ▼	Recommendation ▼	Sales of Selected Items ▼	Linked Sales ▼	% of linked sales ▼	Importance ▼
5	Touring Tire Tube	Touring Tire	897	507	56.52 %	1.96
6	Touring Tire	Touring Tire Tube	582	507	87.11 %	1.44
7	HL Road Tire	Road Tire Tube	463	326	70.41 %	0.93
8	ML Road Tire	Road Tire Tube	533	363	68.11 %	0.92
9	HL Mountain Tire	Mountain Tire Tube	816	552	67.65 %	0.83
10	Road Bottle Cage	Water Bottle	1005	897	89.25 %	0.83
11	LL Road Tire	Road Tire Tube	608	334	54.93 %	0.82
12	Mountain Bottle Cage	Water Bottle	1201	998	83.10 %	0.82
13	ML Mountain Tire	Mountain Tire Tube	661	435	65.81 %	0.78

Figure 2-46 Recommendations report for products without an Item Value selection

The exact method for computing the importance of a recommendation is described in Chapter 11, which discusses the Microsoft Association Rules data mining algorithm used by the Shopping Basket Analysis tool. The importance is directly related to the percentage of linked sales, but it also penalizes a recommendation that links to a very popular product. For example, in the report shown in Figure 2-46, a very high percentage (83.1 percent) of customers who purchased a Mountain Bottle Cage also purchased a Water Bottle. However, the Water Bottle is a very popular item, and many customers are likely to buy this product. Therefore, a recommendation to buy a Water Bottle, although supported by the frequency, is not very interesting.

Tweaking the Tool

As mentioned in the beginning of this discussion, the Shopping Basket Analysis tool looks for bundles of products that appear together, and derives recommendations based on the frequency of products in transactions containing other products.

The tool is looking for the significant bundles of items, as well as for strong recommendations. Thresholds are used both for the significance of bundles and for the strength of recommendations. You can tweak these thresholds by selecting the Advanced option in the Shopping Basket dialog box (shown previously in Figure 2-42). When you do that, a new dialog box similar to the one shown in Figure 2-47 is displayed, allowing you to specify these thresholds.

The first threshold, Minimum Support, states when a bundle of items is significant enough to be taken into account by the analysis. The significance of a bundle is directly linked to the frequency of that bundle in transactions. Therefore, the threshold is a minimum frequency for each bundle. You can specify this minimum frequency as a percentage of the number of transactions, or as an absolute number of transactions. The default option is to ignore bundles that appear in less than 10 transactions.

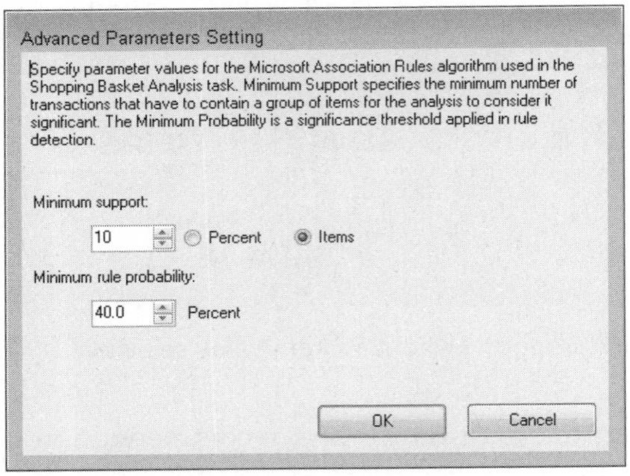

Figure 2-47 Advanced options for the Shopping Basket Analysis tool

The second threshold, Minimum Rule Probability, deals with recommendations. Consider a recommendation of the type, "Transactions containing Beer will likely include Chips." You learned in the beginning of this discussion that such a recommendation is based on the fact that most transactions containing Beer also include Chips. The Minimum Rule Probability threshold states how many Beer transactions have to include Chips before such a recommendation is considered by the tool. The default value, 40 percent, requires that at least 40 percent of the transactions containing Beer must also include Chips.

These thresholds are directly related to the Microsoft Association Rules data mining algorithm used by the Shopping Basket Analysis tool. Chapter 11 provides more details on how these thresholds are used internally by the algorithm.

REMOVING THE SHOPPING BASKET ANALYSIS OUTPUT

The Shopping Basket Analysis tool does not modify your original data. The result of the execution is a set of new spreadsheets added to your workbook. Removing these spreadsheets restores the original state of the workbook.

Summary of the Shopping Basket Analysis Tool

The Shopping Basket Analysis tool is designed to analyze sales transactions to find groups of products that sell together and opportunities for cross-sales. By extension, the tool can be used to analyze any transaction (such as tables) containing many-to-one relationships. The implementation creates temporary mining models using the Microsoft Association Rules algorithm, as discussed in Chapter 11.

Technical Overview of the Table Analysis Tools

The Table Analysis Tools are a pure client application for SQL Server Data Mining. They were developed using exclusively public APIs.

The tools use the ADOMD.NET programming API (described in Chapter 16) to communicate with the Analysis Services server. Certain ADOMD.NET features described in Chapter 16 (such as the concept of rowset parameters) are extensively used by the Table Analysis Tools.

All of these tools function by uploading data from Microsoft Excel to an Analysis Services server. A temporary (also called *session*) mining model is built on the server to analyze the uploaded data. The tools then query the mining model for patterns and predictions and render the results in Microsoft Excel. When Excel is closed (or when the mining model is not used for a long period of time), the temporary objects on the Analysis Services server disappear. These objects are visible only to the user who creates them. Even users with administrative permissions on the database cannot access your models or the data used in training those models. On the other hand, an Analysis Services server administrator *can* see the models and possibly access the data from the moment you start a tool, and until the moment Excel is closed.

The data mining algorithms used by the Table Analysis Tools are present in the SQL Server Standard edition. Certain tools (for example, Forecast) can do a better job when operating on top of SQL Server Enterprise Edition.

During your installation of the Table Analysis Tools, if you also included the Data Mining Client for Microsoft Excel, you can use the Trace option on the Data Mining menu to see all the requests sent from the Table Analysis Tools to the Analysis Services server. You can also use the Browse option on the Data Mining menu to explore the content of the mining models created by the Table Analysis Tools.

The tools are designed to allow people with little or no data mining experience to solve some very general problems and to introduce many users to the possibilities offered by data mining technology in general and SQL Server Data Mining in particular. If you (or your organization) may benefit from this kind of canned data mining solution but would like some more-specialized tools, you will find all the information you need to implement Table Analysis Tools for your specific application later in this book, particularly in Chapter 3, Chapters 6 through 12, and Chapter 16.

Summary

In this chapter, you learned about the SQL Server Data Mining Table Analysis Tools for Microsoft Excel 2007 add-in. These tools provide one-click insights about your data. You learned how to install the add-in and how to connect to an Analysis Services server. You also learned how to use each tool and how to interpret the results generated by them.

The chapters that explore specific algorithms later in the book (Chapters 6 through 12) provide more insight into how the tools actually process data and produce the results.

But first, Chapter 3 introduces the DMX language, your instrument for harnessing all the power behind the SQL Server Data Mining platform.

Data Mining Concepts and DMX

This chapter provides a detailed overview of the query language created by Microsoft for performing data mining operations — Data Mining Extensions to SQL (DMX). In order to review DMX, why it was created, and how it is used to represent and operate a data mining system, this chapter identifies the parts you use to analyze a problem, both on the conceptual level and on an object level. This chapter discusses the mandatory process that must be followed in any data mining implementation, and gives the necessary language constructs (along with many tips and tricks) required for that implementation.

History of DMX

DMX was first introduced in the OLE DB for Data Mining specification authored by Microsoft in conjunction with other vendors in 1999. The goal of this specification was to create a vendor-neutral, programmable interface that leverages concepts already known to the people most able to take advantage of such interfaces — the programmers.

At the time, the target programmer was a database programmer who would do application programming in Visual Basic. The data interface at the time was ActiveX Data Objects (ADO), which was a front end for OLE DB, and the standard language was Standard Query Language (SQL). The OLAP Services team (where SQL Server Data Mining started) decided to capitalize on this developer knowledge and use OLE DB as the application programming interface (API) and create a query language as close to SQL as possible, while still meeting the needs of data mining. Thus was born DMX.

Times have changed and the target developer has expanded to include .NET developers using C# or VB.NET (or any other .NET language), so the importance of the "OLE DB-ness" of the specification has waned. What remains is a flexible and descriptive language that makes discussing, describing, and implementing data mining solutions as easy as (or at least similar to) discussing, describing, and implementing relational solutions. Chapter 16 explains the APIs for implementing DMX solutions in code.

WHAT'S IN A NAME?

The acronym *DMX* was never officially approved by SQL Marketing despite constant haranguing by the development team. For the longest time, the DMX language could only be referred to as "the query syntax described in the OLE DB for Data Mining spec." After months of repeating that tongue twister, the data mining team resorted to guerilla tactics by using the term *DMX* whenever possible, and encouraging customers and partners to do the same. When marketing slipped up and used the term as well, DMX became the official language for the "Syntax formerly described in the OLE DB for Data Mining specification."

Why DMX?

Although data mining technologies have existed since the 1960s in various forms, the field is still relatively immature. There are no standard concepts of mining models, training, or predictions. For many people, data mining is just a set of algorithms, just as in the past when people thought of a database as simply a hierarchical data structure to store data. As such, data mining became a high-end tool available only to specialists who speak the various dialects of jargon known to the field (typically PhDs in statistics or machine learning).

There are many data mining products on the market, and each of these products has its own proprietary ways of describing and building data mining applications. Most data mining packages include their own algorithms, their own formats to browse and store model patterns, their own data-cleansing tool, and even their own reporting tools. Such approaches isolate the data mining systems from the enterprise operational systems, increasing the difficulty and cost of implementing data mining solutions.

The goal of DMX is to define common concepts and common query expressions for the data mining world, similar to what SQL has done for databases. The expression language is designed to be easily understood by database developers (rather than specialists), and to provide an explicit language for which data mining problems can be discussed, independent of algorithms or vendors.

NOTE The first vendor to provide a shipping version of DMX was not Microsoft. It was Megaputer, which shipped its commercial implementation months earlier. Microsoft later shipped an implementation in SQL Server 2000 Analysis Services, and SP1 of SQL Server 2000 provided the source code to its DMX parser and interpreter in the sample OLE DB for the Data Mining provider.

The Data Mining Process

The basic premise of data mining or machine learning is that you show the algorithm some examples and, from those examples, an algorithm can extract patterns that can then later be used for inspection or to deduce information about new examples. The trick to data mining is forming those examples in such a way that the patterns that are extracted are useful, informative, and accurate.

Figure 3-1 shows the data mining process in a nutshell. First you must define the problem and formulate an object, called a *mining model*. This mining model describes what the example data looks like and how the data mining algorithm should interpret the data. Second, you must provide the data examples to the algorithm. The algorithm uses your problem definition (the mining model) as sort of a lens through which to examine the data and extract the patterns. This is called *training the model*. When this is complete, depending on what you are trying to do, you could stop and analyze the patterns found by the algorithm in your examples. For some data mining scenarios, this is all that is necessary, as demonstrated in some of the tools in Chapter 2 (such as Analyze Key Influencers). Finally, you can provide new data, formulated in the same way as the training examples, to perform *predictions* or *deductions* of information about the examples using the patterns discovered by the algorithm.

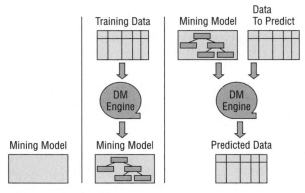

Figure 3-1 The data mining process

This is, of course, a gross simplification of the overall data mining process, which involves data exploration, validation, testing, and other steps. Industry processes, such as CRISP-DM (`www.crisp-dm.org`), give in-depth descriptions of the entire data mining life cycle. This encapsulated process, however, is sufficient for discussing the data mining component of SQL Server.

Key Concepts

A data mining scenario is like a carefully worded question with very specific rules about how to ask it. This section discusses the concepts you need to know to successfully formulate that question and implement a data mining scenario.

Attribute

The most basic part of a data mining question is the *attribute*, which is a single piece of information about an example. Examples include a customer's gender, age, or marital status; a product's category, volume, or color; or a store's square footage, ZIP code, or annual revenue. Other attributes can be whether customers purchased a particular product, or even how much of that product they bought or how much they liked it.

When choosing attributes for data mining, you should be careful to choose attributes that are likely to be relevant to your question and provide information that can be used by the data mining algorithm. Many attributes are not suitable for data mining, at least not in the form that they exist within your data. For example, the street address of a customer is an attribute, but it isn't generally correlatable to other attributes unless it can be first transformed, such as by using geospatial tools to determine distance to a particular landmark.

It is generally useful to create the most specific attributes possible for your question. It is possible to derive uncountable attributes from the attributes present in the data. Attributes such as the maximum purchase price a customer ever spent, the number of weeks a product has been on the market, or the ratio between the store size and number of customers per day could all be useful for your data mining problem. Creatively thinking about the aspects of your problem and the data you have at hand can provide you with a wealth of additional information to mine.

In general, there are two types of attributes. *Categorical* (or *discrete*) *attributes* have a set number of values (such as `male` or `female`, or `ZIP` code). *Continuous attributes* are, by definition, numerical. They can be operated on with standard mathematical operators and use some type of distribution (such as Gaussian). Additional attribute types are based on the main categorical or continuous attributes. For example, *ordered* or *cyclical* types are categorical but have a preset ordering (such as shirt sizes). *Discretized attributes* are another special case of the categorical type. In this case, a continuous attribute is broken into discrete ranges for analysis. This is done either for convenience (sometimes ranges are easier to understand than means and standard deviations), or because the target algorithm does not support continuous types and only works with categorical data (such as association rules).

When choosing which attributes to use in your data mining solution, keep in mind that the more attributes you have, the more examples are needed to elicit information from those attributes. If you have only gender, marital status, and home ownership, you could represent all possible variations in a very small set of data. However, as you add more attributes, the combinations grow, and more data is required to find good patterns. Of course, that is what data mining is for!

State

Associated with each categorical attribute is its set of possible values, or *states*. A marital status attribute may have the states Married and Single. It could also have additional states such as Divorced, Separated, Widowed, or any other combination. Just as with attributes, it is important to limit the states of an attribute to those relevant to the problem.

A data mining algorithm will treat each state with equal bias and will not understand any implied relationships between them. For example, an algorithm will not understand that Divorced and Widowed customers are, in fact, Single. Likewise, it won't understand that Separated is still Married.

If the concepts are important to the problem, include them; if not, simplify them to the greatest extent possible. For example, if you are mining for a business with customers all over the United States, but concentrated in certain areas, you may want to limit the ZIP Code attribute to those values that make up the majority of business. You could then substitute a value such as Other for the ZIP codes that fall outside of that set. Most algorithms have parameters to limit the number of states allowed for any particular attribute.

In SQL Server Data Mining, all attributes have the implied Missing state. This state indicates that the attribute may not be present at all for a particular row in the data. Likewise, there can be attributes with the implied Existing state, which means that the attribute's presence is the only information available, such as the existence of a product in a shopping basket. The Missing state is also frequently used when a previously unseen value is encountered during the prediction phase. If, for example, the algorithm received a request to predict information about someone with the marital status Never Married and had only seen the states previously described, SQL Server will automatically replace that value with the Missing state.

Additionally, even though continuous attributes don't have states, but have only continuous values, they are still considered to have the implicit Missing state. This allows algorithms to operate on data that contains the occasional NULL value.

Case

The *case* is the single most important concept to understand in DMX. If you understand your case, you understand the problem you are asking. If you don't understand your case, you will never get results you may expect or comprehend.

A DMX case is a single example that you provide to the data mining algorithm. It consists of a set of attributes with their associated values. Although this sounds simple, misunderstanding your case is the single most common cause of failure in a data mining implementation.

A case represents the entity you are mining — that thing you are asking the question about. In the simplest situations (and, in fact, most situations), a case is represented by a row in a table, with the table columns representing attributes. In fact, the vast majority of data mining problems are of this form, if for no other reason than the capabilities of earlier data mining tools limited users to posing questions in that form. For example, if your question was about the factors of a customer that impact credit risk, the cases would be the customers themselves and would contain all the information you knew or imputed about the customer.

Even in simple scenarios, it is easy to misunderstand how the case should be represented to ask a question. Say, for example, you want to understand what factors impacted the crime rate in cities. For this situation, the case can very well be the city because you are interested in attributes about cities that impact crime. However, consider a situation where you want to examine how the city itself contributes to the overall crime rate. In this case, the city would be an *attribute* because it becomes one of the independent variables to be used in the analysis. A case in this scenario would be something like a measurement that contains the city name, crime rate, and other attributes.

NOTE One way to identify a case is to think of what is *anonymous* about your analysis. If you are analyzing factors about customers, then the customer is likely the case because the individual customer doesn't matter in the result, only how the properties of that customer behave as compared to properties of other customers.

A more complex scenario involves a situation where you want to analyze relationships between attributes that may or may not exist within a case, and the number of attributes in a case is not known ahead of time. A common example of this is in *market basket analysis*, where you are discovering which products sell together and which product sales are predictive of other product sales. Here you have a transaction table with a column for the transaction ID, a column representing the product item, and potentially other columns for Quantity, OnSale, and so on, as shown in Table 3-1. In this scenario, the rows of the table *do not* represent the case and the columns *do not* represent attributes.

Table 3-1 Transaction Table

TRANSID	PRODUCT	QUANTITY	ONSALE
1	Bread	4	False
2	Milk	3	False
2	Cheerios	1	True
3	Television	1	True
3	Milk	2	False
3	Bread	4	True

In a transaction table, all rows belonging to the same transaction (identified by the transaction ID) comprise the case. The attributes are identified by the item of interest within a transaction row. In the example shown in Table 3-1, the *values* of the Product column generate the possible attributes in the case. The attributes that can be described from this table include Quantity of Milk, Milk was on sale, Quantity of Bread, Bread was on sale, and so on. A special kind of attribute can also be described that is simply the *existence* of the attribute, such as Milk appeared in this case or Bread appeared in this case. When a transaction or transaction-like table appears in a case, it is called a *nested table*. Likewise, any case containing a nested table is often referred to as a *nested case*.

DMX allows for arbitrarily complex cases. A case can contain attributes represented by columns in a row (referred to as *case-level attributes*) and multiple transaction tables (or nested tables) containing *nested attributes*. Figure 3-2 shows a set of cases with both case-level and nested attributes. This flexibility in modeling provides the freedom to include all relevant attributes in your analysis, whereas most commercial and noncommercial mechanisms are limited in complexity by external constraints (such as the number of columns allowed in a database table).

Keys

DMX references two different types of columns as *keys*. These columns have vastly different meanings and implications. The first is the *case key* that indicates the identity of the entity represented by the case. In many implementations, the primary key of a source data table can be used as the case key. Frequently, if there are no nested tables, a case key can simply be the row index or any other arbitrary label.

Key	Name	Gender	Age	Purchases		Movie Ratings	
				Product	Quantity	Movie	Rating
1	Jamie	Male	38	Milk	2	Matrix	5
				Bread	3	The Truman Show	4
				Coffee	1		

Figure 3-2 A nested customer case

The other type of key, the *nested key*, is quite different. Whereas the case key represents the anonymous part of the case, the nested key indicates the named entity of the nested row. For example, in Figure 3-3, the key of the nested table `Purchases` is the product name, indicating that the `Quantity` and `OnSale` columns refer to the item named in that column. Thus, you can derive the attributes `Quantity of Milk` and `Milk was OnSale`. If you mistakenly used the `Quantity` column as the nested key, your attributes would be nonsensical, such as `Milk of 2` and `OnSale of 2`.

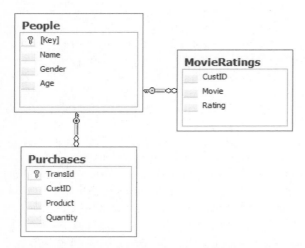

Figure 3-3 Relational schema for a nested relationship

NOTE A common mistake is to use a foreign key as a nested key. This happens primarily because of the naming conventions — individuals believe that because it is called a *key*, it should be a key in the relational sense. However, the nested key is only a key in the context of the nested table for a single entity. The relational foreign key is usually the same value as the case key. Therefore, for the case shown previously in Figure 3-2, using the foreign key as the nested key, in this case the CustId column of the Purchases table, would result in attributes like

"Milk of 1," Quantity of 1, and OnSale of 1. Additionally, because the foreign key is the same for all rows in the transaction, the result is duplicate keys in the nested table. Although this will not cause an error with SQL Server Data Mining, the behavior is undefined — and undesirable! Figure 3-3 shows the relational schema for the case described in Figure 3-2.

Inputs and Outputs

An attribute in DMX can be an input, an output, or both. On the surface, this concept appears simple, but in practice, it can be a source of confusion. In general terms, data mining algorithms use inputs to learn about outputs. However, each algorithm imbues its own interpretations to what exactly that means, which will be explained in each algorithm chapter in this book. As far as DMX is concerned, inputs and outputs are both provided to the algorithm during training. At prediction time, the inputs are provided to the algorithm, and outputs are returned.

In the case of an attribute being both input *and* output, the convention adopted by the Microsoft algorithms is that output attributes are never used to predict themselves. Therefore, the algorithms take steps to ensure the proper separation of information. This is dependent on the algorithm, but it can involve how many networks are created in a neural network, how clusters are computed, and so on. The ability to have multiple outputs in a single model was an innovation in DMX that has allowed the creation of much more complex and interesting scenarios.

The selection and definition of appropriate inputs and outputs are critical to success in a data mining solution, as exemplified in the sidebar, "Log Mining: A Non-obvious Example."

LOG MINING: A NON-OBVIOUS EXAMPLE

An interesting case-development scenario that requires a creative solution is that of mining server logs in order to predict server failure. On the surface, creating a solution appears somewhat straightforward — you have a log table with rows and columns. The rows become cases, and the columns become the attributes that make up the case.

However, the problem quickly becomes somewhat murky. The log doesn't have a column that says The server failed. What does server failure mean anyway? Does it mean that the server actually crashes? Does it mean that queries time out? Does it mean that particular queries run slower? Clearly, log mining does not mean simply taking the logs and mining them directly. One immediate option is to capture information outside of the log and correlate that to the log entries (such as various system performance counters and events).

(continued)

LOG MINING: A NON-OBVIOUS EXAMPLE *(continued)*

Adding the external information still doesn't provide what is needed for a practical data mining solution. Assuming that you define the event of failure and can perform the correlation to the most recent log event, what you have created are cases that can describe events that occur immediately before or coincident with server failure. If you are mining for descriptive purposes, this may be okay. But if you actually want to predict that the server is failing, by the time you could make a prediction with this information, it would already be too late.

Therefore, a different, more creative strategy is needed. The event you are mining for needs to be defined in a more useful manner, such as `The server will fail within the next 30 minutes`, or whatever time period allows the model user to take action. Again, failure means whatever you need it to mean — for example, a system crash, failed queries, excessive memory use, or whatever factors are important to your business. Even with this definition, the log entries by themselves are not usable. What particulars of a single log entry would be indicative of some random failure in the future? The attributes of the case must be creatively constructed (using the log data and other data) to be meaningful in the context of this question.

In this scenario, the case becomes the system state and recent history at a particular point in time. For example, your case could include state information such as the following:

- ◆ Number of queries running
- ◆ Number of users connected
- ◆ Amount of memory in use
- ◆ Percentage of CPU being used

Additionally, your case should include events about recent history. For example, you could include the following information captured over the past hour or two (or both):

- ◆ Number of successful queries
- ◆ Number of failed queries
  - ▪ Number failed because of timeouts
  - ▪ Number failed because of memory
  - ▪ Number failed for reason *X*
- ◆ Average query time
- ◆ Average memory use
- ◆ Average CPU use

(continued)

DMX Objects

The concepts discussed so far are abstract and have no direct representation in DMX, but are critical in understanding how to construct a data mining solution. DMX, however, being an extension of SQL, doesn't deal directly with attributes and cases. DMX is the language that transforms the data you have (that is, the tables with columns and rows) to the data needed by the data mining algorithms (that is, the cases and attributes). There are two major objects that are used to manifest this transformation: the mining structure and the mining model, as described in the next two sections.

Mining Structure

The *mining structure* describes the shape of the problem. It represents the columns of data available to your mining problem as well as information about those columns, and it can contain a cache of the source data used for training and testing your models. Depending on how the structure is created, it can also contain bindings to your data sources so that the structure can be reprocessed without you needing to provide the source data information again. Additionally, a mining structure contains all of the models that are used to analyze the source data of the structure.

A mining structure is defined as a list of columns, with their data types and information describing how they should be handled — essentially, if they are categorical or continuous. The columns in a mining structure do not represent attributes; they are simply the columns of data that will be available when creating models.

Frequently, a mining structure contains more columns than will be used in any one model. For example, you may create many different models with different algorithms to address a particular data mining problem. Because the algorithms have different capabilities, they have different data requirements. For example, the Microsoft Linear Regression algorithm accepts only continuous data, whereas the Microsoft Naïve Bayes algorithm accepts only categorical data. In situations when you need both algorithms to mine the same source data and the data contains types incompatible with one of the algorithms, you would add both continuous and categorical versions of the column to the structure. The categorical version of the column would be divided into discrete buckets. Each of these columns would be bound to the same column during processing.

Likewise, because a mining structure contains the superset of columns that models can use to create attributes, it also contains the superset of rows that models can use to create cases. A mining structure can be constructed to automatically divide your data into training and testing sets, and only the training set will be available to data mining algorithms for machine learning.

When a mining structure is processed, it contains a compressed *cache*, or copy, of the source data. This cache is used to train any models that are subsequently added to the structure. The cache can be queried to return its data or the distinct states that exist in any structure column. The cache is only maintained as a convenience, and can be dropped at any time. However, if models are added or changed, you will have to reprocess the structure to populate the models.

Mining Model

Whereas a mining structure is a container and descriptor, a *mining model* is the object that transforms rows of data into cases and performs the machine learning using a specified data mining algorithm. A mining model is described as a subset of columns from the structure, how those columns are to be used as attributes (that is, whether they are inputs, outputs, or both), along with the algorithm and algorithm parameters that will be used to perform the machine learning on the structure data. Furthermore, a mining model can be described to mine only a subset of data in the structure. The structure data can be arbitrarily filtered (based on the structure columns) to mine only the data appropriate for a specific problem.

For example, if you discover that customers in the state of Washington exhibit significantly different behavior from customers elsewhere, you can create a model with a filter to exclude the other customers without having to create another structure. It is also possible to filter the contents of a nested table from the structure to further refine your questions. For example, you can study only products of a particular category, or only transactions in a particular time period.

When a mining model is processed (or trained), it contains the patterns that the algorithm derived from the data. A model can then be used against new data to predict any output columns that were specified during its creation. Statistics about predictions are available as well, such as the imputed probability of the prediction and other statistics made available by the algorithm. Additionally, the learned patterns themselves can be queried to discover what the algorithm found. These patterns are generally referred to as the *model content*. Many algorithms are able to provide information about what specific pattern was used for a particular prediction, so you can correlate prediction results directly to the content.

DMX Query Syntax

Once you understand the core concepts behind DMX, and you know the problem you are trying to solve and what information you have, you're ready to start DMX. DMX is a command language much like SQL, meaning that you will require some program to execute the statements provided in this section. You can easily use SQL Server Management Studio to execute DMX statements, but you can also write your own program to do this as described in Chapter 16.

This section uses the sample data available for download on this book's companion website (`www.wiley.com/go/data_mining_SQL_2008`). It follows the three basic steps of data mining described earlier:

1. Creation
2. Training
3. Predicting

The file `Chapter3.zip` on the companion website contains supplemental files for use with this chapter. The `Chapter3.zip` file contains the following:

- `Chapter3.bak` — A SQL Server 2008 database backup file containing the data used in the chapter examples.
- `Chapter3.dmx` — A DMX file containing all of the query listings from this chapter.

NOTE The sample data for this chapter is a modified version of a test set used by the SQL Server Data Mining team to verify the DMX parser and interpreter. The data set was originally created in 1999 to test SQL Server 2000, and is still used to help ensure code quality. The data itself is meaningless, other than some names of team members and their children circa 1999.

Creating Mining Structures

Because DMX was designed to be as similar as possible to SQL, creation of mining structures and models is very much like the creation of SQL tables. The syntax is much simpler because there are fewer options, and there are some additional features, but anyone familiar with SQL will easily adjust to the DMX syntax. For example, consider Listing 3-1.

```
CREATE MINING STRUCTURE [People1]
(
        [CustID]    LONG    KEY,
        [Name]      TEXT    DISCRETE,
        [Gender]    TEXT    DISCRETE,
        [Age]       LONG    CONTINUOUS,
        [CarMake]   TEXT    DISCRETE,
        [CarModel]  TEXT    DISCRETE
)
```

Listing 3-1 Simple CREATE MINING STRUCTURE statement

SQL aficionados will easily identify this as a statement creating a mining structure, with the columns CustID, Name, Gender, Age, CarMake, and CarModel. Furthermore, they will see that the CustID column is the key of the structure and that CustID and Age are long integers, while the remaining columns are strings (text). The point where data mining starts to creep in is in what is called the *content type* of the column. The content type tells the data mining engine how to treat the column — for example, whether or not the column should be categorical (that is, DISCRETE) or CONTINUOUS.

The essential elements for the CREATE MINING STRUCTURE statement are the name of the structure and the column list. The most important part is the column list itself. Each column has a name, a data type, a content type, some optional modeling flags, and maybe a flag indicating the distribution of the data.

Table 3-2 shows the data types and content types that are both supported and used by data mining in SQL Server Analysis Services 2008. The additional content types aren't used by any of the built-in algorithms, so those are excluded from this text. Similarly, the Microsoft algorithms accept, but ignore, any distribution flags, so again, those are not addressed. Additionally, the only modeling flag that you can specify on a mining structure column is NOT NULL, and even that is rarely used. If you really need to understand all the unused aspects of the language, they are all well-documented in

Books Online, which can be accessed through the help menus in the Business Intelligence Development Studio or other user interface components of SQL Server.

Table 3-2 Supported (and Used) Data and Content Types

DATA TYPES	
	LONG
	DOUBLE
	TEXT
	DATE
	BOOLEAN
	TABLE
Content Types	
	KEY
	DISCRETE
	CONTINUOUS
	DISCRETIZED
	KEY TIME*
	KEY SEQUENCE**

*KEY TIME is used only with Time Series models.
**KEY SEQUENCE is used only with Sequence Clustering models in nested tables.

Discretized Columns

Of all the content types, the one that bears additional discussion is DISCRETIZED. (The content types KEY TIME and KEY SEQUENCE are discussed in the chapters that reference those types.) *Discretization* (or the operation of breaking continuous values into ranges) is a common operation in data mining for two major reasons.

The first reason is that ranges quite often make more sense than values and variances when you observe the patterns in a model. The second reason is that some algorithms simply don't accept continuous values. Typically, data miners would define ranges (or buckets) to be used for their models, and manually transform their data to those ranges before showing the data to data mining algorithms. SQL Server Data Mining addresses this issue by automatically creating buckets based on the distribution of the data in the column, and then using the bucket number when exposing the data to the algorithm. This has the obvious advantage of not requiring the user to predetermine ranges, but also helps later on during prediction, allowing you to provide the algorithm with values in its native, continuous form, and letting SQL Server Data Mining determine which bucket contains the value.

DISCRETIZED is also the only content type that is parameterized. The default system behavior is to create five buckets by first attempting an equal-areas approach, and, if that fails, using a clustering approach. If there is not enough data to support five buckets, the system will automatically try fewer buckets. You can customize this behavior by selecting both the number of buckets you want to use and the method in which to discover those buckets. Following are the available methods:

- EQUAL_AREAS — Compute ranges such that there are an equal number of values in each range.

- CLUSTERS — Use a single dimensional clustering to find grouped areas of points.

- AUTOMATIC (default) — Use EQUAL_AREAS and, if unsuccessful, use CLUSTERS.

Listing 3-2 demonstrates a mining structure with a customized DISCRETIZED column. Note that the original Age column from Listing 3-1 is still included. This is useful when you want to create models using algorithms that support different content types.

```
CREATE MINING STRUCTURE [People2]
(
        [CustID]      LONG      KEY,
        [Name]        TEXT      DISCRETE,
        [Gender]      TEXT      DISCRETE,
        [Age]         LONG      CONTINUOUS,
        [AgeDisc]     LONG      DISCRETIZED(EQUAL_AREAS,3),
        [CarMake]     TEXT      DISCRETE,
        [CarModel]    TEXT      DISCRETE
)
```

Listing 3-2 Creation with a DISCRETIZED column

Nested Tables

Whereas DISCRETIZED columns are mainly a convenience, nested tables (as indicated by the TABLE data type) allow entirely new types of data mining scenarios to be implemented. A nested table is defined much like the structure itself, with a name and a column list, as shown in Listing 3-3. Unlike the mining structure, it is acceptable (and typical) for a nested table to have only a single column that is the key of the nested table.

```
CREATE MINING STRUCTURE [People3]
(
      [CustID]       LONG       KEY,
      [Name]         TEXT       DISCRETE,
      [Gender]       TEXT       DISCRETE,
      [Age]          LONG       CONTINUOUS,
      [AgeDisc]      LONG       DISCRETIZED(EQUAL_AREAS,3),
      [CarMake]      TEXT       DISCRETE,
      [CarModel]     TEXT       DISCRETE,
      [Purchases]    TABLE
      (
            [Product]      TEXT       KEY,
            [Quantity]     LONG       CONTINUOUS,
            [OnSale]       BOOLEAN    DISCRETE
      ) ,
      [Movie Ratings] TABLE
      (
            [Movie]        TEXT       KEY,
            [Rating]       LONG       CONTINUOUS
      )
)
```

Listing 3-3 Creation with a nested table

The structure in Listing 3-3 represents a case similar to the one in Figure 3-2.

Partitioning into Testing and Training Sets

Mining structures also allow you to automatically divide your source data into testing and training sets. You can specify a percentage of the data to use for testing, a case count, or both (in which case, the lower of the two amounts is used). The data that is not held aside for testing is used for training. The test set is used for validating models after training. Listing 3-4 shows a structure definition that holds out 30 percent, or a maximum of 10,000 cases, for testing.

```
CREATE MINING STRUCTURE [People4]
(
      [CustID]       LONG       KEY,
      [Name]         TEXT       DISCRETE,
      [Gender]       TEXT       DISCRETE,
      [Age]          LONG       CONTINUOUS,
      [CarMake]      TEXT       DISCRETE,
      [CarModel]     TEXT       DISCRETE
) WITH HOLDOUT(30 PERCENT OR 10000 CASES)
```

Listing 3-4 Structure creation with a testing set holdout

> **NOTE** HOLDOUT selects a random set of cases for testing. You can guarantee that the same rows are selected every time by adding the REPEATABLE(<seed>) clause immediately after the HOLDOUT specification. A non-zero seed will cause the same random number sequence to be generated for each processing instance, resulting in the same rows being selected as long as the data hasn't changed. This is useful when testing your scenario to ensure consistent behavior.

Creating Mining Models

After you have your mining structure set up, you can start to add mining models. A mining model differs from a structure in that columns are marked as to whether they are inputs or outputs, and an algorithm (along with any algorithm-specific parameters) is specified. A model can contain any subset of columns from the structure as long as any table included contains that table's key. That is, the mining structure key must be included, along with the keys of any nested tables.

The simplest way to add a model to a structure is the default, specifying a name and algorithm with no columns, as shown in Listing 3-5. In this case, all columns are considered inputs, so this form is really only useful for clustering type algorithms that don't require a predefined output. (Their default output is a cluster label.)

```
ALTER MINING STRUCTURE [People1]
ADD MINING MODEL [PeopleClusters]
USING Microsoft_Clustering
```

Listing 3-5 Simplest form of Alter Mining Structure

In most cases, however, a column list is required because you must specify which columns are the output columns. In fact, the model in Listing 3-5 would likely be inadequate because it uses the Name column from the structure, which at best wouldn't add any information to the model, and at worst would skew the model in unpredictable ways (for example, if there were too many people named Jane).

The options for specifying whether or not a column is input or output (referred to as the *usage* of the column) are the flags PREDICT and PREDICT_ONLY. Any column with no usage flag is considered to be an input.

Listing 3-6 shows the definition of a decision tree model that predicts gender based on the age of a person and the kind of car that person drives. Note that, in this case, the PREDICT flag indicates that the Gender column is both input and output. For decision trees, this is irrelevant because there is only one column marked as output. This is not true for all algorithms, because the exact usage of the flags is dependent on how the algorithm processes data.

```
ALTER MINING STRUCTURE [People2]
ADD MINING MODEL [PredictGender-Tree]
(
    [CustID],
    [Gender] PREDICT,
    [Age],
    [CarModel]
) USING Microsoft_Decision_Trees
```

Listing 3-6 Predicting gender with trees

As discussed earlier, not all algorithms support all content types. Notably, the Microsoft Naïve Bayes and Microsoft Association Rules algorithms do not support continuous types. This is why Listing 3-3 includes an additional Age column, called AgeDisc, using the DISCRETIZED content type. This is convenient in that it is possible to represent the same column with different content types in the same structure. However, when creating models, you generally want to use consistent column labeling. When adding models to your structure, this is accomplished using *column aliasing,* as shown in Listing 3-7. In this example, the AgeDisc column is used in the model, but it's called Age to be consistent with other models in the structure.

```
ALTER MINING STRUCTURE [People2]
ADD MINING MODEL [PredictGender-Bayes]
(
    [CustID],
    [Gender] PREDICT,
    [AgeDisc] AS [Age],
    [CarModel]
) USING Microsoft_Naive_Bayes
```

Listing 3-7 Aliasing a structure column in a model

Nested Tables

So far, the models described have very simple attributes. In these models, each non-key column represents an attribute, and the PREDICT flag indicates which attributes are considered to be outputs. If you only create models without nested tables, rest at ease. You really don't need to worry much about attributes because, for the most part, columns at the case level turn into case-level attributes. All of this changes with nested tables, however.

Consider the model created in Listing 3-8, which represents the case shown in Figure 3-2.

```
ALTER MINING STRUCTURE [People3]
ADD MINING MODEL [PredictGenderNested-Trees]
(
    [CustID],
    [Gender] PREDICT,
    [Age],
    [Purchases]
    (
        [Product],
        [Quantity],
        [OnSale]
    ),
    [Movie Ratings]
    (
        [Movie],
        [Rating]
    )
) USING Microsoft_Decision_Trees(COMPLEXITY_PENALTY=0.5)
```

Listing 3-8 Adding a model with nested tables

In this model, the case has two case-level attributes: Gender (which is both input and output) and Age (which is an input attribute). After that, the case has Quantity and OnSale attributes for all possible products, and Rating attributes for all possible movies. Looking at *only* the values in the single case of Figure 3-2, this gives you the following attributes:

- Purchases(Milk).Quantity
- Purchases(Milk).OnSale
- Purchases(Bread).Quantity
- Purchases(Bread).OnSale
- Purchases(Coffee).Quantity
- Purchases(Coffee).OnSale
- Movie Ratings(Matrix).Rating
- Movie Ratings(The Truman Show).Rating

Thus, in the two nested tables, *eight* attributes that only consider a single case of data are generated from the five columns. Because the supplemental columns in nested tables contain values of the generated attributes, they are referred to as *value* columns.

So, what's the value of this form of mining model expression? Not only are you able to describe models that leverage both simple and transaction tables, you have a concise language to discuss the model you have created. In Listing 3-8, you can say that you are creating a model to predict a person's gender based on that person's age, plus the quantity of product purchases, whether they were purchased on sale, and how the person has rated a selection of movies. DMX provides you with a clean, discrete method to describe and discuss highly complex modeling scenarios.

> **NOTE** When nested tables are used, the total number of attributes is not known until the model is processed. Having many possible values for the key of a nested table can quickly expand the number of attributes and, therefore, the complexity of the data mining problem. As a general rule of thumb, the more attributes you have, the more cases you need to derive the patterns generated by those attributes.
>
> Most algorithms have parameters limiting the number of attributes they will consider during processing. The algorithms use heuristics to determine the attributes most likely to impact the patterns in the models. All of these algorithms have options that enable you to use all of the available attributes, if you so desire.

If the model shown in Listing 3-8 described all of the possible nested-table scenarios, DMX would be an easier language to deal with. However, it would also be incomplete and incapable of modeling many scenarios that are both important and quite common.

Consider Listing 3-9. There is a single nested table marked PREDICT that contains only the table key. The nested attributes in this situation, from the single case, are Purchases(Milk), Purchases(Bread), and Purchases(Coffee). The values of these attributes are simply Existing if they show up in a case, or Missing if they do not. These attributes are referred to as *valueless attributes* because they do not have a separate table column representing their value. This form of nested tables (that is, without supporting columns) is actually the most common in practice, and is often used for market basket analysis.

```
ALTER MINING STRUCTURE [People3]
ADD MINING MODEL [PredictPurchases-Trees]
(
    [CustID],
    [Gender],
    [Age],
    [Purchases] PREDICT
    (
        [Product]
    )
) USING Microsoft_Decision_Trees
```

Listing 3-9 Existence-only nested tables

NOTE Although the contents of a case theoretically contain all of the `Missing` and `Existing` attributes, the implementation is such that the algorithms are provided only with the nested attributes for which there is a key present in the case. This is a radical departure from other data mining packages that assume that each case is identically large. The Microsoft algorithms have been specially written to handle variable-length cases.

The model in Listing 3-9 can be said to predict product purchases based on a customer's gender, age, and other products purchased. This is because the table column is marked PREDICT instead of PREDICT ONLY. As it is marked, each attribute in the table is both input and output. If the table was marked PREDICT ONLY, the model would predict purchases based solely on gender and age.

It is important to understand that it is the *table* that is marked with the usage flag and not the *key*. Why? This question is one that has caused many heated debates in the halls of SQL Server Data Mining over the years. The reason is that a key can't be predicted. When you predict, you are predicting a value of an attribute, and the key is always the key — Milk is always Milk, no matter how much you would want it to be Wine. However, you *can* predict the rows that make up the nested table; therefore, it is the table that accepts the usage flag.

Complex Nesting Scenarios

If you typically require only a single column in a nested table to handle all of the data mining scenarios you are likely to encounter, you can skip this section, because understanding exactly what attributes are generated by a particular model description gets tricky at this point.

Because of the way usage flags work, it is not immediately obvious when valueless attributes are created. A simplifying assumption was made by the DMX designers that the existence of a nested table row can be imputed by the existence of a value in a non-key nested column. In general, this makes sense — it is unlikely you would have a row for Milk and have a NULL value for Quantity. Therefore, you can reasonably assume that if Purchases(Milk).Quantity exists, then Purchases(Milk) also exists. You can argue that there are scenarios where this assumption is not true, but those are fairly limited compared to the cases where the assumption holds, and the benefit of the simplification greatly outweighs the infrequent instances where it fails.

When this assumption is combined with usage flags and the understanding that columns are not attributes, new realizations appear. For example, although you can infer the existence of Milk from the fact that Quantity exists, what happens when the table is predictable but Quantity is not? Fortunately, DMX models such scenarios quite nicely and cleanly, provided you understand a few simple (but difficult to remember) rules.

Consider the models in Listing 3-10. Model (a) describes a nested table that is an input (no usage flag specified) that contains a predictable column that is also an input (marked PREDICT). This model predicts the quantity of products purchased based on the age and gender, and the quantity of other products purchased. Because the table is an input and includes a value column that is also an input, a valueless attribute is not necessary and is not generated.

```
// (a) PredictQuantity
ALTER MINING STRUCTURE [People3]
ADD MINING MODEL [PredictQuantity]
(
    [CustID],
    [Gender],
    [Age],
    [Purchases]
    (
        [Product],
        [Quantity] PREDICT
    )
) USING Microsoft_Decision_Trees

// (b) PredictOnlyQuantity
ALTER MINING STRUCTURE [People3]
ADD MINING MODEL [PredictOnlyQuantity]
(
    [CustID],
    [Gender],
    [Age],
    [Purchases]
    (
        [Product],
        [Quantity] PREDICT_ONLY
    )
) USING Microsoft_Decision_Trees

// (c) PredictOnlyTable
ALTER MINING STRUCTURE [People3]
ADD MINING MODEL [PredictOnlyTable]
(
    [CustID],
    [Gender],
    [Age],
    [Purchases] PREDICT_ONLY
    (
        [Product],
        [Quantity]
    )
) USING Microsoft_Decision_Trees

// (d) PredictOnlyTableQuantity
ALTER MINING STRUCTURE [People3]
```

Listing 3-10 Various table prediction scenarios

```
ADD MINING MODEL [PredictOnlyTableQuantity]
(
    [CustID],
    [Gender],
    [Age],
    [Purchases] PREDICT_ONLY
    (
        [Product],
        [Quantity] PREDICT_ONLY
    )
) USING Microsoft_Decision_Trees
```

Listing 3-10 (*continued*)

However, in model (b), the quantity is only an output, as specified by the PREDICT_ONLY flag. Yet, the table is still marked as an input. Because there are no value columns that can impute the existence of the row as an input, valueless attributes are created for the nested keys representing those rows. This model predicts the quantity of a product purchased based on age, gender, and the existence of other products in the shopping basket.

Likewise, in model (c), the table is PREDICT_ONLY, yet the quantity is only an input. This model predicts what products are likely to be purchased based on age, gender, and the quantity of other items purchased. Because you can't predict quantity in this case, a valueless attribute must be created for the outputs.

Finally, model (d) matches the table usage flag with the value column's usage flag. This model predicts the quantity of products purchased based only on gender and age. Because there is no discrepancy between the usage flags, valueless attributes are not created in this case.

In summary, valueless attributes are created whenever the usage flags of the table column cannot be matched with the usage flags of any of the value columns in the nested table. Although this is a bit confusing, the flexibility of the nested usage scheme provides users with the ability to model and mine a much wider set of scenarios than was previously possible.

ADDITIONAL MODEL CREATION METHODS

Data mining has existed in SQL Server since SQL Server 2000, but mining structures were introduced in SQL Server 2005. Prior to the advent of mining structures, mining models were created via the CREATE MINING MODEL statement, which is still supported and frequently used. With CREATE MINING MODEL, SQL Server Data Mining automatically creates a compatible mining structure using the name of the model with the suffix _Structure.

(continued)

ADDITIONAL MODEL CREATION METHODS *(continued)*

CREATE MINING MODEL requires all of the information required in CREATE MINING STRUCTURE (that is, the data type and content type), plus any usage and modeling flags that you would specify in ADD MINING MODEL. Although creating a model in this fashion is more limiting than first creating a structure and subsequently adding models, it is used throughout this text to describe a single model in a more concise fashion.

Another way to create a model is to use the SELECT INTO statement. SELECT INTO copies the entire definition of a model up to the USING clause. This is very useful if you want to create many identical models with different parameter sets. Additionally, if the source model is already processed, the target model will be processed as well. Here is a sample SELECT INTO statement:

```
SELECT * INTO [PredictPurchasesCP50]
  FROM [PredictPurchasesTrees]
USING Microsoft_Decision_Trees(COMPLEXITY_PENALTY=0.50)
```

Another option is to create temporary models. Temporary models (known as *session models*) exist until you disconnect from the server, and are then automatically deleted. To create session models, use the syntax CREATE SESSION MINING MODEL.

Filters

Just as a model can use a subset of the columns in a structure, a model can also use a subset of the data by defining filters when adding the model. Cases can be filtered using arbitrary filter clauses that can include case-level and nested-level columns. The contents of nested tables can also be filtered. The columns referenced in the filter are structure columns, and do not need to be part of the model definition.

Listing 3-11 demonstrates three different filtering scenarios. Model (a) predicts a car model based on age and gender only for those customers older than 30. The model in (b) performs the same operation as (a), but selects only customers who have purchased coffee on sale. Finally, model (c) acts on all customers to predict purchases based on other purchases, but considers only the products that weren't on sale.

```
// (a) Case filter
ALTER MINING STRUCTURE [People3]
ADD MINING MODEL [FilterByAge]
(
    [CustID],
    [Gender],
```

Listing 3-11 Filtered mining models

```
        [Age],
        [CarModel] PREDICT
) USING Microsoft_Decision_Trees
WITH FILTER(Age > 30)

// (b) Case filter by nested
ALTER MINING STRUCTURE [People3]
ADD MINING MODEL [FilterByCoffee]
(
        [CustID],
        [Gender],
        [Age],
        [CarModel] PREDICT
) USING Microsoft_Decision_Trees
WITH FILTER(EXISTS(SELECT * FROM Purchases
        WHERE Product='Coffee' AND OnSale))

// (c) Case filter by nested
ALTER MINING STRUCTURE [People3]
ADD MINING MODEL [FilterNested]
(
        [CustID],
        [Gender],
        [Age],
        [Purchases] PREDICT
        (
              [Product]
        ) WITH FILTER(NOT OnSale)
) USING Microsoft_Decision_Trees
```

Listing 3-11 (*continued*)

Because a mining structure maintains a cache of the source data, leveraging filters allows you to maximize your server utilization by arbitrarily selecting limited data sets from the structure. The addition of filters in SQL Server 2008 Data Mining also encourages you to add columns that are not necessary for mining. For example, if you wanted to arbitrarily include or exclude particular product brands or categories, you could add those columns to the nested table of the structure and filter on them when you add models in the future.

Populating Mining Structures

After you have determined what your structure and models look like, populating them with data is a relatively simple matter. Of course, it requires that you have access to the source data and know how to query it, but that's a topic for a different book. This section discusses the DMX side of populating your structures and models with data, and then briefly covers how to access the data after it's inside the data mining server.

Again, to maintain the goal of parity with SQL, the DMX designers chose a syntax familiar to SQL developers: INSERT INTO. In fact, INSERT INTO is sufficient to populate structures and models without modification. For example, Listing 3-12 populates the mining structure in Listing 3-1. DMX accesses external data through a named data source that was previously created (see the "About Data Sources" sidebar) using an OPENQUERY statement. The query inside OPENQUERY is in whatever syntax is supported by the data source (SQL in this case), and the columns are matched by order.

```
INSERT INTO MINING STRUCTURE [People1]
([CustID], [Name], [Gender], [Age], [CarMake],[CarModel])
OPENQUERY(Chapter3Data,
   'SELECT [Key], Name, Gender, Age, CarMake, CarModel
   FROM People')
```

Listing 3-12 Basic INSERT INTO statement

When INSERT INTO is executed, SQL Server Analysis Services reads the source data into a cache. DMX coerces source data types into the data types specified in the mining structure. For example, because DMX supports only very basic types such as LONG and DOUBLE, SQL types such as I2 and FLOAT are simply converted. If the data in the source column cannot be converted, the processing will fail. After the cache is processed, any mining models in the structure are then processed from the cache. Therefore, many models can be processed while only reading the source data once! Additionally, if you have the Enterprise Edition of SQL Server, all models are processed in parallel (in addition to any built-in parallelism of the algorithms).

ABOUT DATA SOURCES

Data sources are required for most data mining scenarios, but, unfortunately, DMX does not contain any language constructs for creating data sources. Typically, data sources are created in Business Intelligence Development Studio (BI Dev Studio) or a similar tool, or by using XML for Analysis directly. To make executing the examples in this and other chapters easier and to assist you in managing data services, sample stored procedures are included on this book's website (www.wiley.com/go/data_mining_SQL_2008). The following query will create the data source used in the query in Listing 3-12:

```
CALL ASSprocs.CreateDataSource('Chapter3Data',
     'Provider=SQLNCLI10.1;Data Source=localhost;
     Integrated Security=SSPI;Initial Catalog=Chapter3',
     'ImpersonateCurrentUser','','')
```

(continued)

> **ABOUT DATA SOURCES** *(continued)*
>
> Prior to calling the stored procedure, you first must deploy the stored procedure assembly to the server. You can find instructions on how to do this in the readme file included with the assembly.

Even with the simplest form of INSERT INTO, you need to be aware of some special cases. For example, if you add models to the structure after processing, you can call INSERT INTO on each specific model without any query to process those models. Alternatively, you can call INSERT INTO yet again on the mining structure with no source query, and SQL Server Data Mining will do whatever is necessary to ensure that the structure is fully processed — that is, it will process any unprocessed models it contains.

NOTE A convenient column to add to any structure is a random number that enables you to create models on any arbitrary subset of the cases. However, if you use the SQL RANDOM function, it is evaluated once per query, and returns the same value for each row — not very helpful. Luckily, the NEWID function returns a statistically random GUID (globally unique identifier) for each row. For example, when the following query fragment is inserted into a SQL query, it returns a random value from 0 to 0.999 for each row:

```
CAST((ABS(CHECKSUM(NEWID())) % 1000) AS FLOAT)/1000 AS [Random]
```

To use this technique, add a suitably named (for example, Random) DOUBLE column to your mining structure and populate it using the previous query fragment. Finally, you can filter models or even arbitrary selection queries on the Random column. Note that you will get a different sequence of random values every time you populate your structure this way, but that's what you asked for!

Populating Nested Tables

Of course, everything is simple until you consider nested tables. Actually, nested tables aren't that difficult either. The only tricky part is in shaping the source data — which typically comes from flat tables — to the nested representation required by the mining structure.

DMX uses a subset of the SHAPE syntax that was first implemented by the Data Shaping Service for OLE DB to create hierarchical rowsets. The basic form of SHAPE as supported by DMX is as follows:

```
SHAPE { <rowset> }
APPEND ( { <rowset> } RELATE <master> TO <child> ) AS <alias>
```

This statement takes the first rowset and adds a column (given the name specified with the alias) that contains the results of the second rowset. The association of rows between the rowsets is accomplished with the RELATE directive, which specifies a mapping from a column in the outer rowset to a foreign key column in the nested rowset. The SHAPE syntax allows you to arbitrarily append as many rowsets as you wish — simply keep adding more rowset definitions.

The implementation of SHAPE in SQL Server Data Mining requires that all rowsets be ordered by the columns used to relate them. This is to ensure performance and scalability because, in the vast majority of cases, the data provider is more efficient at sorting data at the source than Analysis Services would be at the destination. This introduces a somewhat artificial limitation preventing the inclusion of nested rowsets that use different foreign keys, but this scenario rarely occurs if your case set is constructed correctly. Listing 3-13 shows how to use INSERT INTO to populate the mining structure of Listing 3-3 and illustrates interesting properties.

```
INSERT INTO MINING STRUCTURE [People3]
([CustID], [Name], [Gender], [Age], [AgeDisc], [CarMake], [CarModel]
 ,[Purchases](SKIP, [Product], [Quantity], [OnSale])
 ,[Movie Ratings](SKIP, [Movie], [Rating])
)
SHAPE   // Case Table
     { OPENQUERY( Chapter3Data,
        'SELECT [Key], Name, Gender, Age, Age, CarMake, CarModel
          FROM People ORDER BY [Key]')
     }
APPEND  // Purchases Nested Table
     ({ OPENQUERY( Chapter3Data,
        'SELECT CustID, Product, Quantity, [On Sale]
          FROM Purchases ORDER BY CustID')
     } RELATE [Key] TO [CustID]
     ) AS Purchases
 ,       // Movie Ratings Nested Table
     ({ OPENQUERY( Chapter3Data,
        'SELECT CustID, Movie, Rating
          FROM MovieRatings ORDER BY CustID')
     } RELATE [Key] TO [CustID]
     ) AS MovieRatings
```

Listing 3-13 Nested INSERT INTO

One of the artifacts of using SHAPE is that each of the nested tables in the input set contains a column representing the foreign key to the case table. However, this column is not present in the mining structure.

To accommodate this requirement of SHAPE, the keyword SKIP was introduced to indicate columns that exist in the source data that will not be used to populate the structure. Although SKIP was introduced expressly for this purpose, it can be used to ignore any column that you don't want to use from the source. Looking at the example in Listing 3-13, this may seem arbitrary. However, there may be cases where you do not have control over the set of columns that are returned (such as a web service call) and do not require all the columns for your mining scenario.

As with a relational INSERT INTO statement, bindings from the data columns to the mining structure column are done by order, not by name. In Listing 3-13, notice that two columns of the structure (Age and AgeDisc) are populated by a single column in the relational source. In order to accomplish this, the column is repeated in the source data query.

NOTE In addition to OPENQUERY and SHAPE, you can use other DMX queries, Multidimensional Expressions (MDX) queries, stored procedure calls, and even rowset parameters as the source data query for INSERT INTO. Using DMX queries allows you to mine the results of previous mining tasks, and using MDX allows you to mine ad hoc OLAP queries. The use of rowset parameters is explained in Chapter 16.

Querying Structure Data

After a structure is processed, you can query the structure to see what the cases of the structure look like. This is generally a good idea (particularly with nested tables) to ensure that you are inserting the data you expect into your structure. Listing 3-14 shows three varieties of the statement you use to access the data in your structure.

```
// (a) Select all cases
SELECT * FROM MINING STRUCTURE People3.CASES

// (b) Select cases as a flat rowset
SELECT FLATTENED * FROM MINING STRUCTURE People3.CASES

// (c) Select only test cases
SELECT * FROM MINING STRUCTURE People3.CASES WHERE IsTestCase()
```

Listing 3-14 Selecting structure cases

Querying Model Data

As with the structure, you can select the data from a model — with some caveats as well as additional features.

First of all, you can only select the cases from models that support *drill-through*. Drill-through is an option that is specified in model creation after the USING clause. It is available only on models built with algorithms that support the drill-through operation. Additionally, you can see only the cases that the model can see. That is, if there is a filter on the model, you will see only the cases that meet the criteria specified in the filter. Finally, by default, you will see only the columns that were used with the models — although there is a way to get the additional columns.

Despite the limitations on seeing the cases, the additional features available in querying model data far outweigh any limitations. On the simple side, you can query the contents of a column to see discrete values or ranges of continuous values used in those columns. You can also directly query the model content to explore the patterns in the data discovered by the algorithms. And, if you have drill-through enabled, you can see how cases from the training data back up the patterns that were found.

Listing 3-15 demonstrates the creation and training of a model with drill-through enabled, the determination of the contents of both discrete and continuous columns, the selection of model content, and a drill-through to a cluster. Figure 3-4 displays some of the information available in the model content.

```
// (a) Create model with drillthrough
ALTER MINING STRUCTURE People3
ADD MINING MODEL ClusterDrillthrough
(
    [CustID],
    [Gender],
    [Age]
) USING Microsoft_Clustering
WITH DRILLTHROUGH

// (b) Populate the new model
INSERT INTO ClusterDrillthrough

// (c) Get possible distinct values
SELECT DISTINCT Gender FROM ClusterDrillthrough

// (d) Get range of continuous or discretized values
SELECT DISTINCT RangeMin(Age), Age, RangeMax(Age)
FROM ClusterDrillthrough

// (e) Get the patterns found in the model
SELECT * FROM ClusterDrillthrough.CONTENT

// (f) Get cases in cluster 1
SELECT * FROM ClusterDrillthrough.CASES WHERE IsInNode('001')
```

Listing 3-15 Creation of a model with drill-through and data selection

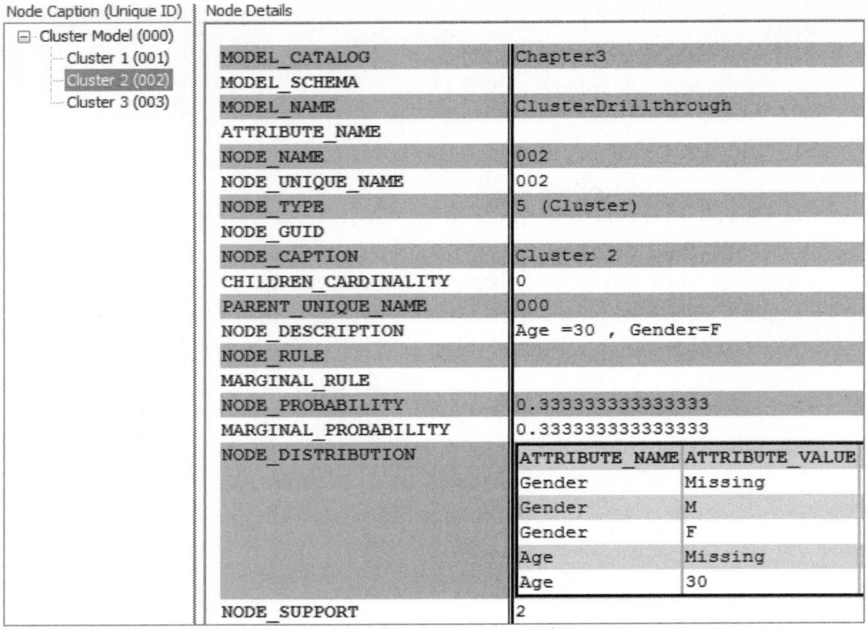

Node Caption (Unique ID) | Node Details

- ⊟ Cluster Model (000)
  - Cluster 1 (001)
  - Cluster 2 (002)
  - Cluster 3 (003)

MODEL_CATALOG	Chapter3	
MODEL_SCHEMA		
MODEL_NAME	ClusterDrillthrough	
ATTRIBUTE_NAME		
NODE_NAME	002	
NODE_UNIQUE_NAME	002	
NODE_TYPE	5 (Cluster)	
NODE_GUID		
NODE_CAPTION	Cluster 2	
CHILDREN_CARDINALITY	0	
PARENT_UNIQUE_NAME	000	
NODE_DESCRIPTION	Age =30 , Gender=F	
NODE_RULE		
MARGINAL_RULE		
NODE_PROBABILITY	0.333333333333333	
MARGINAL_PROBABILITY	0.333333333333333	
NODE_DISTRIBUTION	ATTRIBUTE_NAME	ATTRIBUTE_VALUE
	Gender	Missing
	Gender	M
	Gender	F
	Age	Missing
	Age	30
NODE_SUPPORT	2	

Figure 3-4 Representation of sample model content

ADDITIONAL MANAGEMENT STATEMENTS

DMX also has a variety of statements that you can use to manage your structures and models. They are listed here for your awareness and reference. These statements are straightforward and are detailed in Books Online, so they will not be discussed in detail here.

```
// Rename structure or model
RENAME MINING STRUCTURE People1 TO People

// Clear the cache of cases from a structure
DELETE FROM MINING STRUCTURE People.CASES

// Clear everything (cases and model patterns) from a structure
DELETE FROM MINING STRUCTURE People

// Export structures or models to a file
EXPORT MINING STRUCTURE People2 TO 'C:\temp\People2.abf'
WITH PASSWORD='People2'

// Drop (delete) a structure or model
```

(continued)

Prediction

Prediction in DMX is somewhat loosely defined. In general, *prediction* means applying the patterns that were found in the data to estimate unknown information. Examples of prediction might be predicting if a customer will or will not be good for a loan, estimating a credit score, determining to what cluster a case belongs, determining the likelihood of customers canceling their service, producing a recommended list of products, or predicting future values of a time series.

The actual information that is predicted by a data mining algorithm depends on the capabilities of that algorithm and how your model is defined. The prediction process is often the final goal in any data mining scenario, providing the ultimate benefit of data collection and machine learning, and can drastically change how business is performed. For example, a case study where a SQL Server Data Mining solution was implemented to do product recommendations resulted in a 100-percent increase in sales over the previous "expert" recommendations.

DMX simplifies all these possibilities by using a consistent metaphor for prediction. DMX prediction can be performed in a wide variety of scenarios. Of course, as with traditional data mining systems, predictions can be done in a batch mode with the prediction results being stored in a relational database or some other destination. However, because predictions are efficient, it can also be done in real-time, interactive scenarios.

For example, online advertisers can use customer information plus current web-browsing behavior to predict the most effective advertisement to display while the user clicks through a website. Experiments performed by the SQL Server Data Mining team have shown the capacity to perform more than a billion real-time predictions per day using very complex models handling hundreds of thousands of attributes. DMX encapsulated the entire prediction metaphor using the same constructs, regardless of the type of prediction you require, with only minor variations needed for the particular scenario at hand.

Prediction Join

Assume for a moment that you have a table with a set of columns, such as customer ID, age, first name, and last name, and another table with age, first name, and last name, and street address. If you wanted to determine the street address for each customer ID, you would perform a relational join between the tables on the age and name columns. Performing a prediction leverages this metaphor between data and a mining model. If you stretch your imagination just a bit, you can consider a mining model to be a table that contains all possible combinations of the input and output variables. If you had such a table, determining a predicted result would be a simple lookup (or join) from your source data to this theoretical table.

This metaphor is shown in Figure 3-5. The figure shows that the first customer, being male and 25, would be most likely to purchase a Chevrolet. Of course, a model does not actually contain such a table. Such a table would be impractical at best (considering the number of possible combinations given nested tables), and impossible in any case (considering continuous columns). Models actually contain the patterns learned from the data in the most concise format possible, allowing for quick prediction execution. For example, a decision tree model would have simple predicates to follow, such as "if the customer is male and age 25, then the likely auto choice is Chevrolet."

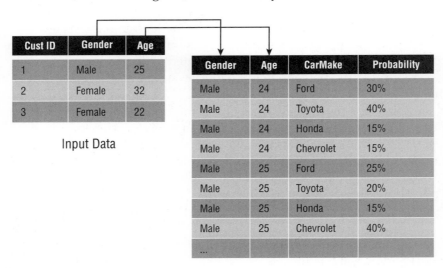

Figure 3-5 Theoretical prediction join

Prediction Query Syntax

As you may have guessed, the DMX query syntax is designed as much as possible to be analogous to SQL query syntax. This approach makes it extremely easy to generate predictive results that can be used in a wide variety of scenarios, from real-time analytics to reporting and more, and occasionally leads to some frustrations, because it looks like SQL and smells like SQL, yet it isn't a full SQL processor and lacks many SQL features. In any case, the flexibility of DMX prediction so dramatically exceeds the scripting languages used by traditional data mining offerings that it allows the integration of data mining into previously unforeseen scenarios.

The complete prediction query syntax is as follows:

```
SELECT [TOP <count>] <column references> FROM <mining model>
[[NATURAL] PREDICTION JOIN
<source-data>
[ ON <mapping clause> ]
[ WHERE <condition clause> ]
[ ORDER BY <order clause> [DESC | ASC] ]]
```

On the surface, the prediction syntax is very simple and straightforward, and for many cases, it is. DMX syntax only grows complex as you add some of the interesting possibilities in the list of column references, such as table returning functions.

For example, look at the basic batch prediction statement in Listing 3-16. This statement applies the model PredictGender-Bayes to each row returned from the specified query, and returns the name from the query and the most likely value for gender based on the Age and CarModel inputs.

```
SELECT t.[Name], Predict([Gender]) AS PredictedGender
FROM [PredictGender-Bayes]
PREDICTION JOIN
OPENQUERY(Chapter3Data,
          'SELECT [Key], [Name], [Age], [CarModel]
          FROM [NewPeople]') AS t
ON [PredictGender-Bayes].[Age]      = t.[Age] AND
   [PredictGender-Bayes].[CarModel] = t.[CarModel]
```

Listing 3-16 Basic prediction query

The details of what occurs during prediction are determined by the algorithm. One rule that is consistent across any algorithm implementation and enforced by DMX is that you can include in your column list any columns from the source data, but only *output* columns (that is, columns labeled PREDICT or PREDICT_ONLY) from the model can be predicted.

Nested Source Data

Nested source data is described in the same fashion as it is with INSERT INTO. However, because joins are bound by column name rather than column order, additional constructs are required for the ON clause. DMX resolves this by requiring a fully qualified descriptor for all the column names in the mapping, as shown in Listing 3-17.

```
SELECT t.[Name], Predict([Gender]) AS PredictedGender
FROM [PredictGenderNested-Trees]
PREDICTION JOIN
SHAPE
    { OPENQUERY( Chapter3Data,
      'SELECT [Key], Name, Age
        FROM NewPeople ORDER BY [Key]')
    }
APPEND
    ({ OPENQUERY( Chapter3Data,
      'SELECT CustID, Product, Quantity, [On Sale]
        FROM NewPeoplePurchases ORDER BY CustID')
     } RELATE [Key] TO [CustID]
    ) AS Purchases
AS t
ON [PredictGenderNested-Trees].Age = t.Age AND
   [PredictGenderNested-Trees].Purchases.Product
        = t.Purchases.Product AND
   [PredictGenderNested-Trees].Purchases.Quantity
        = t.Purchases.Quantity AND
   [PredictGenderNested-Trees].Purchases.OnSale
        = t.Purchases.[On Sale]
```

Listing 3-17 Basic nested prediction query

An interesting aspect demonstrated by this query is that not all inputs as described by the model need to be supplied from the source data. The definition of the model (in Listing 3-8) has an additional nested table called `Movie Ratings` that is not included in the query in Listing 3-17. Any inputs not provided in the source query during prediction are considered `Missing`, and it is up to the individual algorithm to determine exactly how missing data is treated. In general, any algorithm that supports nested tables will also support missing data because it is unlikely that every case will contain all attributes in such circumstances.

Real-Time Prediction

Real-time prediction is when you have an application that uses a model to perform predictions on-the-fly based on data in memory (such as user entry). DMX uses a special form of prediction query called a *singleton query* for real-time prediction. A singleton query contains the source data directly in the text of the query itself, as shown in Listing 3-18. The input is defined by using a SELECT clause and specifying the exact values of each input. In applications, these values are typically specified using parameters (discussed in Chapter 16). Nested rows are grouped together using parentheses and the UNION keyword.

```
// (a) Flat
SELECT Predict([Gender]) AS PredictedGender
FROM [PredictGender-Bayes]
NATURAL PREDICTION JOIN
(SELECT 35 AS Age, 'BMW' AS CarModel) AS t

// (b) Nested
SELECT Predict([Gender]) AS PredictedGender
FROM [PredictGenderNested-Trees]
NATURAL PREDICTION JOIN
(SELECT 35 AS Age,
  (SELECT 'Coffee' AS Product, 2 AS Quantity UNION
   SELECT 'Milk' AS Product, 1 AS Quantity UNION
   SELECT 'Bread' AS Product, 2 AS Quantity)
  AS Purchases) AS t
```

Listing 3-18 Singleton query

Another DMX feature demonstrated in Listing 3-18 is the *natural prediction join*. A natural prediction join matches columns in the source data that have the same name as input columns of the model. Because the input data is explicitly specified in a singleton query, it is convenient to use the same names as model columns. A natural prediction join can be used against any source data input if care is taken to ensure that the names are the same.

NOTE Many users avoid using NATURAL PREDICTION JOIN against arbitrary source data queries because DMX returns no error when columns are not mapped. Using an explicit ON clause guarantees that all of the inputs are mapped and will return errors if referred columns are not present in the data.

Degenerate Predictions

If you have no source data, you can still predict against a model. Predictions performed with no source data are semantically equivalent to prediction with a single row when all inputs are Missing, although each algorithm is free to return whatever results it deems appropriate. Typically, algorithms will return the most likely value for all the population. For example, if 55 percent of your customers were female, the degenerate prediction for gender would be 'female'. A degenerate prediction query has no prediction join clause.

NOTE PREDICTION JOIN accepts a variety of source data, including DMX, MDX, stored procedures, and rowset parameters.

Prediction Functions

DMX provides a variety of functions to support prediction scenarios. The basic function, `Predict`, is polymorphic and the behavior is dependent on whether you supply a scalar (case-level) or table column reference. In many cases, if all you want is to predict the value of a case-level column, you don't need to use `Predict` at all. The act of selecting a predictable column is identical to predicting it — that is, `SELECT [Gender]` is equivalent to `SELECT Predict([Gender])` as long as `Gender` is a predictable column. Additional functions provide supplementary information about the prediction, such as the support, probability (likelihood), or the part of the model that was used to generate the prediction.

`PredictHistogram` is the most comprehensive prediction function for case-level columns. `PredictHistogram` returns a table containing all information available about the prediction of a scalar column. For example, Listing 3-19 shows a call to `PredictHistogram` and Figure 3-6 shows the results.

```
SELECT 'Histogram' AS Label,
       PredictHistogram(CarModel) AS Hist
FROM FilterByAge
```

Listing 3-19 PredictHistogram

Label	Hist
Histogram +	

CarModel	$SUPPORT	$PROBABILITY	$ADJUSTEDPROBABILITY	$VARIANCE	$STDEV
Eclipse	1	0.18333	0.0359	0	0
CRV	1	0.18333	0.0359	0	0
Mustang	1	0.18333	0.0359	0	0
23	1	0.18333	0.0359	0	0
Escort	0	0.13333	0.1333	0	0
	0	0.13333	0.1333	0	0

Figure 3-6 PredictHistogram results

The query contains the label only to demonstrate having both case and nested results in a query. The results of `PredictHistogram` for a categorical (discrete) column are all of the possible states of that column with their associated statistics based on the model's prediction of the value. Following are the columns that are returned:

- `<Target>` — The predicted value.
- `$Support` — How many cases support this fact.

- $Probability — The computed probability of a categorical output. For continuous values, the probability represents the likelihood of a value being present.

- $AdjustedProbability — A modified probability used to boost the likelihood of rare events, frequently used for predicting nested tables.

- $Variance — The variance of a continuous prediction; 0 for categorical predictions.

- $Stdev — The standard deviation of a continuous prediction; 0 for categorical predictions.

What's fascinating about DMX is that when you're dealing with functions such as PredictHistogram that return tables, you can select rows from them like any other table. Consider the queries in Listing 3-20. Query (a) selects all the states of CarModel that have non-zero support. This query also uses the FLATTENED keyword to return a flat rowset rather than a hierarchical rowset. The resulting rowset will have every case-level value copied for every row of the nested table. Query (b) returns the probability associated with the value 'CRV'. Finally, query (c) uses the TopCount function to return the top row of the histogram based on probability, and returns the value for CarModel and the associated probability. DMX doesn't allow TOP and ORDER BY clauses in subselects, so the functions TopCount and BottomCount substitute for this functionality.

```
// (a)
SELECT FLATTENED
    (SELECT CarModel
     FROM PredictHistogram(CarModel)
     WHERE $SUPPORT > 0)
FROM FilterByAge

// (b)
SELECT FLATTENED
    (SELECT $Probability
     FROM PredictHistogram(CarModel)
     WHERE CarModel='CRV')
FROM FilterByAge

// (c)
SELECT FLATTENED
    (SELECT CarModel, $Probability
     FROM TopCount(PredictHistogram(CarModel), $Probability, 1))
FROM FilterByAge
```

Listing 3-20 Subselects

The main operation in query (c) of Listing 3-20 is essentially the same as the Predict function itself — that is, to return the value with the highest probability. Because returning values such as the probability and support are quite common, DMX also has functions that act as shortcuts for these types of queries. The functions PredictProbability, PredictSupport, PredictAdjustedProbability, PredictVariance, and PredictStdev all return their respective values from the most likely row of the PredictHistogram rowset without requiring messy subselect syntax.

All of these functions also allow you to extract the appropriate value for any row of the histogram. This is useful if you must determine the probability of a state, regardless of whether it is the most common state or not. A scenario where this is required is when data is imbalanced such that one state is always predicted. In these cases, it is common that you will consider a true result when the probability is above a particular threshold, despite not being the majority state.

An example is fraud detection. You can determine that fraud is true if, say, it has 10-percent likelihood rather than 50-percent. Using the flexibility of DMX, you can express this simply, as demonstrated in Listing 3-21. This query selects a Boolean expression based on the probability of a particular state, rather than the value itself. The other histogram-based functions can be called in a similar method.

```
SELECT (PredictProbability(Gender, 'Female') > 0.20) AS IsFemale
FROM [PredictGender-Bayes]
```

Listing 3-21 Predicting the non-majority state

NOTE The Predict function assumes that you want a value returned from a query. That is, it assumes that if you are trying to predict 'Age', you actually want a number returned. In some cases, it may be pertinent to your scenario to return NULL values. For example, if you are predicting if people omitted their age, the syntax Predict('Age', INCLUDE_NULL) will return an age if the algorithm determines that an age is likely to be returned. Otherwise, if the algorithm determines it is more likely that this customer skipped that question, it will return NULL.

A reference of all DMX functions supported by SQL Server Data Mining appears in Appendix B.

PredictNodeID

PredictNodeID is a special DMX function that returns an identifier of a node from the model's content used to perform a prediction that can subsequently be used to extract information about that node. This allows you to predict a value, and then determine the reason the model returned the value that it did. Some algorithms such as decision trees have very discrete nodes used for a prediction, whereas other algorithms such as clustering may use several nodes in a single prediction. In the latter case, the model returns what is considered the most influential node for the prediction.

External and User-Defined Functions

DMX also allows the calling of functions defined in stored procedures and, if Microsoft Office is installed on the server machine, select functions from Excel or Visual Basic for Applications (VBA). Excel and VBA functions supported in DMX are listed in Appendix B. The syntax for calling such functions is as follows:

```
SELECT VBA![Log](PredictProbability(Gender)) AS NaturalLog,
        Excel![Log](PredictProbability(Gender)) AS Log10
FROM [PredictGender-Bayes]
```

Predictions on Nested Tables

By far, the most common scenario for prediction with nested tables is a *recommendation engine*. A recommendation engine offers recommended items based on past purchases, the contents of a shopping basket, or merely properties of a customer. Earlier in this chapter, you learned how these models are created by having a predictable nested table with valueless attributes. This section discusses how to perform recommendation-style predictions and other types of predictions when dealing with nested tables.

Recommendation predictions are performed with the PredictAssociation function. The PredictAssociation function takes a predictable nested table and returns a ranked list of results. Consider the queries in Listing 3-22. Query (a) simply returns the top three items based on the default measure, probability. Query (b) is the same, but it uses adjusted probability to rank the items.

```
// (a) Top 3 items
SELECT PredictAssociation(Purchases, 3)
FROM [PredictPurchases-Trees]

// (b) Top 3 items by adjusted probability
SELECT PredictAssociation(Purchases,3,$AdjustedProbability)
FROM [PredictPurchases-Trees]

// (c) all values with 40% probability
SELECT (SELECT * FROM
```

Listing 3-22 PredictAssociation

```
              PredictAssociation(Purchases,
                  INCLUDE_NODE_ID, INCLUDE_STATISTICS)
              WHERE $Probability > 0.40)
   FROM [PredictPurchases-Trees]
```

Listing 3-22 (*continued*)

Adjusted probability is useful in associative predictions because it penalizes items that are too popular in favor of less-popular items. Take an example where 90 percent of your customers buy milk, but for a particular customer, the engine recommends milk with 80-percent likelihood. This is likely still higher than the probability of any other item that could be recommended. However, the engine is actually telling you that, for this customer, the chance of the customer wanting milk is *less* than average. Adjusted probability takes these factors into account and often provides better recommendations than using raw probabilities.

Query (c) in Listing 3-22 is interesting in that it doesn't return an ordered list; instead it returns all items that are recommended with a probability of 40 percent or greater. It also returns the statistics and node ID of the prediction for each item that is returned as indicated by INCLUDE_NODE_ID and INCLUDE_STATISTICS flags.

Predicting Nested Value Columns

Predicting the values of columns in nested tables (rather than the contents of the tables themselves) is a relatively rare scenario, but it's extremely useful when required. For example, imagine a scenario where you need to track the temperature at all thermostats in a building. Your case in this situation would be the time at which measurements were taken, and it would contain a nested table containing each thermostat and that thermostat's current reading. Your prediction task would be to predict the temperature of a particular thermostat given the readings of the other thermostats. This operation requires predicting value columns in a nested table.

Predicting nested value columns, as you would guess, requires more subselect syntax. Given that a value column in a nested table has all of the properties of a case-level column, all of the same case-level prediction functions apply in the nested scenario. This can lead to some complicated-looking, but actually very understandable, queries that can even have multiple levels of nesting involved.

Consider Listing 3-23. Query (a) is a simple query that returns the predicted quantity for each product, assuming each product is purchased. Query (b) returns a list of all products with a predicted quantity of greater than 2. Query (c) returns all the possible products for each case and, in a doubly nested table, returns the probability that the product will *not* be purchased. Finally, query (d) simplifies query (c) by using a scalar function instead of the table-returning `PredictHistogram`, and returns the predicted quantity of all products that are likely to be recommended with a probability of at least 30 percent, phrased in the query as determining that the likelihood of it *not* being recommended is less than 70 percent.

```
// (a)
SELECT (SELECT Product,
               Predict(Quantity)
        FROM Purchases)
FROM PredictOnlyTableQuantity

// (b)
SELECT (SELECT Product
        FROM Purchases
        WHERE Predict(Quantity) > 2)
FROM PredictOnlyTableQuantity

//(c)
SELECT (SELECT Product,
               (SELECT $Probability
                FROM PredictHistogram(Quantity)
                WHERE Quantity=NULL)
        FROM Purchases)
FROM PredictOnlyTableQuantity

// (d)
SELECT (SELECT Product,
               Predict(Quantity)
        FROM Purchases
        WHERE PredictProbability(Quantity, NULL) < 0.7)
FROM PredictOnlyTableQuantity
```

Listing 3-23 Nested value prediction

Summary

The basic concepts you need in order to understand a mining scenario are cases, attributes, and states. How you arrange these concepts into mining structures and set the appropriate flags representing the inputs and outputs is critical to the success of any data mining project. Often, creative license must be taken with the data to extract a set of attributes that will be useful to develop insightful patterns, and you should feel encouraged to experiment.

DMX provides an environment that simplifies such experimentation by providing a clear and concise syntax for describing and discussing data mining scenarios. The concepts covered in this chapter provide you with the tools you need to be successful in implementing a data mining solution from start to finish. Understanding the capabilities and leveraging the nuances of DMX creation, training, and prediction will accelerate your ability to develop predictive solutions.

The next two chapters describe tools used to implement the data mining process through rich user interfaces. Chapter 4 explains the Data Mining Client for Excel 2007, which encapsulates the process in the familiar Excel interface. Chapter 5 shows how to use the tools included with SQL Server 2008 to do the same.

Using SQL Server Data Mining

This chapter reviews the Analysis Services toolset and provides techniques to effectively create and analyze mining models. Before reading this chapter, you should be familiar with the model-building concepts introduced in Chapter 3. In particular, you should understand the concepts of mining structures, mining models, mining model columns, and case and nested tables.

This chapter is designed to help novice users get started, as well as provide experienced users with techniques that will help them get the most out of the toolset. This is not meant to be a substitute or a replacement for the excellent documentation and tutorials found in the product documentation. Rather, it describes and applies the general tools provided with Analysis Services specifically for data mining purposes.

This chapter describes features of Analysis Services through the user interface, and provides step-by-step instructions for creating a set of mining models for illustrative purposes. Feel free to deviate from these instructions and explore the concepts introduced in the chapter. If you stray too far, starting over is not difficult, or you can always pick up the completed project file contained in `Chapter4.zip` on this book's companion website (`www.wiley.com/go/data_mining_SQL_2008`) for examination.

We will be using the `MovieClick` database to exemplify tool usage. This database is described in Appendix A.

This chapter covers the following topics:

- Using the Business Intelligence Development Studio (BI Dev Studio)
- Understanding Immediate mode and Offline mode

- Creating and modifying data sources, data source views, and data mining objects
- Exploring data and evaluating models

Introducing the Business Intelligence Development Studio

Most of your time using SQL Server Data Mining will be spent in BI Dev Studio. This environment is integrated into the Microsoft Visual Studio (VS) shell to provide a complete development experience for business intelligence operations. A data mining project is part of a collection of projects known as a *solution*. Additional projects required for your application can be grouped together into this cohesive solution.

For example, a database administrator (DBA) might create an Integration Services project to pull the data out of your online transaction processing (OLTP) system and transform it into a form suitable for data mining. An analyst could create an Analysis Services project containing models that explored and examined the transaction data. Finally, a developer could create a web service and a website, embedding these models in an end-user application and commercializable service.

All of these projects can be contained inside a single solution that encompasses the entire body of the collaborative work. Furthermore, all aspects of the work can be captured with complete version histories in the source control system.

Understanding the User Interface

BI Dev Studio is designed primarily for developers, with an unstructured approach to solution implementation — which is very different from traditional data mining tools. This approach, along with the added complexity from the fully featured development environment, can be daunting to those familiar with other data mining toolsets. However, after you get past the initial shock of dealing with the myriad of options and windows inherent in VS, creating and analyzing models is fairly simple.

The first step in familiarizing yourself with BI Dev Studio is to understand which of the various parts of the user interface are interesting, and what they are used for. Figure 4-1 shows a typical window layout for BI Dev Studio with elements of interest called out.

Window Tabs   BI Menus   Designer Tabs   Solution Explorer

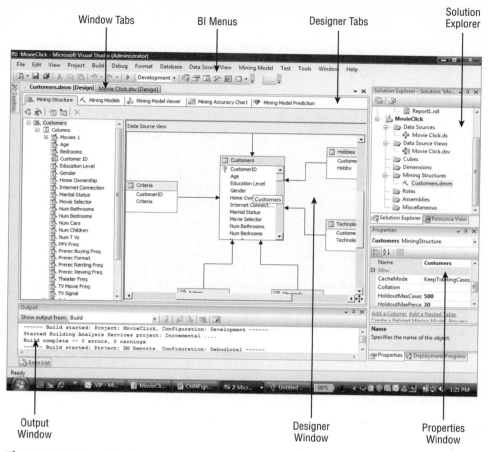

Figure 4-1 BI Dev Studio

Output Window   Designer Window   Properties Window

Following are the most important parts of BI Dev Studio:

- **Solution Explorer** — This is where you manage your solution and projects. All objects are created and managed here. To add objects to your project, you right-click the project name and select Add New Item. Alternately, you can right-click a particular folder and select New. Doing so will launch a dialog box or wizard, allowing you to create the specified object.

- **Window tabs** — These tabs allow you to quickly switch between designer windows. A tab will be displayed for each object or file that is currently open. If more objects are open than can appear in the tab area, you can access additional windows using the down arrow to the right of the tabs.

- **Designer window** — This is where you edit and analyze your objects. Creating a new object or double-clicking an object in Solution Explorer will open that object's specific designer, allowing you to modify and interact with the object.

- **Designer tabs** — Many objects have different aspects that you can edit or interact with. These aspects are indicated by tabs within the Designer window.

- **Properties window** — This is a context-sensitive window that displays properties for the currently selected item, which is a general concept in VS and applies to any type of operation performed within the studio. For example, selecting an object in Solution Explorer causes properties of that object (such as object ID, filename, and so forth) to be displayed. Selecting a column in the Data Mining Designer window causes column properties (such as name and data type) to be displayed. When an item with no properties is selected, the Properties window will be empty.

- **BI menus** — The area on the main menu bar between the Debug menu and the Tools menu is where you will find context-sensitive menus specific to Analysis Services objects. For example, opening the data source view (DSV) editor will cause formatting and data source view (DSV) menus to appear in that area.

- **Output window** — The Output window displays messages when you build and deploy projects. If there are errors in your project, this is where you will find their descriptions.

NOTE To make the environment more suitable for your data mining use, you can reorganize the workspace as you see fit. Clicking and dragging the title bar of any window displays floating icons that will help you float or dock the window. You can even stack these windows on top of each other, causing selectable tabs to appear beneath the windows.

As you experiment with different options in the studio, additional windows may appear. You can always close the windows you are no longer interested in — don't worry, if you need them, they are always available from the View menu. If you want the windows to be readily available, but you're running short on screen space, you can click the pushpin icon on the window's title bar, and the window will slide out of sight when not in use.

Offline Mode and Immediate Mode

BI Dev Studio works in two operating modes. The mode you use is sometimes based on personal preference, and sometimes on necessity. Each mode has its advantages and drawbacks, and it is important to understand the differences between them when working with BI Dev Studio.

Immediate Mode

Working in Immediate mode is generally a more natural experience for data mining users. When you work in Immediate mode, you are connected directly and continually to an Analysis Services server. When you open an object (such as a mining structure), you are opening the object from the server as you would expect. When you change the object and save it, the object is immediately changed on the server. In Immediate mode, your BI Dev Studio project is a link to a database on your server. In Solution Explorer, you see all objects that are currently in that database. If you close and reopen this project, you automatically reconnect to the database. If objects on the database have changed since the last time you opened the project, those changes are present when you open it again.

Although this mode is very intuitive and easy to understand, you should take some factors into consideration during use. Most importantly, it is truly *immediate*. If you have a working model in production, and you modify and save that model, it is instantly changed and becomes unprocessed, causing any queries against that model to fail. Additionally, other users can modify objects while you have them open. You see a warning when you try to save an object if it has been modified. Saving then overwrites any changes that other users have made. Changes to objects on the server are reflected in your project only when you close and reopen the object. New or deleted objects in the database are reflected only when you close and reopen the project itself.

One huge advantage that Immediate mode has over Offline mode has to do with security. Working in Immediate mode allows you to work within the confines of a single database, allowing users with Administrator permissions on the database to create and modify objects. For reasons described in the next section, using Offline mode requires the user to be an administrator for the entire server instance.

Getting Started in Immediate Mode

To get started with Immediate mode in BI Dev Studio, follow these steps:

1. Launch BI Dev Studio.
2. From the File menu, select Open ⇨ Analysis Services Database. The dialog shown in Figure 4-2 will appear.
3. Enter the server name and database name to which you want to connect.
4. Click OK.

You can also create new databases on servers where you have server administrator permissions by selecting Create New Database and specifying the server and database names.

Figure 4-2 Dialog box to connect to a database in Immediate mode

Offline Mode

When you're working in Offline mode, your project contains files that are stored on your client machine. As you make modifications to objects in this environment, the changes are stored in XML format on your hard drive. The models and other objects are not created on the server until you decide to deploy them to the destination server of your choosing. This provides you (as the data mining developer or analyst) with the capability to design and test your models on a test server before deploying them to a live server. Also, these files can be checked into a source control system to track changes in the object metadata over time, and to share among a development team. You can view and edit the source code of these files by right-clicking an object in Solution Explorer and selecting View Code.

When you deploy a project, BI Dev Studio validates the objects in your project, creates a deployment script, and sends that script to the server. The unit of deployment is the entire project, representing an entire Analysis Services database. The tools are smart enough to deploy incremental changes while you are working on a project. However, if you deploy the project to a server that has a database of the same name as the one in your project settings, or if the project is deployed from a different machine, the deployment will completely overwrite the database. Luckily, you will be warned before this situation occurs. Also, because a database is created upon deployment, you must be a server administrator to deploy a project from Offline mode to the server.

Getting Started in Offline Mode

To get started with Offline mode in BI Dev Studio, follow these steps:

1. Launch BI Dev Studio.

2. Select New ⇨ Project from the File menu. The New Project dialog box appears, as shown in Figure 4-3.

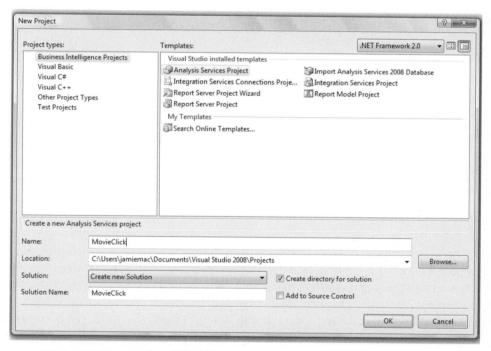

Figure 4-3 New Project dialog box

3. Open the Other Languages node in the Project Types pane if it is not already open.

4. Select Business Intelligence Projects.

5. Select Analysis Services Project from the Templates pane.

6. Give your project a name, and click OK.

7. Select Build ⇨ Deploy to deploy your project to the server, creating your database.

By default, the project will be deployed to the local host server (that is, the server on the same machine as your tools). To change the target server, select Project ⇨ Properties. This launches the Configuration Property Management dialog box, where you can create different deployment configurations and specify the target server and database name for each potential configuration, as illustrated in Figure 4-4.

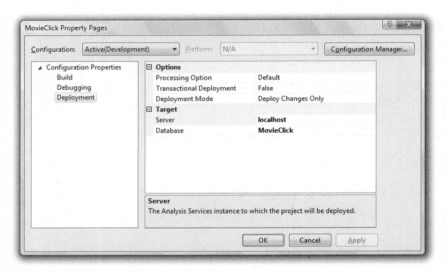

Figure 4-4 Project Properties dialog box

The other important properties on this dialog box to note for deployment are the Processing Option and Deployment Mode. By default, deployment automatically processes any objects that have been created or invalidated by the project changes. The Processing Option property controls this behavior. Again by default, only the incremental changes from the tools are deployed to the server. This can result in errors if the database has been changed from another client, or if a database with the same name already exists on the server. The Deployment Mode property controls this behavior.

NOTE You can change the default deployment server that is set every time you create a new offline project. To do so, open the Options dialog box by selecting Options on the Tools menu. Drill down to Business Intelligence

Designers ➪ Analysis Services Designers ➪ General and set the Default Target Server property to the server instance of your choice. This setting affects only new projects, so you still have to manually change any projects previously created.

Switching Project Modes

You may find yourself in one mode and need to be in the other — such as when you're making a quick update to a deployed project from a different machine, or when you want to save the object metadata of an operational database to source control. Luckily, it is easy and painless to make the switch.

The easiest way to do this is to switch from Offline mode to Immediate mode. You simply go to the File menu, select Open ➪ Analysis Services Database, and select the database you previously deployed. To go the other way (that is, to switch from Immediate mode to Offline mode), you create a new project and select Import Analysis Services 2008 Database in the New Project dialog box (shown previously in Figure 4-3). This launches a wizard where you can specify the server and source database name, and then extract the metadata into a new project. Note that you still must set the deployment options to indicate the target server and database name as necessary.

NOTE You can tell if you are in Immediate or Offline mode by looking at the name of the project in the Solution Explorer. If you are in Immediate mode, the project name will be followed by the server instance name in parenthesis. Additionally, all window tabs will have the text `(Online)` after the object name.

Creating Data Mining Objects

After you open your database or project, the operations performed inside an Analysis Services project are similar, regardless of the operational mode you chose. To perform data mining, you must indicate and describe your source data, and then create mining structures and models.

Setting Up Your Data Sources

Two objects in Analysis Services act as interfaces to your data: the data source and the data source view (DSV). The data source is essentially a connection string indicating data location, whereas the DSV is an abstraction layer that enables you to modify the way you look at data sources, or even define a schema and switch the actual source at a later time. This section discusses how to set up these objects for use in data mining.

Understanding Data Sources

A data source is a rather simple object. It consists of nothing more than a connection string, plus some additional information indicating how to connect. However, two aspects of data sources can easily trip you up and cause general frustration if you don't understand them. Both issues will manifest themselves by allowing you to create objects on the client that will fail to work properly when deployed.

The first issue is *data location*. Unlike most data mining products, SQL Server Data Mining is a server-based solution. This means that when you set up your data sources, the data source must be accessible not only to the client where you used the tools to build the model, but also to the server where the model will be processed.

For example, if you build your model based on an Access database in `C:\My Documents\Northwind.mdb`, your model will fail to process unless the file is located on the same place on the server. Even if the file happens to be present, this is a bad thing, because you have no way of knowing if such a file actually contains the same data or even the same schema as your local version. In general, when mining on local data, you should move the data to a SQL Server database using SQL Server Integration Services (SSIS) before building your models using BI Dev Studio.

The second issue is *security*. It is important to understand the user credentials that are used to access data from Analysis Services. When you set up your connection, you can choose to use *integrated security* (where account credentials are required to access the data) or *simple security* (where a specified username and password are required to access data). Microsoft recommends always using integrated security if it's supported by the source database.

Regardless of the method the source database supports, a data source object contains additional information that tells Analysis Services exactly which security credentials to use (or *impersonate*) when connecting to the database. A data source object can be created with one of the following four impersonation options:

- **Impersonate Current User** — In general, this method is the most secure for data sources accessed through query statements. It causes Analysis Services to use the current user credentials to access the remote data. However, in many implementations, Analysis Services must delegate credentials to the source database machine. For delegation to work correctly, it must be configured by your domain administrators. Consult the Windows Server documentation regarding Kerberos for more information on this topic. This method cannot be used in data sources that are used for processing Analysis Services objects, because it can result in different data being accessed, depending on who processes an object.

- **Impersonate Account** — When Impersonate Current User isn't an option, Impersonate Account is the second-best choice. Impersonate Account allows you to specify the account credentials that will be used to access the data source. The credentials (which consist of a username and password) are stored with Analysis Services, and all access to that data uses those credentials. This method is the most secure if delegation is not an option.

- **Impersonate Service Account** — This option causes all data access to occur under the account that Analysis Services is running. This method exists mainly for testing purposes, and is discouraged for production use. In general, Analysis Services should be running under an account with the most limited privileges possible.

- **Default** — This option causes different credentials to be used, depending on how the data source is accessed. When the data source is used for processing, the service account credentials will be used to access data. If the data source is used for querying, the current user credentials will be used, if possible.

Creating the MovieClick Data Source

To create a data source to the MovieClick database, follow these steps:

1. Download the MovieClick database and install it as described in Appendix A.

2. Right-click the Data Sources folder in the Solution Explorer or Object Explorer and select New Data Source to launch the Data Source Wizard.

3. Skip the introductory page, and click the New Connection button on the second page to launch the Data Link dialog box.

4. Enter the Server name where you installed the database, specify your security settings, and select the MovieClick database.

5. Click OK to exit the Data Link dialog box. Click Next to advance the wizard to the Impersonation Information page.

6. Enter the username and password you want Analysis Services to use to access the MovieClick database, and click Finish to close the wizard.

Using the Data Source View

The DSV is an abstract client-side view of your data. This is where your modeling begins. The DSV is where you select, organize, explore, and in a sense, manipulate the data in the source. In essence, the DSV tells Analysis Services how you want to see the data on the source. Because the object exists on your Analysis Services server and not your relational source, you can perform such manipulations even if you have only read access to the relational server.

When you're creating a DSV for data mining purposes, the most important table to identify is your case table. This is the table that contains the cases you want to analyze. You must also bring in any related tables (such as nested or lookup tables) that provide additional information about your cases.

Creating the MovieClick Data Source View

To create a DSV from the MovieClick data source, follow these steps:

1. Right-click the Data Source Views folder in the Solution Explorer or Object Explorer, and select New Data Source View to launch the Data Source View Wizard.

2. Skip the introductory page. On the next page, the Select Data Source wizard page, the MovieClick data source will be selected by default. Click Next to continue.

3. The Name Matching page performs no function for the data source as imported, so click Next to continue. (This page appears only when relationships are not specified in the source database and allows you to choose how to automatically create relationships based on the key columns of the tables. Because, in this case, the only table without predefined relationships does not have a key, the algorithm it uses does not work.

4. On the Select Tables and Views wizard page, click the >> button to move all tables from the Available Objects list to the Included Objects list.

5. Click Next and then click Finish to exit the DSV Wizard and display the DSV Designer.

6. Right-click the Movie column in the MovieGenre table, and select Set Logical Primary Key.

7. Drag a relationship from the Movie column in the Movies table to the Movies column in the MovieGenre table. After the connection, you can right-click in the Designer window and select Arrange Tables to make the tables easier to see. Your DSV should now look like Figure 4-5.

The DSV Designer initially displays a diagram of the tables in your data source and the relationships between them. If you already know your data, and it is in the proper shape for mining, you can begin creating your mining models at this point. However, if this is not true (which is usually the case), you can use the DSV Designer to explore the data and alter it to the shape you need for your models.

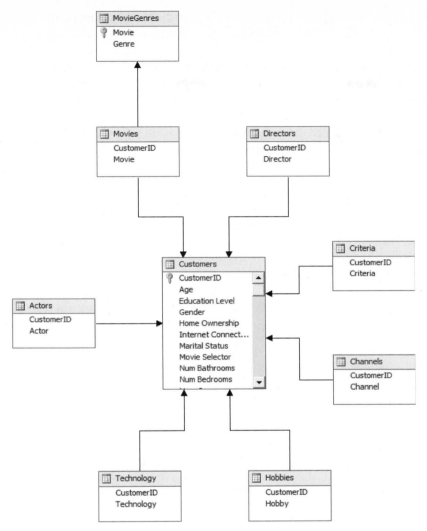

Figure 4-5 Completed MovieClick DSV

Initially, you can simply annotate the tables and columns in your schema to make them easier to understand and more supportable. You can add descriptions to these objects and even change the names to something more readable and understandable. For example, if you had a table named NWSFY03, you could rename it to Fiscal Year 03 Northwest Sales or rename column 014 to Quantity. You do this by selecting the object and typing the description and the friendly name in the Properties window. Additionally, any relationships between tables that were not specified in the source database can be indicated here simply by dragging from the foreign key column in one table to the primary key column in another. All of these modifications occur only in the DSV and do not affect your original data in any way.

> **NOTE** If the relationship between a case table and a nested table does not exist in the database, you must specify it in the DSV, or you will not be able add the nested table to your model.

In addition to annotating your schema, the DSV allows you to create named calculations, named queries, and views to interactively explore your data using pivot charts.

Working with Named Calculations

Named calculations are additional virtual columns on the tables in your DSV, which enable you to mine derived information in your data without having to change your source data. A named calculation consists of name, a SQL expression containing the calculation, and an optional description.

The calculation can be any valid SQL expression. If you are not a SQL expert, here are some types of expressions that are useful in many data mining projects:

- **Arithmetic operations** — Standard SQL supports +, −, *, /, and % (modulo). For example, you could create a `Profit` named calculation with the following formula:

  ```
  [Sales Price] - [Item Cost]
  ```

- **Mathematical functions** — Mathematical functions are useful, especially when data in a column does not follow a uniform distribution. The SQL functions `ABS`, `LOG`, `SIGN`, and `SQRT` are particularly useful. Here are two examples:

  - To flatten out an exponentially increasing variable, you could use the following function:

    ```
    LOG([Sales Quantity])
    ```

  - To create a flag for expenses that are over/under budget, you could use the following function:

    ```
    SIGN([Actual Expenses] - [Budgeted Expenses])
    ```

- **Compositing expressions** — Often, the hypothesis you want to test depends on a variable that is a combination of two of the variables you already have. For example, it may not be interesting that a person is married or has children, but the combination of the two may provide valuable information. A composite expression for this situation could look like this:

  ```
  [Marital Status] + ' ' + [Has Children]
  ```

- **CASE expressions** — CASE expressions are an extremely flexible way to create meaningful variables for data mining. The CASE expression allows you to assign results based on the evaluation of one or more conditions. Useful applications of CASE are to change value labels, manually discretize columns, reduce the number of valid states, and convert an attribute from a nested table to the case level. Here are some examples:

  - To change value labels, you could use the following type of expression:

    ```
    CASE [Category]
        WHEN 1    THEN 'Food'
        WHEN 2    THEN 'Beverage'
        WHEN 3    THEN 'Goods'
    END CASE
    ```

  - To manually discretize a column, you could use the following type of expression:

    ```
    CASE
        WHEN [Age] < 20 THEN 'Under 20'
        WHEN [Age] <= 30 THEN 'Between 20 and 30'
        WHEN [Age] <= 40 THEN 'Between 30 and 40'
        ELSE 'Over 40'
    END
    ```

  - To reduce the number of valid states, you could use the following type of expression:

    ```
    CASE [Marital Status]
        WHEN 'Married'      THEN [Marital Status]
        WHEN 'Never Married' THEN [Marital Status]
        ELSE 'Other'
    END
    ```

  - To convert an attribute from a nested table to a case table, you could use the following type of expression:

    ```
    CASE
        WHEN EXISTS
            (SELECT [Movie] FROM [Movies]
                WHERE [Movie]='Star Wars' AND
                    [Movies].[CustomerID]=[Customers].[CustomerID])
            THEN 'True'
        ELSE 'False'
    END
    ```

    For example, this would be done when you wanted to convert a nested attribute to a case-level attribute. Note that if you still want to use the nested table in the model, you will have to use a named query to filter the attribute from the nested table, as described in the next section.

Creating a Named Calculation on the Customers Table

To create a named calculation to discretize and reduce the number of states in the Num Bedrooms column, follow these steps:

1. Right-click the Customers table and select Create a Named Calculation.

2. Enter the calculation name **Bedrooms** and optionally enter a description.

3. Enter the following expression:

```
CASE
   WHEN [Num Bedrooms] = 1 THEN 'One'
   WHEN [Num Bedrooms] <= 3 THEN 'Two or Three'
   WHEN [Num Bedrooms] >= 4 THEN 'Four or more'
   ELSE 'None'
END
```

4. Close the dialog box.

After the dialog is closed, the DSV Designer will validate your expression and return any applicable errors. You can see the results of your calculation by right-clicking the table and selecting Explore Data.

Working with Named Queries

Because a named calculation is a virtual column on a DSV table, a named query is just a virtual view on your data source. Again, this allows you to change the data you are mining without making any changes to your original data. Even when modifications to the source are possible, creating named queries directly in your DSV is quick and easy, and it allows you to maintain these views alongside the models where they are used (instead of polluting your databases with single-use objects).

The Create/Edit Named Query dialog box provides a standard query builder user interface to assist in creating queries, which is very useful for complicated joins. Note that named queries can be built only on database objects, and not other DSV objects.

Typical queries that are useful for data mining are filtering and joins. Simple row filtering can be accomplished using the built-in case filtering on mining structure columns, but more advanced filtering scenarios require named queries, as shown in the following examples:

▪ To filter out unpopular items from a nested table, you use this type of named query:

```
SELECT [CustomerID], [Movie] FROM [Movies]
WHERE [Movie] IN
  (SELECT DISTINCT
    [Movie]
  FROM [Movies] GROUP BY [Movie]
      HAVING COUNT([Movie]) > 20)
```

■ To join information from a foreign table, you use this type of named query:

```
SELECT
    Customers.*, Education.[Education Level]
FROM Customers JOIN Education
ON Customers.[Education Id] = Education.[Education Id]
```

Creating a Named Query Based on the Customers Table

Let's say you want to create a named query in your DSV based on a Customers table that contains only homeowners. Because this table contains a named calculation, you must manually add the calculation into the query by following these steps:

1. Double-click the Bedrooms named calculation in the Customers table to open the Named Calculation dialog box, and copy the SQL text.

2. Right-click the DSV Designer, and select New Named Query.

3. Enter the query name **Homeowners**, and optionally enter a description.

4. Click the Add Table button, select the Customers table, and close the Add Table dialog box.

5. Select the * (All Customers) check box on the Customers table.

6. Do the following to add the calculated column:

    (a) Enter a comma after Customers.* in the query window, and paste the contents of the clipboard into the second row of the Column column.

    (b) Type **as Bedrooms** after the pasted text.

    The query will expand to replace Customers.* with the list of all the table columns.

7. Do the following to filter on homeowners:

    (a) In the grid control, find the row containing [Home Ownership] in the Column column.

    (b) Clear the check mark in the second row of the Output column.

    (c) Enter = **'Own'** in the criteria column.

8. Your final query should look like Figure 4-6. Click OK to close the dialog box.

Your named query can now be explored from the context menu using Explore Data, like any other DSV table.

NOTE This example is mainly illustrative because simple filters based on column values can easily be done as model filters in a structure.

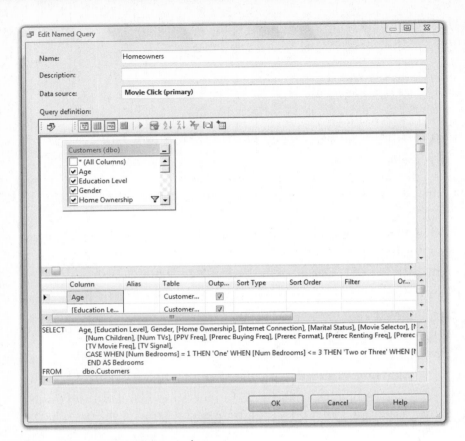

Figure 4-6 Homeowners named query

Organizing the DSV

When a named query is created, any relationships that the original table had are not carried over to the new table. This means that to use those relationships, you must re-create them by dragging from the foreign key to the primary key for each table relationship. When you complete the plethora of crossing relationships in your DSV, it will be very difficult to read and comprehend, as shown in Figure 4-7.

You can remedy this problem by using DSV diagrams. The DSV Designer allows you to create any number of diagrams, allowing you to select a subset of DSV tables and arrange them as you see fit. To create these diagrams, you click the New Diagram button, name the diagram, and drag tables from the list on the left to it. You can also add tables to the view by right-clicking a table that is already in the view and selecting Show Related Tables. After adding tables, you can clean up your arrangement by right-clicking the design area and selecting Arrange Tables.

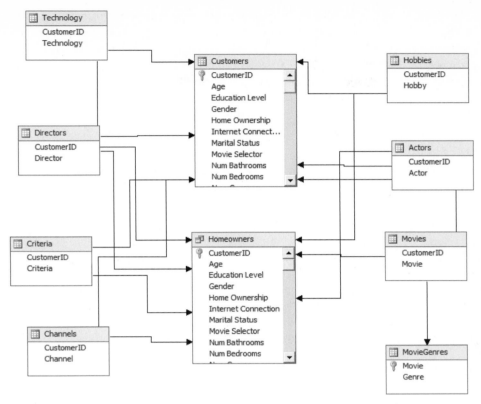

Figure 4-7 DSV with many relationships in the DSV Designer

NOTE Named queries and named calculations rely on the processing power of your relational server. The additional resources required to process the generated queries will have an impact on the initial processing time of your mining models. If this increase becomes too severe, and if you will be frequently repeating these queries, you should consider materializing these views on the relational server.

Exploring Data

Part of any data mining project is learning about and understanding the nature of your data. By leveraging controls from Office Web Components (OWC), the DSV Designer provides the functionality to explore your data in four different views. By right-clicking a DSV table and selecting Explore Data, you can view your data as a table, PivotTable, simple charts, and a PivotChart. By default, the Explore Data component will sample 5,000 points of your data. The option buttons in the upper left of the Explore Data window allow you to change this setting to a maximum of 20,000 points (because of a limitation of the OWC controls).

The tabular views allow you to do a simple exploration of your data. Clever use of the PivotTable will allow you to get a better understanding of the data by arranging, slicing, and aggregating your data in different ways. For example, by exploring a PivotTable on the `Customers` table, you can find the average `Age` and its standard deviation by using the `Bedrooms` column created previously (see Figure 4-8). This is possible because you are exploring the DSV table and not the actual source table as it is in the data. You can explore named queries in the DSV in precisely the same manner.

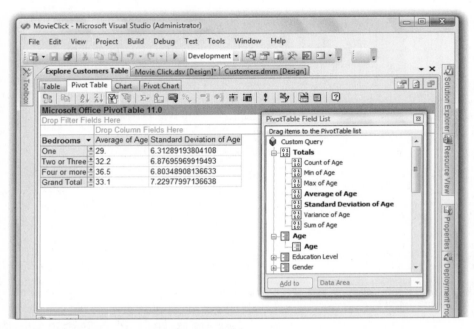

Figure 4-8 Exploring data with the PivotTable

The graphical exploration offers a page of simple column, pie, and bar charts plus a PivotChart view. Using the simple charts, you can see histograms and pies of various attributes side by side. If your data is continuous, the chart divides the continuous range into 10 buckets. The PivotChart, on the contrary, provides a wealth of graphing controls to analyze your data, from your standard line, bar, scatter, column, and pie charts, to more exotic types such as doughnut and radar charts, as shown in Figure 4-9.

The PivotTable and PivotChart have many configuration options to help you analyze your data in different ways. Many of these are available through the context-sensitive Command and Options dialog box, from the Context menu, or from embedded toolbars. Virtually every aspect of the tables and charts can be modified, either by graphically selecting the object, or by using the selection box on the General tab of the dialog box. Describing the full feature set of the OWC could easily fill another book, and mastering the OWC controls for best value will take some practice. With experience, however, you will be able to manipulate the controls to find exactly the right view for you. Additionally, the PivotTable and PivotChart are linked, so you can switch back and forth, make edits, and see how changes in one view affect the other view.

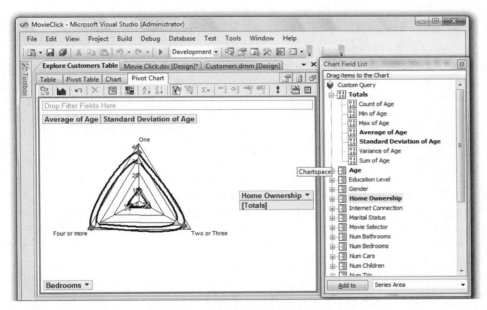

Figure 4-9 Radar chart showing Age by Bedrooms and Home Ownership

One additional feature of the PivotChart that is important for data exploration is graphical named query generation. By clicking the Named Query button on the toolbar, you can use elements of the chart to define a named query. For example, you could select only those homeowners with one bedroom and renters with four or more bedrooms on the chart, and add them to the query. This named query becomes like any other, and can be used as a source for exploring data.

NOTE Although the Explore Data window looks like other document windows, it's actually a tool window like the Solution Explorer and Properties windows. By right-clicking the Window tab, you can change the Explore Data window into a floating or dockable window. You can also open many Explore Data windows on different DSV tables to display charts and tables side by side.

Creating and Editing Models

After you have organized, modified, selected, and understand the data you want to analyze, you can start to create data mining objects. The first step is to run the Data Mining Wizard. After completing it, you can refine the results in Data Mining Designer.

Structures and Models

As detailed in Chapter 3, SQL Server Analysis Services has two major objects that deal with data mining: *mining structures* and *mining models*.

A mining structure defines the domain of a mining problem, whereas a mining model is the application of a mining algorithm to the data in a mining structure. A mining structure contains a list of *structure columns* that have data and content types, bindings to the data source, and some optional flags that control how the data is modeled. Additionally, a mining structure contains a list of mining models that use the columns from the structure.

The definition of a mining model contains an algorithm with its associated parameters, plus a list of columns from the mining structure. Each model in a structure can use a different algorithm, or the same algorithm with different parameters, and/or a different subset of the columns in the structure. For each column in the model, you can assign how it is to be used in that model, as well as algorithm-specific modeling flags. This feature allows you to easily test different hypotheses on the same data set.

Using the Data Mining Wizard

The Data Mining Wizard creates the mining structure that describes the columns and training data you will use for mining, and optionally a mining model, which takes those columns, applies an algorithm, and defines the usage of each column for that algorithm. The wizard wraps the creation of these two objects into one simple set of steps.

The steps of the wizard are:

1. Select your algorithm or choose only a structure.
2. Select the source tables and specify how they are used.
3. Select the columns from those tables and specify how they are used.
4. Finally, specify holdout data and name the structure and model.

At that point, you can process and analyze the results of your model without further ado. Analysis Services makes it that simple to get started. The wizard also allows you to create models from multidimensional — that is, online analytical processing (OLAP) sources. OLAP is covered in Chapter 13, so this chapter will focus only on relational sources.

Using the wizard is simple because it performs several steps automatically, based on the input you provide. As a data miner, it is important that you understand these steps, as well as how and when decisions that impact your model are made.

On the first page in the wizard, Select the Definition Method, you choose whether you are creating a model from a relational or multidimensional source, as shown in Figure 4-10. Although the finished models end up looking the same, regardless of their source, their creation process is slightly different, so there are different wizard paths for each source option. Also, a particular mining algorithm may not support creating models from OLAP sources, so this question is asked first.

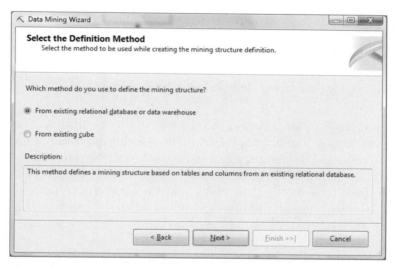

Figure 4-10 Selecting the model definition method in the Data Mining Wizard

The next page, Create the Data Mining Structure, asks you which data mining technique you want to use to create your initial mining model. This is a list of algorithms that is determined by the capabilities of your target server, and may contain all or only some of the algorithms covered in this book. The process used to determine which algorithms are used is described in Chapter 15. If you cannot connect to a server at the time the wizard is run, you get the default list of algorithms provided with SQL Server Data Mining, as shown in Figure 4-11. Choosing which algorithm you are going to use is dependent on the business problem you are trying to solve. The application of each algorithm is described in its respective chapter later in this book.

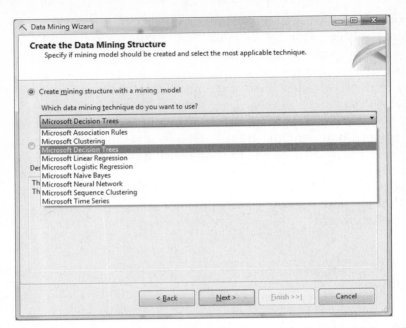

Figure 4-11 The Creating the data mining structure in the Data Mining Wizard

On the next two pages, you indicate the data you will be mining. You choose the DSV containing the tables, and then you specify the actual tables themselves. When choosing the tables, you must specify whether each table is the *case* table or if it is a *nested* table, as shown in Figure 4-12. As described in Chapter 3, the case table is the case that contains the entities you want to analyze, and a nested table contains additional (usually transactional) information about each case.

> **NOTE** Sometimes determining which table is the *case* table can be a bit confusing. For example, if you want to analyze how products are purchased together, you may naïvely choose products as the case table. However, you are actually analyzing the groups of those products that were purchased by a single customer. In this case, the *customer* becomes the case, with the transaction table containing the product purchases as a nested table.
>
> When you have only a transaction table, you can use it as both the case table and the nested table by specifying the transaction ID as the case-level key, and the other columns as columns in the nested table.

On the next two pages of the Data Mining Wizard, you indicate which columns you are using and how you want the mining algorithms to interpret each one. First, you specify which columns are used in the structure and model, plus whether they are *key*, *input*, and/or *predictable*. Then you specify the data and content types for each of the columns. As shown in Figure 4-13, if you check the leftmost check box for each column, but no Input or Predict check boxes, the column will appear in the mining structure, but not in the initial model. Of course, if you are creating only a structure, the Input and Predict check boxes will not be present.

Figure 4-12 Specifying table types in the Data Mining Wizard

You must specify a key for the case table and each nested table in your model. Remember that the key of a nested table in DMX *is not* the foreign key that relates the nested table to the case table. Instead, it is the key in the context that you have it nested. The wizard enforces this relationship by not presenting the foreign key as a choice, and warning the user if a key is not specified.

For example, a nested table representing a customer's shopping cart comes from a table that may have a row ID as a key, plus the transaction ID, product name, quantity, and price. The nested table in this model would have only the product, quantity, and price columns, because the row ID isn't of interest in this model, and the transaction ID is the foreign key to the case table.

In this reduced context, you can see that the quantity and price relate to the *product*, which becomes the key of the nested table. Time series and sequence clustering models have special rules regarding the specification of keys, as described in Chapters 8 and 10, respectively.

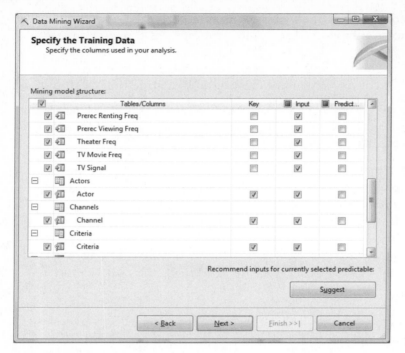

Figure 4-13 Indicating how columns are used and how nested keys are specified in the Data Mining Wizard

NOTE One thing to consider when determining which column should be the nested key is that data mining finds patterns by examining similarities and differences between cases. If you choose a column as a nested key where the values in that column would show up only in a single case, the data mining algorithms would find no patterns relative to that column. This logic summarily dismisses the use of transaction IDs or row IDs as nested keys.

Which columns you specify as Input and which as predictable (Predict) depends on your business problem, the hypothesis you are trying to test, and the algorithm you chose. In general, specifying a column as Input indicates that the algorithm will use that column to determine the columns marked as Predict, or an output. The exact way that each algorithm uses this information varies somewhat, so you should familiarize yourself with the specific semantics detailed in each algorithm chapter. One fact that remains constant among all algorithms is that if you want to be able to select a column from the model in a PREDICTION JOIN statement, the column must be predictable. To predict a nested table, check the box in the Predict column next to its key.

NOTE If you have many columns in your table, it can be difficult to know which to choose as inputs. You can always use all the columns, but this involves

additional processing power and, depending on the algorithm, may make your model difficult to interpret.

The Suggest button on the Specify the Training Data page of the wizard performs a quick entropy-based analysis to indicate which columns are likely to provide information toward a selected output, thereby reducing the number of columns in your final model. Note that this feature considers only case-level columns in its analysis, and is not a guarantee that the selected columns will impact (or that the nonselected columns will not impact) your target variable.

Next, you are presented with the list of columns you have chosen and their respective data and content types, as shown in Figure 4-14. Indicating the correct content type is crucial to the performance and accuracy of your model. For example, if you have an `Income` field marked as `DISCRETE`, the algorithm will assume that each possible income value is a distinct category, and will likely spend extra processing power to learn absolutely nothing. On the flip side, if you have a categorical column where the categories are indicated by integers (such as `1-Blue`, `2-Yellow`, `3-Red`, `4-Green`, and so on) marked as `CONTINUOUS`, the algorithm will assume that it can mathematically compare the categories and measure distances between points, in this case creating the bizarre logic that `Green(4) - Red(3) = Blue(1)`!

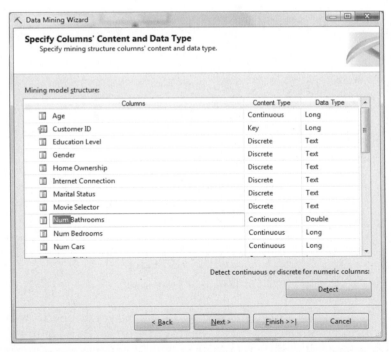

Figure 4-14 Specifying content and data types in the Data Mining Wizard

Luckily, the Data Mining Wizard has the capability to automatically detect whether a numeric column is categorical (discrete) or continuous. Clicking the Detect button on the Specify Columns' Content and Data Type page causes the wizard to sample and analyze the source data and choose an appropriate content type. If a continuous type is determined and your selected algorithm does not support continuous columns, the content type will be specified as DISCRETIZED. You can set discretization parameters in the designer, as specified in the next section. Before moving on with the wizard, you should verify that the content types were assigned correctly, and modify any that were not.

The next page of the wizard, the Create Testing Set page shown in Figure 4-15, allows you to specify a percentage of data up to a maximum that will be randomly set aside for use by the validation methods described later in this chapter. Holding out data for testing is highly recommended, particularly for classification and regression models. Currently, BI Dev Studio does not offer any tools for evaluating the accuracy of models with predictable nested tables, so specifying a testing set for such models isn't useful unless you implement your own accuracy methods.

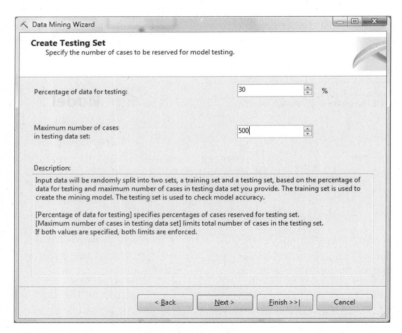

Figure 4-15 Specifying a testing set with a maximum of 500 cases

The final page of the wizard, shown in Figure 4-16, allows you to specify the names of the structure and model, as well as enable the drill-through feature if it is supported by the algorithm. When completed, the wizard creates a mining structure containing a mining model and launches Data Mining Designer.

Figure 4-16 Naming objects in the Data Mining Wizard

Creating the MovieClick Mining Structure and Model

For this discussion, you'll create a mining structure and model that will predict the number of bedrooms for customers who own their homes, based on all of the information you know about them. Follow these steps to create the structure and model using the Data Mining Wizard:

1. Right-click the `Mining Structures` folder in the Solution Explorer or Object Explorer, and choose New Mining Model.

2. Skip the description page and go to the Select the Definition Method page. Because you are building the model from relational data, leave the default option selected and click Next.

3. On the Create the Data Mining Structure page, you can view the list of available algorithms if you are connected to your server. Leave Microsoft Decision Trees selected, and click Next.

4. On the Select Data Source View page, you are presented with the single DSV in this project or database. Click Next to continue.

5. On the Specify Table Types page, you must indicate your case and nested tables. You only want to analyze homeowners, but you want the structure to be able to support a broader range of models, so click the

check box in the `Case` column next to the `Customers` named query. You want to add all of the nested tables, so click the check box in the `Nested` column next to the `Actors`, `Channels`, `Criteria`, `Directors`, `Hobbies`, `Movies`, and `Technology` tables. Click Next to continue.

6. On the Specify the Training Data page, you indicate which columns to use in the model and how they are to be used. Because the key column for the `Homeowners` table was indicated in the DSV, it is already selected as the key of the model. You are predicting `Bedrooms`, so click the check box in the Predict column next to the named calculation `Bedrooms`.

7. You want all other case-level columns to be inputs, except for the `Num Bedrooms` column from which `Bedrooms` is derived. Check the check box in the Input column next to all case columns except `Customer ID` and `Num Bedrooms`.

   > **NOTE** You can use the Shift key to check multiple columns at the same time, or you can click the check box in the Input column header and then uncheck the box next to `Num Bedrooms`.

8. For each nested table, you must indicate the nested key. The wizard automatically filters out the foreign key column, so each nested table is left with a single column. Click the check box in the Key column for each column in each nested table. Check the Input column as well. Click Next to continue.

9. On the Specify Columns' Content and Data Type page, click the Detect button to automatically assign the correct content types. Click Next to continue.

10. On the Create Testing Set page, limit the number of cases in the test set by entering **500** into the Maximum Number of Cases in Testing Data Set edit control. Click Next to continue.

11. On the completion page of the wizard, type **MovieClick** as the name of the structure and **Homeowner Bedrooms** as the name of the model. Then, check the Allow Drill Through box and click Finish to end the wizard.

When you finish the wizard, Data Mining Designer opens to the Mining Structure Editor. Because the model is currently specified to use all cases in the structure, the model definition is not yet finished. You will use Data Mining Designer to complete the definition.

Using Data Mining Designer

Data Mining Designer is where most of the work with your models will take place. It contains the following five panes for editing, browsing, querying, and comparing models:

- The Mining Structure pane
- The Mining Models pane
- The Mining Model Viewer pane
- The Mining Accuracy pane
- The Mining Model Prediction pane

This section focuses only on editing with the Mining Structure and Mining Models panes, leaving the other functionality for the "Using Your Models" section later in this chapter.

Working with the Mining Structure Editor

The Mining Structure Editor allows you to add columns to and remove columns from your mining structure, as well as set the properties of each mining structure column. You must use the structure editor to perform modeling operations that are not possible in the Mining Model Wizard. Even if the wizard-generated structure suits your needs, it is a good idea to inspect your mining structure after running the wizard to be sure that it contains everything you want.

The three components of the mining structure editor are the structure tree, the DSVview, and the Properties window, as shown in Figure 4-17. Clicking columns in the structure tree or the DSV will cause their properties to be displayed in the Properties window. Dragging columns from the DSV to the structure tree will add the column to the Mining Structure. Right-clicking almost any item produces a menu with a list of actions to be performed on that item. You can browse your data and explore your DSV. Note that to edit the DSV, you must return to the DSV Designer.

There are several operations possible in the mining structure editor that can not be accomplished using the Data Mining Wizard. The following modeling tasks are not available in the wizard, but can be performed using the editor:

- **Set discretization properties** — The Mining Model Wizard will automatically set the content type of continuous columns to DISCRETIZED if the selected algorithm does not support continuous attributes. However, you may want to be able to specify the discretization method or the number of buckets that the attribute will be divided into.

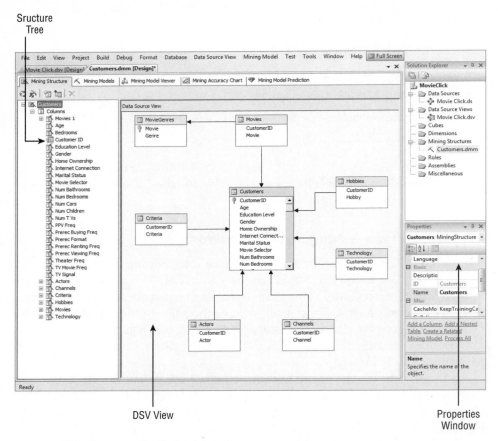

Figure 4-17 Mining Structure Editor in Data Mining Designer

To set these values, click the column you want to modify, and set the `DiscretizationMethod` and `DiscretizationBuckets` properties in the Properties window. The various discretization methods that are available are described in Chapter 3.

▪ **Add a column to the structure multiple times** — A structure may contain multiple models, and you may find that you want to model a specific column in different ways to see how it impacts the results. For example, you may want to compare how Age influences the results when it's treated as a continuous value, or when it's discretized into three, five, or seven buckets. You can add a column to the structure multiple times simply by dragging the source column from the DSV to the structure tree. Each column will be given an incremental name, which you can change in the Properties window.

■ **Add a column that has its values looked up in another table** — If your data is normalized, it is likely that the table you want to mine contains foreign keys to lookup tables instead of the actual data labels you want to appear in the model. Using the structure editor, you can add these columns directly to your model. To add such a column, right-click the table that has the foreign key and select Show Related Tables. The table that contains the primary key will appear in the DSV area of the structure editor. If the relationship is not specified in the DSV, you will have to return to the DSV editor and add it. From this new table, drag the column that contains the data name you want to use in your model to the structure tree.

For example, assume that you are mining a Purchases table that has a Product ID column and another table Products that relates Product ID to Product Name. To create a structure that uses the Product Name column, you would right-click the Purchases table and select Show Related Tables to introduce the Products table. Then you would click and drag the Product Name column to your structure.

NOTE The easiest way to add a nested table to a mining structure is to drag the key of the nested table to the structure tree. When you drop the key, the editor will automatically create a nested table with the key you specified.

Adding the Genre Column to the Movies Nested Table

When you created the DSV earlier in this chapter, you added a lookup table to retrieve genre information for each movie. Follow these steps to add the Genre column to the mining structure:

1. In the mining structure editor, right-click on the DSV surface and select Show Tables.

2. Select the MovieGenres table and click OK.

3. In the Mining Structure tree, click the plus sign on the Movies nested table to expand its children.

4. Drag the Genre column from the MovieGenres table in the DSV to the Columns child of the Movies nested table.

NOTE If you want to use a lookup column as the key of the nested table, you must edit the properties of the structure columns. You must first set the IsKey property of the lookup column to True, and then set the content type to Key. Also, you must set the original key columns IsKey and Content properties appropriately.

Working with the Mining Models Editor

The Mining Models Editor consists of a table that includes the models and their columns, and again displays the Properties window, as shown in Figure 4-18. This configuration allows you to quickly see how each column is used in each model and set properties appropriately.

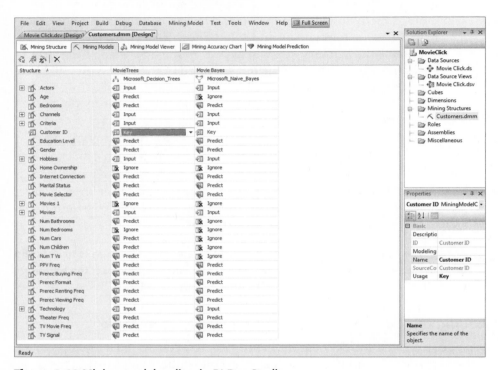

Figure 4-18 Mining models editor in BI Dev Studio

As with the Mining Structure Editor, there are many tasks that you can perform that aren't available in the Data Mining Wizard, including the following:

- **Create multiple models in a structure** — To create multiple models on the same structure, simply select the New Mining Model item in the Mining Model menu. You are prompted to enter a name and select the algorithm, and the editor creates a new mining model in the structure. The new model you create maintains the settings of the model that you selected when you chose the creation operation. The new model will use the same inputs, have the same targets, and use any additional settings that are compatible with the new algorithm you selected.

- **Set algorithm-specific parameters for each model and set algorithm-specific modeling flags on model columns** — To edit and set the model properties, select the mining model itself. You do this by selecting the column header so that the model properties are shown in the Properties window. Here, you can change the model name, set the algorithm used, filter the cases seen by the model, annotate your model with a description, enable drill-through if supported, and set the algorithm parameters. Setting the algorithm parameters brings up a dialog box that lists the available parameters with their defaults and descriptions, as shown in Figure 4-19. See the chapter that corresponds to the algorithm you want to use for a detailed discussion of its parameters.

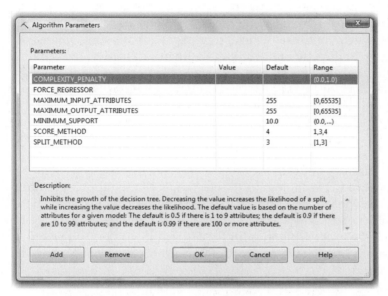

Figure 4-19 Algorithm Parameters dialog box for Microsoft_Decision_Trees

- **Filter the cases seen by a mining model, or the rows in a nested table** — The model you're building in this exercise is on homeowners only, so you must add a filter that eliminates non-homeowners from the model, as follows:

  1. Switch to the mining models editor by clicking the Mining Models tab of Data Mining Designer.

  2. Select the model by clicking the `Bedrooms Tree` column header in the mining model editor.

  3. In the Properties pane, click the `Filter` property and click the ellipses (...) button to bring up the Filter dialog box.

  4. In the Filter dialog box, specify **Home Ownership** for the mining structure column and **Own** as the value.

  5. Click OK to finish.

You can also filter cases based on the contents of a nested table. For example, you can build a model only for those customers who bought science fiction movies. Note that the filtering is performed on mining structure columns rather than on mining model columns. The columns used for filtering do not need to be included in the model to be used as a filter. In fact, in many cases, they should not be. In this case, because you are filtering on a single value of Home Ownership, the column adds no predictive value to the model and can be ignored.

- **Set column properties** — Column properties are set in the same manner as model properties — by selecting the column and using the Properties pane. However, because the usage property is commonly changed, you can change it directly in the editor. Setting the usage of each column involves selecting the column and choosing whether you want this column to be used as Input, Predict, PredictOnly, or Ignore. Selecting Input is analogous to selecting the Input column in the Mining Model Wizard. Selecting PredictOnly is analogous to selecting the Predict column in the wizard. Generally, this usage implies that this column will not be used as input for other predictable targets; however, you should check the chapter that discusses the algorithm you are using for the exact semantics. Selecting Predict is analogous to selecting both the Input and Predict columns in the wizard, and implies that the column will be treated both as an input for other targets and as a target in and of itself. Again, you should check the exact semantics for the algorithm you're using. Setting a column to Ignore creates a model that simply does not contain the specified column.

You can also use the Properties window to set model-specific properties for each column. The properties that are typically changed are algorithm-specific modeling flags, filters for nested tables, and the column name. Typically, you would change the column name when the mining structure contains multiple versions of a column and the model contains only one. For example, if the mining structure contains an Age column and a discretized version called AgeDisc, and the model contains the latter, you can rename the mining *model* column as Age to be consistent with other models in the structure. An aliased column will be indicated in the main view of the editor.

NOTE You can use the Shift and Ctrl keys to select multiple columns simultaneously. This allows you to set properties on many columns at the same time. Because setting a column to Ignore removes it from the model, you can set Ignore only in the column grid and not in the Properties window. Also, you cannot change the usage of any ignored columns in the Properties window.

To change multiple columns to or from Ignore, select them in the column grid using Shift or Ctrl, and then press the F2 key to show the combo box where you can make the change.

You can also change the properties of structure columns in the mining models editor by selecting the column and setting the properties in the Properties window. In this editor, you can also change the properties of multiple structure columns simultaneously, using Shift, Ctrl, and the F2 key as you did with mining columns.

Creating and Modifying Additional Models

Next, you'll set all of the case-level columns of the `Bedrooms Tree` model to be predictable, and then create a new model in the same structure, using the Microsoft Naive Bayes algorithm (discussed in detail in Chapter 6). Follow these steps:

1. Click the row for the `Age` column in the `Movie Trees` model column to select the table cell.

2. While holding down the Shift key, click the row for the `Bedrooms` column in the `Movie Trees` model. Now the usage for both `Age` and `Bedrooms` should be selected.

3. Press the F2 key to bring up a drop-down box where you can select the type of usage.

4. Change the usage to Predict. The usage of all selected will be changed accordingly.

5. Use Ctrl, Shift, and F2 to select the remaining case-level columns and change their usage to Predict.

6. Select New Mining Model from the Mining Model menu.

7. In the New Mining Model dialog box that appears, type **Movie Bayes** for the name and select Microsoft Naive Bayes as the algorithm. Click OK.

8. A warning appears that the `Age`, `Num Bathrooms`, `Num Children`, and `Num TVs` columns contain a content type not supported by the new algorithm, and asks if you want to continue. Click Yes, and the new model will be created with those columns set to Ignore.

At this point, you have a mining structure containing two models. The new model has all of the same columns set to Predict as the first, with the exception of the columns that have a content type not supported by the selected algorithm, which were set to Ignore.

Processing

Chapter 3 described how to train a model using an INSERT INTO statement. Using the tools to train models on the server is called *processing*. SQL Server Data Mining has the capability to process all models in a structure in parallel on a single data read. It does this by creating a compressed cache of the data that is used to train each of the models in the structure. This functionality requires you to set several processing options that control exactly what will be processed when, and to clean up after you're done. The mechanism is described in more detail in Chapter 15.

> **NOTE** Before processing a newly created or edited structure or model, you must first send the object to the server. In Immediate mode, simply saving your work deploys the object. However, in Offline mode, you must first deploy the project. To do so, select Deploy Solution from the Build menu. When you use the default settings, deploying the project will also cause any objects in the project to be processed.

Mining models and structures can have the following three processing states:

- **Processed** — A processed object is completely finished and ready to go.

- **Partially processed** — This is an ambiguous state indicating that part of the object is processed and other parts are not. This may be acceptable for your circumstances — for example, you may have a mining structure with several mining models and only want to process one of the models — so the structure would then be partially processed.

- **Unprocessed** — This implies that the object contains absolutely no data whatsoever.

The processing options for mining structures and models are as follows:

- **Process Full** — This causes the object to be completely reprocessed from the source data. When this option is sent to a mining structure, the structure is processed, and then each model in the structure is processed in parallel (in Enterprise editions of SQL Server). When this option is sent to a model, the source data is read only if the structure has not been processed.

- **Process Default** — Processing an object with Process Default causes the server to do whatever it takes to bring the object to a fully processed state. If the object is already processed, the server will perform no action. For example, if you edit a model within a structure and send Process Default to the structure, the server will process that one model without re-reading the source data.

- **Unprocess** — This causes the object to be completely unprocessed, dropping all data associated with that object. Sending a process command with this option to a structure causes any caches to be cleared, and contained models to be unprocessed.

- **Process Structure** — This option is valid only on a mining structure and causes the structure to read and cache the source data without processing the contained models. Executing subsequent process commands with Process Full and Process Default options on the models will process information from this cache.

- **Process Clear Structure** — Using this option on a structure causes the structure to drop any cached source data, while leaving the contained models processed. This greatly reduces the disk footprint of your mining structure at the cost of having to re-read the data on the next process command. Additionally, drill-through functionality on any contained models will be disabled until the models are reprocessed.

Processing the MovieClick Mining Structure

In this example, you'll process the `MovieClick` mining structure. First, follow these steps in Immediate mode:

1. Save your structure by clicking the Save button on the toolbar.
2. Select Process Mining Structure and All Models from the Mining Model menu, or click the Process button on the Designer toolbar.
3. Click Run in the processing dialog box.

Now follow these steps in Offline mode:

1. Select the Deploy option from the Build menu. By default, deploying the solution will process all objects.
2. If the default has changed, deploy the solution and follow the instructions for Immediate mode.

At this point, the Processing Progress dialog box will appear, providing status information for the processing operation. When the process is complete, you can view details about each step, including the processing time.

Using Your Models

After you have created and processed your models, you need to be able to explore, query, and compare them so that you can understand and apply the information they provide.

Understanding the Model Viewers

Each data mining algorithm provided with Analysis Services has its own associated viewers. The chapters later in this book that address specific algorithms include detailed descriptions of how you can use the corresponding algorithm viewer to interpret the models you create. However, the viewers have some common functionality that is better described outside the context of a specific algorithm.

The Mining Model Viewer pane provides a drop-down control that allows you to select which model you want to view. When you select a model, it is loaded into an algorithm-specific viewer. All of the viewers provided allow you to view multiple aspects of your models, which are indicated by tabs on the top of the viewer.

There are two basic types of model views: diagrams and tables. Each *diagram view* has the basic zoom and size-to-fit buttons on its embedded toolbar. Copying a bitmap of the entire diagram or just the displayed portion is supported through the toolbar or the pop-up menu that appears when you click the right mouse button.

Additionally, there are some special mouse-handling capabilities available for all diagram views. Rolling the mouse wheel will cause the diagram to zoom in and out, and pressing the mouse wheel like a button will bring up a mini-navigator, as shown in Figure 4-20. This will allow you to quickly and easily move to any portion of your view.

Tabular views support a variety of features. Every tabular view supports Copy functionality that copies the table contents in HTML format so that they can be pasted into Word, Excel, FrontPage, or any other application that supports HTML. Headers in many views contain informative tooltips and you can click the headers to sort the view by the information in that column. You can also resize columns by dragging the edges between column headers. Some views also allow you to rearrange columns by dragging and dropping column headers.

You can view the raw data of any model by setting the Viewer control to Microsoft Generic Content Tree Viewer. The Viewer control is also used if you install custom visualizations provided by third parties for the algorithms.

> **NOTE** If you don't like the colors that the viewers use to display graphs, you can always change them. Selecting the Options item from the Tools menu brings up the Visual Studio Options dialog box. Drilling down in the tree control to Business Intelligence Designers ⇨ Analysis Services Designers ⇨ Data Mining Viewers provides a panel where you can customize the color of pretty much any aspect of any data mining chart.
>
> Changing the color will not affect visualizations that are currently open. To see the change, close the mining viewer and reopen it, or switch to a different model.

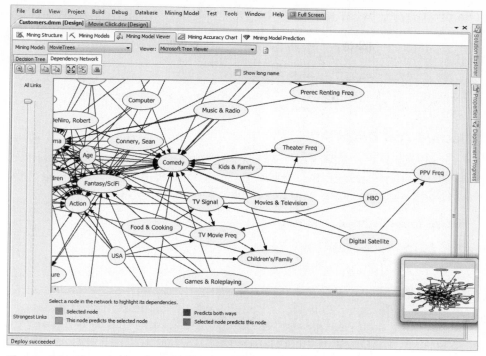

Figure 4-20 The mini-navigator window in the Dependency Network view

Many viewers show statistics about the currently selected item in the Mining Legend. The Mining Legend is a dockable window that automatically appears when a viewer that requires it is displayed.

Using the Mining Accuracy Chart

The Mining Accuracy Chart pane provides the following tools to help gauge the quality and accuracy of the models you create:

- **Accuracy chart** — Performs predictions against your model, and compares the result to data for which you already know the answer.

- **Profit chart** — Performs the same task as an accuracy, except it also allows you to specify some cost and revenue information to determine the exact point of maximum return.

- **Classification matrix** — Shows you exactly how many times the algorithm predicts results correctly, and what it predicts when it is wrong. (This chart is also known as a *confusion matrix*.)

In practice, it's better to hold some data aside when you train your models, to use for testing. Using the same data for testing that you trained your models with may make the model seem to perform better than it actually does.

As you learned in the "Creating and Editing Models" section earlier in this chapter, as of the 2008 version of SQL Server Data Mining, you can specify a percentage of the data to be held in the mining structure for accuracy tests.

Selecting Test Data

To use the accuracy chart, you must specify some source data to be used for testing. The first pane of the Accuracy Chart viewer allows you to select the data to be used for testing. You have the following three options:

- Use mining model test cases
- Use mining structure test cases
- Specify a different data set

In general, the test data should be structurally similar to the data used for training the mining models, and should have the same statistical properties as the training data. The easiest way to use the accuracy chart is against the holdout data preserved in the mining structure. The first two options (model test cases and structure test cases) use this holdout data set.

The first option, model test cases, represents the cases from the mining structure holdout data set that satisfy any filter the model might have. The second option, structure test cases, uses all the holdout data set. If the models you are evaluating have no filter, then these two options result in using exactly the same data set (the full mining structure holdout data set).

To use the accuracy chart with a different data set (an external one), you must select source tables from your DSV (or other data sources) and bind them to your mining structure. If the columns from the tables have the same name, this step is done automatically upon table selection. After you have selected the case and any nested tables and performed the binding, you can optionally filter the cases — this can be done when you have a specific column that indicates if a case is for training or testing, or simply to verify how the model performs for certain populations. For example, does the model perform differently for customers over age 40? Last, you choose which target you are testing and, optionally, the value you are testing for. By default, the accuracy chart selects the same column and value for each model in the structure. However, you can also test different columns at the same time. For example, if you have different discretizations in different models, you might want to see how well predicting Age with five buckets compares to doing the same with seven buckets.

WHY USE AN EXTERNAL DATASET INSTEAD OF THE HOLDOUT SET?

The mining structure holdout options (model test cases and structure test cases) are great ways to evaluate the accuracy of a mining model as soon as it is trained. However, as new data becomes available, the underlying patterns may change. Periodically, you will need to evaluate the performance of your existing model against the most recent data, to see if it is still accurate enough to be used, or if it requires retraining to learn the most recent patterns.

You may also want to use the accuracy chart against an external data set if your model is trained with oversampled data. Fraud detection and fault prediction models often use oversampling for training data, where frauds (or faults) are overrepresented. Evaluating such a model's accuracy against the holdout set of the mining structure (also oversampled) will give you a good idea of the number of faults that go undetected (false negative, or Type II errors), but it will not provide an accurate representation of false alarms raised by the model (false positive, or Type I errors).

Understanding the Accuracy Charts

The type of chart you receive depends on whether the target you chose is continuous or discrete, and whether or not you chose a target value to predict. The latter case is the most common, so let's look at that first.

When you select a discrete target and specify a target value, you receive a standard lift chart. A standard lift chart always contains a single line for each model you have selected, plus two additional lines: an ideal line and a random line. The coordinates at each point along the line indicate what percentage of the target audience you would capture if you used that model against the specified percentage of the audience.

Figure 4-21 shows a standard lift chart. The top line shows that an ideal model would capture 100 percent of the target using 18 percent of the data. This simply implies that 18 percent of the data indicates the desired target — there is no magic here. The bottom line is the random line. The random line is always a 45-degree line across the chart. This indicates that if you were to randomly guess the result for each case, you would capture 50 percent of the target using 50 percent of the data — again, no magic here. The other lines on the chart represent your mining models. Hopefully, all your models will be above the random line. When you see a model's line hovering around the random guess line, this means that there wasn't sufficient information in the training data to learn patterns about the target.

Using the example in Figure 4-21, the Decision Tree model can get about 90 percent of the target using only 35 percent of the data, whereas the Naïve Bayes model can get 90 percent of the target only by using 70 percent of the data. Therefore, in this example, the Decision Tree model performs better than the Naïve Bayes model.

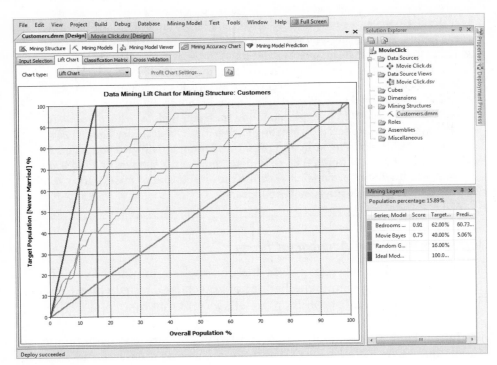

Figure 4-21 Standard lift chart

A simple way to interpret the standard lift chart (for a specific target value) is to imagine that you intend to use the model for a direct marketing campaign. In this scenario, think of the prediction produced by the model for your selected target value as being the prediction that a customer will respond to your marketing campaign. Because your purpose is to get as many responses as possible, you would naturally sort the potential customers in descending order of the probability returned by the model.

Consider now that you have 1,000 potential customers on your list and you know that 160 of those customers (16 percent, just like in Figure 4-21) will actually respond positively to your campaign. When sorting the customers by probability to respond, an ideal model will place these 160 customers on top. A real-life model will produce a number of incorrect predictions and rank some of the nonresponsive customers too high on the list.

If you sort the customers based on the probability predicted by the Decision Tree model in Figure 4-21, you will find 144 of the good customers (90 percent of the 160 target population) in the top 350 (35 percent). If you sort the customers based on probabilities predicted by the Naïve Bayes model, you will find the same number of good customers in the top 700 (70 percent). Therefore, you should use the Decision Trees model because you will need to send less marketing material to get the same result.

The lift chart's legend can be used to find the best probability threshold to use in predictions. For example, in Figure 4-21, the legend reflects the performance of each mining model for the top 16 percent of the test population (or after the top 16 percent of the hypothetical customers we considered). As you can see, 62 percent of the top 16 percent of all customers as sorted by the Decision Tree model are actually the target population. The probability that these customers are a target, as determined by the Decision Trees algorithm, is at least 60.73 percent as indicated in the Mining Legend. This number is the probability threshold required to achieve the performance at the indicated location of the lift chart.). The score associated with a mining model expresses the performance of the respective model as a fraction of the performance of the ideal model. Therefore, the score is always less than or equal to 1 and the performance is better as it gets closer to 1.

Using the Profit Chart

By changing the chart type to a profit chart, you can get a cost perspective of the quality of the model. The profit chart moves closer to the direct marketing campaign simulation that explains the lift chart. It prompts you to enter the initial cost (of the campaign), cost per item (how much it costs you to target one customer), and revenue per successful return (or how much you gain when the model correctly identifies a target customer). It then plots a chart of the profits you will receive, using the models you've created. This can help you decide which model to use and how many people to send mail to.

The profit chart in Figure 4-22 is built for a target population of 1,000 potential customers. The initial cost of the campaign is $500, the individual cost is $10, and the revenue per successful prediction is $50. You can tell that if you only have enough money to mail to less than 5 percent of the population, you should go with the Naïve Bayes model. If you have enough to go up to about 28 percent, the Decision Trees model would be your best bet. Most importantly, it tells you that regardless of how much money you can spend, you will maximize your profits by sending mail to the top 28 percent of the population as sorted by probabilities predicted using the Decision Trees model. Additionally, it tells you how to determine the people to send to.

Clicking on the chart causes a vertical line to appear with statistics about each line at the point displayed in the Mining Legend. In this case, the chart shows that you will maximize your profit by sending a mailing to everyone with a propensity to buy of 13.24 percent or better using the Decision Trees model.

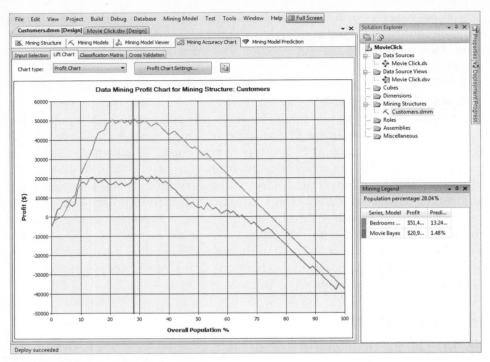

Figure 4-22 Profit chart with a legend

Multiple Target Accuracy Charts

Another type of accuracy chart is produced when you select a discrete target variable but you don't specify which value of the target you are looking for. In this case, you get a modified lift chart that looks a bit like an upside-down standard chart. This chart shows the overall performance of the model across all possible target states. In this version, a line coordinate indicates how many guesses would have been correct had you used that model. The ideal line here is at a 45-degree angle, indicating that if you had used 50 percent of the data, you would have been correct for about 50 percent of the population, or if you had used 100 percent of the data, you would have been correct all the time. The random guess line is based on the most likely state discovered in the training set. For example, if you were predicting gender and 57 percent of your training data was female, you could presume that you would get the best results by guessing female for every case. The random guess line will end at the percentage of the target that was equal to the most likely state in the training set. That is, for the gender example, if the testing set had the same distribution as the training set, the line would end at 57 percent; but if only 30 percent of the testing set was female, the line would end at 30 percent.

Using the Classification Matrix

The Classification Matrix tab of the Mining Accuracy Chart pane shows you how many times a model made a correct prediction and what answers were given when the answers were wrong. This can be important in cases where there is a cost associated with each wrong decision. For example, if you want to predict which class of member card to assign to a customer based on his or her creditworthiness, it would be less costly to misclassify someone who should have received a bronze card than it would to issue that person a platinum card. This view simply shows you a matrix per model, illustrating counts of each pairwise combination of actual values and predicted values.

Scatter Accuracy Charts

The last type of accuracy chart is strictly for continuous values. This chart is a scatter plot, comparing actual values versus predicted values for each case. In a perfect model, each point would end up on a perfect 45-degree angle, indicating that the predicted values exactly matched the actual values. On any other model, the closer the points fall to the 45-degree line, the better.

Figure 4-23 shows a scatter accuracy plot. You can see that this model performed well for most cases, with only one point that was significantly off. The scatter accuracy plot is automatically displayed instead of the lift chart when a continuous target is selected. (The model used in generating the scatter plot in Figure 4-23 is available on this book's companion website at www.wiley.com/go/data_mining_SQL_2008.)

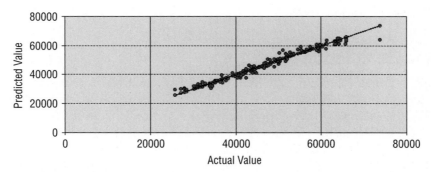

Figure 4-23 Scatter accuracy plot

Creating a Lift Chart on MovieClick

As an example, follow these steps to create a lift chart targeting customers who go to the theater weekly:

1. Switch to the Mining Accuracy Chart pane by clicking the Mining Accuracy Chart icon.

2. Ensure that the Synchronize Prediction Columns and Values option is checked.

3. Select the mining models you want to analyze for accuracy. For this example, select the `Bedrooms Tree` and the `Movies Bayes` model.

4. In the `Predictable Column Name` column, select the `Marital Status` model.

5. In the `Predict Value` column, select the `Never Married` value.

6. In the Select data... area of the Mining Accuracy Chart pane, ensure that you select the option to use the mining model test cases.

7. Click the Lift Chart tab on the top of the pane to switch to the chart view.

   A query is sent to the server and a chart similar to the one shown previously in Figure 4-21 is displayed.

NOTE You may find cases where a model provides significant lift, yet rarely (or possibly never) classifies your specified target correctly. This is because the standard lift chart doesn't actually care if the model predicts correctly. The lift chart sorts the predictions by the highest probability that the prediction hits the target. If the maximum probability for the target in the model is 25 percent, then the model may never actually predict the target. The plot of the lift chart consists of the number of targeted cases that were captured by that ordering. Because the result of the lift and profit chart is simply a probability threshold indicating where you should stop considering customers, it doesn't actually matter if the final prediction was actually correct.

Using CrossValidation

The rightmost pane of the Mining Accuracy Chart view allows you to perform cross-validation on the models in your mining structure. The charts you learned about in the previous section measure the accuracy of a mining model on a test dataset. *Multifold cross-validation* is a technique that allows you to determine whether your model's training data is fit for the task.

Instead of using a validation data set that was not seen by the model during training, the cross-validation technique uses all (or a part) of the model's training data. It splits the training data into a number of partitions (or *folds* — hence the name of the technique) containing the same (or a very similar) number of training cases. The technique consists of building a mining model for each of these partitions. This partition-specific model is built with data from *all the other* partitions and validated against data from the current partition. The validation results for all partition models are returned as a result of running the cross-validation procedure. The validation of the partition models is performed by computing various accuracy measurements.

After executing this procedure, you must investigate the accuracy results for each partition model and look for two things:

- **How good the results are** — If all of the partition models' accuracy results are very good, then using the full data set to train a model will very likely result in a good mining model. If, on the other hand, all of the partition models' accuracy results are very poor, a model trained with the full data set is unlikely to provide much better results.

- **How similar the partition results are** — If the results for each partition are similar, then the training set is good for the current task. If the results vary a lot between partition models, then you probably do not have enough data in your training set. (Differences suggest that partitions have significantly different data distributions.)

In SQL Server Data Mining, the cross-validation stored procedure is executed for all the mining models defined inside the current mining structure. The data set partitioned and used by the procedure is the training data inside the mining structure (so the holdout data does not participate in cross-validation). Note that a model need not be trained for the procedure to work, because it creates model clones (using the same algorithm and parameters) for each partition. Also, the procedure can be configured to run only on a limited subset of data from the mining structure.

Consequently, you can use the cross-validation procedure to find out which algorithm does the best job for the problem you are modeling, without having to train a model for each algorithm, which is a potentially time-consuming task. To do so, follow these steps:

1. Define your mining structure in BI Dev Studio.

2. Add multiple models (using various algorithms, parameters, and filtering configurations) inside the mining structure.

3. Execute the cross-validation stored procedure on all or just a part of the structure training data.

4. Select the models that perform best.

5. Remove the other models.

6. Train the best performing models with all data in the mining structure.

The procedure uses stratified sampling in building the partitions in order to ensure that all partitions have similar data distributions with respect to the target column. Similar data distributions lead to similar patterns. So, if the accuracy results vary wildly between partitions, it means that the sampling produced very different distributions, which happens often if the training set is not large enough.

Follow these steps to evaluate the models in the `MovieClick` project using the cross-validation procedure:

1. Switch to the Cross Validation pane of the Mining Accuracy Chart view.

2. Select the number of folds to be used in the procedure. Use the default of 10.

3. Select the number of training cases to be used in the procedure. The default selection, 0, means that all mining structure training data will be used in the procedure (which may take longer). Since there is a small amount of data in this set, you can leave the default.

4. Select a target attribute and optionally a target state. The state is useful if you are not interested in the overall accuracy of the models, but in how well they predict a certain state of an attribute. For this example, select the `Marital Status` attribute.

5. Click the Get Results button to launch the procedure.

Execution may take a while. The structure in the example contains two models (`Bedrooms Tree` and `Movies Bayes`). The cross-validation procedure will train 10 clones for each of these models, each with 90 percent of the structure training data, and then evaluate the accuracy for these clones. The procedure results are shown in Figure 4-24.

> **NOTE** BI Dev Studio has a `Query Timeout` property that may affect the execution of long-running queries, such as the cross-validation procedure. If execution results in a timeout error, you should increase the query timeout. Select the Tools ⇨ Options menu and, under the Business Intelligence Designers node, change the value of the `Query Timeout` property to either 0, which indicates that the query will never timeout, or a large number (in seconds).

The procedure results are grouped by models in the mining structure. The first set of results describes the `Bedrooms Tree` model, and the second set of results (you will need to scroll down the window to find it) describes the `Movies Bayes` model.

For each model, the result consists of a set of accuracy measurements and their values for each of the folds considered by the procedure. Figure 4-24 presents two such measurements: `Classification — Pass` and `Classification — Fail`.

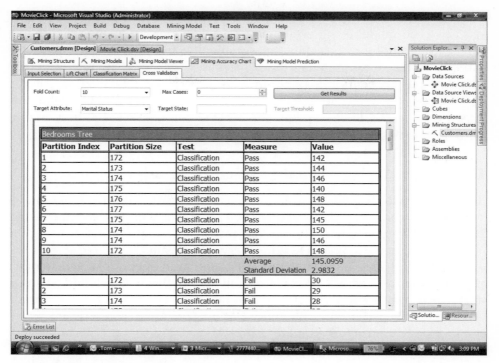

Figure 4-24 Cross-validation results

The first accuracy measure, `Classification – Pass`, tells you how many correct classifications of the target attribute (`Marital Status`) were performed over each partition by its corresponding partition model. The numbers vary between 140 and 150, with an average of about 145 and a standard deviation of almost 3. The absolute number of correct classifications does not tell you much yet, but the standard deviation of 3, compared to the average of 145, means that the partitions differ typically by less than 2 percent, so the results seem reasonably compact. This is good news for the `Bedrooms Tree` model — it seems the training data is enough.

The second set of measurements, `Classification – Fail`, tells you how many incorrect classifications of the target were performed during evaluation. The numbers vary between 24 and 35, with an average of around 29 and a standard deviation of 3.5. The results are not as compact as in the case of correct classification, but they don't vary wildly.

Consequently, it seems that the training data is pretty good for the classification problem at hand (correctly identifying the marital status), and a model trained on the full training set will produce significantly more correct classifications than incorrect ones.

The type of accuracy measurements depends on the type of the algorithm used by each model being evaluated (clustering measurements are different than classification or regression measurements), and also on the type of the target predictable attribute (accuracy measurements for a discrete target are different than those used for a continuous target). For a detailed description of all accuracy tests and measurements executed by the cross-validation procedure, search Books Online (or MSDN) for **Cross-Validation Report (Analysis Services - Data Mining)**.

Using the Mining Model Prediction Builder

The Mining Model Prediction Builder pane in Data Mining Designer allows you to build and edit prediction queries, view the results, and save the results back to a table. The Query Builder has three views that you select using the View button on the toolbar: Design, Query, and Results.

The Design view for building queries is similar to query designers in other products such as Access, so if you are familiar with them, you should feel right at home. The process of selecting input tables is the same as in the Mining Accuracy Chart. The only difference is that you must also indicate which model from the structure you are using. After doing so, you can build your query.

To build the query, drag and drop columns from the model or input tables at the top to the grid at the bottom. In addition to dragging and dropping columns, the grid control allows you to manually specify output columns by clicking empty cells and selecting from drop-down controls that appear, or typing as appropriate.

NOTE You can drag only the columns that are predictable from the model. These columns are marked with a diamond in the Query Builder.

When you're selecting a prediction function, the drop-down list in the Field column contains all the functions that are allowed on the algorithm used by the selected model. You specify the function parameters in the Criteria/Argument column, which contains a description of what type of parameters you can use.

The Query view shows you the query generated by the builder. You can copy and paste this query into your applications if needed, or edit the query here as necessary. This view is very handy for modifying queries to use constructs that aren't supported by the Query Builder. For example, you can use `SELECT TOP n <column> FROM <model> ORDER BY PredictProbability(<column>)` to retrieve the respondents above the threshold you determined using the accuracy charts. Note that the edits you make to the query are not reflected in Design view, so switching back to that view will override your changes.

Switching to the Results view executes your query and displays the results in a table. You can copy the results to other applications, or click the Save Query Result button to export the results to a database table.

NOTE You can export your results to a table, and then add this table to your DSV to perform iterative data mining.

Executing a Query on the MovieClick Model

In this exercise, you execute a query that will return the predicted frequency that a customer goes to movies at theaters, along with the probability that the customer would have done so on a monthly basis. Follow these steps:

1. Switch to the Query Builder by choosing the Mining Query Builder icon in the Data Mining designer.

2. Click Select Case Table on the Select Input Tables window in the top pane of the Query Builder.

3. Select the Homeowners table in the dialog box that appears, and click OK.

4. Drag the Customer ID column from the Homeowners table, and drop it on the grid.

5. Drag the Theater Freq column from the mining model, and drop it on the grid.

6. In the Source column of the last row, select Prediction Function.

7. In the Field column of the last row, select PredictProbability.

8. In the Alias column of the last row, type **ProbMonthly**.

9. Drag the Theater Freq column from the mining model, and drop it into the Criteria/Argument column of the last row.

10. Edit the Criteria/Argument column of the last row by adding **'Monthly'** to the end of the text that's already there.

11. To display the query (and see how much typing you saved), switch to the Query view using the drop-down button on the Query Builder toolbar.

12. Switch to the Results view to execute the query and see the results.

The query is executed on a separate thread, and the results are streamed to the client. This means that the user interface is still active while the query is running, so you can cancel it or perform any other user interface task during this process. When it is complete, you can copy the results or save them to a database.

Creating Data Mining Reports

Another way to access data mining query results and to distribute those results is to use SQL Server Reporting Services. Reporting Services provides a mechanism for creating custom reports containing text and graphics that can be distributed via HTML, e-mail, or in print or Microsoft Office documents. Web-based reports can be made interactive by adding report parameters that modify the report contents. Reporting Services has options to run reports periodically and cache the results to expedite report retrieval, and you can even specify queries to control report distribution. The product documentation has extensive details on Reporting Services functionality, and there are several books on how to create and manage reports, so this discussion only examines how data mining features are integrated.

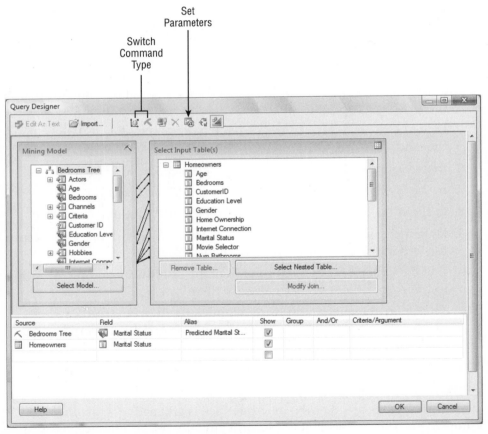

Figure 4-25 Reporting Services Data Mining Query Designer

To use Reporting Services with data mining, you simply create a Reporting Services project with BI Dev Studio, and specify an Analysis Services database as your data source. Depending on the contents of the database, you will be presented with either an OLAP or Data Mining query builder, as shown in Figure 4-25. You can always switch between the two modes by clicking the Switch Command Type button indicated in the figure. The Set Parameters button allows you to create parameters that can be set by Reporting Services. The Edit as Text button allows you to switch into SQL mode so that you can create queries not supported by the Query Builder.

NOTE You can create reports from user-defined functions using the CALL syntax. To do this, you must be in the DMX Query Builder and switch to the SQL mode, where you can type in your CALL statement.

When creating a report from a data mining query, you have all of the Reporting Services functions to work with. For example, DMX does not support grouping operations, but Reporting Services does. You can use the grouping function of Reporting Services against the query described in Figure 4-25 to create a report that is the equivalent of the classification matrix described previously. This report contains a matrix control with the predicted values in the columns, and the actual values in the rows. The cell data contains the expression "=CountRows()". Figure 4-26 shows the result of such a report.

Marital Status	Predicted Never Married	Predicted Married	Predicted Divorced
Actual Married	102	1467	7
Actual Divorced	27	40	14
Actual Never Married	237	76	2
Actual Separated	5	10	2
Actual Other	17	29	5
Actual	3	17	2

Figure 4-26 Classification matrix report

Using SQL Server Management Studio

Management Studio in SQL Server 2008 is an environment familiar to DBAs — it was introduced in SQL Server 2005 to replace Enterprise Manager and Query Analyzer from SQL Server 2000, which are the tools of the trade for many administrators. In SQL Server 2005, this environment has been expanded to cover all SQL Server technologies. One user interface can manage relational databases, OLAP cube, data mining models, Reporting Services, and more. The following tasks pertinent to data mining can be performed in Management Studio:

- Maintain servers
- Create and maintain databases
- Browse models
- Build queries using the prediction builder
- Build queries using the query editor
- Process models and structures
- Assign object permissions
- Backup and restore databases

To perform operations on an Analysis Services database in Management Studio, you must have administrator permissions on the database you are modifying. You do not need to be an administrator of the entire server.

NOTE If you want to set up a database for a nonserver administrator to create mining models, a user with server administrator privileges needs to create a new database in SQL Management Studio and make the nonserver administrator a database administrator for that database. The user will then use BI Dev Studio in Immediate mode to create and edit mining models. The user can also use Offline mode if he or she changes the deployment database to the name of the database created for him or her. Note, however, that this method will overwrite the existing database completely, so users must create their own administrative roles, or they will not be able to modify the database after the first deployment.

Understanding the Management Studio User Interface

The Management Studio interface has the same look and feel as BI Dev Studio. Windows, menus, and toolbars all work the same way in both studios, so you can customize your layout in Management Studio just as you can in BI Dev Studio. The tool windows most pertinent to data mining are the Registered Servers (Server Explorer) window, Object Explorer, and Template Explorer, as shown in Figure 4-27.

Using Server Explorer

The Server Explorer window allows quick access to a number of servers you interact with regularly. To access Analysis Services servers, click the cube icon in the embedded toolbar (shown previously in Figure 4-27). You will perform most of your work in the Object Explorer window, which is described in more detail in the next section. The Template Explorer is hidden by default, and must be selected from the View menu. The Template Explorer contains a set of syntax templates to make it easier to create queries. As in the Server Explorer, you select the corresponding cube icon (shown previously in Figure 4-27) to access the templates specific to Analysis Services.

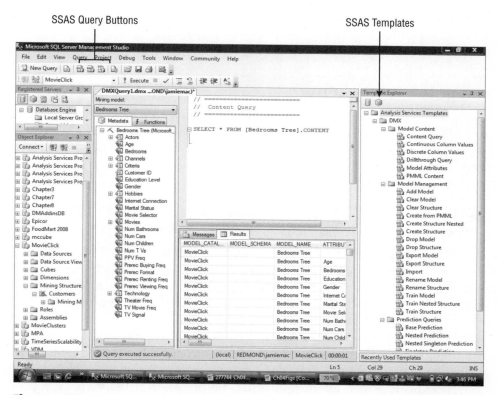

Figure 4-27 Management Studio with Template Explorer shown and Analysis Services Icons indicated

Using Object Explorer

Object Explorer is where the majority of data mining management operations will occur. You can perform most operations by expanding the tree structure to the object of interest, and then right-clicking the object and selecting the desired operation. The most common operations you will perform here are processing, security management, and backing up and restoring databases.

Security management is described in Chapter 15, and backing up and restoring are well-documented in the product documentation. Looking at the object properties from this interface will provide you with the creation date and last processing date.

From Object Explorer, you can also create XML for Analysis (XMLA) scripts that will create, alter, or delete the specified object. Selecting Script Mining Model as Create from the context menu will create an XMLA script to the clipboard, a file, or a Query Editor window. Using XMLA is a quick and convenient way to create objects that differ only slightly by scripting them, changing the object identifiers, and making other edits. XMLA is described in more detail in Chapter 15.

Using the Query Editor

The query editor is designed for advanced users with a solid understanding of DMX syntax. It is a freeform text editor with IntelliSense that allows you to type and execute ad hoc queries. You can then execute these queries directly from the interface and examine the results.

There are two ways to create a DMX query:

- You can click the New DMX Query button on the toolbar
- You can open a template from Template Explorer

When you create a new query window, you will be prompted to connect to a server. The Connection dialog box does not ask you to provide the database name, so after the editor window opens, you need to select the target database in the SQL Editor toolbar. At this point, you can start authoring your queries. In the editor, you have all of the standard VS editing features (such as search and replace, bookmarking, keyword color coding, and IntelliSense). You can use IntelliSense by beginning to type a keyword and pressing Ctrl+Spacebar to see a menu of likely matches. You can have many DMX queries in the same file. To indicate which query to execute, simply select it before pressing the Execute button or pressing F5.

Although the level of flexibility provided by the query editor demands quite a bit of user DMX knowledge, there are ways to jumpstart the query authoring process to make it easier. The first is to use Template Explorer, which provides many syntax examples from which to choose. The other is to use the query builder described earlier in this chapter. You can launch the query builder by right-clicking on a mining model and selecting the query builder from the model's context menu. When you have built enough of your query to get started, you can simply switch to SQL view and copy the text into a query editor window. This automatically creates any source data queries for prediction JOIN statements and frees you from writing lengthy On clauses.

NOTE You can also drag Template Explorer items into existing query windows to add the template contents to your current query.

Summary

In this chapter, you learned about the breadth of tools available for data mining. BI Dev Studio, with its wizards and editors, is where you will perform most of your data mining by creating and examining models either attached to a server or in an offline project. In this environment, you complete a data mining project by creating a data source, a data source view (DSV), and finally a mining structure with its corresponding mining models. All of these objects are fully editable through a combination of custom designers and the property grid. In addition, you can use Data Mining Designer to view models with a variety of custom viewers, and to test models with a variety of accuracy charts.

SQL Management Studio is where models are managed throughout their lifetime. This environment provides tools for security, processing, backing up and restoring databases, and other management functions. The viewers, accuracy charts, and prediction builder that are available in BI Dev Studio are available here as well. Additionally, there is the free-form query editor with a query template library that you can leverage to create ad hoc DMX queries.

These BI Dev Studio and SQL Management Studio tools create the user interface suite for Analysis Services.

Chapter 5 describes a simplified interface for creating and managing data mining structures and models inside Microsoft Excel.

Implementing a Data Mining Process Using Office 2007

In Chapter 4, you learned how to get the best out of SQL Server Data Mining using the tools in the box, such as BI Development Studio (BI Dev Studio) and SQL Server Management Studio. Although it's true that these tools provide the most comprehensive access to the data mining functionality in SQL Server, it is also true that, for most users, they simply are too much to handle. The Data Mining Add-Ins for Office 2007 do not claim to offer fidelity with BI Dev Studio — or even to cover the entire feature set of SQL Server Data Mining — but they do provide a much simpler client interface for performing data mining. Also, because of the nature of the tools themselves, they offer useful and interesting functionality not present in the toolset that comes with SQL Data Mining.

As with Chapter 4, this chapter is not intended to replace Books Online. Instead, this chapter gives you a higher-level overview, lower-level details, and tricks that allow you to exploit the tools to your best advantage.

In this chapter, you will learn about the following:

- The overall data mining process as implemented using the Data Mining Client for Excel 2007

- The different methods for getting data into Excel, and how to prepare the data for mining

- Creating structures and models using Excel data or external data

- Validating models for accuracy

- Applying, browsing, and managing models

- Creating shareable, interactive model visualizations using the Data Mining Templates for Visio 2007

- Getting a jump start on DMX using the Trace dialog box

The examples in this chapter use the `Chapter5.xlsx` file available at `www.wiley.com/go/data_mining_SQL_2008`.

Introducing the Data Mining Client

The Data Mining Add-Ins for Office 2007 comprise three different add-ins. The Table Analysis Tools for Excel 2007 (covered in Chapter 2) are designed for the non-data miner who simply wants to learn more about data without a lot of investment. The Data Mining Client for Excel tool and the Data Mining Templates for Visio tool are designed for the intermediate data miners to expert information workers who know they must do data mining and desire a clean, concise, and appropriate workspace in which to do so.

The Data Mining Add-Ins package is available as a free download from Microsoft. Additional information about the add-ins is available at `www.sqlserverdatamining.com`.

The Data Mining Client is designed to walk you through the data mining process. The basic process in any data mining project is shown in Figure 5-1.

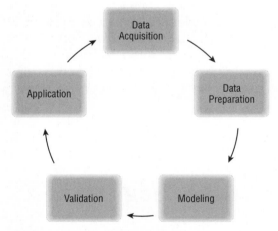

Figure 5-1 Data mining process

Data acquisition tools are provided natively by Excel with the Data Mining Client. The Data Mining Client adds an additional method beyond those. Many users already have data in Excel-accessible formats, and Excel has tools for data importation. The other pieces of the data mining process are supported directly from the Data Mining Client ribbon, as shown in Figure 5-2. Each chunk of the ribbon indicates a step in the process.

Figure 5-2 Data Mining Client ribbon

Although the entire process is necessary for any project, not all steps must be taken by the same individual. For example, it is common for an analyst to develop a data set to be modeled and validated by a data miner. After a model is created, business users may use the model to make predictions against data in their own workbooks. Alternatively, a model created using the Data Mining Client can be deployed in applications as can models created using the BI Dev Studio (for example, using Reporting Services or Integration Services).

Importing Data Using the Data Mining Client

For those who don't already have data in a workbook ready to go, Excel offers several options for importing data. Excel can import data directly from Access, SQL Server (and other databases), text files, and XML files. It can also scrape web pages to turn them into raw data (provided they are well formatted). Additionally, if you are connected to Microsoft SharePoint, your enterprise may have advertised data sources. The data import options are located in the first chunk of Excel's Data ribbon, as shown in Figure 5-3.

Excel saves connection and mapping information in your workbook, so you can refresh your workbook as the data changes without having to go through the import process again. The details of the various data import options of Excel are beyond the scope of this book, but they are included in the Excel documentation.

The Data Mining Client offers a method of importing data from large database tables that may not fit into the 1 million-row limit of Excel, or simply when you want to retrieve only a portion of the data. The Data Preparation chunk of the Data Mining Client (shown in Figure 5-4) contains the Sample Data tool, which offers the option to sample external data. This allows you to use a percentage or a fixed number of rows sampled randomly from a database table or query accessed through Analysis Services. Note that the sampling occurs on the client side, so all of the data will be moved to the client, and the unselected rows will be discarded.

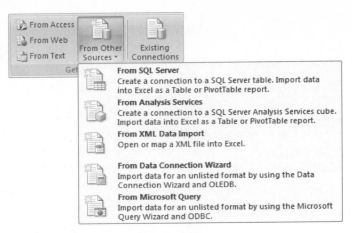

Figure 5-3 Excel Data Import options

Figure 5-4 Data Preparation chunk of the Data Mining ribbon

ACCESSING DATA IN THE DATA MINING CLIENT

All of the Data Mining Client operations allow you to access data in Excel ranges or tables. Most of them also allow you to access external data in databases. The mechanism for importing data is to go through an Analysis Services data source object, meaning that the data you want to use must be accessible to the Analysis Services server to which you are connected.

If your Analysis Services database doesn't already have the necessary data source, you can use the Data Source Query dialog box to create data sources. Because of the wide variety of data sources, the Data Mining Client supports only the creation of data sources and queries to SQL Server databases. You can still query any arbitrary data source if you use BI Dev Studio or another tool to create the data source object, and enter a query manually.

Data Exploration and Preparation

Most (if not all) experts consider data exploration and preparation to be the single most important step in the data mining process. Exploration and preparation is where you begin to form your hypothesis about the problem you are trying to solve. In this step, you understand, shape, and select your data in a way that you believe will be pertinent to the problem at hand. Excel is a great environment for massaging data to look the way you want it to for your problem, and you can exercise creativity in how you manipulate your data because the entire Excel arsenal of data tools is at hand.

The most common manipulation is simply to derive values from other columns in your data. For example, many data sets have Start Date and End Date columns (or their equivalents). The direct interpretation of such data is usually of little value for most data mining applications. However, from these columns, you could easily add an Elapsed Time column that may be much more useful. Furthermore, depending on the nature of the problem and your business, it may be beneficial to create Start Month and End Month columns. Taking the difference, average, sum, ratio, or other operation on row data is very useful in generating attributes that can be informative for mining.

The Data Mining Client adds some additional data exploration and preparation tools that, although useful for most Excel users, are particularly necessary to data miners. Whereas Excel manipulations generally operate across rows, these tools operate on a single column of data, providing summary information and comprehensive changes across the rows.

Discretizing Data with the Explore Data Tool

Many times, it is more convenient to deal with ranges of data, rather than continuous data. For example, instead of considering Age as a continuous number across the range of ages in your data, you could break the ages into discrete sections that are easier to understand. The Explore Data tool is designed to show histograms for discrete and continuous columns, and it has a bonus feature that allows you to materialize continuous histograms into table columns.

Figure 5-5 shows the Explore Data tool displaying a histogram for the Age column divided into six buckets. Clicking the Add New Column button causes the tool to add a new column to the workbook, indicating the specified range for each row. Additionally, you can use the adjacent copy button to copy an image of the chart, which you can then paste into your workbook, retain for documentation purposes, or print out.

Chopping Off the Long Tail

Another frequent scenario occurs when you have a discrete column with many values, but only a few values have any meaningful support. For example, this could happen with a City column for an Employee table. Most employees will live in a few cities close to work, but many people live farther away. The farther away the city, the fewer employees are likely to work there. In situations like these, there are often a large number of cities that have only a few employees or even a single employee living there. For many data mining problems, values with small support don't have significant patterns, and can even act as a source of noise that reduces the overall quality of the model.

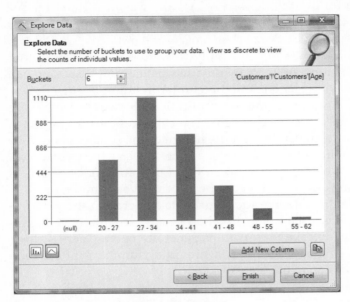

Figure 5-5 Exploring continuous data

The Outliers tool can be used to remove or replace values that occur below a certain threshold. Figure 5-6 shows the Specify Thresholds page of the Remove Outliers wizard, indicating that all values that occur less than 65 times in the column should be removed. The subsequent pages of the wizard offer multiple choices on how to perform the removal. You can replace the values with a set value such as Other, or you can delete the rows containing the values below the threshold. You can also choose to change the data in place, or to create new data with the changes.

NOTE Excel does not support Undo operations for functionality provided by add-in components. Therefore, unless you are absolutely sure and have a backup of your data, you should never choose the option to change the data in place.

Consolidating Meaning

A different reason many distinct values appear in a column is that a single concept can be represented in multiple ways. This can be because of abbreviation, convention, or simply misspelling. For example, a column representing a person's title could have the values Dr. and Doctor, which mean the same to people, but are distinct to the data mining algorithms. Also, there are cases where the values have distinct meanings, but are too detailed for the problem you are trying to solve. A typical example is education. Values can be High School Equivalency, High School Graduate, Some College, Associate's Degree, Bachelor's Degree, Master's Degree, PhD, JD, and so on — the list goes on and on. For the business problem you are interested in, the only point of interest may be whether or not a customer graduated from college without all the details. In both of these cases, the column values should be consolidated to a single value for use by the data mining algorithms.

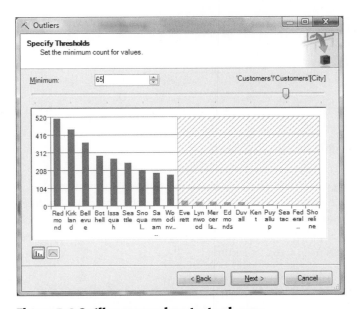

Figure 5-6 Outlier removal on text columns

Figure 5-7 shows the Re-label Data tool being used to consolidate multiple education levels into two values representing a customer's college education. As with the Outliers tool, the results can be changed in place if you're absolutely certain you don't need to undo, or they can be added to the data.

Although the functionality of the Re-label Data tool could be implemented with a series of search-and-replace activities, the ability to change all values in a single place is very powerful. An unexpected usage scenario for Re-label Data appeared when an Analysis Services team member demonstrated the feature at a user conference in Serbia. While on stage, the presenter realized that because he was speaking Serbian, he should be showing data in Serbian as well. He then proceeded to use the Re-label Data feature to quickly and efficiently translate his workbook in front of the audience.

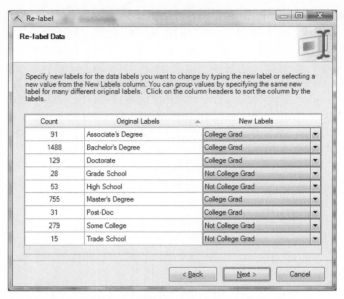

Figure 5-7 Using Re-label Data to consolidate values

NOTE The Data Mining Client will consider a column to have discrete values even if it contains only a single text value. You can use Re-label Data to eliminate the odd text value in a column of otherwise numerical data. Sort the dialog's table by the `Original Labels` column to pop the text values to the top, and blank out or enter a number into the `New Labels` column.

Eliminating Spurious Values

Whenever you have numerical data, it is quite possible that a few values will be far out of the range of the rest of the data. For example, if you had a column containing the net wealth of Microsoft employees, you would have Bill Gates, Steve Ballmer, a handful of other presidents and vice presidents, and then the other 70,000 employees. The wealth figures of those few outliers are not representative of the whole, and have the potential of skewing the results quite a bit. Data errors (such as negative figures when the numbers should always be positive) can also have deleterious effects (although, with the 2008 financial crisis, negative wealth values may be common).

The Remove Outliers tool can be used on continuous columns to ensure that all values are in a reasonable range. As shown in Figure 5-8, the tool shows the data as a curve that you can truncate on either side by setting minimum and maximum values, or by using the sliders. As with the discrete use of the Remove Outliers tool, you have several options on how to resolve the outlying values. However, unlike the discrete scenario, it is often preferable to simply delete entire rows, rather than changing values.

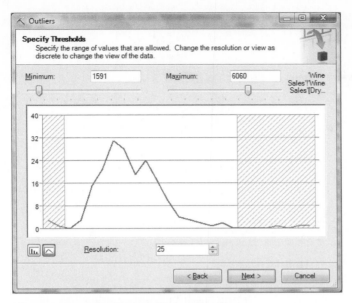

Figure 5-8 Removing continuous outliers

Rebalancing Data

When you're trying to mine for rare events (such as fraud detection), you need to take a different approach. Many algorithms perform poorly when looking for a target that occurs very infrequently in the data. One solution to this problem is to selectively sample data such that the target occurs more often. The core assumption behind this technique is that non-target states are essentially random, and patterns surround the thing you are looking for. You can think of the target as a signal the algorithm is trying to detect, and rebalancing the data is a method of amplifying that signal.

For example, imagine a situation where you are looking for fraudulent transactions, and you have 500,000 rows of data that are marked as to whether they are fraudulent or not. Because fraud is rare, there are only a very few (about 1,000) rows that are marked as fraudulent, giving you a target that's only 0.2 percent of your data. To assist the algorithm, you can rebalance the data to increase the frequency to 5 percent or 10 percent.

In addition to creating small data sets from big ones, you can use the Sample Data tool to rebalance data. When selecting the rebalance option, you select a target column and state, as well as the percentage of target representation and the maximum size of the result set. Figure 5-9 shows a sample of rebalancing such that the value Rent for the Home Ownership column will be present in 30 percent of the columns, and the result set will have no more than 10,000 rows. If there aren't enough rows in the source data to allow for 30-percent representation of Rent, then the result set will be smaller to ensure the correct ratios.

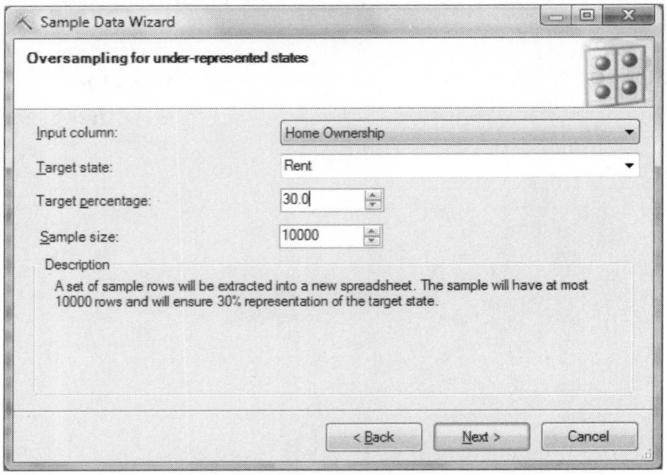

Figure 5-9 Oversampling to rebalance data

You must be careful about interpreting results from models created on rebalanced data sets. Using the data in Figure 5-9 as an example, if you increase the concentration of renters from 3 percent to 30 percent, prediction results will be weighted to reflect that concentration and will have much higher probabilities. For this reason, it is a good idea to use the Sample Data tool to first split the raw data into distinct sets so that you will have representative data to test any models you build.

> **NOTE** With the exception of sampling data from an external data source, all of the data exploration and preparation tools operate on Excel data only. These tools are not functions of the SQL Server Analysis Services server, and execute completely on the client.

Modeling

The *data modeling chunk* is where you build models on your prepared data sets. The data modeling chunk, shown in Figure 5-10, provides options for task-based modeling that trades simplicity for flexibility, and advanced options that provide almost as much functionality as BI Dev Studio.

Task-Based Modeling

Each modeling task on the data modeling ribbon loosely corresponds to the data mining tasks described in Chapter 1 — classification, regression, clustering, association, and forecasting. The tasks are designed to provide an experience that is suitable for a wider range of users than exists within BI Dev Studio. As a result, the tasks sacrifice flexibility and capability for ease of use. For example, each task automatically selects the data mining algorithm and the column types, and presents focused task-based options rather than offering all possibilities.

Figure 5-10 Data modeling chunk of the Data Mining Client ribbon

Table 5-1 shows the algorithms used by each task. This section outlines the modeling process and describes the idiosyncrasies of each step. The algorithms displayed in bold are the default for each task.

Table 5-1 Algorithms Used for Data Modeling Tasks

TASK	ALGORITHMS	DETAILS
Classify	**Decision Trees**	Chapter 7
	Logistic Regression	Chapter 12
	Naïve Bayes	Chapter 6
	Neural Networks	Chapter 12
Estimate	**Decision Trees**	Chapter 7
	Linear Regression	Chapter 7
	Logistic Regression	Chapter 12
	Neural Networks	Chapter 12
Cluster	**Clustering**	Chapter 9
Forecast	**Time Series**	Chapter 8
Associate	**Association Rules**	Chapter 11

Each task launches a wizard that prompts you for information needed to complete the modeling and mining operation. Figure 5-11 shows the basic flow of the modeling task wizards.

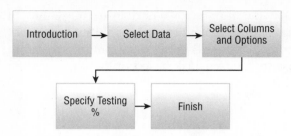

Figure 5-11 Modeling task wizard flow

Introduction

The Introduction page shows helpful text describing the purpose and the use of the task wizard.

Select Data

The Select Data page is identical to the select data pages of the data exploration and preparation tools. All of the tasks (with the exception of Associate) operate on both data inside Excel and data in external databases.

The first three tasks (Classify, Estimate, and Cluster) operate on a standard data format where rows represent each case and columns represent attributes of that case. Advanced features such as nested tables are not available through the Data Mining Client modeling tasks.

Following is a description of the last two tasks:

- **Forecast** — In the Forecast task, each row represents a unit of time, and each column represents the value of an event during that time. Optionally, there can be a column that indicates the value of the time unit (such as the day or month that the events were recorded). If there is a time column, the data must be sorted by that column, as with the Associate task's group column. If there is no time column, the data is assumed to be sorted already.

- **Associate** — In addition to requiring data to be in an Excel worksheet, the Associate task also requires that the data be in a specific format. Each row of data for the Associate task represents one item in a group. Therefore, Associate requires one column to represent the group, and one column to represent the item, and the data must be sorted by the group column. Figure 5-12 shows a sample data layout for the Association task.

Select Columns and Options

This step in the wizard is where the columns used for modeling and the options for each task are specified. Each task also allows for the specification of additional algorithm parameters that are not necessary for completion of the task. This list shows the column selection requirements for each of the data modeling tasks.

	A	B
1	CustomerID	Hobby
2	877687	Business & Investing
3	877687	Travel
4	877687	News & Media
5	877687	Kids & Family
6	877687	Camping & Hiking
7	877687	Science & Technology
8	877723	Other
9	877723	Computer
10	877723	Travel
11	877723	Science & Technology
12	877723	Museums & Art
13	877757	Computer
14	877757	Camping & Hiking
15	877757	Charity and Community Organizations
16	877757	Photography
17	877757	Travel
18	877792	Travel
19	877792	Gardening
20	877792	Home Design/Improvement
21	877792	Kids & Family
22	877792	Autos Boats & Planes
23	877840	Games & Roleplaying
24	877840	Science & Technology
25	877840	News & Media
26	877840	Fitness

Figure 5-12 Transactional data for the Associate task

- **Classify** — For the Classify task, you need to indicate the target — the column you want to classify — and the columns to be used as inputs. You can change the algorithm used for classification by clicking on the Parameters button and choosing a different algorithm.

- **Estimate** — Like the Classify task, Estimate requires that you specify the target and the inputs. However, the Estimate task requires you to specify which columns will indicate regressors — that is, which numerical columns will be used in regression formulas to estimate the target value. The nature of the Decision Tree algorithm (described in Chapter 7) is that the accuracy depends on the specification of proper regressors. The task provides a tool to suggest regressors that seem to add value. When you execute this task, the task actually creates a series of estimation models that try different options, and suggests the columns that are likely to add value. As with the Classify task, this task allows you to change the algorithm used for estimation through the Parameters button. Because only the Decision Tree algorithm requires regressors, the regressor options are unavailable if you change the algorithm.

- **Cluster** — With the Cluster task, you set the columns to use and the number of clusters for the task to find. The number you set is a suggestion — the algorithm may determine that there are actually fewer clusters in the data than you specify.

- **Forecast** — The Forecast task provides the option to select a column representing the time stamp (if there is one) and the columns you want to forecast. Forecasting can provide different results, depending on the edition of SQL Server to which you are connecting. Enterprise editions of SQL Server allow cross-prediction (that is, the ability to determine patterns between the various data series), whereas Standard edition servers forecast based on the independent patterns in each series.

- **Associate** — The Associate task requires you to specify the group column (or transaction ID) and the item column that you want to associate. It also allows you to specify the two critical parameters of the association algorithm: support and probability. The *support* parameter indicates how many times an item or group of items must occur in the data for it to be considered interesting, and the *probability* parameter indicates how likely a coincidence must be for it to be considered a rule. For more details on these parameters, see Chapter 11.

Split Data

The Split Data page is shown for the Classify and Estimate tasks. Specifying an amount of data to set aside for testing your model simplifies the entire data mining process.

Finishing the Task

The Finish page in each task wizard allows you to name the objects that are created and set additional options. On this page, you set the names of the mining structure and mining model that are created, and you can optionally add textual descriptions for these objects as well. If you want to create models with the Data Mining Client, and do not have administrative permissions on an Analysis Services database, you can check the Use Temporary Model box to create temporary models that will be deleted when you disconnect from the server.

Advanced Modeling in the Data Mining Client

If you think the canned modeling tasks are too limiting, or you simply need greater flexibility, there are the advanced modeling tools. The advanced modeling tools allow the explicit definition of a mining structure that can take advantage of almost all the features of SQL Server Data Mining — nested tables being the notable exception. Furthermore, you can add models to any existing mining structure using any algorithm available on the Analysis Services server, including third-party plug-in algorithms.

You can also use the advanced modeling tools to add multiple models to a mining structure. This is necessary if you want to try a variety of scenarios using different algorithms' parameters and compare the results. For example, you can use the Classify task with the default settings, and then use Add Model to Structure to add another model to the created structure via the neural network algorithm to determine if decision trees or neural networks perform better for your algorithm.

The advanced tools allow you to set every possible option on each mining structure and mining model column. However, the user interface for this is quite cumbersome if you have to change more than two or three columns. Also, the interface does not display the settings directly, so you are required to open a dialog box for each column to see if you need to make any changes.

Fortunately, there is an easier way. The workaround is unintuitive and a bit awkward, but it can save a lot of time and frustration.

To quickly change all column settings in the Create Mining Structure and Add Model to Structure task wizards, perform the following steps:

1. Launch the appropriate task wizard from the ribbon.
2. Advance to the Select Columns page, making the choices suitable for your problem along the way (for example, data selection, structure selection, and so on).
3. On the Select Columns page, click the copy button (circled in Figure 5-13).
4. Cancel out of the wizard.
5. Paste the contents of the clipboard into a new sheet in your workbook.
6. Edit the column settings (displayed in Figure 5-13) to what is needed for your modeling task. *Do not* change the sheet columns or row order.
7. Select all of the column settings and copy them to the clipboard.
8. Launch the appropriate task wizard from the ribbon again.
9. Advance to the Select Columns page, again making the suitable choices along the way.
10. On the Select Columns page, click the paste button.

Unfortunately, after completing this procedure, there is no feedback indicating that the pasting of the settings actually happened. You must probe one of the columns you edited to verify that the changes actually were applied.

It is important to change the settings to the exact values that are understood by the wizard, or your changes will be ignored. The best way to determine what the possible settings are is to make a few changes and see how they look when you paste the description of the structure or model in your workbook.

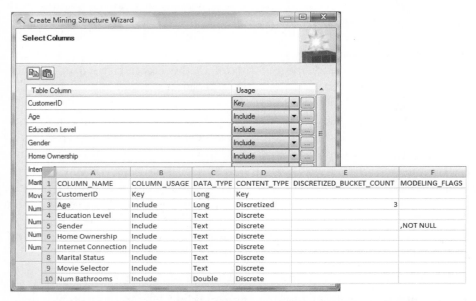

Figure 5-13 Bulk column setting in the Create Mining Structure wizard

This method is the easiest way to add many models to a structure. You can quickly make small changes and run through the Add Model to Structure wizard creating variations on a theme. You can also save the model or structure definition for reuse at a later time.

NOTE Using the copy-and-paste trick is the only way to use the Data Mining Client interface to set the discretized bucket count on a discretized column. Setting this content type with the user interface leaves the count at default values.

Another shortcut in the Add Model to Structure Wizard is to select a mining model on the Select Structure page instead of a mining structure. When you select a mining model, all of the column settings from that model are automatically carried forward to your new model.

When you're adding several models to a structure, deselect the Process Model option on the last page of the Add Model wizard. After adding all of your models, use the Manage Models tool to process the structure and all of the models simultaneously.

Accuracy and Validation

The Accuracy and Validation tools in the Data Mining Client are almost equivalent to the accuracy tools in BI Dev Studio described in Chapter 4. The most obvious exception is that instead of the results being trapped inside the BI Dev Studio environment, they are created as Excel charts. You can use the Accuracy and Validation tools on models and structures that were created with any method, including through BI Dev Studio.

The most significant difference is added functionality in the profit chart. As with the profit chart in BI Dev Studio, you specify a target you want to predict, along with profit parameters such as the base cost of a campaign, the incremental cost of each item, and the return received from a successful prediction. The profit chart in the Data Mining Client allows you to model more complex and realistic profit scenarios where there is a variable cost.

A *variable cost* is when the incremental cost of contacting a customer is reduced after reaching certain volume thresholds. For example, if you are creating a mailing, it may cost $5,000 to design a *brochure*, $3 to print it, and 50 cents to mail. Your printer may offer volume discounts and charge $2 for every copy over 10,000 and $1.50 for every copy over 15,000. Figure 5-14 shows the Profit Chart wizard configured to test this scenario.

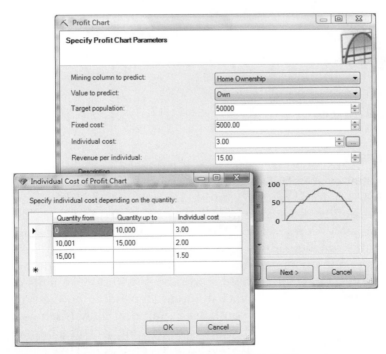

Figure 5-14 Configuring a profit chart for variable cost

Another difference between the Data Mining Client's Accuracy and Valida-tion tools and the corresponding tools in BI Dev Studio is merely cosmetic, but the cosmetic change is so significant that you will always want the Data Mining Client version. Both versions of cross-validation provide detailed reports of a variety of accuracy measurements across all of the validation folds. The Data Mining Client, however, includes an additional summary section at the top of the report that tells you, at a glance, which models performed the best for each measure.

Model Usage

Model usage refers to any action where you view or apply learned patterns in processed models. These can be models you created yourself, or models created by others for which you have been granted permission. The Data Mining Client for Excel 2007 add-in provides tools to view, document, and query (`predict from`) models, as well as cell functions that allow you to create interactive predictive workbooks (see Figure 5-15). The Data Mining Templates for Visio add-in provides renderers that allow you to create annotated diagrams from models that you can save to web formats. This section discusses the model application functionality of the Data Mining Add-Ins, and highlights the sometimes-hidden features that make a difference.

Figure 5-15 Model Usage tools

Browsing Models

The same viewers that exist in BI Dev Studio are used for browsing models in the Data Mining Client for Excel 2007 add-in, so you have exactly the same functionality and flexibility in viewing models. An additional feature in the Data Mining Client is the Copy to Excel button. Although unobtrusive and seemingly simple, this functionality is subtly powerful, and you will likely find it to be a best friend in understanding, explaining, and sharing models.

Copy to Excel creates a new sheet in your workbook with the contents of the current view. What gets copied is very different, depending on the type of view you currently have shown. If you have a graphical view (such as a decision tree or a dependency network), Copy to Excel simply takes a bitmap image and places it in your Excel workbook. However, on tabular style views (such as tornado charts and cluster profiles), Copy to Excel transforms the data from the data mining viewer into a formatted Excel table, complete with color-coded data bars, as shown in Figure 5-16. The resulting tables can be sorted and filtered like any Excel table.

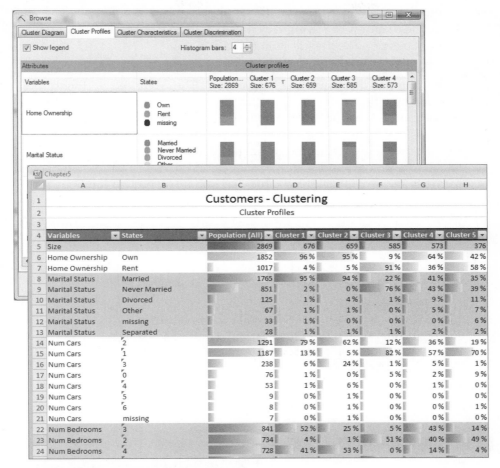

Figure 5-16 Copy to Excel tabular results

After the data mining views are copied to Excel, they can be shared with any other Excel user or via Excel Services without requiring the Data Mining Add-Ins or Analysis Services.

Viewing Models with Visio

Viewing models with Visio is a completely different experience. The Data Mining Templates for Visio add-in is intended for users who want to create interactive, annotatable diagrams of the graphical data mining viewers. The

Visio template has three smart shapes that allow you to generate trees, cluster diagrams, and dependency networks. When dropped on the canvas, each shape launches a wizard that allows you to choose a model and to select a variety of options for your diagram. After your diagram is created, you can use Visio to beautify your diagram by setting themes and adding notes, and then share the diagram by saving it as a web page or PDF document.

The templates provide the following shapes:

- **Decision Tree** — The Decision Tree shape creates both classification and regression tree diagrams (see Figure 5-17). The advanced options allow shading by either support or probability. But if you choose a shading option, you can no longer change the shape color by applying Visio color schemes. Each tree shape contains properties, including all node statistics and rules. Right-clicking on shapes in the tree diagrams allows you to collapse and expand nodes, or move child nodes to additional pages to create more compact, navigable diagrams. The navigation behavior and shape properties are maintained when the diagram is saved as a web page.

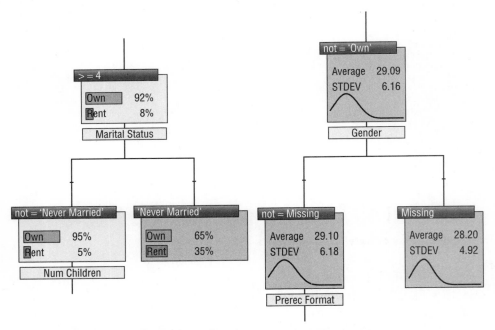

Figure 5-17 Classification and regression examples in Visio

- **Dependency Network** — The Dependency Network shape can be used to create diagrams for models created with a Decision Trees, Naïve Bayes, or Association Rules algorithm. Unlike the built-in viewer, the

Dependency Network shape gives you much more flexibility in what your network displays. By default, the built-in viewer uses a heuristic to display up to 60 nodes, which are typically the most popular items. This is impractical when there is a catalog of thousands of items or more, and the item of interest isn't near the top. By contrast, the Dependency Network shape allows you to select a shape or set of shapes to start your network, and then organically grow the network by fetching shapes that are related to those already in the diagram. Other useful presentation features of the Dependency Network shape that aren't present in the built-in viewers are the ability to show the weight of each edge and to replace the node graphic with any shape of your choice. The result of applying these features generates a much more dynamic diagram to illustrate your model, as shown in Figure 5-18.

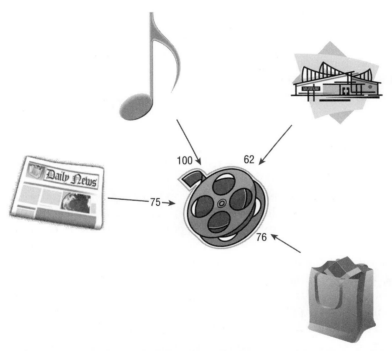

Figure 5-18 Dependency Network with shape replacement showing edge weights

- **Cluster** — The Cluster shape creates Visio diagrams akin to the cluster diagram in the built-in viewers. You can use the Cluster shape on both clustering and sequence clustering models, although it does not create the transition diagrams for sequence clusters. Because a cluster diagram shares the general appearance of a dependency network, the cluster shape shares many of the features of the respective shape. Additionally, you can show characteristic or discrimination diagrams in place of the Cluster shape. Limitations of the canvas, however, make it difficult to use the characteristic or discrimination options with models that contain many attributes.

Querying Models

Querying models is clearly where you get the most value from data mining. This is where the rubber meets the road, so to speak — it's where you get to perform magic on your data and predict the unknown. The Data Mining Client offers two methods for executing prediction queries: the query wizard (allowing basic, advanced, and even more advanced modes) and data mining cell functions (allowing interactive predictions in the workbook).

Query Wizard

The query wizard provides the capability to execute DMX queries against data mining models using Excel data or external data. In its most basic mode, practically no knowledge of DMX is required. You indicate which model you want to query, the source data, and how the columns in the source map to the columns in the model. Then, from a series of lists, you indicate what results you want from the model, as shown in Figure 5-19. If you are querying against Excel data, you can append the columns to the source data, or using any data source, put the result at any arbitrary location. After the query is finished, there is no requirement to retain an Analysis Services connection, so the results can be shared and manipulated as necessary.

When you are querying against external data, you must also select columns from the input to identify the results. Otherwise, if you choose the likelihood a customer is to be a renter, for example, you will get a meaningless column of probabilities with nothing to associate them. This is equally true if you query against Excel data but put the results in a new spreadsheet.

In general, the basic mode is sufficient for most prediction queries using data in Excel. However, the true value of executing queries against external data is reached only when you use the advanced mode. For example, external data may be too large to fit into an Excel workbook. The advanced query editor (which you open by clicking the Advanced button on any page) allows you to execute arbitrary DMX queries, such as those that filter the results or return only the best returns.

Even if you don't have a deep understanding of DMX, you can still use the advanced query editor. Rather than throwing you into a text editor with a link to help files, the advanced mode is a structured query editor where you can interactively click any editable part of a query and enter appropriate values using a suitable user interface. The editor automatically generates the correct DMX syntax. Any settings made so far in the basic mode of the wizard will be reflected in the DMX query. For example, if you selected a model, an input set, mappings, and a prediction column, the query displayed in the query editor will show all of the choices you made.

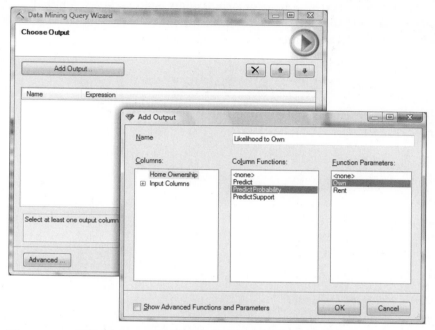

Figure 5-19 Adding an output column using the query wizard

Using the advanced mode, you can select DMX templates for performing top, filtered, and many other types of queries. For example, if you wanted to extract from a database the top 100 customers who were most likely to rent, you could follow these steps:

1. Run the query wizard.
2. Select the model, input data, and mappings.
3. Add the columns from the input you want in the output.
4. Add the predictable columns you want in the output.
5. Click the Advanced button.
6. Select the DMX template for a TOP prediction.
7. Click the `<count>` field and enter **100**.
8. Click the `<expression>` field and specify `PredictProbability([Home Ownership, 'Rent')`, as shown in Figure 5-20.

When you select a DMX template, all preselected fields (such as model name, input source, outputs, and so on) that apply to the new template are automatically moved to the new query.

NOTE If you must execute the same or similar query multiple times, run the query wizard and click Advanced before making any selections. The previously run query will be in the Advanced Query Editor dialog box.

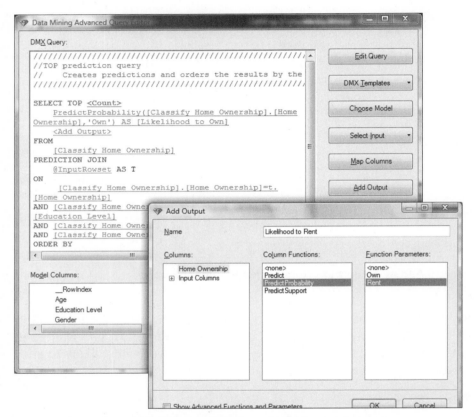

Figure 5-20 Setting the order expression in advanced query mode

The advanced query editor can also be used to execute non–rowset-returning DMX statements. That is, it can be used to execute statements such as CREATE MINING STRUCTURE, INSERT INTO, RENAME MINING MODEL, and the like. Interactive templates exist for most functionality, making the advanced query editor an easy way to execute and learn DMX syntax.

USING NESTED TABLES IN THE DATA MINING CLIENT

All of the tools in the Data Mining Client conveniently ignore the nested tables feature of SQL Server Data Mining. However, with some trickery, you can use the advanced query editor to create, train, and predict nested tables. The editor allows you to specify multiple input rowsets, and provides templates for nested prediction and nested training. For nested creation, and for using more than one nested table, you must edit the query manually by clicking the Edit Query button. This turns off all interactive behavior, and turns the editor into a big text box where you can type arbitrary DMX.

When you're working with nested tables, ensure that all tables are sorted by the case table key. That is, use an ORDER BY clause for external data, and sort Excel tables by the key column.

Data Mining Cell Functions

You can create interactive predictive spreadsheets by using the three data mining cell functions provided with the Data Mining Client. Unlike the other functionality, any user who wants to use a workbook with such embedded functionality will require the Data Mining Add-Ins and a connection to the database containing the model.

DMPREDICT

The DMPredict function allows you to return any predicted result from a model. The function takes a connection, a model, the prediction function, and up to 32 name/value pairs for the input. For example, putting the following function into a cell will create a query that selects the predicted home ownership from the Classify Home Ownership model using the values from cells B2:B4 as inputs:

```
=DMPREDICT("DMAddinsDB",
          "[Classify Home Ownership]",
          "Predict([Home Ownership])",
          "Age",B2,"Education Level",B3,"Gender",B4)
```

Any prediction function can be called in DMPredict. The Predict, PredictProbability, and Cluster() functions are usually the most useful for interactive scenarios.

DMPREDICTTABLEROW

This function is analogous to DMPredict, except that it operates on a table row instead of an arbitrary collection of cells. As such, the function takes a range and a list of ordered mappings. For example, the following function maps the cells from B2:D4 to the columns Age, Education Level, and Gender to generate a result:

```
=DMPREDICTTABLEROW(''DMAddinsDB'',
    ''[Classify Home Ownership]'',
    ''Predict([Home Ownership])'',
    B2:D4, ''Age,Education Level,Gender'')
```

DMPredictTableRow calls the Analysis Services server for every row in its containing table. This can cause large tables to calculate slowly.

DMCONTENTQUERY

DMContentQuery allows you to fetch an arbitrary piece of content from a mining model. Usually, this function is used in conjunction with a cell containing a DMPredict or DMPredictTableRow function call that returns PredictNodeID, allowing you to return the reason for a particular prediction. The function takes the model name, the piece of content to be returned, and the filter clause used to specify the content. The following cell function returns the description of the node identified in cell B7:

```
=DMCONTENTQUERY(''DMAddinsDB'',
    ''[Classify Home Ownership]'',
    ''NODE_DESCRIPTION'',
    ''NODE_UNIQUE_NAME='' & B7)
```

You can submit arbitrarily complex DMX fragments as the return value for any of the data mining cell functions. For example, you can specify subselects from nested return tables such as the following:

```
(SELECT $Support FROM PredictHistogram([Home Ownership]) WHERE
     [Home Ownership]='Own')
```

This extracts the support of the Own state from the home ownership histogram. If a result returns multiple rows or columns, the value in the first row or column is returned.

NOTE One drawback of the data mining cell functions is the reference to the data mining connection. Because the data mining connection information is stored on the machine where Excel is running and not the Excel workbook, anyone who uses the workbook must have the same connection information with the same name. One potential workaround is to leave the connection name as an empty string (' ' ' '). **This causes the cell function to use the current connection, whatever that may be. If the current connection happens to contain a model with the schema required by the cell function parameters, it will just work!**

Model Management

The Manage Models tool launches a dialog that contains many options for managing structures and models. The main reason these tools are included is to allow the user to stay in the Data Mining Client without having to use the SQL Server tools such as Management Studio. Of all the tools that are available, the only ones that require special care are the export and import functions. When issuing an export or import command, you must specify a path relative to the Analysis Services server.

For example, if you send a command to export a structure to C:\MyStructure .abf, the file will end up in the root directory on the Analysis Services server machine, not your local directory. The way to work around this is to share a directory on your client machine, and provide the complete path to the location in the export command.

Trace

The trace function provides a detailed log of every command sent from the Data Mining Add-Ins to the server. For most functions, the commands sent are DMX, making trace a great way to learn DMX syntax for a variety of scenarios. If you use Table Analysis Tools, for example, you can see all of the model creation, training, query, and stored procedure calls made by those tools.

NOTE Uncheck the Use Session Models check box in the trace dialog box to force the Table Analysis Tools to create permanent models. These models can then be browsed and otherwise used from the Data Mining Client or other tools.

Summary

The Data Mining Client for Excel 2007 add-in is designed to walk you through the data mining process. The tools provided with this add-in are similar to those available in BI Dev Studio, but are presented in a more intuitive, actionable fashion, with the added bonus of being inside Excel, where most people work with data anyway. The Data Mining Client usage tools and the Visio data mining templates allow any user to access data mining models as long as the users have permission to do so.

For the most part, the tools presented in this chapter are simplified and limited. However, you can use almost all SQL Server Data Mining functionality through the client with some clever application and knowledge.

The upcoming chapters detail the specific algorithms provided in Analysis Services. Each chapter talks about the concepts, application, and theory behind the algorithm. Chapter 6 begins this analysis with a discussion of Microsoft Native Bayes.

Microsoft Naïve Bayes

Picture a newborn witnessing his first sunset. Being new to this world, he doesn't know if the sun will rise again. Making a guess, he gives the chance of a sunrise even odds and places in a bag a black marble, representing no sunrise, and a white marble, representing a sunrise. As each day passes, the child places in the bag a marble based on the evidence he witnesses — in this case, a white marble for each sunrise. Over time, the black marble becomes lost in a sea of white, and the child can say with near certainty that the sun will rise each day.

This was the example posed by Reverend Thomas Bayes in his 1763 paper establishing the methodology that is now one of the fundamental principles of modern machine learning.

In this chapter, you will learn about the following:

- How to use the Naïve Bayes algorithm
- How to create Naïve Bayes models using DMX
- How to interpret Naïve Bayes results
- The principles of the Naïve Bayes algorithm
- How to tune the Naïve Bayes algorithm using parameters

Examples, data sets, and projects for this chapter may be found in its downloadable companion, `Chapter6.zip`, which is available on the book's website at `www.wiley.com/go/data_mining_SQL_2008/`. The archive contains the following:

- A SQL Server 2008 database backup containing the data sets used in this chapter
- A set of files containing the DMX scripts for this chapter
- An Analysis Services project

The DMX examples for this chapter require the database created by deploying the included Analysis Services project.

Introducing the Naïve Bayes Algorithm

The Naïve Bayes algorithm enables you to quickly create models with predictive abilities and provides you with a new method of exploring and understanding your data. Thinking about the metaphor presented at the beginning of this chapter, it is easy to see how Bayes's technique can be applied to predictive analysis.

Bayes's paper provides a systematic method for learning based on evidence. The algorithm learns the evidence by counting the correlations between the variable you are interested in and all other variables. For example, if you are trying to determine whether a representative in Congress is Republican or Democrat based on his or her voting history, your evidence would be the counts of how Congress members from each party voted on each issue. The algorithm would then use these counts to form a prediction based on the voting history of the Congressional representative you were interested in.

Alternatively, you may really be more interested in learning about what issues differentiate the parties. The counts taken by the Naïve Bayes algorithm can be used to explore the relationships among the various attributes in your model. For example, Figure 6-1 shows the top issues that distinguish Democrats from Republicans in the House of Representatives.

Attributes	Values	Favors Republican	Favors Democrat
Class Action Fairness Act	Y	▬▬▬▬▬	
Fed Up Higher Education Technical ...	N		▬▬▬▬▬
Fed Up Higher Education Technical ...	Y	▬▬▬▬	
Class Action Fairness Act	N		▬▬▬▬▬
Help Efficient Accessible Low Cost Ti...	Y	▬▬▬▬	
Help Efficient Accessible Low Cost Ti...	N		▬▬▬▬
Premanent Death Tax Repeal Act	N		▬▬▬▬
Pension Security Act	N		▬▬▬▬
Premanent Death Tax Repeal Act	Y	▬▬▬	
Consumer Rental Purchase Agreem...	N		▬▬▬
Consumer Rental Purchase Agreem...	Y	▬▬▬	

Figure 6-1 Distinguishing Congressional parties by their 2002 voting records

Using the Naïve Bayes Algorithm

Used in conjunction with the viewers provided in SQL Server Analysis Services 2008, the Naïve Bayes algorithm provides a very effective way to explore your data. The processing phase of the algorithm merely counts the first-order correlations between the inputs and the outputs, so you don't have to worry about picking the correct inputs, and you can simply throw anything you have at it.

This does not hold true when using the algorithm for predictive purposes. When building a predictive model with Naïve Bayes, you must take care that the input attributes are relatively independent. For example, if input A and input B always have the same value, this would have the effect of multiplying the weight of input A by two, which is something you generally want to avoid. Because of this behavior, it is particularly important to evaluate the accuracy of your model with holdout data using the lift chart as described in Chapter 4. Typically, although Naïve Bayes can be a powerful predictor, many people use more sophisticated algorithms such as decision trees or neural networks for prediction when these tools are available.

Exploring a Naïve Bayes model will tell you how your attributes are related to each other in ways that aren't easily discovered when using other methods. Using the previous example of Congressional voting records, you can easily see what the most important votes are for each party. You can see how votes on a particular act are distributed across party lines. You can even see how votes on an act are distributed across the votes of every other act, and how they are related to each other.

This ability to explore the relationships between attributes can be applied to many problems. What are the differences between satisfied and unsatisfied customers? What factors are related to defects in a production line? What differentiates weekly and monthly movie renters? This ability can be combined with the concept of nested tables to provide a further realm of insights. What's the difference between people who bought the movie *Fargo* and those who didn't? How are all products related? Naïve Bayes provides quick and understandable answers to all of these questions.

> **NOTE** A good way to start mining your data is to create a Naïve Bayes model and check both input and predictable on all non-key columns. The resultant model provides you with a better understanding of your data and helps you build better subsequent models.

Creating a Predictive Model

Given the exploratory nature of the Naïve Bayes algorithm, it is often useful to create ad hoc data mining models on arbitrary sets of data. For example, to create a voting model for members of Congress (the problem discussed earlier in this chapter), you would issue a DMX statement such as the one in Listing 6-1.

```
CREATE MINING MODEL VotingRecords
(
    [ID]    LONG   KEY,
    [Party] TEXT  DISCRETE PREDICT,
    [Class Action Fairness Act]    TEXT  DISCRETE,
    [Farm Security Act] TEXT  DISCRETE,
    [Highway Funding Restoration Act] TEXT  DISCRETE,
    [Homeland Security Act] TEXT  DISCRETE
) USING Microsoft_Naive_Bayes
```

Listing 6-1 Creating a Naïve Bayes mining model

You would then train the model with a standard INSERT INTO statement, like the one in Listing 6-2.

```
INSERT INTO VotingRecords
    (
        [ID],
        [Party],
        [Class Action Fairness Act],
        [Farm Security Act],
        [Highway Funding Restoration Act],
        [Homeland Security Act]
    )
    OPENQUERY([Chapter 6],
        'SELECT [ID],
[Party],
[Class Action Fairness Act],
            [Farm Security Act],
            [Highway Funding Restoration Act],
            [Homeland Security Act]
FROM [Voting Record Report]')
```

Listing 6-2 Training a Naïve Bayes mining model

At this point, you can use the model for prediction or browsing. For predicting, you use a standard SELECT statement with a PREDICTION JOIN clause. For example, Listing 6-3 uses parameters to predict party affiliation based on the Farm Security Act and Homeland Security issues.

```
SELECT Predict(Party) FROM VotingRecords
    NATURAL PREDICTION JOIN
    (SELECT @FarmSecurityAct AS [Farm Security Act],
        @HomelandSecurity AS [Homeland Security Act]) as t
```

Listing 6-3 Executing a prediction against a Naïve Bayes mining model

The result will be based on the values specified in the parameters.

Data Exploration

When you are faced with a new data set, a convenient way to start analyzing it is to create a Naïve Bayes model and mark all the non-key columns as both input and predictive. You would do that with a statement such as the one in Listing 6-4.

```
CREATE MINING MODEL VotingRecordsAnalysis
(
        [ID]                                LONG  KEY,
        [Party]                             TEXT  DISCRETE PREDICT,
        [Class Action Fairness Act]         TEXT  DISCRETE PREDICT,
        [Farm Security Act]                 TEXT  DISCRETE PREDICT,
        [Highway Funding Restoration Act]   TEXT  DISCRETE PREDICT,
        [Homeland Security Act]             TEXT  DISCRETE)
                                USING Microsoft_Naive_Bayes
```

Listing 6-4 Creating a Naïve Bayes mining model for data exploration

After the model is trained (using an INSERT INTO statement similar to the one used in the previous section), data exploration can follow a few directions.

The *Dependency Network viewer* (described in the "Exploring a Naïve Bayes Model" section later in this chapter) is a very informative starting point. It presents the strength of correlations between all input columns and all output columns of the model. If your goal is to create a predictive model, you would start by inspecting relationships between all the columns and your prediction target. The next step should be to use the same Dependency Network viewer to inspect correlations between input variables. Strong correlations between two input variables generally indicate that they should probably not be used together to predict the same target. The Dependency Network viewer works with attributes (columns), but it does not provide information about their states (the values in the columns).

If your goal is to better understand the data, the next stop is the *Attribute Profiles* viewer. It presents a matrix of correlations between all states of the inputs and all states of all outputs.

Last, but not least, if you only need to understand similarities and differences between various states of your prediction target, you would use the other two viewing options offered for Naïve Bayes: the *Attribute Characteristics* viewer and *Attribute Discrimination* viewer.

Analysis of Key Influencers

The visualizations offered for the Microsoft Naïve Bayes algorithm suggest a different kind of application: analyzing the key influencers for a specific target. For example, for the voting data set mentioned earlier, you may want to create a report that emphasizes the most-important factors that differentiate between Republican and Democrat members of Congress. Or, in a generic application, you may want to discriminate between states of any column as requested by the user. The Attribute Discrimination viewer for the Microsoft Naïve Bayes algorithm shows exactly the information you need. Furthermore, this information can be obtained programmatically, so that the results may be included in a report or in any application.

To get this report, you would execute a statement such as the one in Listing 6-5.

```
CALL GetAttributeDiscrimination('Voting Record Report', '10000000m',
    'Democrat', 1, 'Republican', 1, 0.0005)
```

Listing 6-5 Discriminating between attribute states in a Naïve Bayes model

The parameters of this statement, as well as the format of the result, are discussed in the "Understanding Naïve Bayes Content" section later in this chapter.

In your report, you will need to use a query such as the one in Listing 6-5 as the data source. In your custom application, you would likely need to create a Naïve Bayes model on-the-fly, train it using application's data, and then execute the discrimination query to get the desired results. Chapter 2 presents such an application: the Analyze Key Influencers tool for Microsoft Excel.

Document Classification

Because the processing phase of the Naïve Bayes algorithm just counts the first order correlations between inputs and outputs, a model's training is done with a single pass over the training data. This behavior makes Naïve Bayes a fast processing algorithm (compared with most of the other data mining algorithms, which execute multiple passes over data), which makes it a good candidate for analysis of large data sets with very large numbers of attributes.

Document classification is such a task, and Naïve Bayes often does a very good job of classifying documents. This derives both from the processing performance of the algorithm and from the nature of the problem. The presence of certain keywords is usually the most important feature in classifying documents. Therefore, document classes are often highly correlated with keywords.

A typical document classification model is created using the nested table feature in SQL Server Data Mining, which allows modeling each training document as a collection of terms. You would create such a model with a statement such as the following:

```
CREATE MINING MODEL DocumentClassification
{
    [DocID]      LONG  KEY,
    [Class]      TEXT  DISCRETE PREDICT, // the class of the document
    [Terms]      TABLE
    (
        [Term] TEXT  KEY, // collection of terms included in the document
    )
} USING Microsoft_Naive_Bayes
```

Training the model requires reading data from two separate tables: one containing the document IDs and the class associated with each training document, and the second containing the list of (multiple) keywords from each document, as shown here:

```
INSERT INTO [DocumentClassification]
  (
    [DocId], [Class],
    [Terms](SKIP, [Term])
  )
SHAPE
  {
    OPENQUERY ([DocTerms],
    'SELECT [DocId], [Class] FROM Documents ORDER BY [DocId]')
  }
  APPEND
  (
    {
      OPENQUERY ([DocTerms],
      'SELECT [DocId], [Term] FROM DocumentTerms ORDER BY [DocId]')
    }
    RELATE [DocId] To [DocId]
  )
  AS [Terms]
```

NOTE Document classification patterns typically change slowly, and such a task is almost never performed on-the-fly. Spending more time during modeling may significantly change the performance of the system. Therefore, you should build multiple models with various algorithms when performing this task. Other algorithms from the SQL Server Data Mining suite also provide very good document classification accuracy, including Microsoft Decision Trees, Microsoft

Logistic Regression, and Microsoft Neural Network. You can find a full example of a document classification model (together with the data set) in Chapter 12, which covers the Neural Network algorithm.

After the model is trained, the prediction operation is used to present the model with the list of keywords and retrieve the most probable document class, as shown here:

```
SELECT Predict(Class) FROM [DocumentClassification]
NATURAL PREDICTION JOIN
  ( SELECT
     (SELECT 'Democrat' AS Term UNION
      SELECT 'Republican' AS Term UNION
      ... // Other terms here
      SELECT 'Independent' AS Term) AS [Terms]
  ) AS T
```

DMX

Because Naïve Bayes is a rather simple algorithm, Naïve Bayes models support standard DMX commands and there is no algorithm-specific extension. The only issue to keep in mind is that the `Microsoft_Naive_Bayes` implementation supports only discrete attributes, so continuous input or output columns must be discretized in order to be used by the algorithm. Creating a Naïve Bayes model with continuous columns will result in an error.

Drill-through

The Microsoft Naïve Bayes algorithm does not support the drill-through functionality. The patterns detected by the algorithm (conditional probabilities) do not intuitively map to distinct subsets of the training set. However, if you want to inspect the support for the cross correlations detected by Microsoft Naïve Bayes, this can be done with a relatively simple query that uses the mining structure drill-through functionality available in SQL Server 2008.

Let's assume that you want to identify the voting records that appear in the training set, and correlate Republican affiliation and positive votes on the bill concerning Homeland Security. You can find those records with a query such as the one in Listing 6-6.

```
SELECT * FROM MINING STRUCTURE VotingRecords_Structure.CASES
WHERE
    [Party] = 'Republican' AND
    [Homeland Security Act]='Y'
```

Listing 6-6 Extracting training cases that support a certain correlation detected by a Naïve Bayes model

> **NOTE** When you create a model using a `CREATE MINING MODEL` statement, a mining structure is automatically created using the specified name appended with `_Structure`.

Understanding Naïve Bayes Content

Naïve Bayes content is laid out in four levels. The first level is simply the model itself. The model node has one child node containing (as a node distribution) the first-level statistics for all the attributes and all their states (that is, the number of occurrences for each attribute state), and then one child node for each of the outputs (predictable targets) of the model. Each output node has as its children the entire set of input attributes with a dependency probability higher than the `MINIMUM_DEPENDENCY_PROBABILITY` parameter. Finally, each input node has a child for each state the input can take, with the distributions of the output attribute states. This arrangement is shown in Figure 6-2.

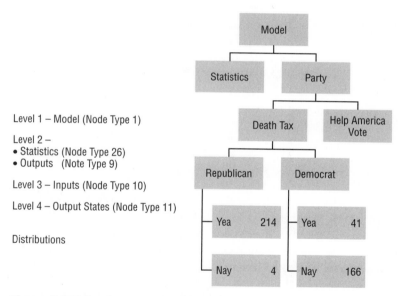

Figure 6-2 Naïve Bayes content hierarchy

Fortunately, for many content-browsing purposes, there are user-defined functions that can condense the Naïve Bayes content into a somewhat more useful form. The Attribute Characteristics view and the Attribute Discrimination view described later in this chapter both receive their data through built-in, system-stored procedures that you can use as well.

As shown in Listing 6-7, `GetPredictableAttributes` returns the list of predictable attributes for a specified model, along with the `NODE_UNIQUE_NAME` (a unique identifier for each node in the model content) for each attribute.

```
CALL GetPredictableAttributes('Voting Record Report')
```

Listing 6-7 Fetching the list of predictable attributes and associated content nodes

After you have the list of attributes, you can call `GetAttributeCharacteristics` to return a table that describes the characteristics of an attribute's value. This function takes as arguments the model's name, the attribute's node unique name, the value of interest, a value type flag, and a threshold value, along with the model name. It returns an ordered list of attributes and values that correlate with the selected attribute value, along with the strength of the correlation.

The value type flag tells the function if the value you are specifying is a value from the model, or the intrinsic missing value. Setting the value type to 1 indicates that the value of interest is a known state of the attribute — for example, Yea or Nay. Setting it to 0 indicates that the value is the intrinsic missing value, which occurs when the attribute does not appear in a case, when it is NULL, or when the specific value is removed from the model by feature selection. The threshold indicates the minimum correlation strength returned by the function, and is used to limit the number of returned rows.

A call to get the characteristics of Democrats from the Voting Records model would look like Listing 6-8.

```
CALL GetAttributeCharacteristics('Voting Record Report', '10000000m',
    'Democrat', 1, 0.0005)
```

Listing 6-8 Extracting the characteristics of a predictable attribute state

A similar function, `GetAttributeDiscrimination`, takes two values of an attribute and returns an ordered list of attributes, along with the strength with which they differentiate the two values. Negative strength numbers indicate that the attribute value pair on the row favors the first specified value, whereas positive strength numbers indicate that the second value is favored. Similar to `GetAttributeCharacteristics`, a value type must be specified for each value. However, an additional value, 2, can be specified to indicate that you want to compare a value against all other possible values. For example, a query to compare Democrats against all other possible parties would look like Listing 6-9.

```
CALL GetAttributeDiscrimination('Voting Record Report', '10000000m',
    'Democrat', 1, 'All other states', 2, 0.0005)
```

Listing 6-9 Discriminating between one state and all other states of a Naïve Bayes predictable attribute

To compare Democrats and Republicans, you would issue the following query (which is the same as the query shown previously in Listing 6-5):

```
CALL GetAttributeDiscrimination('Voting Record Report', '10000000m',
    'Democrat', 1, 'Republican', 1, 0.0005)
```

NOTE You can issue all of these queries using the DMX query editor in SQL Server Management Studio. Training the model requires that a Data Source object representing the Voting Records database described in Appendix A be created using the SQL Server Business Intelligence Development Studio. The DMX statements are available in the `Chapter6.zip` archive for this chapter, found on the book's companion website (`www.wiley.com/go/data_mining_SQL_2008`).

Exploring a Naïve Bayes Model

When you're exploring a trained Naïve Bayes model, it is easier to think of the process as simply exploring your data. Because the Naïve Bayes algorithm does not perform any kind of advanced analysis on your data, the views into the model are basically just a new way of looking at the data you always had.

SQL Server Data Mining provides four different views on Naïve Bayes models that help provide insight into your data. The Naïve Bayes viewer is accessed through either the BI Development Studio or SQL Management Studio by right-clicking on the model and selecting Browse. Following are the available views:

- Dependency Network
- Attribute Profiles
- Attribute Characteristics
- Attribute Discrimination

Dependency Network

The first tab of the Naïve Bayes viewer is the Dependency Network view. The Dependency Network view (shown in Figure 6-3) provides a quick display of how all of the attributes in your model are related. Each node in the graph represents an attribute, whereas each edge represents a relationship. If a node has an outgoing edge (as indicated by the arrow), it is predictive of the attribute in the node at the end of the edge. Likewise, if a node has an incoming edge, it is predicted by the other node. Edges can also be bidirectional, indicating that the attributes in the corresponding nodes predict and are predicted by each other.

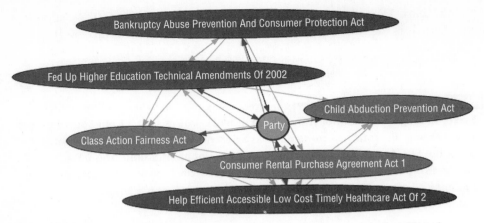

Figure 6-3 Naïve Bayes Dependency Network view with the Party node selected

You can easily hone in on the attributes that interest you by using the Find Node feature. Clicking the Find Node button on the Dependency Network's toolbar provides a list of all attributes appearing in the graph or hidden. Selecting a node from the list will highlight that node in the graph. All connected nodes are also highlighted with a color representing their relationship with the main node selection. Figure 6-3 shows a portion of the Dependency Network view for the Voting Record Report model with the Party node selected. From this view, it is easy to see the relationships that Party has with the other attributes in the model.

In addition to displaying the relationships, the Dependency Network view can also tell you the strength of those relationships. Moving the slider from top to bottom will filter out the weaker links, leaving the strong relationships.

> **NOTE** You will not see all of the possible relationships in your model unless all columns are checked as both predictable and input in the Mining Model Wizard, or marked Predict in the Mining Model Editor. Additionally, some links may be missing if you raise the MINIMUM_DEPENDENCY_PROBABILITY parameter.

Attribute Profiles

The second tab, the Attribute Profiles view, provides you with an exhaustive report of how each input attribute corresponds to each output attribute, one attribute at a time. At the top of the Attribute Profiles view, you select which output you want to look at, and the rest of the view shows how all of the input attributes are correlated to the states of the selected output attribute.

Figure 6-4 shows the attribute profiles for the Party attribute. You can see that the Abortion Non-Discrimination Act vote was approximately even, with Republicans voting Yea and Democrats voting Nay. At the same time, you can see the almost unanimous support for the Child Abduction Prevention Act.

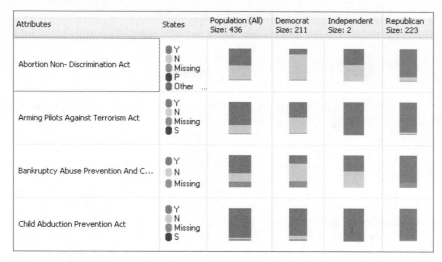

Figure 6-4 Attribute profiles for the Party attribute

You can also use this view to organize your data so it is presented the way you see fit. You can rearrange columns by clicking and dragging on their headers, or you can even remove a column altogether by right-clicking the column header and selecting Hide Column. Additionally, if the alphabetical order doesn't suit you, simply click the header for the attribute state you are interested in, and the row ordering changes based on how important that attribute is in predicting that state.

Attribute Characteristics

The third tab, Attribute Characteristics, allows you to select an output attribute and value and shows you a description of the cases where that attribute and value occur. For example, Figure 6-5 shows the characteristics of Democrats. You can see that, in general, these representatives voted Nay on the healthcare, class action, and rental purchase acts, but voted Yea on the Child Abduction Act.

Attributes	Values	Probability
Help Efficient Accessible Low Cost Timely Healthcare ...	N	
Class Action Fairness Act	N	
Consumer Rental Purchase Agreement Act 1	N	
Child Abduction Prevention Act	Y	
Fed Up Higher Education Technical Amendments Of 2...	N	

Figure 6-5 Characteristics of attributes, values, and probability

When viewing the attribute characteristics, there are two issues you should keep in mind. First, an attribute characteristic does not imply predictive power. For example, if most representatives voted for the Child Abduction Prevention

Act, then it is likely to characterize Republicans as well as Democrats. Second, inputs that fall below the minimum node score set in the algorithm parameters are not displayed.

Attribute Discrimination

The last tab, Attribute Discrimination, provides the answers to the most interesting question: What is the difference between A and B? With this viewer, you choose the attribute you are interested in, and select the states you want to compare. The viewer displays a modified tornado chart indicating which factors favor each state.

Figure 6-6 shows the results that distinguish Republicans and Democrats. Republicans tended to vote for most issues, and Democrats voted against them. When reading this view, you also need to take care in your interpretation. It is *not* implied that no Democrats voted for the Death Tax Repeal Act, but only that these factors *favor* one group over the other.

Attributes	Values	Favors Republican ▽	Favors Democrat
Class Action Fairness Act	Y	▭	
Fed Up Higher Education Technical ...	N		▭
Fed Up Higher Education Technical ...	Y	▭	
Class Action Fairness Act	N		▭
Help Efficient Accessible Low Cost Ti...	Y	▭	
Help Efficient Accessible Low Cost Ti...	N		▭
Premanent Death Tax Repeal Act	N		▭
Pension Security Act	N		▭
Premanent Death Tax Repeal Act	Y	▭	

Figure 6-6 Distinguishing between Republicans and Democrats

NOTE You can determine the unique characteristics of a group by comparing one state to all other states. This will give you a view of what separates that particular group from the rest of the crowd.

When interpreting this view, you must be careful to consider the support level of the attribute before making judgments. Figure 6-7 shows the discrimination between Independents and all other Congressional representatives. Looking at this figure, you could say that a strong differentiator between Independents and Democrats is the support for the Low Cost Healthcare Act. Unfortunately, you would be wrong. When examining the Mining Legend for that issue, you see that there are actually only two Independents in your data set. Obviously, it is not prudent to predicate conclusions based on such limited support.

NOTE If the Mining Legend is not visible, you can display it by right-clicking on the view and selecting Show Legend.

Attributes	Values	Favors Independent	Favors Democrat
Help Efficient Accessible Low Cost Ti...	Y	▬▬▬▬▬▬	
Class Ac			
Abortion			
Consume			
Premane			
To Autho			
Customs			
Help Efficient Accessible Low Cost Ti...	N		▬▬▬▬

Mining Legend			
		Independent	Democrat
Help Efficient Accessible Low Cost Timely Healthcare Act Of 2 = Y		1	14
Help Efficient Accessible Low Cost Timely Healthcare Act Of 2 != Y		1	197

Figure 6-7 Discrimination between Independents and Democrats

Understanding Naïve Bayes Principles

The mathematical method proposed by Bayes uses a combination of conditional and unconditional probabilities. At first glance, the formula may seem a bit daunting, but when you break it down into its principal components, it's really quite easy to understand.

Let's use the Congressional records as an example to build up the Bayes rule. First, suppose that you had to simply guess the party affiliation of a Congressional representative during the 2002 Congressional sessions without any additional information. Given that there were more Republicans in the House than Democrats that year (51 percent to 49 percent), your best guess would be to choose Republican, because it is the most likely choice. In data mining terms, this unconditional probability is called the *prior* probability of a hypothesis, and can be written as P(H). In this case, P(Republican) = 51 percent, and P(Democrat) = 49 percent.

Additionally, you can increase the likelihood of your guess being correct if you know the overall voting records of the House members and those of your representative. Table 6-1 shows the votes by party for selected issues in 2002, and Table 6-2 shows how the representative in question voted.

The numbers in Table 6-1 represent the counts of votes broken down by party affiliation — your target variable. For example, 41 Democrats voted Yea for the Death Tax Repeal Act, and 166 voted Nay. This gives you the percentages in the lower part of the graph: $41/(41 + 166) = 20$ percent Yea and $166/(41 + 166) = 80$ percent Nay. The final column of the table, Party, provides you with the counts and percentages of Democrats and Republicans overall.

The *Naïve* part of Naïve Bayes tells you to treat all of your input attributes as *independent* of each other with respect to the target variable. This may be a faulty assumption, but it allows you to multiply your probabilities to determine the likelihood of each state. For your representative in Table 6-2, the likelihood calculation that this person is a Democrat would be as follows:

$$\text{Likelihood of (D)} = 0.2 * 0.57 * 0.94 * 0.89 * 0.49 = 0.0467$$

Table 6-1 Voting Data by Party Affiliation

	DEATH TAX		HOMELAND SECURITY		HELP AMERICA VOTE		CHILD ABDUCTION		PARTY	
	D	R	D	R	D	R	D	R	D	R
Yea	41	214	87	211	184	172	178	210	211	223
Nay	166	4	114	6	11	36	23	1		
Yea	20%	98%	43%	97%	94%	83%	89%	99.5%	49%	51%
Nay	80%	2%	57%	3%	6%	17%	11%	0.5%		

Table 6-2 Target Representative

DEATH TAX DEATH TAX	HOMELAND SECURITY	HELP AMERICA VOTE	CHILD ABDUCTION	PARTY PARTY
Yea	Nay	Yea	Yea	?

Likewise, the calculation for Republican would be as follows:

$$\text{Likelihood of (R)} = 0.98 * 0.03 * 0.83 * 0.995 * 0.51 = 0.0124$$

You can instantly see that the representative is almost four times as likely to be a Democrat as a Republican, based on this voting behavior. You can convert these likelihoods to probabilities by normalizing their sums to 1, as shown here:

$$P(D) = \frac{0.0467}{0.0467 + 0.0124} = 79\%$$

$$P(R) = \frac{0.0124}{0.0467 + 0.0124} = 21\%$$

The Bayes rule states that if you have a hypothesis H and evidence about that hypothesis E, then you can calculate the probability of H using the following formula:

$$P(H \mid E) = \frac{P(E \mid H) \times P(H)}{P(E)}$$

This simply states that the probability of your hypothesis given the evidence is equal to the probability of the evidence given the hypothesis multiplied by the probability of the hypothesis, and then normalized. Although that may seem pretty complex, it will become clearer if you apply it to the Congressional example.

First, you tackle the probability of the hypothesis given the evidence — which in this case would be the probability that the representative is a Democrat given that he or she voted Yea on the Death Tax Repeal, Help

America Vote, and Child Abduction Acts, and Nay on the Homeland Security Act. To determine this probability, you must compute the probability of the evidence, given that your hypothesis is true. This is simply a lookup from the counts presented in Table 6-1. That is, your evidence states that the representative voted Yea on the Help America Vote Act, and your hypothesis is that the representative is a Democrat. From the table, you see that the probability of this piece of evidence is 94 percent. The probability of *all* the evidence given the hypothesis is simply the product of the probabilities of each individual piece. Next, you multiply by the overall probability (the prior probability) of your hypothesis — which in this case is 49 percent.

Last, you divide by the probability of the evidence. However, in practice, this isn't necessary. Because you will test all possible hypotheses, both Democrat and Republican, this factor is eliminated when you normalize the results.

USING BAYESIAN PRIORS

Using the methodology discussed here can have some undesirable side effects if there is no evidence for an event in the training data. For example, if no Democrat voted Yea on the Death Tax Act, there would be 0-percent probability that your sample case could be a Democrat, regardless of the other votes. Similarly, if no Republican had voted Nay on Homeland Security, there would be 0-percent probability that your sample case could be a Republican.

To resolve this problem, you should consider all available values to be possible. When calculating the likelihoods of each state, you add a nonzero amount to each count. This amount is called a *prior*, and indicates the *prior* belief of each possible output. In practice, you simply add 1 to each count. This provides you with a value that loses significance as the amount of evidence grows, but guarantees that you never run into the 0-percent issue.

Limitations of the Naïve Bayes Algorithm

The Naïve Bayes algorithm belongs to a class of algorithms known as *linear classifiers*. In the multidimensional space defined by the inputs, a linear classifier acts as a hyperplan separating data points that belong to various classes. In the very particular case when there are only two inputs and only two target states, A and B, a linear classifier is effectively a line that separates the plan (data space) into two subspaces: one labeled A, and one labeled B. Consequently, the Naïve Bayes algorithm is not able to correctly classify nonlinearly separable classes (that is, data points that *cannot* be separated by a line, as in the simplified case described earlier).

Figure 6-8 shows an example of such a problem. It consists of two-dimensional points that have X and Y coordinates between 0 and 1. Because

Naïve Bayes cannot handle continuous data, the coordinates are approximated by ranges: [0, 1] and [1,2]. Some of the points are plus signs; the others are squares.

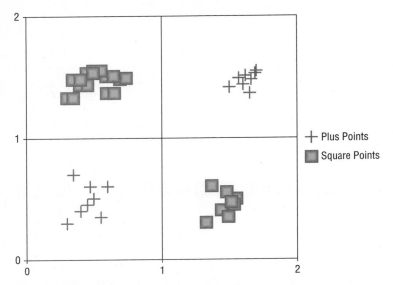

Figure 6-8 A nonlinearly separable classification problem

When trained from this data set, the Naïve Bayes algorithm produces poor classification accuracy. (The data is available in the LinearSeparability.xlsx file included in the Chapter6.zip archive. You can download it from the book's companion website at www.wiley.com/go//data_mining_SQL_2008.)

A simple explanation is that the conditional probabilities linking X and Y to Plus and Square are almost similar, so the algorithm does not have enough evidence to determined whether X in [0,1] favors Plus or Square, and the same applies to all other states of X and Y.

A careful analysis of the trained model may indicate that the Naïve Bayes algorithm is not a good choice for the data set. Here are some of the symptoms that will help you identify such cases:

- The Attribute Discrimination view is empty.

- In the Attribute Characteristics view, certain input attribute states seem to characterize *all* the target attribute states. (In this case, all the input attribute states are related to all target states.)

When these symptoms occur, either Naïve Bayes is not suitable for use with the data set, or the data is not fit for data mining (because the inputs are not related to the output at all). You will have to train models using other algorithms in order to determine whether the data is inappropriate, or the algorithm is not fit for the data.

The Microsoft Logistic Regression algorithm has the same problem with nonlinearly separable classes. Some other algorithms included in SQL Server 2008 (particularly Microsoft Decision Trees and Microsoft Neural Network) do a very good job of handling these types of problems.

Naïve Bayes Parameters

The implementation of Naïve Bayes is fairly straightforward and therefore, isn't heavily parameterized. The parameters that exist ensure that the algorithm is completed in a reasonable amount of time by default. Because the algorithm considers all pairwise attribute combinations, the time and memory usage to process the data is related to the total number of input values multiplied by the total number of output values. In general, the algorithm does a good job of choosing which inputs and outputs are considered when the parameters are applied, and each of them can be turned off to force the algorithm to consider them all.

MAXIMUM_INPUT_ATTRIBUTES

The MAXIMUM_INPUT_ATTRIBUTES parameter determines the number of attributes that will be considered as inputs for training. If there is more than this number of inputs, the algorithm will select the most important inputs and ignore the rest. Setting this parameter to 0 causes the algorithm to consider all attributes.

The default value is 255.

MAXIMUM_OUTPUT_ATTRIBUTES

The MAXIMUM_OUTPUT_ATTRIBUTES parameter determines the number of attributes that will be considered as outputs for training. If there is more than this number of outputs, the algorithm will select the most important outputs (generally the most popular) and ignore the rest. Setting this parameter to 0 causes the algorithm to consider all attributes.

The default value is 255.

MAXIMUM_STATES

MAXIMUM_STATES controls how many states of an attribute are considered. If an attribute has more than this number of states, only the most popular states will be used. States that are not selected will be considered to be missing data. This parameter is useful when an attribute has a high cardinality (such as a

ZIP code). As with the other parameters, setting this parameter to 0 will allow the algorithm to consider all states.

The default value is 100.

MINIMUM_DEPENDENCY_PROBABILITY

The MINIMUM_DEPENDENCY_PROBABILITY is a measure from 0 to 1 of how likely it is that an input attribute is predictive of an output. Using the voting records as an example, assume that 100 percent of the Congressional representatives that voted Yea on issue A also voted Yea on issue B. If only 25 percent of Congress actually voted Yea on B, then issue A provides information. However, if almost everyone voted for B, then the preceding fact is simply superfluous because no information is gained.

Setting the MINIMUM_DEPENDENCY_PROBABILITY parameter does not impact model training or prediction. Instead, it allows you to reduce the amount of content returned by the server from content queries. Setting this value to 0.5 returns only those inputs that are more likely than not to be correlated with the outputs. If you browse a model and do not find any information, try lowering this value until correlations are observed.

The default value is 0.5.

Summary

Naïve Bayes is a machine implementation of the Bayes rule created by the Reverend Thomas Bayes in the eighteenth century, which has become the foundation for many machine-learning and data mining methods. It is a quick, approachable data mining algorithm that you can use to perform predictions and do advanced exploration of your data. The visualizations provided for Naïve Bayes are easy to understand by a wide audience, and are particularly suitable for inclusion in reports.

In Chapter 7, you will learn about a very popular, albeit slightly more complex, data mining algorithm: Microsoft Decision Trees.

Microsoft Decision Trees Algorithm

Put yourself in the place of a loan officer at a bank. A young couple walks in to request a loan. Young, you think — not a good sign. You talk to them. They're married, and that's a plus. He's worked the same job for three years. Job stability is another good sign. A look at their credit reports shows they've missed three payments in the last 12 months — a big negative. From your experience, you've created a tree in your mind that allows you to determine how you rank each loan application. The question remains: Does this couple get the loan? A decision tree can help you solve this puzzle, as you'll see in this chapter.

In this chapter, you will learn about the following:

- Using the Microsoft Decision Trees algorithm
- Interpreting the tree model content
- Understanding the principles of the Microsoft Decision Trees algorithm

You can find the associated files for this chapter in the file `Chapter7.zip` at this book's companion website (`www.wiley.com/go/data_mining_SQL_2008`). `Chapter7.zip` includes the following files

- `Chapter7.abf` — An Analysis Services 2008 backup of the Analysis Services database used in this chapter
- `Chapter7.bak` — A SQL Server 2008 database backup of the tables used in this chapter
- `Chapter7.dmx` — A DMX query file containing the query listings in this chapter

Introducing Decision Trees

The decision tree is probably the most popular data mining technique because of fast training performance, a high degree of accuracy, and easily understandable patterns. The most common data mining task for a decision tree is classification — that is, determining whether or not a set of data belongs to a specific type, or class. For example, loan applicants can be classified as high risk or low risk, and decision trees help determine the rules to perform that classification based on historical data.

The principal idea of a decision tree is to split your data recursively into subsets. Each input attribute is evaluated to determine how cleanly it divides the data across the classes (or states) of your target variable (predictable attribute). The process of evaluating all inputs is then repeated on each subset. When this recursive process is completed, a decision tree is formed.

Decision trees offer several advantages over other data mining algorithms. Trees are quick to build and easy to interpret. Each node in the tree is clearly labeled in terms of the input attributes, and each path formed from the root to a leaf forms a *rule* about your target variable. Prediction based on decision trees is efficient.

The prediction process is like dropping a ball through a pachinko machine (which is a device similar to a vertical pinball machine). As the ball hits each pin, it falls to the left or the right. Finally, it lands, and you can see the score of the slot in which it landed. An input case for a prediction falls through the tree, coming to rest at a leaf, based on the split conditions associated with tree nodes. When the case lands on a leaf node, the predicted value of this case is based on the statistics stored at the node.

There are several options that control how a tree grows. You can use a variety of criteria to determine how to split the data. The tree can have a thin shape or a bushy shape. A tree can be made to grow deep or remain shallow.

Decision trees can perform regression tasks to predict continuous variables. For example, in addition to predicting whether a couple is at high or low risk for a loan, a tree can be built to predict the exact interest rate that should be charged to the customer. Developed by a Microsoft research team, the Microsoft Decision Trees algorithm is a hybrid decision tree algorithm that supports classification and regression tasks. One of the unique features of the Microsoft Decision Trees algorithm is that it can also be applied for association analysis, which will be explained later in this chapter.

WHY TREES?

The algorithm is named Microsoft Decision *Trees* instead of Microsoft Decision *Tree* for a couple of reasons. First, the parameter settings can be tweaked such

(continued)

WHY TREES? *(continued)*

that the resulting trees can be very different in terms of node splits and tree shapes, or even splitting criteria — so much so that they can be considered different decision tree algorithms. Second, the Microsoft Decision Trees algorithm allows for the creation of multiple trees targeting multiple attributes in a single model. A tree model may contain hundreds or thousands of trees, depending on the shape of the data. These trees can be visually linked through a dependency network for further analysis.

Using Decision Trees

In this section, you will learn how to use the Microsoft Decision Trees algorithm, including how to create a model, write DMX queries, and perform model interpretation.

Creating a Decision Tree Model

Let's start by creating a simple tree model based on the `College Plans` data set. The table `CollegePlans` contains data about 8,000 high school students, including Parent Encouragement, Parent Income, Gender, IQ, and whether or not the student plans to attend college. `College Plans` is a binary attribute and has two states: `Plans to Attend` and `Does not plan to attend`. You can use the Decision Trees algorithm to create a mining model, predicting the `College Plans` attribute based on the four other attributes.

The model is easy to build in BI Dev Studio using the Data Mining Wizard as described in Chapter 4, or by importing the data into Excel and using the Classify task as described in Chapter 5.

DMX Queries

The Microsoft Decision Trees algorithm can be used for three different data mining tasks: classification, regression, and association. It is a very flexible and powerful algorithm. In this section, you will build three different models using DMX to illustrate these usage scenarios.

Classification Model

The first model predicts `College Plans` based on `Gender`, `IQ`, `ParentIncome`, and `ParentEncouragement`. Listing 7-1 shows the DMX for creating this model.

```
CREATE MINING STRUCTURE CollegePlan_Structure
(    StudentId          LONG KEY,
     Gender             TEXT DISCRETE,
     ParentIncome    LONG CONTINUOUS,
     IQ                 LONG CONTINUOUS,
     ParentEncouragement TEXT DISCRETE,
     CollegePlans       TEXT DISCRETE
)
WITH HOLDOUT (10 PERCENT)

ALTER MINING STRUCTURE CollegePlan_Structure
ADD MINING MODEL CollegePlan
(    StudentId,
     Gender,
     ParentIncome,
     IQ,
     ParentEncouragement,
     CollegePlans    PREDICT
)
USING Microsoft_Decision_Trees
```

Listing 7-1 CollegePlan model creation

After creation, you can process the model using the statement shown in
Listing 7-2.

```
INSERT INTO CollegePlan_Structure
(StudentId, Gender, IQ, ParentEncouragement,
   ParentIncome, CollegePlans)
OPENQUERY(CollegePlans,
 'SELECT StudentId, Gender, IQ, ParentEncouragement,
   ParentIncome, CollegePlans FROM CollegePlans')
```

Listing 7-2 Training the CollegePlan model

Listing 7-3 shows how to apply the model to predict the College Plans for
new students.

```
SELECT t.StudentID, CollegePlan.CollegePlans,
       PredictProbability(CollegePlans) AS [Probability]
FROM CollegePlan
   PREDICTION JOIN
   OPENQUERY(CollegePlans,
    'SELECT StudentID, Gender, IQ, ParentEncouragement, ParentIncome
       FROM NewStudents') AS t
```

Listing 7-3 Predicting College Plans

```
ON CollegePlan.ParentIncome = t.ParentIncome AND
   CollegePlan.IQ = t.IQ AND
   CollegePlan.Gender = t.Gender AND
   CollegePlan.ParentEncouragement = t.ParentEncouragement
```

Listing 7-3 (*continued*)

This query returns three columns: StudentID, CollegePlans, and Probability.

As explained in Chapter 3, a data mining query result may contain nested tables, and sometimes even multiple levels of nesting. The query in Listing 7-4 returns the histogram of the CollegePlans predictions in the form of a nested table.

```
SELECT t.StudentID,
       PredictHistogram(CollegePlans) AS [CollegePlans]
FROM CollegePlan
   PREDICTION JOIN
   OPENQUERY(CollegePlans,
   'SELECT StudentID, Gender, IQ, ParentEncouragement, ParentIncome
       FROM NewStudents') AS t
ON CollegePlan.ParentIncome = t.ParentIncome AND
   CollegePlan.IQ = t.IQ AND
   CollegePlan.Gender = t.Gender AND
   CollegePlan.ParentEncouragement = t.ParentEncouragementn
```

Listing 7-4 Returning a prediction histogram

The result of the query is shown in Table 7-1. The histogram column embeds a nested table. In addition to the College Plans column, there is a set of predefined columns in the nested table, including $Support, $Probability, $AdjustedProbability, and so on. Each row represents a state of the College Plan, and the last row represents the missing state.

Regression Model

Regression models predict continuous variables using linear regression formulas based on *regressors* that you specify. Each regressor must have a continuous content type. Normally, a regression formula contains one or more regressors that have coefficients in the regression formulas. When none of the specified regressors is deemed suitable by the algorithm, the resultant tree contains a constant in that particular node. (The "Regression" section later in this chapter provides more details on this topic.)

Table 7-1 Query Results

STUDENTID	COLLEGEPLANS				
8001	CollegePlans	$Support	$Probability	$AdjustedProbability	....
	Plans to attend	767	0.75847	0.0831	
	Does not plan to attend	249	0.24513	0.0004	
	Missing	0	0	0.	
8002	CollegePlans	$Support	$Probability	$AdjustedProbability	....
	Plans to attend	352	0.60169	0.0001	
	Does not plan to attend	233	0.39831	0.0439	
	Missing	0	0	0	
8003	...				

The DMX shown in Listing 7-5 creates and trains a model to predict
ParentIncome using IQ, Gender, ParentEncouragement, and CollegePlans. IQ
is used as a regressor. The training statement simply indicates that the model
should be trained using the cases already present in the mining structure.
Although it is not really viable to predict parents' income based on the
intelligence of their children, this serves as a relevant syntax example.

```
//Create model
ALTER MINING STRUCTURE CollegePlan_Structure
ADD MINING MODEL ParentIncome
(     StudentId,
      Gender,
      ParentIncome PREDICT,
      IQ            REGRESSOR,
      ParentEncouragement,
      CollegePlans
)
USING Microsoft_Decision_Trees

// Train model
INSERT INTO ParentIncome
```

Listing 7-5 Creating and training a regression model

The query in Listing 7-6 predicts the `ParentIncome` for new students and the estimated standard deviation for each prediction. The returned deviation is the deviation of the target variable in the decision tree node from which the prediction arose. In general, the smaller the deviation, the more accurate the prediction is. However, the accuracy assumes that the input regressors are in the same range as the regressors seen during training. For example, if you provided a case with $IQ = 2,000$, it could dramatically skew the results.

```
SELECT t.StudentID, ParentIncome.ParentIncome,
       PredictStdev(ParentIncome) AS Deviation
FROM ParentIncome
PREDICTION JOIN
OPENQUERY(CollegePlans,
    'SELECT StudentID, Gender, IQ, ParentEncouragement,
        CollegePlans FROM NewStudentsPI') AS t
ON ParentIncome.CollegePlans = t.CollegePlans AND
    ParentIncome.IQ = t.IQ AND
    ParentIncome.Gender = t.Gender AND
    ParentIncome.ParentEncouragement = t.ParentEncouragement
```

Listing 7-6 Continuous prediction using a decision tree

When you apply the `PredictHistogram` function on the continuous column, it returns two rows in the nested table (one for the predicted mean value, and one for the missing state), each with its associated probability. Table 7-2 shows the result of calling `PredictHistogram` on a continuous column.

Association

As mentioned in the previous section, you can use the Microsoft Decision Trees algorithm for association tasks. The model uses a predictable nested table, builds a set of trees for each unique key in the table, and calculates the relationship among these trees.

Listing 7-7 shows an example of an associative trees model built on a movie data set.

```
CREATE MINING MODEL MovieAssociation
(
    CustomerID          LONG  KEY,
    Gender              TEXT  DISCRETE,
    MaritalStatus       TEXT  DISCRETE,
    Movies              TABLE PREDICT
```

Listing 7-7 Creating an associative trees model

```
      (
        Movie               TEXT KEY
      )
  )
  USING Microsoft_Decision_Trees
```

Listing 7-7 (continued)

This query analyzes the associations among all movies, together with the customer's gender and marital status. It builds a decision tree for up to 255 movies. Each movie is considered an attribute with binary states — existing or missing. Trees may have splits on movie name, gender, and marital status. You can change the number of trees that are created by setting parameters described later in this chapter.

Because the model contains a nested table, the training statement involves the Shape statement, as shown in Listing 7-8.

```
INSERT INTO MovieAssociation
( CustomerId, Gender, MaritalStatus,
  Movies (SKIP, Movie))
SHAPE
{
 OPENQUERY (MovieSurvey,
  'SELECT CustomerId, Gender, [Marital Status]
   FROM Customers ORDER BY CustomerID')
}
APPEND
(
 {OPENQUERY (MovieSurvey,
            'SELECT CustomerId, Movie
             FROM Movies ORDER BY CustomerID')}
 RELATE CustomerID TO CustomerID
) AS Movies
```

Listing 7-8 Training an associative trees model

Suppose that there is a married male customer who likes the movie *Terminator*. The query shown in Listing 7-9 returns the other five movies this customer is most likely to find appealing. The Predict call instructs the algorithm to return the results by the adjusted probability, rather than the true probability. This allows less popular movies that have a higher lift based on the input to be recommended.

Table 7-2 Query Result

STUDENTID	HISTOGRAM	ParentIncome	$Support	$Probability	$AdjustedProbability	$Variance	$Stdev
8001		38018	1624	0.99947	0	194993736	13964
		Missing	0	0.0006	0.0006	0	0
		ParentIncome	$Support	$Probability	$AdjustedProbability	$Variance	$Stdev
8003		35082	3254	0.9997	0	219019156	14799
		Missing	0	0.0003	0.0003	0	0
...							

```
SELECT
  t.CustomerID,
  Predict(MovieAssociation.Movies,5, $AdjustedProbability)
      AS Recommendation
FROM
  MovieAssociation
NATURAL PREDICTION JOIN
(SELECT '101' AS CustomerID, 'Male' AS Gender,
  'Married' AS MaritalStatus,
  (SELECT 'Terminator' AS Movie)
      AS Movies) AS t
```

Listing 7-9 Associative singleton query

Table 7-3 shows the result of the query in Listing 7-9, with Recommendation as a nested table containing the five recommended movies.

Table 7-3 The Five Recommended Movies

CUSTOMERID	RECOMMENDATION
101	*Terminator 2: Judgment Day*
	Shawshank Redemption, The
	A Beautiful Mind
	Matrix, The
	Saving Private Ryan

Model Content

Figure 7-1 shows the layout of a tree model. The top level is the model node. The children of the model node are its tree root nodes. If a tree model contains a single tree, there is only one node in the second level. The nodes of the other levels are either intermediate nodes (or leaf nodes) of the tree. The probabilities of each predictable attribute state (or regression coefficients, in the case of a regression model) are stored in the distribution rowsets, as shown in Figure 7-1.

Interpreting the Model

Figure 7-2 shows the Microsoft Decision Tree viewer, displaying the classification tree model of CollegePlans. The tree is laid out horizontally with the root node on the left side. Each node contains a histogram bar with different colors, representing various states. In this case, there are two colors in the histogram bar. The darker color shown in Figure 7-2 represents College Plan = Plans to attend, and the lighter color represents College Plan = Does not plan to attend. The bottom part of the screen is a dockable window that displays the node legend of the selected node.

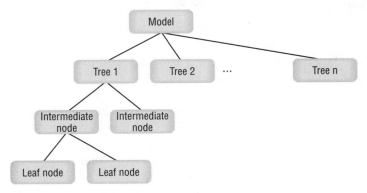

Figure 7-1 Content for a decision tree model

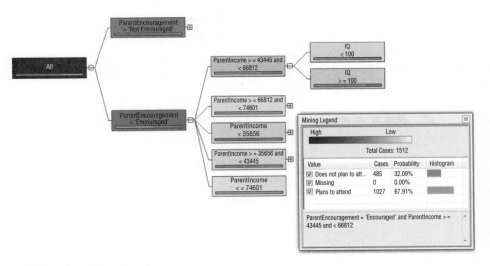

Figure 7-2 Decision Tree viewer

The decision tree patterns are very easy to interpret. Each path from the root to a given node forms a rule. In Figure 7-2, the selected node represents the node path: ParentEncouragement = 'Encouraged' and ParentIncome >= 43445 and < 66812 and IQ >= 100. From the Node Legend window, you can see that there are 1,016 cases classified to this node, and the probability of College Plan = Plans to attend in this node is 75.49 percent.

There are several buttons and drop-down lists on the toolbar, including buttons for Zoom in, Zoom out, and Zoom to fit. You use the Tree drop-down list to make tree selections. (Remember, a model may contain a set of trees.) The left bar in this drop-down list tells you the size of the associated tree. The Histograms combo box allows you to specify the number of states (colors) to display in the histogram bar of each tree node. For example, if a predictable attribute has 10 states, you can use this drop-down list to display the five states that are most important. The other states are all grouped and shown in gray.

Let's say you want to find the nodes representing the highest probability of `College Plan = Plans to attend`. You can do this by looking at the histogram bar of each node. But when there are many states of the predictable attribute, it is not obvious which nodes you need. The Background drop-down list is very useful for this purpose. It controls the background color of the tree nodes. By default, the tree node background color represents the number of cases classified in each node. The darker a node, the more cases it contains. You can also pick a particular state of the predictable attribute in this drop-down list — for example, `College Plan = Plans to attend`. In this case, the background color represents the probability for the selected state. If a node is a dark color, it has a high probability associated with the given state.

All Microsoft data mining viewers in SQL Server 2008 have multiple tabs, which display the patterns from different angles. Figure 7-3 shows a section of the Dependency Network pane for the `MovieAssociation` model. The dependency network displays the relationships among attributes derived from decision tree model's content.

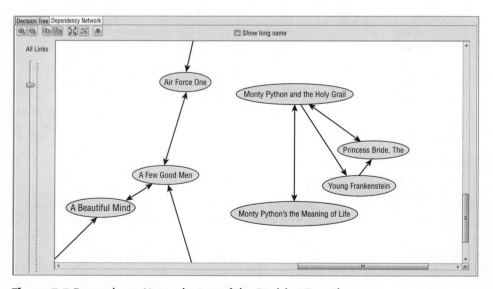

Figure 7-3 Dependency Network pane of the Decision Tree viewer

Each node in Figure 7-3 represents one attribute, and each edge represents the relationship between two nodes. An edge has a direction, pointing from the input attribute (node) to the predictable attribute (node). An edge can be bidirectional, which means two nodes can predict each other. In Figure 7-3, *Monty Python and the Holy Grail* predicts and is predicted by *The Princess Bride* and *Monty Python's the Meaning of Life*, but predicts and is not predicted by *Young Frankenstein*. An edge has a weight, which is associated with the slider at the left side. The heavier the weight, the stronger the predictor is. The weight is derived from the tree's statistics, mainly based on the split score. In this example, if you moved the slider down, you would see that the strongest relationship is between the two Monty Python movies, and the weakest relationship is between *Young Frankenstein* and *The Princess Bride*.

The Dependency Network viewer is very useful in situations like the `MovieAssociation` model where there are lots of predictable attributes, particularly from a predictable nested table. In this case, each node in the dependency network represents a tree. This graph is like a bird's-eye view over a forest. It provides extremely useful information for exploratory data analysis.

NOTE In most cases, not all of the input attributes are used for splitting a tree. The unselected attributes generally have less impact than the predictable attribute has, and they are not displayed in the dependency network.

Be careful, though. In some cases, important attributes don't appear in the tree split. For example, suppose that a tree predicts `HouseOwnership`. The `Education` and `Income` attributes have a major impact on `HouseOwnership` and are highly correlated. For example, higher education is always associated with high income. When the tree splits on one attribute, it is almost equivalent to splitting on the other. After the split on the `Income` attribute, `Education` is not an important attribute in subtrees. As a consequence, there is no tree split based on `Education`. Thus, `Education` is not displayed in the dependency network, even though it is a good predictor for `HouseOwnership`. This is a weakness of the greedy search mechanism used by decision trees. To compensate for this, you should build an additional model using the Naïve Bayes algorithm, which will show relationships hidden by trees.

Figure 7-4 shows a regression tree model predicting `ParentIncome`. The regressor is `IQ`. The overall view of the regression tree is similar to that of a classification tree. However, the tree nodes are different. There is no histogram bar in a regression tree. Instead, it contains a diamond bar representing the distribution of predictable variables (continuous values). The diamond represents the value distribution of the given node. The diamond is centered on the mean of the predictable attribute of those cases that are classified in the current node. The width of the diamond is twice the standard deviation. If the diamond is thin, the prediction on this node is more precise.

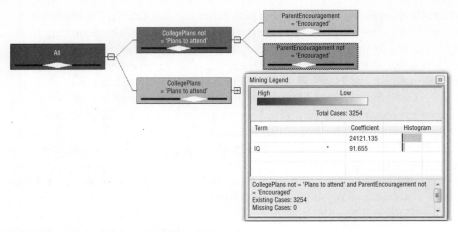

Figure 7-4 Visualizing a regression tree

As explained previously, each node of a regression tree model contains a regression formula. For example, the selected node in Figure 7-4 contains the following regression formula:

```
Parent Income = 32,634.510 + 91.655*(IQ-92.885)
```

NOTE The Decision Tree viewer renders regression formulas in a rather odd manner. Most people are familiar with the format $y = mx + b$, but the Decision Tree viewer shows formulas like $y = b + a(x-m)$. The intercept (*b*) is modified so that you can see the mean value of the regressor at the selected node (*i*). In the node selected in Figure 7-4, the mean value of IQ is 92.885. The intercept (*b*) as shown in the Decision Tree viewer can be interpreted as the value of the target attribute when all input regressors are at their mean values.

Decision Tree Principles

This section takes a closer look at the principles of the Microsoft Decision Trees algorithm.

Basic Concepts of Tree Growth

The basic idea of a decision tree algorithm is fairly straightforward. This discussion describes the algorithm by going through an example based on the college scenario described previously in this chapter. The table contains 8,000 students with information about their IQ, gender, parents' income, and parental encouragement. The predictable attribute is College Plan, a binary column indicating if the student is planning to attend college.

The first step is to build a correlation count table as displayed in the top part of Figure 7-5. Each column in the correlation count table is an attribute/value pair of input attributes. Each row is a state value of a predictable attribute. The cells in the table are the counts of correlations of input attribute values and predictable states.

		IQ			Parent Encouragement		Parent Income		Gender	
		High	Medium	Low	Yes	No	High	Low	Male	Female
College Plan	Plans	300	500	200	700	300	400	600	500	500
	Does not Plan	100	1000	900	400	1600	400	1600	1100	900

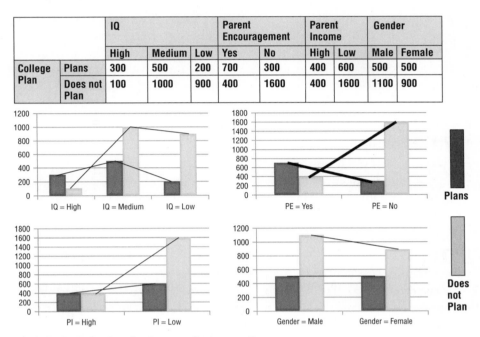

Figure 7-5 Selecting the best attribute to split

From the table, you can see that there are 400 high-IQ students — 300 of them are associated with `College Plan = Plans to attend`, and 100 of them are associated with `College Plan = Does not plan to attend`. The bottom part of Figure 7-5 contains four bar charts graphically displaying the information in the correlation count table. The dark bars represent `College Plan = Plans to attend`, and the light bars represent `College Plan = Does not plan to attend`.

The decision tree algorithm will first pick an attribute to split at the root level. The selection criteria for the subsets after the split should be very different in terms of the predictable attribute value. From the four bar charts in Figure 7-5, you can identify that `Parent Encouragement` is the most significant attribute. If `Parent Encouragement = Yes`, the dark bar is longer. If `Parent Encouragement = No`, the light bar is much longer. You can also see from the last bar chart that the `Gender` doesn't contain much useful information related to `College Plan` in the overall data set. Whether the `Gender` = `Male` or `Female`, the `College Plan` distributions are the same.

Although you can easily pick the best attribute to split by examining these bar charts, the decision tree algorithm can't view these charts. However, you can measure the information contained in these bar charts by using some formal criteria (math formulas). Two frequently used criteria are *entropy* (or *information value*) and *Bayesian score*. The details of Bayesian score were discussed in Chapter 4. This section explores the concept of entropy.

You must find a math formula to measure the purity of a data set on a given attribute (predictable attribute). In the `CollegePlans` example, this formula must satisfy the following criteria:

- In a data set, if all the cases have `College Plan` = `Plans to attend` (or `Does not plan to attend`), the no information can be gained — thus the formula returns 0.

- In a data set, if the number of cases of `College Plan` = `Plans to attend` and the number of cases of `College Plan` = `Does not plan to attend` are the same, the information reaches the maximum — thus the formula returns the maximum value.

- Predictable attributes may have multiple states. For example, in a bank loan analysis scenario, the predictable attribute `CreditRisk` has three states: `High`, `Medium`, and `Low`. In this case, you have two choices for decision making. You can make the decision in a single step for each state, or you can make the decision in two steps. The first step is to consider `CreditRisk` = `High` or `Not High`, and the second step is to consider `CreditRisk` = `Medium` or `Low`. The amount of information in both cases should be equivalent.

Conveniently, the following formula satisfies all the three criteria:

```
Entropy (p₁, p₂,...,pₙ) = -p₁log₂p₁ -p₂log₂p₂... -pₙlog₂pₙ
Where p₁, p₂,...,Pₙ are the probability of each state on the predictable
attribute, p₁+ p₂...+Pₙ= 1.
```

In the college example, there are only two predictable states (`Plans` and `Does not Plan`), so $n = 2$. Using the preceding formula, you can calculate the entropies of the splits on the four input attributes as follows:

- Split on `ParentEncouragement`:

  ```
  Entropy(700, 400) + Entropy(300, 1600) = 0.946 +0.629 = 1.571
  ```

- Split on `IQ`:

  ```
  Entropy(300, 100) + Entropy(500, 1000) + Entropy(200, 900) =0.814
     + 0.918 0.684 = 2.416
  ```

■ Split on `ParentIncome`:

Entropy(400,400) + Entropy(600,1600) = 1.0 + 0.845 = 1.845

■ Split on `Gender`:

Entropy(500, 1100) + Entropy(500, 900) =0.896 + 0.941 = 1.837

Based on these calculations, you find the subsets after the splits on `ParentEncouragement` have the lowest entropy. Thus, the most significant attribute to split at the root level is `ParentEncouragement`. After the data is split into two subsets, the algorithm repeats the same process on each leaf node to grow the tree. Figure 7-6 shows the new correlation count table on the subset where `ParentEncouragement = Yes`.

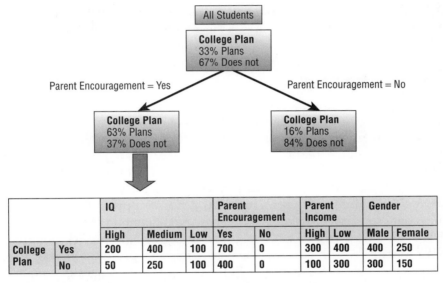

		IQ			Parent Encouragement		Parent Income		Gender	
		High	Medium	Low	Yes	No	High	Low	Male	Female
College Plan	Yes	200	400	100	700	0	300	400	400	250
	No	50	250	100	400	0	100	300	300	150

Figure 7-6 Recursive application of the correlation count

Working with Many States in an Attribute

For classification trees, a reasonable number of states of an input attribute would be less than 100, but this is not always the case in a real data set. Some attributes may have thousands of states (for example, the ZIP code), and some decision tree algorithms simply ignore these attributes even though they can contain useful information. For example, customers living in certain ZIP codes may have a higher credit risk than customers living in other ZIP codes.

There are different techniques to resolve this issue — for example, grouping similar states to reduce the total number of states. The grouping method is accurate, but it is very time-consuming because the algorithm must repeat it at each split. The Microsoft Decision Trees algorithm deals with this issue through dynamic grouping. At each split, the algorithm (by default) considers only 100 states, with 99 of the most popular states plus one state representing all of the remaining states. After each split, the popular states vary across subsets. Of course, this is based on a heuristic assumption that the more-popular states have a larger impact on the prediction than less-popular states do.

Alternatively, you can solve this problem before processing the model. You can visualize the impact of the states by using data-visualizing tools such as bar charts during the data exploration stage, and then manually grouping similar states. Most of the less-important states can be grouped into one single value. With the Data Mining Client for Excel add-in, you can easily perform this task using the Re-label Data tool, as described in Chapter 5.

NOTE For discrete predictable attributes, the recommended number of states is less than 10. If you have too many states in the predictable attributes, you should consider grouping some states.

Avoiding Overtraining

As explained in the previous sections, the Decision Trees algorithm grows the tree recursively. As a result, you can sometimes end up with a fairly large tree. These trees have many levels and branches, and thus contain many rules.

However, the size of the tree has no direct relation to the quality of prediction. As a matter of fact, when the tree becomes too deep, it tends to overrepresent the training cases instead of generalizing rules. Such a model does a great job of classifying the training data set. However, it has bad prediction accuracy for the new data set. This problem is called *overtraining* or *overfitting*.

There are many ways to deal with the overtraining issue. Some decision tree algorithms contain two processing steps: growing and pruning. During the *growing step* you develop the tree, and in the *pruning step* you cut tree nodes and branches, thus making the rules more generally applicable.

Microsoft Decision Trees performs what is called *forward pruning*. The tree growth is controlled by using the Bayesian score, which avoids splitting when there is not enough information to justify a split. This is controlled by a COMPLEXITY_PENALTY parameter, which has values from 0 to 1. If this parameter value is set high, more restrictions are imposed during the tree growth, making the tree size smaller. Tree growth is also controlled by the MINIMUM_SUPPORT parameter, which prevents nodes from splitting unless there is a certain amount of data to justify the split. (These parameters are discussed in greater detail later in this chapter.)

Incorporating Prior Knowledge

In many cases, you have prior information about events. For example, when flipping a coin, you know that you are most likely to see 5 heads in 10 flips. This sort of prior information can be integrated with the training data set to make sure the model is more objective. The Microsoft Decision Trees algorithm automatically adds priors (counts) at each tree node for each state of the predictable attribute. The predicted probability is calculated with priors added.

For the example of `College Plan`, if there is a tree node that contains only those students with `College Plan = Plans to attend`, the probability of `College Plan = Does not plan to attend` is not 100 percent, because the algorithm adds one count of `College Plan = Does not plan to attend` as prior knowledge.

Feature Selection

Data mining algorithms can be very sensitive to the number of attributes you include. Too many attributes requires extensive CPU and memory resources for processing. Also, not all attributes are equally important in terms of the prediction accuracy. *Feature selection* is a process that selects a subset of attributes so that the processing time can be substantially reduced, but with no (or limited) sacrifices on the model accuracy.

The basic idea of feature selection is quite simple. You use statistical functions (such as the Bayesian score or entropy) to calculate the potential impact of each input attribute related to the predictable attribute, and then select the most significant attributes for the model.

Feature selection is applied not only to input attributes, but also to output (predictable) attributes. Some models may have lots of predictable attributes. For example, if a model contains a nested table, and the nested table is predictable, all of the nested keys are modeled as predictable attributes. In the case of a retail store's market basket model, the nested table key is often the product. However, there could be thousands of products in a store. The algorithm can't efficiently deal with that many trees in the model, so a feature selection technique is applied to speed up model building. For those output attributes that are filtered out, the prediction is based on simple probability.

A feature selection component is used internally by all Microsoft data mining algorithms. Users don't need to invoke this process explicitly. Different algorithms have different feature selection criteria. Two algorithm parameters control the feature selection thresholds: `Maximum_Input_Attributes` and `Maximum_Output_Attributes`. (These two attributes are discussed in more detail later in this chapter.)

Using Continuous Inputs

One of the content types for numeric attributes is *continuous* (as opposed to *discrete*). Although continuous attributes must be numeric, not all numeric attributes are necessarily discrete (such as a ZIP code). Continuous variables can be used as input for the classification tree. Suppose that the `ParentIncome` column in the `College Plan` data set contains continuous numbers instead of `High` and `Low`, as in the previous example. You cannot use the same approach you would use for discrete attributes to measure the tree split score. There are simply too many different states. Also, the split condition should recognize the ordered nature of a continuous variable (for example, by using less than and greater than operators).

The Microsoft Decision Trees algorithm deals with continuous inputs in a unique way. It first bins the continuous input into large buckets based on the equal range. Then the algorithm merges the buckets based on the same measurement you use for a discrete attribute such as `Entropy`. If merging two buckets can increase the split score, those two buckets are combined. This process is calculated recursively. At the end, you have a set of buckets with an optimized split score. This score is then compared with other discrete or continuous input attributes, and the attribute with the best score will be selected for the split.

Regression

Regression is similar to classification. The only difference is that regression predicts continuous attributes. Although the basic task of a decision tree algorithm is classification, it can be used for regression as well. The Microsoft Decision Trees algorithm added support for regression in SQL Server 2005.

Regression models use regressors to calculate the output variable. A *regressor* is a continuous input attribute that is used to model the continuous predictable attribute in a linear way. For example, suppose `IQ` is the continuous predictable attribute and `ParentIncome` is the regressor. The following is a classic linear regression formula:

```
IQ = a + b*ParentIncome + e
```

The residual `e` represents the noise, with a mean of 0 (zero). The coefficients `a(intercept)` and `b(slope)` are determined by the condition that the sum of the square residuals is as small as possible.

A regression model can have as many regressors as you specify in the model definition. The algorithm will automatically choose which regressors provide the most information to the output attribute at each node in the tree.

The Microsoft Decision Trees algorithm contains a linear regression formula at each leaf node. One advantage of using a regression tree instead of simple linear regression is that a tree can represent both linear and nonlinear relationships. For example, if the relationship between `IQ` and `ParentIncome` is very different for male students and female students, the regression tree will have a split on the gender and return two different formulas — one for each gender. When there is no tree split, the regression tree reverts to a linear regression. Likewise, when there are no suitable regressors at a node, the tree predicts a constant value.

MICROSOFT LINEAR REGRESSION ALGORITHM

To make the linear regression feature of the Microsoft Decision Trees algorithm more visible, SQL Server Analysis Services 2005 added a new algorithm: Microsoft Linear Regression. It is based on the Microsoft Decision Trees algorithm, but instead of splitting the data, the regression formula is based on the entire data set.

Association Analysis with Microsoft Decision Trees

One of the unique features of the Microsoft Decision Trees algorithm is that it can be used for association analysis. A mining model may contain a forest of trees. If a model contains a nested table, and the nested table is predictable, all the nested keys are considered to be predictable attributes. The Microsoft Decision Trees algorithm builds trees for each nested key that is a selected feature.

Figure 7-7 illustrates a set of trees to predict movie relationships. The top-left tree predicts the popularity of the movie *Stargate*. The dark bar in the histogram represents the probability of a viewer not liking *Stargate*, and the white bar represents the probability of a viewer liking *Stargate*. The first split is on the *Star Wars* attribute. If a person likes *Star Wars*, there is a high probability that he or she is going to like *Stargate*. The second split shows that a person who likes *Star Trek* also has a high probability of liking *Stargate*.

There are multiple trees in the model. From each tree, you can find a set of movies that is correlated with the predictable movie. For example, based on the *Stargate* tree, you can say that fans of *Star Wars* and *Star Trek* are likely to enjoy *Stargate* with certain weights (calculated based on the probability gain). Based on the *Terminator* tree, you can predict that *Matrix* and *E.T.* fans will also like *Terminator*. By going over the entire forest of trees, you can derive all the relationships among the movies. These relationships are, in fact, association rules, and can be used for making associated predictions. For example, if a person likes *Star Wars*, you can recommend *Stargate* and *Matrix* to him or her.

Using Microsoft Decision Trees for association analysis is very interesting — associated items are displayed in the tree form and dependency network form. However, there are also limitations to this association task. Because it builds a decision tree for each item, this may take time and resources when there are lots of items. The default maximum number of trees is 255. If there are more than 255 items, the algorithm uses feature selection techniques to select the important features.

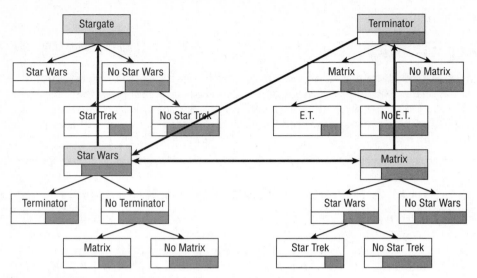

Figure 7-7 Association using Microsoft Decision Trees

NOTE The Microsoft Decision Trees algorithm does association analysis by combining all the trees and deriving the correlations among the tree roots. It is best when the number of items for association analysis is limited; otherwise, the algorithm must build a large number of trees. This is time- and resource-consuming.

The other issue is that the Microsoft Decision Trees algorithm doesn't return item sets and rules like an association rules algorithm does. The user must figure out the relationship using a content viewer. Our recommendation is to build models with both the decision tree and association rules algorithms — you may find complementary information. If you have a large number of items, you should use an association rules algorithm.

Parameters

The Microsoft Decision Trees algorithm has a number of parameters. These parameters are used to control the tree growth, tree shape, and the input /output attribute settings. By adjusting these parameter settings, you can fine-tune your model's accuracy. The following sections examine the Decision Trees algorithm parameters.

COMPLEXITY_PENALTY

COMPLEXITY_PENALTY is a floating point number with the range [0,1]. The concept behind forward pruning of decision trees is that the simpler answer is usually better, and this parameter controls how much penalty the algorithm applies to complex (or large) trees.

When the value of this parameter is set close to 0, there is a lower penalty for the tree growth, and you may see large trees. When its value is set close to 1, the tree growth is penalized heavily, and the resulting trees are relatively small. Generally speaking, large trees tend to have overtraining issues, whereas small tree may miss some patterns.

The recommended way to tune the model is to try multiple trees with different settings, and then use cross-validation to see where you get the highest and the most stable accuracy. The default setting is related to the number of input attributes. If there are fewer than 10 input attributes, the value is set to 0.5; if there are more than 100 attributes, the value is set to 0.99. If you have between 10 and 100 input attributes, the value is set to 0.9.

MINIMUM_SUPPORT

MINIMUM_SUPPORT is used to specify the minimum size of each node in a tree. For example, if this value is set to 20, any split that would produce a child node containing less than 20 cases is not accepted. The default value for MINIMUM_SUPPORT is 10. Often, if the training data set contains lots of cases, you will need to raise the value of this parameter to avoid overtraining.

SCORE_METHOD

SCORE_METHOD is used to specify the method for determining a split score during tree growth. There are three possible values for SCORE_METHOD:

- SCORE_METHOD = 1 instructs the algorithm to use an entropy score for tree growth.

- SCORE_METHOD = 2 instructs the algorithm to use the Bayesian with K2 Prior method, meaning it will add a constant for each state of the predictable attribute in a tree node, regardless of the node level of the tree.

- SCORE_METHOD = 3 instructs the algorithm to use the Bayesian Dirichlet Equivalent with Uniform Prior (BDEU) method, which is the default value and adds weighted support to each predictable state based on the node support and level in the tree. The weight of the root node is higher than that of the leaf node; thus, the assigned prior (knowledge) is larger.

SCORE_METHOD = 2 in previous versions of SQL Server specified a method called orthogonal that did not perform well and is no longer supported.

SPLIT_METHOD

SPLIT_METHOD is used to specify the tree shape — for example, whether the tree shape is binary or bushy. Following are the methods used:

- SPLIT_METHOD = 1 means the tree is split only in a binary way. For example, assume Education is an attribute with three states: high school, undergraduate, and graduate. If the tree split is set to be binary, the algorithm may split the tree into two nodes with the criteria Education = undergraduate and Education = Not undergraduate.

- SPLIT_METHOD = 2 indicates that the tree should always split completely on each attribute. In this case, a split on the assumed Education attribute would produce three nodes, one corresponding to each educational state.

- SPLIT_METHOD = 3, the default method, specifies both of the previous two methods. That is, the decision tree will automatically choose the better of these methods to create the split.

MAXIMUM_INPUT_ATTRIBUTES

MAXIMUM_INPUT_ATTRIBUTES is a threshold parameter for feature selection. When the number of input attributes is greater than this parameter value, feature selection is invoked implicitly to select the most significant input attributes.

MAXIMUM_OUTPUT_ATTRIBUTES

MAXIMUM_OUTPUT_ATTRIBUTES is another threshold parameter for feature selection. When the number of predictable attributes is greater than this parameter value, feature selection is invoked implicitly to select the most significant attributes. A tree is built for each of the selected attributes.

FORCE_REGRESSOR

FORCE_REGRESSOR allows you to override the regressor selection logic in the decision tree algorithm and always use a specified regressor (or set of regressors) in the regression equations in regression trees. It forces the regression to use specified attributes, no matter how small the relationship to the target attribute.

This parameter is typically used in price elasticity models. For example, suppose that you have a model to predict Sales using Price and other attributes. If you specify FORCE_REGESSOR = Price, you get regression formulas using Price and other significant attributes for each node of the tree.

Stored Procedures

The Decision Tree viewer uses a set of system-stored procedures, shown in Listing 7-10, to help you compile the mining content in a meaningful way. You can use these stored procedures in your applications as you see fit.

```
CALL System.GetTreeScores('MovieAssociation')

CALL System.DTGetNodes('MovieAssociation')

CALL System.DTGetNodeGraph('MovieAssociation', 60)

CALL System.DTAddNodes('MovieAssociation', '36;34',
                       '99;282;20;261;26;201;33;269;30;187')
```

Listing 7-10 Decision tree stored procedures

GetTreeScores is the procedure that the Decision Tree viewer uses to populate the drop-down tree selector. It takes a name of a decision tree model as a parameter and returns a table containing a row for every tree on the model and the following three columns:

- ATTRIBUTE_NAME is the name of the tree.
- NODE_UNIQUE_NAME is the content node representing the root of the tree.
- MSOLAP_NODE_SCORE is a number representing the amount of information in the tree. This number is roughly related to the number of nodes in each tree.

DTGetNodes is used by the decision tree Dependency Network viewer when you click the Add Nodes button. It returns a row for all potential nodes in the dependency network and has the following two columns:

- NODE_UNIQUE_NAME1 is an identifier that is unique for the dependency network but is not necessarily related to the NODE_UNIQUE_NAME in the model content.
- NODE_CAPTION is the name of the node.

DTGetNodeGraph takes a model name and a number of nodes to display in the dependency network. If there are more nodes in the model (representing both input and output attributes) than the number specified, the stored procedure balances the result set so that a fair number of both inputs and outputs are represented, and an attractive graph can be rendered.

The DTGetNodeGraph procedure returns four columns:

- The NODE_TYPE column has either the value 1 or 2, and effectively divides the result into two sections.
- When a row has NODE_TYPE = 1, it contains a description of the nodes and the remaining three columns have the following interpretation:
  - NODE_UNIQUE_NAME1 contains a unique identifier for the node, as described in DTGetNodes.
  - NODE_UNIQUE_NAME2 contains the node caption.
  - MSOLAP_NODE_SCORE is unused in this section.
- When a row has NODE_TYPE = 2, it represents a directed edge in the graph and the remaining columns have these interpretations
  - NODE_UNIQUE_NAME1 contains the node name of the starting point of the edge.
  - NODE_UNIQUE_NAME2 contains the node name of the ending point of the edge.
  - MSOLAP_NODE_SCORE contains the relative weight of the edge. This value is used to show and hide edges with the slider is moved in the Dependency Net.

DTAddNodes allows you to add new nodes to an existing graph. It takes a model name, a semicolon-separated list of the IDs of nodes you want to add to the graph, and a semicolon-separated list of the IDs of nodes already in the graph. This procedure returns a table similar to the NODE_TYPE = 2 section of DTGetNodeGraph, but without the NODE_TYPE column. The rows in the result set contain all the edges between the added nodes, and all of the edges between the added nodes and the nodes specified as already in the graph.

Summary

This chapter covered the Microsoft implementation of one of the most important data mining algorithms: The Microsoft Decision Trees algorithm. This implementation performs three distinct data mining tasks — classification, regression, and association. After reading this chapter, you should now understand (and be able to explain) the usage scenarios of decision trees, as well as the basic concepts of how decision trees work. You should also have a basic understanding of how to interpret a decision tree model using the Decision Tree viewer.

This chapter also covered in some depth the variety of options available for creating and accessing decision tree models through DMX (including creation, training, and prediction), as well as custom model parameters and stored procedures that access the content shown in the Decision Tree viewer.

Chapter 8 covers an evolution of the core Decision Trees algorithm as it is used for forecasting in the Microsoft Time Series algorithm.

Microsoft Time Series Algorithm

Suppose you are running a retail store and are managing the inventory of each of the products you stock. You know that at the end of the week, people buy more wine, so you put in an extra order and tell your supplier to send the same amount each week. Approaching Valentine's Day, you know that there will be some extra demand, so you order even more for that period. A new, promising winery has only been on the shelves a few weeks, but you see how other wineries from the same region are doing, so you guesstimate how much of that brand to order as well. Also, as wine sales increase, so do sales of cheeses, breads, and gourmet foods, so you increase those orders by a similar amount.

In each of these cases, you are doing time series analysis. You are using the past sales history of product sales to predict future inventory needs. You automatically apply seasonality, including weekly periods and annual events — you even adapt behavior of existing product sales to predict the volume of new sales.

The ability to accurately forecast time series is essential to running almost any business. The Microsoft Time Series algorithm provides a unique approach to time series forecasting that is both intuitive and accurate. This chapter covers the following topics:

- An overview of the Microsoft Time Series algorithm
- The usage and application of the Time Series algorithm
- DMX syntax for time series scenarios
- Details on how the algorithm works and its parameters

To assist with this chapter, content files are included in the `Chapter8.zip` archive available at `www.wiley.com/go/data_mining_SQL_2008`. This archive contains the following files:

- `Chapter8DMX.dmx` — Contains all the DMX queries used in this chapter
- `Chapter8.bak` — Backup of the SQL Server database referenced in the chapter
- `MSFT.xlsx` — Excel file referenced in the chapter
- `Wine.xls` — Excel file referenced in the chapter

Overview

A *time series* consists of a series of data collected over successive increments of time or other sequence indicator. For example, the closing price of Microsoft stock is a time series, as shown in Figure 8-1. The monthly sales of carbonated beverages is also a time series. You could even create a time series by recording your distance from your kitchen every five minutes. Any sequence of numbers recorded over time (regardless of how trivial) forms a time series.

Figure 8-1 Time series showing Microsoft stock price history for 12 years

In most time series, a value at a given time is related to its values at preceding times. For example, the closing price of Microsoft stock on May 10 is strongly related to its closing price on May 8 and May 9. If you were driving on the road, your distance from your kitchen would grow progressively closer or farther in every five-minute increment.

Generally speaking, the time increments in a time series may be discrete or continuous — that is, the distance between measurements can be the same or variable. In addition, the observed values in a time series may be discrete or continuous. For example, stock values, sales, and distances are all continuous, whereas weather reports composed of values such as sunny, cloudy, or rainy are discrete. Usually, people use the term *time series* to refer to the cases where the series is discrete (evenly spaced) with continuous measurements, and the term *sequence* when the series is continuous but the observations are discrete. In this sense, the Microsoft Time Series algorithm deals with time series, whereas sequences are considered by the Microsoft Sequence Clustering algorithm described in Chapter 10.

Usage

The main purpose of the Microsoft Time Series algorithm is to forecast future series points based on past history. The algorithm is configured to do the best job possible with a minimum of information — in general, the data you have should be enough to provide accurate and informative predictions. Time series data can be presented in two formats, as shown in Figure 8-2. The first format (A) is more like a spreadsheet view, and displays the time series in columns, with the rows representing distinct time events. The second format (B) is a little different, in that there are multiple rows for each time series, and an additional column indicates to the series to which the value column belongs. Microsoft literature offers no official terminology for these formats, so this discussion will refer to them as *columnar* (part A in Figure 8-2) and *interleaved* (part B in Figure 8-2).

(a)

Date	Red Sales	White Sales	Red Volume	White Volume
Jan 2008	$8,425	$12,563	932	1105
Feb 2008	$8,782	$11,725	978	1076
Mar 2008	$9,653	$11,278	1012	1053

(b)

Date	Type	Sales	Volume
Jan 2008	Red	$8,425	932
Jan 2008	White	$12,563	1105
Feb 2008	Red	$8,762	978
Feb 2008	White	$11,725	1076
Mar 2008	Red	$9,653	1012
Mar 2008	White	$11,278	1053

Figure 8-2 Time series data formats A (columnar) and B (interleaved)

Even though the different data formats represent exactly the same data (in this case, the monthly sales of red and white wines), they have various advantages and disadvantages in practical use. Columnar data is more intuitive, because it looks like a spreadsheet, which most people who deal with time series data work with for a large part of their days. However, columnar data is limited in that every time you want to add a new product, you must add a new column. This may not seem like much of a limitation for many cases, but when you need to forecast 100, 1,000, or even 25,000 series, this format becomes unusable. Even when you have a small set of series, each series addition is a schema change and will require you to rebuild your mining objects from scratch.

The interleaved format is a bit more difficult to interpret visually, but it has an advantage in that the series names come directly from the data. Adding a new product is as simple as adding the rows for that product to your table. You can mine new series without changing your schema and therefore, your model definition. The disadvantages of the interleaved format are reduced flexibility and increased complexity. For example, if you use the columnar format in the data set in Figure 8-2, you can set different usage flags on the different columns (such as making red wines predictable and white wines input-only). On the other hand, if you use the interleaved format, all product types will share the same column settings. Additionally, the DMX for getting predictions for a particular series is much simpler in columnar format than in interleaved format, as demonstrated later in this chapter.

INTERPRETATION OF TIME SERIES DATA

The Microsoft Time Series algorithm assumes that you are providing a discrete series (that is, a series of data points evenly spaced in time). However, the algorithm does not enforce this, and you are free to provide series that have varying distances between points. For example, you could provide daily data recorded only on workdays — the algorithm doesn't particularly care that weekends and holidays are missing.

However, the algorithm does have some restrictions on how you can present data. By default, time series are assumed to be complete. This means that for each series, there is a non-NULL data point for every time slice starting when the series begins until the last time slice provided by the data. The different series can have ragged starts, but they must continue without holes through the end. In reality, many series are not complete and (for a variety of reasons) they do have holes. For example, a model that contains daily closing prices of various foreign stock indexes would obviously not have closing prices for all indexes on all days. In this case, it is correct to simply replace the missing data with the closing price of the previous day. The algorithm parameter

(continued)

> **INTERPRETATION OF TIME SERIES DATA *(continued)***
>
> MISSING_VALUE_SUBSTITUTION **(described in more detail later in this chapter) offers an option for automatically replacing holes with imputed data.**
>
> **Another restriction on the data is that the data must be presented to the algorithm *in time order*. If you're querying from a database, this simply means that you need to add an** order by **clause to your source data query. If you are sourcing data from an application, the data must be ordered before sending it to an Analysis Services server. If you are using BI Dev Studio to create time series models, Analysis Services automatically generates the correct query to order your data.**
>
> **A side effect of how the Microsoft Time Series algorithm interprets series data is that it doesn't really matter what you use to indicate the *time* aspect of the series. The time is only used to indicate the *time slice* to which a data point belongs; therefore, it can be any data type — even if it's simply an integer indicating the ordinal of the slice.**

Time Series Scenarios

As with all Microsoft algorithms, the Time Series algorithm is designed to be highly flexible in how it can be applied, so you can use it for a variety of time series analysis scenarios.

Performing a Simple Forecast

The most obvious application of the time series algorithm is simple forecasting — that is, creating a model, showing it some data, and asking it for predictions of future values. As noted previously, the algorithm is designed such that you can do simple forecasts with little intervention — simply create your model, add data, and then perform a forecasting query.

However, there are situations where additional tweaking can provide better results. The most frequent and useful tweak you can provide is specifying the seasonality of the data. For example, if you are providing quarterly data, you can specify a seasonality of 4, indicating that the algorithm should look back one year (that is, four quarters) for indicative patterns. Likewise, you could specify 24 for hourly data, 5 or 7 for daily data (depending on how many days you are counting for a week), or even 60 for minute-by-minute data.

You can also specify multiple periodicities for your data. For example, if you have monthly data, an obvious periodicity is 12 for annual patterns. However, if you suspect that you have quarterly or semi-annual periods as well, you could also specify 3 and 6, indicating the number of months for each period.

Predicting Interdependent Series

The Microsoft Time Series algorithm can examine many series in a single model. Whereas this is merely a convenience feature in many time series implementations, the Microsoft implementation finds relationships where they exist between series and will use these relationships in forecasting. For example, if you have a variety of red wines with a particular sales behavior, but the overall sales of red wines stays constant, then it must be that when sales of one variety goes up, the sales of another variety goes down. Rather than treating these series independently, Microsoft Time Series treats them together and discovers the interplay among the data.

Given the flexibility of the SQL Server Data Mining platform, you can use prediction flags on a per-series basis to indicate how the series should be handled. Marking a series as INPUT indicates that it cannot be forecasted and will be considered only as to its impact on other series. Marking a series as PREDICT_ONLY, on the other hand, indicates that the series can be forecasted, but will not be considered by other series.

NOTE Although the prediction flags seem to mean the same as they do for other algorithms, in reality, they have quite different interpretations. Even though you mark a series as PREDICT ONLY, the values of that series still serve as inputs for itself. Likewise, even though you mark a series as INPUT, that series will still be forecasted internally so that any output series depending on that input will be able to be forecasted perpetually.

Understanding Your Time Series

Like other Microsoft algorithms, the time series algorithm not only applies discovered patterns for prediction, but the patterns are also browsable. For example, you can explore the individual patterns that are being used for prediction and see if the previous month's sales or the previous year's sales have a larger impact on future behavior.

The Microsoft Time Series algorithm presents patterns in multiple ways. In one sense, a series prediction is simply a regression formula, but even a regression formula can tell you how strong or weak any factor is in forecasting. In another sense, because the Time Series algorithm is based on the decision tree implementation used in the Microsoft Decision Trees algorithm, you can get more descriptive rules about your data.

For example, Figure 8-3 shows a portion of a model for forecasting sales of red wine that demonstrates the use of multiple series. Here you can see that when the preceding month (Red.Sales -1) sold more than 2,447 units, a forecast is negatively impacted by the sales of fortified wines from six months ago, the previous month's red wine sales, and Rosé sales from two months ago. Conversely, it is positively impacted by the previous two years of red wine sales. Time series models provide you with enough information to see how your data interacts so that you can make sound business decisions. For example, this information implies that if you force red wine sales higher for a month, you have a good chance of drawing down sales for the month after.

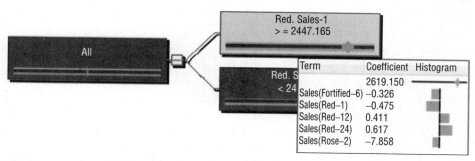

Figure 8-3 Time series model showing a tree and histogram

NOTE Cross-prediction is supported only in Enterprise and Developer editions of SQL Server Analysis Services. In the Standard edition, all predictable columns must be marked PREDICT_ONLY.

What-If Scenarios

After you build your time series models and forecast future values, you can ask additional questions of the model to explore what the future would hold if you change certain points. In the model described in Figure 8-3, for example, you could see exactly what will happen to the forecast if you boost red wine sales by 100 units for a month. How much is the next month impacted? How are related series impacted?

Predicting New Series

A common problem in time series prediction is that you need a significant amount of consistent historical data in order to build a model. So, what do you do when you have only a few data points and want to predict?

The Microsoft Time Series algorithm allows you to use an existing model on data not seen during training to give you an idea of how the series will behave in the future. For example, say you start selling a new type of white wine and have only seven months of sales data — not enough to create a reasonable forecasting model. If you believe that the behavior of this wine will be similar to other white wines, you can build a time series model on the aggregate sales of all your white wines, and then apply that model to the seven months of data for the new wine. The algorithm will use the general patterns discovered in the model to the specific data of your new product to forecast sales for the upcoming months.

DMX

In models built on top of other algorithms, each row of input data represents a *case of data*. A model built using the Microsoft Time Series algorithm (that is, a time series model) treats the input data in a different way, and therefore, the application of DMX to time series is substantially different than with other models. With time series, a row of data typically represents a slice of time rather than a case. In fact, the term *case* doesn't really apply to time series — with time series, it's pretty much just *data*. This section explains and demonstrates how DMX is applied under these circumstances.

Model Creation

The input rows for time series models have a different semantic meaning than with other algorithms, so mining structures created for this purpose are essentially incompatible with non–time series algorithms. Although it is possible to construct a mining structure that can be used both for time series and non–time series analysis, the practical use of such a structure is so limited that it is, at best, an academic effort to do so.

The main element that differentiates a mining structure used for time series from other structures is the inclusion of a KEY TIME column. The KEY TIME content type indicates that a column is a KEY as well as the time slice representing the row. Listing 8-1 describes a mining structure for creating time series models based on Australian wine sales.

```
CREATE MINING STRUCTURE [Wine Sales]
(
      [Month]         DATE KEY TIME,
      [Fortified]     DOUBLE CONTINUOUS,
      [Dry White]     DOUBLE CONTINUOUS,
      [Sweet White]   DOUBLE CONTINUOUS,
      [Red]           DOUBLE CONTINUOUS,
      [Rose]          DOUBLE CONTINUOUS,
      [Sparkling]     DOUBLE CONTINUOUS,
      [Average Red]   DOUBLE CONTINUOUS,
      [Average White] DOUBLE CONTINUOUS
)
```

Listing 8-1 Creating a time series mining structure in columnar format

Notice that there is no holdout specified for a testing set. Although it is syntactically correct (and possible) to add holdout to such a structure, it is semantically incorrect to do so. The holdout mechanism randomly selects top-level rows from the structure, so adding a holdout clause to a time series structure would simply mean that you are deleting points of data, not separating cases for testing.

Earlier in this chapter, Figure 8-2 showed the two different formats for time series data. Each of these formats requires the creation of a different type of mining structure. The interleaved format includes the series type in each row, where the type of series is not an input or predictable column, but is an integral part of the key. In fact, mining structures in interleaved format can be said to have a compound key consisting of the time slice and the series label. The additional category column is used for filtering, as you can see when you add models to the structure. Listing 8-2 shows the creation statement for the wine structure in interleaved format.

```
CREATE MINING STRUCTURE [Wine Sales Interleaved]
(
     [Month]        DATE KEY TIME,
     [Series]       TEXT KEY,
     [Category]     TEXT DISCRETE,
     [Sales]        DOUBLE CONTINUOUS
)
```

Listing 8-2 Creating a time series mining structure in interleaved format

When you create a mining model in either the interleaved or columnar structure, you must be cognizant of the form of the data. The most striking difference between the two formats is the way you select which series are included in the model, and how prediction flags are applied. Listing 8-3 shows how you would create models in each scenario on a subset of the series. For columnar models, you simply add the columns representing the series of interest. For interleaved models, on the other hand, you must apply a filter to select the series you want.

```
// (a) Adding a columnar model
ALTER MINING STRUCTURE [Wine Sales]
ADD MINING MODEL [Reds]
(
     [Month],
     [Fortified]    PREDICT,
     [Red]          PREDICT,
```

Listing 8-3 Adding models to the time series mining structures

```
    [Rose]          PREDICT
) USING Microsoft_Time_Series
WITH DRILLTHROUGH

GO

// (b) Adding an interleaved model
ALTER MINING STRUCTURE [Wine Sales Interleaved]
ADD MINING MODEL [Reds Interleaved]
(
    [Month],
    [Series],
    [Sales]         PREDICT
) USING Microsoft_Time_Series
WITH DRILLTHROUGH,
    FILTER([Category] = 'Red')
```

Listing 8-3 (*continued*)

NOTE It is practically required that all time series models be created with drill-through enabled. Although it is possible and legitimate to create time series models without drill-through, the Time Series viewer will not be able to browse charts on such a model without drill-through because it will not be able to access the historical data from DMX queries. All of the Microsoft data mining tools (that is, BI Dev Studio and Data Mining Client for Office) automatically select drill-through for time series models.

Model Processing

To process structures built for time series models, you use the straightforward INSERT INTO syntax. However, because of the differences in the columnar and interleaved formats accepted by the algorithm, the queries needed to populate the structures are quite different. Although the structure format is simple, populating an interleaved structure with raw and aggregate data requires significantly more difficult SQL, as demonstrated in Listing 8-4.

```
// (a) Processing columnar structure
INSERT INTO MINING STRUCTURE [Wine Sales]
( [Month],
  [Fortified], [Red], [Rose], [Average Red],
  [Dry White], [Sweet White], [Sparkling], [Average White])
OPENQUERY ([Chapter8Data],
  'SELECT
```

Listing 8-4 Processing time series mining structures

```
        Month,
        [Fortified], [Red], [Rose],
            ([Fortified] + [Red] + [Rose]) / 3,
        [Dry White], [Sweet White], [Sparkling],
            ([Dry White] + [Sweet White] + [Sparkling]) / 3
        FROM [Wine Sales]
        ORDER BY [Month]')

// (b) Processing interleaved structure
INSERT INTO MINING STRUCTURE [Wine Sales Interleaved]
( [Month], [Series], [Category], [Sales] )
OPENQUERY ([Chapter8Data],
 'SELECT * FROM
  (SELECT [Month],
          [Type],
          CASE [Type] WHEN ''Red'' THEN ''Red''
                      WHEN ''Rose'' THEN ''Red''
                      WHEN ''Fortified'' THEN ''Red''
                      ELSE ''White''
          END AS [Category],
              [Sales]
    FROM [Wine Sales2]
    UNION ALL
    SELECT [Month], ''Red Average'' AS [Type],
            ''Red'' AS [Category], SUM(Sales)/3 AS [Sales]
    FROM [Wine Sales2] t
    WHERE t.[Type] IN (''Red'', ''Fortified'', ''Rose'')
    GROUP BY [Month]
    UNION ALL
    SELECT [Month], ''White Average'' AS [Type],
            ''White'' AS [Category], SUM(Sales)/3 AS [Sales]
    FROM [Wine Sales2] t
    WHERE t.[Type] IN (''Dry White'', ''Sweet White'', ''Sparkling'')
    GROUP BY [Month]) t
    ORDER BY [Month], [Type]')
```

Listing 8-4 *(continued)*

This listing demonstrates some important details. First, ordering source data by the month for columnar data sources, and by month and series name, is required for interleaved data sources. Also, ensure that you double any single quotation marks used inside source data queries so that the DMX engine interprets the quotation mark as part of the string, and not the end of it.

Another important consideration when processing mining models is missing data. Series can have ragged starting points, but the Microsoft Time Series algorithm requires that, unless otherwise specified, all series must end at the same point and have no missing data after they start. Missing data is generally indicated by NULL values in columnar structures and by missing rows in interleaved data. You can use the `MISSING_DATA_SUBSTITUTION` parameter to handle missing data, as described later in this chapter.

TIME SERIES FROM OLAP CUBES

Because generating the proper series from SQL may be difficult and time-consuming, DMX also allows input directly from MDX queries against OLAP cubes. The following queries create a model consisting of all product categories and their total, and train it from the Adventure Works sample cube using an MDX query:

```
// Create model
CREATE MINING MODEL MDXModel
(
     MonthID       LONG KEY TIME,
     Category      TEXT KEY,
     Sales         DOUBLE CONTINUOUS PREDICT
) USING Microsoft_Time_Series
WITH DRILLTHROUGH


// Train Model from MDX
INSERT INTO MDXModel(Category, MonthID, Sales)
WITH MEMBER Product.Category.[All Products].[Total]
                  AS [Product].[Category].[All Products]
SELECT [Measures].[Reseller Sales Amount]
    ON COLUMNS,
NONEMPTY([Date].[Month Number].[Month Number].MEMBERS *
        [Product].[Category].[Category].ALLMEMBERS)
    ON ROWS
FROM [Adventure Works]
```

The MDX query result is flattened from its normal multidimensional format to a tabular format before being fed to the data mining engine. Notice that the query uses the `[Month Number]` property rather than the month itself. Because the `KEY TIME` column requires a numeric value, you should always add a monotonically increasing member to each level of your OLAP date hierarchy for which you may create time series. Data mining integration with OLAP is described in more detail in Chapter 13.

Forecasting

The most important piece of time series analysis is also the simplest. Time series prediction (also known as *forecasting*) consists of a single function — `Predict-TimeSeries` — that returns a table of the forecasted results. Of course, there's a little maneuvering to be done to support the different time series formats, but the singular function remains. Furthermore, because you are generally forecasting the time series from which a model was trained, there is no source data to provide and thus no PREDICTION JOIN clause, which simplifies the base case even more. Listing 8-5 shows queries for each of the two models that forecast monthly red wine sales for the next year (created previously in Listing 8-3).

```
// (a) Columnar
SELECT FLATTENED PredictTimeSeries([Red], 12) AS Forecast
  FROM [Reds]

// (b) Interleaved
SELECT FLATTENED PredictTimeSeries([Sales], 12) AS Forecast
  FROM [Reds Interleaved]
  WHERE [Series] = 'Red'
```

Listing 8-5 Simple forecasting queries

Each of these queries returns two columns: a time column called Forecast.$Time and a column for the resultant values. In the result for the query in Listing 8-5a, the column is titled Forecast.Red, and in the result for the query in Listing 8-5b the column is Forecast.Sales. The time column (Forecast.Red) represents the time slice for each row. It is important to understand that although the Microsoft Time Series algorithm predicts future series values with great accuracy, it doesn't do quite the same for the time column. The time slice values are computed by taking the average of the distance between the time slices in the source data and repetitively adding that amount to the last time slice value from the source data. This may or may not produce the results that you want because your slices may be irregular in absolute time (for example, the first day of each month). You should use the time column only as an ordering for the results and not try to interpret the contents as having any particular business value.

Note that in the columnar query, you simply select the series you want to predict, whereas in the interleaved query, you specify the series name in the query's where clause. If you leave off the where clause, you will receive a 12-step forecast for every series in the model. This is often an easy way to generate all possible predictions, but you will need to specify the column that represents the series name in the select list to disambiguate the results.

Returning Supplemental Statistics

As with classification or regression queries, often the resulting value is not enough for your solution. With forecasting in particular, the variance in the output is generally more important than with other prediction techniques. The form of time series prediction and the models you use for that prediction make obtaining such results nonintuitive until you get the hang of it, but it holds together once you gain familiarity with the system.

Listing 8-6 shows how to retrieve the standard deviation, variance, and content node ID for each forecasted prediction. By default, each forecast prediction uses two nodes from the model to compute the predicted result. One component of the prediction is static and always uses the same node, depending only on the series you are predicting. The other component is specific to the individual circumstance of the prediction. It is this latter component that is returned as the predict node ID, because the former component can easily be determined by examination. The content layout of a time series model is discussed in detail later in this chapter.

```
SELECT FLATTENED
    (SELECT *, PredictStdev([Red]) AS [Stdev],
            PredictVariance([Red]) AS [Variance],
            PredictNodeID([Red]) AS [NodeID]
        FROM PredictTimeSeries([Red], 12))
    AS Forecast
    FROM [Reds]
```

Listing 8-6 Returning additional prediction information from time series

Changing the Future — Executing a What-If Forecast

Predictive forecasts are great in that they provide a method for determining future values that are more accurate than guesses. However, whenever a forecast is delivered, the question always arises: "What if I could do better?" For example, if you pushed hard to sell an extra 10 percent of goods next month, how would that impact future sales? Even more interesting (because Microsoft Time Series uses hidden relationships between series) is what impact would changing a value have on other series? Continuing with the wine example, if you promoted your Rosé wines next month, what would the impact be on sales of other red varietals?

SQL Server 2008 introduces the capability to supplement series data to execute what-if scenarios by supplying input data using a PREDICTION JOIN clause. Listing 8-7 demonstrates predicting future values of Red after specifying the next two months of sales.

```
SELECT FLATTENED
    PredictTimeSeries([Red], 3, 12, EXTEND_MODEL_CASES)
    FROM [Reds]
```

Listing 8-7 What-if forecasting query

```
NATURAL PREDICTION JOIN
(SELECT 1 AS [Month], 4520 AS [Red]
 UNION SELECT 2 AS [Month], 4000 AS [Red]) as t
```

Listing 8-7 (*continued*)

This query demonstrates a few features of the `PredictTimeSeries` function. First, this query specifies a range of time slices rather than a count. The query will return 10 slices starting at time slice 3 and continuing through time slice 12. Second, the query uses the flag `EXTEND_MODEL_CASES` to specify that the data provided in the `PREDICTION JOIN` clause is to be appended to the data that the model was trained with. `EXTEND_MODEL_CASES` is the default behavior, so specifying this flag is optional.

Finally, the input data in this query is written as a singleton to show that the `KEY TIME` column must be provided along with any column values. As with the training data, the value of the `KEY TIME` column is simply used to order the rows and has no inherent meaning.

This last factor is subtly the most important piece to understand. Because there is no inherent meaning to the numbers, the query could have used 1 and 3, 2 and 5, or even 1,000 and 1 million in the `Month` column, and the algorithm would still interpret the values as the next two values in the series. However, if you wanted to specify the first and the *third* future values, you would need to add a `NULL` valued row in between, such as the following:

```
SELECT 2 AS [Month], NULL AS [Red]
```

The data type used for the `KEY TIME` columns is also irrelevant, provided it can be converted to the same type as defined in the mining structure. Because `KEY TIME` is numeric, you are always safe using integers. If the range or count specified in `PredictTimeSeries` overlaps the data you provide, the model will echo the input data for the overlapping time slices.

Figure 8-4 shows the result of the query in Listing 8-7. The dashed grey line represents the original forecast, and the black line shows the modified forecast.

Forecasting with Little Data – Applying Models to New Data

Often, forecasting must be applied to time series where there isn't sufficient history to create a model. This is particularly true for new products. If the product has been on the market for six weeks, how can you predict its sales for the next 52 weeks? If you believe that a series is likely to behave like a different series for which you can build a model, you can use that model to forecast your short series. For example, it is reasonable to assume that future sales of a new red varietal will behave much like other red wines. Therefore, you could use a series based on the average sales of reds to forecast a new product given the small amount of data you have on hand.

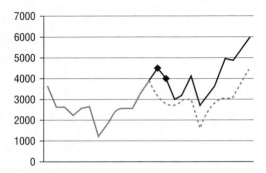

Figure 8-4 What-if forecasting results showing historical (grey solid), forecasted (grey dashed), and modified forecasted (black solid) results with the modified points indicated by black diamonds

Listing 8-8 demonstrates forecasting two years of sales from a new wine based on sales from only six months of the new product. This query uses the REPLACE_MODEL_CASES flag of PredictTimeSeries to indicate that the specified data is used in place of the original series data. In this case, the last point of data ordered by the KEY TIME column replaces the last point of data in the series, and it works backward from there.

```
SELECT FLATTENED
     PredictTimeSeries([Average Red], 24, REPLACE_MODEL_CASES)
FROM [Average Sales]
PREDICTION JOIN
(SELECT 1 AS [Month], 109 AS [New Varietal]
  UNION SELECT 2 AS [Month], 123 AS [New Varietal]
  UNION SELECT 3 AS [Month], 154 AS [New Varietal]
  UNION SELECT 4 AS [Month], 165 AS [New Varietal]
  UNION SELECT 5 AS [Month], 225 AS [New Varietal]
  UNION SELECT 6 AS [Month], 230 AS [New Varietal]
) AS t
ON [Average Sales].Month = t.Month AND
   [Average Sales].[Average Red] = t.[New Varietal]
```

Listing 8-8 Forecasting a short series based on a different model

Figure 8-5 shows the result of forecasting this new varietal based on the historical average sales of red wine. Even though there is only a short history for the new wine, the two-year forecast shows the seasonal traits of the overall wine sales.

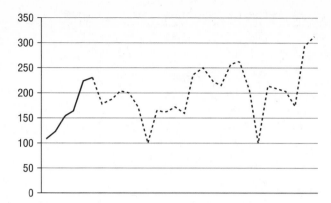

Figure 8-5 Forecast of new varietal using an average sales model and showing actual (solid) and predicted (dashed) values

CHANGING THE PAST TO PREDICT THE FUTURE

Given the capability to replace past values with new ones, you may think that you can use this to implement what-if scenarios of the type, "What if I sold 50 percent more last month?" Although this is technically possible, it is not semantically correct. The model was built with the full set of data and will predict based on the patterns from the full set of data.

The more correct method is to create a new model that includes the data only up to the point you want to change. Then, use the `EXTEND_MODEL_CASES` method of what-if analysis to explicitly specify the first prediction the way you want. You create such a model by adding a copy of the `KEY TIME` column as a continuous column, and filtering on that, as shown here:

```
// Create mining structure with extra month column
CREATE MINING STRUCTURE [Red With Filter]
(
        [Month]        DATE KEY TIME,
        [Month Filter] DATE CONTINUOUS,
        [Red]          DOUBLE CONTINUOUS
)

// Add time filtered model
ALTER MINING STRUCTURE [Red With Filter]
ADD MINING MODEL [Reds Before 1990]
(
  Month,
  Red PREDICT
) USING Microsoft_Time_Series
WITH DRILLTHROUGH,
    FILTER([Month Filter] < '1/1/1990')
```

(continued)

CHANGING THE PAST TO PREDICT THE FUTURE *(continued)*

```
// Process the structure and the model
INSERT INTO MINING STRUCTURE [Red With Filter]
    ([Month], [Month Filter], [Red])
OPENQUERY([Chapter8Data],
    'SELECT [Month], [Month] AS [Filter],
           [Red]
      FROM [Wine Sales] ORDER BY [Month]')
```

Drill-Through

With most algorithms, drill-through is used to find supporting cases for a rule or content node, and is usually an optional part of the data mining process. With time series, however, drill-through is used to return the data on which the model was trained — which is required if you want to display the forecast along with the historical data, as is done in the Time Series viewer. Listing 8-9 demonstrates using drill-through and the Lag function to return the final two years of data in both the columnar and interleaved scenarios.

```
// (a) columnar
SELECT [Month], [Red] FROM [Reds].CASES WHERE Lag() < 24

// (b) interleaved
SELECT [Month], [Sales] FROM [Reds Interleaved].CASES
   WHERE Lag() < 24 AND [Series] = 'Red'
```

Listing 8-9 Returning the last 24 months of red wine sales in (a) columnar and (b) interleaved formats

Principles of Time Series

The Microsoft Time Series algorithm is an encapsulation of two different machine-learning algorithms. The first algorithm, *autoregressive tree with cross prediction (ARTxp)*, was introduced in SQL Server 2005 and has been shown to be the most accurate algorithm for predicting the next value in a series. The second algorithm, introduced in SQL Server 2008, is *autoregressive integrated moving averages (ARIMA)*, which is an industry-standard forecasting algorithm. The default behavior of the Microsoft Time Series algorithm is to blend the results of both algorithms to achieve optimal forecasts.

Autoregression

Regression is a process of determining a value x in terms of other attributes, as shown here:

```
X = f(W,X,Y,Z) + ε
```

In this example, W, X, Y, and Z represent regressors in the input. The last term is an epsilon (ε), which represents noise. If the function f is a linear function, you have a simple linear regression, such as the following:

```
X = aW + bX + cY + dZ + ε
```

Here, a, b, c, and d represent the regression coefficients. The job of a linear regression algorithm is to determine those coefficients.

Autoregression differs from standard regression in that the value x is considered at a particular time (t) and is expressed in terms of its value at previous times. Therefore, if you consider *n* previous times, you end up with a function such as the following:

$$X_t = a_1X_{t-1} + a_2X_{t-2} + a_3X_{t-3} +... + a_nX_{t-n} + ε_t$$

The job of the algorithm is to determine the autoregression coefficients *a1* through *an*.

One of the key steps of autoregression is to transform a time series into multiple cases internally. Figure 8-6 shows the process. The left table in the figure contains two time series (sales of red and rosé wines) in columnar format. The job of the transformation is to create a single row that will allow an algorithm to compute a value based on past values. To transform the left table to the table on the right, the transformation creates a row for every row in the source data and looks back *n* values to populate the columns of that table. In this case, you see that for March of 1980, there is a row that contains January's sales in the Red(-2) columns and February's sales in the Red(-1) columns, with March's sales in the Red(0) columns. After transforming data in this way, you could theoretically use any algorithm to predict the Red(0) columns based on all of the other columns — the previous data.

Periodicity

Most time series have periodic or seasonal patterns. For example, monthly retail sales figures peak in December, the temperature is cooler at night than during the day, and so on. To obtain an accurate forecast, it is important that the algorithm understands the various periodicities in the data.

The algorithm uses the periodicity of the data to generate additional input terms. For example, if you are mining monthly data with a periodicity of 12, in addition to generating the terms for t-1, t-2, and so on, the algorithm will use the terms t-12, t-24, and so on. Because a series may have multiple periodicities, the algorithm will generate these terms for all periods required. By default, a fast Fourier transform (FFT) is applied to the series to automatically detect periodicities in the data, although they can be specified as a parameter as well.

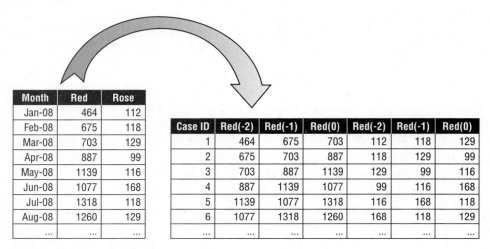

Figure 8-6 Case transformation

NOTE You will generate a superior model if you specify known periodicities. Always specify them if you know them.

Autoregression Trees

ARTxp is essentially the regression tree algorithm included in Microsoft Decision Trees, combined with the autoregression data preparation described earlier. All columns that represent previous time slices are considered regressors and inputs for the model, whereas the t0 components are the predictable outputs.

The algorithm regresses up to eight historical terms for each periodicity — that is, it will build cases using previous values xt-(p*8), xt-(p*7), ... xt-p for each periodicity p, plus the standard periodicity of 1. All time series within the same mining model are converted to columns in the same table.

For example, when you use decision tree techniques to predict Red(0), all other columns (regardless of whether they are from red or rosé wines) are considered input columns. This allows the model to cross-predict values based on other series. Part of the intelligence of the algorithm is to determine, out of all of the possible inputs, which ones are actually useful in determining the output.

The impact of applying decision trees to the autoregressive problem is that, rather than computing a simple regression against the inputs, the result is a piece-wise linear regression split at the points of non-linearity. That is, the algorithm does its best job to fit a regression formula to the data, and when it can't, it looks to split the data such that it can find a regression that fits.

In time series, this comes into play when patterns change. For example, you may have a series that exhibits a downward trending behavior until it hits a certain threshold, but then turns around. Frequently, patterns change as time progresses. You may find that after a certain point in time, the patterns up to that point don't make sense any more. The Microsoft Time Series algorithm always considers time itself as an input to handle the case of dramatic pattern changes over time.

Figure 8-7 shows a hypothetical tree model for predicting red wine. Each leaf node of the tree (represented in white) contains a regression formula for the transformed cases that reach that node. In this example, a prediction will execute one regression formula if the previous value of Rose was greater than 135. A different formula will be used when the value is less than 135 — in fact, it will use the highlighted formula based on the previous values of Red and Rose wines. The regression formula in the other node, where Month < Mar 1990, will never be executed in a standard forecast because future times are all greater than March 1990. The only case where the regression formula in that node will be executed is when you use PredictTimeSeries with REPLACE_MODEL_CASES.

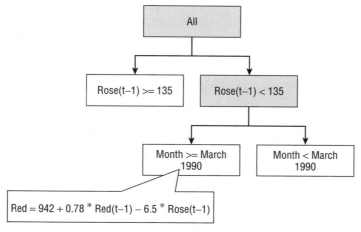

Figure 8-7 Regression tree on time series data

ARIMA is a general algorithm for predicting time series. It considers a number of historical terms, a number of differences in those terms, and a number of error factors in predicting terms. In other words, it predicts values in the series and uses the differences between the actual values and the predicted values as factors for the algorithm. ARIMA models are written as ARIMA(p,d,q) where p, d, and q represent the number of terms, number of differences, and number of errors, respectively.

The SQL Server 2008 implementation of ARIMA goes beyond the basic ARIMA implementation. Primarily, this implementation automatically determines the optimal ARIMA parameters so you do not have to do so yourself. Secondly, this version of ARIMA is a seasonal model (documented in literature as SARIMA) that adds seasonal components to the model. The seasonal ARIMA actually generates separate ARIMA terms for each periodicity in the source data.

Prediction

An autoregressive tree (ART) algorithm has the benefit of being highly optimized for predicting the next step in a series. To predict further out, the algorithm assumes the predicted value is the actual value, and then predicts the next value, and so on. In theory, this seems sound, but in practice, predicted values can very easily become unstable, with the predicted values growing or dropping exponentially or oscillating wildly. To optimally predict further out, the algorithm would have to create separate models for each possible step. That is, if you wanted to use this method to predict 10 steps out, you would have to create trees for the first step, the second step, the third step, and so on, until you got to 10. This quickly becomes slow and impractical, and eventually impossible, because you run out of data to predict any further.

For this reason, SQL Server 2008 added the ARIMA algorithm. Although ARIMA can exhibit instability, it is much more stable in the long-term predictions than ART. Forecasts are made by predicting a value using each of the algorithms and blending the results. The blended result is an average of the results weighted by how far away the prediction is. Near-term predictions will be weighted toward the ART result, whereas long-term predictions are weighted toward ARIMA, eventually reducing the ART component to essentially 0, as shown in Figure 8-8.

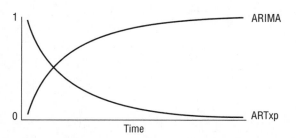

Figure 8-8 Contribution of ARTxp and ARIMA to prediction results over time

Parameters

In general, the Microsoft Time Series algorithm is self-tuning and does not require much tweaking with parameters. Typically, you'll need only the parameters that set the periodicity of the series and handle missing values. The parameters are presented in this section in (approximately) their order of usefulness.

MISSING_VALUE_SUBSTITUTION

This is the parameter that will keep you awake at night if you forget about it. If you leave MISSING_VALUE_SUBSTITUTION unset and have any blanks in your data (even just one), your model processing will fail. Luckily, it will fail with an error message informing you to set the MISSING_VALUE_SUBSTITUTION parameter, so you can get some sleep.

Experience has proven that no matter how many time series models you create, you will undoubtedly forget to set this at the wrong time and come back to an unprocessed model. This begs the question, "Why isn't MISSING_VALUE_SUBSTITUTION set by default?" The answer is that the handling of missing values in time series can have a dramatic effect on the resultant model. Therefore, the safe route is to inform you of the discrepancy and force you to take the corrective action. One corrective action is to change the source data series such that there are no holes. The other is to set this parameter to one of the following values.

- Previous — This setting causes the algorithm to use the prior value whenever there is missing data. This option is correct for a variety of scenarios, such as stock closing prices, which can be assumed to be the same as the previous day for days that the stock didn't trade.

- Mean — This setting replaces missing data with the mean of the entire series. This option isn't really correct in any scenario, but is useful when you simply want to replace values with a value that's not likely to sway the series too much.

- A number — Specifying a numerical value will cause the algorithm to replace missing values with exactly that number. This option is correct in scenarios where such a number can be known, and usually that number will be 0. For example, if you have a series of product sales figures, a missing value likely indicates that the product didn't sell during that period and thus, the value should be 0.

When you use this parameter, remember that a value is only considered missing if the time slice was actually provided to the algorithm. For example, if you are using the interleaved format and there are no values for any series during a particular time slice, that means that the time never happened, and missing value substitution will not kick in.

PERIODICITY_HINT

PERIODICITY_HINT is the second most important parameter to understand after MISSING_VALUE_SUBSTITUTION. Because knowing the correct periodicity can make the difference between a good model and a bad model, you should always set the periodicity if you know it. The format of PERIODICITY_HINT is n [, ...], meaning you can specify as many periodicities as you wish. For example, monthly revenue data may have both a quarterly and an annual period. In that case, you would specify the PERIODICITY_HINT as 3, 12 to indicate the number of months in a quarter and in a year.

AUTO_DETECT_PERIODICITY

AUTO_DETECT_PERIODICITY controls how aggressive the algorithm is in finding the natural periodicities in the data. Setting this value close to 1 will cause the algorithm to find even the slightest periodicities, whereas if you set it close to 0, only the strongest periodicities (if any) will be detected.

When PERIODICITY_HINT is set, AUTO_DETECT_PERIODICITY is automatically set to a very low number so as to honor the user periodicities, while still detecting any strong periodicities unspecified by the user. The algorithm will always honor any explicit settings of AUTO_DETECT_PERIODICITY.

MINIMUM and MAXIMUM_SERIES_VALUE

These two parameters simply allow you to limit the range for valid predictions. For example, if you are predicting inventory on a declining series, it will eventually cross 0. Because it's impossible to have less than zero of any physical item, this simply doesn't make sense. Setting the MINIMUM_SERIES_VALUE parameter to 0 causes any negative predictions to be truncated to 0. Note that because of cross-prediction from other series, a forecasted series that hits either its minimum or maximum limit can still change in future predictions.

FORECAST_METHOD

FORECAST_METHOD indicates which algorithm to use to perform predictions. By default, this parameter is set to MIXED, indicating that it will use both algorithms and blend the prediction results. Additional options are ARIMA and ARTXP to specify exclusive use of a single algorithm. Setting this parameter to ARTXP will simulate SQL Server 2005 Time Series behavior.

PREDICTION_SMOOTHING

PREDICTION_SMOOTHING controls the balance of the blend between ARTxp and ARIMA. The closer this value is to 0, the more ARTxp will be used, and the higher the likelihood of instability. The closer to 1, the more ARIMA is used. This parameter has no effect if FORECAST_METHOD is set to anything other than MIXED.

INSTABILITY_SENSITIVITY

INSTABILITY_SENSITIVITY was an internal parameter in SQL Server 2005 that was made public because of massive customer feedback. Because of the long-term instability of ARTxp, the development team implemented some code that would predict when the forecast was growing unstable and stop returning values, assuming that no values were better than wildly out-of-range values. This parameter puts this control in your hands. The default value of 1 is equivalent to the SQL Server 2005 behavior and is the strongest cutoff for instability. If you set this parameter to 0, instability detection will be completely turned off. This parameter is valid only when FORECAST_METHOD is set to ARTXP. Instability for MIXED mode is controlled through the PREDICTION_SMOOTHING parameter.

HISTORIC_MODEL_COUNT and HISTORIC_MODEL_GAP

Accuracy determination for a time series model is a difficult prospect. The general method of determining accuracy by holding out test cases and validating against a trained model doesn't apply to the Microsoft Time Series algorithm. The way to validate time series is to consider how well the model predicts compared to real results. However, if you need to wait until next month's sales figures roll-in to see if the model worked well, it's too late.

Another option is to use REPLACE_MODEL_CASES to replace the series with all of the historical data, save the last few points, predict those points, and compare them with the actual results. Unfortunately, this doesn't actually provide you with a good answer either. Because the model was trained with those data points, it has a much greater capability to predict them than if it did not actually see them.

HISTORIC_MODEL_COUNT and HISTORIC_MODEL_GAP are designed to fix this problem. When you use these parameters, the Microsoft Time Series algorithm creates a number of additional models equal to the HISTORIC_MODEL_COUNT parameter. Each of these models is trained with a truncated series. The HISTORIC_MODEL_GAP parameter determines how much of the data is truncated for each model. You set the gap parameter based on how far you need to predict with your model. For example, if you need to check the accuracy of a monthly model predicting six months into the future, you would set `HISTORIC_MODEL_GAP = 6`.

Figure 8-9 shows an example of how these parameters are applied for `HISTORIC_MODEL_COUNT = 3` and `HISTORIC_MODEL_GAP = 4`. When processing is completed, the model contains four models for this series.

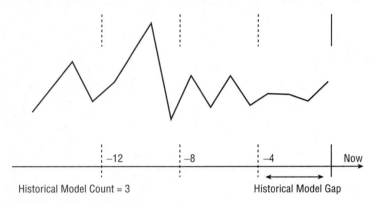

Figure 8-9 Historical models

The first model contains all the data, the second has the data truncated by 4 points, the third by 8 points, and the last by 12 points. You can determine the reliability of the historical models by using the prediction functions with negative numbers. For example, to retrieve all the predictions covering the period indicated in Figure 8-9, you would use the function `PredictTimeSeries (-15, 0)`. The algorithm automatically picks the most relevant model for the prediction (that is, from time slices `-15` to `-12`). It will use the oldest model and then seamlessly transition to the next model for slices `− 11` to `-8`, and so on. You can then compare predicted values and deviations to the actual values in the series to get an approximate idea of how well the algorithm will predict the series in the future.

Although this is a very good way of determining how well the model fits your scenario, it is important to understand that you are actually comparing how *different* models perform against *different* data. It may be that the older models are using patterns that are no longer valid at the end of the series. Or, older models may not have enough data to produce good predictions. In any case, the results of using `HISTORICAL_MODEL_COUNT` and `HISTORICAL_MODEL_GAP` can give you an *idea* of how accurate the algorithm *settings* work on your particular data to predict a particular distance into the future.

COMPLEXITY_PENALTY and MINIMUM_SUPPORT

The `COMPLEXITY_PENALTY` and `MINIMUM_SUPPORT` parameters are rarely used. They are artifacts of the decision tree subsystem in the ARTxp algorithm and have no effect on the ARIMA portion of the Microsoft Time Series algorithm.

As with the Microsoft Decision Tree algorithm, these parameters control the growth of the tree. In practice, increasing the values of these parameters reduces the size of the generated trees, thus reducing the inherent long-term instability of ARTxp models while potentially reducing short-term accuracy.

Because SQL Server 2008 controls long-term instability through blending ARTxp and ARIMA, these parameters are less necessary than they were in the 2005 version. An interesting fact about the MINIMUM_SUPPORT parameter is that it is specified in terms of transformed cases (rather than the raw cases that are fed to the algorithm), because decision trees operate on the transformed case set.

Model Content

Because of the dual nature of the Microsoft Time Series algorithm, each series in a model has two independent root nodes representing the ARTxp and ARIMA components of the series model. Each ARTxp tree is identical to the decision tree nodes, with the exception that interior tree nodes do not contain regression formulas. Regressions are found only at the leaf nodes. Additionally, all regression formulas are in autoregressive terms as well.

ARIMA models have three major components. The root node of the ARIMA model contains the found periodicities and intercept of the model, along with the complete ARIMA equation for the series. The children of the root break down the individual seasonal (or periodic) ARIMA model component. Each seasonal component contains the orders of the model — in terms of the ARIMA(p,d,q) discussed earlier, plus child nodes representing the autoregressive (AR) and moving average (MA) components of the seasonal ARIMA model. These leaf components contain their respective coefficients. The overall structure of the Microsoft Time Series model is shown in Figure 8-10.

Summary

The Microsoft Time Series algorithm has changed dramatically between SQL Server 2005 and SQL Server 2008. The new algorithm allows you to use the highly optimized ARTxp algorithm or the industry-standard ARIMA algorithm, or blend the results to take advantage of what both algorithms have to offer. New DMX constructs allow you to use the Microsoft Time Series algorithm in what-if and new product scenarios that weren't previously possible.

The format of your source data has a direct impact on the flexibility and scalability of your models, as well as the complexity of the queries required to populate the models. So, you must take care to make the tradeoffs for your particular scenario. With the Microsoft Time Series algorithm, more than any other algorithm, using OLAP as a data source can have great advantages in data preparation.

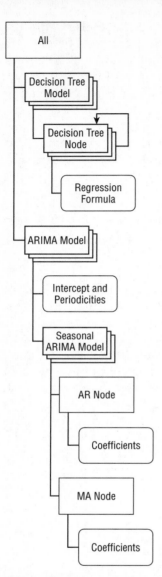

Figure 8-10 Microsoft Time Series model content

This chapter outlined the various scenarios that are possible using the Microsoft Time Series algorithm, and provided examples that are directly applicable to model business problems.

Chapter 9 changes directions and discusses the Microsoft Clustering algorithm, which is significantly different in nature and usage from the algorithms as yet discussed.

Microsoft Clustering

Imagine yourself as a child sitting on the floor with a bag of marbles. You undo the leather strap and let the marbles spill out onto the floor. Instantly you notice that you have four different colors — red, blue, yellow, and green. You separate the marbles by color until you have four groups, but then you notice that some of the marbles are regulars, some are shooters, and some are peewees. You decide that the peewees can stay with the regular marbles, but the shooters belong in a separate group, because only one will be used per player. You look at the organization and are happy with your groups. You have just performed a clustering operation.

Continuing with this marble scenario, when you look at the clusters again, you see that not only do you have solid color marbles, but also cats-eyes, starburst, crystals, steelies, and genuine agates. Some of your marbles are in perfect condition, but others are scuffed. Some are so chipped they don't roll straight. Now you are confused. Should you keep your simple groupings based on size and color, or should you add factors of style, material, and condition? (Most likely, you just go ahead and play marbles.)

Clustering is a simple, natural, and even automatic human operation for dealing with a small set of attributes. However, as the number of attributes grows, the problem becomes increasingly difficult and eventually impossible for the human mind to handle. It is possible for people with particular domain expertise and a deep understanding of the data to create clusters in up to five or six dimensions, but modern data sets typically contain dozens (if not hundreds) of dimensions, leaving you with the impossible task of creating groupings when you can't even conceive of the possible relationships between the attributes.

This chapter contains the following topics:

- An overview of the Microsoft Clustering algorithm
- The usage and application of the Clustering algorithm
- DMX syntax for cluster scenarios
- Details on how the algorithm works and parameters

To assist with this chapter, content files are included in the `Chapter9.zip` archive available at `www.wiley.com/go/data_mining_SQL_2008`. This archive contains the following files:

- `Chapter9 Project` — A folder containing a project with the model used in this chapter
- `Chapter9.dmx` — A DMX file containing the query listing for this chapter
- `2 dimensional cluster text.xlsm` — A macro-enabled workbook used in generating some of the images in this chapter
- `ScoringSample.dmx` — A DMX file provided as an additional example that shows how to create a clustering model on a sample of data and then apply the model to the full data set

Overview

The Microsoft Clustering algorithm finds natural groupings inside your data when these groupings are not obvious. In other words, it finds the *hidden variable* that accurately classifies your data. For example, you may be part of a large group of people picking up bags at the baggage claim. You notice that a significant percentage of the travelers are wearing shorts and have suntans, whereas the rest are bundled up in sweaters and coats. You deduce a hidden variable that one group returned from a tropical climate, and the other group arrived from some cold, wet place.

This capacity for determining the common thread that holds people together makes clustering a popular data mining technique for marketing. You can use clustering to learn more about your customers in order to target your message to specific groups. For example, a movie retailer may find a group of customers that purchases family movies on a regular basis, and another group that purchases documentaries less frequently. Sending monthly coupons for Disney films to the latter group obviously wouldn't be a wise choice. The ability to define and identify your market segments gives you a powerful tool to drive your business.

Identifying natural groups in your data frees you from simply analyzing your business based on the existing organization. Otherwise, you are limited to the groups that you can imagine, which may not have any bearing on how your customers contribute to your business. Do I sell more family favorites or documentaries? Does more profit come from the Northwest or the Southeast? Are renters better for my business than buyers? You could group your data in an almost limitless number of ways, but very few (if any) will provide any deep insight into your business. The unseen organization hidden inside your data is a powerful tool for business analysis. Furthermore, when a retailer knows the groups its customers fall into, he or she can track sales to those groups on a regular basis.

Figure 9-1 shows hypothetical revenue for the movie retailer by region — a typical method of organizing and analyzing sales data. This view shows a healthy growth in business, as well as how each region contributes to that growth. Not all regions are equal, and there are slight differences in the growth for each region. However, there is not much *actionable* information here — nothing that tells you what can you do to increase the overall revenue of your company.

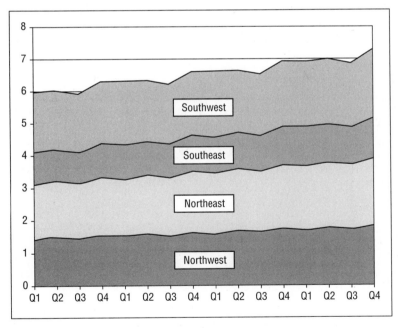

Figure 9-1 Quarterly revenue by region

Figure 9-2 shows the same hypothetical revenue divided by clusters automatically found in the retailer's data. You still see the same growth in the company overall, but now you have a completely different breakdown of that information. You see that you have done an excellent job of catering to the Frequent Viewers segment of your customers, but revenue has decreased in the Family Buyers and Single Moviegoers segments. Breaking down the revenue this way gives you the actionable information you need to affect your business. Where are those Family Buyers going? How can you get them back? Do you worry about the Single Moviegoers, or do you sacrifice that business to focus on segments that contribute more to the bottom line? Clustering finds the hidden dimension that is unique to your data and your data alone — which provides information in a way that is impossible to achieve for the predefined organizations typically employed to examine your data.

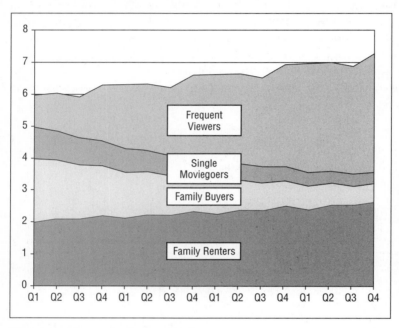

Figure 9-2 Quarterly revenue by cluster

Usage of Clustering

Clustering models are great models to throw your data at just to see what comes out the other side. However, as with all data mining techniques, you get the best answers when you ask your questions the right way. Do you want to group your salespeople by total sales, or by the ratio of sales in each category? Is it important that your clustering model understands income as a continuous value, or do you need to break it down into categories first? The Microsoft Clustering algorithm is very flexible in that it supports all of the possible data and content types available to DMX, but you still need to provide data to the algorithm in the form that is most interesting to solve your problem.

For example, let's say a large company issues an annual employee satisfaction survey to determine an Organizational Health Index (OHI). The results are a percentage for each category — for example, 65 percent for the set of compensation questions. You could simply cluster all of these results for all of your employees, but could you understand the results? Is 65 percent in compensation a good response, a bad response, or neutral? In this case, you could transform your data into buckets of High, Medium, and Low by considering High to be higher than half of a standard deviation above the average response and Low to be lower than the same amount. Now, when you examine resultant clusters, the results will be easier to read — it's easy to pick out the cluster of people who love their job but want to get paid more. You can increase the buckets to the granularity you want to explore. You can perform this kind of transformation in data source view (DSV), or by using SQL Server Integration Services (SSIS) as described in Chapter 14.

The Microsoft Clustering algorithm has some special behavior associated with the column usage flag on the mining model. When you set the column usage to Input or Predict, the algorithm acts as described — the difference being that the predictable columns are selectable from the model during predictions but the input columns are not. When you set the column usage to Predict Only, the column is treated specially. Predict Only columns in the clustering algorithm are not used during the clustering phase of the model training. When the model is completely trained, the algorithm takes another run over the training data and assigns the values of these attributes based on how the training cases fall into the clusters. Using the previous OHI example, to ensure that the company complies with federal guidelines regarding workforce diversity, it may be important to determine the distribution of gender and race among the clusters. Maybe you want to consider only the answers to the survey when you create the clusters, but ultimately you need to know that there is the same ratio of men to women in that group of happy, underpaid employees as there is in the rest of the company.

Performing a Clustering

The most common usage of the Microsoft Clustering algorithm is to simply perform a *clustering* — that is, to use the algorithm to detect the clusters in the data and then label the data with the clusters that are discovered. After the data is labeled, you can use it for reporting and analysis as you would any other attribute of your data. This is so common that many data mining products do this automatically in a single step without much user intervention, as in the Detect Categories tool for Office 2007 described in Chapter 2. With Detect Categories, the model is actually discarded after the clustering is performed, so you're finished with that model after the source data is labeled. Because SQL Server 2008 is a toolset rather than an application, no such assumptions are made as to how you want to apply your cluster model. Therefore, there are some additional steps you must perform to accomplish this task.

In many cases, you simply need to create a cluster model on your data, examine the cluster model to determine the meaning of the clusters, and then assign the labels back to the data. There are, however, cases where it is not so simple. For example, assume you have 15 million rows of data to cluster, and each row is fairly complex — say 40 or more values that are mixed numeric and categorical. In this case, training a cluster model can be very expensive because of the calculations and iterations necessary for the algorithm to analyze the data. However, it turns out that in almost all cases, you don't really need to analyze all the data you have. You can train the clustering model from a small sample (use the arbitrary sampling trick in Chapter 4 to make this easy), and then apply those results to the larger data set.

For example, the following DMX code creates and trains a model on a sample of the data, and then applies the model to the full data set:

```
// Create a cluster model based on three columns
CREATE MINING MODEL ClusterSample
(
    [ID]            LONG KEY,
    MaritalStatus   TEXT DISCRETE;
    Gender          TEXT DISCRETE,
    TotalChildren   LONG CONTINUOUS
) USING Microsoft_Clustering

GO


// Train the model with 70% of the source data, skipping
// the random column
INSERT INTO ClusterSample
([ID], MaritalStatus, Gender, TotalChildren, SKIP)
OPENQUERY(AW,
  'SELECT * FROM
      (SELECT CustomerKey,
        MaritalStatus,Gender,TotalChildren,
        (CAST((ABS(CHECKSUM(NEWID())) % 1000) AS FLOAT)/1000) as Random
      FROM DimCustomer ) as t
  WHERE  Random >= 0.300')

GO


// Apply the model to all data in the table
SELECT t.CustomerKey,Cluster() FROM
ClusterSample
NATURAL PREDICTION JOIN
OPENQUERY(AW,'SELECT * FROM DimCustomer') AS t

GO
```

Clustering as an Analytical Step

Clustering is frequently used as a step in a larger analytical project. By grouping similar data, you can create better supplemental models to explain deeper questions. Returning to the example introduced in Figure 9-2, the decline in revenue among Family Buyers has most likely occurred for a different reason than that of the decline among Single Moviegoers. By analyzing the data along the lines of these clusters, you are able to more tightly focus on the exact reasons for the revenue loss. Perhaps you want to create a tree model to predict whether a customer will repeat business within a month. Creating a model on all of your customers will provide valuable information, but it will be a model that is generalized to the entire data set (see Figure 9-3). Training the tree models only on the areas that clustering has demonstrated as being where the revenue has declined, you can focus on where the problem lies.

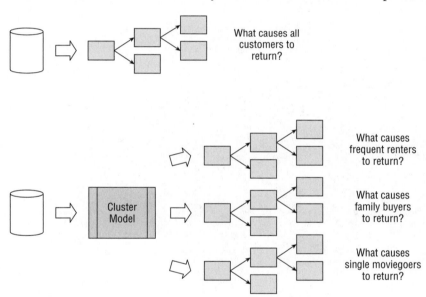

Figure 9-3 Clustering as a preprocessing step for decision trees

Anomaly Detection Using Clustering

Clustering is interesting in that it forms nice groupings of data, and then allows you to ask what group new data fits into. When issuing a query to a cluster model, the model determines the likelihood that each case belongs to each cluster. But what happens when a case doesn't really belong to any cluster? Leveraging the properties of the clustering algorithm, you can determine not only where clusters *are*, but also where they *aren't*. You can then use that information to detect anomalies or other forms of bad data.

Anomaly detection using clustering lets you simultaneously analyze multiple dimensions of your data to see if the combination of values fits in a cluster. The right side of Figure 9-4 shows the probability of each point in space existing within a cluster model built on the data in the left side of the figure. The peaks represent areas where you can say you are confident data is part of the model, whereas the valleys are areas where such combinations of the input data were never seen before, and seem unlikely. Figure 9-4 was created using the `PredictCaseLikelihood` function described later in this chapter and the 2-`Dimensional Cluster Test.xlsx` file included on this book's website (`www.wiley.com/go/data_mining_SQL_2008`).

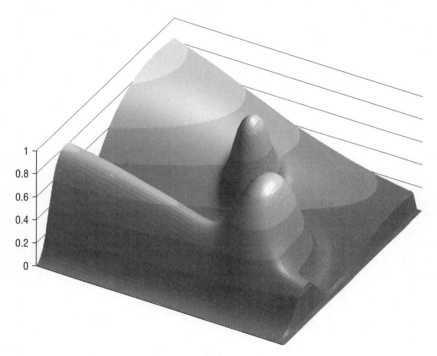

Figure 9-4 Likelihood of points according to a cluster model

In addition to determining the validity of a case, you can determine which case value is the most likely cause for the case to be anomalous. For discrete variables, this is fairly simple. You just take the ratio of the probability of the case value (the actual data value you have) and the probability of the value the model *thinks* the case should have. The DMX fragment would look something like this for each attribute of the case:

```
SELECT (PredictProbability(MyColumn, 'MyValue')
    /PredictProbability(MyColumn)) AS MyColumnRatio ...
```

Obviously, if the actual value matched the predicted value, this ratio would be 1, and it will be lower than 1 for all values that do not match the prediction. After you perform this calculation for all columns, the column that has the smallest ratio is the column that is most likely to be causing the case to be an anomaly. Note that you must apply some reasonable business logic to interpret what that exactly means. For example, the data could be perfectly valid but you simply haven't encountered it before, or the indicated column may be fine and the second or third most likely column could be the problem.

This technique works for discrete variables, but what about continuous values? You obviously cannot get a probability for a continuous value. Even if you could, how would you compare it? With a continuous prediction, you get a value and a variance, which at face value don't give you anything to compare to the probabilities of the discrete values. However, using the actual value, the predicted value, and the variance, you can compute a ratio of probability *distributions*, which is comparable to probability ratios. The probability ratio is determined by the following equation, where *a* is the actual value, *p* is the predicted value, and *v* is the predicted variance:

$$ratio = e\frac{-(a-p)^2}{2 \bullet v}$$

But you don't have to worry about the math. — You can use the following C# snippet (as a stored procedure or otherwise) to compute the ratio, and call it using the following DMX fragment:

```
[SafeToPrepare(true)]
public double GetProbabilityDistribution(double actual,
        double predicted, double variance)
{
    if (Context.ExecuteForPrepare)
        return 0;
    return Math.Exp(-Math.Pow((actual-predicted),2)/(2* variance));
}

SELECT ClusterHelpers.GetProbabilityDistribution(MyActualValue,
    Predict(MyContinuousColumn), PredictVariance(MyContinuousColumn)) ...
```

DMX

Clustering supports all content and data types, as well as prediction, so all of the DMX language that is not specific to other algorithms can be used to query cluster models. This section focuses on DMX constructs unique to and frequently used with clustering models.

Model Creation

As with most algorithms, the Microsoft Clustering algorithm models typically will not use all of the columns that are available in your data set. However, unlike other algorithms, you frequently will want access to the additional columns in your query results. For example, you may want information such as the names and phone numbers of individuals within a cluster, even though you obviously don't want to cluster on names. To accomplish this, you create a mining structure containing the additional columns but don't use those columns in your mining model, as shown in Listing 9-1.

```
// Create a structure with additional columns
CREATE MINING STRUCTURE Customers
(
    [ID]            LONG KEY,
    MaritalStatus   TEXT DISCRETE,
    Gender          TEXT DISCRETE,
    TotalChildren   LONG CONTINUOUS,
    FirstName       TEXT DISCRETE,
    LastName        TEXT DISCRETE,
    Phone           TEXT DISCRETE
)

GO

// Add a cluster model using only relevant columns
ALTER MINING STRUCTURE Customers
ADD MINING MODEL CustomerClusters
(
    [ID],
    [MaritalStatus],
    [Gender],
    [TotalChildren]
) USING Microsoft_Clustering WITH DRILLTHROUGH

GO

// Train the structure and the model
INSERT INTO MINING STRUCTURE Customers
    ([ID],MaritalStatus,Gender,
    TotalChildren,FirstName, LastName, Phone)
OPENQUERY(AW,
  'SELECT CustomerKey,
        MaritalStatus,Gender,TotalChildren,
        FirstName, LastName, Phone FROM DimCustomer')
```

Listing 9-1 Mining structure containing the additional columns

Drill-through

To access the data that comprises a particular cluster, you need to perform a *drill-through* query to the model cases. To do this, you use the `IsInNode` function combined with the `StructureColumn` function, as in Listing 9-2.

```
SELECT *, StructureColumn('FirstName'),
         StructureColumn('LastName'),
         StructureColumn('Phone')
FROM CustomerClusters.CASES WHERE IsInNode('001')
```

Listing 9-2 IsInNode function combined with the StructureColumn function

Cluster

The `Cluster` function returns the cluster that is most likely to contain a particular case. For example, to retrieve all cases from an input set that belong to `'Cluster 2'`, you would use the syntax shown in Listing 9-3.

```
SELECT t.* FROM CustomerClusters
NATURAL PREDICTION JOIN
OPENQUERY(AW, 'SELECT * FROM DimCustomer') AS t
WHERE Cluster() = 'Cluster 2'
```

Listing 9-3 Retrieving all cases from an input set that belongs to Cluster 2

The `Cluster` function can also be used as a column reference for functions that take such references as parameters. `$Cluster` can be used as a synonym for `Cluster()`.

ClusterProbability

`ClusterProbability` returns the probability that a case belongs to a particular cluster. Calling `ClusterProbability` without specifying a parameter returns the probability of the primary cluster. The query in Listing 9-4 returns the *cluster ID* for each case, and the probability that the case is in that cluster:

```
SELECT t.*, Cluster(), ClusterProbability() FROM CustomerClusters
NATURAL PREDICTION JOIN
OPENQUERY(AW, 'SELECT * FROM DimCustomer') AS t
```

Listing 9-4 Returning the cluster ID for each case, and the probability that the case is in that cluster

You can also use the `ClusterProbability` function with a parameter to determine the likelihood that a particular case is in a particular query. The query in Listing 9-5 returns the probability that the specified case is in `'Cluster 2'`:

```
SELECT ClusterProbability('Cluster 2') FROM CustomerClusters
NATURAL PREDICTION JOIN
(SELECT 'F' AS Gender, 'S' AS MaritalStatus, 0 AS TotalChildren) AS t
```

Listing 9-5 Returning the probability that the specified case is in Cluster 2

Note that you can always parameterize this query to specify any case values, or even the cluster caption for interactive or real-time cluster analysis.

PredictHistogram

`PredictHistogram` is not specific to the Microsoft Clustering algorithm, but when you specify it using the `Cluster` function as the column reference, it returns a histogram of the likelihood of the input case existing in each of the model's clusters. The query in Listing 9-6 returns a table with a nested table containing the top three likely clusters for each case, along with associated statistics:

```
SELECT t.*, TopCount(PredictHistogram(Cluster()),$Probability,3)
FROM CustomerClusters
NATURAL PREDICTION JOIN
OPENQUERY(AW, 'SELECT * FROM DimCustomer') AS t
```

Listing 9-6 Returning a table with a nested table containing the top three likely clusters for each case

PredictCaseLikelihood

`PredictCaseLikelihood` returns a measure from 0 to 1 that indicates how likely an input case is to exist, considering the model learned by the algorithm. This measure is very useful for anomaly detection because it quickly and easily tells you if new data is similar to any data seen before. This function operates in two modes: normalized and nonnormalized.

In the nonnormalized mode, the value of the measure is the raw probability of the case (that is, the product of the probabilities of each of the attributes in the case). For example, if the probability of `Home Ownership = 'Yes'` is 40 percent, and the probability of `Occupation = 'Craftsmen'` is 10 percent, then the probability of the case is 40 percent × 10 percent, or 4 percent.

Nonnormalized likelihoods can be useful, because as you increase the number of attributes in a case, the probability of the case becomes increasingly small. Additionally, as a user, you cannot understand if a 4-percent probability for a certain combination of attributes is a good thing or a bad thing.

The normalized likelihood of a case is computed by dividing the probability of the case using raw statistics — that is, the probability of each of the attributes multiplied together — into the probability of the case as determined by the clusters in the model. This provides a *lift* number that is normalized between 0 and 1 using the formula (lift)/(lift + 1). This is interpreted to mean that cases with likelihood values greater than 0.5 have positive lift and are more likely than random to occur, and that values less than 0.5 have negative lift and are less likely than random to occur. For continuous attributes, the probability distribution is used for this computation.

Listing 9-7 returns the normalized case likelihood for each case in the input set.

```
SELECT t.*, PredictCaseLikelihood()
FROM CustomerClusters
NATURAL PREDICTION JOIN
OPENQUERY(AW, 'SELECT * FROM DimCustomer') AS t
```

Listing 9-7 Returning the normalized case likelihood for each case in the input set

Listing 9-8 returns the nonnormalized case likelihood for each case in the input set:

```
SELECT t.CustomerKey, PredictCaseLikelihood(NONNORMALIZED)
FROM CustomerClusters
NATURAL PREDICTION JOIN
OPENQUERY(AW, 'SELECT * FROM DimCustomer') AS t
```

Listing 9-8 Returning the nonnormalized case likelihood for each case in the input set

Model Content

The content of a clustering model is very easy to understand. It contains the following:

- One row for the model, indicated by node type `MiningNodeType.Model` (value 1)
- One row for each cluster, indicated by node type `MiningNodeType.Cluster` (value 5)

Each row contains general information about the node, plus the distributions of all of the attributes that are contained in the node that the row represents. The model node contains the global distributions, and the cluster nodes contain the distributions particular to those individual clusters.

The first row of the model content contains a score for the model in the MSOLAP_NODE_SCORE column of the model content. This score is the average case likelihood for each of the training cases, and represents how well the model describes the training data.

Listing 9-9 returns the model score.

```
SELECT TOP 1 MSOLAP_NODE_SCORE FROM CustomerClusters.CONTENT
```

Listing 9-9 Returning the model score

Each cluster row contains the cluster caption and an algorithm-generated textual description of the clusters. Listing 9-10 retrieves the caption and description for each cluster.

```
SELECT NODE_CAPTION, NODE_DESCRIPTION FROM CustomerClusters.CONTENT
    WHERE NODE_TYPE=5
```

Listing 9-10 Retrieving the caption and description for each cluster

The cluster captions can also be set through DMX. The default caption for clusters simply assigns a numeric value. Listing 9-11 changes the caption for cluster 2 of the model.

```
UPDATE CustomerClusters.CONTENT SET NODE_CAPTION= 'Single males'
    WHERE NODE_UNIQUE_NAME= '002'
```

Listing 9-11 Changing the caption for cluster 2

CLUSTER NAMES AND CAPTIONS

The function `IsInNode` takes a unique node name as a parameter. Luckily, cluster node names are always represented as three-digit integers starting with `001` to make them easy to find.

Other functions return and take a cluster caption as a parameter. You can get an easy mapping from names to captions using the following query:

```
SELECT NODE_UNIQUE_NAME, NODE_CAPTION FROM CustomerClusters.CONTENT
```

Understanding Your Cluster Models

Clustering is very good at taking data with scores of attributes and distilling them down into a handful of groupings. But comprehending what the resultant groups mean can be quite a challenge. This is particularly difficult because each cluster cannot be considered in isolation — a cluster can only be understood given its relationship to all other clusters.

The naming convention used by the Microsoft Clustering algorithm is simply the word `Cluster` followed by a cluster index. When you're presenting your model to others, or even referring to it for your own personal use, you will need to choose appropriate labels for each cluster. With models built on dozens or even hundreds of attributes, a short label seems like a tall promise. The most effective labels come from your personal understanding of the business problem you are trying to solve, combined with the patterns uncovered by the clustering engine.

SQL Server Analysis Services provides a Cluster viewer with tabs that show different views of the same model. A single view will not provide you with enough insight to get a complete understanding of your clusters, but when used together, these views are effective in understanding and labeling your clusters. The basic strategy for doing this is as follows:

1. Get a high-level overview of your clusters.

2. Pick a cluster and determine how it is different from the general population.

3. Determine how that cluster is different from nearby clusters.

4. Verify that your assertions about the cluster are true.

5. Label the cluster.

6. Repeat 2 through 5 for all remaining clusters.

The following sections review these steps in detail, using a model built on the `MovieClick` database of the `MovieClusters` project. It is contained in the `Chapter9.zip` archive, which you can download from this book's website (`www.wiley.com/go/data_mining_SQL_2008`).

Get a High-Level Overview

The first two tabs of the viewer provide a high-level overview of clusters: the Cluster Profiles view and the Cluster Diagram view. Cluster Profiles provides too much information, and Cluster Diagram provides too little, but together they provide the topology of your cluster model.

The Cluster Profiles view displays a column for each cluster in your model and a row for each attribute. This setup makes it easy to see interesting differences across the cluster space. Using this view, you can choose an attribute of interest and visibly scan horizontally to see its distribution across all clusters. When an item catches your interest, you can look at neighboring cells or other cells of the same cluster to learn more about what that cluster means.

Figure 9-5 shows a portion of the Cluster Profiles view on the Customer Clustering model. Cluster 4 clearly contains younger people who like TNT and other non-premium movie channels. In contrast, clusters 5 and 6 seem to avoid those channels, and the members of cluster 6 are a bit older.

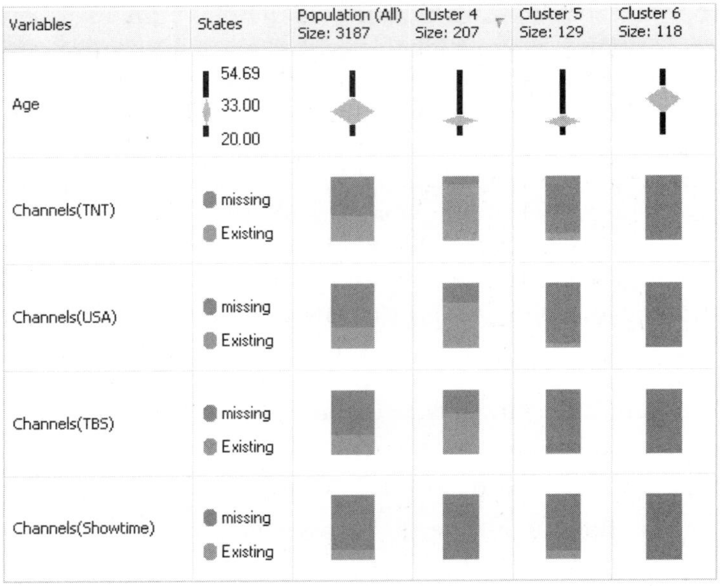

Variables	States	Population (All) Size: 3187	Cluster 4 Size: 207	Cluster 5 Size: 129	Cluster 6 Size: 118
Age	54.69 / 33.00 / 20.00				
Channels(TNT)	missing / Existing				
Channels(USA)	missing / Existing				
Channels(TBS)	missing / Existing				
Channels(Showtime)	missing / Existing				

Figure 9-5 Continuous and binary attributes in the Cluster Profiles view

TIP You can drag clusters by their headers for an easy, side-by-side comparison.

The Cluster Profiles view displays everything in your model in a manner that is easy to see. Binary and continuous attributes are particularly easy to discern, as are discrete attributes with a small number of states. Clicking any cell in the grid provides details on the information contained in the mining legend. Exploring your clusters through the Cluster Profiles view is a good way to find a starting point for further exploration.

The Cluster Diagram view, as shown in Figure 9-6, on the other hand, displays each cluster as a single node. These nodes are scattered across a field and group automatically based on similarities. The resultant view is a diagram indicating which clusters are similar or dissimilar and the relative strength of these similarities.

Using the Cluster Diagram view, it is easy to expand on the exploration begun in the Cluster Profiles view. Using the shading feature of the view, it is easy to ask some more targeted questions about your model. You can ask, "In which clusters are customers who like the Arts & Entertainment channel?"

Or, "Where are my customers who are between the ages of 20 and 25?" Furthermore, you can determine which clusters are very similar by moving the link slider down to remove weak links, leaving only the strongest links (Figure 9-6).

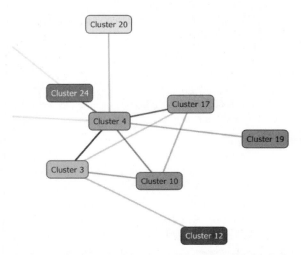

Figure 9-6 Cluster diagram showing strong (dark) links between clusters

Continue to explore the Cluster Profiles and Cluster Diagram views until you feel comfortable with the overall layout of your model.

Pick a Cluster and Determine how It Is Different from the General Population

Choose a cluster for further analysis. At this point, it really isn't important which cluster you choose. One method for picking a cluster is determining which clusters have the strongest link and choosing one of them; another method is to pick a cluster that seems far removed from the rest. You may simply have found an interesting cluster during your initial exploration.

The first thing you need to do is look at the Cluster Characteristics view, which is the third tab in the Cluster viewers. This view describes the characteristics of the cluster cases by displaying attributes in decreasing probability. Figure 9-7 shows the top characteristics for cluster 10. You see that members of this cluster are male married homeowners that own DVD and VHS players, but prefer the DVD format. It may seem like this is enough information to choose an adequate label for the cluster. However, how do you know that this information is the most important? It may be true that customers in this group own DVD players, but all of the customers outside this group may own DVD players as well, which makes that fact uninteresting.

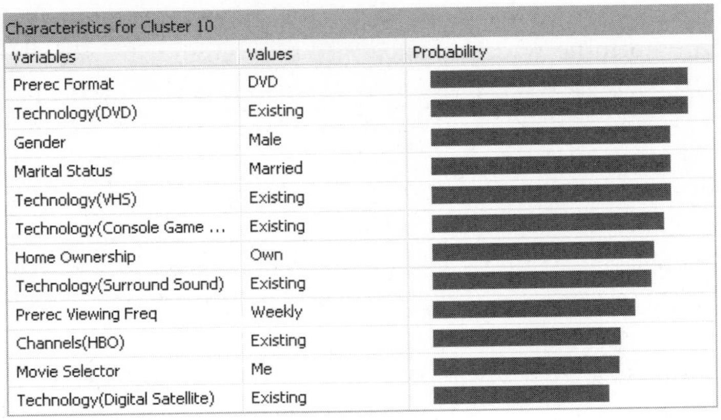

Characteristics for Cluster 10		
Variables	Values	Probability
Prerec Format	DVD	████████████████
Technology(DVD)	Existing	████████████████
Gender	Male	███████████████
Marital Status	Married	██████████████
Technology(VHS)	Existing	██████████████
Technology(Console Game ...	Existing	█████████████
Home Ownership	Own	████████████
Technology(Surround Sound)	Existing	████████████
Prerec Viewing Freq	Weekly	███████████
Channels(HBO)	Existing	██████████
Movie Selector	Me	██████████
Technology(Digital Satellite)	Existing	█████████

Figure 9-7 Cluster characteristics

You can determine what is specifically important about the cluster by comparing it to everything outside the cluster. Figure 9-8 shows the comparison of cluster 10 to everything outside cluster 10 — its complement — using the Cluster Discrimination view, the last tab of the Cluster viewer. Here you see that DVD or VHS ownership isn't quite so important for describing the cluster, but digital satellite technology is. You can also infer that members of this cluster have children and are either married or have been in the past. Your picture of who the customers of cluster 10 are is becoming clear.

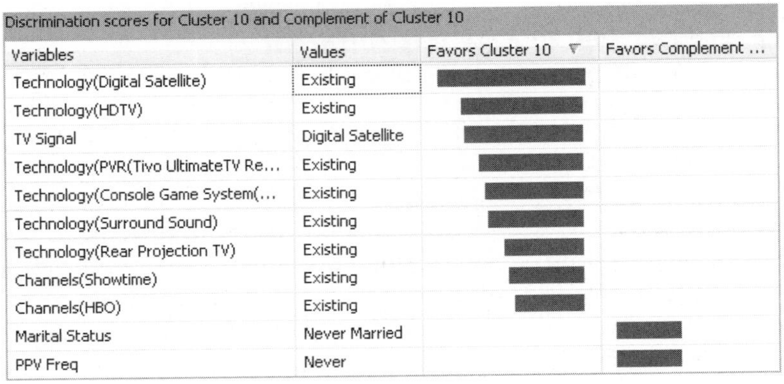

Discrimination scores for Cluster 10 and Complement of Cluster 10			
Variables	Values	Favors Cluster 10 ▽	Favors Complement ...
Technology(Digital Satellite)	Existing	████████████	
Technology(HDTV)	Existing	██████████	
TV Signal	Digital Satellite	██████████	
Technology(PVR(Tivo UltimateTV Re...	Existing	████████	
Technology(Console Game System(...	Existing	████████	
Technology(Surround Sound)	Existing	████████	
Technology(Rear Projection TV)	Existing	██████	
Channels(Showtime)	Existing	██████	
Channels(HBO)	Existing	██████	
Marital Status	Never Married		██████
PPV Freq	Never		██████

Figure 9-8 Cluster discrimination versus complement

Determine how the Cluster Is Different from Nearby Clusters

You may now have enough information to accurately label your cluster. However, this cluster may be very similar to other clusters, and any labeling you do at this point may also apply to them. Therefore, you should use due diligence and compare your chosen cluster to its nearest neighbors. To accomplish this, go to the Cluster Diagram view and determine which clusters are close to the cluster of interest. If no links to the cluster are very strong, it is probably safe to stop. For any clusters that are close, you must switch back to the Cluster Characteristics view to compare those clusters one by one. Through this process, you will refine the view of your chosen cluster. For example, comparing cluster 10 to clusters 12 and 3 may indicate that the most important differences involve age and number of children, respectively.

NOTE The bars of the Cluster Discrimination view indicate which cluster the attribute *favors*. It does *not* indicate that the other cluster doesn't contain the attribute.

Verify that Your Assertions Are True

At this point, you probably have a pretty good idea about the members of your chosen cluster. Switching back to the Cluster Characteristics view allows you to ensure that none of the other views misled you about the cluster. This can happen particularly when refining your cluster understanding by comparing it to neighboring clusters. A difference between the clusters that appeared important in the Cluster Discrimination view may be caused by an attribute that is uncommon in both but is simply less uncommon in one.

Label the Cluster

Labeling the cluster is a simple matter of switching to the Cluster Diagram view, right-clicking the cluster node, and selecting Rename Cluster. The labels you create can have an important impact on the understanding and future use of your model. So which attributes should your labels identify? This depends on your business knowledge of the data you are clustering, and which attributes are interesting to the intended audience of the model. For example, you might label cluster 10 `Digital Satellite Junkies` or `Technology Aficionados` or any number of other monikers, depending on how you want to display your model and how you want others to perceive it.

Principles of Clustering

You now know when and how to use the Microsoft Clustering algorithm, but you also need to know how to tweak the outcome of the clustering by modifying the algorithm parameters. This is important — otherwise, all your clusters will provide is good background information.

Clustering relies on guessing and lying. You guess about the organization of data and create a set of clusters, arbitrarily deciding the set of attributes and values that belongs in each cluster. Then you lie to yourself and assert that your guess is correct. Now that you've created this model of the world, you can take each case from your training data and assign them to clusters as they fit that model.

Next, you adjust your model of the world by looking at how well it fits the data of the world — you move the clusters. Again, you lie and say you believe this new model correctly describes the world, and again you take the world's data and throw it at the model. This time, not all of the same cases fall into the same clusters. You repeat this process of updating your guess and assuming it's true until it either becomes true (cases no longer switch clusters) or you don't believe that you are going to get a better solution.

Figure 9-9 demonstrates this procedure in one dimension. The top chart shows the point distribution on the X-axis, along with your initial guess. In this case, you chose clusters evenly spaced across the range of data with similar distributions. You consider the cluster borders to be the midpoints between the cluster centers. Based on this model, you assign each data point to a cluster, and subsequently set the cluster centers to the mean of the data in each cluster. The second chart shows the new cluster centers and borders after performing this operation. You repeat this operation until the data stops moving between clusters, when the model is *converged*, or until you decide that the model will simply not improve with further iterations.

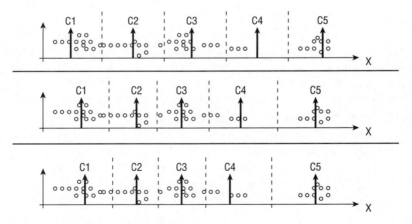

Figure 9-9 Basic clustering procedure

In practice, clusters are initialized randomly along all of the dimensions of the data. The clustering methodology is very sensitive to the starting points, and can converge at local solutions that may not be an optimal global solution. For this reason, you initialize several candidate models and train them simultaneously. When the models have converged, or you have otherwise finished, you pick the best model from the candidates.

Hard Clustering versus Soft Clustering

One of the most important differentiators in a clustering algorithm is the way the algorithm decides how to assign cases to clusters. The Microsoft Clustering algorithm allows two distinct methods of cluster assignment: *K-means* and *Expectation Maximization* (EM).

The K-means method assigns cluster membership by distance. As shown previously in Figure 9-9, an object belongs to the cluster whose center it is closest to (which is measured using a simple Euclidean distance). When all objects have been assigned to clusters, the center of the cluster is moved to the mean of all assigned objects, thus the name K-means — K being the typical denomination for the number of clusters to look for. This technique is considered *hard clustering* because each object is assigned one and exactly one cluster. The clusters are disjoint and do not overlap.

The EM cluster-assignment method uses a probabilistic measure (rather than a strict distance measure) to determine which objects belong to which clusters. Instead of choosing a point for each dimension and computing a distance, the EM method considers a bell curve for each dimension with a mean and standard deviation. As a point falls within the bell curve, it is assigned to a cluster with a certain probability. Because the curves for various clusters can (and do) overlap, any point can belong to multiple clusters, with an assigned probability for each. This technique is considered *soft clustering* because it allows clusters to overlap with indistinct edges. This method permits the clustering algorithm to find non-disjoint clusters, such as the dense regions shown in Figure 9-10.

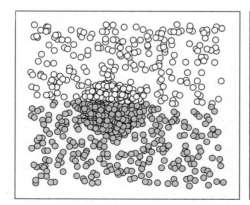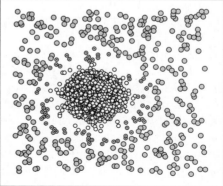

Figure 9-10 Clustering of a dense region using K-means (left) and EM (right)

The dot size in Figure 9-10 refers to the probability that each dot is in its respective cluster. Note that the dot sizes are uniform in the K-means diagram, whereas they are reduced in size near the cluster borders in the EM diagram. These diagrams were created with the 2 Dimensional Cluster Test.xlsm spreadsheet included on this book's website (www.wiley.com/go/data_mining_SQL_2008).

Discrete Clustering

So far, you've seen how clustering works in terms of numerical values. These values are easy to compare and relate, computing distances and whatnot, but what happens when the objects you are trying to cluster do not have attributes that can be easily compared? The marble size could potentially be represented by its diameter, but what value would you assign to a marble's material or color?

Luckily, the Microsoft Clustering algorithm can also handle discrete variables. As you assign random points along each dimension for continuous attributes, you can also assign random distributions for each discrete attribute. For example, if you have an equal number of red, blue, green, and yellow marbles, your global distribution for each color would be 25 percent. As you initialize each cluster, you could assume random distributions such as those shown in Table 9-1.

Table 9-1 Discrete Cluster Distribution Initializations

COLOR	CLUSTER 1	CLUSTER 2	CLUSTER 3	CLUSTER 4
Red	5 percent	70 percent	35 percent	0 percent
Blue	15 percent	5 percent	45 percent	30 percent
Green	50 percent	25 percent	0 percent	25 percent
Yellow	30 percent	0 percent	20 percent	45 percent

For example, with EM clustering, you can pick a green marble and say that it is in cluster 2 with 25 percent likelihood. As you determine all of the probabilities across all of the discrete attributes of a case, you can compute the probability that it exists in each cluster, and assign its values accordingly to each cluster of which it could be a member.

Because it is distance-based, K-means clustering does not fit as naturally in this model of probabilistic measures, and traditionally it isn't used for clustering discrete attributes. K-means can still be applied if you can infer some sort of distance to the cluster. The Microsoft Clustering implementation measures the distance from a value to a cluster as 1 minus the probability of that value in the cluster. For example, a green marble in cluster 2 would be $(1-.25) = .75$ color units away from cluster 2. This distance factors into the distance calculation as would any continuous value.

You can use discrete clustering not only for multi-valued attributes (such as the color of an object), but also to cluster attributes that appear in nested tables. Using the previous movie retailer example, you could cluster your customers not only by their demographics and movie watching behavior, but also by the actual movies they watched. For such attributes, the clustering algorithm treats each movie as having two possible values — existing and missing — and considers them in a manner similar to other discrete attributes.

Scalable Clustering

One of the problems in clustering data is that it requires multiple iterations over the training data set to determine an appropriate segmentation. In small data sets, this is not a problem, because iterating over data in memory is very fast. However, if the data grows to the point where it can no longer fit into memory, the performance of clustering degrades to the point where it is no longer feasible to compute. In this case, the Microsoft Clustering algorithm provides a *scalable framework* for clustering that allows you to efficiently cluster data sets, regardless of the size of the data.

The principle of the scalable framework is that particular data points that are not likely to change clusters can be compressed out of the data you are iterating over, providing room to load more data. This way, the entire data stream is loaded once, one chunk at a time. Additionally, it is possible for the model to converge at each chunk of data, completing the clustering operation without even seeing all of the data.

The basic procedure for using the scalable framework implemented in the Microsoft Clustering algorithm is as follows:

1. Initialize a set of candidate models to random initialization points.
2. Collect a sample of the source data to fill a memory buffer.
3. For each model, perform the following scalable steps:
   (a) Perform a clustering iteration as described earlier in this chapter.
   (b) Add information gathered from previous scalable steps.
   (c) Reinitialize any clusters that disappear or merge.

   Repeat this step until convergence, or until you have sufficiently iterated the models.
4. If models have converged since the last scalable step, or if you have run out of data, you are finished. You can now choose the best model from the candidates.

5. Select and remove data from buffer, adding sufficient statistics to each model.

6. Repeat from step 2.

NOTE The scalable clustering framework was created to solve the problem of too little memory to maintain the entire case set in memory. However, if you have enough memory, you can set the SAMPLE_SIZE parameter (described later in this chapter) to 0 to tell the algorithm to use as much memory as necessary.

Clustering Prediction

You can also use the Microsoft Clustering algorithm to predict values as well as to provide natural groupings. This may seem like a natural and obvious application, but traditionally clustering hasn't been used for such purposes. The Microsoft Clustering algorithm employs two tricks to accomplish this. First, it considers missing values to be uninformative. For example, if you have a new marble and you don't know the color, you won't use the fact that the color value is missing to determine which cluster the marble belongs to. Instead, the algorithm will use only the information for which it knows the values.

After the cluster membership has been determined, the second trick is to simply read off the values from the cluster. For example, if you find the aforementioned marble in cluster 2 from Table 9-1, you can say that it is 70 percent likely to be a red marble. Of course, with soft (EM) clustering, you would generally find that this marble belongs to only a single cluster, rather than a set of clusters with a particular probability for each. In this case, you can composite the result based on the contribution of each member cluster.

Parameters

You can tune the behavior of the Microsoft Clustering algorithm by tweaking its various parameters. The defaults handle most situations, but under certain circumstances, you may find you get better results by manipulating one or more of the parameters described in this section.

CLUSTERING_METHOD

The CLUSTERING_METHOD parameter indicates which algorithm is used to determine cluster membership. The vanilla versions of each algorithm eschew the scalable framework described previously and operate on only one sample of the data. Following are the possible values for this parameter:

- 1 — Scalable EM (default)
- 2 — Vanilla (non-scalable) EM

- 3 — Scalable K-means
- 4 — Vanilla (non-scalable) K-means

CLUSTER_COUNT

CLUSTER_COUNT tells the algorithm how many clusters to find. Set this parameter to a number that makes sense for your business problem. If you can comprehend eight clusters, set it to eight and see what you find. In practice, the more attributes you have, the more clusters you need to describe your data correctly. If you have too many attributes, you may want to pre-organize your data such that the number is reduced. Using the previous movie retailer example, instead of clustering by individual movies that your customers watched, you could cluster by the genres of those movies. This technique substantially reduces the attribute cardinality and creates models that are much more meaningful.

Setting CLUSTER_COUNT to 0 will cause the algorithm to perform a *heuristic* to guess the correct number of clusters in the data. The heuristic creates many models based on a small subset of the data, and generates a measure for each model that indicates how well that number of clusters represents the data. Then, a curve is applied to the results to favor cluster counts of around 10 clusters. Chart (a) in Figure 9-11 shows a hypothetical graph of a cluster score versus the number of clusters. This score indicates that the highest score is around 4 or 5. Chart (b) applies a curve, which generates the modified score shown in chart (c). The modified score indicates that, in this case, 10 clusters will be used to train the model. This heuristic is particularly important with discrete clustering, which tends to favor either very few or very many clusters, neither of which is particularly useful.

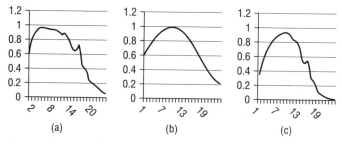

Figure 9-11 Application of the cluster count detection heuristic

The default value for CLUSTER_COUNT is 10.

MINIMUM_CLUSTER_CASES

MINIMUM_CLUSTER_CASES controls when a cluster is considered empty and is discarded and reinitialized. You will typically not need to modify this parameter, except in certain cases when business rules apply. For example, for privacy reasons, you may not want to create clusters smaller than 10 people. Note that this number is used internally only, and because of the nature of soft clustering, you may have clusters reporting membership lower than this amount after training. Setting this number too high can create bad results.

The default value is 1.

MODELLING_CARDINALITY

MODELLING_CARDINALITY controls how many candidate models are generated during clustering. Each candidate model starts with a different random starting point. Reducing this value will increase performance, at the potential cost of reducing accuracy. Typically you can reduce this by half without significantly impacting accuracy. If you are running the Enterprise or Developer edition of SQL Server 2008, each candidate model will be processed on separate threads, allowing you to take advantage of better hardware investments.

The default value is 10.

STOPPING_TOLERANCE

STOPPING_TOLERANCE is used by the algorithm to determine when a model has converged. It represents the maximum number of cases that can change membership before you consider a model converged. This value is checked at each iteration of the internal clustering loop, as well as at the outer scalable step. Increasing this number will cause the algorithm to converge more quickly, resulting in looser clusters (shown at the top of Figure 9-12), and decreasing this number will result in tighter clusters (shown at the bottom of Figure 9-12). If you have a small data set or very distinct clusters, you can set this value to 1.

The default value is 10.

SAMPLE_SIZE

SAMPLE_SIZE indicates the number of cases used in each step of the scalable framework. When you're using the vanilla versions of the algorithm, SAMPLE_SIZE indicates the total number of cases seen. Reducing this value can cause the algorithm to converge early without seeing all of the data, especially when coupled with a large STOPPING_TOLERANCE. This can be useful for creating a quick clustering on a large data set.

Setting this value to 0 will cause the algorithm to use as much memory as is necessary to load the data set. If there is not enough memory to materialize the data set in memory when SAMPLE_SIZE is set to 0, processing will return an error.

The default value is 50,000.

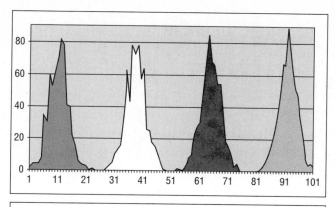

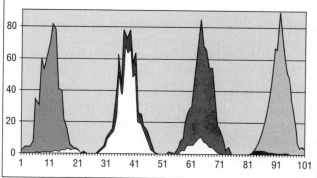

Figure 9-12 Stopping Tolerance = 1 (top) and Stopping Tolerance = 10 (bottom) in one-dimensional EM

CLUSTER_SEED

CLUSTER_SEED is the random number seed used to initialize the clusters. This parameter allows you to test the sensitivity of your data to the initialization point. If your models stay relatively stable when you change this value, you can be sure that the segmentation of your data is correct.

The default value is 0.

MAXIMUM_INPUT_ATTRIBUTES

MAXIMUM_INPUT_ATTRIBUTES controls how many attributes can be considered for clustering before automatic feature selection is invoked. If there are more than this number of attributes in your data set, feature selection will choose the most popular attributes from the set. The non-selected attributes are ignored during clustering. This limit exists because the number of attributes has a significant impact on performance.

The default value is 255.

MAXIMUM_STATES

MAXIMUM_STATES controls how many states one particular attribute can have. If an attribute contains more than this number of states, the most popular states are used by the algorithm and the remaining states are grouped into a state called "other". This limit exists because of the impact of high cardinality attributes on performance and memory.

The default value is 100.

Summary

Clustering is a very important part of your data mining repertoire. Using the Microsoft Clustering algorithm effectively can make the difference between understanding and misunderstanding your data. Opportunities to use this algorithm show up in every industry, and the results of clustering can be instrumental in changing how an organization conducts its business. You can deploy clustering models by simply dumping results to SQL tables, interactively using singleton queries to determine cluster membership on the fly to take immediate action, as part of a data mining dimension in an OLAP cube, or as an essential part of an SSIS package. Additionally, through clever use of DMX, you can embed clustering directly into your applications to leverage query parameters, including rowset parameters that will allow you to cluster application data on the fly. Experiment with clustering — your understanding of the data and the flexibility of your applications will grow tremendously!

Chapter 10 explores a modification of this technology that was originally designed to mine the behavior of web site users: the Microsoft Sequence Clustering algorithm. This algorithm combines clustering with sequencing technologies to group cases based not only on their attributes, but also on a sequence of events.

Microsoft Sequence Clustering

Imagine that you are a marketing manager of a popular online retailer site. You sell various categories of products, including books, magazines, electronics, cookware, office products, and so on. Every day, thousands of web customers come to your site, navigating among different domains of your portal. In a physical shop, you can visually identify those departments and products that attract most customers and the customer interactions on various products. In a virtual store, you don't see your customers.

However, you still want to learn more about your customers to provide them with better services. You want to find out how your customers are using your site and the list of products for which they have shown interest. You also want to know the natural groups among these customers, based on their navigation patterns. For example, one group of customers shops for all sorts of products on your website, and others visit only certain categories of books and magazines.

This information not only gives you a clear picture of your customers' behaviors in your virtual shop, but also allows you to provide personalized shopping guidance to each customer, based on his or her profile. In this chapter, you will learn how to use the Microsoft Sequence Clustering algorithm to analyze navigation sequences and organize sequences into natural groups based on their similarities.

In this chapter, you will learn about the following:

- The principles of the Microsoft Sequence Clustering algorithm
- Using the Microsoft Sequence Clustering algorithm
- Interpreting the model's content

Examples, data sets, and projects for this chapter may be found in its downloadable companion, `Chapter10.zip`, which is available on the book's website at `www.wiley.com/go/data_mining_SQL_2008/`. The archive contains the following:

- A SQL Server 2008 database backup containing the data sets used in this chapter
- A file containing the DMX scripts for this chapter
- An Analysis Services project

The DMX examples for this chapter require the Analysis Services database created by deploying the included Analysis Services project.

Introducing the Microsoft Sequence Clustering Algorithm

As the name suggests, the Microsoft Sequence Clustering algorithm is a hybrid of sequence and clustering techniques. It is designed to analyze a population of cases that contains sequence data, and group those cases into more or less homogeneous segments based on the similarity of those sequences.

A *sequence* is a series of discrete events (states). Usually, the number of discrete states in a sequence is finite. Sequence data is ubiquitous in the real world. Lots of information is encoded in sequence form. For example, a DNA sequence is a series of four discrete states: A (adenosine), G (guanine), C (cytosine), and T (thymidine). The list of courses a student takes at a university forms a sequence. The series of URL clicks of a web user is a sequence. In a shopping basket example, if you don't care about the order of the product purchases, the business problem of market basket analysis is an association task. If you do care about the order of the product purchases, the purchase data forms a sequence, and this problem is a sequence task.

Figure 10-1 shows a weather forecast sequence.

Showers   Partly Cloudy   Partly Cloudy   Light Rain   Mostly Sunny

Figure 10-1 A weather sequence

Using the Microsoft Sequence Clustering Algorithm

The Sequence Clustering algorithm can be applied in many areas such as click stream analysis, customer purchase analysis, bioinformatics, and so on. In this section, you will learn about creating mining models and writing DMX queries using the Sequence Clustering algorithm. You will also learn how to interpret the model using the Sequence Clustering viewer.

In addition to the standard content types supported by other algorithms, the Microsoft Sequence Clustering algorithm supports a special type of nested table designed to represent sequences of states. In such a nested table, the entries are indexed by their ordinal (or sequence) number. Therefore, the nested table has the following two columns:

- A *key sequence* column, which contains the sequence numbers (such as 1, 2, and so on, or the ordinal of a state inside the sequence)

- A non-key column, which contains an identifier for the sequence (typically a string, such as the name of the discrete DNA state or the URL clicked by a user during a browsing session)

NOTE Sequence data must be stored in a nested table. The Microsoft Sequence Clustering algorithm doesn't support multiple sequence tables in a model. Neither does it support more than one non-key attribute in the sequence table.

Creating a Sequence Clustering Model

Suppose you have two tables as shown in Figure 10-2: Customer and ClickPath. The Customer table contains customer profiles about web usage on a portal site. ClickPath is a transaction table. It contains the following three columns:

- CustomerGuid is the foreign key to the Customer table.

- URLCategory is the state of the sequence.

- SequenceID is a numeric column that stores the web click sequence number 1, 2, 3 . . . *n*.

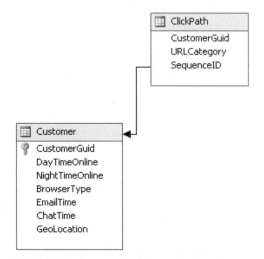

Figure 10-2 Customer and ClickPath tables

The sequence is the series of web clicks on the URLCategory in this model, such as News ⇨ News ⇨ Sports ⇨ News ⇨ Weather. A sequence may have various lengths because some customers stay longer and visit various URL categories.

As previously mentioned, the Customer table is a case table with CustomerGuid as the key, and ClickPath is a nested table with SequenceID as nested key. In order to enable predictions of the next steps in a sequence, the nested table containing the key sequence column must be marked as predictable.

DMX Queries

The statement shown in Listing 10-1 creates a mining model using the Microsoft Sequence Clustering algorithm.

```
CREATE MINING MODEL WebSequence
(
    CustomerGuid    TEXT KEY,
    GeoLocation     TEXT DISCRETE,
    ClickPath       TABLE PREDICT
    (
        SequenceID  LONG KEY SEQUENCE,
        URLCategory TEXT DISCRETE PREDICT
    )
)
USING Microsoft_Sequence_Clustering
```

Listing 10-1 A Sequence Clustering mining model for analyzing sequences of web clicks

The model can be trained with the statement shown in Listing 10-2.

```
INSERT INTO WebSequence
(
    CustomerGuid, GeoLocation,
    ClickPath (SKIP, SequenceID, URLCategory)
)
SHAPE {
 OPENQUERY([Web Data],
        'SELECT CustomerGuid, GeoLocation
            FROM CUSTOMER ORDER BY CustomerGuid')
} APPEND (
   {OPENQUERY([Web Data],
        'SELECT CustomerGuid, SequenceID, URLCategory
            FROM ClickPath ORDER BY CustomerGuid, SequenceID')}
RELATE CustomerGuid TO CustomerGuid) As ClickPath
```

Listing 10-2 Training the sequence model

NOTE The data used to train the sequence model is included in the `Chapter10.zip` archive, which is available for download on this book's companion website (`www.wiley.com/go/data_mining_SQL2008`), and contains one day of visits on the MSNBC website.

As a result of training, the customers are grouped into a set of clusters based on their geographic location and the sequence of clicks they executed on the website.

Executing Cluster Predictions

As with the Microsoft Clustering algorithm described in Chapter 9, the Microsoft Sequence Clustering algorithm supports prediction. For cluster membership prediction, you can use the `Cluster()` function, which returns the cluster ID for each case.

The query shown in Listing 10-3 returns the cluster ID for each input case.

```
SELECT  t.CustomerGuid,  Cluster()
From WebSequence PREDICTION JOIN
SHAPE {
  OPENQUERY([Web Data],
   'uSELECT  CustomerGuid, GeoLocation
    FROM Customer ORDER BY CustomerGuid')}
  APPEND ({
  OPENQUERY([Web Data],
   'SELECT CustomerGuid, SequenceID, URLCategory
    FROM ClickPath ORDER BY CustomerGuid, SequenceID')}
    RELATE CustomerGuid TO CustomerGuid)
    AS ClickPath AS t
ON
  WebSequence.CustomerGuid = t.CustomerGuid AND
  WebSequence.GeoLocation = t.GeoLocation AND
  WebSequence.ClickPath.URLCategory = t.ClickPath.URLCategory AND
  WebSequence.ClickPath.SequenceID = t.ClickPath.SequenceID
```

Listing 10-3 Cluster predictions using the newly created mining model

The query shown in this listing returns a table of two columns: the `CustomerGuid` and the predicted cluster number for each case.

Executing Sequence Predictions

The Sequence Clustering algorithm allows you to predict the subsequent states of a given sequence. The sequence table must be marked as predictable for this to work. Because the nested `ClickPath` table is marked as predictable in Listing 10-1, you can execute sequence predictions on the model. DMX contains a special function for sequence predictions, called `PredictSequence`, which can be invoked in one of the ways shown in Listing 10-4.

```
PredictSequence(ClickPath) : Returns the next (predicted) sequence
state
        for the ClickPath sequence table.

PredictSequence(ClickPath, 3) : Returns the next three (predicted)
        sequence states for the ClickPath sequence table.

PredictSequence(ClickPath, 2, 4) : Returns a range of predictions (the 2
        nd to the 4th) for the sequence states for the ClickPath sequence
table.
```

Listing 10-4 Various flavors of the PredictSequence syntax

The PredictSequence function always returns a table result. The table contains one computed column, $Sequence, which includes the ordinal of the predicted sequence step as well as the other sequence table columns. In the previous examples applied to the ClickPath table defined in Listing 10-1, the resulting table looks like Table 10-1.

Table 10-1 Result of PredictSequence Invocations

$SEQUENCE	SEQUENCEID	URLCATEGORY
1		Sport
2		Sport

The example shown in Listing 10-5 predicts the next two steps for a hypothetical customer who has already visited the Insurance, Loan, and Kits sections (in this order) of the website.

```
SELECT PredictSequence(ClickPath, 2) AS Sequences
FROM WebSequence NATURAL PREDICTION JOIN
(SELECT ( SELECT 1 AS SequenceID, 'Insurance' AS URLCategory UNION
        SELECT 2 AS SequenceID, 'Loan' AS URLCategory UNION
        SELECT 3 AS SequenceID, 'Kits' AS URLCategory)
        AS ClickPath) AS T
```

Listing 10-5 Sequence predictions for a new customer

Note how the input contains the ordered sections already visited by the customer. The order is specified by the SequenceID field of the input nested table.

The statement in Listing 10-5 returns the results shown in Table 10-2. The predicted sequence states are stored in a nested table. The nested table contains the following three columns:

- $Sequence is the generated column. It is an integer indicating the future steps, with ordinal numbers 1, 2, 3, and so on. "1" is, therefore, the first predicted sequence step.

- SequenceID has the same data type as the sequence column. If the sequence key is a date type, it returns the consecutive dates. The Microsoft Sequence Clustering algorithm doesn't fill this column.

- URLCategory is the predicted state of the sequence.

Table 10-2 Nested Prediction Results for Listing 10-5

SEQUENCES		
$Sequence	SequenceID	URLCategory
1		Relationship
2		Pets

You can simplify the result by using the FLATTENED keyword and the sub-select feature of DMX, as shown in Listing 10-6.

```
SELECT FLATTENED
 (
     SELECT $SEQUENCE, URLCategory FROM PredictSequence(ClickPath, 2)
 ) AS Sequences
FROM WebSequence NATURAL PREDICTION JOIN
(SELECT (SELECT 1 AS SequenceID, 'Insurance' AS URLCategory UNION
         SELECT 2 AS SequenceID, 'Loan' AS URLCategory UNION
         SELECT 3 AS SequenceID, 'Kits' AS URLCategory)
       AS ClickPath) AS T
```

Listing 10-6 Using FLATTENED and sub-select to simplify the prediction results

Extracting the Probability for the Sequence Predictions

Listing 10-1 marks the nested non-key column, URLCategory, with the PREDICT attribute. As a result, URLCategory supports DMX constructs specific to predictable columns, such as PredictProbability and PredictHistogram. The statement in Listing 10-7 returns the next predicted sequence steps, together with the probability of the prediction.

```
SELECT  FLATTENED
 (
     SELECT $SEQUENCE, URLCategory, PredictProbability(URLCategory)
             FROM PredictSequence(ClickPath, 2)
 ) AS Sequences
FROM WebSequence NATURAL PREDICTION JOIN
(SELECT (SELECT 1 AS SequenceID, 'Insurance' AS URLCategory UNION
          SELECT 2 AS SequenceID, 'Loan' AS URLCategory UNION
          SELECT 3 AS SequenceID, 'Kits' AS URLCategory)
         AS ClickPath) AS T
```

Listing 10-7 Returning the next predicted steps together with the prediction probability

The probability of the predicted next sequence step may serve as a threshold if any action is to be taken based on the prediction. For example, as a web server developer, you may want to display certain options, or emphasize certain page components, based on the predicted next clicks for the current user. The predicted probability will let you know if the predicted step is likely enough for you to take action.

Using the Histogram of the Sequence Predictions

During sequence predictions, the algorithm ranks all the possible next steps based on their probability in the current state, and then returns the top one. For example, if a user is on a web page in the News category, he or she might go next to Sports (with a 0.3 probability) or to another News page (with a 0.29 probability). Invoking the PredictSequence function will always return the most probable next step — in this case, Sports. The PredictHistogram function shown in Listing 10-8 provides you with a clearer picture of the possibilities at each step in the prediction.

```
SELECT FLATTENED
 (
     SELECT $SEQUENCE,
           PredictHistogram(URLCategory) AS Histogram
       FROM PredictSequence(ClickPath, 2)
 ) AS Sequences
FROM WebSequence NATURAL PREDICTION JOIN
...
```

Listing 10-8 Extracting the prediction histogram from PredictSequence

The result is a rather complex rowset with two levels of nested tables, as shown in Table 10-3.

Table 10-3 Query Result of the PredictHistogram Function

SEQUENCES			
$Sequence	Histogram		
1	URLCategory	$Support	$Probability ...
	Relationship	19	0.18
	Shopping Computer	16	0.15
	News Australia	16	0.15
	...		
2	URLCategory	$Support	$Probability ...
	Pets	19	0.09
	News Local	19	0.09
	Shopping Electronics	12	0.06
	...		
...			

Now, Table 10-3 is difficult to use and interpret because of the multiple levels of nested tables. However, only the top few values in the histogram are typically needed for analysis. Listing 10-9 shows a query that returns only the top two predictions for each step, together with the prediction probability for each.

```
SELECT FLATTENED
  (
    SELECT $SEQUENCE,
      (SELECT URLCategory, $PROBABILITY FROM
         TopCount(PredictHistogram(URLCategory), $PROBABILITY, 3)
       WHERE URLCategory<> NULL
      ) AS TopURLCategories
      FROM PredictSequence(ClickPath, 2)
  ) AS Sequences
FROM WebSequence NATURAL PREDICTION JOIN
...
```

Listing 10-9 Extracting the top two most likely URLCategories for each predicted sequence step

The code in Listing 10-9 is a rather complex DMX statement, so it deserves a bit of analysis. The skeleton of the code is the histogram query shown previously in Listing 10-7. Given that you need only the top two most probable predictions for each prediction step, the occurrence of `PredictHistogram` in the query is replaced with `TopCount(PredictHistogram(URLCategory), $Probability, 3)`. The DMX `TopCount` function sorts a table argument (the first argument, the result of the `PredictHistogram` invocation) based on the columns specified in the second argument (`$probability`), and returns the top N rows, where N is the value of the third argument (`3`, in this example). In general, this can be achieved with a SELECT TOP N FROM statement. However, as of SQL Server 2008, DMX does not support TOP qualifiers in sub-selects, so the use of `TopCount` is the only way to sort the histogram table.

A NULL `URLCategory` (signifying the end of the sequence, or the fact that the user has left the site) may appear with a high probability. Because you are interested in the predicted next sequence steps within the site, you select the top three most probable URL categories, and then filter out any NULL that may appear.

Table 10-4 shows the flattened result.

Table 10-4 Top Two Most Likely URL Categories for Each Predicted Sequence Step

$ SEQUENCE	TOPURLCATEGORIES	$PROBABILITY
1	Relationship	0.179
1	Shopping Computer	0.152
2	Pets	0.093
2	News Local	0.091

The rows in Table 10-4 are grouped by the `$Sequence` and sorted by the probability of the prediction.

As you have learned, a NULL `URLCategory` denotes the end of the sequence. Using the specialized query shown in Listing 10-10, you can find out how likely a user is to leave the site in the next few steps.

```
SELECT FLATTENED
  (
     SELECT $SEQUENCE,
               PredictProbability(URLCategory, NULL)
               AS ProbabilityToLeaveSite
            FROM PredictSequence(ClickPath, 2)
  ) AS Sequences
FROM WebSequence NATURAL PREDICTION JOIN
  ...
```

Listing 10-10 Determining the probability that the current user will leave the site in the next two clicks

Detecting Unusual Sequence Patterns

The clustering part of the Microsoft Sequence Clustering algorithm allows another interesting usage scenario. You can employ models built with this algorithm to detect unusual sequence patterns. An *unusual sequence pattern* (depending on the application context) may identify a customer who cannot find his or her pages of interest on your website or, if you are analyzing sequences of network activity, a possible virus.

For this example, let's use a customer who browses through pages in the following categories (in this order): Insurance, Loan, and Kits. The query in Listing 10-11 allows you to evaluate the likelihood of such a navigation sequence. In Chapter 9, you learned about the `PredictCaseLikelihood` function, which can be used to detect anomalies. Microsoft Sequence Clustering also supports `PredictCaseLikelihood`. The case likelihood results are closer to 1 if the presented case is similar to other data points in the model, and closer to 0 if the presented case is uncommon.

```
SELECT PredictCaseLikelihood()
 FROM WebSequence NATURAL PREDICTION JOIN
(
 SELECT (SELECT 1 AS SequenceID, 'Insurance' AS URLCategory UNION
         SELECT 2 AS SequenceID, 'Loan' AS URLCategory UNION
         SELECT 3 AS SequenceID, 'Kits' AS URLCategory) AS ClickPath
)
AS T
```

Listing 10-11 Detecting an unusual sequence with Microsoft Sequence Clustering

The result of the query in Listing 10-11 is a small number, 1.84e-07, denoting a very small likelihood for such a navigation sequence. Note that the anomaly derives from the sequence, and not from any URLCategory appearing in the sequence. For example, if you change the last entry in the sequence from 'Kits' to 'Sports', the likelihood changes to 0.31. Note also that the 'Kits' category is not unlikely by itself. If you remove the first two visited URL categories ('Insurance' and 'Loan') and evaluate the likelihood of the 'Kits' section, the result is a likelihood of 0.46, significantly better than the result of Listing 10-11.

Consequently, while Insurance, Loan, and Kits are all common URL categories, a click sequence in this order is unlikely.

Interpreting the Model

After the sequence clustering model is defined and processed, you can browse the content of the model using the Sequence Clustering viewer. The Sequence Clustering viewer contains the following five tabs:

- Cluster Diagram
- Cluster Profiles
- Cluster Characteristics
- Cluster Discrimination
- State Transitions

The overall design of this viewer is similar to the Clustering viewer design (described in Chapter 9), except for the Sequence Transition tab, which graphically displays the transition matrix for each cluster.

Cluster Diagram

Figure 10-3 shows the Cluster Diagram pane. This tab is the same as in the Clustering viewer. Clusters are layouts based on relationships. Similar clusters (that is, clusters with similar probability distributions, such as Cluster 1, Cluster 5, Cluster 7, and Cluster 10 in the figure) are closer to each other. The default node background represents the size of the cluster. For example, Cluster 9 is a large cluster and Cluster 12 is much smaller. You can also use the node color-coding to represent other attribute values, including a sequence state (for example, Weather). For this, select URL Category in the Shading Variable list, and the Weather category in the State list. The clusters representing high probabilities of the user clicking on the Weather page are highlighted with a darker color.

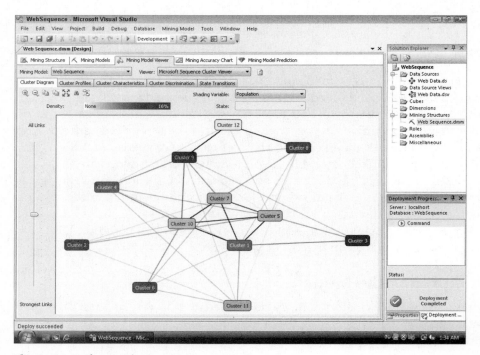

Figure 10-3 Cluster Diagram pane

Cluster Profiles

Figure 10-4 shows the Cluster Profiles pane. Each column represents a cluster, and each row represents an attribute. For example, the URLCategory row represents the sequence attribute, and each cell in this row contains a histogram of sequences. Each line in the histogram represents a sample case in this cluster, and a line is composed of a series of sequence states. Each sequence cell displays about 20 cases — these are the sample sequences from the training cases.

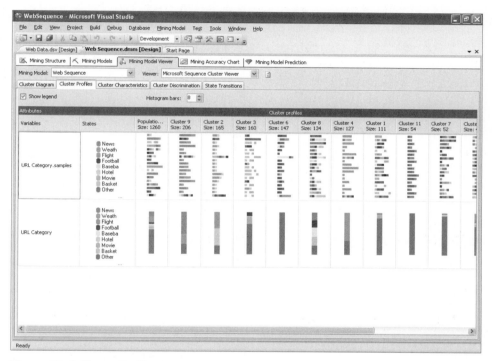

Figure 10-4 Cluster Profiles pane

The Mining Legend shown in Figure 10-5 provides more insight into the histogram of sequences for each cluster. Click inside one cluster column to load the sequence histogram in the Mining Legend window. (If the Mining Legend is not visible, right-click inside the viewer and select Show Legend.) The second histogram in Figure 10-5 shows users who clicked five times in the News North America section of the site, and then once in the Weather section.

Cluster Characteristics

Figure 10-6 shows the characteristics of each cluster as represented in the Cluster Characteristics pane. Each row represents the frequency (probability) of an attribute/value pair in the selected cluster. Each sequence state (including the Start and End events) is considered a distinct value for the sequence attribute. The list of attribute values is sorted based on the frequency. For example, the most likely attribute value in Cluster 1 is Start ⇨ Music, which means that most of the web visitors in Cluster 1 start with the Music page. Movie is another popular URL that Cluster 1 individuals like to visit.

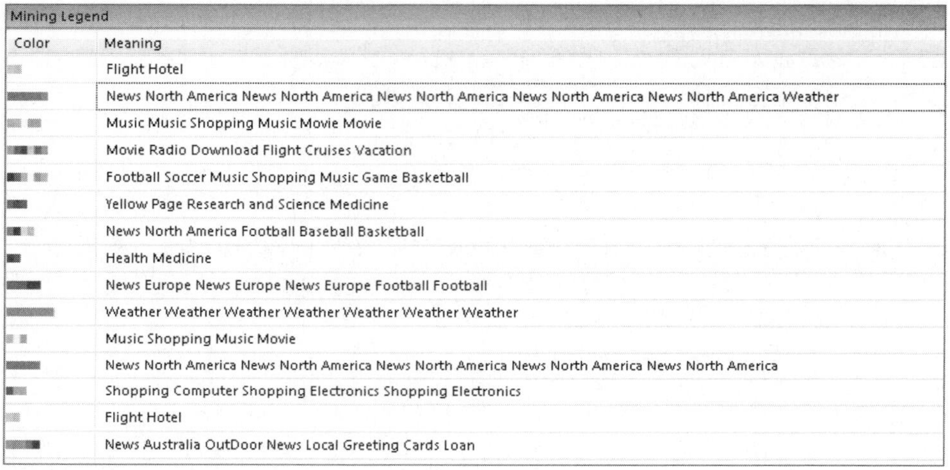

Mining Legend	
Color	Meaning
	Flight Hotel
	News North America News North America News North America News North America News North America Weather
	Music Music Shopping Music Movie Movie
	Movie Radio Download Flight Cruises Vacation
	Football Soccer Music Shopping Music Game Basketball
	Yellow Page Research and Science Medicine
	News North America Football Baseball Basketball
	Health Medicine
	News Europe News Europe News Europe Football Football
	Weather Weather Weather Weather Weather Weather Weather
	Music Shopping Music Movie
	News North America News North America News North America News North America News North America
	Shopping Computer Shopping Electronics Shopping Electronics
	Flight Hotel
	News Australia OutDoor News Local Greeting Cards Loan

Figure 10-5 Sequence histograms in the Mining Legend window

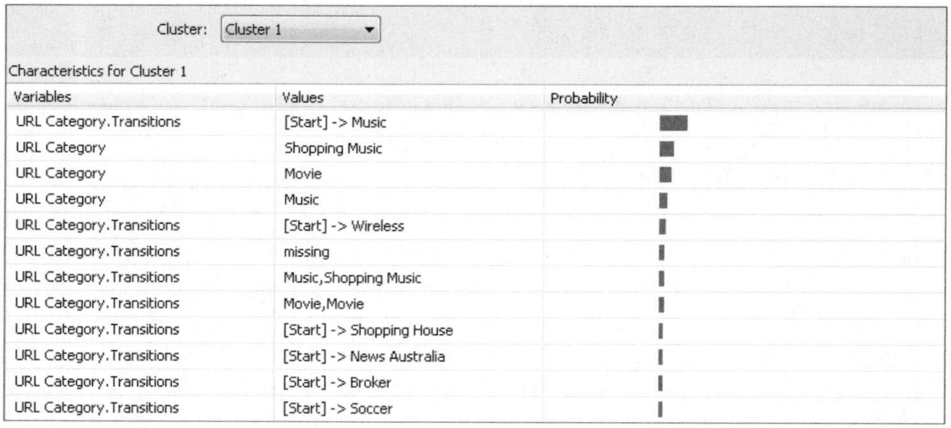

Cluster: Cluster 1 ▾

Characteristics for Cluster 1		
Variables	Values	Probability
URL Category.Transitions	[Start] -> Music	
URL Category	Shopping Music	
URL Category	Movie	
URL Category	Music	
URL Category.Transitions	[Start] -> Wireless	
URL Category.Transitions	missing	
URL Category.Transitions	Music,Shopping Music	
URL Category.Transitions	Movie,Movie	
URL Category.Transitions	[Start] -> Shopping House	
URL Category.Transitions	[Start] -> News Australia	
URL Category.Transitions	[Start] -> Broker	
URL Category.Transitions	[Start] -> Soccer	

Figure 10-6 Cluster Characteristics pane

Cluster Discrimination

Figure 10-7 shows the Cluster Discrimination pane. This pane is designed to compare any two clusters, or to compare a cluster with the whole population or its complement. As you can see in the figure, a significant difference between Cluster 1 and Cluster 8 is that Cluster 8 customers end their navigation on a page in the Soccer section, whereas Cluster 1 customers end their navigation in the Radio section. Cluster 1 customers are interested in Diet and Medicine pages, whereas Cluster 8 customers favor sports URLs (such as those in the Tennis and Hockey sections).

Discrimination scores for Cluster 1 and Cluster 8			
Variables	Values	Favors Cluster 1	Favors Cluster 8
URL Category.Transitions	Soccer-> [End]		▆▆
URL Category.Transitions	Loan-> Yellow Page		▆▆
URL Category.Transitions	Diet-> Medicine	▆▆	
URL Category.Transitions	Pets-> Game		▆▆
URL Category.Transitions	Tennis-> Hockey		▆▆
URL Category.Transitions	Radio-> [End]	▆▆	
URL Category.Transitions	Shopping Car-> Shopping House		▆▆
URL Category.Transitions	Football-> Hotel	▆▆	
URL Category.Transitions	Shopping Electronics-> Insurance	▆▆	
URL Category.Transitions	Loan-> Broker	▆▆	
URL Category.Transitions	Pets-> Wireless	▆▆	
URL Category.Transitions	Wireless-> Shopping Computer		▆▆
URL Category.Transitions	Shopping Electronics-> [End]		▆▆
URL Category.Transitions	News Australia-> [End]		▆▆
URL Category.Transitions	Diet-> [End]		▆▆

Figure 10-7 Cluster Discrimination pane

State Transitions

Figure 10-8 shows the State Transitions pane. It is designed to display the sequence navigation patterns of each cluster. Each node is a sequence state, and each edge is the transition between these two states. Each edge has a direction and weight. The weight is the transition probability. As you can see in the figure, the main interests of customers in Cluster 1 are Music, Shopping Music, and Movie, because those nodes are colored with the highest density. There is a strong link from Music toward Shopping Music. Among those customers who are in the Shopping Music URL category, 50 percent will navigate to a Movie site next.

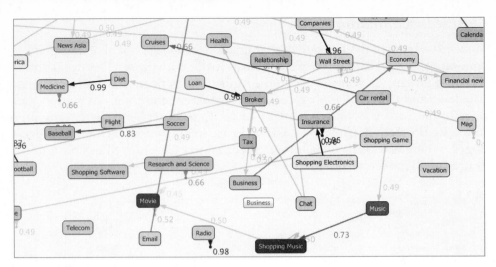

Figure 10-8 State Transitions pane

Microsoft Sequence Clustering Algorithm Principles

Before learning about the inner workings of the algorithm, let's explore a new concept: the Markov chain.

As stated previously, sequence clustering works by merging two technologies: clustering and sequence analysis. The clustering is similar to what was discussed in Chapter 9, but the sequence analysis is something new — a *Markov chain model*.

Understanding a Markov Chain

Andrey Markov was a famous Russian mathematician born in 1856. He was a professor at St. Petersburg University, and is remembered in particular for his study of Markov chains. A Markov chain is a sequence of random variables in which the future variable is determined by the present variable, but is independent of the way in which the present state arose from its predecessors.

Figure 10-9 shows an example of a Markov chain of the DNA sequence. A Markov chain contains a set of states. Most states emit events, but some states (such as Begin and End) are silent.

A Markov chain also contains a matrix of transition probabilities. The transitions emanating from a given state define a distribution over the possible next states. The equation $P(x_i = G | x_{i-1} = A) = 0.15$ means that, given the current state A, the probability of the next state being G is 0.15.

The Microsoft Sequence Clustering algorithm models sequence events based on the Markov chain model.

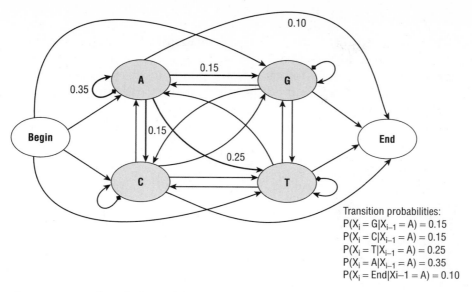

Transition probabilities:
$P(X_i = G|X_{i-1} = A) = 0.15$
$P(X_i = C|X_{i-1} = A) = 0.15$
$P(X_i = T|X_{i-1} = A) = 0.25$
$P(X_i = A|X_{i-1} = A) = 0.35$
$P(X_i = End|X_{i-1} = A) = 0.10$

Figure 10-9 Markov chain model

Order of a Markov Chain

One of the important properties of a Markov chain is the order. In a Markov chain, the order n specifies the probability of a state, depending on the previous n states. The most common Markov chain is *first-order*, which means the probability of each state xi depends only on the state of xi_{-1}. You can build high-order Markov chains using more memory to remember the previous n states.

An *nth*-order Markov chain over k states is equivalent to a first-order Markov chain over kn states. For example, a second-order Markov model for DNA can be treated as a first-order Markov model over the following states: AA, AC, AG, AT, CA, CC, CG,CT, GA, GC, GG, GT, TA, TC, TG, and TT. The total number of states is 4^2. The higher the order of a Markov chain, the more memory and time required for the processing.

Based on the Markov chain, for any given length L sequence x {x_1, x_2, x_3,...,xL}, you can calculate the probability of a sequence as follows:

```
P(x)  =  P(xL . xL-1,...,x1)
      =  P(xL| xL-1,...,x1) P (xL-1|xL-2,...,x1)...P(x1)
```

In the case of a first-order Markov chain, the probability of each xi depends only on xi_{-1}, so the preceding formula is equivalent to the following:

```
P(x)  =  P(xL . xL-1,...,x1)
      =  P(xL|xL-1) P(xL-1|xL-2)...P(x2|x1) P(x1)
```

State Transition Matrix

A Markov chain remembers the transition probabilities among different states. Figure 10-10 graphically displays a state transition matrix of a first-order Markov chain. Each cell in the table corresponds to the probability of the transition. The probability in the grid is encoded by the gray scale; higher probabilities are brighter.

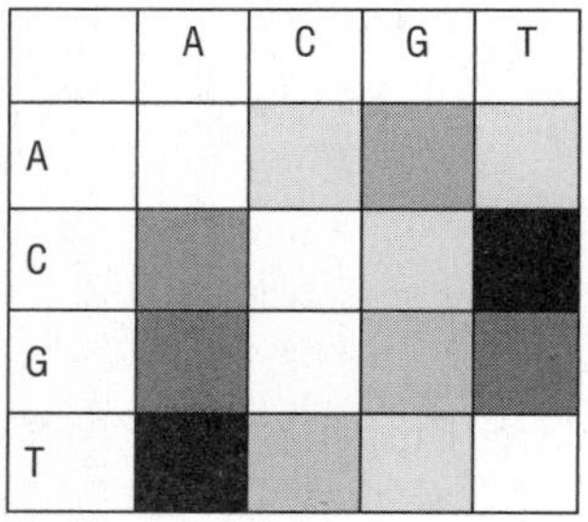

Figure 10-10 State transition matrix

The transition matrix for the first-order Markov model is an $M*M$ square matrix, where M is the number of states in the sequence. When M is large, the size of the transition matrix can be significant. When there are too many states, many cells in the matrix are dark, signifying a low transition probability. One of the ways to optimize the matrix storage is to store only those probabilities that are above a certain threshold.

UNDERSTANDING THE HIDDEN MARKOV MODEL

You may have heard the term *Hidden Markov Model (HMM)*. The difference between an HMM and a normal Markov chain model is that the state sequence of the model is hidden. You know only the observed sequence of outputs. There are five attributes of an HMM:

- ◆ The set of states
- ◆ The output alphabet $\{O_1, O_2, \ldots OT\}$
- ◆ The probabilities of initial states at t_0
- ◆ The state transition probabilities
- ◆ The output probabilities of each given state

For example, say that you have *n* biased coins (the coins are the states of the HMM), and the output alphabet is $\{H, T\}$. You know the transition probabilities among these coins and the output probabilities of *H* and *T* for each coin. You also know the initial probabilities of the coins to flip. But you don't know

(continued)

UNDERSTANDING THE HIDDEN MARKOV MODEL (continued)

exactly which coin is used to produce the output at each step, because the state sequence is hidden from you. Based on the sequence of observed outputs, you can figure out the following:

◆ What is the probability of observed outputs $O_1, O_2, \ldots OT$ given the model, for example $P(O_1, O_2, \ldots OT|model)$?

◆ At each step, what state is most likely given the model and outputs? That is, find the sequence $q_1, q_2, \ldots qT$ such that $P(q_1, q_2, \ldots qT \mid O_1, O_2, \ldots OT, model)$ is maximized.

◆ Given an HMM structure and observed data, find the model parameters that maximize $P(O_1, O_2, \ldots OT|model)$.

HMM is used in many applications, from voice recognition to DNA analysis. The Microsoft Sequence Cluster algorithm is based on an observable Markov chain, not on HMM.

Clustering with a Markov Chain

The Microsoft Sequence Clustering algorithm learns a mixture of Markov chains, where each mixture component corresponds to a particular cluster. To understand what a *mixture model* is, it is useful to understand how a mixture model generates data.

A single case is generated from a mixture model as follows:

1. A particular component (cluster) is randomly selected using a probability distribution over the clusters.

2. Depending on which cluster is selected, a sequence is generated from the Markov chain corresponding to that cluster. (Each cluster or component corresponds to a different Markov chain.)

Given data, the Microsoft Sequence Clustering algorithm learns the parameters of the mixture model: the mixture weights (the probability distribution over the clusters) and the parameters of each Markov chain. Note that the algorithm never sees the cluster identities of any case.

As explained in Chapter 9, Expectation-Maximization (EM) is an iterative algorithm that finds parameters corresponding to local optima for a model, or parameters that locally maximize the likelihood of the data. The overall process of the clustering algorithm is as follows:

1. Initialize the model parameters somehow (for example, at random).

2. Given the current model parameters, each case is assigned to each of the K clusters with some probability. (This is the E step.)

3. Reevaluate the model parameters based on the weighed assignment of each case. (This is the M step.)

4. Check whether the model has converged. If not, return to step 2 for a new iteration.

Chapter 9 discussed the method to calculate the probability and likelihood of a scalar attribute in each cluster. For the sequence attribute, the model parameters have the sequence state transition matrix for each cluster. For a given sequence x, you know its probability in a given cluster C is calculated using the following formula:

```
P(x|C) = P(xL|xL-1) P(xL-1|xL-2)...P(x2|x1) P(x1)
```

where `P(xj|xi)` is the transition probability of states i to j in cluster C.

You can then use the Bayes rule to calculate the cluster membership probabilities of x in cluster C:

```
P = (xi = G | xi-1=A)=0.15
```

where $P(C)$ is the marginal probability of cluster C (for example, the weight of cluster C over the whole population).

The Microsoft Sequence Clustering algorithm supports both sequence and non-sequence attributes. Non-sequence attributes can be scalar attributes or nested attributes, as explained in Chapter 9. Sequence data is stored in a nested table. The sequence nested table must contain a column modeled as the *key sequence*. This column is the key of the sequence. The sequence key can be of any data type that can be used as ordinals (such as date, integer, and string types).

In some cases, your data may have multiple sequence attributes. For example, you may want to group your customers by a sequence of web pages that he or she visited, and a sequence of products that he or she bought. However, multiple sequences in a single model are not supported in SQL Server 2008.

It is possible to build a sequence model without any sequence data. In this case, the model becomes a simple clustering model. Non-sequence and sequence attributes are assumed to be mutually independent given cluster identity.

What's the cost of processing and clustering a Markov chain? Supposing that the number of clusters in the model is K, the number of cases is N, the average length of each sequence is L, and the number of states in the sequence is M, the cost of each iteration is $O(KNL + LM^2)$. The first part, $O(KNL)$, is the cost to assign each sequence to a cluster with a membership probability. The second part, $O(LM^2)$, is the cost to calculate the transition matrix after each iteration. In many applications (such as a DNA sequence), M is relatively small. This complexity can be reduced to $O(KNL)$, which means the total run time of the algorithm scales linearly in both N and K.

Cluster Decomposition

The number of natural groups in a sequence clustering model is different from the number of such groups in a normal clustering model. In normal clustering, a common approach is to build the clustering model with $k < 10$ clusters. When the number of clusters is too large, it is difficult to interpret the final results. If a really large number of distinct groups exist, you can build clustering models in multiple steps, and, in each step, break the population into a handful of groups.

In the sequence clustering model, when the number of states in the sequence is large, there could be many distinct clusters. For example, in a web navigation scenario, there may be more than 60 URL categories in a portal site. The first group of web customers mainly navigates through News; the second group of customers focuses on Music and Movies; and the third group of customers is interested in front pages and Weather. While clustering these customers, you may end up getting a larger number of clusters, compared to the non-sequence cluster model. It is relatively easy to interpret these models based on their sequences of states.

One step during the Sequence Clustering algorithm processing is *cluster decomposition*. If a user specifies a small number of clusters, and there are different types of sequences in a cluster, the algorithm will decompose the cluster into multiple clusters. For example, if a cluster contains two sets of sequences — such as Movie ⇨ Music ⇨ Download and News ⇨ News ⇨ Weather — the algorithm breaks it into two clusters at the final stage of the model processing.

Model Content

The content of a sequence clustering model is laid out in four levels, as shown in Figure 10-11.

The root node represents the model. The second level is the cluster level. Each node except the last one represents a cluster discovered by the algorithm. The last node in the second level is a transition matrix, which represents the state transition probabilities of the overall population. The transition matrix has a set of children, where each child represents a row in the transition matrix. Because of content size, the matrix stores only those items with a probability greater than 0. Each cluster node also has a transition matrix as its child, which represents the transition probability of the given cluster. Therefore, there are four levels in the content of a sequence clustering model.

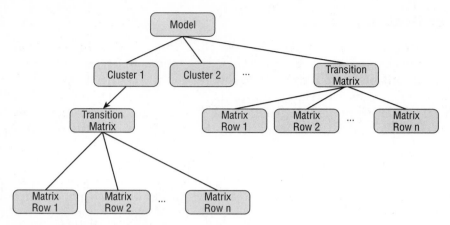

Figure 10-11 Content of a Sequence Clustering model

Algorithm Parameters

There are a few parameters for the Microsoft Sequence Clustering algorithm. These parameters are used to control the cluster count, sequence states, and so on. By adjusting these parameter settings, you can fine-tune the model's accuracy. The following sections detail the algorithm parameters.

CLUSTER_COUNT

The definition of CLUSTER_COUNT in the Microsoft Sequence Clustering algorithm is the same as in the Microsoft Clustering algorithm. It defines the number of clusters a model contains. Setting this value to 0 will cause the algorithm to automatically choose the best number of clusters for predictive purpose. The default value for CLUSTER_COUNT is 0.

MINIMUM_SUPPORT

The definition of MINIMUM_SUPPORT in the Microsoft Sequence Clustering algorithm is the same as in the Microsoft Clustering algorithm. It is an integer. It specifies the minimum number of cases in each cluster to avoid having clusters with too few cases. The default value is 10.

MAXIMUM_STATES

The definition of MAXIMUM_STATES is the same as in the Microsoft Clustering algorithm. This parameter specifies the maximum number of states of a clustering algorithm attribute. This parameter is an integer type. The default value is 100, and attributes with more than 100 states invoke feature selection.

MAXIMUM_SEQUENCE_STATES

MAXIMUM_SEQUENCE_STATES defines the maximum number of states in the sequence attribute. It is an integer type, with a default value of 64. Users can overwrite this value. If the sequence data has more states than MAXIMUM_SEQUENCE_STATES, feature selection is invoked, and the selection is based on the popularity of the states in the marginal model.

NOTE Suppose that there is a total M of distinct sequence states. Each cluster content contains an $M*M$ matrix. The processing time is proportional to M^2. If M is large, it may take a long time to process the model. You should make M no more than 100. If there are too many states (for example, hundreds of pages on your website), you can reduce M by grouping web pages into categories.

Summary

Lots of information can be modeled as sequences, including weather, web clicks, purchases, and so on. This chapter taught you how to build clustering models on sequence data. PredictSequence is a DMX function specifically introduced to predict the consequent states of a sequence attribute. In this chapter, you learned the syntax and query result format of this function.

Furthermore, you learned to use the Microsoft Sequence Clustering viewer, a very powerful tool that helps you explore and interpret the Sequence Clustering model. In this chapter, you also learned about the basic concepts of the Markov model and its application on sequence data. In addition, you learned the principles of clustering based on sequenced attributes and non-sequenced attributes.

In Chapter 11, you will learn about the Microsoft Association Rules algorithm, a very powerful tool frequently used for shopping basket analysis.

Microsoft Association Rules

Beep ... beep ... Good afternoon, sir. Did you find everything you need? ... beep ... beep ... bacon, eggs ... beep ... coffee, sugar ... beep ... milk, cookies ... ketchup, mustard, hot dogs ... beep ... cake mix ... Did you forget the frosting? I thought so! Service to aisle nine, could you bring over a can of frosting? ... Would you like any help out today, sir?

Every purchase a customer makes builds patterns about how products are purchased together. You can use these patterns to learn more about your customers' shopping behaviors in order to optimize product layout and cross-promote the right products to the right customers.

You can find these patterns (called *market basket analysis*) by using the Microsoft Association Rules algorithm, as described in this chapter.

In this chapter, you will learn about the following:

- How to use the Microsoft Association Rules algorithm
- How to create Microsoft Association Rules models using DMX
- How to interpret Microsoft Association Rules mining models
- The principles of the Microsoft Association Rules algorithm
- How to tune the algorithm by using parameters

You can find examples, datasets, and projects for this chapter in its downloadable companion, `Chapter11.zip`, which is available on the book's website (`www.wiley.com/go/data_mining_SQL_2008/`). The archive contains the following:

- A SQL Server 2008 database backup containing the data sets used in this chapter
- A file containing the DMX scripts for this chapter
- An Analysis Services project

The project uses data from the included database, as well as from the SQL Server `AdventureWorksDW2008` sample database. To download and install the sample database, go to the CodePlex website at `www.codeplex.com/MSFTDB-ProdSamples`, select SQL Server 2008 Product Samples, and then locate and install the `SQL2008.AdventureWorks_DW_BI_v2008.x86.msi` package. Be sure to select the Restore AdventureWorksDW2008 (Data Warehouse) option during setup to get the sample database ready.

For the DMX examples for this chapter to function, you will need to open (in Visual Studio) and deploy the Analysis Services project included in the downloadable companion, `Chapter11.zip`

Introducing Microsoft Association Rules

Put yourself in the role of a supermarket manager. One of your many responsibilities is to ensure that you sell the highest volume of product. Your goal is to sell more and be more profitable than your peers who are managing other stores in the chain. Understanding the purchasing patterns of your customers is the first step toward reaching this goal.

By using the Microsoft Association Rules algorithm to perform market basket analysis on your customers' transactions, you can learn which products are commonly purchased together, and how likely a particular product is to be purchased along with another. For example, you might find that 5 percent of your customers have bought ketchup, pickles, and hot dogs together, and that 75 percent of those customers that bought ketchup and hot dogs also bought pickles. Now that you have this information, you can take action. You could change the product layout to increase sales. You could use the insight to manage stock levels. You could determine whether baskets containing pickles, hot dogs, and ketchup are more or less profitable than those without. If they're more profitable, you could run a special to encourage this kind of shopping.

Additionally, you may want to learn more about the customers who shop at your store. With your courtesy cards and video club cards, you have collected several bits of information. You may learn that 15 percent of your female customers have video cards, and 75 percent of those customers rent their homes and live close to the store. Although it is possible to derive such patterns from standard SQL queries, you would have to write hundreds or thousands of queries to explore all possible combinations. This type of data exploration is made easier with the Microsoft Association Rules algorithm.

Using the Association Rules Algorithm

The Microsoft Association Rules algorithm is designed specifically for *association analysis*, a methodology typically used for shopping basket analysis. Given the large size of sales databases, the Association Rules algorithm is optimized for fast training over large data sets, and this makes it an interesting choice for other problems as well.

The algorithm detects *rules* governing the layout of your data. A rule is a statement such as ``If it walks like a duck and quacks like a duck it is (probably) a duck``. More formally, this can be represented as the following logical proposition:

$$P_1 \text{ AND } \ldots P_2 \Rightarrow \text{ AND } P_n \; P_{n+1}$$

In the logical proposition, a set of one or more *predicates* (P_i), when simultaneously satisfied, imply another predicate (P_{n+1}). Such a rule is detected by the algorithm after analyzing the training data and detecting that many (or all) the animals that walk like a duck and quack like a duck are actually ducks. A predicate is a simple condition (such as ``walks like a duck``) that describes the value of one of the attributes of the objects being analyzed. In the product purchasing scenario presented at the beginning of this chapter, a predicate is the presence (or absence) of a product in a shopping basket. Therefore, "milk, cake mix ... beep..." can be interpreted as a collection of the following two predicates:

```
Milk = Existing (in the shopping basket)
Cake Mix = Existing (in the shopping basket)
```

A rule may be discovered that says that, when `Milk` and `Cake Mix` are present, then `Frosting` is likely to be present as well. Such a rule will lead the clerk to suggest to customers that they buy frosting.

A predicate that participates in a rule is called an *item*. Consequently, a set of such predicates is called an *itemset*. Therefore, a rule can be described as a pair containing a left-hand itemset (the condition) and a right-hand itemset (the conclusion). Note that any rule is also a larger itemset that may appear on the left-hand side of another rule. For example, `Milk`, `Cake Mix`, and `Frosting` may be frequently associated with `Soda`.

Data Exploration Models

The algorithm works by counting frequent combinations of various model attributes' states. To the extent that it counts correlations, the Association Rules algorithm is somewhat similar to the Naïve Bayes algorithm. However, the approach is quantitative (it is based on the raw number of occurrences of attribute states combinations) and not qualitative, as it is for Naïve Bayes (which computes all the conditional probabilities). Also, the correlation matrix is not completely computed (which it is for Naïve Bayes). As you will see in the "Association Rules Principles" section later in this chapter, only the significant correlations are retained.

Some of the frequent combinations (those that exceed certain probability thresholds) are strong enough to have predictive value, and are exposed by the algorithm as rules.

The similarity with Naïve Bayes suggests the Association Rules algorithm as a good choice for data exploration mining models. The approach is similar — create a mining model and mark all the columns as predictable, as shown in Listing 11-1.

```
CREATE MINING MODEL VotingRecordsAnalysis
(
    [ID]    LONG   KEY,
    [Party] TEXT   DISCRETE PREDICT,
    [Class Action Fairness Act]          TEXT   DISCRETE PREDICT,
    [Farm Security Act]             TEXT   DISCRETE PREDICT,
    [Highway Funding Restoration Act]       TEXT   DISCRETE PREDICT,
    [Homeland Security Act]         TEXT   DISCRETE,
    ...
) USING Microsoft_Association_Rules
```

Listing 11-1 An Association Rules mining model intended for data exploration

Note that the Association Rules algorithm doesn't accept continuous attributes because it is a counting engine that counts the correlations among discrete attribute states. You must make the continuous attributes in the mining model discrete or discretized.

The Association Rules viewer provides multiple data exploration options, including the following:

▪ A listing of frequent combinations of attribute states

▪ A listing of rules (the frequent combinations that have predictive values)

▪ The capability to browse a dependency network that intuitively displays relationships between attribute states

Figure 11-1 shows the Dependency Net view for the model defined in Listing 11-1. As you may notice, the relationships are not between model attributes, but instead are between attribute states.

A Simple Recommendation Engine

A recommendation engine should be able to make recommendation for items that are likely to be purchased by a customer based on previous purchases by the same customer. (In the simplest case, this may mean the current content of the shopping basket for the respective customer.) To make these

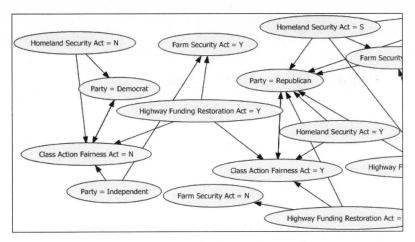

Figure 11-1 Association Rules Dependency Net view used to explore relationships between attribute states

recommendations, the engine must learn frequent purchase patterns from existing sales transactions data.

Suppose that sales transactions are identified by order numbers and, for each transaction, the individual items are recorded. Additional information (such as category or brand) may be available for the products in the catalog (you'll use this information in the next section). Listing 11-2 defines a mining structure to describe this problem space.

```
CREATE MINING STRUCTURE SalesData
(
    [Order Number] TEXT KEY,
    Products TABLE
    (
        Product TEXT KEY,
        Category TEXT DISCRETE
    )
)
```

Listing 11-2 A mining structure describing a sales transaction table

To train the mining structure, you must provide data for both a case-level column and the nested columns, as shown in Listing 11-3. In general, this requires two tables. However, given that all you need for the case-level column is the list of distinct values of the key ([Order Number]), you can substitute a SELECT DISTINCT statement for one of the tables. For the SHAPE construct to work, note how the two data queries must return results sorted by the primary key and foreign key, respectively.

```
INSERT INTO [SalesData]
  (
    [Order Number],
    [Products](SKIP, [Product], [Category])
  )
SHAPE
  {
    OPENQUERY ([Adventure Works DW2008],
    'SELECT DISTINCT [OrderNumber]  AS [Order Number]
          FROM     dbo.[vDMPrep]
          WHERE    FiscalYear = ''2004''
          ORDER BY [OrderNumber]')
  }
  APPEND
  (
    {
      OPENQUERY ([Adventure Works DW2008],
      'SELECT [OrderNumber] AS [Order Number],
              [Model] AS [Product],
              [EnglishProductCategoryName] AS [Category]
        FROM dbo.[vDMPrep]
        WHERE    FiscalYear = ''2004''
        ORDER BY [OrderNumber]')
    }
    RELATE [Order Number] To [Order Number]
  )
  AS [Products]
```

Listing 11-3 Training a mining structure from sales transactions data

Note how the [Order Number] column in the second data query is used only to relate items to the transaction, and is not actually used in the mining structure — hence the SKIP placeholder in the column mapping section of the INSERT INTO statement.

The next step is to create a mining model that will learn purchase patterns and be able to recommend purchases based on previous ones, as shown in Listing 11-4. The Products nested table (which describes the purchases for each transaction) must be both input and predictable. The model will detect products that sell together often, and make recommendations based on products already in the shopping basket.

```
ALTER MINING STRUCTURE SalesData
ADD MINING MODEL Recommendations
```

Listing 11-4 Creating and training a mining model for shopping basket analysis in the SalesData structure

```
(
    [Order Number],
    Products PREDICT
    (
        Product
    )
)USING Microsoft_Association_Rules(MINIMUM_SUPPORT=10,
        MINIMUM_PROBABILITY=0.4)
GO


INSERT INTO Recommendations
GO
```

Listing 11-4 (*continued*)

You can now use the Association Rules viewer to browse the patterns detected by the model. Furthermore, the model can produce recommendations. The statement in Listing 11-5 requests five recommendations based on a hypothetical shopping basket.

```
SELECT FLATTENED Predict(Products, 5) FROM Recommendations
NATURAL PREDICTION JOIN
(
    SELECT (
            SELECT 'Cycling Cap' AS Product UNION
        SELECT 'Sport-100' AS Product) AS Products
) AS T
```

Listing 11-5 Using the Association Rules model for product recommendations

Advanced Cross-Sales Analysis

Association Rules models may be used to analyze the cross-sales driven by a subset of products. For example, you may want to perform such an analysis when planning a promotion for a certain product or brand. You may also want to do this when simply exploring the cross-sales potential of various product categories.

Conceptually, this is a matter of labeling certain products as input, and the others as exclusively predictable. However, because of the nested table nature of most association data sets, this is not as simple as in the case of top-level columns. New DMX features in SQL Server 2008 allow an intuitive partitioning of the items in a nested table for an analysis task such as this.

For example, assume you want to analyze the cross-sales driven by bicycle products. Bicycles always belong to the `Bikes` category. The goal is to build an Association Rules model that uses `Bikes` products as input, but recommends any other product. The statement in Listing 11-6 does exactly this.

```
ALTER MINING STRUCTURE [SalesData]
ADD MINING MODEL CategoryRecommendations
(
    [Order Number],
    Products AS [Bike Products]
    (
        Product
    ) WITH FILTER(Category='Bikes' ),
    Products AS OtherProducts PREDICT_ONLY
    (
        Product
    ) WITH FILTER(Category<>'Bikes'
)
)USING Microsoft_Association_Rules(MINIMUM_SUPPORT=4,
    MINIMUM_PROBABILITY=0.2)
GO

INSERT INTO CategoryRecommendations
GO
```

Listing 11-6 An Association Rules model to analyze cross-sales driven by Bike Products

The DMX statement in Listing 11-6 uses the table of products twice in the mining model. However, the first copy (under the `[Bike Products]` alias) considers only those products (nested table rows) that belong to one of the `Bike` categories, whereas the second copy considers only the other rows and is marked as `PREDICT_ONLY`. As a result, items that are not bikes will never appear on the right-hand side of a recommendation. Figure 11-2 shows the rules detected by such a model.

PREDICTIVE ASSOCIATION RULES MODELS

The Association Rules algorithm may be used as a predictive algorithm (for example, to perform a classification task). In general, this algorithm is not a good predictor, at least when compared against the other predictive algorithms in the SQL Server 2008 suite. If you decide to try this, however, one trick may help: increase the value of the `MINIMUM_PROBABILITY` algorithm parameter, which is discussed in detail later in this chapter. The default value, `0.4`, is good for many associative tasks, but too low for classification. Bumping up the value of this parameter to at least `0.5` will improve the classification performance.

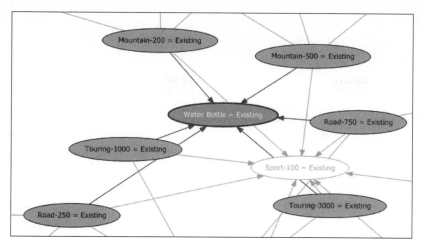

Figure 11-2 Rules detected by a model that analyzes cross-sales driven by Bike Products

DMX

Suppose that you have two tables: Customer and Purchase. The Customer table contains customer demographic information. It includes attributes such as gender, age, marital status, profession, and so on. The Purchase table is a transaction table containing the list of movies each customer purchased in the store. There are two columns in the Purchase table: Customer_ID and Movie_Name. In this section, you build an association model to analyze the relationships among movies and demographics.

Listing 11-7 creates a model for associative analysis using Gender, Marital_Status, and the purchased movies.

```
CREATE MINING STRUCTURE MovieAssociation (
    Customer_Id LONG KEY,
    Gender TEXT DISCRETE,
    Marital_Status TEXT DISCRETE,
    MoviePurchase TABLE(
        Movie_Name TEXT KEY
    )
)
GO

ALTER MINING STRUCTURE MovieAssociation
ADD MINING MODEL MovieAssociation (
    Customer_Id,
```

Listing 11-7 Association Rules model analyzing relationships between movies and demographics

```
   Gender PREDICT,
   Marital_Status PREDICT,
   MoviePurchase PREDICT (
       Movie_Name
   )
)
USING Microsoft_Association_Rules(Minimum_Support = 0.02,
     Minimum_Probability = 0.40)
GO
```

Listing 11-7 *(continued)*

As you already know, a model training statement mainly depends on the model structure, not the algorithm on which the model is based. Listing 11-8 shows the training statement for the `MovieAssociation` model.

```
INSERT INTO MINING STRUCTURE [MovieAssociation]
  (
    Customer_Id, Gender, Marital_Status,
    MoviePurchase (SKIP, [Movie_Name])
  )
SHAPE
  {
    OPENQUERY ([Chapter 11],
    'SELECT CustomerId, Gender, [Marital Status] FROM Customers
         ORDER BY CustomerId')
  }
  APPEND
  (
    {
      OPENQUERY ([Chapter 11],
      'SELECT CustomerID, Movie FROM Movies
          ORDER BY CustomerID')
    }
    RELATE CustomerId To CustomerId
  )
AS Movie_Purchase
```

Listing 11-8 Training a mining structure containing demographics and movie purchases

After the model is processed, you can issue queries to retrieve itemsets (Listing 11-9) and rules (Listing 11-10) from the content. You do this by filtering the content on the node types for itemsets and rules, which are 7 and 8, respectively.

```
SELECT Node_Description FROM MovieAssociation.CONTENT
WHERE Node_Type = 7
```

Listing 11-9 Retrieving all frequent itemsets

```
SELECT Node_Description FROM MovieAssociation.CONTENT
WHERE Node_Type = 8
```

Listing 11-10 Retrieving all rules

If you have only customer demographic information and you want to give movie recommendations based on `Gender` and `Marital_Status`, you can use the prediction query shown in Listing 11-11.

```
SELECT T.CustomerID, Predict(MoviePurchase, 5) AS Recommendation
FROM MovieAssociation
NATURAL PREDICTION JOIN
   OPENQUERY([Chapter 11],
      'SELECT CustomerID, Gender, Marital_Status FROM NewCustomer') AS T
```

Listing 11-11 Retrieving recommendations based on demographics

`Predict(MoviePurchase, 5)` returns the top five movies in a table column based on probability. This kind of prediction is called an *associative prediction*.

Sometimes, you not only know the customer demographics, but you also know a few movies a customer has already purchased. You can use the prediction query in Listing 11-12 to give more accurate recommendations.

```
SELECT T.CustomerID, Predict(MoviePurchase, 5) AS Recommendation
FROM MovieAssociation
PREDICTION JOIN
SHAPE
  {
    OPENQUERY ([Chapter 11],
    'SELECT CustomerId, Gender, [Marital Status] FROM Customers
        ORDER BY CustomerId')
  }
```

Listing 11-12 Retrieving recommendations based on demographics and transaction history

```
  APPEND
    (
    {
      OPENQUERY ([Chapter 11],
      'SELECT CustomerID, Movie FROM Movies
          ORDER BY CustomerID')
    }
      RELATE CustomerId To CustomerId
    )
  AS Movie_Purchase   AS T
  ON
      MovieAssociation.Gender = t.Gender
  AND  MovieAssociation.Marital_Status = t.[Marital Status]
  AND  MovieAssociation.MoviePurchase.Movie_Name = t.Movie_Purchase.Movie
```

Listing 11-12 (*continued*)

**PREDICT, PREDICTASSOCIATION, AND PARAMETERS FOR
RECOMMENDATION QUERIES**

If the first argument is a predictable nested table, then the DMX `Predict`
function is actually an alias for the `PredictAssociation` function. This may
take a variable number of parameters and flags. Flags are included in
the query in the same way that you include parameters. Their presence
affects the query result, but their order does not. All flavors will take a
mandatory first parameter — the name of the nested table. A possible second
parameter, the number of desired recommendations, was previously discussed.
Here are some flags that may be useful for your recommendation queries:

♦ `EXCLUSIVE`, `INCLUSIVE`, or `INPUT_ONLY` — An invocation such as
   `Predict(MoviesPurchase, 5, INCLUSIVE)` may return the movies that
   appear in the input if they are recommended by other movies in the input.
   Such an invocation may be used in evaluating the accuracy of the recommendation engine. `INPUT_ONLY` limits the results to the attributes present
   in the input. Although this is not very useful for a recommendation system, it is extremely useful when the nested table contains other predictable
   columns (for example, predicting the user rating for the movies in a shopping basket). The default behavior, `EXCLUSIVE`, guarantees that the list of
   recommendations does not contain any input.

♦ `$ADJUSTEDPROBABILITY`, `$PROBABILITY`, or `$SUPPORT` — This sorting
   criterion for recommendations determines the measure used in ranking
   recommendations before selecting the ones to be returned. The default is
   `$ADJUSTEDPROBABILITY`.

(continued)

- ◆ INCLUDE_STATISTICS — When this flag is present, the query result includes support, probability, and adjusted probability for each recommendation.

- ◆ INCLUDE_NODE_ID — This is the identifier of the content node that leads to the recommendation. When this flag is present, the query result includes a new column, $NODEID, which contains the NODE_UNIQUE_NAME of the content node describing the left-hand itemset (for those recommendations derived from rules) or NULL (for recommendations based on frequent items popularity). This flag may be particularly useful when you want to identify recommendations that are derived from rules and not item popularity.

The statement in Listing 11-3 returns five recommendations, sorted by probability (and not the usual adjusted probability) with all additional information that can be extracted.

```
SELECT FLATTENED PredictAssociation(
          MoviePurchase,
          5,
          $PROBABILITY,
          INCLUDE_STATISTICS,
          INCLUDE_NODE_ID)
FROM MovieAssociation NATURAL PREDICTION JOIN
( SELECT      'Male' AS Gender,
          'Married' AS Marital_Status,
          ( SELECT 'Alien' AS Movie_Name UNION
            SELECT 'Raiders of the Lost Ark' AS Movie_Name)
              AS MoviePurchase) AS T
```

Listing 11-13 Using Predict flags to get additional information about the recommendation results for a new customer

Model Content

Figure 11-3 shows the content of an association model. The top level has a single node that represents the model. The second level contains nodes that represent qualified itemsets and rules. The relationships between rules and itemsets are presented for a rule that recommends Empire Strikes Back when Attack of the Clones and Return of the Jedi are present.

For any itemset content node (identified by a value of 7 for the NODE_TYPE property), the Distribution rowset contains detailed information about the itemsets, with each row representing an individual item. Other interesting columns of the itemset nodes include the following:

- NODE_UNIQUE_NAME — This is a unique content identifier for this itemset, used as a reference from the rule nodes.
- NODE_SUPPORT — This is the support for this itemset.
- NODE_DISTRIBUTION rows — Each row represents an attribute/value pair that is part of the itemset.

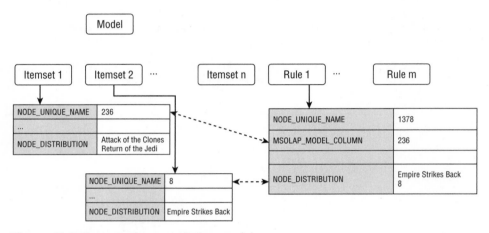

Figure 11-3 Content of an association model

For any rule content node (a value of 8 for the NODE_TYPE property), the Distribution rowset contains the predicted item on the right-hand side of the rule, and the node identifier for the itemset on the left-hand side of the rule. If you decide to write your own Association Rules browser, the following properties of a rule content node may also be useful:

- NODE_PROBABILITY — This is the probability of the rule represented by the current content node.
- MSOLAP_MODEL_COLUMN — This contains the NODE_UNIQUE_IDENTIFIER for the itemset that represents the left-hand side of the rule.
- MSOLAP_NODE_SCORE — This contains the rule's importance.
- NODE_SUPPORT — This is the support for the rule.
- NODE_DISTRIBUTION — The first row is the attribute and state that are on the right-hand side of the rule.

- NODE_DISTRIBUTION — The second row is the NODE_UNIQUE_NAME of the 1-itemset (itemset of length 1) that represents the right-hand side of the rule.

Interpreting the Model

After the association model is processed, you can browse the contents of the model using the Association Rules viewer. This viewer contains three tabs: Itemsets, Rules, and Dependency Network.

The Itemsets tab (shown in Figure 11-4) displays the frequent itemsets discovered by the Microsoft Association Rules algorithm. The main part of the screen is a grid that shows the list of frequent itemsets and their supports and sizes. If Minimum_Support is set too low, this list can be quite long. The Itemsets view includes drop-down lists that enable you to filter these itemsets based on support and itemset size. You can also use the Filter Itemset drop-down option to filter the itemsets. For example, you could select only the itemsets that contain Gender=Male.

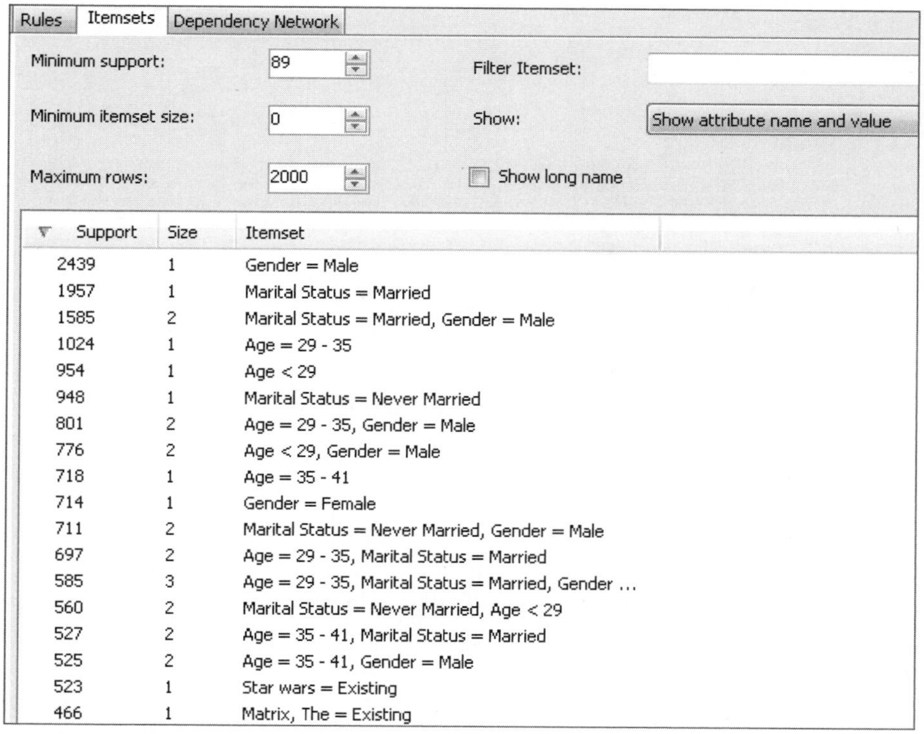

Support	Size	Itemset
2439	1	Gender = Male
1957	1	Marital Status = Married
1585	2	Marital Status = Married, Gender = Male
1024	1	Age = 29 - 35
954	1	Age < 29
948	1	Marital Status = Never Married
801	2	Age = 29 - 35, Gender = Male
776	2	Age < 29, Gender = Male
718	1	Age = 35 - 41
714	1	Gender = Female
711	2	Marital Status = Never Married, Gender = Male
697	2	Age = 29 - 35, Marital Status = Married
585	3	Age = 29 - 35, Marital Status = Married, Gender ...
560	2	Marital Status = Never Married, Age < 29
527	2	Age = 35 - 41, Marital Status = Married
525	2	Age = 35 - 41, Gender = Male
523	1	Star wars = Existing
466	1	Matrix, The = Existing

Minimum support: 89 Filter Itemset:
Minimum itemset size: 0 Show: Show attribute name and value
Maximum rows: 2000 Show long name

Figure 11-4 Frequent itemsets

FILTERS AS REGULAR EXPRESSIONS

The filters are actually regular expressions — the itemsets that match the regular expression are included in the Itemsets report. The language used is the .NET Framework Regular Expression Language, which is documented on the MSDN library (available at `msdn.microsoft.com`). The regular expression language allows more advanced filters. An expression such as `.*Godfather.*` will return all itemsets that include one of the movies in the *Godfather* series.

The Rules tab (shown in Figure 11-5) displays the qualified association rules. The main part of the tab is the rule grid. It displays all qualified rules, their probabilities, and their importance scores. The importance score is designed to measure the usefulness of a rule. The higher the importance score, the better the quality of the rule is. Similar to the Itemsets tab, the Rules tab contains some drop-down lists and text files for filtering rules. For example, you can select all rules that contain `Gender=Male` on the right side.

Figure 11-5 Association rules

The third tab of the association is the Dependency Net view (shown in Figure 11-6). As discussed in the "Data Exploration" section earlier in this chapter, each node in this view represents an item (for example, `StarWars = Existing` or `Gender = Male`). Each edge represents a pairwise association rule. The slider is associated with the importance score. By default, it displays up to 60 nodes. You may add hidden nodes to the graph using the Search button in the toolbar. You can also filter out the weak edges using the slider. If you want to show more nodes and edges in the Dependency Net view, you can lower the value of `Minimum_Probability` and reprocess the model.

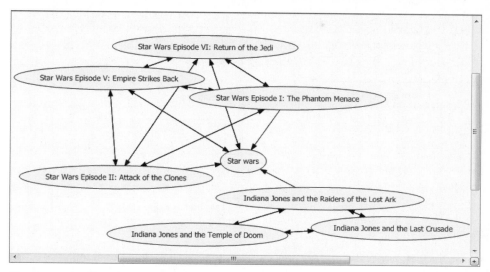

Figure 11-6 Dependency Net view

Association Algorithm Principles

An association algorithm is nothing more than a correlation counting engine. The Microsoft Association Rules algorithm belongs to the Apriori association family, which is a very popular and efficient algorithm for finding frequent itemsets (common attribute value sets). There are two steps in the Microsoft Association Rules algorithm, as illustrated in Figure 11-7. The first step of the algorithm, a calculation-intensive phase, is to find frequent itemsets. The second step is to generate association rules based on frequent itemsets. This step requires much less time than the first step does.

Understanding Basic Association Algorithm Terms and Concepts

The following sections define the basic terms and association-algorithm concepts you will need to understand before implementing the Microsoft Association Rules algorithm principles.

Finding frequent itemsets

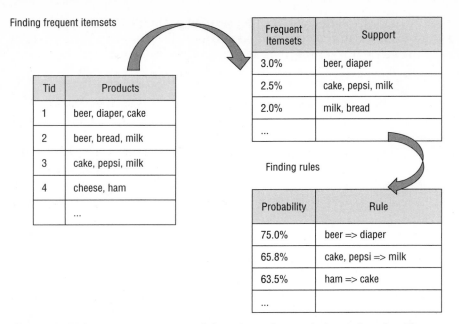

Figure 11-7 The two-step process of the Microsoft Association Rules algorithm

Itemset

An *itemset* is a set of items. Each item is an attribute value. In the case of market basket analysis, an itemset would contain a set of products such as cake, Pepsi, and milk. In the case of customer demographic exploration, an itemset would contain a set of attribute values such as {Gender = 'Male', Education = 'Bachelor'}. Each itemset has a size, which is the number of items contained in the itemset. The size of itemset {Cake, Pepsi, Milk} is 3.

Frequent itemsets are those itemsets that are relatively popular in the data set. The popularity threshold for an itemset is defined using *support*, which is discussed in the next section.

NOTE To be more precise, cake, Pepsi, and milk are all attributes. Their values are binary: Existing or Missing. For simplicity, you use {Cake, Pepsi, Milk} to denote {Cake = Existing, Pepsi = Existing, and Milk = Existing}.

Support

Support is used to measure the popularity of an itemset. Support of an itemset {A, B} is made up of the total number of transactions that contain both *A* and *B*, and is defined as follows:

```
Support ({A, B}) = NumberofTransactions(A, B)
```

`Minimum_Support` is a threshold parameter you can specify before processing an association model. It means that you are interested in only the itemsets and rules that represent at least minimum support of the data set. The parameter `Minimum_Support` is used to restrict the itemset, but not rules.

NOTE `Minimum_Support` **represents the number of cases for the frequency threshold of an itemset. However, many people find it handy to have a percentage value instead of actual counts for this parameter. For example,** `Minimum_Support=0.03` **means that the threshold for support is 3 percent. In the Microsoft Association Rules algorithm, if a user specifies this parameter with an integer number, the algorithm considers the actual case count to be the threshold. If a user inputs a floating number (less than 1.0) for this parameter, the algorithm considers it the percentage threshold.**

Probability (Confidence)

Probability is a property of an association rule. The probability of a rule `A=>B` is calculated using the support of itemset `{A,B}` divided by the support of `{A}`. This probability is also called *confidence* in the data mining research community.

`Probability` is defined as follows:

```
Probability (A => B) = Probability (B|A) = Support (A, B)/ Support (A)
```

`Minimum_Probability` is a threshold parameter you can specify before running the algorithm. It means that the user is interested in only the rules that have a high probability, rather than a minimum probability. `Minimum_Probablity` has no impact on itemsets, but it does impact rules.

NOTE **As you learned in the previous section, the popularity of itemsets is measured by their Support. However, an itemset probability can be defined as below (although it cannot be used as a threshold with the Microsoft Association Rules algorithm):**

```
Probability ({A, B}) = NumberofTransactions (A, B)/
    TotalNumberofTransactions
```

Importance

Importance is also called the *interesting score* (or the *lift* in some literature). Importance can be used to measure itemsets and rules.

The importance of an itemset is defined using the following formula:

```
Importance ({A,B}) = Probability (A, B)/(Probability (A)*
    Probability (B))
```

If importance = 1, A and B are independent items. It means that the purchase of product A and the purchase of product B are two independent events. If importance < 1, A and B are negatively correlated, which means that if a customer buys A, it is unlikely he or she will also buy B. If importance > 1, A and B are positively correlated, which means that if a customer buys A, it is very likely he or she also buys B.

For rules, the importance is calculated using the following formula:

```
Importance (A => B) = log (p(B|A)/p(B|not A))
```

An importance of 0 means that there is no association between A and B. A positive importance score means that the probability of B goes up when A is true. A negative importance score means that the probability of B goes down when A is true.

Table 11-1 gives the correlation counts of donut and muffin derived from a purchase database. Each cell value represents the number of transactions. For example, 15 out of 100 transactions include a customer purchasing both donuts and muffins.

Table 11-1 Correlation Count for Donut and Muffin

	DONUT	NOT DONUT	TOTAL
Muffin	15	5	20
Not muffin	75	5	80
Total	90	10	100

In the following calculations, the previous definitions are used to determine the support, probability, and importance of related itemsets and rules for Donut and Muffin:

```
Support({Donut}) = 90
Support({Muffin}) = 20
Support ({Donut, Muffin}) = 15
Probability({Donut}) = 90/100 = 0.9
Probability({Muffin}) = 20/100 = 0.2
Probability({Donut, Muffin}) = 15/100 = 0.15

Probability(Donut|Muffin) = 15/20 = 0.75
Probability(Muffin|Donut) = 15/90 = 0.167

Importance({Donut, Muffin}) = 0.15/(0.2*0.9) = 0.833
```

The rule importance formula used here may lead to calculation errors if either of the conditional probabilities is 0, which is likely to happen if two items are perfectly correlated. To avoid this issue, all the counts used in computing conditional probabilities are incremented with 1. This alteration has no impact on the relative importance of the rules, particularly for rules supported by many training cases. It has the advantage of providing a uniform treatment for all rules detected by the system. The altered correlation numbers used in computing the rules' importance are presented in Table 11-2.

Table 11-2 Altered Correlation Count for Donut and Muffin, Used in Computing the Rules' Importance

	DONUT	NOT DONUT	TOTAL
Muffin	15 + 1 = 16	5 + 1 = 6	22
Not muffin	75 + 1 = 76	5 + 1 = 6	82
Total	92	12	104

Using the altered counts, the rules' importance is computed as shown here:

```
Importance (Muffin=>Donut) = log10(Probability(Donut|Muffin)
    /Probability(Donut|Not Muffin))= log10( (16/22) / (76/82)) =
        -0.105302438
Importance(Donut=>Muffin) = log10(Probability(Muffin|Donut)
    /Probability(Muffin| Not Donut)) = log10((16/92) / (6/12) ) =
        -0.45864
```

From the importance of the itemset {Donut, Muffin}, you can see that Donut and Muffin are negatively correlated — it is rather unlikely for someone who buys a donut to also buy a muffin.

Finding Frequent Itemsets

Finding frequent itemsets is the core part of using the Microsoft Association algorithm. First, you must specify the frequency threshold using the Minimum_Support parameter (for example, Minimum_Support = 2%). This means that you are interested in analyzing only the items that appear in at least 2 percent of all shopping baskets.

The algorithm finds all frequent itemsets with size = 1 in the first iteration (the popular products with support greater than Minimum_Support). The algorithm does this by scanning the data set and counting the support of each item. The second iteration finds the frequent itemsets of size = 2. Before starting the second iteration, the algorithm generates a set of candidate itemsets of size 2 based on the result of first iteration (frequent itemsets of size = 1). Again, the algorithm scans the data set and counts the supports for each generated candidate itemset. At the end of the iteration, it selects the candidates with support greater than or equal to Minimum_Support to get the list of frequent itemsets with sizes equal to 2.

The algorithm repeats the same procedure to find frequent itemsets with sizes 3, 4, 5, and so on, until no more itemsets meet the `Minimum_Support` criteria.

Figure 11-8 illustrates the process of identifying frequent itemsets. The `Minimum_Support` is set to 250/1000. At the first iteration, `cheese` and `cake` are filtered out. At the second iteration, the candidate {`diaper, milk`} is disqualified. At the third iteration, the candidate {`beer, diaper, bread`} has enough support, whereas the candidate {`beer, milk, bread`} is filtered out.

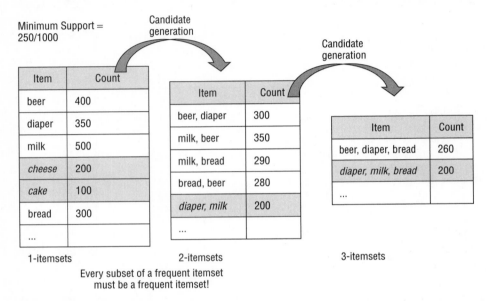

Figure 11-8 Finding frequent itemsets

The following pseudocode is the main procedure for generating frequent itemsets:

```
F: result set of all frequent itemsets
F[k]: set of frequent itemsets of size k
C[k]: set of candidate itemsets of size k
SetOfItemsets generateFrequentItemsets(Integer minimumSupport){
F[1] = {frequent items};
   for (k =1, F[k] >0; k++) {
      C[k+1] = generateCandidates(k, F[k]);
      for each transaction t in databases {
          For each candidate c in C[k+1] {
            if t contains c then c.count++
         }
   } //Scan the dataset.
      for each candidate c in C[k+1] {
```

```
        //Select the qualified candidates
        if c.count >=Minimum_Support F[k+1] = F[k+1] U {c}
      }
   }
   //Union all frequent itemsets of different size
   while k>=1 do {
      F = F U F[k];
      k--;
   }
   return F;
}
```

After you have your frequent itemsets, the `generateCandidates` function returns all of the candidate itemsets with `size = k + 1`. Every subset of a frequent itemset must itself be a frequent itemset as well. For example, if {beer, diaper, bread} is a frequent itemset, then {beer}, {diaper}, {bread}, {beer, diaper}, {beer, bread}, and {diaper, bread} must also be frequent itemsets.

To generate candidate itemsets `Ck+1` from frequent itemsets `Fk`, you use the following SQL join statement:

```
Insert into Ck+1
Select x1.a1, x1.a2, ..., x1.ak, x2.ak
From Fk as x1, Fk as X2
Where
   //match the itemset prefixes of size k-1
     x1.a1 = x2.a1 And
   x1.a2 = x2.a2 And
   ...
   x1.ak-1 = x2.ak-1 And
//avoid duplicates
   x1.ak <> x2.ak
```

This SQL statement generates candidate itemsets of size k having prefixes of itemsets size `k-1`. However, it doesn't guarantee that all the subsets of candidate itemsets are frequent itemsets. So, you must prune the candidates containing infrequent subsets by using the following procedure:

```
Boolean hasInfrequentSubset(Itemset c, SetofItemsets F) {
   For each (k-1) subset s of c {
      If s not in F then return true;
   }
 return false;
}
```

The generation of candidate itemsets and the counting of their correlation are time-consuming tasks. In some cases, this can generate a huge number of candidate sets. For example, suppose that there are 10,000 products (a medium-sized supermarket). If the minimum support is low enough, the algorithm will generate up to 10^8 candidate 2 itemsets. Many optimization techniques are available in this phase. For example, the Microsoft Association Rules algorithm stores the itemsets in a tree data structure to save space.

Some association algorithms generate frequent itemsets without any candidate generation.

FACTORS AFFECTING EFFICIENT PROCESSING

Association algorithm processing is very sensitive to the `Minimum_Support` parameter. When its value is set too low (less than 1 percent), the processing time and required memory become exponential. This is because of the large number of qualified frequent itemsets and frequent itemset candidates.

For large data sets with lots of distinct items, you should avoid setting this parameter too small.

The number of items is also critical to the performance of the processing. When there are too many unique items, consider grouping them into categories. For example, your store may have a dozen different jelly beans. You could group them all into a single `JellyBeans` category, which will not only reduce the total number of items, but also the model processing time.

Generating Association Rules

The next step in the association algorithm process is to generate association rules. You're looking for rules of the form `cake ➪ milk`, or `milk ➪ cake` and you're interested in rules that have a high correlation. To generate these rules, you need the count for the `{cake, milk}` itemset, as well as the counts for cake and milk (the 1-itemsets). In general, you need the itemsets to the left of the arrow (the left-hand side), along with the itemset that includes all items in the rule.

As rules are generated from the itemset, each item in the rule automatically satisfies the minimum support condition. The following procedure generates all of the qualified association rules:

```
For each frequent itemset f, generate all the subset x and its
      complimentary set y = f - x
If Support(f)/Support(x) > Minimum_Probability, then x => y is
      a qualified association rule with probability =
      Support(f)/Support(x)
```

NOTE The Microsoft Association Rules algorithm doesn't generate multiple items on the right side of the rule. However, if you want to have multiple recommendations, you can use a prediction query against an association model, which can return multiple items.

Prediction

In an association model, if a column is used for input, its values can be used only in frequent itemsets and on the left side of association rules. If a column is used to make predictions, the column's states can be used in frequent itemsets and on the left and right sides of the association rules. If a column is predict_only, its states can appear in frequent itemsets and on the right side of rules.

Many association algorithms in commercial data mining packages stop at finding itemsets and rules. The Microsoft Association Rules algorithm can perform predictions using these rules. The results of the predictions are usually a set of items to recommend.

You can build an association model not only based on shopping baskets, but also based on customer demographics. For example, you can include gender, marital status, and home ownership as case-level attributes in the mining structure, and include the shopping basket as a nested table in the same structure. In this case, you analyze the shopping patterns not only based on the relationship of itemsets, but also based on the demographics. For example, you may find a rule that predicts that 65 percent of male customers who purchase beer also purchase diapers in the same transaction, and that 20 percent of male customers who purchase diapers also purchase wine.

These rules can be applied for prediction. For a male customer, you may recommend a list of wines. If a male customer has already bought beer in the shopping cart, you may recommend both wine and diapers.

However, not every itemset is associated with a rule. For example, there is no rule that has the itemset {beer, diaper, bread, milk} on the left side. What would the recommendation list be for a customer who bought beer, diapers, bread, and milk? Here is the method the Microsoft Association Rules algorithm uses to execute associative prediction:

1. Given a list of items, find all rules with the left side matching the given items, or any subsets of the given items. Apply those rules to get the list of recommendations.

2. If there is no appropriate rule, or there are too few recommended items, apply marginal statistics to predict and return the *n* most popular items.

3. Sort the items from steps 1 and 2 based on probability.

NOTE The number of qualified association rules is based on the parameter Minimum_Probability. (Of course, each item in a rule must be a frequent item.) For example, when Minimum_Probability is set to 30 percent, this means 30 percent of customers who purchase A also purchase B (A = > B). This is a qualified rule. Rule generation is a relatively fast process, and you may lower the probability to have more rules. In a sparse data set like the shopping transaction table, you may set `Minimum_Probability` to 5–10 percent and get reasonable rules. In a dense data set like a customer demographic table, you need to raise this parameter to 40–50 percent; otherwise, you may get contradictory rules (for example, `High IQ => Gender = Male` and `High IQ => Gender = Female`).

Algorithm Parameters

As indicated throughout this chapter, the association algorithm is very sensitive to the algorithm parameter settings. This section outlines parameters for the Microsoft Association Rules algorithm.

MINIMUM_SUPPORT

`Minimum_Support` is a threshold parameter. It defines the minimum support requirement that items must meet to qualify as a frequent itemset. Its value is within the range of 0 to 1. If this value is set too low (for example, `0.001`), the algorithm may take much longer to process and require much more memory.

The default value is `0`, and the algorithm uses a heuristic to determine a good minimum support threshold.

If `Minimum_Support` is set to more than 1, it is considered to be the threshold for the number of cases instead of a percentage.

MAXIMUM_SUPPORT

`Maximum_Support` is a threshold parameter. It defines the maximum support threshold of a frequent itemset. Its value is within the range of 0 to 1. The default value is `0.03`. This parameter can be used to filter out those items that are too frequent.

If `Maximum_Support` is set to more than 1, it is considered to be the threshold for the number of cases instead of a percentage.

MINIMUM_PROBABILITY

`Minimum_Probability` is a threshold parameter. It defines the minimum probability for an association rule. Its value is within the range of 0 to 1. The default value is `0.4`.

MINIMUM_IMPORTANCE

`Minimum_Importance` is a threshold parameter for association rules. Rules with importance less than `Minimum_Importance` are filtered out.

MAXIMUM_ITEMSET_SIZE

Maximum_Itemset_Size specifies the maximum size of an itemset. The default value is 0, which means that there is no size limit on the itemset. Reducing the maximum itemset size reduces the processing time because the algorithm can save further iterations over the data set when the candidate itemset size reaches this limit.

MINIMUM_ITEMSET_SIZE

Minimum_Itemset_Size specifies the minimum size of the itemset. The default value is 0. However, you may not always care about the smaller itemsets. For example, you may be interested only in itemsets with sizes greater than 4.

Reducing Minimum_Itemset_Size will not reduce the processing time because the algorithm has to start with itemset size 1 and increase the size step by step.

MAXIMUM_ITEMSET_COUNT

Maximum_Itemset_Count defines the maximum number of itemsets. If this is not specified, the algorithm generates all itemsets based on Minimum_Support. The Maximum_Itemset_Count parameter avoids generating a large number of itemsets. When there are too many itemsets, the algorithm will keep only the top n itemsets based on their importance scores.

OPTIMIZED_PREDICTION_COUNT

Optimized_Prediction_Count defines the number of items to be cached to optimized predictions. The default value of this parameter is 0, meaning that the algorithm will produce as many predictions as requested in the query. Models having this parameter set to a value larger than 0 will expose better prediction performance. However, for those models, queries will return at most the number of predictions specified by the parameter value.

AUTODETECT_MINIMUM_SUPPORT

This parameter represents the sensitivity of the algorithm used to autodetect minimum support. Setting this value to 1.0 will cause the algorithm to automatically detect the smallest appropriate value of minimum support. Setting this value to 0 turns off autodetection, and the algorithm operates on the actual value of minimum support. This parameter is used only when MINIMUM_SUPPORT is set to 0.0.

Summary

This chapter provided you with an overview of the Microsoft Association Rules algorithm and its main usages. You learned the key terms of association algorithms, including itemset, rule, support, probability, and importance. The chapter also taught you the principles of association algorithm processing. There are two steps in this algorithm: identifying frequent itemsets and generating rules. Rules can be used for prediction.

You also learned the DMX queries to use with the association model. These queries generate recommendations based on probabilities or adjusted probabilities. The results of these queries can be used in cross-selling applications.

By now, you should be able to do market basket analysis and advanced data exploration using the Microsoft Association Rules algorithm.

In Chapter 12, you will learn about the Microsoft Neural Network algorithm and its close relative, Microsoft Logistic Regression — two of the most powerful predictive algorithms included in SQL Server Data Mining.

Microsoft Neural Network and Logistic Regression

Imagine the way the human mind works when presented with a problem. At first, the problem's facts are analyzed and weighed at some sensorial level. Next, these facts are passed through neural paths, which act as filters and are based on previously known patterns. This leads to conclusions, which may be possible solutions to the problem or may serve as additional facts for a new iteration over the neural paths.

Artificial *neural networks* are mathematic models for the process just described. The Microsoft Neural Network algorithm is such an artificial neural network. It works by creating and training artificial neural paths (relationships between inputs and outputs) that are used as patterns for further predictions. The algorithm does a better job than other algorithms in detecting very complex relationships between inputs and outputs. Detecting such relationships is a more intricate process than in most of the other algorithms, and training a neural network is generally more time-consuming than using any other model.

In this chapter you will learn about the following:

- How to use Microsoft Neural Network and Microsoft Logistic Regression
- How to interpret models using these algorithms
- The principles of the Microsoft Neural Network

Examples, data sets, and projects for this chapter may be found in its downloadable companion, `Chapter12.zip`, which is available on the book's companion website at www.wiley.com/go/data_mining_SQL_2008/. The archive contains the following:

- A SQL Server 2008 database backup containing the data sets used in this chapter
- A file containing the DMX scripts for this chapter
- An Analysis Services project

The DMX examples for this chapter will function only in the Analysis Services database created by deploying the included Analysis Services project.

Same Principle, Two Algorithms

The complexity of the analysis performed by Microsoft Neural Network derives from two factors. First, any and all of the inputs may be related somehow to any or all of the outputs, and the network must consider this in training (and, consequently, analyze all possible relationships). Second, different combinations of inputs may be related differently to outputs.

Imagine a chessboard. The color of each square is determined not by the row or column number, but by the combined parity of the row and column number. You have inputs that are not directly related to the output (row and column number), which aggregate in combinations (the combined parity) that determine the color of the squares.

The relationships detected by the Microsoft Natural Network algorithm may span on up to two levels. In the *single-level case*, input facts are connected directly to the outputs. In the *two-level case*, input combinations effectively become new inputs, which are then connected to the outputs. The level that transforms certain input combinations into new inputs is referred to as a *hidden layer*. Because it is not directly visible in the data, it is also detected by the algorithm.

The Microsoft Logistic Regression algorithm is a particular case of a neural network — one with a single level of relationships. The logistic regression technique has been used extensively by statisticians to model and predict the probability of events based on inputs. The classic logistic regression learning technique is not based on artificial neural networks. However, the mathematical model is identical to the one mathematical model of a Microsoft Neural Network model, which does not contain a hidden layer. This particular kind of network shares many of the qualities of the more general neural network and is less expensive to train. This reason (together with the intention to make it more discoverable for users who are familiar with the logistic regression technique) leads to the introduction of the separate Microsoft Logistic Regression algorithm.

Note that using a single level of relationships does not necessarily make the logistic regression algorithm a weaker predictor than a full network. In certain cases, logistic regression may prove to be a better predictor than a network with a hidden layer. One reason for this is that the hidden layer adds complexity (and the risk of overtraining) to the algorithm.

The Microsoft Logistic Regression algorithm is implemented by forcing the hidden layer of a neural network to have zero nodes and is manifest only in the internal structure of the algorithm. The two algorithms behave similarly and can be used for the same kinds of problems. Therefore, for the remainder of this chapter, Microsoft Neural Network and Microsoft Logistic Regression are used interchangeably (unless an explicit difference is emphasized).

Using the Microsoft Neural Network

The patterns detected by Microsoft Neural Network are usually not well-suited for exploration because, as you will see in the "Principles of the Microsoft Neural Network Algorithm" section later in this chapter, they consist mostly of numbers (weights connecting inputs and input combinations to outputs).

Text Classification Models

Document classification problems constitute one area where the Neural Network and Logistic Regression models very often yield much better results than other algorithms. The mining structure shown in Listing 12-1 holds the United States presidents' State of the Union address data.

```
CREATE MINING STRUCTURE [StateOfTheUnionAddress]
(
    [Year] LONG KEY,
    [Political Party] TEXT DISCRETE,
    [Address Terms] TABLE
    (
        [Term] TEXT KEY
    )
) WITH HOLDOUT(50 CASES)
```

Listing 12-1 A mining structure holding the State of the Union addresses

The mining structure leaves out the name of the president delivering the address and contains (for each State of the Union document) the list of terms appearing in the address, as well as the political affiliation of the respective president. The list of terms in each address is contained in the Address Terms nested table. As you can see in the mining structure definition, 50 cases are left out of training (to be used later for model validation). You would train the structure with a statement such as the one shown in Listing 12-2. The data used to populate the mining structure can be downloaded from `www.infoplease.com/t/hist/state-of-the-union/`.

```
INSERT INTO MINING STRUCTURE [StateOfTheUnionAddress]
(
     [Year],
     [Political Party],
     [Address Terms]( SKIP, [Term] )
)
SHAPE
  {
    OPENQUERY ([Chapter 12],
    'SELECT [Year], [Political Party] FROM [StateOfTheUnion]
         ORDER BY [Year]')
  }
  APPEND
   (
    {
      OPENQUERY ([Chapter 12],
      'SELECT [Year], [Term] FROM [StateOfUnionTermsTable]
           ORDER BY [Year]')
    }
     RELATE [Year] To [Year]
   )
   AS [TermsTable]
```

Listing 12-2 Training statement for a mining structure containing a nested table with terms appearing in each document

You can create a text classification model that tries to predict the political affiliation of a president based on the terms he used in his State of the Union address. It may not be the best way to detect the political affiliation of a president, but this will work as an example of a text classification task. To do this using the Microsoft Logistic Regression algorithm, you have to issue a statement like the one shown in Listing 12-3.

```
ALTER MINING STRUCTURE [StateOfTheUnionAddress]
ADD MINING MODEL PoliticalParty_LogReg
(
     [Year],
     [Political Party] PREDICT_ONLY,
     [Address Terms]
```

Listing 12-3 A Microsoft Logistic Regression mining model to predict the political affiliation of a president based on the terms used in the State of the Union address

```
        (
            [Term]
        )
)USING Microsoft_Logistic_Regression
GO


INSERT INTO PoliticalParty_LogReg
GO
```

Listing 12-3 (*continued*)

You can use a single call like the one shown in Listing 12-4 to evaluate the accuracy of the mining model.

```
CALL SystemGetAccuracyResults( StateOfTheUnionAddress,
    PoliticalParty_LogReg,
    2, 'Political Party')
```

Listing 12-4 Evaluating the accuracy of the text classification mining model

This call takes the following parameters:

- The name of the mining structure containing the models to be evaluated.

- (Optional) The name(s) of the mining model(s) being evaluated.

- A flag indicating which data is to be used in evaluation. A value of 1 indicates the structure training data, 2 is the structure test data (if a hold-out is specified), and 3 indicates all the structure data (training and testing). Listing 12-4 uses the 2 flag value (the test cases — the 50 left out of training when you created the structure).

- The target attribute being evaluated.

NOTE If your target model contains filters, a set of additional flags are available for filtered evaluation data. Values of 5, 6, and 7 denote filtered training, filtered testing, and all filtered data, respectively.

The result of the call is a table containing the results of various accuracy tests applied to the mining model. The most intuitive results are the number of correct and incorrect classifications, presented in Table 12-1 for the Microsoft Logistic Regression you've just built (that is, a partial view of the results returned by the stored procedure).

As you can see in the table, the Microsoft Logistic Regression algorithm correctly classifies the documents in 24 cases out of 50 — or 48 percent. You should note that, out of 219 addresses, only 171 were delivered by presidents who were either Democrats or Republicans, so a random guess would be right only in about 39 percent of the cases (48 addresses were delivered by presidents representing the Democratic-Republican, Whig, or Federalist party, or no party at all). In this context, 48 percent represents a significant lift over the random guess.

Table 12-1 Accuracy Results (Partial) for a Logistic Regression Text Classification Model

TEST	MEASURE	VALUE
Classification	Pass	24
Classification	Fail	26

The results are not great, and this is often the case. A text classification model rarely produces satisfying accuracy on the first try. You may wonder if a different algorithm would do a better job. With the data already loaded in the mining structure, it is easy to try different algorithms. One candidate is the full Microsoft Neural Network algorithm. For good measure, the Decision Trees and Naïve Bayes algorithms should also be considered. Listing 12-5 contains the DMX code for adding a sibling Microsoft Neural Network model.

```
ALTER MINING STRUCTURE [StateOfTheUnionAddress]
ADD MINING MODEL PoliticalParty_NNet
(
    [Year],
    [Political Party] PREDICT_ONLY,
    [Address Terms]
    (
        [Term]
    )
)USING Microsoft_Neural_Network
GO

INSERT INTO StateOfTheUnionAddress
GO
```

Listing 12-5 A Microsoft Neural Network mining model to predict the political affiliation of a president based on the terms used in the State of the Union address

With the Neural Network and Logistic Regression models trained, the time-consuming part of the analysis is behind you. Changing Listing 12-5 to add Decision Trees and Naïve Bayes models should be an easy and relatively quick task.

A slightly modified version of the accuracy call is shown in Listing 12-6. It is almost identical to the call in Listing 12-4, but it skips one parameter: the model name. Therefore, the evaluation is performed on all the structure's models that have a predictable `Political Party` attribute. Because the structure now contains a few extra models, the result set contains an accuracy measure for all models.

```
CALL SystemGetAccuracyResults( StateOfTheUnionAddress,
                          2, 'Political Party')
```

Listing 12-6 Evaluating the accuracy of all the text classification mining models

Table 12-2 shows the (partial) accuracy results for text classification models built with different algorithms. As you can see, Neural Network and Logistic Regression provide a relatively similar accuracy, followed by Naïve Bayes and then Decision Trees (a victim of the `MINIMUM_SUPPORT` algorithm parameter, which will prevent the tree from having leaves with fewer than 10 cases — not much of a chance for the eight Whig-delivered addresses!).

Table 12-2 Accuracy Results (Partial) for Multiple Text Classification Models

ALGORITHM	TEST	MEASURE	VALUE
Logistic Regression	Classification	Pass	**24**
Logistic Regression	Classification	Fail	26
Neural Network	Classification	Pass	**26**
Neural Network	Classification	Fail	24
Naïve Bayes	Classification	Pass	**23**
Naïve Bayes	Classification	Fail	27
Decision Trees	Classification	Pass	**18**
Decision Trees	Classification	Fail	32

In general, Microsoft Logistic Regression and Microsoft Neural Network algorithms do a better job than other algorithms in text classification tasks (as well as in other tasks where classification depends on many attributes). However, this relative performance boost is not guaranteed (in the preceding example, Naïve Bayes is following very closely) and comes at a cost (processing is time-consuming for a neural network). If speed is your priority, then Naïve Bayes is the choice — it is really fast! If you want to get the best accuracy, then you should try at least the four algorithms mentioned here (maybe with different parameters, particularly with higher-than-default values for `MAXIMUM_INPUT_ATTRIBUTES`). The Logistic Regression algorithm is a promising middle-path choice — it's not as time-consuming as the Neural Network, yet it's likely to produce the best (or close to the best) results.

Utility Models

The Microsoft Neural Network algorithm has the capability to handle both continuous and discrete data as both input and predictable attributes. The Microsoft Decision Trees algorithm has the same capability, but its greedy approach (combined with the requirement that each node must be supported by a minimum number of cases) makes it not very suitable for small data sets. The Logistic Regression algorithm is used for many of the utility models built by the Table Analysis Tools for Excel (such as Fill from Example, Scenario Analysis, and Prediction Calculator).

DMX Queries

The Microsoft Neural Network supports most of the tasks that Microsoft Decision Trees can do, including classification and regression. The association using the Microsoft Neural Network is time- and resource-consuming; hence, it is not supported. Consequently, a nested table cannot be used as a predictable column in a Microsoft Neural Network or Microsoft Logistic Regression mining model. The DMX statements for decision trees and neural networks are the same in terms of model creation, training, and prediction. The only differences are the algorithm name and parameter settings. Also, Microsoft Neural Network and Microsoft Logistic Regression do not support drill-through (that is, training cases cannot be linked to various patterns detected by the algorithm).

Listing 12-7 creates and trains a mining structure for customer information data. Various demographic attributes are included in the structure, together with a list of technologies that customers currently use. You'll use this mining structure as support for various DMX statements on Microsoft Neural Network mining models.

```
CREATE MINING STRUCTURE CustomerStructure(
    CustomerID LONG KEY,
    Gender TEXT DISCRETE,
    [Marital Status] TEXT DISCRETE,
    Age LONG CONTINUOUS,
    [Education Level] TEXT DISCRETE,
    [Home Ownership] TEXT DISCRETE,
    TechnologyUsage TABLE
    (
        [Technology] TEXT KEY
    )
)
GO
```

Listing 12-7 A mining structure holding customer data and technology usage information

```
INSERT INTO MINING STRUCTURE [CustomerStructure]
(
    [CustomerID], [Gender], [Marital Status],
    [Age], [Education Level], [Home Ownership],
    [TechnologyUsage]( SKIP, [Technology] )
)
SHAPE
  {
    OPENQUERY ([Chapter 12],
    'SELECT       [CustomerID], [Gender], [Marital Status],
                  [Age], [Education Level], [Home Ownership]
      FROM [Customers] ORDER BY [CustomerID]')
  }
  APPEND
  (
    {
      OPENQUERY ([Chapter 12],
      'SELECT [CustomerID], [Technology] FROM [Technology]
          ORDER BY [CustomerID]')
    }
    RELATE [CustomerID] To [CustomerID]
  )
  AS [TechUsage]
GO
```

Listing 12-7 (*continued*)

The Neural Network algorithm has no specific modeling flags. For regression-type models where the target is a continuous attribute (either Logistic or Neural Network), you don't need to mark columns with the REGRESSOR modeling flag, as you need to do for the Microsoft Decision Trees and Microsoft Linear Regression algorithms. All the input values are mapped to numbers and used as regressors (regression is a built-in feature of neural networks). Listing 12-8 builds a Neural Network mining model that predicts both a discrete target (Home Ownership) and a continuous (Age) target.

```
ALTER MINING STRUCTURE CustomerStructure
ADD MINING MODEL VariousPredictions(
    CustomerID,
    Gender,
    [Marital Status],
    [Age] PREDICT,
```

Listing 12-8 A Neural Network mining model for predicting both continuous and discrete targets

```
        [Education Level] PREDICT,
        [Home Ownership] PREDICT
)
USING MICROSOFT_NEURAL_NETWORK
GO

INSERT INTO VariousPredictions
GO
```

Listing 12-8 (*continued*)

You can also include a nested table in a neural network algorithm, as long as it is not marked as predictable. For example, the model in Listing 12-9 predicts Age based on the customer demographic data, as well as the technology items that the customer is currently using.

```
ALTER MINING STRUCTURE CustomerStructure
ADD MINING MODEL NestedTableInput(
    CustomerID,
    Gender,
    [Marital Status],
    [Age] PREDICT,
    [Education Level],
    [Home Ownership],
    TechnologyUsage
    (
        Technology
    )
)
USING MICROSOFT_NEURAL_NETWORK
GO

INSERT INTO NestedTableInput
GO
```

Listing 12-9 A Neural Network mining model using nested table input

You can use the trained models for executing predictions, just like models created with any other algorithms. There are no prediction functions specifically for neural networks. You can use algorithm-independent prediction functions, such as Predict and PredictProbability /PredictStdDev; however, PredictAssociation cannot be used because Microsoft Neural Network does not support predictable nested tables. Also, PredictNodeId cannot be used because drill-through is not supported either.

The query shown in Listing 12-10 exemplifies the usage of Neural Network models in predictions with the algorithm-independent prediction functions `Predict` and `PredictProbability`. The query identifies those training cases where the Neural Network generates a prediction different from the actual data by applying the `PREDICTION JOIN` operator against the structure cases and filtering only those rows where the prediction result is different from the actual training value. The statement also extracts the predicted probability for the actual training value.

```
SELECT     T.CustomerID,
           T.[Home Ownership] AS Actual,
           Predict([Home Ownership]) AS Predicted,
           PredictProbability([Home Ownership], T.[Home Ownership])
               AS ProbOfActual
FROM VariousPredictions NATURAL PREDICTION JOIN
(SELECT * FROM MINING STRUCTURE CustomerStructure.CASES) AS T
WHERE VariousPredictions.[Home Ownership] <> T.[Home Ownership]
```

Listing 12-10 A DMX query using algorithm-independent prediction functions on a Neural Network mining model

Model Content

A Neural Network model has one or more subnets. The model content describes the topologies of these subnets. It also stores the weights of each edge of the neural network.

Figure 12-1 shows the layout of the Neural Network model's content. The root node contains a set of child nodes, with one special child representing the input layer node. Each input neuron in a neural network is a child of the input layer node.

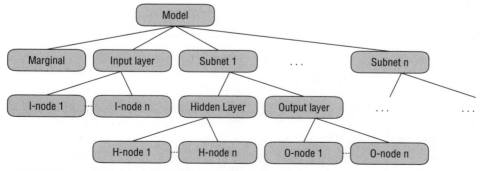

Figure 12-1 Content of the Neural Network model

> **NOTE** The different nodes of a neural network are described in more detail in the "Principles of the Microsoft Neural Network Algorithm" section later in this chapter.

Apart from the input layer node and marginal statistics node, the root node contains a set of subnet nodes. Each subnet node represents a neural network associated with one or more predictable attributes. If the model contains only one predictable attribute, there is only one subnet in the content.

Each subnet has two children: one for the hidden layer and one for the output layer. Each hidden node is a child of the hidden layer. It has incoming edges from one or more of the input nodes. These input node IDs (and their associated weights) are stored in the hidden node distribution rowsets. Each row in the distribution rowsets stores one weight. For example, to represent the weight of the edge from input node i (Gender = Male) to the hidden node h, there is a row in the distribution rowsets of h where Attribute name = i and Attribute Value = weight ih. Each output node is a child of the output layer. It has incoming edges from hidden nodes. These hidden node IDs and their associated weights are stored in the output node distribution rowsets.

The marginal statistics node contains the marginal distributions of all the attributes in the model. For discrete attributes, it lists the support for each state. For continuous attributes, it lists the mean and standard deviations.

WHY MULTIPLE SUBNETS?

The algorithm can analyze complex relationships between multiple inputs and multiple outputs. However, the network cannot simultaneously analyze multiple attributes that are both input and predictable (such as Education Level and Home Ownership in Listing 12-8). Therefore, multiple subnets are created, one for each input and predictable attribute. As you would probably expect, an attribute that is both input and predictable does not appear in the list of inputs for the subnet that analyzes it.

The algorithm may also decide to build multiple subnets when the number of outputs exceeds a large threshold, for scalability reasons.

Interpreting the Model

After your Neural Network or Logistic Regression model is processed, you can browse its content using the Neural Network viewer. The Neural Network viewer is different from other Microsoft data mining content viewers in the sense that it is mainly prediction-based. It does not display the information derived from the model content schema rowsets, and there is no graphical display of the trained neural network's layout. The main purpose of the viewer is to display the impact of attribute/value (AV) pairs related to the predictable attribute.

Figure 12-2 shows the Neural Network viewer. This is a single-tab viewer with three parts. The top-left part is the input grid, where you can specify the values of input attributes. When no input is specified in this grid, the viewer displays the information of all the input AVs related to the predictable states. The top-right part is for the output selection. You can select any two states of a predictable attribute using the drop-down list. For the continuous attribute, the drop-down list provides five ranges based on the mean and standard deviation.

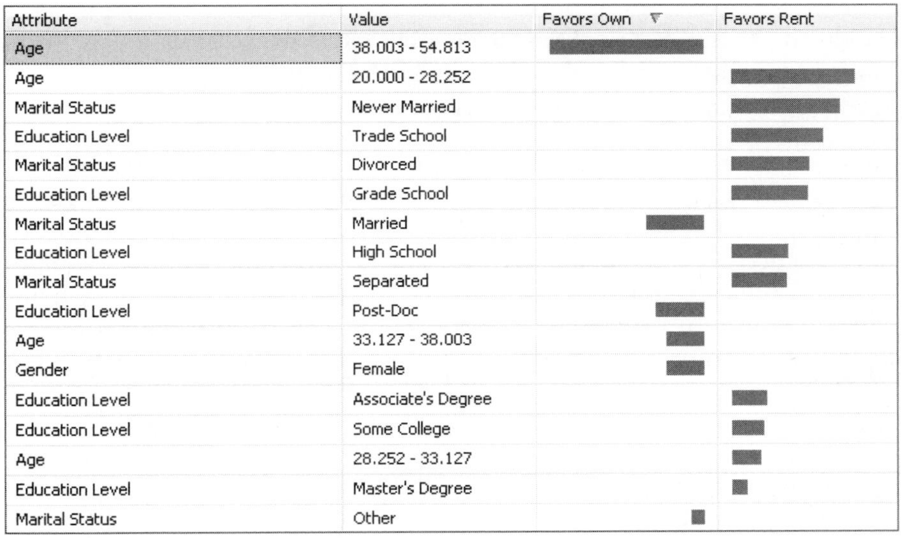

Attribute	Value	Favors Own ▽	Favors Rent
Age	38.003 - 54.813	▆▆▆▆▆▆	
Age	20.000 - 28.252		▆▆▆▆▆▆
Marital Status	Never Married		▆▆▆▆▆
Education Level	Trade School		▆▆▆▆▆
Marital Status	Divorced		▆▆▆▆
Education Level	Grade School		▆▆▆▆
Marital Status	Married	▆▆▆	
Education Level	High School		▆▆▆
Marital Status	Separated		▆▆▆
Education Level	Post-Doc	▆▆	
Age	33.127 - 38.003	▆▆	
Gender	Female	▆▆	
Education Level	Associate's Degree		▆▆
Education Level	Some College		▆▆
Age	28.252 - 33.127		▆▆
Education Level	Master's Degree		▆
Marital Status	Other	▆	

Figure 12-2 Neural Network viewer

The main part of the screen is the grid that displays the impact of AV pairs related to the predictable states. For example, Figure 12-2 shows that the most important AV that favors owning a house is the age range between 38 and 54, and the most important AV that favors renting a house is the age range between 20 and 28.

The Neural Network viewer is similar to the Attribute Discrimination tab of the Naïve Bayes viewer. It evaluates the impact of each AV related to the predictable states and then sorts based on the following score:

```
Score = P(AV |Predictable_State_1)/ P(AV|Predictable_State_2)
```

The Neural Network algorithm can quickly calculate `P(Predictable_State|AV)`. The method used to get this probability is to set all the other input attributes as `Missing` and the AV as the only input neuron. The neural network then calculates the probability of a predictable attribute state. Because you have the marginal states of P(Predictable State 1), P(Predictable State 2), and P(AV), you can derive P(AV | Predictable State 1) using the Bayes rule as follows:

```
P(AV | Predictable State 1) =
    P(Predictable State 1 |AV) * P(AV) / P(Predictable State 1)
```

NOTE The scores shown in the bars' tooltips are slightly different from the scores described here. The scores are applied to the log scale and are also normalized based on all the AV scores. The grid displays only the top 50 AVs and their scores.

Also note that Microsoft Neural Network doesn't return the score of P(Predictable_State|AV). Instead, it returns the score P(Predictable_State|(AV),all other attributes missing).

You can also specify multiple AVs as input. For example, in Figure 12-3, the user specifies the Age to be [33.127, 38.003] and the Education Level to be Some College. In this case, the viewer displays the impacts of AVs of other attributes related to Home Ownership, given the two other input AV pairs. The Neural Network algorithm calculates P(Predictable_State|AV) by fixing the neuron for Age to be in the [33.127, 38.003] range and the neuron for Education Level to be Some College. The rest of the calculation is the same as described previously.

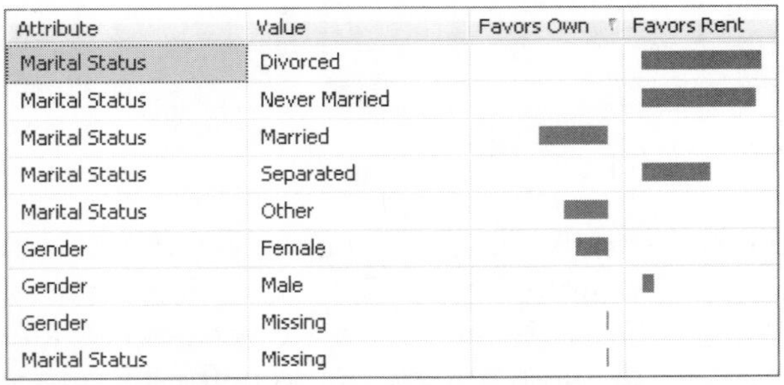

Attribute	Value	Favors Own	Favors Rent
Marital Status	Divorced		▬▬▬▬
Marital Status	Never Married		▬▬▬▬
Marital Status	Married	▬▬	
Marital Status	Separated		▬▬▬
Marital Status	Other	▬	
Gender	Female	▬	
Gender	Male		▪
Gender	Missing		
Marital Status	Missing		

Figure 12-3 Specifying input attributes in the Neural Network viewer

Principles of the Microsoft Neural Network Algorithm

The origin of the Neural Network algorithm can be traced to the 1940s, when two researchers, Warren McCulloch and Walter Pits, tried to build a model to simulate how biological neurons work. Though the focus of this research was on the anatomy of the brain, it turns out that this model introduced a new approach for solving technical problems outside of neurobiology.

During the 1960s and 1970s, with the advance of computer technology, researchers implemented some prototypes of the models based on the work of McCulloch and Pitts. In 1982, John Hopfield invented *backpropagation*, a method to adjust the weights of a neural network in a backward direction based on the learning error, as explained later in this chapter.

Since the 1980s, the theories of neural networks have matured, and the computing power of modern computers has enabled the processing of large neural networks within a reasonable time frame. Neural network technologies are applied to more and more commercial applications (for example, voice and handwriting recognition, fraud detection of credit card transactions, and customer churn analysis).

Neural networks mainly address the classification and regression tasks of data mining. Like decision trees, neural networks can find nonlinear relationships among input attributes and predictable attributes. Neural networks, however, find smooth (rather than discontinuous) nonlinearities. On the negative side, it usually takes longer to learn to use a neural network than it does to use decision trees and Naïve Bayes. Another drawback of neural networks is the difficulty in interpreting results. A neural network model contains no more than a set of weights for the network. It is difficult to see the relationships in the model and why they are valid.

Neural networks support discrete and continuous outputs. When the outputs are continuous, the task is regression. In fact, classic regression techniques (such as logistic regression) can be represented as special cases of neural networks.

Although typically used for classification and regression, feed-forward neural networks can also be applied to segmentation when used with a bottleneck configuration (small hidden layer).

What Is a Neural Network?

Neural networks are pattern-learning instruments that are more sophisticated than decision trees and Naive Bayes. Figure 12-4 shows a couple of examples. A neural network contains a set of *nodes* (neurons) and *edges* that form a network. There are three types of nodes: input, hidden, and output. Each edge links two nodes with an associated weight. The direction of an edge represents the data flow during the prediction process. Each node is a unit of processing.

Input nodes form the first layer of the network. In most neural networks, each input node is mapped to one input attribute (such as age, gender, or income). The original value of an input attribute must be massaged to a floating number in the same scale (often between −1 and 1) before processing.

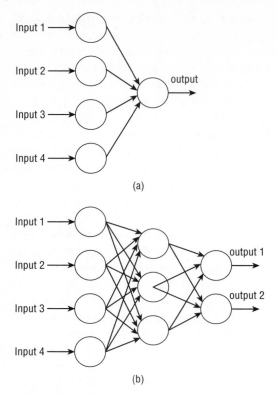

Figure 12-4 Example of a neural network

Hidden nodes are the nodes in the intermediate layers. A hidden node receives input from nodes in the input layers or precedent hidden layer. It combines all the input based on the weight of associated edges, processes some calculations, and emits a result value of the processing to the subsequent layer.

Output nodes usually represent the predictable attributes. A neural network may have multiple output attributes, as displayed in Figure 12-4 (b). It is possible to separate the output nodes to several different networks. However, in most cases, combining several output nodes in the same network reduces the processing time because such networks can share the common cost of scanning the source data. The result of the output node is often a floating number between 0 and 1.

The prediction for a neural network is straightforward. The attribute values of an input case are normalized and mapped to the neurons of the input layer. Then, each hidden layer node processes the inputs and triggers an output for the layers that follow. At the end, the output neurons start to process and generate an output value. This value is then mapped to the original scale (in terms of a continuous attribute) or original category (in terms of a discrete attribute). Although processing a neural network is time-consuming, making predictions against a trained neural network is rather efficient.

As displayed in Figure 12-4, the topologies of the neural networks may vary. Figure 12-4 (a) shows a very simple network. It has one output attribute without a hidden layer. All the input neurons connect to the output neuron directly. Such a neural network is exactly the same as logistic regression.

Figure 12-4 (b) is a network with three layers: input, hidden, and output. There are three neurons in the hidden layer. Each neuron of the hidden layer is fully connected to the input of the precedent layer. The hidden layer is a very important aspect of a neural network. It enables the network to learn nonlinear relationships.

> **NOTE** Neural Networks can be classified as "feed-forward" and "recurrent" (or non–feed-forward). Recurrent neural networks have directed cycles in their topology or architecture. That is, while following the direction of edges in a neural network, you can return to the same node. The Microsoft Neural Network is a feed-forward network.

After the topology of a neural network is configured (that is, the number of hidden nodes is specified), the training process involves finding the best set of weights for the edges in the network. This is a time-consuming task. Initially, the weights are randomly assigned. During each training iteration, the network processes the training cases to generate predictions on the output layer based on the current network configurations. It then calculates the error for the outputs. Based on these errors, it adjusts the weights of network using backward propagation. Details of the neural network learning process are discussed in the following sections.

Combination and Activation

Each neuron in the neural network is a basic processing unit. A neuron has a number of inputs and one output. It combines all the input values (combination), does certain calculations, and then triggers an output value (activation). The process is similar to the activity performed by the biological neuron.

Figure 12-5 shows the structure of a neuron. It contains two functions: a combination of inputs and a calculation of outputs. The combination function combines the input values into a single value. There are different ways to combine inputs. The most popular method is the *weighted sum*, meaning that the sum of each input value is multiplied by its associated weight. Other combination functions include *mean*, *max logical OR*, and *logical AND* of the input values. The Microsoft Neural Network uses the weighted sum approach. The output of combination is then passed through the activation function.

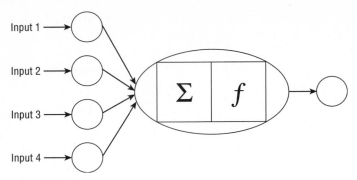

Figure 12-5 A basic processing unit

Similar to the way that a biological neuron works, when using the activation function, small changes of the input value sometimes trigger large output changes, and sometimes large changes of the input value have insignificant impact on the output. In particular, the output is sensitive to the input only when the input is in its midrange. This property enhances the neural network's ability to learn as it introduces the nonlinearity into the network. Several math functions satisfy this property. The most well-known functions are sigmoid (logistic) and tanh. These are nonlinear functions and result in nonlinear behavior. Following are the definitions of sigmoid and tanh:

```
sigmoid: O = 1/(1+eᵃ)
tanh: O = (eᵃ -e⁻ᵃ )/(eᵃ + e⁻ᵃ)
```

In these definitions, a is the input value and o is the output value.

Figure 12-6 shows the distribution of the sigmoid and tanh functions. The X-axis is the input value, and the Y-axis represents the output it triggers. The output value of the sigmoid function is between 0 and 1, whereas the output value for tanh is between -1 and 1. When the input value is close to 0, the output is very sensitive to slight changes in the input. When the absolute value of the input gets larger, the output becomes less sensitive.

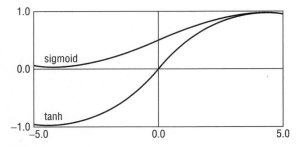

Figure 12-6 Activation function

Microsoft Neural Network uses `tanh` as the activation function in the hidden nodes. For output nodes, it uses the `sigmoid` function.

Backpropagation, Error Function, and Conjugate Gradient

The core part of processing a neural network is *backpropagation*. The training of a neural network is an iterative process. At each iteration, the algorithm compares the output values with the actual known values to get the errors for each output neuron. The weights pointing to the output neurons are modified based on the error calculations. These modifications are then propagated from the output layer through the hidden layers down to the input layer. All the weights in the neural network are adjusted accordingly.

The core process of neural network training is described in the following steps:

1. The algorithm randomly assigns values for all the weights in the network at the initial stage (usually ranging from −1.0 to 1.0).

2. For each training example (or each set of training examples), the algorithm calculates the outputs based on the current weights in the network.

3. The output errors are calculated, and the backpropagation process calculates the errors for each output and hidden neuron in the network. The weights in the network are updated.

4. Step 2 is repeated until the condition is satisfied.

Some neural networks update the weights after examining each case. This is called *case[online] updating*. Other neural networks update the weights until all sample cases are analyzed. This is called *epoch[batch] updating*. One interaction through the training data set is called an *epoch*. The Microsoft Neural Network uses epoch updating because it is more robust for regression models.

The neural network needs a measure to indicate the quality of the training. This measure is the error function (also called a *loss* function). The whole purpose of neural network training is to minimize the training errors.

There are many different choices for error functions, such as the squared residual (the square of the delta between the predicted value and the actual value) or the binary threshold for binary classification (if the delta between the output and the actual value is less than 0.5, then the error is 0; otherwise, it is 1).

The following formula gives one of the common methods for calculating the error for neurons at the output layer using the derivative of the logistic function. (Microsoft Neural Network uses a sum-of-squares error for a continuous attribute and cross-entropy for a discrete attribute.)

$$Err_i = O_i(1 - O_i)(T_i - O_i)$$

In this case, O_i is the output of the output neuron unit i, and T_i is the actual value for this output neuron based on the training sample.

The error calculation of the hidden neuron is based on the errors of the neurons in the subsequent layers and the associated weights. The formula is as follows:

$$\text{Err}_i = O_i(1 - O_i)\sum_j \text{Err}_j w_{ij}$$

Here, O_i is the output of the hidden neuron unit i, which has j outputs to the subsequent layer. Err_j is the error of neuron unit j, and w_{ij} is the weight between these two neurons.

After the error of each neuron is calculated, the next step is to adjust the weights in the network accordingly, using the following method:

$$w_{ij} = w_{ij} + l*\text{Err}_j*O_i$$

Here, l is a value ranging from 0 to 1.

The variable l is called *learning rate*. If the value of l is smaller, the changes on the weights are smaller after each iteration, signifying slower learning rates. The value of l usually decreases during the training process. At the initial stage of training, l is large, which allows the neural network to move quickly toward the optimum solution. Afterward, it decreases, so you can fine-tune the network to search for the best solution.

Many neural networks apply a method called the *conjugate gradient* in the process of adjusting the weight after each iteration. The conjugate gradient method is an algorithm for finding the nearest local minimum. The gradient method uses a derivative (gradient) to find the next direction. Conjugate takes into account the previous direction when it calculates the next direction so that it can avoid a zig-zag problem (in other words, taking a shortcut).

Because the search space for the best set of weights is huge (with many local optimal points), researchers apply different nonlinear optimization methods to guide the training process. There are many optimization algorithms, such as genetic algorithms, simulated annealing, iterative improvement, and so on.

A Simple Example of Processing a Neural Network

The best way to explain the neural network training process is with a simple example. This example uses a weighted sum as the combination function and the sigmoid as the activation function. Figure 12-7 shows the topology of a simple neural network with six neurons. The initial weights of the edges are displayed in the figure.

This example has three input nodes and one output node, which are mapped to the four attributes of a sample case. Suppose that the sample case is (1, 1, 0, 1), where the last digit is the output.

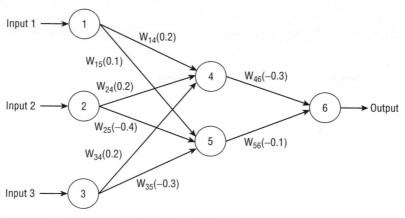

Figure 12-7 An example of neural network training

The first step is to calculate the outputs of each hidden and output neuron, as shown in Table 12-3.

Table 12-3 Calculation of Outputs for Hidden and Output Neurons

NEURON	INPUT	OUTPUT
4	0.2 + 0.2 + 0 = 0.4	1/(1 + e0.4) = 0.401
5	0.1-0.4 + 0 = -0.3	1/(1 + e-0.3) = 0.574
6	-0.3*0.401 + (-0.1)* 0.574 = -0.694	1/(1 + e-0.694) = 0.667

You get the output value of neuron 6, which is 0.667. The actual value is given by the sample as 1. You can thus calculate the error of the output neuron. Using the backpropagation method, you can derive all of the errors for all output and hidden neurons, as shown in Table 12-4.

Table 12-4 Calculation of Errors for Hidden and Output Neurons

NEURON	ERROR
6	0.667*(1-0.667)*(1-0.667) = 0.074
5	0.574*(1-0.574)*0.074*(-0.3) = -0.005
4	0.401*(1-0.401)*0.074*(-0.1) = -0.002

The sample neural network uses the case updating method. After the errors are calculated, you can adjust the weights accordingly. Table 12-5 gives the new set of weights after the first training case. The step size is a constant with a value of 0.8.

Table 12-5 Calculation of New Weights

WEIGHT	NEW WEIGHT
W_{46}	$-0.3 + 0.8{*}\ 0.074{*}0.401 = -0.276$
W_{56}	$-0.1 + 0.8{*}\ 0.074{*}0.574 = -0.066$
W_{14}	$0.2 + 0.8{*}(-0.002){*}1 = 0.198$
W_{15}	$0.1 + 0.8{*}(-0.005){*}1 = 0.096$
W_{24}	$0.2 + 0.8{*}(-0.002){*}1 = 0.198$
W_{25}	$-0.4 + 0.8{*}(-0.005){*}1 = -0.404$
W_{34}	$0.2 + 0.8{*}(-0.002){*}0 = 0.2$
W_{35}	$-0.3 + 0.8{*}(-0.005){*}0 = -0.3$

Normalization and Mapping

The neural network requires the value of input variables to be normalized in the same value scale; otherwise, those variables with a large value scale will dominate the training process.

There are a dozen different methods to normalize continuous input attributes, including z-score, z-axis, log score, and so on. The simplest method is the following:

```
V = (A - Amin)/(Amax - Amin)
```

In this method, `A` is the value of the attribute, `Amin` is its minimum value, and `Amax` is its maximum value.

However, this simple method has some issues. For example, if extreme minimum or maximum values exist in the distribution, the normalized result will be skewed. Suppose that the attribute you want to normalize is income, and the majority of the households have income less than $200,000. If there is a household with more than $1,000,000 income, the majority of the families will be mapped to the first 10–20 percent of the range. In this case, the log score is a better solution because it maps all the values to the log space first to reduce the scale issue.

For discrete variables, the easiest method is to map it to equal space points from 0 to 1. For example, let's say that there are five states for `Education`: partial high school, high school, undergraduate, graduate, and Ph.D. These values can be mapped to `0, 0.25, 0.50, 0.75,` and `1.0`, respectively.

Working with the Microsoft Neural Network, you would use the following method for input attribute normalization:

$$V = (x - \mu)/\sigma$$

For continuous input, μ is mean and is the standard deviation. For discrete input, $\mu = $ p (probability of a state) and $\sigma^2 = $ p * (1−p).

The relationship between the attribute and neurons is 1 to n. An attribute is mapped to n neurons. The Microsoft Neural Network maps a continuous attribute to two nodes: one representing the value and the other representing the Missing state. It maps a discrete attribute into $n + 1$ nodes, with n being the number of distinct states and 1 representing the Missing state. If the attribute is binary with two states — Missing or Existing — it is modeled as a single node.

Figure 12-8 shows an example of input normalization and mapping. The top table is the training input data. The bottom table displays the data after the normalization and mapping process. You can see from the figure that the four input columns (not counting the ID) are mapped to 10 input neurons. If Gender, Income, and IQ are the input attributes and Plan is the predictable attribute, there are seven input neurons and three output neurons.

ID	Gender		Income	Age	Owner
1	Male		46500	33	No
2	Male		39600	40	No
3	Male		63400	34	Yes
4	Female		40400	43	No

ID	Gender			Income		Age		Owner		
	-	M	F	-	val	-	val	-	Y	N
1	0	0.58	-0.58	0	-.09	0	-.91	0	0	1
2	0	0.58	-0.58	0	-.71	0	.56	0	0	1
3	0	0.58	-0.58	0	1.44	0	-.77	0	1	0
4	0	-1.73	1.73	0	-.64	0	1.12	0	0	1

Figure 12-8 Input normalization and mapping

Topology of the Network

The topology of the neural network must be fixed before processing. The number of input and output neurons is fixed with a training data set. The options are mainly related to the configuration of the hidden layers, such as the number of hidden layers and the number of hidden neurons at each hidden layer.

A neural network could have any number of hidden layers. The capacity of a network is a complicated function of the number of nodes and the number of layers. So, multiple hidden layers may increase the learning capacity. The network will also increase the processing time. The other drawback is potential overtraining. With too many hidden layers and hidden nodes, the network tends to remember the training cases instead of generalizing the patterns (similar to the oversplit issue in decision trees). It has been proven that, in most cases, one hidden layer is sufficient. The Microsoft Neural Network doesn't allow more than one hidden layer.

The number of neurons in the hidden layer is also very important. Using too few neurons will starve the network of the resources it needs to solve the problem. Using too many neurons will increase the training time. Researchers propose a rough guideline for choosing the number of hidden neurons: $c*sqrt(m*n)$, where n is the number of input neurons, m is the number of output neurons, and c is a constant. The optimal number varies from problem to problem. You should experiment with the number of nodes. In the Microsoft Neural Network, the default value for c is 4.

Similar to other Microsoft algorithms, a mining model based on the Microsoft Neural Network can have multiple predictable attributes. This results in multiple sub-neural networks. For example, if there are two predictable attributes, Age and Home Ownership, you must create two separate neural networks — one to predict each predictable attribute. However, if these two attributes are predict_only, they can share the same network.

Each input attribute will be mapped to multiple input neurons. Sometimes this can result in a large number of input neurons if there are many discrete attributes with many distinct values. By default, the total number of output neurons per subnetwork is limited to 500 in the Microsoft Neural Network algorithm. It will build multiple neural networks in case the number of output neurons is over 500.

When there are lots of input attributes, the Microsoft Neural Network algorithm invokes the feature selection process. The feature selection process selects the most important 255 input attributes.

> **NOTE** Having multiple predictable attributes results in multiple neural networks. This causes performance issues during the processing. You should carefully select your predictable attributes in neural network models.

Training the Ending Condition

The training process for neural networks is iterative. Depending on the complicity of patterns in the sample data set, it may take hundreds or even thousands of iterations through the data. What is the stop condition for a neural network? The following is a list of possible stop criteria:

- **Sufficient accuracy on a holdout set** — The misclassification rate is below a given threshold.

- **Maximum iteration** — The training process has reached the high limit of the number of iterations.

- **Convergence of the weights** — The change on the weights after each iteration falls below a threshold.

- **Time out** — The number of iterations exceeds the limit.

The Microsoft Neural Network uses the first three conditions as the stop criteria. The training stops when any of the top three conditions is satisfied.

Nonlinearly Separable Classes

In Chapter 6, you learned about a particular type of problem that cannot be properly solved by the Naïve Bayes algorithm because Naïve Bayes is a *linear classifier*. The problem is illustrated in Figure 12-9, which consists of two-dimensional points that have their X and Y coordinates between 0 and 1. The coordinates are approximated by ranges: [0, 1] and [1,2]. Some of the points are plus signs, and the others are squares.

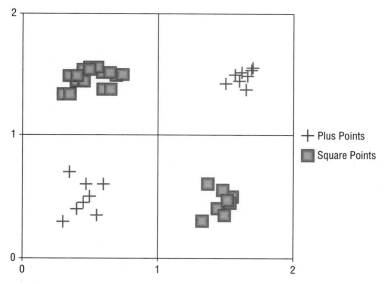

Figure 12-9 A nonlinearly separable classification problem

The data used for rendering Figure 12-9 is available in the LinearSeparability.xlsx file included in the Chapter12.zip archive, which is downloadable from this book's companion website (www.wiley.com/go/data_mining_SQL_2008). You may remember from Chapter 6 that the problem resides in the inability of any single attribute to be strongly correlated with one of the classes of points (Plus Points or Square Points).

As you may have noticed in Figure 12-9, a decision can be made only when both attributes (`Range X` and `Range Y`) are taken into account. As you would expect, Microsoft Neural Network is able to perform this kind of analysis because it analyzes complex relationships between the input combinations and the outputs. A Microsoft Neural Network will have perfect (or near perfect) accuracy for this problem.

A logistic regression model, on the other hand, links inputs directly to outputs, without the hidden layer that considers combinations of inputs. Consequently, the accuracy of the logistic regression algorithm is much lower (and depends on the actual number of Plus Points and Square Points associated with each range). Logistic Regression is also a linear classifier. Interestingly enough, the Microsoft Neural Network viewer (used by both algorithms) has trouble emphasizing the difference as well, because it is based on the probability of the target conditioned by one attribute at a time.

Luckily, any accuracy measurement (stored procedure, lift chart, or classification matrix) emphasizes these kinds of problems very quickly, and the solution is to build multiple models, using a few different algorithms.

Algorithm Parameters

The following sections describe the parameters for the Microsoft Neural Network and Microsoft Logistic Regression algorithms.

MAXIMUM_INPUT_ATTRIBUTES

`Maximum_Input_Attributes` is a threshold parameter for feature selection. When the number of input attributes is greater than this parameter setting, feature selection is invoked implicitly to pick the most significant attributes.

MAXIMUM_OUTPUT_ATTRIBUTES

`Maximum_Output_Attributes` is a threshold parameter of feature selection. When the number of predictable attributes is greater than this parameter setting, feature selection is invoked implicitly to select the most significant attributes.

MAXIMUM_STATES

`Maximum_States` specifies the maximum number of attribute states that the algorithm supports. If the number of states that an attribute has is greater than the maximum number of states, the algorithm uses the attribute's most popular states and treats the remaining states as `Missing`.

HOLDOUT_PERCENTAGE

Holdout_Percentage specifies the percentage of holdout data. The holdout data is used to validate the accuracy during the training. The default value is 0.1.

HOLDOUT_SEED

Holdout_Seed is an integer for specifying the seed for selecting the holdout data set.

HIDDEN_NODE_RATIO

Hidden_Node_Ratio is used to configure the number of hidden nodes. The unit of hidden node numbers is $sqrt(m*n)$, where n is the number of input neurons and m is the number of output neurons. If Hidden_Node_Ratio is equal to 2, the number of hidden nodes is equal to 2 * $sqrt(m*n)$. By default, Hidden_Node_ratio is equal to 4. This parameter is not available for the Microsoft Logistic Regression algorithm.

SAMPLE_SIZE

Sample_Size is the upper limit of the number of cases used for training. The default value is 10000.

MICROSOFT LOGISTIC REGRESSION ALGORITHM

The Microsoft Logistic Regression algorithm is based on Microsoft Neural Network algorithm implementation by setting the parameter Hidden_Node_Ratio to 0. If you use Microsoft Neural Network to build a model without a hidden layer, you get exactly the same result as using Microsoft Logistic Regression. The reason it is packaged as a separate algorithm is to make it easily discoverable for the users.

Summary

This chapter provided an overview of the Microsoft Neural Network algorithm and its main uses: classification and regression. It covered the basic concepts of a neural network and how its training process works, as well as the advantages and disadvantages of a neural network versus other algorithms. As you learned in this chapter, Microsoft Neural Network is a nonlinear algorithm that is able to discover complex patterns that Decision Trees and Naïve Bayes algorithms may miss. You should start with the Decision Trees algorithm because it is simpler to interpret the patterns than it is to interpret the output from the Microsoft Neural Network. You should try a neural network only when the accuracy of other algorithms is not satisfactory.

You should now be able to build mining models using the Microsoft Neural Network algorithm.

This chapter concludes the set of chapters dedicated to the various algorithms in SQL Server Data Mining. In Chapter 13, you will learn how to use the power of these algorithms on top of OLAP cubes.

Mining OLAP Cubes

You may have already heard of (or even have experience with) Online Analytical Processing (OLAP). E. F. Codd, the originator of the relational data model, wrote a white paper in 1994 that introduced the term *Online Analytical Processing* into the lexicon of database users. OLAP is the current term for systems that were formerly called decision-support systems (DSS) or multidimensional databases.

OLAP plays an important role in today's business intelligence (BI) market. An OLAP database contains a number of cubes, similar to the way a relational database contains a number of tables. As you will see in this chapter, a *cube* has a set of well-defined dimensions and measures. A *dimension* is an analytical object that provides axes on which you can ask questions, whereas a *measure* is a numerical value that exists at a coordinate in a cube.

For example, almost all analytical cubes have a Time dimension, and a supermarket chain's sales cube may have additional dimensions, such as Store, Product, and Customer. Each dimension can also have one or more *hierarchies*. The Product dimension may have a category and subcategory hierarchy. Individual members in these dimensions identify a coordinate where you can examine measures, such as Unit Sales, Store Sales, Profit, and Cost. For example, you could ask the value of Profit in the Redmond store for Canned Vegetables during August of 2008 — the dimensions Store, Product, and Time specify the coordinate for the measure Profit.

OLAP and data mining are two complementary technologies for BI. Large cubes often have millions of members in some dimensions, and fact tables can contain billions of transaction records. Finding useful information in such a large space is challenging. There is definitely a requirement to apply data mining techniques to dig for patterns from these cubes.

In this chapter, you will learn about the following:

- The principles of OLAP
- The relationship between OLAP and data mining
- How to apply data mining on OLAP cubes

In this chapter, you will see a few sample models demonstrating some popular scenarios. You will learn how to create OLAP mining models using SQL Server 2008 UI tools and Analysis Object Models (AMO).

To assist with this chapter, content files are included in the `Chapter13.zip` archive available at `www.wiley.com/go/data_mining_SQL_2008`. This archive contains the following files:

- `Chapter13 DMX.dmx` — Contains all the DMX queries used in this chapter
- `Chapter13 MDX.mdx` — Contains all the MDX queries used in this chapter
- `Chapter13 code.txt` — Contains code snippets from this chapter
- `foodmart.zip` — Contains a SQL Server backup of a modified foodmart database
- `Foodmart 2008` — An Analysis Services project containing the OLAP cube and models referenced in this chapter

Introducing OLAP

OLAP is used for decision-support systems to analyze aggregated information for sales, finance, budget, and many other types of applications, whereas Online Transaction Processing (OLTP) is mainly used to record transactions of daily operations, such as updating an account balance for a bank transaction.

An OLTP database schema is not organized in a manner that can easily provide the summarized information required by managers at different levels of an organization. Managers need aggregated data from which they can view reports and analyze the trends. They need to know the key indications that affect their business success in order to make critical decisions. They need to find how their enterprise's workload is affected by seasonal and yearly trends so that they can plan and optimize resources.

The OLTP system is not designed for these kinds of decision-support queries for two reasons. The first is performance. Getting the summarized information requires querying a large amount of transaction data with joins among many different dimension tables. These queries may take hours for a relational database system to compute. Meanwhile, the OLTP system has heavy operational duties. The second reason is the schema. The database schema in the OLTP system is not designed to answer decision-support questions. Extensive numbers of joins among OLTP tables are required to generate the reports that managers need.

An OLAP cube is built for decision-support queries. A cube is a multidimensional database. A typical cube contains a set of well-defined dimensions, such as Customer, Product, Store, and Time. Each dimension contains many members. For example, each product and each product category are members of the Product dimension. Dimension members are organized in hierarchies. For example, the hierarchy in the Product dimension is All Products ⇨ Category ⇨ SubCategory ⇨ Product Name. You can query aggregated values on different levels of a hierarchy.

A cube has a set of measures, such as Store Sales and Unit Sales. Measures come from a transaction table (a fact table), where details of each transaction are stored. These measures are preaggregated (or partially preaggregated) based on the dimension hierarchies. For example, the store sales of beverage products in 2008 in all stores in the state of Washington are calculated during the cube-processing stage. When a user queries this information, the result can be retrieved very fast thanks to the precalculation and the multidimensional index structure.

In summary, OLAP is about aggregating measures based on dimension hierarchies and storing these precalculated aggregations in a special data structure. With the help of preaggregations and special indexes, you can query aggregated data and get decision-support query results back in real time, which traditionally had to be done in batches and in offline mode.

Microsoft initially introduced OLAP Services in SQL Server 7.0 and enhanced it (in terms of functionality) in the SQL Server 2000 and SQL Server 2005 releases. The SQL Server 2008 release significantly improved the OLAP scalability and flexibility. This chapter describes the key OLAP concepts, using the Sales cube as an example. The Sales cube contains sales data of an imaginary supermarket chain — FoodMart — that specializes in food products. The data originally shipped as an Analysis Services sample database in SQL Server 7.0 and SQL Server 2000 but is modified for this chapter.

For more detailed technical information about OLAP, refer to SQL Server Books Online and OLAP-specific books.

Understanding Star and Snowflake Schemas

A *star schema* is a database schema with a star shape. The heart of the schema is the *fact table*, which records the details of each transaction. The fact table contains a large amount of records, and it is the largest table in the database. Surrounding the fact table is a set of dimension tables that describe the properties of each dimension.

Figure 13-1 shows the star schema of the FoodMart retail store database. Sales_Fact is the fact table that contains every sales transaction from all

FoodMart stores. `Product`, `Customer`, `Time_by_day`, `Store`, and `Promotion` are all dimension tables. The fact table is fully normalized. It links to the dimension tables through foreign keys. In addition to foreign keys, a fact table contains a set of numeric columns, which are the measures. A star schema is a typical schema in a database warehouse.

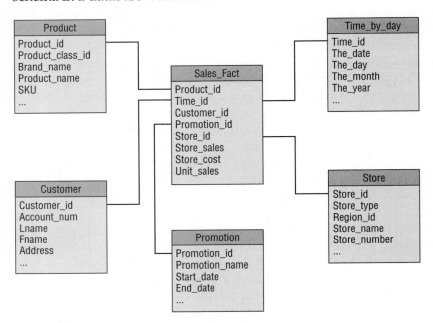

Figure 13-1 Star schema of the FoodMart database

Sometimes a dimension table is partially normalized. For example, in the `Customer` table, the `Education` attribute contains the educational level of a customer (such as `Bachelors`, `Masters`, and so on). To normalize this attribute, you can create a separate `Education` table that contains two columns: `Education_id` and `Description`. The `Education` attribute in the `Customer` table is changed to `Education_id`, which is a foreign key from `Education` table. `Education` becomes a lookup table for the `Education_id` attribute of the `Customer` table. You can create more lookup tables for other attributes in the dimension table. The snowflake shape formed by these relationships is called a *snowflake schema*.

Star schemas can be considered special kinds of snowflake schemas, where there is no lookup table. Both the star schema and the snowflake schema are popular schemas in data warehouse design.

Understanding Dimension and Hierarchy

Each cube contains a number of *dimensions*. The Sales cube in FoodMart contains five dimensions: Product, Customer, Time, Store, and Promotion.

A dimension has dimension members. Each dimension member is a uniquely identifiable unit within a dimension. For example, each customer is identified by `Customer_id` in the Customer dimension. `Customer_id` is the dimension key. A dimension may contain a large number of members. For example, the FoodMart supermarket may have millions of customers.

A *dimension member* has a set of *attributes*. In the Customer dimension, a member has attributes such as gender, education, state, city, country, and so on. Each column in the dimension table could be a member attribute.

Attributes may contain relationships among them. For example, a country has a number of states, and a state has a number of cities. These relationships form *hierarchies*, as shown in Figure 13-2.

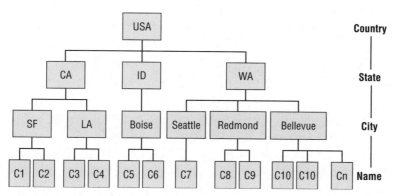

Figure 13-2 Dimension hierarchy

Each hierarchy has a name. The geography hierarchy in Figure 13-2 is named Geo in the Customer dimension. Country, State, City, and Name are the levels of the hierarchy. USA is a member in the Country level. CA, ID, and WA are members in the State level. The lowest level in the Geo hierarchy is Name. Each customer is a member in the Name level.

Hierarchy is a very important concept in OLAP. The hierarchy level is the basic unit of aggregation. Users can query aggregated data at different levels of the hierarchy (for example, to obtain the total beverage sales in the state of Washington).

The Geo hierarchy is a *natural hierarchy* — the relationships among levels exist naturally. You can also define an attribute hierarchy without having a natural relationship. For example, you can build a hierarchy Gender ⇨ Education ⇨ Name. Based on this hierarchy, the customers are separated first by their gender and then by their educational level. You can query aggregated data about store sales to male customers with bachelor's degrees based on this hierarchy.

Analysis Services allows each dimension to have multiple hierarchies.

Understanding Measures and Measure Groups

Measures are the numeric values to be aggregated by the cube. They are based on the numeric columns of the fact table. There are three measure columns in `Sales_Fact`: `Store_Sales`, `Unit_Sales`, and `Store_Cost`. Measures are the numeric data of primary interest to end users browsing a cube. Each measure specifies an aggregate function that determines how values in the measure's source column are aggregated. This function also determines how measured values for sibling members are aggregated to produce a value for their parent. The aggregation functions include `Sum`, `Min`, `Max`, `Average`, `Distinct Count`, and so on.

A cube contains a special type of dimension that contains a member for each measure. This dimension is called the *Measures dimension*. The Measures dimension doesn't contain hierarchies. It is always flat with one level. While browsing the cube, you can slice by a member in the Measures dimension to display values for the selected measure. You can also place the Measures dimension on an axis to view all measures of the cube.

The fact table stores the value of each measure of each transaction. Before SQL Server 2005, each cube could have only one fact table. In SQL Server 2005 and SQL Server 2008, a cube can have multiple fact tables. For example, a cube can store both sales information and inventory information, with one sales fact table and one inventory fact table. Because a fact table is a physical table in a data warehouse and not an OLAP object, the term *measure group* was created for the OLAP representation of the groups of measures and related attributes. A cube may have multiple measure groups.

Understanding Cube Processing and Storage

A cube contains a set of dimensions and measures. There are two steps to processing a cube: dimension processing (if a dimension hasn't been processed previously) and cube processing. *Dimension processing* reads dimension data from underlying dimension tables, builds the dimension structure, creates hierarchies, and assigns members to proper levels of the hierarchy. After all dimensions are processed, cube processing can be started.

The main task of *cube processing* is to precalculate aggregations based on the dimension hierarchies. When there are many dimensions and each dimension contains several levels and many members, the total number of aggregations could be exponential. One of the challenges of cube processing is to choose the optimal number of aggregations to precalculate. Other aggregated values can be derived from those precalculated measures efficiently. For example, if the monthly `Store_Sales` values are preaggregated, quarterly and yearly `Store_Sales` values can be derived easily.

Both dimension processing and cube processing have the options of *full processing* and *incremental processing*. During the processing stage, Analysis Services also builds bitmap indexes that allow efficient access to the aggregated cells.

Analysis Services allows a cube to be separated into different partitions. For example, for the FoodMart Sales cube, each month's fact data can be separated into a partition. Partitions can be processed individually. By the end of each month, only the newest partition needs to be processed. Because a partition can contain a huge amount of aggregations, Analysis Services provides the following three different storage modes for these partitions:

- **Multidimensional OLAP (MOLAP)** — The data of a partition is stored in the special format of Analysis Services, which allows efficient retrieval of multidimensional data. MOLAP is by far the most common storage format.

- **Relational OLAP (ROLAP)** — All data is stored in a relational database management system (RDBMS). Additional tables are created to store precalculated aggregations. ROLAP has the advantage of scalability as compared to the MOLAP structure. However, the performance of ROLAP is less than optimal.

- **Hybrid OLAP (HOLAP)** — The HOLAP partition stores the fact table in an RDBMS. All aggregations are stored in the special format of Analysis Services (just like MOLAP). When your query requires aggregated data, Analysis Services can return these aggregations efficiently because they are stored in its special format. When your query requires atomic-level facts, Analysis Services generates SQL to query the fact table in the RDBMS.

Using Proactive Caching

The OLAP server is an efficient counting engine that calculates all aggregations based on the dimension definitions. A cube can be considered simply as a cache that stores precalculated aggregations. MOLAP is the most popular storage mode because it has a special structure that is optimized for analytical queries. MOLAP has good performance, but it requires the cube to be processed. This is in conflict with the real-time concept. A ROLAP cube, on the other hand, directly queries the relational data source. It lets users immediately browse the most recent changes in a data source, but it can have significantly poorer performance than MOLAP storage.

You may have applications in which your users need to see recent data, but you want the performance advantages of MOLAP storage. The *proactive caching* feature first introduced in Analysis Services 2005 can provide a balance between the enhanced performance of MOLAP storage and the immediacy of ROLAP storage.

With proactive caching, queries against an OLAP object are made against either ROLAP storage or MOLAP storage, depending on whether recent changes have occurred in the data. The query engine directs queries against source data in MOLAP storage until changes occur in the data source. After these changes occur, cached MOLAP objects are dropped and querying switches to ROLAP storage, while the MOLAP objects are rebuilt in cache. After the MOLAP objects are rebuilt and processed, queries are switched again to the MOLAP storage. The cache refresh can occur extremely quickly for a small partition.

Caching may also be used without dropping the current MOLAP objects. Queries then continue against the MOLAP objects while data is read into and processed in a new cache. This method provides better performance, but may result in queries returning old data while the new cache is being built.

Proactive caching features simplify the process of managing data obsolescence. If a transaction occurs on the source database (such as the addition of a new dimension member or new fact transaction), the existing cache becomes obsolete. The proactive caching settings determine how frequently the multidimensional cache is rebuilt, whether the outdated MOLAP storage is queried while the cache is rebuilt, and whether the cache is rebuilt on a schedule or based on changes in the database.

Querying a Cube

After a cube is processed, you can query it to retrieve aggregated information. The OLE DB for OLAP specification has defined a query language for querying OLAP cubes. The language is called Multidimensional Expressions (MDX). MDX is similar to SQL in the sense that it follows the Select ... From ... Where framework. But that is where the similarity ends. MDX is not an extension of SQL, and its syntax is much more complicated than SQL. SQL deals only with two-dimensional data, whereas MDX allows for data to be queried with a theoretically unlimited number of dimensions.

In SQL, the Select clause is used to define the column layout for a query, and the Where clause is used to define the row layout. In MDX, the Select clause can be used to define several axis dimensions, and the Where clause is used to restrict multidimensional data to a specific dimension or member. MDX also contains hundreds of functions, which helps users specify dimension navigations and calculations. The detailed syntax of MDX can be found in SQL Server Books Online.

Listing 13-1 is a simple example of an MDX query to retrieve the total Unit Sales and Store Sales of beverage products.

```
Select NON EMPTY
    {Measures.[Unit Sales], Measures.[Store Sales]} on columns,
      {Store.Stores.members} on rows
From [Sales]
Where Product.Drink.Beverages
```

Listing 13-1 Simple MDX query

Table 13-1 shows the result of Listing 13-1.

Table 13-1 Results of an MDX Query to Retrieve Beverage Product Sales

	UNIT SALES	STORE SALES
Store 1	2085	4018.15
Store 2	3898	8002.32
Store 3	3985	8123.68

Performing Calculations

A cube stores aggregated information. The aggregated values are based on the measures in the measure group. The most common arithmetic operator is sum. However, other arithmetic functions may be applied to measures as well (for example, min, max, count, average, and so on).

A cube may also contain *calculated measures*, which are measures that are derived from other basic measures. For example, you can create a calculated measure Profit based on Store Sales and Store Cost using the following MDX expression:

```
Profit = [Store Sales] - [Store Cost]
```

From the user's point of view, Profit is just another measure similar to Store Sales and Store Cost. Calculated measures are evaluated during query processing, whereas other measures are aggregated during the cube processing stage.

Apart from calculated measures, you can also create calculated members for dimensions. However, because a measure is a special kind of dimension, a calculated measure is a special type of calculated member. For example, Listing 13-2 creates two calculated members (1st Half Sales and 2nd Half Sales) in the Time dimensions and asks for the store sales for these two calculated members.

```
WITH
    MEMBER [Time].[Time].[1st Half Sales] AS'Sum({[Time].[Time].[Q1],
            [Time].[Time].[Q2]})'
    MEMBER [Time].[Time].[2nd Half Sales] AS'Sum({[Time].[Time].[Q3],
            [Time].[Time].[Q4]})'
SELECT
        {[Time].[Time].[1st Half Sales], [Time].[Time].[2nd Half Sales]}
            ON COLUMNS
FROM Sales
WHERE [Measures].[Store Sales]
```

Listing 13-2 Calcluated members in MDX

A cell in a cube can also contain calculations. These cells are called *calculated cells*. With a calculated cell, you can define an MDX formula that can be used to supply a new value for each cell in a specific group of cells. These cells are evaluated during query processing by the MDX formula engine. For example, you can define the next year's new sales quota for the Northwest region (a subcube) as the actual value multiplied by 120 percent. In Analysis Services 2005, the calculated cell feature was enhanced to use *MDX scripts*, which enable users to write calculation scripts with MDX statements and debug the calculations step by step.

Browsing a Cube

There are a dozen OLAP client tools available in the market that allow the interactive querying of OLAP cubes and the generation of dynamic reports. These tools include three Microsoft Office family products — Excel, Office Web Components (OWC), and ProClarity — as well as many third-party OLAP client tools (such as Panorama). These products provide more sophisticated browsers for visualizing cube data in either numeric format or graphic format. Users can easily slice and dice the cube to generate reports with these tools. Figures 13-3 and 13-4 show examples of how you can use Excel to browse the Sales cube. Figure 13-3 analyzes store sales for females and males. Figure 13-4 analyzes product sales during a Sale Days promotion.

Understanding Unified Dimension Modeling

Data is stored in various data sources (for example, heterogeneous relational databases, text files, Excel, and OLAP cubes), and because the data models for relational and multidimensional data are different, you must use different APIs to access these data types. To address this issue, Analysis Services 2005 introduced the *Unified Dimension Model* (*UDM*). UDM provides a bridge between the user and the data source and allows the user to define a single metadata model for dimensions and facts from various sources.

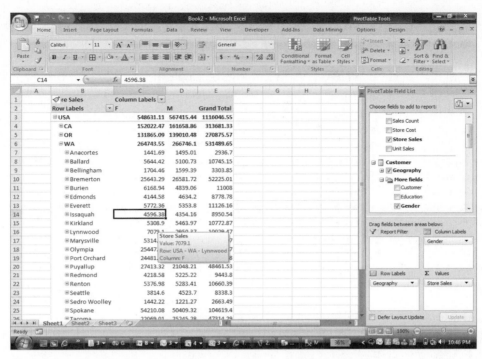

Figure 13-3 Browsing the Sales cube to analyze store sales for female and male customers

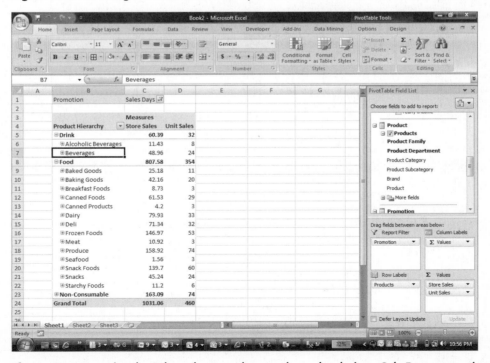

Figure 13-4 Browsing the Sales cube to analyze product sales during a Sale Days promotion

The following are some key benefits of UDM:

■ **Provides a standard model for all BI applications** — There are various types of BI components for enterprise applications (for example, data warehouse, OLAP, data mining, reporting, and so on). UDM provides a standard model that all these BI technologies can understand, and they all benefit from its richness. This reduces the number of data models in an enterprise. Figure 13-5 shows an example of UDM. The left side presents the contents of the UDM, including a few measures and a set of dimensions. The right side shows those elements included in the current query.

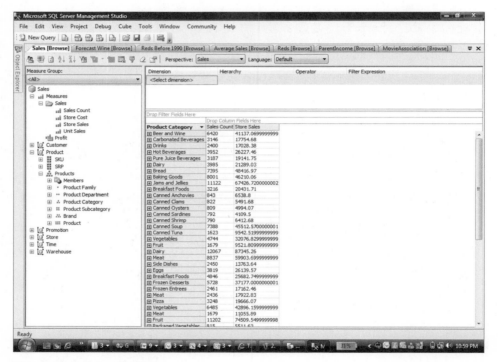

Figure 13-5 A simple UDM

■ **Provides a rich data-modeling tool** — Dimensions contain hierarchies. For example, the Product dimension contains the hierarchy All Product ⇨ Product Category ⇨ Product SubCategory ⇨ Product SKU. You can perform analyses based on such hierarchies, first viewing totals by category, and then drilling down to their subcategories, and subsequently to the lowest SKU level. UDM allows the definition of such hierarchies. Each hierarchy is simply a sequence of attributes that can then be used in queries to ease such drill-down/drill-up scenarios. A dimension may contain multiple hierarchies. For example, the Time dimension contains two hierarchies: fiscal time and calendar time. Figure 13-6 shows an example of dimension modeling. The Warehouse dimension contains a set of attributes and four hierarchies. The source table for this dimension has two tables: `warehouse` and `warehouse_class`.

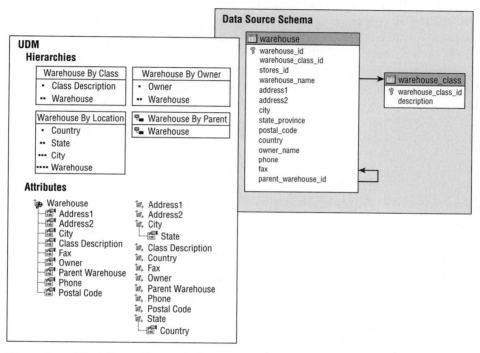

Figure 13-6 UDM dimension example

- **Provides high query performance** — A UDM may contain one or more cubes. In most cases, cube aggregations are preprocessed. This allows user queries to be executed rapidly.

- **Provides advanced analytics** — UDM not only provides simple aggregations, it also allows you to define advanced calculations based on the powerful MDX and DMX. In many cases, you want to know more than just aggregations. For example, you may want to know the three-month moving average for each time period, the year-on-year growth in each period, the sales and inventory forecast, and so on. With MDX and DMX, you can perform sophisticated calculations on UDM.

- **Supports closing the loop** — UDM not only enables you to visualize information, it also allows you to act on the data. From the aggregated values, you can drill-through the source data and make changes. In addition, it is possible to update summary numbers. For example, consider a budgeting scenario. Although the budgeted amount might eventually be known down to a detailed level (for example, by team and account), values might be known only at a more summarized level (such as by department and account type) until that point.

Figure 13-7 shows the overall architecture of UDM. Consumer applications (most often BI applications) can access the Analysis Services UDM via the XML for Analysis (XMLA) protocol. The XMLA commands embed the DMX, MDX, or SQL queries. UDM gets these queries and then executes the query directly against itself or forwards it to other sources (such as an RDBMS or text files), depending on the query type and data that the UDM contains. The result is mapped back in an XML rowset format to the client application. In this way, various client applications can use the same API to query the same data model and get back either relational or multidimensional query results.

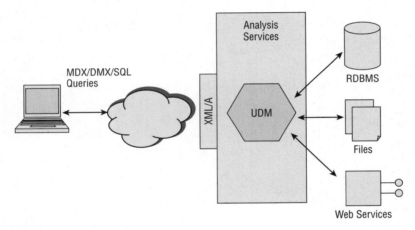

Figure 13-7 Architecture of UDM

IS UDM JUST A CUBE?

UDM is a broader concept than just a cube. It's more about dimension modeling than aggregation in that it integrates both relational and mutlidimensional technologies. You can think of a UDM as a combination of cubes and dimensions. You can create a UDM without actually building a cube. In this case, the UDM will forward queries to the relational source during query processing, although the performance may not be as fast as having a cube serve as the aggregation cache. It is also possible for a UDM to contain multiple cubes, although in most cases, a UDM contains a single cube that has one or more measure groups.

Understanding the Relationship between OLAP and Data Mining

Both OLAP and data mining are important analytical technologies in the BI family. OLAP is good at aggregating a large amount of transaction data based on the dimension definitions. The following are some typical questions answered by OLAP:

- What is the total sales amount of beverage products in the past three months in the Northwest region?
- What are the top 10 products sold in all stores last month?
- What are the store sales for male and female customers, respectively?
- What is the daily sales difference during a promotional period versus a normal period?

The core technique of OLAP is aggregation calculation. An OLAP server is a special kind of database server that deals with multidimensional data. It has most of the challenges that RDBMS has, including indexing, querying, persistence, data caching, and so forth. However, because of its multidimensional nature, an OLAP server can't just simply apply relational technology without major enhancements. For example, OLAP indexing requires indexes based on multidimensional coordinates. It uses a specially designed data structure based on a bitmap index. MDX is more complicated than SQL is. It has many predefined functions for dimension navigation.

Data mining is good at finding the hidden patterns of a data set by analyzing correlations among attribute values. As explained in Chapter 1, there are two kinds of data mining techniques: supervised and unsupervised. *Supervised data mining* requires the user to specify a target attribute and a set of input attributes. The typical supervised data mining algorithms include decision trees, Naïve Bayes, and neural networks. An *unsupervised data mining* technique doesn't have to have a predictable attribute. Clustering is a good example of unsupervised data mining. It groups heterogeneous data points into subgroups so that data points in each subgroup are more or less homogeneous.

The following are typical questions answered by data mining:

- What is the profile of customers who like to buy the newest model of digital cameras?
- What products should be recommended to this particular customer?
- What's the estimated sales amount for digital cameras in the next three months?
- How should the customer base be segmented?

Whereas most of OLAP techniques come from the database family, data mining techniques come from three academic fields: statistics, machine learning, and database technology.

One of the fundamental processes of data mining is to analyze correlations among attributes and their values. Statisticians have been working on this issue for centuries. There are many profound statistical theories that still apply today. Most data mining algorithms use more or less statistical techniques, such as Naïve Bayes and clustering.

Machine learning has introduced many new algorithms for information discovery, some of which can be applied to data mining. The most common algorithms are decision trees and neural networks. Other algorithms, such as genetic algorithms and fuzzy logic, are also included in some data mining packages.

Although traditional statisticians don't pay too much attention to data volume, the database community knows how to deal with large amounts of data. For example, many popular association algorithms for analyzing product associations of large transaction tables were proposed by database researchers.

Mining Aggregated Data

Both OLAP and data mining are key members of the BI technology family. They are complementary and can benefit from each other's characteristics to provide deep analysis. OLAP can help data mining tasks with the data transformation step, thanks to its data aggregation engine. In many cases, patterns can be found only in aggregated data. It is difficult to discover patterns directly from the fact table. For example, analyzing the sales of snow tires at the city level can be challenging for many data mining algorithms because there are too many cities. However, when data is aggregated to the state level, these algorithms may easily discover a pattern, such as "the most important factor for sales of snow tires is region; people in the Northeast are more likely to purchase snow tires."

NOTE A large retail customer asked us to do a data mining project. They gave us a fact table with tens of millions of transactions from the past few years. Their dimension tables contained thousands of items and hundreds of stores. The business problem was to forecast weekly sales for each item at each store. With a relational database, it took about 1 hour for the computer to pull out related sales information about an item (for thousands of items!). Using a cube, it took about 3 seconds to get the same information. If you have a large amount of transaction data and your mining model requires aggregated data, you should consider using OLAP technologies for data transformation.

OLAP Pattern Discovery Needs

A cube is a well-structured database. There are often millions of members in a dimension and tens of millions of aggregated values in a cube. Like any relational database, a cube contains hidden patterns such as sales trends, product associations, customer segments, and so on. An OLAP cube needs data mining techniques to discover the inside information. The following is a list of typical business questions about OLAP cubes that require data mining techniques:

- **Market basket analysis about products** — Market basket analysis of product associations is a frequent marketing problem. Store managers want to know which products sell together in order to do promotional cross-selling.

- **Customer segmentation** — Store managers also like to group customers into segments using customer demographic information, as well as aggregated measures (for example, monthly spending at the store). Segmentation can be done on dimensions other than the Customer dimension. For example, the marketing department of a retail chain may want to cluster its stores based on store attributes and sales.

- **Customer classification** — Based on the customer attributes in the Customer dimension and measures, it is possible to build a classification-type mining model to analyze the customer information. For example, a store manager might want to know the profile of customers who are interested in applying for a gold membership card.

- **Sales trend analysis** — Based on historical product sales, a store manager might like to know projected future sales amounts. For example, what are the potential sales of all beverages in all stores in the state of Washington next month?

- **Target promotion** — Suppose that a store ordered a product — for example, a new kind of beer. The store manager wants to know which customers are most interested in buying this product. The store manager can apply data mining techniques to discover the profile of customers who are interested in buying beer and send mailings to those people with similar profiles.

OLAP Mining versus Relational Mining

The fundamentals of OLAP mining and relational mining are the same. The OLAP mining model and the relational mining model use the same set of data mining algorithms. The only difference is the mining column's binding. Instead of being bound to table columns, the mining columns are bound to dimension attributes, measures, and measure groups.

Because the OLAP cube contains precalculated aggregations, attributes bound to measures can be accessed very efficiently. This information can be derived from relational tables as well. However, this requires extra data transformation steps. In addition to aggregated data, dimensions contain hierarchies in a cube. This hierarchy information defines relationships among attributes and can be used during data mining processing for attribute roll-up.

In SQL Server 2000, mining models built on OLAP cubes had different structures and metadata than those built on relational tables. In SQL Server 2005 and 2008, there are almost no differences between OLAP mining models and relational mining models. In this chapter, *OLAP mining model* refers to a mining model built on OLAP cubes, and *relational mining model* refers to a mining model built on relational data tables.

The OLAP mining model often contains nested tables. The case table of an OLAP mining model is always one of the dimensions, and nested tables always come from one of the fact tables using another dimension attribute as the nested key.

Probably the best way to understand the OLAP mining model is to think in a relational way. Figure 13-8 provides a relational view of an OLAP mining model. The model analyzes customer segmentation based on customer profiles such as age, gender, the list of products they purchased, and the associated quantity. Some mining model attributes come directly from relational tables (dimension tables), such as gender and age. Some attributes come from nested tables (the fact table), such as quantity (the aggregated value of unit sales). `Product Name` is an attribute that comes indirectly from the `Sales_fact` table, by joining the `Product` dimension table through the lookup key (`Product_id`).

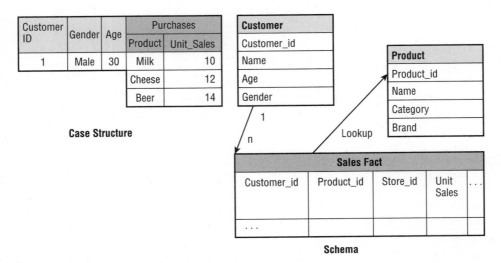

Figure 13-8 Relational view of an OLAP mining model

Building OLAP Mining Models Using Wizards and Editors

You have just learned about the basic concepts of OLAP, the relationship of OLAP and data mining, and a few business problems for which data mining techniques can be applied to OLAP cubes. In this section, you build a few typical mining models on a cube. The best tools for creating OLAP mining models are the Data Mining Wizard and the Data Mining Designer. Note that you can build an OLAP mining model only if it is based on a cube located in the same Analysis Services database.

Using the Data Mining Wizard

The Data Mining Wizard is a handy and powerful tool to help you build data mining models. There are two branches in the wizard based on the types of the data source: the relational branch and the multidimensional branch. Chapter 4 showed you how to build mining models using the data mining wizard on relational tables. Now, you will use the other half of the wizard to build a few OLAP mining models. The source cube is the Sales cube of the FoodMart database, as described earlier in this chapter.

Building the Customer Segmentation Model

The first model to build is about customer segmentation. You want to group customers based on their demographics (Occupation, Marital Status, Member Card, and so forth), as well as the total Store Sales for the segmentation. The demographics are dimension attributes, and Store Sales is a measure that contains the aggregated value of each transaction for each customer. In this model, the case table is the Customer dimension, and there is no nested table.

To invoke the Data Mining Wizard, access the context menu by right-clicking the `Mining Structures` folder in the Solution Explorer window of BI Dev Studio. Because the source data is a cube, select the From Existing Cube option in the Select the Definition Method page, as shown in Figure 13-9.

After selecting the cube as the data source, select the Microsoft Clustering algorithm as the mining technique for this model.

The next two steps are to select the source cube dimension and specify the case key from the source cube dimensions. For the OLAP mining model, a case key is a dimension attribute, and the dimension that contains the case key is the case dimension. The case key may or may not be a dimension key. For example, you can select Last Name as the case key. You can even choose Gender as the case key if you want only two cases for the training data: Male and Female. In this example, because you want to segment all customers, choose Customer (the dimension key) as the case key (see Figure 13-10).

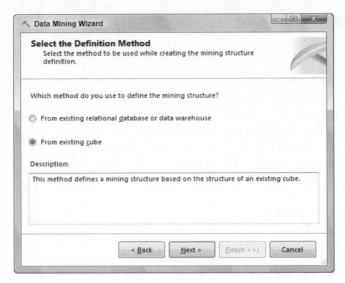

Figure 13-9 Selecting an existing cube as the data source

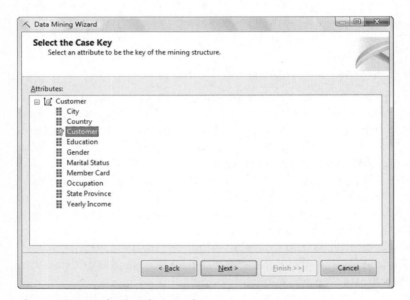

Figure 13-10 Selecting the case key

After you specify the case key, the Data Mining Wizard asks you to select case-level attributes from a set of related attributes and measures.

For this example, select the following attributes (see Figure 13-11):

- Marital Status
- Member Card

- Num Cars Owned

- Num Children At Home

- Occupation

- Yearly Income

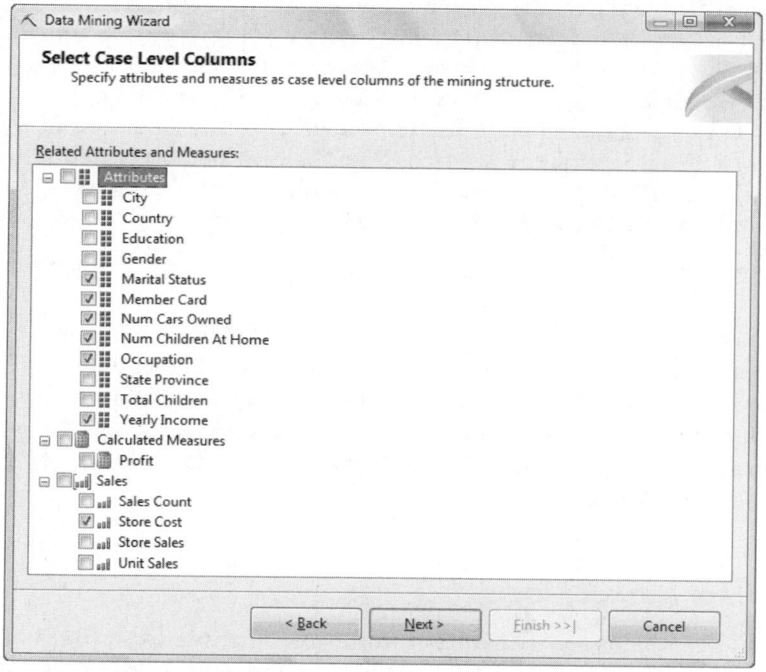

Figure 13-11 Selecting case-level attributes and measures

Select Store Cost as the measure (also shown in Figure 13-11).

Because a clustering algorithm doesn't require a predictable attribute, specify all the selected columns as input on the Specify Mining Column Usage Wizard page.

You have now defined the mining model. All you have left to do is name the mining structure and model on the last page of the wizard and then process the model.

CHOOSING DIMENSION PROPERTIES

In this example, you use the dimension key Customer as the case key. Because all of the dimension properties have a 1-*n* relationship with the dimension key,

(continued)

CHOOSING DIMENSION PROPERTIES *(continued)*

you can choose any other properties as case-level attributes for the mining model.

You can choose dimension properties other than the dimension key as the case key (such as City). In this case, your model will cluster cities based on the attributes you specified in the model. Most attributes in the Customer dimension (such as Gender and Occupation) don't have a 1-*n* relationship with City. It doesn't make sense to select these attributes to cluster City. However, if there is an attribute hierarchy, such as Country ➪ State ➪ City ➪ Customer, you can select Country and State as input attributes to the cluster City. Country and State are both at a higher level in the hierarchy than the case key City is, and they have 1-*n* relationships to City. So, the wizard allows you to select Country and State after you specify City as the case key.

NOTE You may have noticed that the number of training cases in an OLAP mining model is not exactly the same as the number of cases in a relational mining model built directly on the dimension table. This is because there is always an additional member, called Unknown, in an OLAP dimension. This also affects the prediction probability slightly.

Creating a Market Basket Model

Market basket analysis is a popular data mining task. In this example, you will do some market basket analysis of customer purchases in the state of Washington based on the Sales cube. The algorithm to use for this task is Microsoft Association Rules.

Before starting to build the model, you must define the basket and item. Because the model is for analyzing customer purchase behavior, the unit of a basket is a customer. A customer buys a set of products, and the purchase details are modeled as a nested table. In an OLAP mining model, a case table is mapped to a case dimension, and a nested table is mapped to a measure group dimension. The dimension (which serves as a lookup table for the measure group) is called a *nested dimension*. In this example, the case dimension is the Customer dimension and the nested dimension is Product.

You use the Data Mining Wizard to define the model. Similar to the customer segmentation model in the previous example, choose Customer as the case dimension and the Customer attribute as the case key. Don't select any attribute other than this case key in the case level. (You may select properties in the Customer dimension if needed.) After selecting the case key, the mining structure is displayed, as shown in Figure 13-12.

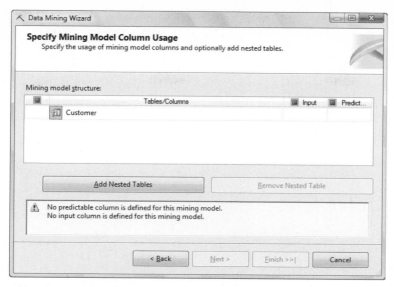

Figure 13-12 Specifying mining model column usage

Add the nested table by clicking the Add Nested Tables button shown toward the bottom of Figure 13-12. A pop-up wizard appears, as shown in Figure 13-13. You use this pop-up wizard to add nested tables for the mining structure. In this example, you are creating associations between product types, so your nested dimension is Product, and the nested key is the attribute Product Subcategory. If you wanted to see associations of individual products, you could instead choose the dimension key Product to be the nested key.

NOTE If you are mining a cube with several measure groups, ensure that you select the key attribute from the appropriate measure group containing the relationship you want. For example, if Product appears in a Sales measure group and an Inventory measure group, you would choose the nested key from the Product dimension in the Sales measure group to analyze sales.

Because this model is purely for analyzing the relationships among products, you don't need to include any other attributes in the nested table, nor do you need to add other nested tables. The mining structure is shown in Figure 13-14. The nested table is named as the measure group by default, and the nested key for your model is Product Subcategory. You specify the nested table as predictable by clicking the Predict box for the Product nested table.

Now that you've defined the mining structure, the Data Mining Wizard asks you to slice the source cube if necessary. Your market basket model is for analyzing the cross-selling patterns in the state of Washington. Use the cube slice to slice the customers based on the Country ⇨ State Province ⇨ City ⇨

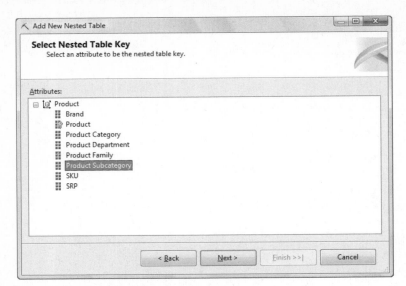

Figure 13-13 Adding the nested table key

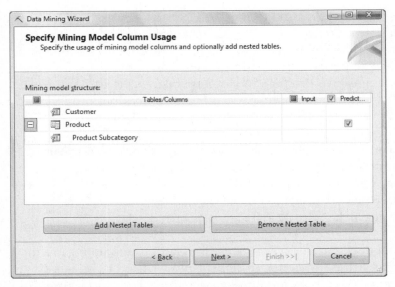

Figure 13-14 Mining structure for market basket analysis

Customer hierarchy, and use the Filter expression drop-down list to select WA at the State level, as shown in Figure 13-15.

On the next page, specify how much data is held out for testing. Because there is no built-in associative model evaluation in SQL Server 2008, you can set the holdout percentage to 0. On the next and final page, it is often a good

Figure 13-15 Slicing the cube

idea to check the Enable Drill through box when you're creating OLAP mining models. This will allow you to inspect the cases to ensure they contain exactly what you expect. Finally, name the structure and model, and then click Finish.

WORKING WITH TRANSACTIONS

The model you just defined analyzes the products that customers tend to purchase together. If a customer bought a case of beer in March, and then purchased some diapers in September, this model considers beer and diapers to be correlated because no time constraints are specified. This may not satisfy the marketing department's business requirements. There are two ways to address this issue.

The first method is to use cube slices to limit the purchases to a given day. But you may miss some patterns because your analysis is based on only one day.

The second method is to add a transaction dimension on the cube so that each row in the fact table contains a transaction ID. You then specify the case dimension as `Transaction` and the nested dimension as `Product`. In this way, you analyze the purchase patterns within each transaction. If the same

(continued)

WORKING WITH TRANSACTIONS *(continued)*

customer completed three transactions in the cube, these transactions are considered three independent cases.

Market basket analysis is not limited to customer purchases. You can model different business problems by specifying the correct sets of cases and nest tables and/or dimensions. For example, if you want to analyze the series of stores in which a customer tends to shop, you can set `Customer` as the case dimension and `Store` as the nested dimension. If you want to analyze the relationship among various promotions each store runs, you can set the `Store` as the case dimension and `Promotion` as the nested dimension.

Creating a Sales Forecast Model

Forecasting is yet another important data mining task. A cube usually contains a time dimension. It is natural for cube users (those who consume cube information through queries and reports) to ask to forecast cube measures. For example, you may want to forecast how many bottles of red wine will be sold in Washington stores over the next three months, or how much revenue each store can make over the next two years.

In this example, you build a mining model using the Microsoft Time Series algorithm on the Sales cube. The objective of the model is to perform a monthly forecast about the `Unit Sales`, `Store Sales`, and `Store Cost` for each store.

Because the model is for forecasting each store's sales, the case dimension is Store. Choose the dimension key `Store` as the case key, as shown in Figure 13-16.

You learned in Chapter 8 that there are different ways to model time series data. Because the case dimension Store doesn't contain time information, the time information is modeled in the nested table. Click the Add Nested Tables button in the Mining Model Column Usage page, as shown in Figure 13-17.

Clicking this button launches a mini-wizard where you specify the settings for a nested table based on a related dimension. On the first page, select the Time dimension to be the nested dimension. On the next page you specify a dimension attribute to be the nested key. It is important that you choose a time attribute that is unique across time. For example, if you choose the `Month` attribute, your series will have only 12 values, regardless of how many years of data are available in the cube. The values for each measure will be the aggregate values across all years. For example, the value of `Unit Sales` for January will be the sum of all `Unit Sales` that happened in January of every year. Therefore, for the purpose of time series forecasting, you add the time attribute `Year Month` — which is a concatenation of the year and the month — so you have a unique value to use as the nested key. This modified version of the FoodMart model is available on this book's companion website (`www.wiley.com/go/data_mining_SQL_2008`). Figure 13-18 shows the selection of the `Year Month` attribute as the nested key.

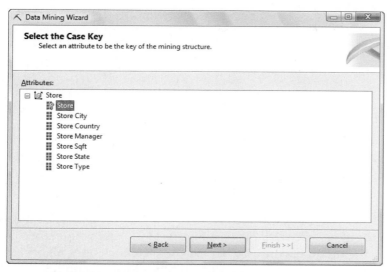

Figure 13-16 Selecting Store as the case key

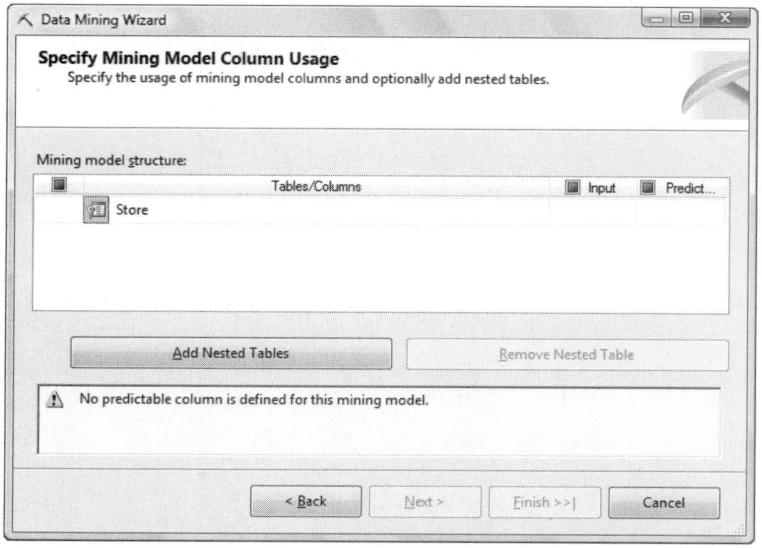

Figure 13-17 Mining model columns

Figure 13-18 Specifying Year Month as the nested table key

On the Select Nested Table Columns page, select the cost and sales measures to be both input and predictable (see Figure 13-19). As you learned in Chapter 8, one of the unique features of the Microsoft Time Series algorithm is cross-prediction among series. For example, if the previous month's `Store Sales` has a strong correlation with this month's `Store Cost`, the algorithm will discover this pattern and use `Store Sales` to forecast `Store Cost`.

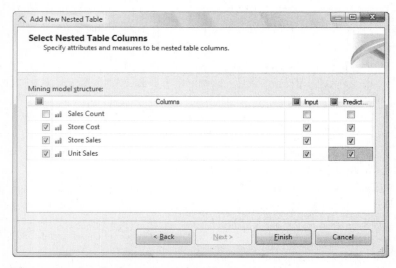

Figure 13-19 Selecting measures as time series

Figure 13-20 shows the mining structure for the forecasting model. The case key is `Store`, the nested key is `Year Month`, and the three measures are included in the nested table. There are two dozen stores in the Store dimension of the Sales cube, and each store has three selected measures. There are a total of 72 time series in this forecast model.

Figure 13-20 The mining structure for a time series

Before creating the forecasting model, you must specify the time frame for the training data. A cube may contain many years of data, and you don't need to use all of the historical data for model training. Some data may be too old and won't have any impact on the forecast. For example, consider sales data. If a product has been sold for more than 10 years, the initial five years of data is mostly likely useless for prediction. You can slice the cube on the time dimension, using only two years of data, as shown in Figure 13-21.

NOTE Most cubes have time dimensions. Most time dimensions contain members that represent future time units. Slicing the cube on the time dimension is a necessary step for time series models. If you don't slice the time dimension, you will have future time members included in the training data. Because there are not yet values for these future members, these null values are replaced with 0 by default during the processing of OLAP mining models. If you don't slice the cube, the model you build will not be the one that you really want.

Figure 13-21 Slicing the cube to specify a time frame

Using the Data Mining Designer

After defining the mining model in the Data Mining Wizard, the Data Mining Designer opens with a view of the mining structure created by the wizard. Chapter 4 explained how to build mining structures and models using the Data Mining Designer. Figure 13-22 shows the Data Mining Designer with the market basket model you just defined on the Sales cube.

Working with the designer on OLAP mining structures is very similar to working on structures built on tables — the difference is in the Structure pane on the right. It displays the OLAP cube in a relational way, similar to the right part of Figure 13-8. There are two "tables" for this model. The case "table" on the left represents the case dimension Customer, with all Customer properties and a set of measures. The nested "table" on the right represents the fact table. It has many more attributes than the original fact table. The original fact table contains a set of foreign keys and measures. The nested table in the editor displays all the dimension attributes under the dimension keys and the set of measures. You can add these dimension attributes to the nested table of your mining structure.

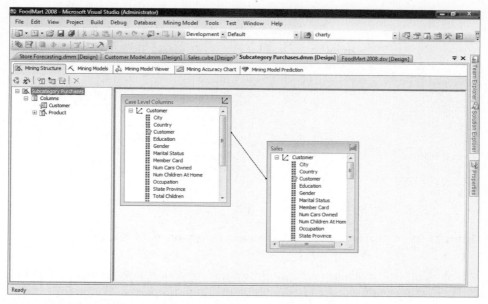

Figure 13-22 Data Mining Designer showing an OLAP mining structure

Understanding Data Mining Dimensions

You may have noticed that on the last page of the Data Mining Wizard, there is an option to create a data mining dimension. So, what is a data mining dimension?

Each algorithm chapter discussed the schema representation specific to that algorithm. After processing a model, the pattern discovered by the algorithm is persisted in the `Model_Content` schema rowset. In a decision tree model, each tree node is stored as a row in this schema rowset. In a clustering model, each cluster is a row in this schema rowset. The `Model_Content` schema rowset is like a parent-child dimension, where each node has a parent node.

If you create a data mining dimension in the Data Mining Wizard, Analysis Services processes the mining model and creates a new dimension based on that model's content. For example, the data mining dimension has two levels for a clustering model: the `All` level and individual cluster levels. For a decision tree model, the dimension hierarchy structure is tree-shaped. Meanwhile, the server creates an internal index structure, which maps each case in the case dimension to the members in the data mining dimension, as shown in Figure 13-23.

On the last page of the Data Mining Wizard, you can also ask the server to create a new cube that contains the set of existing dimensions in the source cube, plus the data mining dimension. You can browse the new cube by slicing and pivoting the data mining dimension.

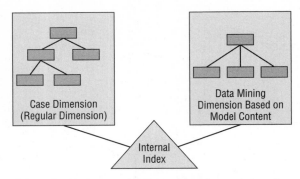

Figure 13-23 Internal indexes for a data mining dimension and a case dimension

Not all algorithms support data mining dimensions. For example, it doesn't make business sense to create a data mining dimension for a time series model. Three algorithms currently support this feature: Microsoft Clustering, Microsoft Decision Trees, and Microsoft Association Rules.

The following is a special type of DMX query designed for the data mining dimension feature:

```
SELECT * FROM myModel.DIMENSION_CONTENT
```

The query result is similar to the query `SELECT * FROM myModel.CONTENT`. However, it has only a subset of content columns and may contain a slightly modified set of rows. For example, the `NODE_DISTRIBUTION` column is not included, and the content may be modified so it more appropriately maps to an OLAP dimension. The query result represents the parent-child structure of the data mining dimension. For example, for a clustering model with 10 clusters, the query contains 11 rows (1 for the model root, and 10 for each individual cluster). The root node is the parent of the 10 individual cluster nodes. When creating a data mining dimension based on this cluster model, the new dimension contains a parent-child hierarchy: `All` and `Node_Unique_Name`. The `All` level represents all clusters in which `Node_Unique_Name` represents an individual cluster.

INTERPRETING MEMBERS OF A DATA MINING DIMENSION

The interpretation of the data mining dimension members depends on the algorithm that the source model uses.

(continued)

INTERPRETING MEMBERS OF A DATA MINING DIMENSION *(continued)*

For clustering, the dimension members represent each cluster, so slicing by the dimension restricts the output to cases in each cluster.

For decision trees, the dimension members represent the tree nodes, so slicing by the dimension divides your data by the rules that are most important in determining the target variable of the model.

For association rules, the dimension members represent the size 1 itemsets found in the model. Slicing by this type of data mining dimension allows you to determine sales and profit figures from *baskets* containing a particular item, as opposed to the sales and profits of that item alone.

Table 13-2 shows the list of columns returned by the `model.DIMENSION _CONTENT` query and the usage of each column in the data mining dimension.

Table 13-2 Columns Returned by the model.dimension_content Query

COLUMNS	DATA MINING DIMENSION FUNCTION
ATTRIBUTE_NAME	Dimension attributes
NODE_NAME	Dimension attributes
NODE_UNIQUE_NAME	Dimension key attribute
NODE_TYPE	Dimension attributes
NODE_CAPTION	CaptionColumn for key attribute
CHILDREN_CARDINALITY	Dimension attributes
PARENT_UNIQUE_NAME	RelatedAttribute for key attribute (ParentAttribute in parent-child hierarchy)
NODE_DESCRIPTION	Dimension attributes
NODE_RULE	Dimension attributes
MARGINAL_RULE	Dimension attributes
NODE_PROBABILITY	Dimension attributes
MARGINAL_PROBABILITY	Dimension attributes
NODE_SUPPORT	Dimension attributes

NOTE After you create a data mining dimension based on a customer segmentation model, the new dimension doesn't contain each customer as a dimension member. This is so because the data mining dimension is purely based on model content and doesn't drill-through to the individual training cases.

However, the internal index maps the relationship of the content node and training cases. You can still find the customers for each cluster and their related measures by slicing the cube based on the data mining dimension.

Using MDX within DMX Queries

DMX is the SQL language for data mining. You have seen many examples throughout this book. Up to now, all DMX prediction query examples have been prediction join statements with a trained mining model and a relational SQL query.

DMX is much enhanced in the latest SQL Server releases and supports prediction join statements with a MDX query. When embedded inside a DMX query, the MDX query returns rowsets instead of a multidimensional cellset. The rowsets may be nested, depending on the query.

The mining model is not required to be an OLAP mining model. You can use PREDICTION JOIN in a relational mining model with a MDX query, as long as your query specifies the mapping between the mining model columns and the columns returned by your MDX query.

The query in Listing 13-3 returns the cluster ID for each member in the Customer dimension. The prediction is based on three member properties (Occupation, HouseOwner, and Member Card) and one measure (Store Sales).

```
SELECT
  t.[[Measures]].[Customer]]],
  Cluster()
FROM
  [Customer Clusters]
PREDICTION JOIN
(
WITH
MEMBER MEASURES.Customer
      AS Customer.Customer.MEMBER_CAPTION
MEMBER MEASURES.Occupation
      AS Customer.Customer.PROPERTIES(''Occupation'')
MEMBER MEASURES.[Member Card]
      AS Customer.Customer.PROPERTIES(''Member Card'')
MEMBER MEASURES.[Marital Status]
      AS Customer.Customer.PROPERTIES(''Marital Status'')
SELECT { MEASURES.Customer,
        MEASURES.Occupation,
        MEASURES.[Member Card],
        MEASURES.[Marital Status],
        MEASURES.[Store Cost] } ON COLUMNS,
```

Listing 13-3 PREDICTION JOIN using MDX as input

```
Customer.Customer.Customer.MEMBERS ON ROWS
FROM [Sales]) AS t
ON
    [Customer Clusters].Occupation
        = t.[[Measures]].[Occupation]]]
AND [Customer Clusters].[Member Card]
        = t.[[Measures]].[Member Card]]]
AND [Customer Clusters].[Marital Status]
        = t.[[Measures]].[Marital Status]]]
AND [Customer Clusters].[Store Cost]
    = t.[[Measures]].[Store Cost]]]
```

Listing 13-3 (*continued*)

Take care when referencing MDX column names in the DMX query. Because the MDX column names contain bracket characters, the brackets must be escaped correctly through doubling. Note that the query in Listing 13-3 contains three closing brackets at the end of each MDX column to properly close the column name.

DETERMINING MDX COLUMN NAMES

When performing a PREDICTION JOIN operation against an MDX query, the MDX engine flattens the multidimensional result set using built-in mechanisms. It isn't always obvious how the flattened result will look or what the resulting column names will be. Because your PREDICTION JOIN statement will require columns from the MDX result to be mapped to the mining column names, you need to know a priori what those names will be.

Luckily, there is a trick that uses DMX syntax to elicit the format of the flattened rowset as well as the generated column names. By selecting all of the columns from the input into the output, and nothing from the mining model, you can perform a NATURAL PREDICTION JOIN between any mining model and any MDX query to see how the result looks. The query in Listing 13-4 demonstrates this technique.

```
SELECT
  t.*
FROM
  [Customer Clusters]
NATURAL PREDICTION JOIN
(SELECT { MEASURES.[Store Cost] } ON COLUMNS,
Customer.Customer.Customer.MEMBERS AS Customer ON ROWS
FROM [Sales]) as t
```

Listing 13-4 Flattening MDX using DMX

Using Analysis Management Objects for the OLAP Mining Model

In Chapter 16, you learn to program with Analysis Management Objects (AMO). There, you will find code examples for creating mining models on relational tables. In this section, you learn how to use AMO to create a mining model based on a cube. You may want to read Chapter 16 and then revisit this section after learning the basics of AMO.

In SQL Server 2000, relational mining models and OLAP mining models are two different types of objects. In SQL Server 2005 and SQL Server 2008, you no longer need this separation. The term *OLAP mining model* is still used as a short notation to indicate that the mining model is created and processed based on a cube. Mining models that are defined based on a relational source and a multidimensional source have the same structure and metadata. The only difference is the way the models are bound to data and processed. In fact, a model created and processed with relational tables can be reprocessed with new bindings to a cube. The only functional difference between an OLAP mining model and other mining models is that OLAP mining models can be used to create data mining dimensions and can be referenced in the MDX `Predict` function.

To create a mining model based on a cube, you must define bindings to cube attributes, measures, and fact tables. This section shows you some sample code for defining mining structure columns based on cube attributes and measures.

The `CreateMiningStructureColumn` procedure in Listing 13-5 creates a `ScalarMiningStructureColumn` based on a dimension attribute. It has two parameters: a dimension attribute and a Boolean value that indicates whether or not the column is a key column.

```
public static ScalarMiningStructureColumn
    CreateMiningStructureColumn(CubeAttribute attribute, bool isKey)
{
  ScalarMiningStructureColumn column = new
      ScalarMiningStructureColumn();
  column.Name = attribute.Attribute.Name;
  //cube attribute is usually modeled as discrete except for key column
  column.Content = (isKey ? MiningStructureColumnContents.Key :
  MiningStructureColumnContents.Discrete);
  column.IsKey = isKey;
  //bind column source to a cube dimension attribute
  column.Source = new CubeAttributeBinding(attribute.ParentCube.ID,
                  ((CubeDimension)attribute.Parent).ID,
```

Listing 13-5 CreateScalarMiningStructureColumn

```
                    attribute.Attribute.ID,
                AttributeBindingType.Name);
  //Get the column data type from the attribute key column binding.
  column.Type = MiningStructureColumnTypes.GetColumnType
  (attribute.Attribute.NameColumn.DataType);
   return column;
  }
```

Listing 13-5 (*continued*)

In addition to dimension attributes, an OLAP mining model may have measures as input columns. The following `CreateMiningStructureColumn` procedure has one parameter: a cube measure. It creates a mining structure column and binds it to a cube measure.

```
public static ScalarMiningStructureColumn
     CreateMiningStructureColumn(Measure measure)
{
 ScalarMiningStructureColumn column = new ScalarMiningStructureColumn();
 column.Name = measure.Name;
 //Set the content type to continuous for measures.
 column.Content = MiningStructureColumnContents.Continuous;
 column.Source = new MeasureBinding(measure.ID);
 column.Type =
     MiningStructureColumnTypes.GetColumnType(measure.Source.DataType);
 return column;
}
```

Using the previous two procedures based on AMO, you can create the customer segmentation model of the previous section programmatically. In Listing 13-6, the `CreateProcessSegmentationModel` procedure creates a mining structure and a clustering mining model based on two dimension attributes (`Member Card` and `Total Children`) and one measure (`Store Sales`) of the FoodMart cube.

```
 Public void CreateProcessSegmentationModel()
 {
  //connecting the server and database
  Server myServer = new Server();
  myServer.Connect("DataSource=localhost;Catalog=FoodMart");
  Database myDatabase = myServer.Databases["FoodMart"];
  Cube myCube = myDatabase.Cubes["FoodMart 2000"];
  CubeDimension myDimension = myCube.Dimensions["Customer"];
  MiningStructure myMiningStructure =
        myDatabase.MiningStructures.Add
```

Listing 13-6 CreateProcessSegmentationModel creates a mining structure and a clustering mining model based on two dimension attributes

```
        ("CustomerSegement","CustomerSegement");
    //Bind the mining structure to a cube.
    myMiningStructure.Source = new CubeDimensionBinding(".",

                        myCube.ID, myDimension.ID);

    // Create the key column.
    CubeAttribute customerKey =
            myCube.Dimensions["Customer"].Attributes["Customer"];
    ScalarMiningStructureColumn keyStructureColumn =
            Utilities.CreateMiningStructureColumn(customerKey, true);
    myMiningStructure.Columns.Add(keyStructureColumn);

    //Member Card attribute
    CubeAttribute memberCard =
            myCube.Dimensions["Customer"].Attributes["Member Card"];
    ScalarMiningStructureColumn memberCardStructureColumn =
            Utilities.CreateMiningStructureColumn(memberCard, false);
    myMiningStructure.Columns.Add(memberCardStructureColumn);

    //Total Children attribute
    CubeAttribute totalChildren =
            myCube.Dimensions["Customer"].Attributes["Total Children"];
    ScalarMiningStructureColumn totalChildrenStructureColumn =
            Utilities.CreateMiningStructureColumn(totalChildren, false);
    myMiningStructure.Columns.Add(totalChildrenStructureColumn);

    //Store Sales measure
    Measure storeSales = myCube.MeasureGroups[0].Measures["Store Sales"];
    ScalarMiningStructureColumn storeSalesStructureColumn =
            Utilities.CreateMiningStructureColumn(storeSales);
    myMiningStructure.Columns.Add(storeSalesStructureColumn);

    //Create a mining model from the mining structure. By default, all the
    //structure columns are used. Nonkey columns are with usage input
    MiningModel myMiningModel = myMiningStructure.CreateMiningModel(true,
            "CustomerSegment");
    //Set the algorithm to be clustering.
    myMiningModel.Algorithm = MiningModelAlgorithms.MicrosoftClustering;

    //Process structure and model
    try
    {
      myMiningStructure.Update(UpdateOptions.ExpandFull);
      myMiningStructure.Process(ProcessType.ProcessFull);

    }
```

Listing 13-6 (*continued*)

```
catch (Microsoft.AnalysisServices.OperationException e)
{
   string err = e.Message;
}


}
```

Listing 13-6 (*continued*)

An OLAP mining model may contain nested tables. In an OLAP mining model, a case table is always bound to a dimension, while a nested table is always bound to a measure group and/or fact table. For example, in the market basket analysis model created earlier in this chapter, the case table is bound to the Customer dimension, and the nested table is bound to the `Sales Fact` table. In AMO, you can create a `TableMiningStructureColumn` and then bind the column to the measure group, as shown in the following code example:

```
public static TableMiningStructureColumn
      CreateMiningStructureColumn(MeasureGroup measureGroup)
{
 TableMiningStructureColumn column = new TableMiningStructureColumn();
 column.Name = measureGroup.Name;
 column.SourceMeasureGroup = new MeasureGroupBinding(".",
 ((Cube)measureGroup.Parent).ID, measureGroup.ID);
 return column;
}
The following code creates a Market Basket Analysis model based on a cube:
private void CreateMarketBasketModel()
{
cubeAttribute basketAttribute;
CubeAttribute itemAttribute;

Server myServer = new Server();
myServer.Connect("DataSource=localhost;Catalog=FoodMart");
Database myDatabase = myServer.Databases["FoodMart"];
Cube myCube = myDatabase.Cubes["FoodMart 2000"];
CubeDimension myDimension = myCube.Dimensions["Customer"];
MiningStructure myMiningStructure =
          myDatabase.MiningStructures.Add("MarketBasket",
          "MarketBasket");
myMiningStructure.Source = new
CubeDimensionBinding(".", myCube.ID, myDimension.ID);

basketAttribute = myCube.Dimensions["Customer"].Attributes["Customer"];
itemAttribute = myCube.Dimensions["Product"].Attributes["Product"];

//basket structure column
ScalarMiningStructureColumn basket =
```

```
            Utilities.CreateMiningStructureColumn(basketAttribute, true);
    basket.Name = "Basket";
    myMiningStructure.Columns.Add(basket);

    //item structure column - nested table
    ScalarMiningStructureColumn item =
            Utilities.CreateMiningStructureColumn(itemAttribute, true);
    item.Name = "Item";
    MeasureGroup measureGroup = myCube.MeasureGroups[0];
    TableMiningStructureColumn purchases =
            Utilities.CreateMiningStructureColumn(measureGroup);
    purchases.Name = "Purchases";
    purchases.Columns.Add(item);
    myMiningStructure.Columns.Add(purchases);

    MiningModel myMiningModel = myMiningStructure.CreateMiningModel();
    myMiningModel.Name = "MarketBasket";
    myMiningModel.Columns["Purchases"].Usage = MiningModelColumnUsages.PredictOnly;
    myMiningModel.Algorithm = MiningModelAlgorithms.MicrosoftAssociationRules;
    }
```

Summary

In this chapter, you learned about several important OLAP concepts, including cubes, dimensions, hierarchies, measures, and UDM. You also learned about the relationship between OLAP and data mining. They are both powerful tools for data analysis with different focuses, and they are complements of each other.

The second half of the chapter taught you how to apply data mining on a cube. You learned how to build OLAP mining models using the Data Mining Wizard and Designer. You saw several examples of models that represent some popular scenarios in OLAP mining. The chapter also discussed data mining dimensions, which enable you to optimize your dimension hierarchy designs and allow you to perform more advanced cube explorations.

The last part of the chapter taught you how to build OLAP mining models programmatically using AMO. Now it's time for you to apply these techniques to discover patterns on your own cubes.

Chapter 14 shows you how to combine SQL Server Data Mining with SQL Server Integration Services (SSIS) — the extract, transform, and load (ETL) piece for SQL Server BI.

Data Mining with SQL Server Integration Services

In a typical data mining project, the most resource-consuming step is data preparation. Creating and tuning mining models may represent only 20 percent of the total project effort. However, before you create these models, your data must be in the right format. Data preparation consists of multiple steps, including data gathering, cleaning, and transformation. You can prepare the data using SQL scripts, but there is a better tool for this: SQL Server Integration Services (SSIS).

SSIS provides a workflow environment for you to build data transformation packages. You can extract data from different data sources and perform a sequence of operations on the data. Many such operations are predefined and provided as components in the SSIS Toolbox. You can enrich this set with your own custom operations. After transforming your data, you can use it to process a data mining model, or execute prediction queries directly inside the SSIS environment.

This chapter begins with an overview of the SSIS components and continues by explaining how to perform data mining tasks in an SSIS environment.

In this chapter, you will learn about the following:

- The basic concepts of SSIS, including control flow and data flow
- Performing data mining–related transformations and tasks in SSIS
- The text mining solution based on Term Extraction and Term Lookup transformations

Examples, datasets, and projects for this chapter are included in `Chapter14.zip`, which you can download from the book's website (`www.wiley.com/go/data_mining_SQL_2008/`). The archive contains the following:

- A SQL Server 2008 database backup containing the datasets used in this chapter
- An Analysis Services solution containing multiple projects that exemplify the concepts described in this chapter

The projects use data from the included database, as well as from the SQL Server `AdventureWorksDW2008` sample database. To download and install the sample database, go to the Codeplex website at `www.codeplex.com/MSFTDB-ProdSamples`, select SQL Server 2008 Product Samples the `SQL2008.AdventureWorks_DW_BI_v2008.x86.msi` package. Be sure to select the Restore AdventureWorksDW2008 (Data Warehouse) option during setup to get the sample database ready.

Next, deploy the `ASProject`, `DataFlow_ASProject`, and `AS_TextMining` Analysis Services projects. These projects create the mining models and structures discussed in this chapter.

SSIS packages require a level of protection for sensitive information, such as connection strings and/or query strings. Therefore, the sample SSIS projects associated with this chapter have their protection level set to `EncryptSensitiveWithPassword`. The password is `DM`.

An Overview of SSIS

SSIS belongs to the extraction, transformation, and loading (ETL) product family. ETL was first introduced in SQL Server at version 7.0 in 1997 under the name Data Transformation Services (DTS). The product went through a major change in the 2005 version of SQL Server and got a new name: SQL Server Integration Services

Today, more and more enterprises have data warehouses. ETL is an indispensable tool for loading data from Online Transaction Processing (OLTP) databases into data warehouses on a regular basis. In the first two releases (SQL Server 7.0 and SQL Server 2000), the SQL Server ETL product mainly focused on data extraction and loading to or from multiple data source. Starting with SQL Server 2005, the product was re-engineered and enhanced. The resulting SSIS is a control flow environment that allows execution of various tasks in sequential order, loops, or branches conditioned by the execution result of previous tasks.

Data flow was a new concept introduced in SQL Server 2005. It is also called a *pipeline*. It mainly addresses the issue of data transformation. A data flow is composed of a set of predefined transformations. The starting point of a data flow is usually a *data source* (for example, a source table). The ending point of a data flow is usually a *data destination* (for example, a destination table). You can think of data flow execution as a pipeline process with each row of data as the part to be processed and each transformation as the processing unit in the assembly line.

Starting with SQL Server 2005 (and continuing in SQL Server 2008), a number of incremental improvements have been made to SSIS in the area of scripting and performance. The new script engine is based on Visual Studio Tools for Applications (VSTA). VSTA is a .NET-based application customization technology, which makes it easy for developers to write reliable, robust, and secure customizations. Developers can use C# as a scripting language inside data flow and task flow. The data flow engine (together with a number of transformations, such as Lookup and Merge) performs better because of smart caching and improved run-time design.

Figure 14-1 shows the SSIS Designer. You can invoke the SSIS Designer by launching Business Intelligence Development Studio (BI Dev Studio) and creating an Integration Services project. A Toolbox window on the left contains predefined control flow tasks and data flow transformations.

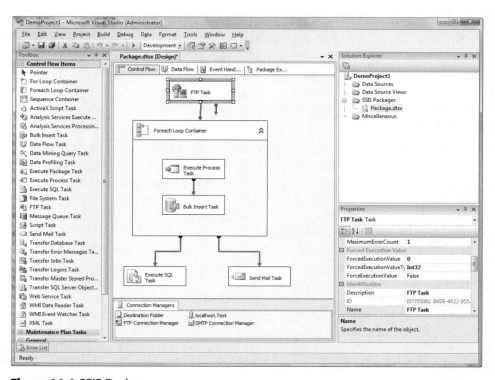

Figure 14-1 SSIS Designer

The middle view pane contains four views:

- **Control Flow** — This view provides a design environment for building control flows using the control flow items in the Toolbox.
- **Data Flow** — This view provides a design environment for building data transformation pipelines using the data flow items in the Toolbox.
- **Event Handlers** — This view allows you to define follow-up actions triggered by certain execution events.
- **Package Explorer** — This provides a tree-style view of the flow.

Understanding SSIS Packages

A *package* is the basic deployment and execution unit of an SSIS project. All the work performed by SSIS tasks occurs within the context of the package. An SSIS package is the container for SSIS flows. You can create an SSIS package by right-clicking the SSIS Package folder in the Integration Services project folder and selecting the New SSIS Package menu item.

An SSIS project may contain multiple packages. A package contains only one control flow, which may contain one or more data flows.

In addition to control flow and data flow, a package contains SSIS connections and package variables. Variables can have different scopes (for example, global to the whole package or local to a sequence of tasks).

The connections and variables are displayed in the tray, located in the lower portion of the SSIS Designer (shown previously at the bottom of Figure 14-1). The connection can be to a relational database, to an Analysis Services database, or even to a file containing data.

Task Flow

An SSIS package contains one control flow, which is composed of a set of tasks. These tasks define the job of the package (such as loading the data, executing SQL statements, processing scripts, or invoking other processes). Tasks are listed in the SSIS Toolbox. You can add a task to the package by dragging it from the Toolbox and dropping it into the package designer (the middle pane shown previously in Figure 14-1).

A package usually contains multiple tasks in a task flow. Multiple tasks are organized in sequential order with precedence constraints. *Precedence constraints* link two tasks in a sequence, where the result of executing the first task determines whether the second task is run. You can use precedence constraints to build conditional branches in a workflow. Multiple precedence constraints can be combined and evaluated as one constraint.

Standard Tasks in SSIS

Table 14-1 lists some of the prebuilt tasks and their descriptions in the SSIS task flow.

Table 14-1 SSIS Tasks

TASK	DESCRIPTION
Bulk Insert	Loads large amounts of data from a text file into a SQL Server table.
Data Flow	Supports the copying and transformation of data between heterogeneous data sources. A data flow task contains a data flow pipeline.
Execute Package	Runs sub-packages.
Execute Process	Runs a program or a batch file as part of a package.
Execute SQL	Runs SQL statements during package execution and optionally saves the results of those queries.
File System Task	Performs file system operations.
File Transfer Protocol	Downloads data files from a remote server or an Internet location as part of a package workflow.
Message Queue	Uses message queuing to send and receive messages between SSIS packages.
Script	Uses a script to perform functions that are not available in prebuilt SSIS tasks. The Script task enables you to write script code in Visual Basic .NET and C# using the Microsoft VSTA environment.
Send Mail	Sends an e-mail message.
XML	Merges, filters, and transforms data in XML documents.
Data Profiling	Analyzes (and maintains) the data quality. Provides column value distributions and statistics.

In addition to the tasks listed in Table 14-1, SSIS provides simple APIs that you can use to develop your own tasks. After you register these tasks, they will appear in the Toolbox and can be used in the task flow just like any prebuilt task.

Containers

Containers are SSIS objects that provide structure to a package. Each package has a container, which stores the flows of a package. A package container may have other types of containers, such as a sequence container, `Foreach` loop container, and `For` loop container, which are available in the Control Flow Toolbox (shown previously on the left side of Figure 14-1). You can define a sub-flow in these containers. Containers enrich the run-time execution model of control flow. For example, not all the tasks are executed in sequential order. The sub-flow within a `Foreach` loop container will be executed multiple times based on the iterator defined in the container.

Debugging

As of SQL Server 2005, you can debug the SSIS control flow. You can set a breakpoint by simply pressing F9 while selecting a task in the SSIS Designer. Debugging enables you to examine the values of package variables and the states of a task during the execution. Breakpoints can be set based on the events. For example, you can set one or more breakpoints on the following events of a task:

- OnPreExecute
- OnPostExecute
- OnError
- OnWarning
- OnProgress

The SSIS run-time routine pauses during the package execution when it reaches a breakpoint event. The experience is similar to debugging your C# code in Visual Studio.

Exploring a Control Flow Example

Figure 14-2 shows an example of a simple control flow. It starts with an FTP task to download compressed data files. After the files are downloaded, the run-time routine reaches a Foreach loop container that has two tasks inside: an Execute Process task (which calls the Unzip application to unzip the data file) and a Bulk Insert task (which inserts the data file data into SQL Server). The loop stops when the data file is unzipped and the data is loaded into SQL Server. If there is an error during the loop, the flow will execute the Send Mail task to send an e-mail to the database administrator. If every task is executed correctly, it will execute a SQL task to create some views on the new dataset. A breakpoint is set on the Execute SQL task at OnPreExecute event so that the administrator can verify the data before creating views.

Data Flow

Whereas control flow is an old concept that has existed since the release of DTS in SQL Server 7.0, data flow is a relatively new concept introduced in SQL Server 2005. A *data flow* is a workflow that is specific to data operations.

As previously mentioned, a data flow is also called a *pipeline*. You can think of a data flow as an assembly line that contains multiple operations in sequential order. Each node in the data flow is called a *transformation*. A data flow usually starts with a source transformation and ends with a destination transformation. In between, predefined data flow transformations are applied to the data in a sequential order.

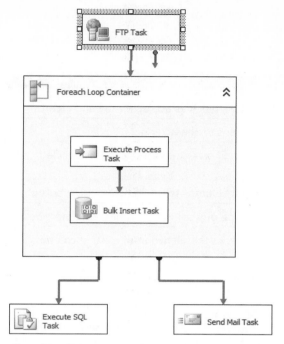

Figure 14-2 A control flow example

Some transformations are *synchronous* (for example, Lookup, Conditional Split, and Data Conversion). These synchronous transformations can be executed in parallel. After a transformation has been applied to a data row, the next transformation can start to operate on it without waiting until the entire data set is processed in the upstream transformation.

Some transformations are *asynchronous* (for example, Aggregation and Sort). These transformations need to get all rows from the previous output in order to process and produce outputs for subsequent transformations.

In addition to the prebuilt transformations, SSIS provides APIs to help you build your own data flow transformations. For example, you can build a Numeric Processing transformation to apply mathematical calculations and transformations on the pipeline data.

Data flow is always included in a task flow. There is one special task named *Data Flow* that is a container to host a data flow. You must add the Data Flow task to the SSIS Designer before building a data flow.

Transformations

Whereas tasks are the basic components of task flows, transformations are the basic components of data flows. Transformations are predefined data operations. They are the machines in an assembly line that operate on the input data. Table 14-2 lists popular transformations in the SSIS data flow environment.

Table 14-2 SSIS Transformations

TRANSFORMATION	DESCRIPTION
Aggregate	Performs aggregations (such as average, sum, and count).
Character Map	Applies string functions to character data.
Conditional Split	Routes data rows to different outputs based on specified criteria.
Copy Column	Adds copies of input columns to the transformation output.
Data Conversion	Converts the data type of a column to a different data type.
Derived Column	Generates new columns that derive from existing columns using expressions.
Dimension Processing Destination	Processes Analysis Services dimensions.
Fuzzy Grouping	Performs data-cleansing tasks by identifying rows of data that are likely to be duplicates and by choosing a canonical row of data to use in standardizing the data.
Fuzzy Lookup	Looks up values in a reference table using a fuzzy match.
Lookup	Looks up values in a reference table using an exact match.
Merge	Merges two sorted data sets.
Merge Join	Joins two sorted data sets using a FULL, LEFT, or INNER join.
Multicast	Distributes data sets to multiple outputs.
Partition Processing Destination	Processes Analysis Services partitions.
Pivot	Creates a less normalized version of a normalized table.
Sort	Sorts pipeline data.
Union All	Creates a union of multiple data sets.
UnPivot	Creates a more normalized version of a nonnormalized table.

Viewers

Viewers are designed for data flow debugging purposes. You can use viewers to visualize the rows that traverse the pipeline during flow execution. You can also attach viewers on the lines between transformations. To add a viewer, simply right-click a line and select Data Viewers from the context menu that appears. The default viewer is Grid. You can also add histogram, scatter plot, and column charts as graphic viewers. If these predefined viewers don't satisfy your needs, you can even build your own viewers.

Exploring a Data Flow Example

Figure 14-3 shows a data flow example. The flow starts with an OLE DB Source transformation, which loads a fact table containing retail sales transactions. The second transformation is Lookup, which looks for the first and last names of a customer in the customer dimension table. These two columns are added to the pipeline data. The next transformation is Derived Column, which creates a new `Full Name` column based on the first and last names. Then the data enters the Aggregate transformation, which sums the total sales for each customer. Based on the sales amount, the Conditional Split transformation routes the customer to two destination tables: one for important customers (spending large amounts) and the other for regular customers (spending average amounts).

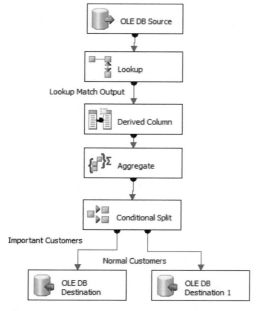

Figure 14-3 A data flow example

Working with SSIS in Data Mining

SSIS provides a flow environment for data extraction, transformation, and loading (ETL) with a set of built-in tasks and transformations.

As you have already learned, the most resource-consuming work in a data mining project is data cleaning and transformation. Naturally, SSIS can be a good complement to a data mining project. You can use this powerful tool to load data from various sources, combine these data sources, normalize column values, remove dirty records, replace missing values, split data into training and testing data sets, and so on.

But SSIS is more than just an ETL tool for data mining — it actually provides a few built-in data mining components in the control flow and data flow environment. Table 14-3 lists some data mining–specific tasks and transformations provided by SSIS.

Table 14-3 SSIS Tasks and Transformations for Data Mining

DATA MINING TASK	DESCRIPTION
Data Mining Query	Runs prediction queries based on data mining models.
Analysis Services Processing	Processes analytic objects, such as cubes, dimensions, partitions, and data mining models.
Analysis Services Execute DDL	Runs Data Definition Language (DDL) code that can create, modify, delete, and process analytic objects.
Data Mining Data Flow Components	
Data Mining Model Training Destination	Processes data mining models using the pipeline data as input.
Data Mining Query Transformation	Executes data mining prediction queries.
Text Mining Transformations	
Term Extraction	Processes the textual column to extract the key terms (either a single word or a short noun phrase). Extracted terms can be used as the dictionary for a Term Lookup transformation.
Term Lookup	Searches and extracts the key terms from the input textual column based on a dictionary. The result of Term Lookup can be used as the training data for text mining.

Data Mining Tasks

This section examines a few tasks related to data mining.

Data Mining Query Task

The Data Mining Query task is used for executing data mining queries, mainly prediction queries in the SSIS control flow. It works against a mining model or structure already deployed on an Analysis Services server.

NOTE For the sample projects associated with this chapter to function correctly, you must deploy the ASProject Analysis Services project first. That project creates the mining models and structures used in this chapter's examples. Note also that the SSIS packages require a level of protection for sensitive information, such as connection strings and/or query strings. The protection level is set to EncryptSensitiveWithPassword for all sample SSIS projects in this chapter, and the password is DM.

To use the Data Mining Query task, start by launching Visual Studio and creating a new Integration Services project in the Business Intelligence Projects group. In the newly created project, drag and drop the Data Mining Query Task item from the Toolbox onto the Control Flow surface, and then double-click the task to edit its properties.

The first thing you need to do in this task is specify a connection to the Analysis Services instance that contains the model or structure you intend to query. Click the New button next to the Connection drop-down list to create a new connection. When the Connection Manager dialog box appears, select the Microsoft OLE DB Provider for Analysis Services 10.0 option located under the .Net Providers for OleDb collection of providers. After selecting the provider, create a new connection by indicating the server (and, if necessary, the instance name) where the model you intend to query is hosted.

Select the mining structure that contains the model you intend to query, as shown in Figure 14-4.

After your model and structure are selected, you specify the query to be executed. To do this, you input the data mining query statement in the Query tab of the Data Mining Query Task Editor, as shown in Figure 14-5. You can write the query directly in the text box, or you can click the Build New Query button to invoke the Query Builder. The Query Builder provides a graphic environment that helps you build the DMX query. You learned how to use this tool in Chapter 4.

Your DMX query may contain parameters. You can use the Parameter Mapping tab shown in Figure 14-6 to map these parameters to SSIS variables. For example, you could write a query that identifies customers whose probability of buying a bicycle is greater than a given value and stores the threshold value in an Integration Services package variable (such as User::Threshold). You can change the prediction query in Figure 14-5 to use a threshold by appending the construct shown in Listing 14-1.

Figure 14-4 Selecting the mining model in the Data Mining Query Task Editor

Figure 14-5 Building a query in the Data Mining Query Task Editor

Figure 14-6 Mapping DMX query parameters to Integration Services package variables

```
...WHERE   PredictProbability([TM_Decision_Tree].[Bike Buyer]) >
          @MinimumProbability
```

Listing 14-1 Changing the DMX query of the Data Mining Query Task Editor to use a threshold parameter

NOTE Changing the DMX query as in Listing 14-1 requires you to manually edit the statement in the Build Query box shown in Figure 14-5. If you try to insert a new line by pressing the Enter key, you will notice that the dialog box goes away. Use Ctrl+Enter to insert a new line in the Query Builder.

In the Parameter Mapping subtab of the Query dialog box, associate the MinimumProbability DMX parameter with the User::Threshold package variable, as shown in Figure 14-6.

The last subtab of the Query dialog box, Result Set, provides you with an option to map the result to an SSIS variable, such as a collection.

EXECUTING ARBITRARY DMX STATEMENTS IN THE DATA MINING QUERY TASK

Apart from DMX prediction queries, you can also execute other types of DMX statements in the Data Mining Query Task. For example, you can type the following content query:

SELECT * from TM_Decision_Tree.CONTENT WHERE NODE_TYPE=3

(continued)

EXECUTING ARBITRARY DMX STATEMENTS IN THE DATA MINING QUERY TASK *(continued)*

You can also call a stored procedure as follows:

CALL System.GetModelAttributes('TM_Decision_Tree')

In addition, you can specify a DMX CREATE or INSERT INTO statement in a Data Mining Query task, and then use this task to create and process a mining model.

The Output tab of the Data Mining Query Task Editor shown in Figure 14-7 allows you to specify the connection destination database where the query result will be stored. You must also give name of the result table.

Figure 14-7 Specifying the output for the Data Mining Query task

NOTE Your DMX query may produce nested results. For example, if you use the PredictHistogram function in your Select clause, the Data Mining Query task will automatically flatten the nested rowsets and insert the query result in a single table.

The configuration of the Data Mining Query task is now complete. You can execute the task (right-click and select Execute) or the whole package.

Analysis Services Processing Task

You can use the Analysis Services Processing task to process major objects in the Analysis Services database. The objects can be dimensions, cubes, mining structures, and mining models.

To use the task, just drag it from the Toolbox and drop it on the Control Flow surface. Double-click the task to edit its settings. Figure 14-8 shows the Analysis Services Processing Task Editor for this task. You can select objects using the Add button shown in the middle of Figure 14-8. You can also specify the process options and settings in the Process Options column.

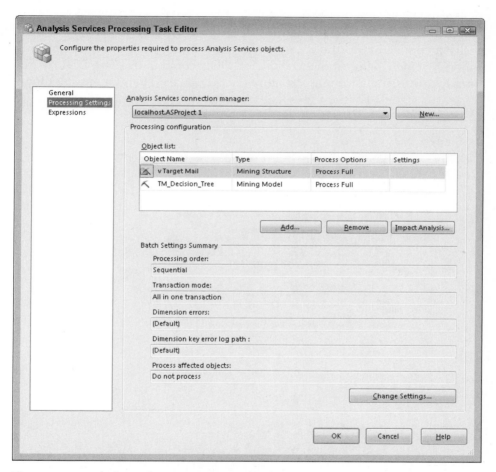

Figure 14-8 Analysis Services Processing Task Editor

Analysis Services Execute DDL Task

As you will learn in detail in Chapter 15, all communication with Analysis Services is performed via the Analysis Services Scripting Language (ASSL), also known as Data Definition Language (DDL). All objects in Analysis Services (mining models, mining columns, dimensions, cubes, roles, and so on) are defined using DDL.

In addition to object definitions, DDL contains a set of commands. These commands facilitate creating, updating, processing, and deleting objects.

When you use graphic tools such as mining model editors to create mining models, these tools produce DDL scripts that are sent to the server.

At times, you may want to create or update these objects without using data mining editors. You can copy or write the DDL scripts and execute them with the Execute DDL task.

Figure 14-9 shows the editor for the Execute DDL task. First, you must specify a connection to the Analysis Services. Then, click the `SourceDirect` property, which invokes a text box for DDL commands. The DDL in the figure is processing a mining structure (`v Target Mail`) and a mining model (`TM_Decision_Tree`) in the `ASProjects` database.

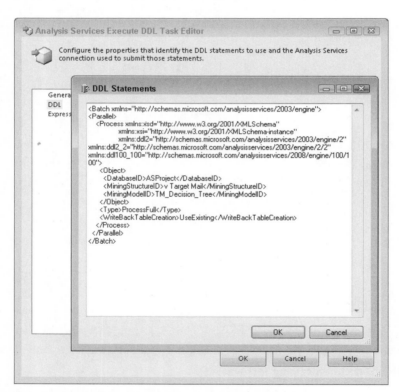

Figure 14-9 Analysis Services Execute DDL Task Editor

> **NOTE** You do not have to include the DDL command to be sent to the server in the editor. The Execute DDL task can use a file or an Integration Services variable as an argument.

You can also use the Execute DDL task to execute DMX statements. DMX is not really DDL but, as you will learn in Chapter 15, *all* communication between the client and the server happens through DDL, so there must be a way to place DMX inside DDL. Listing 14-2 shows how this is done.

```
<Statement>
    UPDATE MyModel.CONTENT SET NODE_CAPTION='My Cluster Label'
        WHERE NODE_UNIQUE_NAME='001'
<Statement>
```

Listing 14-2 The Execute DDL task can execute DMX statements wrapped in DDL

You can use this mechanism for various Analysis Services maintenance tasks, such as processing a mining model, renaming clusters, exporting or importing mining models or structures, and so on.

Data Mining Transformations

This section examines data flow transformations related to data mining. The data flow components can be categorized in three large groups, depending on their position in the data flow:

- **Data flow sources** — Components that appear at the top of a data flow pipeline. They act as data producers.

- **Data flow transformations** — Components that appear in the middle of a data flow pipeline. They actually transform the data.

- **Data flow destinations** — Components that appear at the end of a data flow pipeline. The data produced by the sources and transformations in the pipeline ends up being used by the data flow destinations.

In this section, you will learn how to use data mining components in each of these groups. The most common uses of SSIS for data mining prepare the data for the actual modeling. Therefore, you will first learn how to train a mining model at the end of a dataflow pipeline, on top of the transformed or cleaned-up data.

Data Mining Model Training Destination

The Data Mining Model Training destination is used for processing a mining structure and its associated mining models in the data flow environment. It is a data flow destination transformation.

You can also achieve this processing by using one of the control flow components. You just learned how to use the Analysis Services Processing task. However, the processing task uses the bindings in the definition of the mining object. Consequently, as far as the data preparation is concerned, it does not provide much flexibility over the BI Dev Studio.

During the execution of a data flow, the DM Training destination pushes data from the pipeline to Analysis Services. The pipeline data is wrapped by the DM Training destination in an XML rowset format before it is sent to the Analysis Services Server.

Figure 14-10 shows a very simple data flow that trains a mining model using a sample of data from a table. The data flow uses an OLE DB relational data source, applies one Integration Services transformation to the data (for sampling), and pushes the resulting dataset into an Analysis Services mining structure for training. All mining models in the structure are processed as a result of this operation. The remainder of this section explains the steps you must take to create such a data flow.

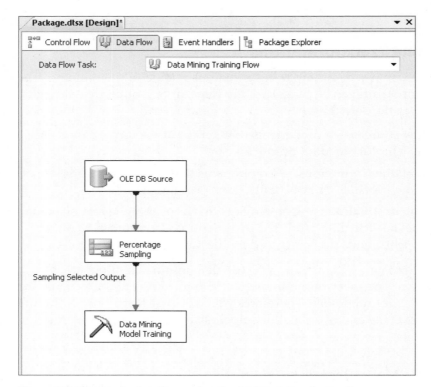

Figure 14-10 Simple data flow using the DM Training destination

To create the data flow, start by adding a Data Flow task to the Control Flow surface, and then double-click the data flow task to edit the pipeline. In the Data Flow editor, drag and drop an OLE DB data source transformation onto the surface. Edit the transformation properties to point to the relational database that contains the data to be transformed.

After you've added a data source to the data flow, you can start using various Integration Services transformations to alter data from that source.

The example in Figure 14-10 uses Percentage Sampling, a very simple transformation. After your transformation process is completed, you will typically make use of the transformed data in the pipeline by configuring a destination transformation. Drag and drop the DM Training transformation from the Toolbox onto the Data Flow surface and connect the output of the pipeline to the training transformation.

Double-click the DM Training transformation to edit its properties. Figure 14-11 shows the Connection tab of the Properties dialog box for the DM Training transformation. In this tab, you specify the connection to an Analysis Services server database and select the mining structure you want to process using the pipeline data.

Figure 14-11 DM Training transformation Connection tab

You can also create a new mining structure using the New button. Clicking this button launches the Data Mining Wizard. The wizard walks you through the model-creation process in the same way as it does in the Data Mining Editor environment. However, there are a few differences.

First, the columns are from a pipeline, not from a relational table. Certain features (such as the autodetect content type and correlation suggestions) are not available. This is because these features require scanning and a sample of the input data, which is not feasible in the pipeline environment.

Figure 14-12 shows the Columns tab of the DM Training destination editor, where you specify the mappings between pipeline columns and mining structure columns. By default, the tool maps pipeline columns to model columns automatically based on column names.

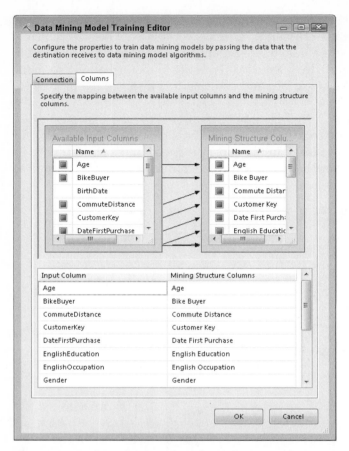

Figure 14-12 The Columns tab of the DM Training destination editor

NOTE Although the DM Training transformation allows you to create a model, it is rather difficult to edit it (for example, to change the model parameters).

One solution is to have two BI projects in the same solution: the SSIS project and the Analysis Services project. In this case, you can use the Mining Model Editor in the Analysis Services project to fully edit the mining models before training them from the Integration Services pipeline.

Data Mining Query Transformation

The Data Mining Query transformation (or DM Query transformation), as the name suggests, is a transformation for executing data mining queries. You learned about the various types of DMX queries in Chapter 3 (including prediction, content, model creation, and model training). Among them, the prediction query is the most common.

To execute a prediction query, you need a trained mining model and an input data set. In the pipeline environment, the input data set is pushed from the pipeline. The DM Query transformation wraps the input data from the pipeline into XML rowsets and sends them to the Analysis Services server through the XML for Analysis (XMLA) protocol. The Analysis Services server executes the query and returns XML results to the transformation. The transformation then unwraps the results and pushes them into the pipeline for the next transformation to consume. When the input data is large, this process is done in chunks each time a set of rows is sent to the Analysis Services server for prediction.

NOTE Data travels through the pipeline in batches (also called *buffers*). The size of such a buffer (and, implicitly, the number of rows) is a parameter of your Integration Services project. Depending on the buffer size, one or more data mining queries are actually executed. Therefore, it is very important that the data mining query applies only to data in a batch. Accordingly, the DM Query transformation supports *only* data mining queries that contain the PREDICTION JOIN DMX operator (which applies the model patterns to the input data, in this case, the rows in the batch). Queries that do not relate strictly to the input data (such as certain Time Series Forecasting queries or DMX content queries, etc.) are not allowed in the DM Query transformation.

To use the DM Query transformation, drag it from the Toolbox, drop it on the Data Flow surface, and then edit its properties.

Figure 14-13 shows the Mining Model tab of the transformation editor, where you specify the connection to a database of a live Analysis Services server. You must also select a mining structure and one of its models.

After configuring the Analysis Services connection, you must specify the data mining query to be executed. Figure 14-14 shows the Query tab of the transformation editor, where you specify a DMX query. You can either manually write the query, or click the New button to launch the Query Builder. The input table for the prediction is the pipeline input, which is denoted as @InputRowset. Your DMX query result may contain nested results, but those will be flattened so they can be used in the pipeline. For example, you could use the PredictionHistogram function in the Select statement. In this case, the nested rowsets will automatically be flattened.

NOTE In SQL Server 2008, SSIS data flow doesn't support nested rowsets natively. This creates technical challenges for data mining training and prediction, which may require nested inputs and produce nested outputs. To address this issue, the DM Query transformation will automatically flatten the results if there are nested rowsets. However, for nested input, it is more problematic. You should use the DM Training task and DM Query task when your model or query requires nested input.

Figure 14-13 The Mining Model tab of the DM Query transformation editor

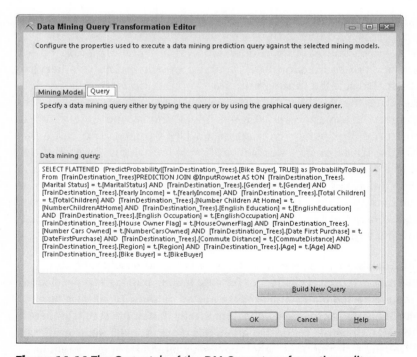

Figure 14-14 The Query tab of the DM Query transformation editor

In the simplest form, the DM Query transformation augments data in the pipeline by adding new columns inferred by the mining model. In this form, the number of rows in the pipeline does not change — each row gets one or more new columns based on the query results. However, the transform can be used in a couple of very different ways, as follows:

- You can filter out rows based on the prediction result. For example, your query may look like Listing 14-3.

```
SELECT FLATTENED
   (PredictProbability([TrainDestination_Trees].[Bike Buyer], TRUE))
        as [ProbabilityToBuy]
From
   [TrainDestination_Trees]
PREDICTION JOIN
 @InputRowset AS t
ON
   [TrainDestination_Trees].[Marital Status] = t.[MaritalStatus] AND
...
WHERE PredictProbability([TrainDestination_Trees].[Bike Buyer],
     TRUE) > 0.5
```

Listing 14-3 Using the DM Query transformation to filter out rows with low predicted probability

Note that this query does not change the shape of a pipeline row. Instead, it filters out rows resulting in a low confidence prediction.

- You can increase the number of rows in the pipeline by flattening nested data mining query results. Listing 14-4 shows an example.

```
SELECT FLATTENED
 (
   SELECT [Bike Buyer], $PROBABILITY FROM
     TopCount(PredictHistogram([Bike Buyer]), $PROBABILITY, 2)
 )
FROM TrainDestination_Trees PREDICTION JOIN
 @InputRowset AS t
ON
   [TrainDestination_Trees].[Marital Status] = t.[MaritalStatus] AND
...
```

Listing 14-4 Using the DM Query transformation to increase the number of rows in the pipeline through flattening

Each row in the original pipeline gets transformed to two new rows. Each new row contains the information of the original row, plus two new columns: `Bike Buyer` predictions and the associated confidence.

Example Data Flows

Figure 14-15 shows examples of how data flows use data mining transformations. The pipeline starts with an OLE DB source transformation, which loads a table containing new customers. The second transformation is DM Query, which uses a trained decision tree model to predict the likelihood that a new customer will purchase a bicycle. The result of the prediction is sent to the Conditional Split transformation, which splits the data into three pipeline branches based on the likelihood value. The left branch contains the customers who are very likely to buy a bike (where the predicted probability exceeds 85 percent), the middle branch contains customers who are likely to buy a bike (probability exceeds 50 percent), and the right branch contains new customers who are unlikely to buy a bicycle. Each branch leads to an OLE DB destination transformation, which stores the customers' names and e-mail addresses in three separate tables.

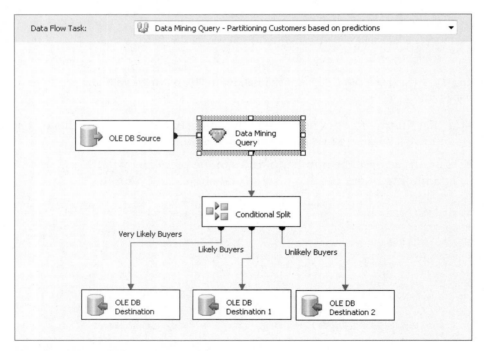

Figure 14-15 Data flow example with prediction

This example also demonstrates that data mining techniques can be applied as advanced ETL processes. It enables data splitting not only based on the existing attributes, but also based on predictable attributes.

> **REMOVING OUTLIERS IN A DATA FLOW**
>
> You can apply data mining techniques to remove outliers in a data flow. As explained in Chapter 9, the Microsoft Clustering algorithm provides a function called `PredictCaseLikelihood` that returns the likelihood of a case being fit in a given model. The cases with very low likelihood scores are likely anomalies. You can use the DM Query transformation to execute prediction queries against the pipeline data and filter out the anomalies based on the query result. You can change the DM Query transformation to something like what is shown in Listing 14-5 in order to compute the likelihood for each row in the pipeline. After the likelihood is computed, you can use either a `WHERE` clause in the DMX query or a Conditional Split transformation in the pipeline to extract the outliers.

```
SELECT FLATTENED
   PredictCaseLikelihood() AS CaseLikelihood
From
   [Customer Clusters]
PREDICTION JOIN
 @InputRowset AS t ON
   [Customer Clusters].[Marital Status] = t.[MaritalStatus] AND
...
```

Listing 14-5 Using the Data Mining Query transformation to detect outliers in a pipeline

Using Non-Predictive Data Mining Queries in an Integration Services Pipeline

As mentioned in the previous section, the DM Query transformation can only be used to execute PREDICTION JOIN DMX statements, which apply the patterns in a mining model against chunks of data in the pipeline. However, a mining model (or any arbitrary Analysis Services query) can be a data source by itself. The Integration Services data flow is a great tool for processing any Analysis Services result set, including mode content rowsets. For example, the result of the query in Listing 14-6 can be used to extract rules for each node in a decision tree.

```
SELECT NODE_DESCRIPTION, NODE_SUPPORT
FROM TrainDestination_Trees.CONTENT
```

Listing 14-6 A DMX statement returning the rules represented by each node in a decision tree model

In order to use Analysis Services as a regular data source, you must perform the following steps:

1. Add a new OLE DB data source transformation to your data flow.

2. Ensure that your OLE DB data source uses the Microsoft OLE DB Provider for Analysis Services 10.0 option (located under the .Net Providers for OleDb'' collection of providers).

3. Set the Data Access Mode property of your Data Source to SQL Command, which allows you to type in your query.

4. Type in an Analysis Services query (such as the DMX statement in Listing 14-6).

5. Click the Parse Query button to ensure the validity of the statement.

Now you can use the new OLE DB data source just like any other data source and apply any data flow transformations on top of the results returned by Analysis Services.

Text Mining Transformations

This section examines two particularly interesting data flow transformations that facilitate text mining: Term Extraction and Term Lookup.

SQL Server Data Mining supports the TEXT data type, but that data type is not enough to perform meaningful text analysis. From the algorithm's perspective, columns having the TEXT data type are treated just like discrete columns that have the LONG data type — as a collection of various distinct states, without any way to directly access the content of a text value.

To perform text mining with SQL Server Data Mining, you must first bring the text to some form that can be consumed by the algorithms. The solution included in the product is to represent each piece of text as a collection of words and phrases, and perform data mining based on the occurrence of certain key words and phrases inside a certain document (and possibly some frequency-related scores). Therefore, a document is modeled very similarly to a shopping basket that contains (or does not contain) certain items (which happen to be key words and phrases).

After each document is represented as a collection of key phrases, you can perform data mining using one of the following model types:

- Classification models that use the key words and phrases nested table as input to predict the class of a document

- Clustering models that find similar documents based on common occurrences

- Association models that detect cross-correlations between key words and phrases

The process of text mining usually consists of at least the following three phases:

1. Build a dictionary of key words and phrases over a collection of representative documents. This task is usually accomplished using the Term Extraction transformation.

2. Based on the dictionary, extract the list of significant key words and phrases for each document to be analyzed. This task is usually accomplished using the Term Lookup transformation.

3. Train mining models on top of the transformed data.

NOTE If you intend to perform predictions on the mining models built in phase 3, you must convert any new document to the same representation (that is, run the Term Lookup transformation on new documents using the same dictionary used in training the mining model or models).

Term Extraction Transformation

You use the Term Extraction transformation to build a glossary of key words and phrases for a specific domain. This is usually the first step of a text mining project. The transformation applies to a pipeline that already contains one column with text data of type `ntext` or `nvarchar`. The purpose of the transformation is to analyze this column and build a dictionary of key terms based on its content. The output of the transformation is a table with a single column. Extracting key terms is not a trivial task because it involves sophisticated techniques, such as word stemming and grammar parsing. The transformation extracts nouns and noun phrases, such as *data mining*.

You can download the data used for the examples in this section from `www.infoplease.com/t/hist/state-of-the-union/`. This download contains the text for 219 State of the Union addresses of U.S. Presidents between 1790 and 2006.

The user interface of the Term Extraction transformation is quite simple. In the first tab of the Term Extraction Transformation Editor shown in Figure 14-16 (Term Extraction), you must specify the textual column. You can also name the output columns for key terms and their associated scores. The score is based on Term Frequency and Inverse Document Frequency (TFIDF). This is a statistical technique used to evaluate how important a word is to a document. The importance increases proportionally to the number of times a word appears in the document, but it's offset by how common the word is in all of the documents in the collection.

The Exclusion tab shown in Figure 14-17 provides the option to specify inclusion and exclusion terms. You may already have a list of predefined terms that must be included, as well as a list of terms that you don't want extracted. You can specify these two term lists in this tab.

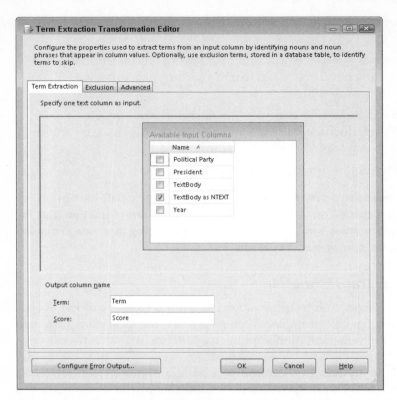

Figure 14-16 The Term Extraction tab in the Term Extraction Transformation Editor

The Advanced tab of the Term Extraction Transformation Editor (shown in Figure 14-18) also provides options for the terms. For example, you can specify that terms must be single words or noun phrases. In the case of a noun phrase, you can specify the maximum length. You can also choose the type of score to be computed (Frequency or TFIDF), as well as a minimum frequency threshold and the maximum length (in words) of any single term (phrase). In addition, you can choose whether the term extraction should be case-sensitive or not (the default setting is case-insensitive).

After you have configured the term extraction transformation, you should bind its output (in the pipeline) to a relational table destination that will store the dictionary of terms. The table will contain two columns: one containing the terms and the other containing the score associated with each term. Figure 14-19 shows the full transformation used to extract the terms from the State of the Union addresses. The Data Conversion transformation that appears in the pipeline before the Term Extraction transformation converts the text from the original database format (ASCII text) to one of the formats supported by Term Extraction (UNICODE text).

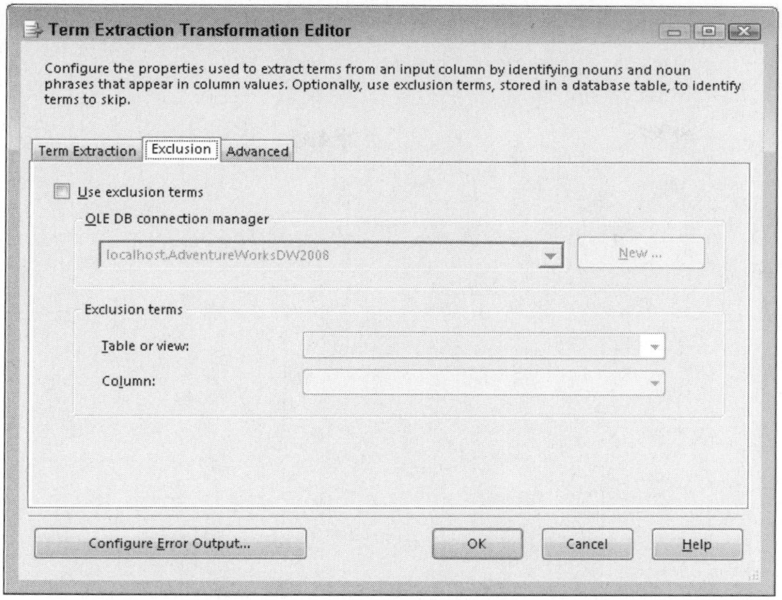

Figure 14-17 The Exclusion tab in the Term Extraction Transformation Editor

Term Lookup Transformation

After a dictionary is built using the Term Extraction transformation, each document to be analyzed must be transformed to a collection of terms, based on that dictionary. The Term Lookup transformation is used to search for key terms from the input textual column, based on a dictionary. The dictionary is usually generated by the Term Extraction transformation. Because the dictionary is just a table, you can write SQL queries to modify the list by adding or removing terms when necessary.

Just like the Term Extraction transformation, the Term Lookup transformation requires the input text column in the pipeline to have the `ntext` and/or `nchar` data types. The editor for the Term Lookup transformation is quite simple. The first tab, Reference Table, is used for specifying the reference table (that is, a dictionary produced by the Term Extraction transformation), as shown in Figure 14-20.

The Term Lookup tab shown in Figure 14-21 is used to specify the column mapping (for mapping the input text column to the Term column dictionary). You can also pass through some input columns, such as `President` and `Year` in this example. Pass-through columns are accessible to the rest of the data flow. Note that the actual input text column (`TextBody ASNTEXT` in this example) does not need to be passed through.

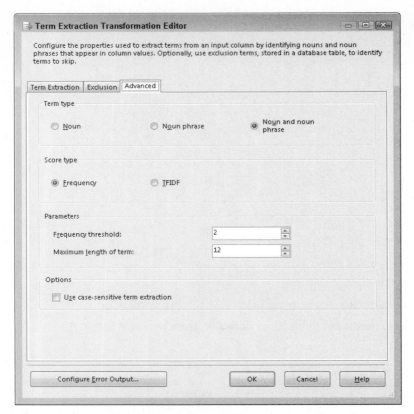

Figure 14-18 The Advanced tab in the Term Extraction Transformation Editor

The Advanced tab of the Term Lookup Transformation Editor allows you to specify whether the lookup should be case-sensitive or not. Just like the Term Extraction transformation, Term Lookup is case-insensitive by default.

The Term Lookup transformation produces two new columns as output: Term and Frequency. You can think of the output of this transformation as a fact table with a large number of rows containing the document ID, key terms, and associated frequency. Figure 14-22 shows the full transformation used to look up terms from the State of the Union addresses.

> **NOTE** If your data flow destination is a relational table that holds the terms associated with each document, then you must ensure that a document key appears in that table (such as a document ID column or the Year column in the current example). This key will be used later in modeling the nested table relationship between the documents table and the terms table.

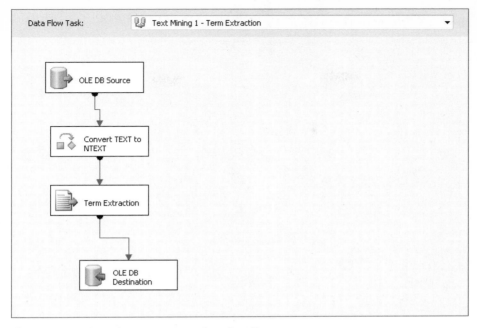

Figure 14-19 Complete term extraction data flow

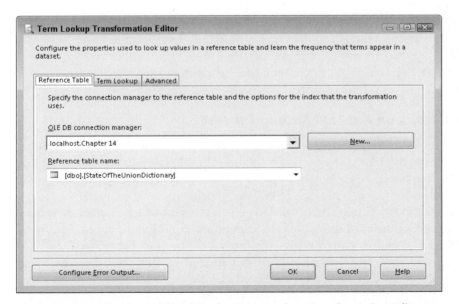

Figure 14-20 Reference Table tab in the Term Lookup Transformation Editor

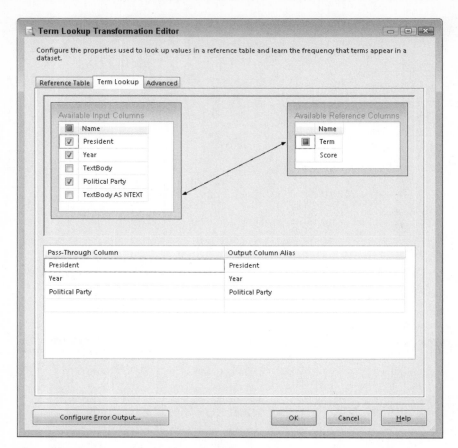

Figure 14-21 Tem Lookup Tab in the Term Lookup Transformation Editor

More Details on the Text Mining Process

Let's review the steps performed using the Term Extraction and Term Lookup transformations. You started with a relational table containing one large text column, the `TextBody` column, plus some additional columns, as shown in Table 14-4.

The Term Extraction transformation selected a set of significant terms from the `TextBody` column of the table. The dictionary contains the most significant terms and a score associated with each term, as shown in Table 14-5.

In the next step, the Term Lookup transformation detected the significant terms in each document (based on the dictionary in Table 14-5) and placed them in a new table, together with the document identifier (in this case, the `Year` column was used as a document key). Table 14-6 shows a fragment of the resulting table.

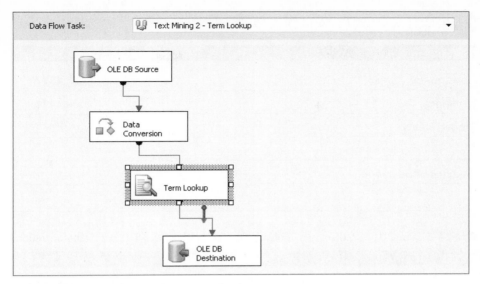

Figure 14-22 Complete term lookup data flow

Table 14-4 Original StateOfTheUnion Table

PRESIDENT	YEAR	TEXTBODY	POLITICAL PARTY
George Washington	1790	I embrace with great satisfaction . . .	No party
George Washington	1790 Dec	In meeting you again I feel . . .	No party
. . .			
Jimmy Carter	1981	To the Congress of the United States: . . .	Democratic
Ronald Reagan	1982	Mr. Speaker, Mr. President, Distinguished . . .	Republican
. . .			

The StateOfTheUnionTerms table can now be used as a nested table in a model that analyzes the documents in the original StateOfTheUnion table.

Figure 14-23 shows an example of a mining structure designed to perform text mining on this data set. The structure uses the StateOfTheUnion table as a case table (using Year as the key column and Political Party as a case level column) and the StateOfTheUnionTerms table generated by the Term Lookup transform as a nested table. For simplicity, the frequency of a term in a State of the Union address is not included in the model.

Table 14-5 StateOfTheUnionDictionary Table Generated by the Term Extraction Transformation

TERM	SCORE
government	4877
Congress	4471
United States	3697
. . .	
Careful consideration	52
. . .	

Table 14-6 StateOfTheUnionTerms Table Generated by the Term Lookup Transformation

TERM	FREQUENCY	YEAR
Constituent	1	1790
Society	1	1790
Common defense	1	1790
. . .		
Metropolitan area	1	1965
truth	2	1965
New approach	1	1965
. . .		

In the mining structure, you can now add multiple models that apply different analysis techniques to the documents. Figure 14-24 shows the output of an Association Rules mining model that analyzes the cross-correlations of terms in State of the Union addresses.

Summary

In this chapter, you learned the basic concepts of another important SQL Server component: SQL Server Integration Services (SSIS). You were introduced to control flow and data flow, and learned about a few important tasks and transformations. SSIS is an important tool for data cleaning and transformation, which is a time-consuming step for any data mining project.

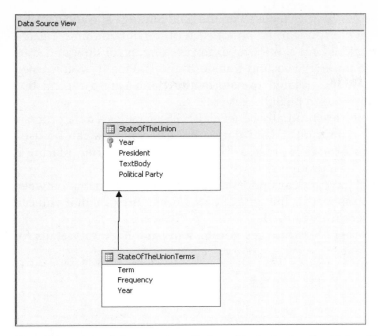

Figure 14-23 A mining structure designed to text mine the State of the Union data set

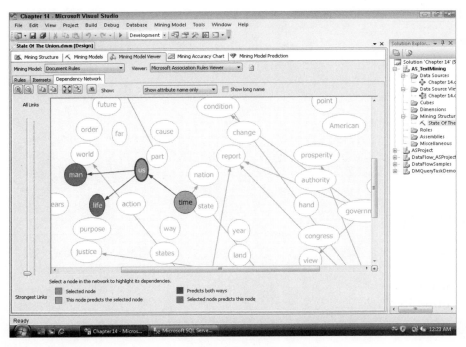

Figure 14-24 Output of an Association Rules mining model

The second half of the chapter focused on the data mining–specific features in the SSIS environment. You learned about each of the data mining–related tasks and transformations and saw some examples of control flow and data flow using these data mining tasks and transformations. Finally, you learned about the two text mining–related transformations and saw a typical text mining project example based on SQL Server 2008.

Data mining and SSIS are mutually beneficial. SSIS provides a data processing environment for data mining, and data mining techniques can be used as part of a data transformation process. This makes SSIS smarter, placing it ahead of other classic ETL products.

By now you should have a clear understanding of the relationship between SSIS and data mining, as well as the type of data mining projects that you can complete in the SSIS environment.

Stay tuned, as Chapter 15 introduces you to some architectural details for SQL Server Data Mining.

SQL Server Data Mining Architecture

This chapter discusses the architecture of Analysis Services, particularly the data mining side of things. It covers the communication mechanisms used between the client and the server, the server components and how they are used, server configuration, and how different options impact memory and disk usage. This chapter is intended for those who will be administering a data mining server, or programming against it. If you are interested only in performing analysis with SQL Server Data Mining, you can skip this chapter.

In this chapter, you will learn about the following:

- The Analysis Services architecture
- Using XML for Analysis (XMLA)
- How data mining processing works
- Prediction architecture
- Server administration
- Data mining security

Examples, datasets, and projects for this chapter are included in Chapter15.zip, which you can download from this book's website (www.wiley.com/go/data_mining_SQL_2008/). The archive contains the following:

- A SQL Server 2008 database backup containing the data set used in this chapter
- A set of files containing the DMX and XMLA scripts for this chapter
- An Analysis Services project

In order to try out the DMX and XMLA examples for this chapter, you must first build and deploy, from BI Development Studio, the included Analysis Services project.

Introducing Analysis Services Architecture

Analysis Services works in a simple client/server architecture, allowing clients to connect either through a LAN TCP/IP connection, or through IIS, using HTTP over the Internet. Analysis Services provides a variety of clients, such as OLE DB, ADOMD.NET, and more. Instead of introducing a new communication mechanism for each client, each client is merely a thin shim that communicates with the server by producing and consuming the core Analysis Services interface, which is *XML for Analysis* (*XMLA*). XMLA is a simple XML protocol for communicating with analysis servers, regardless of the source or destination platform.

When a request is received by the server, Analysis Services determines whether the request is an Online Analytical Processing (OLAP) request or a data mining request, and routes the request appropriately. In the end, a data mining request is either handled by the common data mining infrastructure or transmitted to a data mining algorithm, which can be an algorithm created by Microsoft (and included with the product) or a custom third-party plug-in algorithm loaded into the Analysis Services server. Additionally, a user-defined stored procedure can be invoked that uses a server-side version of the client ADOMD.NET interface to access server objects and model content directly.

Figure 15-1 shows the Data Mining Client architecture. The shaded boxes represent components that are part of Analysis Services, and, where appropriate, identify the files necessary to use the component. Chapters 16 and 17 explain how to program with these components.

XML for Analysis

XMLA is an XML application programming interface (API) based on the Simple Object Access Protocol (SOAP) designed to standardize and facilitate the interaction between clients and data providers across the Web. Traditional data access technologies require the installation of client components that are tightly coupled to the data provider. This coupling creates limitations such as platform- and language-dependence, as well as versioning issues between the client and server components. XMLA is built on the open standards of HTTP, XML, and SOAP. Therefore, it is not bound to any specific language or platform.

XMLA defines the mechanism for communicating with analytical data providers (such as data mining or OLAP providers) over the Web. It takes the concepts defined in other specifications (such as OLE DB, OLE DB for Data Mining, and OLE DB for OLAP) and extends them to be accessible via XML. Because of the flexibility this allows, XMLA is the core communications protocol to the Analysis Services server for all clients.

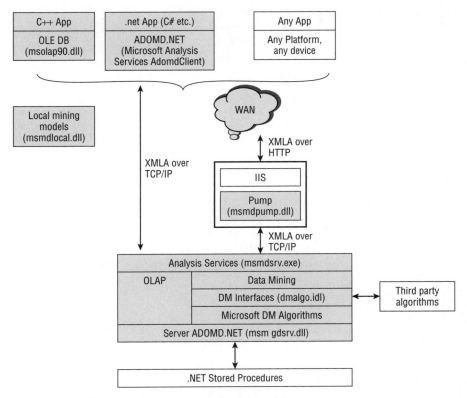

Figure 15-1 Analysis Services communication architecture

This discussion covers only the basic aspects of XMLA. If you want to learn more, the complete specification is available at www.xmla.org. The architecture diagram shown earlier in Figure 15-1 demonstrates how all client interfaces communicate through the XMLA protocol.

XMLA APIs

XMLA accomplishes all that it does with only the following two APIs:

- `Discover` retrieves schema information from the data provider.
- `Execute` executes queries or commands on the server.

You can execute the XMLA examples in this section in SQL Server Management Studio by choosing File ➪ New ➪ Analysis Services XMLA Query. The query window allows you to send XMLA statements directly to the server and displays the server response, also using the native XMLA format.

Discover

The `Discover` method allows the caller to receive information about the capabilities and the state of the data provider. The caller indicates the type of information requested, and the provider returns that information in the form of a rowset (analogous to a schema rowset in OLE DB or ADO).

The prototype for a `Discover` call is as follows:

```
Discover(IN RequestType as EnumString,
         Restrictions as Array,
         Properties as Array,
    OUT Resultset as Rowset)
```

The `RequestType` indicates the requested schema. This can be any of the schemas defined in the OLE DB for Data Mining or OLE DB for OLAP specification. Or it can be one of the six XMLA specific schemas from the XML specification, such as `DISCOVER_DATASOURCES` (which enumerates the data sources the XMLA provider is exposing).

The `Restrictions` parameter contains an array of restrictions. The possible restrictions for each schema are exposed through the `DISCOVER_SCHEMA_ROWSETS` schema (which describes all the other schemas). Listing 15-1 shows a request for the mining columns' schema rowset (`DMSCHEMA_MINING_COLUMNS`) that is restricted to the `Customers` mining model.

```
<Discover xmlns=''urn:schemas-microsoft-com:xml-analysis''>
  <RequestType>DMSCHEMA_MINING_COLUMNS</RequestType>
  <Restrictions>
    <RestrictionList>
      <MODEL_NAME>Customers</MODEL_NAME>
    </RestrictionList>
  </Restrictions>
  <Properties>
    <PropertyList>
      <Catalog>Customers</Catalog>
      <Format>Tabular</Format>
      <Content>SchemaData</Content>
    </PropertyList>
  </Properties>
</Discover>
```

Listing 15-1 XMLA Discover for mining columns

The `Properties` parameter contains an array of properties — the possible options indicated in the `DISCOVER_PROPERTIES` schema. Listing 15-1 shows a properties array, indicating that you are accessing the `Customers` database. Additionally, the code specifies that the results should appear in tabular format (the only option for schema rowsets) and that they contain the schema that was used plus the data returned.

After the request is submitted, the server returns an XMLA rowset. The rowset contains a schema section (describing the columns returned) and a data section (containing the data). If the schema is known, you can set the Content property to Data to eliminate the schema section from the response. Listing 15-2 shows a fragment of the response from the query in Listing 15-1 that contains a single row. You can see that a row simply contains the column names as tags with the column data as the text.

```
...
<row>
    <MODEL_CATALOG>Customers</MODEL_CATALOG>
    <MODEL_NAME>Customers</MODEL_NAME>
    <COLUMN_NAME>Age Disc</COLUMN_NAME>
    <ORDINAL_POSITION>2</ORDINAL_POSITION>
    <COLUMN_HAS_DEFAULT>false</COLUMN_HAS_DEFAULT>
    <COLUMN_FLAGS>16</COLUMN_FLAGS>
    <IS_NULLABLE>true</IS_NULLABLE>
    <DATA_TYPE>20</DATA_TYPE>
    <NUMERIC_PRECISION>10</NUMERIC_PRECISION>
    <CONTENT_TYPE>DISCRETIZED(AUTOMATIC,0)</CONTENT_TYPE>
    <IS_RELATED_TO_KEY>false</IS_RELATED_TO_KEY>
    <IS_INPUT>true</IS_INPUT>
    <IS_PREDICTABLE>false</IS_PREDICTABLE>

    <PREDICTION_SCALAR_FUNCTIONS>RangeMax,RangeMid,RangeMin
      </PREDICTION_SCALAR_FUNCTIONS>
    <IS_POPULATED>true</IS_POPULATED>
    <PREDICTION_SCORE>0</PREDICTION_SCORE>
    <SOURCE_COLUMN>Age Disc</SOURCE_COLUMN>
    <FILTER />
</row>
...
```

Listing 15-2 Excerpt from the Discover response

Execute

Whereas Discover retrieves information about the server, Execute allows you to send queries or commands. The function prototype is as follows:

```
Execute (IN   Command as String,
              Properties as Array,
         OUT  Resultset as Resultset)
```

The parameters for Execute are simply the command string and the properties array. The latter is identical to that of a Discover call. The command string is generally one XMLA node containing one command and the parameters for that command. Examples of such commands are Create, Alter, and Process. One special command is Statement, which encapsulates generic DMX or MDX commands that are included as text inside the XMLA element. Listing 15-3 uses Statement to issue a singleton prediction query to predict theater-going frequency based on marital status and number of children. The resultant rowset is identical to that of a Discover call.

```
<Execute xmlns=''urn:schemas-microsoft-com:xml-analysis''>
  <Command>
    <Statement>
      SELECT Flattened
      PredictHistogram([Theater Freq])
      FROM [Customers]
      NATURAL PREDICTION JOIN
      (SELECT 'Married' as [Marital Status],
      '2' as [Num Children])
      AS T
    </Statement>
  </Command>
  <Properties>
    <PropertyList>
      <Catalog>Customers</Catalog>
      <Format>Tabular</Format>
      <Content>SchemaData</Content>
    </PropertyList>
  </Properties>
</Execute>
```

Listing 15-3 XMLA Execute package

NOTE The Template Explorer in SQL Management Studio contains XMLA templates that you can use to perform common operations against Analysis Services.

XMLA and Analysis Services

XMLA is the core communication mechanism for Analysis Services. Regardless of which API you are using to connect to the server, the payload of the request and the response is essentially XMLA, as shown in Figure 15-1. In the case of OLE DB and ADOMD.NET, these clients enhance XMLA with compression and encryption and allow communication with binary XML.

Because XMLA is platform- and language-independent, and XMLA is the one native protocol, all the functionality of the server is accessible from any platform. No limitations are imposed on any client running on any device using any operating system and language.

Analysis Services extends XMLA to include the Data Definition Language (DDL) it uses to create server objects. This DDL is directly accessible and editable in both Business Intelligence Development Studio (BI Dev Studio) and SQL Server Management Studio. To access the DDL of an object in BI Dev Studio, right-click the object in the Solution Explorer and choose View Code. To access an object's DDL from SQL Server Management Studio, right-click in Object Explorer and choose Script Database as ▷ CREATE To, as shown in Figure 15-2.

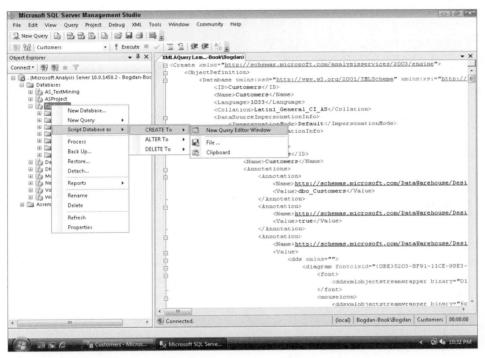

Figure 15-2 Scripting a database in SQL Server Management Studio

SQL Server Management Studio does not require a full `Execute` statement for a query to be valid. If the XMLA fragment in the editor does not start with `Execute` or `Command`, these elements are automatically added around the fragment. Also, the properties array (describing, among others, the current database) is added automatically. This is very useful for certain XMLA commands. XMLA DDL commands (such as `Create` or `Alter`) do not require a current database, because all object references contain a full path (including the catalog of the respective object).

However, `Statement` commands typically must be executed in a certain database. As you can see from the XMLA syntax in Listing 15-3, the property that describes the target catalog (the `Catalog` property) is included in an XMLA element on the same level as the Command element (outside of the Statement body). Consequently, any Statement command should use the full syntax and include both the Command\Statement elements and the Properties element.

> **NOTE** After you become familiar with the syntax of DDL, many edits are faster to accomplish in the DDL rather than with the user interface. Using SQL Server Management Studio, you can easily modify existing objects (with ALTER) or clone objects with small modifications by editing the DDL and submitting the altered DDL to the server.

Processing Architecture

SQL Server Data Mining is built from the ground up for performance and scalability, sharing many components with the OLAP portion of Analysis Services. Processing occurs in the following four stages:

1. Prepare the mining structure and its storage.
2. Query the source data.
3. Select the data to be used in training.
4. Use the model definition and the data mining algorithms to train your mining models.

Whenever a mining structure is created, a specialized OLAP cube (which is not user-accessible) is built by Analysis Services to hold the training data for the mining structure. Each non-continuous mining structure attribute (column) appears as an attribute in a cube dimension. Continuous columns from the training data are added as measures in the specialized cube.

There are multiple reasons for this architecture. Analysis Services must temporarily store the training data during model processing for algorithms that require multiple passes over data. Collecting relational data in a cube is a natural operation inside Analysis Services, and the data mining subsystem takes advantage of this. Data inside an OLAP cube is stored in a *tokenized* format — that is, distinct values for dimension attributes are represented numerically (one number for each distinct value), which is the format required by the data mining algorithms. Also, this storage mechanism provides unified data access for OLAP mining structures (on top of existing cubes) and relational mining structures (on top of specialized cubes generated during processing).

The first phase of mining structure processing fetches data from the source database and stores it in the specialized cube previously mentioned. Multiple source database queries may be executed at the same time to populate different components of the specialized cube. As the engine queries the data, it builds an index of all discrete and discretized columns in the mining structure. Additionally, another query is issued if there are any continuous-valued columns in the structure.

For models with nested tables, Analysis Services first issues one query per discrete-valued column in each nested table to generate an index, and then issues an additional query per nested table in the mining structure to process the relationships between the nested tables and the case table.

> **NOTE** Analysis Services issues many queries against the source database. You can limit the number of simultaneous queries to your relational store by setting the server property `OLAP\Process\DatabaseConnectionPoolMax` in SQL Server Management Studio. (See the "Server Configuration" section later in this chapter.)

After the data is fetched into the specialized cube, Analysis Services may start the data mining–specific processing. The second phase of processing consists of building the holdout store. SQL Server 2008 introduces the concept of *holdout cases* inside the mining structure — data points that should not be used in processing but are held out for ulterior validation of the models in the current structure. A data point from the original data source may belong to the training partition (that is, it should be visible to mining models during training), or to the holdout partition (that is, it should not be visible during training but kept for validation). The *holdout store* is an index of all the source data and the partition to which it belongs. This store is preserved in a file with the `hld.partition` extension in the `data` folder of the Analysis Services server.

WHAT'S A CASE?

A *case* (also referred as a *mining case* or a *training case*) represents one data point to be presented to the mining model for training (or prediction). In simple mining models with no nested tables, a mining case is one data row. In models with one or more nested tables, a mining case is the row in the main table, together with the associated rows from the nested tables (linked to the main table via the foreign key).

The third phase of processing is the actual model processing. In the Enterprise Edition of SQL Server, multiple models may be trained in parallel (depending on the available resources), whereas in the Standard Edition, they are trained serially. For each model, this phase consists of three distinct operations.

The first operation determines the raw statistics of the training data. First-level statistics (such as histograms for discrete attributes, and mean and standard deviation for continuous attributes) are computed for each mining model based on the training set of that mining model. Within the same structure, the raw statistics may be different between models, as a result of various filters defined for models.

The second operation consists of presenting the model with training cases and collecting patterns. From the perspective of Analysis Services, each mining algorithm is a data consumer. The server provides an algorithm with an interface for traversing the cases, and the algorithm is responsible for iterating the cases as many times as necessary and detecting patterns. More details on how an algorithm handles training cases are presented in Chapter 17, which covers extending data mining with various components (including plug-in algorithms). For now, you'll learn how the cases are prepared for model consumption from the server's perspective.

The data that aggregates in a mining training case may come from different components of the specialized OLAP cube built as a result of querying the data source. Case-level attribute values are typically stored in a cube dimension. An additional dimension is included in the cube for each nested table. Continuous attribute values are stored as measures. A component of the data mining processing architecture, the *case processor*, has the role of aggregating values from these different sources and presenting them as a single case to the mining algorithm. The case processor issues a query to each of the distinct cube components involved in building a model training case. These queries are executed on multiple threads, and a coordinator thread collects the results and merges them in actual training cases.

Figure 15-3 shows the case processor. After a case is materialized, it must go through two validation steps before being presented to the mining model. First, the case should be included in the training partition (and not one of the cases held out for verification). The identity of the partition to which a case belongs is preserved in the holdout store. Then, a mining case must match the filter associated with the mining model (if the mode has a filter). Cases that fail either of these validations are skipped by the case processor and not presented to the model during training.

WORKING WITH MULTIPLE THREADS

As you can see in Figure 15-3, multiple threads are used in preparing the mining cases for training a single model. If your model has many nested tables, this may lead to *thread starvation* (not enough threads are available to complete the processing), which is an unpleasant situation where processing

(continued)

WORKING WITH MULTIPLE THREADS *(continued)*

basically hangs. The minimum number of threads required to process a mining model can be computed as follows:

```
<Number of nested tables> + 1 (for the main table) + 1
```

For example, in a model with seven nested tables, nine concurrent tasks may be executed at one time. By default, Analysis Services is configured to execute at most four concurrent tasks per CPU. On a single CPU machine, four tasks are not enough to process a model with seven nested tables. The default configuration can be changed. The "Server Configuration" section later in this chapter explains how to access the Analysis Server Properties dialog box. Changing the following properties in this dialog box will solve the thread starvation problem:

◆ `CoordinatorExecutionMode` — Change the default value of −4 to −16. This will allow 16 concurrent tasks to be run per CPU, enough to complete the processing of a model with seven nested tables.

◆ `ThreadPool\Process\MaxThreads` — Change the default value of 64 to 128.

◆ `ThreadPool\Process\Concurrency` — Change the default value of 2 to −4.

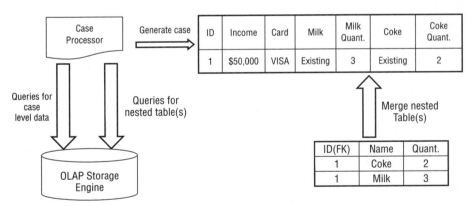

Figure 15-3 Case preparation during mining model processing

The third and last operation during the model processing phase is building the drill-through store (if the algorithm supports drill-through, and the mining model has that option enabled). During this operation, all cases in the mining structure (both training and holdout partitions) are presented to the mining model to be associated with one or more content nodes (patterns).

Once the algorithm training is completed, the patterns are saved and model processing is complete.

Predictions

As you learned previously, the mining algorithms see only a tokenized (numeric) view of the data during training. Consequently, during predictions, data must be mapped to the same numeric space to be used by algorithms. Prediction results (generated in the numeric space) must be mapped back to the original data space before being returned. Figure 15-4 shows the steps that are executed during a prediction query.

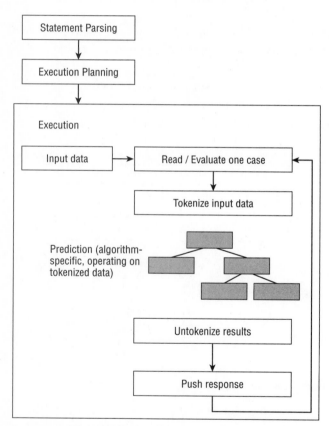

Figure 15-4 Data mining prediction

As you can see in Figure 15-4, each prediction query goes through two initial phases: parsing and execution preparation. After the execution is prepared, a prediction is typically generated for each mining case in the input. (An exception to this rule is the Time Series algorithm, which generates a block of predictions for all input cases.) To generate the prediction, Analysis Services converts the input mining case to the numeric space over which the algorithm was trained, presents the tokenized case to the algorithm for prediction, and then converts the predictions back to the original data space before pushing the result back to the user that issued the prediction query.

A direct consequence of this behavior is that a singleton prediction statement takes more time to execute (on average, per row) than a prediction statement against an OPENQUERY fragment. In the OPENQUERY case, parsing and execution preparation happen only once for all rows returned from the data source.

If you need to execute singleton prediction statements, then the parsing time can be reduced by using named parameters for input values, rather than typing the values as strings.

For example, the statement in Listing 15-4 would generally execute faster than the statement in Listing 15-5. Named parameters can be strongly typed in the client application, and this saves parsing and type conversion time on the server. The performance difference is generally not very significant for a single input row. However, for predictions based on many inputs, a table parameter (a feature described in Chapter 16) is significantly faster than a large singleton statement comprising many input rows linked with UNION constructs.

NOTE Parameterized queries can only be executed programmatically, not from SQL Server Management Studio. Examples of such queries are presented in Chapter 16.

```
SELECT PredictProbability([Theater Freq], 'Weekly')
    FROM Customers NATURAL PREDICTION
    JOIN(SELECT @numChildren as [Num Children], @age as Age) AS T
```

Listing 15-4 Singleton prediction query with strongly typed parameters as input

```
SELECT PredictProbability([Theater Freq], 'Weekly')
    FROM Customers NATURAL PREDICTION
    JOIN(SELECT 1 as [Num Children], 35 as Age) AS T
```

Listing 15-5 Singleton prediction query with inline values as input

Data Mining Administration

Most administration information is well-documented in Books Online, accessible through the Help menu of BI Dev Studio or SQL Server Management Studio. However, the topics of server configuration (as it relates to data mining) and data mining security warrant special attention here.

Server Configuration

The variables that control server behavior are modified in SQL Management Studio. To access server properties, you must connect to the server in Object Explorer, and then right-click the server and select Properties from the context menu. This action will launch the Analysis Server Properties dialog, presented in Figure 15-5.

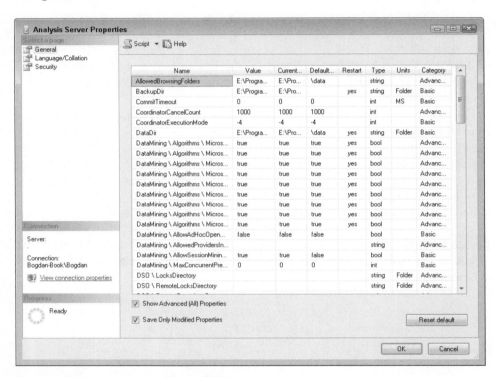

Figure 15-5 Analysis Server Properties dialog box

Modifying these properties allows you to tune your server for the way you use it, and also to control how the server is used by clients for security issues. Properties are divided into two categories: basic and advanced.

By default, in the dialog you will see only the basic server properties. To see the advanced properties, you must check the Show Advanced (All) Properties check box at the bottom of the Properties window. All data mining–specific entries start with `DataMining`.

The properties `AllowAdHocOpenRowsetQueries` and `AllowedProviders InOpenRowset` enable you to control ad hoc access to OLE DB providers during prediction or training (`INSERT INTO`) queries. Because OLE DB providers are loaded directly into the server's memory space, it is theoretically possible for a security hole in the provider to manifest in Analysis Services. Setting

`AllowAdHocOpenRowsetQueries` to `true` allows the execution of `OpenRowset` queries by those who are not server administrators, but opens a potential security hole. Leaving this property set to `false` (the default value) limits your users to browsing models, executing singleton queries, and executing statements containing `OPENQUERY` clauses against data sources for which they have permission.

If you choose to allow ad hoc `OPENROWSET` access, you still can limit your security exposure. The advanced property `AllowedProvidersInOpenRowset` enables you to select exactly which OLE DB providers can be loaded. This parameter takes a comma-delimited list of providers, or you can specify `[All]` to indicate that all installed providers are allowed. It is recommended that you set this property to the specifically allowed providers if you turn on `AllowAdHocOpenRowsetQueries`.

The `MaxConcurrentPredictionQueries` property enables you to control the load on the server caused by predictions. The default value, `0`, allows the server to simultaneously process as many queries as are allowed by the edition of SQL Server Analysis Services that is installed (that is, five for Standard Edition, and unlimited for Enterprise Edition). Queries sent to the server beyond this number are serialized and may time out.

Two sections of advanced properties control which algorithms are available to users and what their default parameters are. The first section, `Algorithms`, enables you to control which algorithms are available. For example, if you want only analysts to use a particular server for Time Series analysis, you could enforce this by setting the `Enabled` flag for all other algorithms to `0`.

Changing certain properties (such as the enabled state of algorithms) may require a server restart.

Data Mining Security

When the word *security* is used in conjunction with data mining, it has a tendency to raise some eyebrows. The Data Mining Moratorium Act of 2003 introduced by Senators Russell Feingold and Ron Wyden exemplifies the level of mistrust that much of the populace has toward this rather innocent technology. This being the case, Analysis Services has many options for controlling access to the information stored inside mining models.

Table 15-1 describes the types of permissions that can be assigned.

NOTE If you want to expose a model directly as a web service through XMLA for predictive purposes, you can protect the content of your model by assigning Read permission but not Browse permission. Also, ensure that only authorized users have the Drill Through permission on mining structure objects.

Security in Analysis Services is *role-based* — that is, you create a role that defines a set of permissions you want to provide, and then you assign users to that role. All users in a role have all the permissions of that role. You can automatically update their permissions by modifying the role permissions using the Create Role dialog box shown in Figure 15-6. You can create or edit roles in both the BI Dev Studio and SQL Server Management Studio.

Table 15-1 Data Mining Permissions

PERMISSION	EFFECT
Read	User can perform prediction queries on the mining model
Read/Write	User can update node captions in the model content
Browse	User can access the learned content of the model
Drill Through	User can access the source data from which the model or structure was trained
Read Definition	User can see the DDL representing the model metadata
Process (mining structure only)	User can process the mining structure

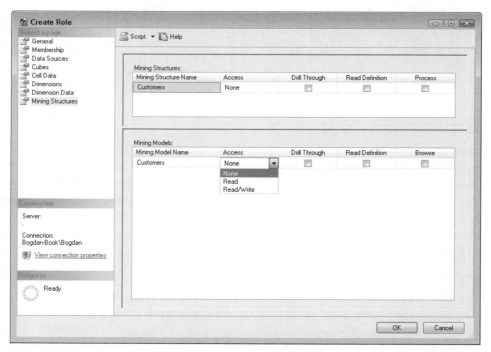

Figure 15-6 Create Role dialog box showing Mining Structures and Mining Models permissions

NOTE Analysis Services has only the capability to permit access, not to deny access (as the SQL Server relational engine does). Therefore, a user inherits the access permissions (but not restrictions) from all of the roles to which the user belongs. For example, Mary belongs to the Database Processors role, which allows her to process all database objects but not query them. She also belongs to the Data Miners role, allowing her to query models but not process them. Mary has the permission to both process and query models.

Additionally, permissions are nested, meaning that a role must have the same permission (if applicable) on the parent object to perform that action on the target object. For example, the Data Miners role must have Access Read permissions on the database and the mining structure containing the mining model to be queried, as well as permission on the model itself.

Security Requirements for Creating and Training Mining Objects

The permissions listed previously in Table 15-1 allow a database administrator to configure other users' access to existing mining models and structures. In general, in order to create a mining structure or model, you must be a member of a role with administrative permissions on the database.

Session mining structures and models (temporary objects that exist for the duration of the client session) are an exception to this rule. Such models can be created by users who do not have administrative permissions on a database.

The support for session mining models is governed by a global server property that can be changed only by a server administrator. After support for session mining models is enabled on an Analysis Services server, any user can create such objects as long as he or she has at least Read permissions on an Analysis Services database. Session mining objects can be queried and browsed by their creators without any additional permission.

Other areas of concern are stored procedures and plug-in algorithms. Although users must be administrators to install either one, you should check the source of the code to ensure that the authors are security-conscious.

Security for Various Deployment Scenarios

As you learned in Chapter 4, SQL Server Data Mining uses Data Source objects to access data in relational databases (for model training or for executing predictions). Data source access is governed by the ImpersonationMode property of the Data Source object, and this property determines what account is used (impersonated) while accessing the data source.

Selecting the right impersonation mode depends on the physical implementation of your solution, as well as the location of the database server and the Analysis Services server. Another important factor is the authentication scheme supported by your relational database.

If the database supports Basic Authentication and password, then all you need to secure is access to Analysis Services. Then, create a `Data Source` object using the correct username and password. Typically, you can use the `ImpersonateAnonymous` value for the `ImpersonationMode` property, because the username and password are already specified in the connection string. You can then grant users Read permissions on that `Data Source`.

On the other hand, if your database is configured to use Integrated Authentication (also known as Windows Authentication), things may get a bit more complex. The remainder of this section deals only with the Integrated Authentication model, because the Basic Authentication model can be easily configured using the Analysis Services security model.

First, you should keep in mind that the `ImpersonateCurrentUser` value for the `ImpersonationMode` property cannot be used for processing operations. The reason for this limitation is that the permission to process an Analysis Services object is a relatively weak permission — scheduled jobs or agents may need to periodically process objects, and these agents typically do not need access to the source database. `ImpersonateCurrentUser`, however, can be used in queries. That means you can use it in any prediction statement (via the `PREDICTION JOIN` operator), as well as in `INSERT INTO` training statements.

Additionally, Integrated Authentication does not work over multiple hops unless you configure Kerberos on your network. Without Kerberos, if you connect from machine A to machine B (which is running Analysis Services), then that instance of Analysis Services cannot forward your credentials to machine C running the SQL Server database. For more details on the Windows security protocols, read "Accessing SQL Server Using Windows Integrated Security" at `http://msdn.microsoft.com/en-us/library/aa984236.aspx`.

In this discussion, you will learn about some common deployment scenarios and the security and impersonation requirements for these scenarios. In the scenarios, *local* means on a desktop machine where you are either the administrator or can contact an administrator to configure the right settings. It also means that you need to secure access only for yourself. The term *intranet* in these scenarios refers to machines that are part of a Microsoft Windows network (either in the same Windows domain or in trusted domains), which means that you need to configure Analysis Services for multiple users.

Local Database and Analysis Services

This is the easiest scenario to configure. Typically, you need to ensure that the account used by Analysis Services has permissions to access the relational database on your machine, and then use the Impersonate Service Account option.

Alternatively, you could run Analysis Services under any account and create a `Data Source` object with the `ImpersonateAccount` value for the `ImpersonationMode` property. Then, configure the data source to use your username and password, and Analysis Services will have the same level of access to the SQL Server database as you do.

Local Analysis Services and a Remote Database

This is very similar to the previous scenario, with one notable exception. If Analysis Services is running under a local computer account (such as NETWORK SERVICE or LOCAL SYSTEM), you will not be able to set up Integrated Security access to a remote database, because the remote system will not accept the credentials of your local machine accounts.

For this scenario, you will have to either set up Analysis Services to run under a domain account (which has permissions on the SQL Server database), or use a `Data Source` that is configured with the `ImpersonateAccount` value for the `ImpersonationMode` property and specify an account that has permissions on the SQL Server database.

Intranet Analysis Services and Databases on the Same Server

When a user connects to Analysis Services, the first level of security is the database permission. The user will see only the Analysis Services databases that he or she has permissions to use. The Analysis Services permission model allows you to easily restrict user access to any mining structure or mining model.

When building your mining structures, you would typically use a `Data Source` with the `ImpersonateAccount` value for the `ImpersonationMode` property and specify an account that has permissions on the SQL Server database. This guarantees that any user with Read permissions on the data source and Process permissions on the mining structure can process the structure (and the models).

You can set up another `Data Source` (possibly pointing to the same relational database) for querying and executing predictions. This second `Data Source` could either impersonate a different account (with more restrictive data access permissions), or use the `ImpersonateCurrentUser` value for the `ImpersonationMode` property.

In this dual `Data Source` deployment, the users typically belong to the following three roles:

- A privileged role containing only Analysis Services database administrators. Members of this role may access either `Data Source`.

- A Processing Users role containing a service account (or maintenance users) that allows the members to process the mining structure and models using the first `Data Source`. Members of this role cannot access the `Data Source` directly, nor can they browse or query the models or structure.

- A Model Users role that can use the model to execute singleton predictions (against their own data), or batch predictions against the second data source (impersonated). Members of this role can access only data they are entitled to in the SQL Server database. Depending on your deployment requirements, you may choose to merge the Model Users role with the Processing Users role.

Note that the `ImpersonateCurrentUser` value will work only if the SQL Server database is installed on the same machine as Analysis Services, or if the Kerberos protocol is configured for the network. If these conditions are not met, then the second data source (used for querying) should be configured to use a low privilege account that can be safely used by all members of the Model Users role.

Analysis Services and Databases behind an HTTP Endpoint in an Internet Deployment

Analysis Services provides a way to use an HTTP endpoint to access it. Details on configuring the HTTP access are presented in "Configuring HTTP Access to SQL Server 2005 Analysis Services on Microsoft Windows Server 2003" at `www.microsoft.com/technet/prodtechnol/sql/2005/httpasws.mspx`. Although this document was published for SQL Server 2005, it applies to SQL Server 2008 as well. It explains how an HTTP connection to the endpoint is mapped to a TCP connection from IIS to Analysis Services. The document also describes how to configure the credentials of the account used to open the TCP connection.

Depending on your choices in configuring the HTTP endpoint, your TCP connection may impersonate the credentials of the remote user or a fixed account used by IIS to process the HTTP request.

If IIS is configured to use Basic Authentication (recommended only over HTTPS/SSL), or if IIS requires client certificates that are mapped one-to-one to Windows accounts, then the TCP connection uses distinct Windows credentials for each user who accesses the HTTP endpoint (specifically, the credentials associated with that user). Consequently, the scenario becomes similar to the intranet scenario described earlier. This solution requires that each user either has a distinct account in the domain where Analysis Services is running or has a certificate that is mapped to a distinct account in that domain. Analysis Services database permissions will ensure that each user sees only the Analysis Services databases he or she is entitled to.

You can assign users to groups, with each group using a specific database (or set of databases). You can also create one database per user and make each user an administrator in his or her own database to get complete isolation. (Again, a user must be a database administrator to create mining objects, and a database administrator has access to all objects in a database.)

You may want to offer some level of Analysis Services access to users who do not have an account in your domain. In this case, IIS cannot use Basic Authentication and will always impersonate the same account. You will do this either to offer access for everybody on the Internet (not a usual requirement, but a valid one for demo applications) or for a limited set of users. You can restrict access to a set of privileged users by providing each of them with a certificate and configuring IIS to require a client certificate and perform a many-to-one mapping of the certificates (and mapping them all to the same user account).

Even after limiting the clients by requiring client certificates, there is no way for Analysis Services to distinguish between the remote clients, so they will all have the same permissions (those of the account used to map the client certificates or the account used by IIS to handle requests).

This scenario should be implemented when the whole Analysis Services HTTP experience can be configured for multiple members of the same role (for example, a sales staff). The account used by IIS can be configured to have query permissions on certain mining models, and if necessary for predictions, to have read permissions on `Data Sources` impersonating low privilege accounts. The account used by IIS could also be granted the Database Administrator permission (by including it in a role that has this permission), which allows users to create mining models (but keep in mind that they will also be able to see each other's models).

Configuring Analysis Services for Use with Data Mining Excel Add-Ins over HTTP

This scenario is very similar to the previous Internet deployment scenario. However, it includes some additional options because the Microsoft SQL Server 2008 Data Mining Add-Ins for Excel can provide a full experience via session mining models.

As you have learned, if Basic Authentication can be used, the scenario is similar to the Internet scenario. However, if Basic Authentication is not an option, then you will need to create an Analysis Services database and grant Read permissions to the account used by IIS to execute requests. You must then enable Analysis Services support for session mining models. After you do this, users can connect to your HTTP endpoint using the Table Analysis Tools for Excel 2007 add-in. They can also use the Data Mining Client for

Excel add-in, but you will need to instruct them to always create session mining models.

If you want to provide some relational database access (for example, a sample database to be used with the add-ins), you will need to create a Data Source object in the Analysis Service database and point it to your relational data using a *low-privileged account*.

> **NOTE** Using a low-privileged account to access relational databases is very important in this scenario. A Data Source object with Read permissions allows a user to execute any DMX statement against that data source. A polite user will execute something like CALL SystemOpenQuery([DS], 'SELECT * FROM MyData'). A malicious user may try to execute CALL SystemOpenQuery([DS], 'DROP TABLE MyData').
>
> Analysis Services sends the strings blindly to the relational data source, so the only protection is to connect to the data source using an account with low privileges.

You may also choose to make the account used by IIS a member of a role with administrative privileges in the Analysis Services database used for this scenario. This will allow your users to create persistent mining objects, but they will also see all the models in the database.

The HTTP access can be load-balanced by providing your users with different HTTP endpoints on different servers, or on the same server, but using different Analysis Services database.

Summary

In this chapter, you learned where SQL Server Data Mining fits into Analysis Services. The native protocol of Analysis Services is XML for Analysis (XMLA), which allows clients on any device, on any platform, and using any language to connect and perform analytical queries. Analysis Services comprises many APIs, but all client communication (including management) has XMLA at its root.

You also learned about what happens in Analysis Services during model processing and prediction, the special configuration options of SQL Server Data Mining and how to set them, and the various security options that are available to secure your models.

In Chapter 16, you will learn about the programmability interfaces that allow you to build highly flexible and customized solutions using the SQL Server Data Mining platform.

Programming SQL Server Data Mining

The concept of data mining as a platform technology opens up the doors for the possibility of a new breed of intelligent applications. An *intelligent application* is one that does not need custom code to handle various circumstances. Instead, it learns business rules directly from the data. Additionally, as business rules change, intelligent applications are updated automatically by reprocessing the models that represent the business logic.

Examples of intelligent applications are cross-sales applications that provide insightful recommendations to your users, call center applications that show only customers with a reasonable chance of making a purchase, and order-entry systems that validate data as it is entered without any custom code. These are just the tip of the iceberg. The flexibility and extensibility of the SQL Server Data Mining programming model will excite the creativity of the developer, leading to the invention of even more types of intelligent applications.

Chapter 15 explained that the core communication protocol for Analysis Services is XML for Analysis (XMLA). This protocol provides a highly flexible, platform-independent method for accessing your data mining server. Everything that can be done between the client and the server can be done through XMLA. However, just because you can do it the hard way doesn't mean that you have to.

This chapter reviews programming interfaces and object models that make it easy to write data mining applications using Analysis Services. All the examples use Visual C# .NET to demonstrate how to implement typical data mining tasks with the appropriate interface for each task, and how to use some special features of SQL Server data mining to exploit data mining programming to the fullest.

Sample code and data sets for this chapter are included in `Chapter16.zip`, which you can download from the book's companion website (`www.wiley.com/go/data_mining_SQL_2008/`). The archive contains the following:

- A SQL Server 2008 database backup containing the data sets used in this chapter
- Three projects demonstrating the different APIs presented in this chapter

In this chapter, you learn about the following:

- APIs and their application to data mining
- Using Analysis Services APIs
- Creating and managing data mining objects using Analysis Management Objects (AMO)
- Data Mining Client programming with ActiveX Data Objects (Multidimensional) (ADO MD) for .NET (ADOMD.NET)
- Writing server-side stored procedures with Server ADOMD.NET

Data Mining APIs

If you were to list the various application programming interfaces (APIs) for SQL Server Data Mining, you would get a dizzying array of acronyms. To make things even more confusing, many of the names were chosen not because of their functions, but to provide brand affinity with existing technologies. Table 16-1 describes the major APIs used in Analysis Services programming.

NOTE See Books Online for full documentation and samples of all APIs used by Analysis Services.

ADO

ADO was created to assist the Visual Basic programmer in accessing data residing in databases. The ADO libraries wrap the OLE DB interfaces into objects that are easier to program against. Because OLE DB for Data Mining specifies that a data mining provider must be an OLE DB provider, ADO can be used to execute data mining queries just as it does relational database queries.

Table 16-1 SQL Server Mining APIs

API	COMPLETE NAME	DESCRIPTION
OLE DB	OLE for Databases	Microsoft standard API for accessing database objects from within any application that supports COM/ActiveX technology. It is typically used in native languages such as C++. It is supported via the Microsoft OLE DB Provider for Analysis Services 10.0.
ADO	ActiveX Data Objects	Friendly and easy-to-use wrapper on top of OLE DB. It provides access to data objects (including data mining) from native languages such as Visual Basic. It works on top of any OLE DB provider, in particular on top of the Microsoft OLE DB provider for Analysis Services 10.0.
ADO.NET	ActiveX Data Objects for .NET	.NET (managed) version of the ADO library. It is a friendly and easy-to-use managed wrapper on top of OLE DB. Just like its native counterpart (ADO), it works on top of any OLE DB provider, including Microsoft OLE DB Provider for Analysis Services 10.0.
ADOMD.NET	ActiveX Data Objects (Multidimensional) for .NET	.NET (managed) dedicated provider for Analysis Services. It works only with Analysis Services and does not use OLE DB. It has the same ease of access as ADO.NET, but it is optimized for Analysis Services operations, and offers various specific classes and interfaces. It provides access to Analysis Services data objects from managed languages such as Visual Basic .NET, C#, and J#.
Server ADOMD .NET	Server ActiveX Data Objects (Multidimensional)	Provides access to Analysis Services data objects from user-defined functions running inside the server.
AMO	Analysis Management Objects	A management interface for Analysis Services that provides objects for performing operations such as creation, processing, and so on.
DMX	Data Mining Extensions	Extensions to SQL to support data mining operations.

(continued)

Table 16-1 (*continued*)

API	COMPLETE NAME	DESCRIPTION
OLE DB/DM	Object Linking and Embedding for Databases for Data Mining	The name of the specification that defines the DMX language. It introduces the concept of data mining models as database objects.
XMLA	XML for Analysis	A communication protocol and XML format for communicating with an analytical server independent of any platform. It is supported by Microsoft Analysis Services and constitutes the main communication protocol between any client API and the server.

ADO reduces the complexity of OLE DB interfaces to the following three essential objects:

▪ The *connection object* is used to connect to the server and issue schema rowset queries.

▪ The *command object* is used to execute DMX statements and optionally retrieve their results.

▪ The *record set object* contains the result of any data-returning queries.

ADO.NET

ADO.NET is the managed data access layer. It was created to allow managed languages (such as Visual Basic .NET and C#) to access data, much as ADO was created for native languages. The philosophy of ADO.NET is somewhat different from that of ADO in that ADO.NET is designed to work in a *disconnected* mode, where data can be accessed and manipulated without maintaining an active connection to the server. When work is completed, a connection can be established, and all the appropriate updates will be propagated to the server (providing that there is server support for such behavior).

ADO.NET is more modular than ADO. ADO works in one way and that way only and contains special code to interact with the SQL Server provider better than other providers. ADO.NET provides generic objects that work with any OLE DB provider and allows providers to create their own managed providers for data interaction. For example, SQLADO.NET contains objects optimized for interacting specifically with SQL Server, and similar managed providers can be written for any data source.

ADO.NET contains connection and command objects, which is similar to ADO. However, ADO.NET introduces the data set object for data interaction.

A *data set* is a cache of the server data contained in a set of data tables that can be independently updated or archived as XML. You would typically use data adapters to load data sets — either the generic adapter that is supplied with ADO.NET or a provider-specific adapter such as SQLDataAdapter. For direct data access, ADO.NET uses a data reader (similar in concept to the ADO record set) returned from its command object.

ADOMD.NET

ADOMD.NET is a managed data provider that implements the data adapter and data reader interfaces of ADO.NET specifically for Analysis Services, making it faster and more memory-efficient than the generic ADO.NET objects. In addition to the standard ADO.NET interfaces, ADOMD.NET contains data mining and OLAP-specific objects, making programming Data Mining Client applications easier.

The `MiningStructure`, `MiningModel`, and `MiningColumn` collections make it easy to extract the metadata that describes the objects on the server. The `MiningContentNode` object allows for the programmatic browsing of mining models, and can be accessed from the root of the content hierarchy or randomly from any node in the content.

NOTE There is also a native version of ADOMD.NET, appropriately named ADOMD. This interface is maintained mostly for backward compatibility with SQL Server 2000 and does not contain any objects or interfaces for data mining programming.

Server ADOMD.NET

Server ADOMD.NET is a managed object model for accessing Analysis Server objects (both data mining and OLAP) directly on the server. It is intended for use in user-defined functions and stored procedures, described later in this chapter.

AMO

AMO is the main management interface for Analysis Services. It replaces the SQL Server 2000 interface, Decision Support Objects (DSO), which is still maintained for backward compatibility but has not been updated to take advantage of all the new features of SQL Server 2005 and SQL Server 2008.

Like ADOMD.NET, AMO contains the `MiningStructures`, `MiningModels`, and `MiningColumns` collections, and the like. However, whereas ADOMD.NET is for browsing and querying, AMO is for creating and managing. You can use AMO to perform programmatically all the operations you perform in the user interfaces of Business Intelligence Development Studio (BI Dev Studio) or SQL Server Management Studio. In fact, the management operations of both user interfaces were written using AMO.

NOTE You should use ADOMD.NET when writing Data Mining Client applications except when .NET is not available. Otherwise, use ADO (or OLE DB) for Windows applications, or plain XMLA for thin client applications. For applications in which you will be creating new models or managing existing models, use AMO. Note that AMO does not allow the execution of queries (such as prediction queries).

Using Analysis Services APIs

Whenever you need to access any of the APIs for Analysis Services, you must ensure that you add the appropriate references to your project. Table 16-2 lists many of the APIs with the required references.

Table 16-2 Analysis Services References

API	TYPE	REFERENCES
ADO	Native	Microsoft ActiveX Data Objects
ADOMD.NET	Managed	Microsoft.AnalysisServices.AdomdClient
Server ADOMD.NET	Managed	Microsoft.AnalysisServices.AdomdServer
AMO	Managed	Microsoft.AnalysisServices Microsoft.DataWarehouse.Interfaces

To make your coding easier, add a library reference at the top of your source files so that you don't have to specify the fully qualified name for every object. For VB.NET, add the following:

```
Imports Microsoft.AnalysisServices
```

Or for C#, add the following:

```
Using Microsoft.AnalysisServices
```

Using Microsoft.AnalysisServices to Create and Manage Mining Models

In this section, you will learn how to use AMO to create and manage data mining objects (models and structures). The examples use the MovieClick dataset and the goal is to analyze the way different generations of customers use various channels.

If your programming interest lies only in embedding data mining into client applications, you can skip this section.

The simplest way to create mining models is to use DMX statements such as CREATE MINING MODEL and INSERT INTO with any of the command interfaces such as ADO, ADO.NET, or ADOMD.NET. Although that method has the advantage of simplicity, features such as custom column bindings and OLAP mining models (among others) are not accessible through the command-based APIs. Therefore, to ensure that your application can take advantage of all that SQL Server Data Mining has to offer, the recommended API for creating complex mining models is AMO. In fact, the creating, editing, and managing tools included in BI Dev Studio and SQL Server Management Studio were written with AMO.

Figure 16-1 shows the major AMO objects used for data mining programming. These objects will be used in the code samples throughout the AMO section of this chapter.

AMO Basics

AMO is a straightforward object model placed on top of the XML representation of Analysis Services objects. In addition to providing a convenient API, AMO provides basic validation and methods to update, change, and monitor objects on the server.

> **NOTE** To add AMO code to your project, you must add references to two assemblies: `Microsoft.AnalysisServices` and `Microsoft.DataWarehouse.Interfaces`. Add the following line of code to the top of your source files so that you don't have to specify the fully qualified name for every object. For VB.NET, add:
>
> ```
> Imports Microsoft.AnalysisServices
> ```
>
> **Or for C#, add:**
>
> ```
> Using Microsoft.AnalysisServices
> ```

Every object in AMO implements the NamedComponent interface, which supplies Name, ID, and Description properties as well as a Validate method. An object's ID is its immutable identifier that cannot be changed after it is set. This is useful when you're developing user applications with fixed objects. It allows users to arbitrarily change object names for their own needs, while providing a consistent way for your code to reference objects.

MajorObject inherits NamedComponent. MajorObject adds the Update and Refresh methods to update the server with local changes. NamedComponent refreshes the local model with the server contents. Additionally, Major-Objects has methods to access referring and dependent objects, and contains an Annotations collection for arbitrary user extensions. The Role object is an example of a MajorObject.

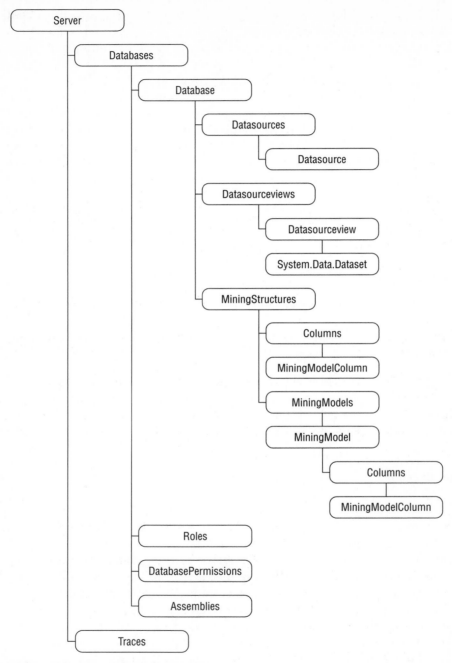

Figure 16-1 Partial AMO object hierarchy

`ProcessableMajorObject` inherits `MajorObject`, adding methods and properties to process the object and determine the processed state and last processed time. `MiningStructure` is an example of a `Processable-MajorObject`.

AMO Applications and Security

Because AMO is generally a management API, certain permissions must be present for users to use any AMO-based application. Obviously, any user with administrative permissions (members of the server Administrator role) will have access through AMO, but users with more restrictive permissions can also have limited access.

> **NOTE** To perform certain operations, such as iterating objects, using AMO, you may need a higher level of permission than when using a command API, such as ADOMD.NET. This is because ADOMD.NET and other APIs use database schemas to access objects, rather than metadata definitions.

Table 16-3 describes the permissions necessary for a user to perform any function through AMO.

Table 16-3 AMO Permissions

FUNCTION TO PERFORM	PERMISSION REQUIRED
Iterate objects	Access and Read Definition
View object definitions	Access and Read Definition
Modify objects	Administrator
Process objects	Access, Read Definition, and Process
Add or delete objects	Administrator
Set permissions	Administrator
Receive traces	Administrator

> **NOTE** You can test security in your application by impersonating roles or specific users. Set the `Effective Roles` property in your connection string to a comma-delimited set of roles you want to impersonate, or set the `Effective Username` connection string property to the name of the user. Note that only server administrators can connect with these properties.

For example, you could use the following:

```
svr.Connect("location=localhost;" _ &
    "Initial Catalog=MyDatabase;Effective Roles=LimitedAccessRole")
```

Object Creation

To create mining models programmatically using AMO, you perform all the same steps you would perform if you were creating and managing the models in the user interface. That is, create a database, data source, data source view, mining structure, and mining model.

To create any object on the server, you generally perform the following steps:

1. Instantiate the object.
2. Set the object Name and ID properties.
3. Set the object-specific properties.
4. Add the object to its parent container.
5. Call Update to the object or its parent.

For example, Listing 16-1 demonstrates how to connect to a local server and create a database.

```
// Connect to the Analysis Service server
Server svr = new Server();
svr.Connect("localhost");
CreateDatabase();


Database CreateDatabase()
{
    // Create a database and set the properties
    Database db = new Database();
    db.Name = "Chapter 16";
    db.ID = "Chapter 16";

    // Add the database to the server and commit
    svr.Databases.Add(db);
    db.Update();

    return db;
}
```

Listing 16-1 Database creation

NOTE For simplicity, the rest of the listings in this chapter that include AMO sample code assume that **svr** is a member variable containing a connected Analysis Services server object.

Creating Data Access Objects

After you have an Analysis Services database object, the next step is to create Datasource and DatasourceView (DSV) objects. The Datasource object is fairly trivial, consisting of little more than a connection string to your database. The DSV is a bit more complicated. The main element of the DSV is the *schema*, which is a standard Dataset object augmented with custom properties.

To load a schema into a DSV, you create data adapters for each of the tables you want to load and add their schemas into a data set. You then add any relationships necessary, and finally add the data set to a DSV, which is then added to the AMO database.

Listing 16-2 demonstrates this procedure by creating a Datasource object for the MovieClick data (which is included in the Chapter 16 sample database, available in the Chapter16.zip archive for this chapter at www.wiley.com/go/ data_mining_SQL_2008) and a DSV that can be used to create mining models with a nested table needed for analysis of movie channels.

```
void CreateDataAccessObjects(Database db)
{
    // Create a relational data source
    // by specifying the name and the id
    RelationalDataSource ds = new RelationalDataSource("MovieClick",
      Utils.GetSyntacticallyValidID("MovieClick", typeof(Database)));
    ds.ConnectionString = "Provider=SQLNCLI10.1;Data Source=localhost;
        Integrated Security=SSPI;Initial Catalog=Chapter 16";
    db.DataSources.Add(ds);

    // Create connection to datasource to extract schema to a dataset
    DataSet dset = new DataSet();
    SqlConnection cn = new SqlConnection("Data Source=localhost; Initial
        Catalog=Chapter 16; Integrated Security=true");

    // Create data adapters from database tables and load schemas
    SqlDataAdapter daCustomers = new SqlDataAdapter(
                "SELECT * FROM Customers", cn);
    daCustomers.FillSchema(dset, SchemaType.Mapped, "Customers");

    SqlDataAdapter daChannels = new SqlDataAdapter(
                "SELECT * FROM Channels", cn);
    daChannels.FillSchema(dset, SchemaType.Mapped, "Channels");

    // Add relationship between Customers and Channels
    DataRelation drCustomerChannels = new DataRelation(
            "Customer_Channels",
```

Listing 16-2 Data access object creation

```
                dset.Tables["Customers"].Columns["SurveyTakenID"],
                dset.Tables["Channels"].Columns["SurveyTakenID"]);
        dset.Relations.Add(drCustomerChannels);

        // Create the DSV, ad the dataset and add to the database
        DataSourceView dsv = new DataSourceView("SimpleMovieClick",
                            "SimpleMovieClick");
        dsv.DataSourceID = "MovieClick";
        dsv.Schema = dset.Clone();
        db.DataSourceViews.Add(dsv);

        // Update the database to create the objects on the server
        db.Update(UpdateOptions.ExpandFull);
    }
```

Listing 16-2 (*continued*)

TIP The ID of a `MajorObject` (database, data source, mining model, and others) must respect a set of syntactic restrictions. For example, certain special characters such as ? or ! cannot appear in a valid object ID. The `Utils.GetSyntacticallyValidID` function included in AMO generates a syntactically valid identifier starting from a given name and should always be used in real applications to generate valid IDs. It is only for simplicity reasons that this function is not used in the other code samples in this chapter.

The DSV in Listing 16-2 contains the `Customers` table and the `Channels` table, but the models you want to build need more specific information than is present in the raw data — in particular, the generation that the customers belong to (such as Baby Boomer or GenX) and a list of the premium movie channels they watch. To accomplish this, you must modify the code to add a calculated column to the `Customers` table, and swap out the `Channels` table with a named query that returns only the limited set of channels you are interested in.

Listing 16-3 contains `CreateDataAccessObjects` modified with a named calculation and named query.

```
void AddNewDataAccessObjects(Database db)
{
    // Create connection to datasource cto extract schema to a dataset
    DataSet dset = new DataSet();
    SqlConnection cn = new SqlConnection("Data Source=localhost;
```

Listing 16-3 Creating calculated columns and named queries

```
                Initial Catalog=Chapter 16; Integrated Security=true");

// Create the Customers data adapter with the calculated appended
SqlDataAdapter daCustomers = new SqlDataAdapter(
        "SELECT *, " +
        "(CASE WHEN (Age < 30) THEN 'GenY' " +
        " WHEN (Age >= 30 AND Age < 40) THEN 'GenX' " +
        "ELSE 'Baby Boomer' END) AS Generation " +
        "FROM Customers", cn);
daCustomers.FillSchema(dset, SchemaType.Mapped, "Customers");
// Add Extended properties to the Generation column indicating to
// Analysis Services that it is a calculated column
DataColumn genColumn = dset.Tables["Customers"].Columns
  ["Generation"];
genColumn.ExtendedProperties.Add("DbColumnName", "Generation");
genColumn.ExtendedProperties.Add("Description",
  "Customer generation");
genColumn.ExtendedProperties.Add("IsLogical", "true");
genColumn.ExtendedProperties.Add("ComputedColumnExpression",
                "CASE WHEN (Age < 30) THEN 'GenY' " +
                "WHEN (Age >= 30 AND Age < 40) THEN 'GenX' " +
                "ELSE 'Baby Boomer' END");

// Create a 'Pay Channels' data adapter with a customer query
// for our named query
SqlDataAdapter daPayChannels = new SqlDataAdapter(
    "SELECT * FROM Channels " +
    "WHERE Channel IN ('Cinemax', 'Encore', 'HBO', 'Showtime', " +
    "'STARZ!', 'The Movie Channel')", cn);
daPayChannels.FillSchema(dset, SchemaType.Mapped, "PayChannels");
// Add Extended properties to the PayChannels table indicating to
// Analysis Services that it is a named query
DataTable pcTable = dset.Tables["PayChannels"];
pcTable.ExtendedProperties.Add("IsLogical", "true");
pcTable.ExtendedProperties.Add("Description",
                "Channels requiring an additional fee");
pcTable.ExtendedProperties.Add("TableType", "View");
pcTable.ExtendedProperties.Add("QueryDefinition",
    "SELECT * FROM Channels " +
    "WHERE Channel IN ('Cinemax', 'Encore', 'HBO', 'Showtime', " +
    "'STARZ!', 'The Movie Channel')");

// Add relationship between Customers and PayChannels
DataRelation drCustomerPayChannels = new DataRelation(
    "CustomerPayChannels",
    dset.Tables["Customers"].Columns["SurveyTakenID"],
```

Listing 16-3 (*continued*)

```
                    dset.Tables["PayChannels"].Columns["SurveyTakenID"]);
        dset.Relations.Add(drCustomerPayChannels);

        // Access the data source and the DSV created previously
        // by specifying the ID
        DataSourceView dsv = new DataSourceView("MovieClick", "MovieClick");
        dsv.DataSourceID = "MovieClick";
        dsv.Schema = dset.Clone();
        db.DataSourceViews.Add(dsv);

        // Update the database to create the objects on the server
        db.Update(UpdateOptions.ExpandFull);
    }
```

Listing 16-3 (*continued*)

Creating the Mining Structure

The next step in the data mining program is to create the mining structure that describes the domain of the problem in terms the data mining engine understands. You must create MiningStructureColumns and specify their data types, content types, and data bindings to their source columns in the DSV. Listing 16-4 contains the code to create a mining structure that will allow you to analyze the relationships between generation and premium channels.

```
MiningStructure CreateMiningStructure(Database db)
{
    // Initialize a new mining structure
    MiningStructure ms = new MiningStructure(
            "PayChannelAnalysis", "PayChannelAnalysis");
    ms.Source = new DataSourceViewBinding("MovieClick");

    // Create the columns of the mining structure
    // setting the type, content and data binding

    // User Id column
    ScalarMiningStructureColumn UserID = new
        ScalarMiningStructureColumn("UserId", "UserId");
    UserID.Type = MiningStructureColumnTypes.Long;
    UserID.Content = MiningStructureColumnContents.Key;
    UserID.IsKey = true;
    // Add data binding to the column
    UserID.KeyColumns.Add("Customers", "SurveyTakenID",
        System.Data.OleDb.OleDbType.Integer);
```

Listing 16-4 Creating the mining structure

```
        // Add the column to the mining structure
        ms.Columns.Add(UserID);

        // Generation column
        ScalarMiningStructureColumn Generation = new
            ScalarMiningStructureColumn("Generation", "Generation");
        Generation.Type = MiningStructureColumnTypes.Text;
        Generation.Content = MiningStructureColumnContents.Discrete;
        // Add data binding to the column
        Generation.KeyColumns.Add("Customers", "Generation",
            System.Data.OleDb.OleDbType.WChar);
        // Add the column to the mining structure
        ms.Columns.Add(Generation);

        // Add Nested table by creating a table column and adding
        // a key column to the nested table
        TableMiningStructureColumn PayChannels = new
            TableMiningStructureColumn("PayChannels", "PayChannels");
        PayChannels.ForeignKeyColumns.Add("PayChannels", "SurveyTakenID",
            System.Data.OleDb.OleDbType.Integer);

        ScalarMiningStructureColumn Channel = new
            ScalarMiningStructureColumn("Channel", "Channel");
        Channel.Type = MiningStructureColumnTypes.Text;
        Channel.Content = MiningStructureColumnContents.Key;
        Channel.IsKey = true;
        // Add data binding to the column
        Channel.KeyColumns.Add("PayChannels", "Channel",
            System.Data.OleDb.OleDbType.WChar);
        PayChannels.Columns.Add(Channel);
        ms.Columns.Add(PayChannels);

        // Add the mining structure to the database
        db.MiningStructures.Add(ms);
        ms.Update();

        return ms;
    }
```

Listing 16-4 (*continued*)

NOTE You may wonder why you specify that the column content is `Key` and also have to set the `IsKey` property to `True`. This is because of the extensibility in the content types defined in the OLE DB for Data Mining specification. Currently, Analysis Services supports three types of keys: `Key`, `Key Time`, and `Key Sequence`. Having a separate `IsKey` property allows you to take advantage of this extensibility in the future.

Creating the Mining Models

Finally, you are at the point where you can create the models you want to use to analyze your customers. In addition to a collection of columns, a structure contains a collection of models. For each model, you add the columns you want from the structure and set their usage to `Key`, `Predict`, or `PredictOnly`. Columns without a specified usage are assumed to be `Input`, so you do not need to explicitly set them. For columns that you want the algorithm to ignore, you simply do not add them to the model.

Listing 16-5 demonstrates how to create two models inside the structure you previously built. A parameterized cluster model is created, and then a tree model is built from a copy of that model.

```
void CreateModels(MiningStructure ms)
{
    MiningModel ClusterModel;
    MiningModel TreeModel;
    MiningModelColumn mmc;

    // Create the Cluster model and set the algorithm
    // and parameters
    ClusterModel = ms.CreateMiningModel(true,
            "Premium Generation Clusters");
    ClusterModel.Algorithm = "Microsoft_Clustering";
    ClusterModel.AlgorithmParameters.Add("CLUSTER_COUNT", 0);

    // The CreateMiningModel method adds
    // all the structure columns to the collection


    // Copy the Cluster model and change the necessary properties
    TreeModel = ClusterModel.Clone();
    TreeModel.Name = "Generation Trees";
    TreeModel.ID = "Generation Trees";
    TreeModel.Algorithm = "Microsoft_Decision_Trees";
    TreeModel.AlgorithmParameters.Clear();
    TreeModel.Columns["Generation"].Usage = "Predict";
    TreeModel.Columns["PayChannels"].Usage = "Predict";

    // Add an aliased copy of the PayChannels table to the trees model
    mmc = TreeModel.Columns.Add("PayChannels_Hbo_Encore");
    mmc.SourceColumnID = "PayChannels";
    mmc = mmc.Columns.Add("Channel");
    mmc.SourceColumnID = "Channel";
    mmc.Usage = "Key";

    // Now set a filter on the PayChannels_Hbo_Encore table and use it
```

Listing 16-5 Adding mining models to the structure

```
          // as input to predict other channels
          TreeModel.Columns["PayChannels_Hbo_Encore"].Filter =
              "Channel='HBO' OR Channel='Encore'";

          // Set a complementary filter on the payChannels predictable
          // nested table
          TreeModel.Columns["PayChannels"].Filter =
              "Channel<>'HBO' AND Channel<>'Encore'";

          ms.MiningModels.Add(TreeModel);

          // Submit the models to the server
          ClusterModel.Update();
          TreeModel.Update();
      }
```

Listing 16-5 (*continued*)

Processing Mining Models

The code for processing an object is trivial, consisting only of the `Process` method called with the appropriate options. In the example program, you could process an individual model, the mining structure, or the entire database as you choose. However, because processing can be a rather lengthy task, it would be nice to receive progress messages from the server for the duration. Luckily, the AMO contains a `Trace` object to handle this type of server interaction. Listing 16-6 demonstrates setting up a progress trace for a processing operation.

```
void ProcessDatabase(Database db)
{
    Trace t;
    TraceEvent e;
    // create the trace object to trace progress reports
    // and add the column containing the progress description
    t = svr.Traces.Add();
    e = t.Events.Add(TraceEventClass.ProgressReportCurrent);
    e.Columns.Add(TraceColumn.TextData);
    t.Update();

    // Add the handler for the trace event
    t.OnEvent += new TraceEventHandler(ProgressReportHandler);
    try
    {
        // start the trace, process of the database, then stop it
        t.Start();
```

Listing 16-6 Processing the database with progress reports

```
            db.Process(ProcessType.ProcessFull);
            t.Stop();
        }
        catch (System.Exception /*ex*/)
        {
        }

    }

    void ProgressReportHandler(object sender, TraceEventArgs e)
    {
        Console.WriteLine(e[TraceColumn.TextData]);
    }
```

Listing 16-6 *(continued)*

DETERMINING SERVER CAPABILITIES

When you're creating models on the server, it is useful to understand exactly what kinds of models you can create. Besides the built-in algorithms, there may be plug-in algorithms installed as well. Additionally, each algorithm supports a variety of parameters whose default values may vary depending on the server configuration, for example between the Standard and Enterprise editions of SQL Server.

The MINING_SERVICES and MINING_PARAMETERS schema rowsets exposed by Analysis Services contain descriptions of the available algorithms and their capabilities. You can use any client command API to access these schemas, or even better, you can use the object model provided in ADOMD.NET to iterate quickly through the server's data mining capabilities. The following code demonstrates how to iterate through the mining services and their respective parameters:

```
public void DiscoverServices()
{
    AdomdConnection connection = new AdomdConnection(
        "Data Source=localhost");
    connection.Open();
    foreach( MiningService ms in connection.MiningServices)
    {
        Console.WriteLine("Service: " + ms.Name);
        foreach( MiningServiceParameter mp in
            ms.AvailableParameters)
        {
            Console.WriteLine("  Parameter: " + mp.Name +
                "  Default: " + mp.DefaultValue);
        }
    }
    connection.Close();
}
```

Deploying Mining Models

After creating your models, you may find that you need to move them around to different servers. For example, you may need to move them from an analytical server to a production server for embedding into line-of-business applications, or maybe simply to share a model with a colleague who cannot physically access your servers.

Analysis Services provides a robust backup-and-restore API in AMO. However, these APIs are geared more toward OLAP objects than toward data mining objects. The APIs contain many options that are unnecessary for data mining and operate solely at the database level, which is generally too coarse for most data mining operations.

Because of the mismatch in the functionality provided and the functionality required in AMO, the deployment of data mining objects is handled through DMX via a command API. Using the DMX EXPORT and IMPORT commands, you can select the single model that performs best out of the forest of candidate models you created and deploy it alone, rather than deploying the entire database.

Listing 16-7 demonstrates how you can use ADOMD.NET to transfer individual models from your current server to your production server.

```
public void TransferModel()
{
    // Create connections to the source and destination server.
    AdomdConnection cnSource = new AdomdCommand(
     "Data Source=localhost; Initial Catalog=Chapter 16");
    AdomdConnection cnDest = new AdomdCommand(
     "Data Source=ProductionServer; Initial Catalog=Chapter 16");
    try
    {
        // Export the model to a share on the destination server.
        AdomdCommand cmdExport = new AdomdCommand();
        cmdExport.Connection = cnSource;
        cmdExport.CommandText =
    "EXPORT MINING MODEL GenerationTree " +
     "TO '\\\\ProdutionServer\\Transfer\\GenerationTree.abk' " +
    "WITH PASSWORD= 'MyPassword'";
        cnSource.Open();
        cmdExport.ExecuteNonQuery();

        // Import the model into the current database on the
        // destination server.
        AdomdCommand cmdImport = new AdomdCommand();
        cmdImport.Connection = cnDest;
        cmdImport.CommandText = "IMPORT FROM " +
            " 'c:\\Transfer\\GenerationTree.abk' " +
```

Listing 16-7 Exporting and importing mining models

```
                " WITH PASSWORD= 'MyPassword' ";
        cnDest.Open();
         cmdImport.ExecuteNonQuery();
    }
    catch(Exception /*ex*/)
    {
    }
    cnSource.Close();
    cnDest.Close();
}
```

Listing 16-7 (*continued*)

In this example, you simply move one model between servers. The EXPORT command is flexible enough to export multiple models or entire mining structures as well. If you need to reprocess the models on the destination server, you can append INCLUDE DEPENDENCIES to the EXPORT command, and the necessary Datasource and DSV objects will be included in the export package.

NOTE Because OLAP objects do not support object-level importing and exporting, you cannot use the EXPORT command to export OLAP mining models.

Setting Mining Permissions

After the models are built, processed, and deployed, you must assign permissions so that they can be accessed by client applications. Permissions in Analysis Services are managed by the coordination of two objects: a Role object (which belongs to the database and contains a list of members) and a Permission object belonging to the protected object (which refers to a role and specifies the access permissions of that role). Listing 16-8 demonstrates the creation of a role and assigning permissions.

```
void SetModelPermissions(Database db, MiningModel mm)
{
    // Create a new role and add members
    Role r = new Role("ModelReader", "ModelReader");

    r.Members.Add(new RoleMember("redmond\\jamiemac"));
    r.Members.Add(new RoleMember("redmond\\zhaotang"));
    r.Members.Add(new RoleMember("redmond\\bogdanc"));

    // Add the role to the database and update
```

Listing 16-8 Assigning mining model permissions

```
      db.Roles.Add(r);
      r.Update();


      // Create a permission object referring the role
      MiningModelPermission mmp = new MiningModelPermission();
      mmp.Name = "ModelReader";
      mmp.ID = "ModelReader";
      mmp.RoleID = "ModelReader";

      // Assign access rights to the permission
      mmp.Read = ReadAccess.Allowed;
      mmp.AllowBrowsing = true;
      mmp.AllowDrillThrough = true;
      mmp.ReadDefinition = ReadDefinitionAccess.Allowed;


      // Add permission to the model and update
      mm.MiningModelPermissions.Add(mmp);
      mmp.Update();
}
```

Listing 16-8 (*continued*)

Browsing and Querying Mining Models

Creating and deploying models is only the beginning. The real fun starts when you take the power of the learned knowledge of your models and embed that directly into your applications. You can recommend products, manage inventory, forecast revenue, validate data, and perform countless other tasks limited only by your data and your imagination.

Predicting with ADOMD.NET

Let's start with an example of a basic prediction query using ADOMD.NET. Listing 16-9 demonstrates a typical example of query execution. Readers familiar with ADO.NET will notice that the only differences between the APIs thus far are the names of the data access classes. In fact, it is equally possible to use the ADO.NET classes to perform simple queries against Analysis Services. However, ADOMD.NET is optimized to work with the Analysis Services server and allows you to take advantage of additional Analysis Services features.

```
public void SimplePredictionQuery()
{
    AdomdConnection connection = new AdomdConnection();
    connection.ConnectionString =
        "Data Source=localhost; Initial Catalog=Chapter 16";
    connection.Open();

    AdomdCommand cmd = connection.CreateCommand();
    cmd.CommandText =
        "SELECT Predict(Generation) FROM [Generation Trees] " +
        "NATURAL PREDICTION JOIN " +
        "( SELECT   " +
        "    (SELECT 'Cinemax' AS Channel UNION " +
        "     SELECT 'Showtime' AS Channel) AS PayChannels " +
        ") AS T ";

    // execute the command and display the prediction result
    AdomdDataReader reader = cmd.ExecuteReader();
    if (reader.Read())
    {
        string predictedGeneration = reader.GetValue(0).ToString();
        Console.WriteLine(predictedGeneration);
    }
    reader.Close();
    connection.Close();
}
```

Listing 16-9 Executing a simple singleton prediction query

For simplicity, the rest of the code samples in this chapter assume that the containing class has a `connection` member variable of type `AdomdConnection`, which holds an initialized connection.

Use `ExecuteReader` when executing queries that return multiple columns or rows, as shown in Listing 16-10. This performs the same prediction as in Listing 16-9, but it returns the flattened result of `PredictHistogram` so that you can see the likelihood of all possible prediction results.

```
public void MultipleRowQuery()
{
    AdomdCommand cmd = connection.CreateCommand();

    cmd.CommandText =
        "SELECT FLATTENED PredictHistogram(Generation) " +
        "FROM [Generation Trees] " +
        "NATURAL PREDICTION JOIN " +
        "( SELECT   " +
```

Listing 16-10 Iterating a multiple-row result

```
"        (SELECT 'Cinemax' AS Channel UNION " +
"         SELECT 'Showtime' AS Channel) AS PayChannels " +
") AS T ";
AdomdDataReader reader = cmd.ExecuteReader();
try
{
    for (int i = 0; i < reader.FieldCount; i++)
    {
        Console.Write(reader.GetName(i) + "\t");
    }
    Console.WriteLine();

    while (reader.Read())
    {
        for (int i = 0; i < reader.FieldCount; i++)
        {
            object value = reader.GetValue(i);
            string strValue = (value == null) ?
                string.Empty : value.ToString();
            Console.Write(strValue + "\t");
        }
        Console.WriteLine();
    }
}
finally
{
    reader.Close();
}
}
```

Listing 16-10 (*continued*)

NOTE If your application reuses an `AdomdConnection` object for multiple queries, then you should ensure that any `AdomdDataReader` object is closed. A connection cannot execute a command while a reader is opened on that connection, and an exception thrown while reading data (and not handled properly) may lead to a leaked open reader that makes the connection unusable. The `finally` block at the end of the iteration in Listing 16-10 guarantees that the `connection` member variable is still available and in a valid state, even if reading from the reader throws an exception.

In the preceding example, you flatten the results of a nested table query for ease of iteration. In some situations, however, flattening the results is not practical. For example, this is not practical if you have a query that returns multiple nested tables, or even nested tables inside nested tables. Listing 16-11 demonstrates how to iterate the results of the previous example with the FLATTENED keyword removed.

```
while (reader.Read())
{
    for( int i = 0; i < reader.FieldCount; i++)
    {
        // Check for nested table columns
        if (reader.GetFieldType(i) == typeof(AdomdDataReader))
        {
            // fetch the nested data reader
            AdomdDataReader nestedReader = reader.GetDataReader(i);
            while (nestedReader.Read())
            {
                for (int j = 0; j < nestedReader.FieldCount; j++)
                {
                    object value = nestedReader.GetValue(j);
                    string strValue = (value == null) ?
                    string.Empty : value.ToString();
                    Console.Write(strValue);
                }
                Console.WriteLine();
            }
            // close the nested reader
            nestedReader.Close();
        }
    }
}
```

Listing 16-11 Iterating the Attribute column of the nested PredictHistogram result

Everything that you've done thus far could also have been done with ADO.NET (albeit, less efficiently). Next, you'll expand your application's functionality by using a parameterized query to change the prediction input. ADO.NET does not support named parameters for providers other than the SQL Server relational engine. To use named parameters in your data mining query, you must use ADOMD.NET, as demonstrated in Listing 16-12.

```
cmd.CommandText =
    "SELECT Predict(Generation) FROM [Generation Trees] " +
    "NATURAL PREDICTION JOIN " +
    "( SELECT   " +
    "    (SELECT @Channel1 AS Channel UNION " +
    "     SELECT @Channel2 AS Channel) AS PayChannels " +
    ") AS T ";

AdomdParameter p1 = new AdomdParameter();
p1.ParameterName = "Channel1";
```

Listing 16-12 Data mining query with named parameters

```
p1.Value = "Cinemax";
cmd.Parameters.Add(p1);

AdomdParameter p2 = new AdomdParameter();
p2.ParameterName = "Channel2";
p2.Value = "Showtime";
cmd.Parameters.Add(p2);
```

Listing 16-12 *(continued)*

Listing 16-12 assumes that you allow and require only two channels to perform the prediction. Obviously, this is not always the case. ADOMD.NET allows you use a parameter to pass an entire table as the input data source. This enables you to easily perform predictions using data that is on the client or otherwise unavailable to the server. Multiple table parameters may be shaped together to represent nested tables. Listing 16-13 demonstrates how you can use shaped table parameters as prediction input.

```
AdomdCommand cmd = connection.CreateCommand();

cmd.CommandText =
    "SELECT Predict(Generation) FROM [Generation Trees] " +
    "NATURAL PREDICTION JOIN " +
    "SHAPE { @CaseTable } " +
    "  APPEND( { @NestedTable } RELATE CustID TO CustID) " +
    "  AS PayChannels " +
    "AS T ";

DataTable caseTable = new DataTable();
caseTable.Columns.Add("CustID", typeof(int));
caseTable.Rows.Add(0);

DataTable nestedTable = new DataTable();
nestedTable.Columns.Add("CustID", typeof(int));
nestedTable.Columns.Add("Channel", typeof(string));
nestedTable.Rows.Add(0, "Cinemax");
nestedTable.Rows.Add(0, "Showtime");


AdomdParameter p1 = new AdomdParameter();
p1.ParameterName = "CaseTable";
p1.Value = caseTable;
cmd.Parameters.Add(p1);


AdomdParameter p2 = new AdomdParameter();
```

Listing 16-13 Data mining query with table parameters

```
    p2.ParameterName = "NestedTable";
    p2.Value = nestedTable;
    cmd.Parameters.Add(p2);

    // execute the command and display the prediction result
    AdomdDataReader reader = cmd.ExecuteReader();
    if (reader.Read())
    {
        string predictedGeneration = reader.GetValue(0).ToString();
        Console.WriteLine(predictedGeneration);
    }
    reader.Close();
```

Listing 16-13 (*continued*)

NOTE The SHAPE statement builds a hierarchical rowset out of two flat rowsets, based on a parent-child relationship between the two rowsets. In Listing 16-13, the parent-child relationship links the CustID column in the top rowset (the CaseTable parameter) to the CustID column in the child rowset (the NestedTable parameter). A value of 0 is used in both rowsets to link Cinemax and Showtime together as nested table rows for a single top-level data row.

More on Table-Valued Parameters in ADOMD.NET

Listing 16-13 introduced table-valued parameters (in the form of DataTable objects) and used them for predictions. Table-valued parameters (also called *rowset parameters* in Books Online and various Analysis Service materials) are a very powerful feature of SQL Server Data Mining, because they allow data mining on any kind of application data.

Table-valued parameters may be used in prediction queries (such as in Listing 16-13), as well as in training mining structures and models (in conjunction with the DMX INSERT INTO statement). This allows applications to build mining models on-the-fly, without the need to stage the data in a relational database first. This feature is extensively used in the Table Analysis Tools for Excel 2007 add-in discussed in Chapter 2.

Note that a table-valued parameter need not be a .NET DataTable object. In .NET, a table-valued parameter may also be an implementation of the IDataReader interface, commonly implemented by various data access tools (such as ADO.NET). This allows Analysis Services to perform data mining on relational data that is not accessible because of network constraints.

Consider the scenario shown in Figure 16-2. An application has access to a local database and also to an Analysis Services HTTP endpoint, which resides outside of the local network. In this configuration, it is not possible to define binding on the Analysis Services server (bindings pointing to the local database). Therefore, the standard AMO method of building mining models cannot be used.

Figure 16-2 Data mining query with table parameters

However, the application may use table-valued parameters to upload training data from the local database to the Analysis Services instance. Listing 16-14 shows the code required to do this.

```
// Prepare one connection for each of the queries
SqlConnection relationalCnTop = new SqlConnection(
    "Data Source=localhost; Initial Catalog=Chapter 16;" +
    "Integrated Security=true");
SqlConnection relationalCnNested = new SqlConnection(
     "Data Source=localhost; Initial Catalog=Chapter 16;" +
    "Integrated Security=true");
// Open the local relational connections
relationalCnTop.Open();
relationalCnNested.Open();
SqlCommand cmdTop = relationalCnTop.CreateCommand();
SqlCommand cmdNested = relationalCnNested.CreateCommand();

// Prepare the relational queries
cmdTop.CommandText =
    "SELECT [SurveyTakenID], "+
    "   (CASE WHEN (Age < 30) THEN 'GenY' "+
    "      WHEN (Age >= 30 AND Age < 40) THEN 'GenX' "+
    "    ELSE 'Baby Boomer' END) AS Generation " +
    "FROM Customers " +
    "ORDER BY [SurveyTakenID]";


cmdNested.CommandText =
"SELECT * FROM Channels " +
"   WHERE Channel IN ('Cinemax', 'Encore', 'HBO',  " +
"                    'Showtime', 'STARZ!', " +
                    "'The Movie Channel') " +
```

Listing 16-14 Uploading training data with table-valued parameters

```
" ORDER BY [SurveyTakenID] ";

// Create an Adomd command for Analysis Services
AdomdCommand cmd = connection.CreateCommand();

// Unprocess the mining structure, to make sure INSERT INTO
        will work
cmd.CommandText = "DELETE FROM PayChannelAnalysis";
cmd.ExecuteNonQuery();

// Now prepare the INSERT INTO command
cmd.CommandText = "INSERT INTO PayChannelAnalysis( " +
"UserId, Generation, PayChannels( SKIP, Channel) ) " +
"SHAPE { @CaseTable } " +
"    APPEND( { @NestedTable } RELATE SurveyTakenID TO
        SurveyTakenID) " +
"AS PayChannels";


// Add table valued parameters to the Adomd command
// The parameters are added as IDataReader objects
AdomdParameter p1 = new AdomdParameter();
p1.ParameterName = "CaseTable";
p1.Value = (IDataReader)cmdTop.ExecuteReader();
cmd.Parameters.Add(p1);

AdomdParameter p2 = new AdomdParameter();
p2.ParameterName = "NestedTable";
p2.Value = (IDataReader)cmdNested.ExecuteReader();
cmd.Parameters.Add(p2);

// Execute the training query
cmd.ExecuteNonQuery();

// close the relational connections
relationalCnTop.Close();
relationalCnNested.Close();
```

Listing 16-14 (*continued*)

Listing 16-14 uses two relational connections (to a local relational database) to execute two queries: one for the top-level data and one for the nested table data. The query results are passed to the AdomdCommand object as IDataReader objects, a forward-only interface that does not cache all the rows in memory (as in the case of a data table). Therefore, large volumes of data may be uploaded to Analysis Services without overloading the memory of the client application.

Browsing Models

ADOMD.NET provides a rich object model for browsing the content and metadata of the mining objects on a server that are otherwise accessible only through schema rowsets. Figure 16-3 shows the major data mining objects of ADOMD.NET.

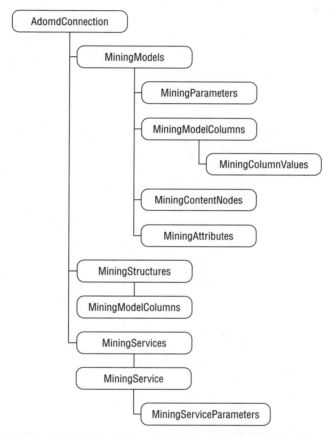

Figure 16-3 Data mining object hierarchy in ADOMD.NET

As you can see from the object model, you can simply connect to the server and iterate over any of the data mining objects without having to resort to schema queries. A nice benefit to application developers is that if a connected user does not have access to a particular object, that object will simply not appear in its collection (as if it didn't exist).

The most interesting thing you gain by using the ADOMD.NET object model is the capability to iterate mining model content in a natural, hierarchical manner using objects instead of trying to unravel the flat schema rowset form. Using this object model makes it easy to write complex programs to explore or display the content to your users. For example, an interesting problem for the Microsoft Decision Trees algorithm is to find all of the trees that contain a split on a given attribute.

Listing 16-15 demonstrates how you can use the content object model to explore trees and find splits on a specified attribute. First, you identify all child nodes of the root that represents trees, and then recursively check the children of the trees to see whether their marginal rule contains the requested attribute. By looking at the node type rather than at the algorithm used, this function will work against any model that contains trees, whether it uses the Microsoft Decision Trees algorithm, the Microsoft Time Series algorithm, or any third-party tree-based algorithm.

```csharp
// Identify all the attributes that split on a specified attribute
public void FindSplits(string ModelID, string AttributeName)
{
    // Access the model and throw an exception if not found
    // The error text will be propagated to the client
    MiningModel model = connection.MiningModels[ModelID];
    if (model == null)
    {
        throw new System.Exception("Model not found");
    }

    // Look for the attribute in all model trees
    foreach (MiningContentNode node in model.Content[0].Children)
    {
        if (node.Type == MiningNodeType.Tree)
        {
            FindSplits(node, AttributeName);
        }
    }
}

// Recursively search for the attribute among content nodes
// return when children are exhausted or attribute is found
private void FindSplits(MiningContentNode node, string AttributeName)
{
    // Check for the attribute in the MarginalRule
    // and add row to the table if found
    if (node.MarginalRule.Contains(AttributeName))
    {
        Console.WriteLine(node.Attribute.Name);
        return;
    }
```

Listing 16-15 Exploring content using ADOMD.NET

```
        // recurse over child nodes
        foreach (MiningContentNode childNode in node.Children)
        {
            FindSplits(childNode, AttributeName);
        }

    }
```

Listing 16-15 (*continued*)

You can also use the `PredictNodeId` function to find the reason for a prediction. For example, you can use the following query to retrieve the ID of the node used to generate the prediction:

```
SELECT Predict(Generation), PredictNodeId(Generation) ...
```

You can then feed the result of this query into a function such as the one shown in Listing 16-16.

```
public string GetPredictionReason(string ModelID, string NodeID)
{
    // return the node description
    if (connection.MiningModels[ModelID] == null)
        throw new Exception("Model not found");
    MiningContentNode node =
     connection.MiningModels[ModelID].GetNodeFromUniqueName(NodeID);
    if( node == null )
        throw new Exception("Node not found");
    return node.Description;
}
```

Listing 16-16 Using ADOMD.NET to find the reason behind a prediction

Stored Procedures

ADOMD.NET provides an excellent object model for accessing server objects and browsing content. However, there are some major drawbacks.

For the `FindSplits` method in Listing 16-15, you must bring the entire content from the server to the client to determine the list. A model with 1,000 trees and 1,000 nodes per tree would require the marshaling of more than 1,000,000 rows, even if only a handful of trees referenced the desired attribute. Also, in the `GetPredictionReason` function, even though you can access the desired node directly using `GetNodeFromUniqueName`, you are still causing a round trip to the server on each call. Performing this operation in batch mode is not recommended.

There is a solution to these problems. Analysis Services, starting with SQL Server 2005 (and continuing in SQL Server 2008) supports stored procedures that can be written in any managed language such as C#, VB.NET, or managed C++. The object model is almost identical to the object model of ADOMD.NET, making conversion between the two models simple. The clear advantage of Server ADOMD.NET is that all of the content is available on the server, and you can return only the information you need to the server. You can call user-defined functions (UDFs) by themselves, using the CALL syntax or as part of a DMX query. For example, the following query calls a stored procedure directly and simply returns the result:

```
CALL Chapter16SP.TreeHelper.FindSplits('Generation Trees','HBO')
```

The following query calls a stored procedure for every row returned from the prediction query:

```
SELECT Predict(Generation),
  [Chapter16SP].TreeHelper.GetPredictionReason(PredictNodeId(Generation))
  ...
```

In this case, the query will return the prediction result, plus the explanation of the result for every row.

CALLING VBA AND EXCEL FUNCTIONS AS STORED PROCEDURES

If you have Microsoft Office installed on the same machine as your Analysis Services server, you can leverage the functions of Visual Basic for Applications (VBA) and Excel as stored procedures inside your DMX queries.

For example, you can convert the prediction output to lowercase like this:

```
SELECT LCase(Predict([Generation])) FROM [Generation Trees]
PREDICTION JOIN ....
```

If a function exists in both Excel and VBA, you must prefix the function name with the name of the function. For example, to get the base 10 log of a prediction from Excel, and the natural log of the prediction from VBA, you would issue a query like this:

```
SELECT Excel!Log(Predict(Sales)), VBA!Log(Predict(Sales))
From MyModel ....
```

If an Excel function or VBA function also exists in MDX or DMX, or contains a $ character, you must escape the function name with square brackets ([ ]). For example, to format a prediction as currency (such as $20.56), you would issue a query like this:

```
SELECT [Format](Predict(Sales), '$d.dd') FROM MyModel ....
```

The supported VBA and Excel functions are listed in Appendix B.

Writing Stored Procedures

After you reference the required assembly (`Microsoft.AnalysisServices` `.AdomdServer`), you have access to a global object called `Context`. This object is similar to the ADOMD.NET connection object in that it contains all collections of major objects (such as `MiningModels`) that you can access in your stored procedure. The server-side `Context` object exposes a property, `CurrentMiningModel`, with no correspondent in the client side object model. This property provides the model that is the subject of the query and can be used in user-defined functions, as you will see in one of the procedures in Listing 16-17.

Stored procedures can take any simple type as a parameter and can return simple types or even a `DataTable` or `DataSet` in response. A client using `CALL` to call a stored procedure that returns a simple type will not receive a value, although the stored procedure will be executed. A client calling a stored procedure inside a prediction query that returns a `DataTable` or `DataSet` will receive a nested table containing the returned rows.

SENDING COMPLEX TYPES TO STORED PROCEDURES

If you need to send complex types (such as structures or arrays) to a stored procedure, you can serialize them using the `System.Xml.` `Serialization.XmlSerializer` object on the client and send them as a string. On the server side, deserialize the structure or array and call an overloaded function using the complex types you are interested in. For example, you may have a function that requires an array of the following type:

```
public struct MyType
{
    public int a;
    public string b;
}
```

You could write the following function to serialize the array into an XML string and send that string as a parameter to a stored procedure:

```
public string SerializeMyTypeArray(MyType[] arr)
{
    System.Xml.Serialization.XmlSerializer s =
      new System.Xml.Serialization.XmlSerializer(arr.GetType());
    System.IO.StringWriter sw = new System.IO.StringWriter();
    s.Serialize(sw, arr);
    string str = sw.ToString();
}
```

On the server side, you would need to duplicate the type definition and write a stub function to deserialize the array and call the real function, as follows:

```
public DataTable MySProc(string xmlString)
{
```

(continued)

SENDING COMPLEX TYPES TO STORED PROCEDURES *(continued)*

```
      MyType[] arr = null;
      System.Xml.Serialization.XmlSerializer s =
          new System.Xml.Serialization.XmlSerializer(typeof
              (MyType[]));
      System.IO.StringReader sr = new
              System.IO.StringReader(xmlString);
      arr = s.Deserialize(sr);
      return MySProc(arr);
  }
  protected DataTable MySProc(MyType[] arr)
  {
  ...
  }
```

This strategy will allow you to pass complex types and will prepare you for future versions that may allow complex types to be naturally passed.

Depending on the complexity of your data, you may want to use built-in .NET data types that support serialization (such as a DataSet object).

Stored Procedures and Prepare Invocations

When writing a procedure to be executed on the server, you need to know when you are being called to return a result versus when you are being called simply to gather schema information during a prepare call. Additionally, you need to indicate that your procedure is safe to call during a prepare operation and that calling it won't have any undesirable side effects. You wouldn't want to create the same object twice, for example.

The Context object contains an ExecuteForPrepare property that you can check before performing any time-consuming operations in your procedure. If you are returning a DataTable or DataSet, you should fully define the objects and return them empty of data so the client will know the schema. In general, you should not raise errors during preparation, especially for missing objects, because the prepare call could be used during a batch query, and the objects may exist by the time the procedure is called to return a result.

To indicate that your procedure does not have any unwanted side effects, you must add the custom attribute SafeToPrepare.

A Stored Procedure Example

Listing 16-17 demonstrates a stored procedure written in C#. The methods are the same as in Listing 16-15 and 16-16, but they are modified to operate on the server, take into account the presence of the Context object, and properly handle situations where the procedure is called during a prepare operation.

```
    [SafeToPrepare(true)]
public DataTable FindSplits(string ModelID, string AttributeName)
{
    // Create the result table and add a column for
    // the attribute
    DataTable tblResult = new DataTable();
    tblResult.Columns.Add("Attribute", typeof(string));

    // If this is a Prepare statement, return the empty table
    // for schema information
    if (Context.ExecuteForPrepare)
        return tblResult;

    // Access the model and throw an exception if not found
    // The error text will be propagated to the client
    MiningModel model = Context.MiningModels[ModelID];
    if (model == null)
    {
        throw new System.Exception("Model not found");
    }

    // Look for the attribute in all model trees
    if (model.Content.Count > 0)
    {
        foreach (MiningContentNode  node in model.Content[0].Children)
        {
            if (node.Type == MiningNodeType.Tree)
            {
                FindSplits(node, AttributeName, ref tblResult);
            }
        }
    }
    // return the table containing the full result
    return tblResult;
}

private bool FindSplits(MiningContentNode node, string AttributeName,
        ref DataTable tblResult)
{
    // Check for the attribute in the MarginalRule
    // and add row to the table if found
    if (node.MarginalRule.Contains(AttributeName))
    {
        string[] row = new string[]{node.Attribute.Name};
        tblResult.Rows.Add(row);
        return true;
```

Listing 16-17 Data mining stored procedure

```
        }

        // recurse over child nodes
        foreach (MiningContentNode childNode in node.Children)
        {
            if( FindSplits(childNode, AttributeName, ref tblResult) )
            {
                return true;
            }
        }

        return false;
    }


    [SafeToPrepare(true)]
    public string GetPredictionReason(string NodeID)
    {
        // return immediately if executing for prepare
        if (Context.ExecuteForPrepare)
            return string.Empty;

        // return the node description
        return        Context.CurrentMiningModel.GetNodeFromUniqueName(NodeID)
                .Description;
    }
```

Listing 16-17 (*continued*)

SUMMARY OF SIGNIFICANT DIFFERENCES BETWEEN ADOMD.NET AND SERVER ADOMD.NET

Following is a summary of significant differences between ADOMD.NET and Server ADOMD.NET:

◆ Many of the functions of the client-side `Connection` object are covered by the `Context` object.

◆ There is no `Console.WriteLine` or any direct output on the server side. Results must be collected in a `DataTable` before being returned to the caller.

◆ Server-side code should handle statement preparation (the `SafeToPrepare` attribute).

◆ The server-side object model uses the concept of a `CurrentMiningModel`, which identifies the model targeted by the current query.

Executing Queries inside Stored Procedures

A common use of a stored procedure is to encapsulate a query for easy reuse. For example, if your application needs to predict Generation, but you need the flexibility to change the model being used or add more business logic, you could write a procedure that executes the query and redeploy the procedure as necessary without changing the application layer.

Server ADOMD.NET allows you to execute DMX queries using the same objects that you would use with ADOMD.NET. The only exception is that you do not have to specify a connection, because you are already connected. You can copy the results from the query into a DataTable, or you can simply return the DataReader returned by ExecuteReader.

Listing 16-18 demonstrates the query from Listing 16-9 implemented as a UDF.

```
using Microsoft.AnalysisServices.AdomdServer;
using System.Data;
...
[SafeToPrepare(true)]
public IDataReader PredictGeneration()
{
    // Create a new AdomdCommand object
    // Note how it does NOT use a connection. The command is implicitly
    // connected to the database on which the stored procedure is invoked
    AdomdCommand cmd = new AdomdCommand();

    // Use an empty table to create a reader with the same shape
    // as the result for Prepare
     if (Context.ExecuteForPrepare)
     {
         DataTable tbl = new DataTable();
         tbl.Columns.Add("Generation", typeof(string));
         return tbl.CreateDataReader();
     }

    // Initialize the command with a query
     cmd.CommandText =
         "SELECT Predict(Generation) FROM [Generation Trees] " +
         "NATURAL PREDICTION JOIN "+
         "( SELECT   " +
         "    (SELECT 'Cinemax' AS Channel UNION " +
         "     SELECT 'Showtime' AS Channel) AS PayChannels " +
         ") AS T ";
     return cmd.ExecuteReader();
}
```

Listing 16-18 Executing a DMX query inside a stored procedure

In this example, if you want to change the model that's performing the prediction, you could just change the query inside the stored procedure, without having to change queries embedded inside your application. Of course, you can also parameterize your query as previously demonstrated in Listing 16-12.

> **NOTE** Stored procedures cannot be used to implement security in Analysis Services. The security context of the current user determines the access to the objects inside the Analysis Services server. That is, any user who calls a procedure that queries a mining model but who does not have Read permission on that model will receive a permission error. Similarly, a user who calls the `GetPredictionReason` UDF from Listing 16-17 but who does not have Browse permission on the model will also receive a permission error.

Returning Data Sets from Stored Procedures

Server-side procedures used as UDFs inside a query may return tabular- or scalar-type data. Procedures invoked with CALL typically need to return tabular content (that is, a `DataTable` or an `IDataReader` implementation).

Server-side stored procedures also have the ability to return `DataSet` objects (including multiple data tables and possibly various relationships defined between tables). `DataSet` results cannot be displayed in tabular result viewers (such as SQL Server Management Studio, which treats them as strings), but can be used programmatically. Listing 16-19 shows a server-side stored procedure that returns a `DataSet` object, and Listing 16-20 shows the client-side ADOMD.NET code that consumes the `DataSet` results.

```
public DataSet GetSimpleDependencyNet(string ModelID)
{
    // define the first table in the data set
    // It has two columns, AttributeID(int) and AttributeName (string)
    DataTable tblAttributes = new DataTable();
    tblAttributes.Columns.Add("AttributeID", typeof(int));
    tblAttributes.Columns.Add("AttributeName", typeof(string));

    // define the second table in the data set. Each row indicates a
    // dependency in the net (an arrow).
    // It has two numeric columns, each indicating the source attribute
    // and the second indicating the target
    DataTable tblRelationships = new DataTable();
    tblRelationships.Columns.Add("From", typeof(int));
```

Listing 16-19 Stored procedure that computes a dependency network and returns it as a DataSet object

```
tblRelationships.Columns.Add("To", typeof(int));


// Access the model and throw an exception if not found
// The error text will be propagated to the client
MiningModel model = Context.MiningModels[ModelID];
if (model == null)
{
    throw new System.Exception("Model not found");
}


// Build a hash table which contains all attributes and their IDs
Dictionary<string, int> dictAttributes = new
        Dictionary<string, int>();
foreach (MiningAttribute att in model.Attributes)
{
    dictAttributes.Add(att.Name, att.AttributeID);
}


// Now traverse all the predictable attributes, call the FindSplits
// procedure and insert the results in the table
foreach (MiningAttribute att in model.Attributes)
{
    // Add one row to tblAttributes for each model attribute
    object[] attributeRow = new object[2];
    attributeRow[0] = att.AttributeID;
    attributeRow[1] = att.ShortName;
    tblAttributes.Rows.Add(attributeRow);


    DataTable tblSplitsOnThisAttribute =
            FindSplits(ModelID, att.ShortName);
    // add one row to tblRelationships for each attribute that
    // depends on the current one
    object[] relationshipsRow = new object[2];
    relationshipsRow[0] = att.AttributeID;
    foreach (DataRow row in tblSplitsOnThisAttribute.Rows)
    {
        // FindSplits returns a 1-column table containing
        // attribute names
        string dependentAttribute = row[0] as string;
        relationshipsRow[1] = dictAttributes[dependentAttribute];
        tblRelationships.Rows.Add(relationshipsRow);
    }
}
```

Listing 16-19 (*continued*)

```
        // Add both tables to a data set object
        DataSet ds = new DataSet();
        ds.Tables.Add(tblAttributes);
        ds.Tables.Add(tblRelationships);

        // define a relationship inside the dataset
        ds.Relations.Add("FromAttributeName",
                tblAttributes.Columns["AttributeID"],
                tblRelationships.Columns["From"]);
        ds.Relations.Add("ToAttributeName",
                tblAttributes.Columns["AttributeID"],
                tblRelationships.Columns["To"]);

        // return the data set
        return ds;
}
```

Listing 16-19 (*continued*)

```
        AdomdCommand cmd = connection.CreateCommand();
        DataSet resultDS = null;
        // Invoke the DataSet returning stored proc
        cmd.CommandText =
            "CALL [Chapter16SP].GetSimpleDependencyNet('Generation Trees')";

        // The first value returned by the query is the data set
        AdomdDataReader rdr = cmd.ExecuteReader();
        if (rdr.Read())
        {
            object obj = rdr.GetValue(0);
            if (obj is DataSet)
                resultDS = (DataSet)obj;
        }
        rdr.Close();

        DataTable tblAttributes = resultDS.Tables[0];
        DataTable tblRelationships = resultDS.Tables[1];

        DataRelation fromAttName = resultDS.Relations["FromAttributeName"];
        DataRelation toAttName = resultDS.Relations["ToAttributeName"];

        foreach (DataRow relRow in tblRelationships.Rows)
        {
                string attFrom =
```

Listing 16-20 Using ADOMD.NET to consume the DataSet results from a stored procedure

```
        relRow.GetParentRow(fromAttName)["AttributeName"] as string;
    string attTo =
        relRow.GetParentRow(toAttName)["AttributeName"] as string;
    Console.WriteLine(string.Format("{0} -> {1}", attFrom, attTo));
    }
```

Listing 16-20 (*continued*)

The stored procedure presented in Listing 16-5 traverses all attributes in a mining model and invokes the previously defined FindSplits procedure to detect all attributes that depend on the current attribute (effectively building a dependency network of all attributes in the mining model). The dependency network is serialized in a data set that contains two tables: a table of the attributes' IDs and names, and a table of edges (directed dependencies between attributes).

Deploying and Debugging Stored Procedure Assemblies

After you have compiled and built your stored procedure, you must deploy the procedure to your Analysis Server so that you can call it from DMX. To add a .NET assembly to your Analysis Services project, right-click the Assemblies folder in Solution Explorer and select New Assembly Reference.

When deploying an assembly, you will need to select some security-related options, such as Permissions and Impersonation information. The defaults are functional for most scenarios. However, the discussion in this section provides some details on these options.

The Permissions property specifies the code access permissions that are granted to the assembly when it's loaded by Analysis Services. The recommended (and default) value is Safe. Table 16-4 shows the possible values and their implications. As a developer of stored procedures, you may need less-restrictive permissions (such as network access, if your stored procedure attempts to connect to an external data source). As a system administrator, you will need to decide what permissions would be best to balance your system's safety and functionality.

You can use the Impersonation property of an assembly when you require the stored procedure code to run under certain credentials. However, you cannot use Impersonation to control access to the internal object model. Object model access is always performed under the credentials of the current user. However, if your stored procedure connects to a remote database, you may need to require your assembly to impersonate the current user.

When you deploy your project, your assembly is encoded and sent to Analysis Server, where it is available for use in the project database. When you need to update your assembly, you can simply redeploy it. If you are using a live project, the assembly is immediately deployed on the server. To update an assembly in a live project, delete the assembly and add it back to the project.

Table 16-4 Permissions for Stored Procedure Assemblies

VALUE	DETAILS
Safe	This is the most restrictive and safest permission set. The code executed by the assembly cannot access external system resources (files, the network, or the registry).
External access	The assembly code may access files, the network, and the registry.
Unrestricted	The assembly code is completely unrestricted and may call any managed or unmanaged code.

If you have a general-purpose assembly that you want to access across all databases on the server, you can use SQL Server Management Studio to deploy it at the server level. In Object Explorer, right-click the Assemblies collection of the server, select Add Assembly, and then select the assembly you want to add.

Debugging assemblies is best done when you're running the server and client on the same machine. You can use a development license of SQL Server for this purpose. To debug the assembly in Visual Studio, select Attach to Process from the Debug menu. Select the executable msmdsrv.exe from the list, and ensure that the dialog box displays Common Language Runtime as the Attach To option. After you have followed these steps, you will be able to set breakpoints in your stored procedures.

Summary

In this chapter, you learned about the variety of APIs that you can use to access the functionality of Analysis Services programmatically. Although many APIs are supported, the two most important APIs are AMO and ADOMD.NET. You can use AMO to programmatically create, process, and manage your mining models, structure, and servers. ADOMD.NET is the general client API for browsing and prediction queries.

Using these APIs, you can create intelligent applications of your own. The logic of your application can involve dynamically creating mining models to solve user-defined problems. It can apply the predictive power of the data mining algorithms or examine the learned content of the mining models to provide new insights and new abilities to your users. You can also leverage your server in your application by writing UDFs that have access to all of the server resources through a .NET programming model.

The sample code for this chapter is available at www.wiley.com/go/data _mining_SQL_2008. It consists of three projects that exemplify AMO (the AMO-Management project), ADOMD.NET (the ADOMD-BrowseAndQuery project), and Server ADOMD.NET (the Chapter16SP project). The ADOMD.NET sample application depends on the mining models and structure created by the AMO application, as well as some stored procedures included in the Server ADOMD.NET sample project. Therefore, the sample projects should be built and deployed in this order: AMO, Server ADOMD.NET, and then ADOMD.NET.

In Chapter 17, you will learn how to extend the set of features that are built into Analysis Services, such as custom data mining algorithms and viewers.

Extending SQL Server Data Mining

One of the drawbacks of any data mining tool is that no matter how many features and algorithms the tool provides, it becomes useless the moment you require features and algorithms not provided by the tool. SQL Server Data Mining addresses this problem by providing extensibility mechanisms and allowing you to augment the functionality of the server and tools. There are four main ways to extend the SQL Server Data Mining system:

- Using stored procedures to add business logic or enhanced intelligence on top of SQL Server Data Mining

- Using the Visual Studio extensibility mechanisms to extend and enhance the data mining tools

- Developing plug-in algorithms that extend the algorithm set available on the server

- Writing new viewers to visualize data mining models

The use and implementation of stored procedures is detailed in Chapter 16. Extending Visual Studio is beyond the scope of this book — details, white papers, and samples are available at `http://msdn.microsoft.com/vstudio/extend`.

This chapter briefly describes the potential of and mechanisms used in developing plug-in algorithms and viewers. It covers the topics in enough detail for you to understand the basic architecture of each extensibility method, as well as how and why you would use such methods. The precise details of the interfaces involved are described in white papers and tutorials that are available in the SQL Server Books Online, or by visiting the SQL Server Data Mining Web site at `www.sqlserverdatamining.com` and selecting the Tutorials and the Whitepapers and Articles sections of the site.

Plug-in Algorithms

Starting with the 2005 version, the SQL Server data mining product has been considered unique in that it provides the mechanisms for third parties to develop and integrate their own algorithms that run inside Analysis Services. The Analysis Services tools and server architecture are arranged in such a way that they are agnostic to the actual algorithms that exist on the server.

Using the configuration management mechanism, you can disable server algorithms. You can also add new algorithms to each server. These algorithms operate using essentially the same interfaces as the built-in algorithms provided by Microsoft, so they can take advantage of all the platform features provided by the server, and with no performance penalties. You may want to build such a plug-in algorithm to do one or more of the following:

- Use your highly specialized data mining technique in the Microsoft Business Intelligence (BI) ecosystem.

- Rapidly prototype your newest idea without worrying about data loading and model management.

- Load models trained using a different tool and saved in the Predictive Model Markup Language (PMML) format.

A *plug-in algorithm* is a COM object that implements and understands a set of interfaces specified by the SQL Server Data Mining team. From an end-user perspective, plug-in algorithms are no different than the built-in algorithms. They appear in the tools as an algorithm that you can select to build a model. Their functions are included in the query builders' function lists. You can add them to your mining structures and compare them using the standard lift charts.

If you are just an end user of plug-in algorithms, you can stop reading this chapter here. However, if you're interested in implementing your own plug-in algorithm, read on.

You don't have to be familiar with COM to create an algorithm. Starting with SQL Server 2005 Service Pack 2 (and continuing in SQL Server 2008), you can implement a plug-in algorithm as a managed class library, using a .NET language such as Visual C# or Visual Basic .NET. You will need to download the managed API package, which you can find by searching the Web for **Data Mining Managed Plug-in Algorithm API for SQL Server 2005**, or by typing the following (rather complex) URL in your web browser and then scrolling to the bottom of the page.:

```
http://www.microsoft.com/downloads/details.aspx?familyid=
DF0BA5AA-B4BD-4705-AA0A-B477BA72A9CB
```

The managed plug-in API consists of a set of base classes and interfaces to derive from and use in your code. These classes and interfaces do the COM interoperability weightlifting, allowing you to focus on the data mining task.

Whether you use COM or a managed language, the objects involved in a plug-in algorithm are the same. Because the managed code is easier to follow, this chapter uses Visual C# and the managed interfaces to exemplify concepts.

Plug-in Algorithm Framework

The plug-in algorithm framework makes it very easy to create and deploy fully functional, enterprise-ready data mining algorithms. Because algorithm development takes place at the lowest possible level, the algorithm developer gets (for free!) all the platform capabilities of SQL Server Data Mining. The framework takes care of the following:

- DMX language processing
- Transaction management
- Object management
- Security
- Data access and tokenization
- Modeling
- Backup, restore, and synchronization
- Integration with other components of the Microsoft BI suite, including the following:
  - Data Mining Client for Excel add-in
  - BI Development Studio (BI Dev Studio)
  - SQL Server Management Studio
  - Online Analytical Processing (OLAP)
  - Integration Services
  - Reporting Services

Lifetime of a Plug-in Algorithm Instance

Before getting into the details of plug-in algorithm components, you should become familiar with the lifetime of such an object.

When you create a mining model (by using either BI Dev Studio or the DMX language), you must choose the algorithm you want to use. Depending on the algorithm, you have a set of parameters, modeling flags, and column properties to configure. For example, most of the built-in algorithms require a predictable column (not a requirement for the Microsoft Clustering algorithm). Also, some algorithms (for example, Microsoft Decision Trees and Neural Network algorithms) support continuous columns, whereas other algorithms (for example, Microsoft Association Rules and Naïve Bayes algorithms) cannot handle such content. The server contains a `Metadata` object that describes each available algorithm and provides information such as the name, description, supported content types, modeling flags, and parameters. After the model is deployed on the server, it is just a definition, with no actual data.

Typically, creation is followed by training. During training, the `Metadata` object instantiates an actual algorithm instance. The mining model presents the algorithm with the data contained in the mining structure. The algorithm typically iterates the data (once or multiple times) in order to learn patterns. After training is completed, you will have a processed model that contains patterns. The `Algorithm` object saves its state (the complete collection of patterns and additional information) as the last step of training. Multiple instances of the same algorithm may exist in the same mining structure (usually with different parameters) or in the same database.

A trained model can be used for prediction against new data. During prediction, each new data entry is presented to the `Algorithm` object for evaluation, and the result of evaluation is returned to the user who initiated the prediction.

The `Algorithm` object may expose its patterns (as you learned in previous chapters that discuss specific algorithms) through content queries. It may also implement specific functions, such as `Cluster` and `PredictCaseLikelihood` for the Microsoft Clustering algorithm, or `PredictTimeSeries` for the Microsoft Time Series algorithm.

When a model is deleted (or replaced by a newer version), the algorithm instance (together with the patterns it detected and saved) also goes away.

In addition to explicitly creating a mining model using a specific algorithm, you can use the `CREATE MINING MODEL ... FROM PMML` statement to load a mining model from a saved PMML document. Note that Analysis Services supports only version 2.1 of PMML (see `http://dmg.org/pmml-v2-1.html` for details).

A PMML document is parsed in the following two phases.

1. The server analyzes the document and determines the structure (columns) of the mining model, as well as the algorithm being used.

2. The server instantiates an algorithm object of the kind specified in the PMML document and delegates the content parsing to that algorithm.

The result of this parsing is a set of algorithm-specific patterns and an `Algorithm` object that can expose the patterns or use them to perform predictions. The whole training phase is replaced (in the case of PMML models) with loading patterns directly from the document.

NOTE Because the whole training phase is skipped in the PMML scenario, you can write a plug-in algorithm that does not implement training and can only be

used to handle PMML documents. This is a solution for deploying models trained using a different data mining tool in order to take advantage of all the operational features of the SQL Server platform.

Conceptual Overview

As mentioned previously, at least two distinct objects are involved when you're working with a data mining algorithm. The first exposes the capabilities of the algorithm and is used to instantiate `Algorithm` objects. If you're using the COM API, this object derives from two COM interfaces: `IDMAlgorithmMetadata` and `IDMAlgorithmFactory`. In the managed API, the two interfaces are merged in a single base class (which also provides the COM interoperability code): `AlgorithmMetadataBase`. The second object is the algorithm itself. Analysis Services creates one instance of an `Algorithm` object for each mining model using that algorithm. This object is responsible for handling processing, prediction, and content navigation requests, and contains the in-memory representation of the learned content of the mining model. In COM, the `Algorithm` object derives from the `IDMAlgorithm` interfaces (and possibly from other interfaces, as you will see later in this chapter). When you're using the managed API, you derive your algorithm from the `AlgorithmBase` class.

At the most basic level, a plug-in algorithm receives a stream of data from which it must extract patterns, and then stores these patterns onto disk. It receives requests to describe these patterns and apply them to new data streams to perform predictions.

The data stream that is provided to the algorithm is a stream of attribute-value pairs representing a set of cases. This stream is called the *case set*, and from the algorithm point of view, it's the same for all data sources. Regardless of whether the streams are relational or OLAP, streams from Integrations Services, and so on, they are all delivered to the algorithm using the same mechanism. An attribute can be either numerically valued or nominally valued. Attribute-value pairs for numeric attributes (such as income) contain an attribute index and a double containing the value. Attribute-value pairs for discrete (nominal) attributes (such as gender) contain the attribute index, along with an index representing the state of the attribute.

The set of attributes that are available to an algorithm, along with their metadata, are described in the *attribute set*. Figure 17-1 shows an example of a potential case set and attribute set. Your plug-in algorithms generally need not care about the actual attribute names and their values, but only about the view of the attribute space offered by the attribute set.

The data stream illustrated in Figure 17-1 demonstrates many issues that algorithm developers should be aware of. For example, it contains both numerical and nominal data. The data set has a case table with four attribute columns (and a key column that doesn't show in the data stream), and a nested table containing a single key column. When you're implementing an algorithm, you need to keep in mind the capabilities of your algorithm and accurately represent your functionality by exposing the correct algorithm `Metadata`. Algorithms such as Microsoft Decision Trees and Microsoft Clustering support all content types and expose them in their `Metadata`. If your algorithm cannot handle numerical data, do not indicate that it supports `CONTINUOUS` as a content type. If your algorithm can't handle nominal data, don't indicate `DISCRETE` or `DISCRETIZED`. If your algorithm does not understand cases of varying lengths, don't support the `TABLE` content type.

Case Set

1	2	2	34	3	35000	4	2	8	1	10	1		
1	1	2	25	3	24000	4	1	5	1	7	1	9	1
1	1	2	47	3	75500	4	3	8	1	6	1		
1	2	2	31	3	52300	4	1						

Attribute Set

Index	Name	DataType	Content Type	Cardinality	States
1	Gender	Text	Discrete	3	Missing, Male, Female
2	Age	Long	Continuous	2	Missing, Value
3	Income	Long	Continuous	2	Missing, Value
4	Marital Status	Text	Discrete	5	Missing, Never Married, Married, Divorced, Widowed
5	Milk	Text	Key	2	Missing, Existing
6	Bread	Text	Key	2	Missing, Existing
7	Cereal	Text	Key	2	Missing, Existing
8	Eggs	Text	Key	2	Missing, Existing
9	Bacon	Text	Key	2	Missing, Existing
10	Coffee	Text	Key	2	Missing, Existing

Figure 17-1 Case set and attribute set

The data mining infrastructure validates models based on your `Metadata` implementation to ensure that the user model conforms to the basic requirements of your algorithm. Additionally, your algorithm `Metadata` class is called to validate the attribute set when you have more complex requirements that can't be represented by metadata. For example, if you have an algorithm that requires two continuous inputs and one discrete output, you can guarantee that the model will meet your algorithm requirements. You define all of these validation components by implementing the various methods of your `Metadata` object.

After a model is processed, an algorithm must be able to respond to prediction and content navigation requests. All requests are handled in the context of the attribute set. In prediction requests, the server infrastructure converts the input data to the same format used in training. The converted data is presented to the algorithm to produce the actual prediction query results. The algorithm is required to evaluate the inputs and return a data structure containing the predicted results with supporting statistics.

Content is assumed to be a set of nodes organized in a tree hierarchy and is navigated by Analysis Services in a preordered fashion (that is, first the content of one node is requested, and then Analysis Services will request all children of that node). Whenever a content query is executed, the server requests a `Content navigator` object from the algorithm. A *content navigator* is an interface for traversing the set of model patterns. More details about the content navigator are provided in the "Content Navigation" section later in this chapter

Two sets of objects are involved when you're building a plug-in algorithm:

- Objects exposed by the server to be used in your algorithm (as shown in Table 17-1)
- Objects that must be implemented by your algorithm to be used by the server (as shown in Table 17-2)

Model Creation and Processing

From an algorithm's perspective, model creation begins when Analysis Services calls the `Metadata` object to validate the model structure against the `Metadata` implementation in your plug-in, specifically the `ValidateAttributeSet` method of this object. In `ValidateAttributeSet`, your algorithm receives an unpopulated attribute set that describes the structure of the model. This attribute set contains the descriptions of the attributes as described by the model metadata. For example, you will be able to tell what the content type and usage of each attribute is, and if there is a nested table, but you won't be able to determine the number of states of each discrete attribute, or even the total number of attributes when there is a nested table.

When a process command is sent to a mining model, the `Metadata` object is called to instantiate a new `Algorithm` object, through the `CreateAlgorithm` method.

Algorithm processing begins when Analysis Services calls the algorithm's `InsertCases` method with a case set parameter (a `PushCaseSet` object in the managed API) and a collection containing the model parameters, as specified by the creator of the model.

Table 17-1 Objects Exposed by the Server

COM INTERFACE	.NET API WRAPPER	DESCRIPTION
IDMModelServices	ModelServices	Provides access to the properties of the current model that uses your algorithm.
IDMContextServices	ContextServices	Provides access to the properties of the current model that uses your algorithm.
IDMMarginalStats	MarginalStats	Training set statistics computed by the server.
IDMPersistenceWriter	PersistenceWriter	Used to save the patterns discovered by your algorithm.
IDMPersistenceReader	PersistenceReader	Used to load patterns previously saved by your algorithm.
IDMPushCaseSet	PushCaseSet	An object encapsulating the training case set for a mining model.
IDMAttributeSet	AttributeSet	The collection of attributes in your model, together with methods for transforming data from training format to the internal format and back.
DM_ATTRIBUTE_STAT	AttributeStatistics	Statistics for one attribute. This object is returned by MarginalStats or is created as a prediction result or to describe a content node.
DM_STATE_STAT	StateStatistics	Statistics for a state of an attribute. This object is used in conjunction with AttributeStatistics.
DM_STATE_VALUE	StateValue	Describes the value of an attribute state during training, prediction, or content navigation.
DM_PROGRESS_ NOTIFICATION_EVENT	TaskProgressNotification	Encapsulates progress notifications.

Table 17-2 Objects to Be Implemented by a Plug-in Algorithm for Consumption by the Server

COM INTERFACE	.NET API WRAPPER BASE CLASS	DESCRIPTION
IDMAlgorithmMetadata	AlgorithmMetadataBase	Describes the properties of a plug-in algorithm
IDMAlgorithmFactory	AlgorithmMetadataBase	Allows instantiation of an Algorithm object
IDMAlgorithm	AlgorithmBase	The algorithm object
IDMCaseProcessor	ICaseProcessor	Processes (individually) each case in the training set
IDMClusteringAlgorithm	AlgorithmBase	Clustering-specific extensions to the Algorithm object
IDMSequenceAlgorithm, IDMTimeSeriesAlgorithm, IDMTimeSeriesAlgorithm2	Not supported	Other specific extensions to the Algorithm object
IDMCustomFunctionInfo	AlgorithmMetadatabase	Describes custom functions supported by your algorithm
IDMDispatch	AlgorithmBase	Allows invocation of the custom functions supported by your algorithm
IDMAlgorithmNavigation	AlgorithmNavigationBase	Implements content navigation for patterns detected by your algorithm

NOTE Before `InsertCases` is invoked, Analysis Services iterates once over the training set to compute the first-level statistics. The mean and standard deviation are computed for continuous attributes in your model, and a histogram of all states is computed for each discrete or discretized attribute. These statistics are available to the algorithm code through the `MarginalStats` property of the `AlgorithmBase` object. If your algorithm does not need first-level statistics, your `Metadata` class may instruct the server to skip this step.

Inside `InsertCases`, your algorithm will process any algorithm parameters, and then use the `PushCaseSet` object to start the flow of training cases.

The `PushCaseSet` object encapsulates the process of preparing training cases and presenting them to the algorithm. It exposes a single method, `StartCases`, which performs a full iteration over all the training cases. The method takes a single parameter, a `CaseProcessor` object, which encapsulates all the processing code for each training case. You must provide your own implementation of a case processor, by deriving from the `ICaseProcessor` (or `IDMCaseProcessor`, when you're using COM) and implementing the `ProcessCase` method.

As `PushCaseSet` streams cases from the source, it calls `ProcessCase` for each case it reads. It is up to the algorithm to determine how to process each case. For example, an algorithm can update its learned model as each case is fed, or it can cache a subset of the case set to process a larger number of cases at one time, or to set cases aside for validation purposes.

Often, the `Algorithm` object also implements the case processor interface. However, when multiple processing phases require very different operations, it is convenient to have multiple case processor implementations.

In the following code, you can see the typical processing sequence in a plug-in algorithm:

```
class Algorithm : AlgorithmBase, ICaseProcessor

{
    protected override void InsertCases(
      PushCaseSet caseSet,
      MiningParameterCollection trainingParameters)
    {
        // Handle the trainingParameters collection here

        bool success = true;
        bool completed = false;

      while(!completed)
        {
           caseSet.StartCases(this);
               if( !NeedsOneMoreIteration() )
           completed = true;
        }
    }
    ...
}
```

As you can see, the algorithm may iterate the training cases as many times as necessary, by invoking `StartCases` on the `PushCaseSet` object. The previous code fragment assumes that the `Algorithm` object also implements the case processor interface. Your `ProcessCase` code may decide to terminate iteration before traversing all the training cases, by throwing an exception specific to your algorithm. You may catch your own exceptions in the training loop and depending on their severity, start a new iteration or terminate training with an error.

NOTE Do not catch exceptions that are not issued from your plug-in code. An invalid model state may result from doing so (for example, catching an internal exception thrown by `StartCases`).

The server-side implementation of `StartCases` works as described by the pseudo-code shown here:

```
class PushCaseSet
{
    public void StartCases(CaseProcessor processor)
    {
      StartMaterializingTrainingCases();
      while(!EndOfCases)
        {

            long nextCaseId;
          MiningCase nextCase;
          WaitToMaterializeNextCase(nextCaseId, nextCase);
          processor.ProcessCase(nextCaseId, currentCase);
          }
    }
  ...
}
```

The `StartMaterializing...` and `WaitToMaterialize...` statements in this pseudo-code are not actual functions, but represent states of the Analysis Services engine during model processing. The training set materialization happens asynchronously, because data may be collected from multiple nested tables in order to produce a single training case.

The design of `PushCaseSet` allows training to happen without ever fully materializing the training set in memory. If your algorithm can take advantage of this design and perform the processing without attempting to load the whole training set, then it can theoretically handle any data volume, regardless of the size. (The only limits are the disk space and the memory used by the patterns collected during training.)

The `ProcessCase` method must iterate the attributes in each mining case. As you saw in Figure 17-1, the cases may contain different numbers of attributes (if the model contains a nested table). If your model does not include a nested table, then all mining cases have the same length. An attribute containing NULL in the training data will be marked with the `Missing` state in the mining case (as an explicit `Missing` attribute). If your model includes one or more nested tables, then your mining cases are likely to have different lengths (for example, one customer may purchase more products than another customer). Attributes that are implicitly missing from a mining case (as in the previous example, where attributes that represent products are missing from one customer's shopping basket) should be treated just like attributes that have the `Missing` state.

> **NOTE** Your algorithm may decide to handle explicit `Missing` values (from the case-level attributes) in a different way than it handles implicit `Missing` values (from nested table attributes). For example, the absence of a product from a shopping basket may be less significant than the fact that one customer does not want to specify a home city.

The following code shows the basic components for a typical implementation of `ProcessCase`:

```
class Algorithm : AlgorithmBase, ICaseProcessor
{
 ...
    public void ProcessCase(
            long caseId,
            MiningCase currentCase)


    {
        // use the MiningCase as an iterator to
        // collect attributes
        // and their respective values
        bool bContinue = currentCase.MoveFirst();
        while (bContinue)
        {
            // Find the current attribute
            UInt32 currAttribute = currentCase.Attribute;
            // Find its value

            if (currentCase.Value.IsDouble)
            {
                double d = currentCase.Value.Double;
              // Use this continuous attribute value
          ...
      }
            else if (currentCase.Value.IsIndex)
            {
                UInt32 index = currentCase.Value.Index;
              // Use this discrete attribute value


          ...

      }
            else
            {
                Debug.Assert(currentCase.Value.IsMissing);
              // currAttribute ha an explicit Missing value
          ...
      }
         // Move to next attribute in the mining case
```

```
                    bContinue = currentCase.MoveNext();
          }
       }
    ...
 }
```

The preceding code skeleton can handle both dense mining cases (having the same length) and sparse ones (containing implicitly `Missing` attributes).

During `ProcessCase`, your algorithm is also responsible for periodically sending feedback notifications through the progress notification mechanism exposed by the `Algorithm` object. Note that the Analysis Services data mining architecture allows for an unlimited number of attributes and an unlimited number of discrete states per attribute. Because many data mining algorithms are very sensitive to these cardinalities, it is up to your implementation to gracefully handle circumstances where high cardinalities would indicate undesirable memory usage or processing time. One way to alleviate this problem is with intelligent feature selection, or by simply returning descriptive error conditions.

By the end of `InsertCases`, your algorithm should have all of its learned content stored in memory allocated from the model context, and should have freed any temporary memory allocated using the execution context. If your `InsertCases` implementation does not throw an exception, Analysis Services invokes the `SaveContent` method of your `Algorithm` object to archive the in-memory representation of your model. You should use a forward-compatible file format for this so that future versions of your algorithm will be able to load the models.

If any part of the processing procedure fails (including saving the models), the architecture will automatically roll back the transaction to preserve the server state.

Prediction

The primary method for predicting attribute values is via the `Predict` function implemented in your `Algorithm` object. The plug-in architecture also allows for algorithm-specific prediction methods in custom interfaces such as using the `ClusterMembership` function to determine cluster membership in clustering-type algorithms, or other custom functions for your algorithm needs (discussed later in the "Custom Functions" section later in this chapter). The main `Predict` function is used for predicting a specific attribute value, retrieving statistics about a predicted value, retrieving statistics about all possible predicted values (as in `PredictHistogram`), and predicting sets of attributes (as in predicting nested table membership).

Regardless of the method used, all prediction works in a similar way. Analysis Services parses DMX statements and prepares input cases in a manner similar to training. For each input row, Analysis Services calls `Predict` or the appropriate function as indicated by the DMX statement. `Predict` indicates that the algorithm provided predictions for a group of attributes, specifies how many predictions to return and how many states to return for each prediction, and provides a set of modifiers to control how the algorithm should return the values.

The COM and managed API white papers (referenced in the "Plug-in Algorithms" section earlier in this chapter) and plug-in tutorials provide in-depth implementation details for `Predict`.

> **NOTE** Regardless of the API used to build a plug-in algorithm, each input data case is converted by Analysis Services to the attribute/value (A/V) format used during training. This makes things simpler for the algorithm, which already has the patterns in the same format. However, this behavior raises certain issues. A categorical attribute value that was never seen during training is always mapped to the `Missing` state of that attribute. Therefore, if the `Education` contains (at training time) `Bachelor` and `Associate`, and a prediction join is performed against an entry with `Graduate` education, the algorithm will see `Missing` as the value for `Education`, without any way of detecting whether it is an actual `NULL` in the data or a new value, and also without any way of retrieving the actual value.
>
> Continuous (numeric) attributes preserve their actual value, regardless of whether that value was seen or not during training.

Content Navigation

The final required area of implementation detail is content navigation. As described throughout this book, SQL Server Data Mining exposes learned content as a parent-child nested rowset. Each row represents a node in the model's content, and specifies (among other things) the node's unique ID, parent ID, node type, and a set of distributions in a nested table. This schema allows for a wide range of content types to be represented in a generic way.

How your algorithm represents its content is a personal design decision. If you are implementing algorithms with structures similar to the Microsoft algorithms, it is recommended that you mimic the content structure of those algorithms as closely as possible. Doing so will allow models built using your algorithm to be browsed using the standard Microsoft viewers. The viewers and associated stored procedures are tolerant (in some degree) to variations in content.

Content navigation is initiated by a call to your algorithm's `GetNavigator` implementation to return a derivative of the `AlgorithmNavigationBase` class. Because many clients may be browsing a model simultaneously, this method should create a new object every time it is called. As mentioned previously, navigating the entire model content is done in a preordered fashion, but navigation can be initiated from any node in the model.

When you're designing your content layout and data structures to store the in-memory representation of your model, it is important to keep in mind how the content is exposed to the user, especially for performance reasons. For example, the initial design of the Microsoft Association Rules algorithm considered each rule as the child of the left-side itemset. However, the design team soon discovered that this hierarchy made it extremely expensive to retrieve a simple list of rules. The final design treats all itemsets and rules as children of the model root node.

Although the content layout is entirely your decision, the following practices are followed by most (or all) of the built in algorithms:

- The top-level content node has the `NodeType.Model` node type. This identifies it as a root of the rowset.

- The full set of marginal statistics (pre-computed by Analysis Services) are exposed either in the top-level node or in the first descendent of this node (as part of the `NODE_DISTRIBUTION` content column).

Custom Functions

Custom algorithm-specific functions allow the developer to transcend the limitations of the DMX language and fully expose the power of algorithms. However, the functions are invoked through DMX. Therefore, implementing a custom function does have the following requirements:

- The syntax of the custom functions must be exposed by your plug-in algorithm (in the `Metadata` implementation) so that DMX can parse them.

- The `Algorithm` object must expose a way to invoke the functions on a trained algorithm instance.

The .NET API greatly simplifies the task of implementing custom functions. All you have to do is add a public method to your `Algorithm` object and decorate it with the `MiningFunction` attribute.

Depending on the usage scenario for the function and the signature it should use in DMX, there are two distinct functions categories:

- Functions that expose patterns detected by the algorithm which cannot be easily represented through content navigation. Such functions typically operate directly on a trained mining model and do not appear in a `PREDICTION JOIN` DMX statement. Following is an example of such a function:

```
SELECT ExtendedInformation(HairColor) FROM MyModel
```

▪ Functions that perform predictive analysis that cannot be easily covered by the `Predict` function (for example, assigning multiple cluster labels to a data row). Following is an example:

```
SELECT MultiCluster() FROM MyModel PREDICTION JOIN ...
```

The main difference between these two function categories is that the former does not use a data point to analyze against the training results.

The following code shows the function signatures (as they should be implemented in the `Algorithm` object) for the examples used previously:

```
class Algorithm : AlgorithmBase
{
  ...
    [MiningFunction(''Returns extended attribute information'')]

    public object ExtendedInformation(
          AttributeGroup targetAttribute )
    {
      ...
    }

    [MiningFunction(''Returns Multiple Cluster Labels'')]
    public DataTable MultiCluster(
          MiningCase inputCase)
    {

      ...
    }
```

The preceding fragment illustrates the following properties of the custom algorithm functions:

▪ A model column referred to in the DMX invocation of the function is represented internally as an `AttributeGroup` object (a collection of attributes). If the column represents a scalar attribute (such as `HairColor`), then the collection contains the identifier of that attribute. If the column represents a set of attributes (such as `Products`, the name of a nested table), then all the attributes are included in the group.

▪ A custom function intended to match a new data point against learned patterns (that is, to be used in a `PREDICTION JOIN` statement) must take a `MiningCase` parameter. This object contains the representation (in the format defined by the attribute set and used during training) of the data point being currently evaluated. This parameter does not appear in the DMX syntax for invoking the function.

▪ Custom functions may return scalar results or tables. A table-returning function returns a nested table in the result of the DMX statement.

PMML

As mentioned earlier in this chapter, plug-in algorithms may generate and consume PMML documents. As a plug-in developer, you will do this by implementing (in your algorithm class) code for reading and rendering PMML fragments.

The PMML documents typically consist of at least two sections: a data dictionary section (defining the attributes in the model) and an algorithm-specific section (containing the serialized patterns in an XML format).

Analysis Services parses the data dictionary part to create a mining model and an attribute set. If a statistics section is present in the PMML document, Analysis Services loads that section and exposes it to the plug-in algorithm through the `MarginalStats` object.

The task of parsing patterns (the algorithm-specific part of a PMML document) is delegated to the plug-in algorithm through the `LoadPMMLContent` method, which you also need to implement in your algorithm in order for it to consume PMML documents. When a model is created from a PMML document, the whole training phase (`InsertCases`) is skipped. Consequently, you can write plug-in algorithms that do not support actual training, and are used only to load patterns from PMML documents produced outside of Analysis Services.

The same task partitioning happens when PMML content is generated from an Analysis Services model. The server takes care of rendering the data dictionary section, as well as the statistics section, and the algorithm is responsible for rendering the patterns by implementing the `RenderPMMLContent` method.

Managed vs. Native Plug-ins

As described earlier in this chapter, a plug-in is a COM object. A pure COM implementation (using a native language such as Visual C++) gives the developer full control over code execution, allows very good integration with the server memory-management mechanism, and provides the best performance. There is no fundamental difference between the functioning of built-in algorithms and a plug-in developed in native C++ using COM

It is possible to wrap the COM interfaces with .NET and write managed plug-ins in languages such as C# and Visual Basic.NET. Microsoft even provides a sample wrapper to facilitate the development of managed plug-ins, which greatly simplifies the coding effort.

However, the ease of development provided by .NET does not come without cost. There are performance penalties in training and prediction related to the cost of marshalling data between native C++ and managed code, although the Microsoft-supplied wrappers do their best to alleviate this. Additionally, all memory used by a managed plug-in is allocated using the .Net memory management functions and not allocated using the Analysis Services allocators. As a result, the server is not aware of the memory used by the plug-in and may not be to optimize memory utilization under stress situations.

For these reasons, the decision to create and use managed plug-ins in a production environment should be made only after careful consideration, and only after extensive testing using simulated server loads.

Installing Plug-in Algorithms

To install a COM plug-in algorithm, you must register it as aCOM server and update the Analysis Services server's `.ini` file. Details on the exact registry and `.ini` file settings are specified in the tutorials and sample plug-ins mentioned previously in this chapter.

The managed API for developing plug-in algorithms contains a setup and deployment project that, in addition to registering your libraries and adding them to the global assembly cache, connects to the Analysis Services server of your choice and updates the server's `.ini` file programmatically.

Where to Find Out More about Plug-in Algorithms

Raman Iyer provides a high-level overview of the architecture and benefits of plug-in data mining algorithms in "Add Custom Data Mining Algorithms to SQL Server 2005" at `http://msdn2.microsoft.com/en-us/library/aa964125.aspx`.

A lower-level overview is provided in the "SQL Server Data Mining: Plug-In Algorithms" article at `http://technet.microsoft.com/en-us/library/ms345133.aspx`. There is also a full tutorial for developing a COM plug-in algorithm using Visual C++ at `http://technet.microsoft.com/en-us/library/ms345112.aspx`, developed by Max Chickering and Raman Iyer.

The managed plug-in API contains a help file and a step-by-step tutorial for building a very simple algorithm, as well as extending it with all the features supported by the framework. (Instructions for downloading this package are included at the beginning of this chapter.)

The managed API contains the full source code for a wrapper class library (`DMPluginWrapper`) that includes the interoperability layer between COM and .NET. Fragments of the wrapper code can be used in COM plug-ins as sample code for working with the server memory allocators and manipulating the data sources that are part of the API.

Data Mining Viewers

Another way of extending SQL Server Data Mining is to add data mining visualizations. The visualization architecture in Data Mining Designer allows you to add viewers for any or all algorithms. For example, you could write an additional viewer for the Microsoft Decision Trees algorithm that displays line charts for continuous targets, or you could create a viewer for the Microsoft Neural Network algorithm that displays the actual nodes of the network. Of course, you can also add viewers specifically designed to display your custom plug-in algorithms.

Interfaces to Be Implemented

The Microsoft-supplied visualization controls are just .NET `WinForm` controls that implement the `IMiningModelViewerControl` interface. To implement your own visualization, you simply need to launch Visual Studio, create a new .NET class library, and add the controls you want to your class. BI Dev Studio initializes your controls by setting the `MiningModelName` and `ConnectionString` properties of the `IMiningModelViewerControl` interface, and then calling `LoadViewerData`.

SQL Server 2008 adds a new interface, `IMiningModelViewerControl2`. If your viewer implements this new version, then it can share a connection (OLE DB or ADOMD.NET) with the application that hosts the control. This is particularly useful if the application hosting the viewer control is also used to create session mining models (like the Data Mining Add-Ins for Excel). Such temporary models are not visible to a new connection, even when using the same connection string. In order for your viewer to work in all scenarios, it should implement `IMiningModelViewerControl2`. When a hosting application uses `IMiningModelViewerControl2`, it typically sets the connection to be shared and then calls `LoadViewerData`.

Your implementation of `LoadViewerData` uses the shared connection, or opens a connection to the server (using the connection string), and queries the model for at least enough information for the initial display of the model. For example, the Decision Tree viewer retrieves the list of trees in the model, plus the complete first tree. Depending on the expected time to load, your interface should indicate that loading is occurring.

Rendering the Information

The actual information rendering in the viewer is completely up to the developer. As an example, the following code shows an implementation of `LoadViewerData` that populates a list box with the unique name and caption of all model nodes:

```
public  bool LoadViewerData(object context)
{
    ADOMDConnection connection = new ADOMDConnection();
    ADOMDCommand command = new ADOMDCommand();
    ADOMDDataReader reader;

    // Open a new connection to the server.
```

```
connection.ConnectionString = this.ConnectionString;
connection.Open();

// Initialize the command.
string commandText = string.Format("SELECT NODE_UNIQUE_NAME, " +
    "NODE_CAPTION FROM [{0}].CONTENT",
    this.MiningModelName);
command.Connection = connection;
command.CommandText = commandText;

// Execute the command
reader = command.ExecuteReader();

// Extract information from the schema here.
while (reader.Read())
{
    string uniqueName = " ";
    string caption = " ";

    if (!reader.IsDBNull(1))

        uniqueName = reader.GetString(1);
    if (!reader.IsDBNull(2))
        caption = reader.GetString(1);

    ListBox1.Add(uniqueName + " " + caption);
}
reader.Close();
connection.Close();

return true;
}
```

If you used the connection string to open the connection to the server, it is up to you whether that connection is kept open or closed and reconnected only as necessary to fetch additional data based on user interaction. If you maintain a live connection, your code should handle a situation where the connection is dropped, and be sure to close the connection when the control is destroyed.

However, if the viewer does not own the connection (it was shared by the hosting application through the `IMiningModeViewerControl2`), then your viewer should not close the connection because this may produce undesirable side effects in the application.

Retrieving Information from Analysis Services

The patterns detected by the mining model during training are exposed in the model content. Therefore, content queries should be enough for your

`LoadViewerData` implementation. However, often the viewer shows an aggregated view of the patterns. When this happens, you have the option to download the full model content in the memory of the hosting application and perform the aggregations, but this may raise significant performance problems.

Server-side stored procedures (discussed in Chapter 16) provide the solution for these problems. The whole model content is already loaded in the server memory. A server-side stored procedure can traverse it on the server without creating an additional copy on the client and returns only the aggregated results in a form that makes rendering easy for `LoadViewerData`.

If the algorithm behind your model implements custom functions to return information that cannot easily be included in the parent-child format of the content, your viewer may call those functions directly.

In your viewer, you may also want to use the actual properties of the training data. Certain clustering visualizations project some or all the training set using the model columns as axes. The Microsoft Time Series viewer uses the time stamp as the horizontal axis and the actual series values as the vertical axis, and projects the training data to present the historical evolution of the series. Then, it uses the same axes for the forecasted values for the series.

To get the actual training data, your viewer may require the model to support the drill-through feature. If the underlying algorithm does not support drill-through (such as the Microsoft Neural Network algorithm), the viewer can use the new SQL Server 2008 mining structure drill-through to get access to the training cases with a query like the one shown here, if the mining model does not use a filter:

```
SELECT * FROM MINING STRUCTURE <MyStructure>.CASES WHERE

    IsTrainingCase()
```

Registering the Viewer

After you implement your viewer, you need to strongly name your assembly, and register and place your viewer. This involves a number of steps, which are detailed in the data mining viewer tutorial included with the plug-in sample mentioned at the beginning of this chapter. If your viewer (like the Microsoft viewers) makes use of custom stored procedures, your installation procedure will have to include installing these procedures on servers you intend to access with the viewer. You can use SQL Server Management Studio to generate the DDL required to deploy the necessary assemblies.

Where to Find Out More about Plug-in Viewers

"A Tutorial for Constructing a Plug-in Viewer," by Jesper Lind and Scott Oveson, is available at `http://technet.microsoft.com/en-us/library/ms345129`

.aspx. This document provides all the details for registering a plug-in viewer. Unfortunately, the document is based on SQL Server 2005, and an updated 2008 version is not available, so you will need to adjust the registration information in order to use the tutorial with SQL Server 2008.

Summary

This chapter examined the basic concepts behind extending SQL Server Data Mining. In addition to extending the server by creating stored procedures as described in Chapter16, or extending Visual Studio as described at http://msdn.microsoft.com/vstudio/extend, you can add your own custom data mining algorithms and viewers to SQL Server Data Mining. The concepts discussed in this chapter enhance and extend the plug-in white papers and tutorials provided in the Analysis Services samples.

In this chapter (as well as in Chapter 16), you learned about the programming interfaces offered by the SQL Server Data Mining platform. In Chapter 18, you will learn how to use some of these interfaces to build a cross-selling web application.

Implementing a Web Cross-Selling Application

Cross-selling is a very common business problem. It involves suggesting a list of new products based on those in the customer's current or previous shopping basket. For example, if you go to Amazon.com and put a book in your shopping cart, you get a set of other book recommendations. This list is based on the market basket analysis of thousands of customers with similar purchases. Good recommendations improve customers' shopping experiences and, thus, increase the overall sales. Bad recommendations annoy customers and eventually drive them away. The major challenge of cross-selling is how to give each customer the right set of recommendations. If the shop product catalog is small, it is relatively easy to give suggestions based on marketing experiences. However, when the number of distinct products is large, the problem is pushed to a new dimension.

Suppose that you are the owner of MovieClick.com, a fictional online retail store that sells movies. You have thousands of movies at MovieClick.com. You want to increase movie sales by giving online shoppers personalized suggestions. This chapter will help you solve this business problem using data mining techniques.

In this chapter, you will learn about the following:

- Source data descriptions
- Building recommendation models with the Microsoft Decision Trees and Microsoft Association Rules algorithms
- The difference between Microsoft Decision Trees and Microsoft Association Rules for cross-selling
- Integrating your predictions within web applications

To assist with this chapter, content files are included in the `Chapter18.zip` archive available at `www.wiley.com/go/data_mining_SQL_2008`. This archive contains the following files:

- `Chapter 18 code.txt` — Contains code snippets from the chapter
- `Chapter 18 DMX queries.dmx` — Contains DMX query listings from the chapter

Source Data Description

Figure 18-1 shows the partial schema of the `MoviePick.com` data mart. Two tables are shown in the figure: `Survey` and `Movies`. The `Survey` table contains the customer demographic information such as age, education, gender, income, and so on. It is a dimension table. The `Movies` table stores the historical transactions of the customer's previous purchases. It is a fact table with two columns: `SurveyTakenID` and `Movie`. Each customer has bought a set of movies. The relationship between these two tables is 1 to *n*.

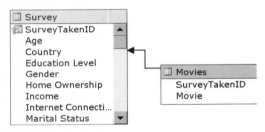

Figure 18-1 Schema of MovieClick.com

Building Your Model

The first step in a data mining project is to understand the business requirement and identify the proper data mining task for this business problem. The list of data mining tasks includes classification, regression, association, segmentation, forecasting, and so on. Most of the data mining algorithms in SQL Server 2008 can be applied to multiple tasks. After you identify the data mining task, you can apply the set of algorithms that is suitable for this task to build mining models.

Identifying the Data Mining Task

Before building any mining models, you must identify the type of data mining task for the business problem. In this case, the goal is to analyze the movies that customers tend to buy together. After you get these patterns, you can use them for making recommendations. Based on the problem spaces that were laid out in Chapter 1, this problem belongs to the data mining association task. There are a few Microsoft data mining algorithms that you can apply to the association task. The two most suitable ones are Microsoft Decision Trees and Microsoft Association Rules, which you will use to build the models in this chapter.

Using Decision Trees for Association

In Chapter 7, you learned how decision trees can be applied to association analysis. Usually, there is a predictable nested table in the association model. Each nested key is modeled as a predictable attribute, and a decision tree is built for each of the nested keys during the process.

NOTE Nested tables need to be set as `Predict` if you want to analyze the relationship among the nested keys (Movies, Products, and so on). If you set the nested table to `Predict_Only`, you won't find splits based on other movies in the Microsoft Decision Trees algorithm, and you won't find rules with other movies on the left side of the Association Rules algorithm.

Figure 18-2 shows the model definition. The model has only one case-level attribute, which is the case key `Customer ID`. `Purchase` is a nested table, with `Movie` modeled as the nested key. The model will analyze the movie associations based purely on each customer's shopping cart. You can also include demographic information in the mining structure. The model will then analyze the associations among all the movies, as well as the demographic information.

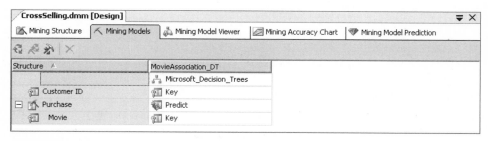

Figure 18-2 The decision tree model for movie association

After processing the model, you get a set of decision trees. Figure 18-3 shows the decision tree for predicting the movie *Jaws*. Only about 2 percent of the customers purchase this movie. The first tree split is on *Jurassic Park*. Among those who like *Jurassic Park*, about 20 percent also like *Jaws*. This gives a lift of 10 times compared to the overall population. Among those who don't like *Jurassic Park* but like *E.T.*, about 10 percent also like *Jaws*. This tree tells you that *Jurassic Park* and *E.T.* are good predictors for *Jaws*. You can quantitatively measure the relationship between these predictors and the predictable attribute (Jaws) based on the tree-splitting scores at each level.

Figure 18-3 Decision tree for Jaws

Figure 18-4 shows the dependency network of the tree model. This can be thought of as a bird's-eye view from the top of the forest. Each node is a decision tree or an input attribute. Each edge represents the relationship between two attributes. Each edge has a direction, which indicates the direction of the prediction. Each edge also has a weight, which represents the strength of the prediction. For example, the figure shows that *Jurassic Park* predicts *Jaws* and that *E.T.* and *Jaws* predict each other. All information displayed in the Dependency Network view is derived from source trees.

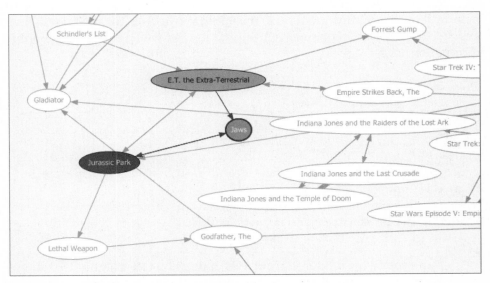

Figure 18-4 Dependency Network view of a decision tree model

By default, the mining model builds 255 trees, even though there may be thousands of different movies. These 255 movies are chosen by the feature selection component in the Microsoft Decision Trees algorithm. As explained in Chapter 7, you can raise this limit by setting higher values in the MAXIMUM_INPUT_ATTRIBUTES and MAXIMUM_OUTPUT_ATTRIBUTES parameters. However, the processing time and tree loading time will be longer. If your decision trees don't have enough splits because the data is sparse, you can reduce the value of Complexity_Penalty to create reasonably sized trees. The default setting for Complexity_Penalty tends to be high when the data is not dense.

When there are thousands of different movies, the Microsoft Decision Trees algorithm is clearly not the best choice.

In SQL Server 2008, the feature selection component is part of the algorithm. Different algorithms have different feature selection criteria.

NOTE Depending on which algorithm you are using, the feature selection algorithm may be different.

The Microsoft Naïve Bayes and Clustering algorithms use an entropy-based score, which tells how an attribute would be interesting.

The Microsoft Decision Trees algorithm uses the same interestingness score for output attribute feature selection, and then calculates the split score for each input attribute versus the selected output attributes. Input feature selection is based on the calculated split score. This effectively tells you which input attributes are worth consideration and which ones are not, based on selected output attributes.

The Microsoft Association Rules algorithm doesn't have a built-in feature selection component. However, you can specify feature selection by setting MINIMUM_SUPPORT and MINIMUM_PROBABLITY values.

Using the Association Rules Algorithm

The Microsoft Association Rules algorithm is an efficient counting algorithm. It counts the support of each frequent itemset, meaning the number of distinct customers who purchase both Movie *A* and Movie *B*. This is the algorithm designed for market basket analysis.

Based on the same mining structure displayed in Figure 18-1, you can create a related mining model using the Microsoft Association Rules algorithm. As explained in Chapter 11, you usually specify the two threshold parameters before processing the model to get the best results. The first parameter, MINIMUM_SUPPORT, is used to filter unpopular itemsets. The other parameter is MINIMUM_PROBABILITY, which is used to restrict rules. Rules will be used for prediction. Rules are generated based on the frequent itemsets. The Association Rules algorithm is very sensitive to MINIMUM_SUPPORT. If this parameter is set too high, there won't be enough itemsets and rules. If this parameter is set too low, the model processing time will increase exponentially.

In this example, you set the MININUM_SUPPORT to 0.01, which means you are interested in only those itemsets that appear in at least 1 percent of all shopping carts. Set the MINIMUM_PROBABILITY to be 0.30, which means that if 30 percent of the customers who purchase Movie *A* also purchase Movie *B*, you consider A=>B as a qualified rule. Figure 18-5 shows the model.

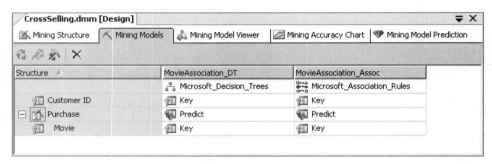

Figure 18-5 Association model for movie association

The Microsoft Association Rules model and the Microsoft Decision Trees model share the same mining structure. Because the mining structure is processed while training the tree model, the source data has already been tokenized and the correlations among movies have been counted. This saves much time for Association Rules model processing.

Figure 18-6 shows the Dependency Network view of the Association Rules model. The dependency network is generated based on the pairwise rules. Usually, an association model has more rules than those displayed in the dependency network. By default, the dependency network displays only 60 popular nodes. The strength of each link represents the importance of the rule. Lowering the value of MINIMUM_PROBABILITY and MINIMUM_SUPPORT results in the model returning more rules.

Comparing the Two Models

Both the Microsoft Decision Trees algorithm and the Microsoft Association Rules algorithm find the relationship among the movies. The discovered patterns are represented in different forms: one with decision trees, and the other with a set of frequent itemsets and rules. So which technique should you use for the cross-selling model?

Table 18-1 provides a general comparison of the Microsoft Decision Trees algorithm and the Microsoft Association Rules algorithm for association tasks.

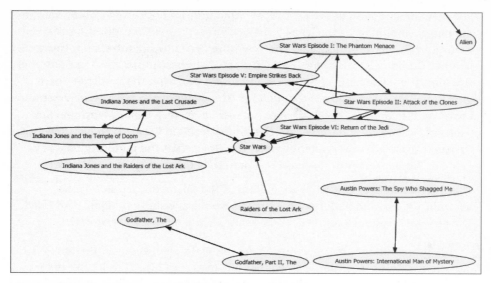

Figure 18-6 Dependency network for movie association

Table 18-1 Comparison of Microsoft Decision Trees and Association Rules Algorithms for the Association Task

	MICROSOFT DECISION TREES	MICROSOFT ASSOCIATION RULES
Pros	More detailed patterns for each item	Fast, scalable
	Supports continuous input	
Cons	Not scalable to large catalogs	Very sensitive to the algorithm parameters

The Decision Trees algorithm has the advantage of showing deeper correlations. It is rather easy for the user to visualize all the patterns related to a given movie by browsing the decision tree. The Decision Trees algorithm also supports continuous inputs. For example, you can add continuous attributes such as age and income to the model. The drawback of using the Decision Trees algorithm is its scalability, because it builds one tree per movie.

The biggest advantage of the Microsoft Association Rules algorithm is its performance and scalability. The drawback is that the algorithm is sensitive to the threshold parameter settings. You must adjust these parameter values to have a good model.

NOTE In many cases, the Microsoft Decision Trees algorithm performs well for association tasks. However, the Decision Trees algorithm may ignore patterns in some cases.

For example, the movies *The Godfather*, *The Godfather II*, and *The Godfather III* are highly correlated. In the tree of *The Godfather III*, the first split is on *The Godfather II*. *The Godfather* and *The Godfather II* are highly correlated. Those who like *The Godfather II* also like *The Godfather*. Because the split on *The Godfather II* is almost equivalent to splitting on *The Godfather*, after the first split, there aren't any further splits on *The Godfather*. The dependency network is generated based on the top three levels of decision tree splits. As a consequence, no link exists between *The Godfather* and *The Godfather III* in the dependency network. For associative prediction queries given *The Godfather*, the predicted results won't contain *The Godfather III*, because this pattern is covered by *The Godfather II*.

This phenomenon is caused by the nature of the Microsoft Decision Trees algorithm. It may hide information if some input attributes are highly correlated. The general recommendation is to try using several different algorithms.

NOTE In addition to the Microsoft Decision Trees algorithm and the Microsoft Association Rules algorithm, a few other techniques of SQL Server 2008 can be applied for the association task. These techniques include the Microsoft Naïve Bayes, Neural Network, and Clustering algorithms. Generally speaking, any algorithm except a time series algorithm (such as Microsoft Time Series) that allows nested tables to be predictable can be used for associative analysis. In the case of the Naïve Bayes algorithm, the conditional probabilities are calculated for each movie given other movies during training. During prediction, the algorithm uses conditional probabilities to predict other associated movies for each movie in the shopping basket of the input case, and returns the top *n* most likely ones based on the probabilities.

In general, you should use the Microsoft Decision Trees algorithm or the Microsoft Association Rules algorithm for cross-selling because of scalability and accuracy. However, if you have a small data set with a limited number of items (catalog) in the nested key, you can try the different techniques described in this sidebar.

Making Predictions

After the models are processed, you can use their patterns to predict the movies that new customers may be interested in.

Making Batch Prediction Queries

MovieClick.com has two tables: NewCustomer and NewCustomerPurchase. NewCustomer contains a list of new customers with their demographic information. NewCustomerPurchase contains a list of movies that each new customer has purchased recently. As the store manager, you plan to do a mailing campaign, sending these customers a set of personalized movie recommendations.

You can get the best recommendations for your customers by using the prediction query shown in Listing 18-1.

```
SELECT
  t.CustomerID,
  Predict(Movies, $AdjustedProbability, 5) AS Recommendation
FROM
  MovieAssociation
PREDICTION JOIN
  SHAPE {
  OPENQUERY([Movie Click],
    'SELECT
      CustomerID
    FROM
      Customers
     ORDER BY
      CustomerID')}
  APPEND ({
  OPENQUERY([Movie Click],
    'SELECT Movie, CustomerID
    FROM
      Movies
    ORDER BY
      CustomerID')}
    RELATE
      CustomerID TO CustomerID)
    AS
      NewCustomerPurchase AS t
ON
  MovieAssociation.Movies.Movie = t.NewCustomerPurchase.Movie
```

Listing 18-1 Associative batch prediction

You can generate the query shown in this listing using the Prediction Query Builder in the BI Dev Studio. Figure 18-7 shows the results of this prediction query.

NOTE Predict(Purchase, 5) returns the five most likely products based on the probability. Sometimes items with the highest probabilities may not be the best ones to recommend. For example, if every customer likes *Star Wars*, recommending *Star Wars* may not be necessary. For this purpose, you can use AdjustedProbability Predict(Purchase, $AdjustedProbability, 5) instead. AdjustedProbability is derived from probability, but it penalizes items with high popularity. You should try both Probability and AdjustedProbability in your prediction query, and pick the one that makes more sense for your application.

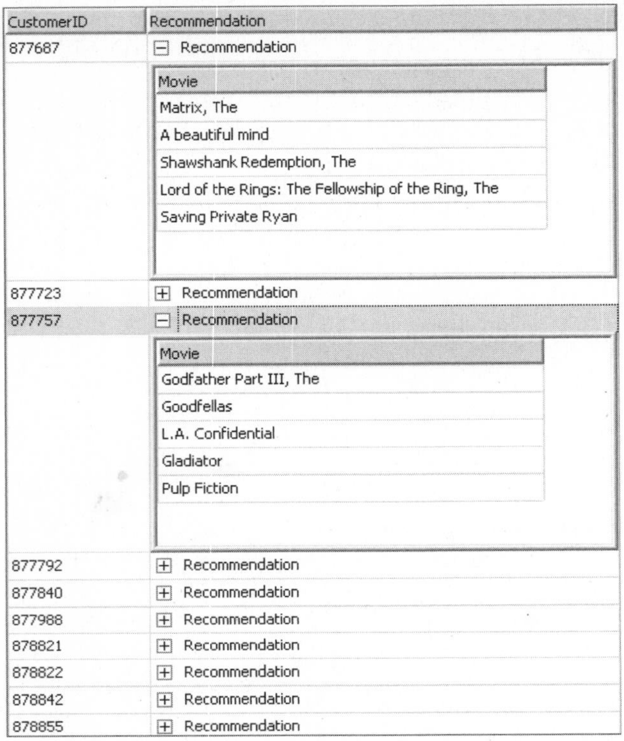

CustomerID	Recommendation
877687	⊟ Recommendation
	Movie
	Matrix, The
	A beautiful mind
	Shawshank Redemption, The
	Lord of the Rings: The Fellowship of the Ring, The
	Saving Private Ryan
877723	⊞ Recommendation
877757	⊟ Recommendation
	Movie
	Godfather Part III, The
	Goodfellas
	L.A. Confidential
	Gladiator
	Pulp Fiction
877792	⊞ Recommendation
877840	⊞ Recommendation
877988	⊞ Recommendation
878821	⊞ Recommendation
878822	⊞ Recommendation
878842	⊞ Recommendation
878855	⊞ Recommendation

Figure 18-7 Query result for movie recommendations

Using Singleton Prediction Queries

In many cases, the information about new customers has not yet been stored in the database. For example, if a web customer visits `MoviePick.com` to purchase movies, you want to give the customer recommendations in real time based on what he or she has selected in the shopping cart. To do this, you can use a DMX singleton query as shown in Listing 18-2.

```
SELECT FLATTENED
    (Predict(Movies, 6)) AS [Recommendation]
FROM
  MovieAssociation
NATURAL PREDICTION JOIN
  (SELECT  ((SELECT 'Jaws' AS Movie)
   UNION (SELECT 'Matrix' AS Movie))
        AS Movies)
  AS NewCustomer
```

Listing 18-2 Singleton associative prediction

Integrating Predictions with Web Applications

You have explored association patterns from the historical data of
MoviePick.com using the Microsoft Decision Trees and Association Rules
algorithms. You have also seen the prediction queries you need to get movie
recommendations for each customer. In the next step, you add the recommendation feature to the website. This section discusses the details of integrating
data mining prediction features in a web application.

Understanding Web Application Architecture

A web application usually has *multiple* tiers, as shown in Figure 18-8. A
customer uses a web browser to connect to the Internet Information Server
(IIS), which is a web server integrated inside a Windows server. then requests
an Active Server Pages (ASP) web page. The ASP page connects to the SQL
Server relational database to display the list of movies so that the customer
can pick one. After the customer selects a movie, an ASP page generates a
singleton prediction query based on the contents of this customer's shopping
cart. The ASP page then connects to SQL Server Analysis Services through
ADO.NET, ADOMD.NET, or OLE DB directly, and sends the prediction query
against a given mining model. The results of the prediction are displayed in
the web page as recommendations. A singleton prediction can be executed
in real time.

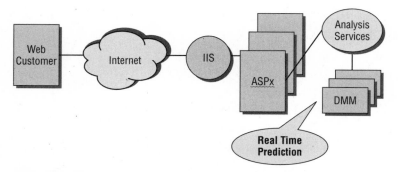

Figure 18-8 Architecture of a web-based cross-selling application

The cross-selling mining model is retrained regularly (for example, once
every two weeks). Although the content of the model changes after each
update, the model definition remains the same. Thus, the prediction query
generated by the ASP page is always valid. No matter how frequently the
model is reprocessed, you don't need to update the query embedded in ASP
pages.

Setting the Permissions

After you create the mining model, you must assign the proper permissions for your web customers. First, you create a new database role in the Analysis Services server named "ASP". As this role is only to be used to query a single model, you don't need to provide any general permissions to this role. You can use the Create Role dialog box in the SQL Server Management Studio environment to do this, as shown in Figure 18-9.

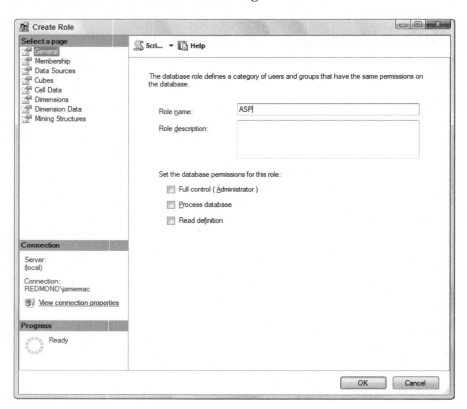

Figure 18-9 Creating a new role in the Analysis Services database

After you create the ASP role, you need to assign the permission on the mining model for this new role. In the Movie.com example, web customers only query the model for recommendations, so you assign only the Read permission for the ASP role as shown in Figure 18-10. Because ASP pages execute only prediction queries, you don't need to add Browse and Drill Through permissions for the role.

The last step is to associate users to the newly created role. Because ASP has only the Read permission, you can assign the account that ASP.NET runs under, WebApplicationAccount, to this role as shown in Figure 18-11.

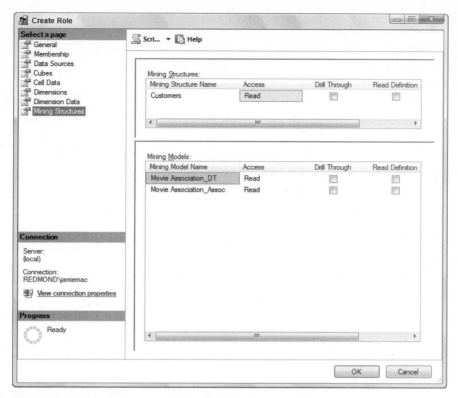

Figure 18-10 Assigning permissions on a mining model

Figure 18-11 Associating users to the new role

Examining Sample Code for the Web Recommendation Application

This section takes a closer look at how to build a web application that includes the recommendation feature. The code presented here is written in C#, and is embedded in the ASP.NET page.

Listing 18-3 connects to Analysis Services through ADOMD.NET.

```
using System;
using Microsoft.AnalysisServices.AdomdClient;
using System.Data;

AdomdConnection con;

static bool CreateADOMDConnection()
{
  con = new AdomdConnection("Data Source=ASServer;
        Catalog=MovieAssociation; Integrated Security=SSPI");
  try
  {
     con.Open();
  }
  catch (System.Exception e)
  {
     Log(e.Message);
     return false;
  }
   return true;
}
```

Listing 18-3 Connecting to Analysis Services through ADOMD.NET

The web application will dynamically generate a DMX singleton prediction query. The = GenerateDMX function in Listing 18-4 is invoked each time a customer selects a movie in the shopping cart. SelectList is a list box for storing the list of movies the customer picked. When there is more than one movie in the shopping cart, the singleton query uses the Union operator to construct multiple rows of the table column Movies.

```
public string GenerateDMX()
{
    static string DMX1 = "Select Flattened Predict(Purchase,5) From
       MovieAssociation Natural Prediction Join (Select (";
    static string DMX2 = ") as Purchase) as input";
    int Count = SelectedList.Items.Count;
    string DMX = "";
    for (int i=0; i<Count; i++)
    {
    string movieName = SelectedList.Items[i].Text;
        DMX += "select '" + movieName + "' as Movie ";
```

Listing 18-4 Generating a singleton query in C#

```
            if (i<Count-1)
                    DMX += "UNION ";
    }
    DMX = DMX1 + DMX + DMX2;
    return DMX ;
}
```

Listing 18-4 (*continued*)

The `ExecuteAndFetchSQL` function in Listing 18-5 executes the prediction query through an `AdomdCommand` object and fetches the query result using a `DataReader` object. Each predicted item in the record set is displayed in a list box of the recommendations web page.

```
public bool ExecuteAndFetchSQL(string strCommand)
{
AdomdCommand cmd = (AdomdCommand)
con.CreateCommand();
cmd.Text = strCommand;
IDataReader dr = null;
try
{
    dr = cmd.ExecuteReader();

}
catch(Exception e)
{
    Log(e.Message);
    return false;
}
    ...
//display the result in the listbox
while(dr.Read())
{
    string val = dr.GetString(0);
    SuggestedList.Items.Add(val);
}
...
return true;
}
```

Listing 18-5 ExecuteandFetchSQL Results

Figure 18-12 shows the `MoviePick.com` sample website as demonstrated at `SQLServerDataMining.com` with a cross-selling feature integrated. When a customer picks a movie from the movie list (for example, *The Lord of the Rings: The Fellowship of the Ring*), he or she immediately sees a list of movie suggestions below the shopping cart. The recommendations are purely based on other customers' shopping patterns in similar cases. These patterns are stored in either a Decision Trees model or an Association Rules model.

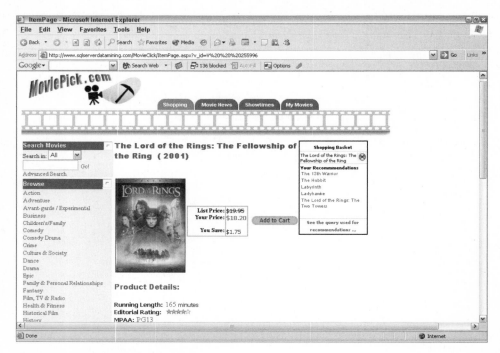

Figure 18-12 MoviePick.com website

The customer can then pick movies directly from the suggested list. Again, when an item is added to or removed from the shopping cart, a new singleton prediction query is executed against the model, which returns a new set of recommendations.

Summary

In this chapter, you learned how to build mining models to do market basket analysis. Several algorithms in SQL Server 2008 can be applied for data mining association tasks. The recommended algorithms for this purpose are Microsoft Decision Trees and Microsoft Association Rules. You learned the pros and cons of these two algorithms.

The second half of the chapter talked about how to write associative prediction queries and how to integrate these queries into a web cross-selling application. You learned about the architecture of web applications that execute data mining predictions.

Chapter 19 reviews the material covered in this book, including a reminder of why data mining is a compelling technology, and provides some additional resources.

Conclusion and Additional Resources

This book provides you with a valuable resource for learning about the data mining features of SQL Server 2008, finding examples that highlight both basic and more complex usage scenarios, and gaining some deeper insight into the peculiarities of SQL Server Data Mining (and how to apply them). This chapter reviews the highlights of data mining features in SQL Server 2008, examines the new business opportunities in data mining, and points you to other resources for further reading and discussion.

Recapping the Highlights of SQL Server 2008 Data Mining

This book covers a wide range of data mining topics and features. Starting with an overview of what data mining means, the early chapters demonstrate how any Excel user (with or without any knowledge of data mining) can take advantage of powerful predictive technology in everyday data usage. From that point, the discussions turn to the basic concepts of SQL Server Data Mining through the Data Mining Extensions (DMX) to SQL language, and how to use data mining tools in SQL Server 2008 and Excel. The discussions provided an in-depth look at each usage and application of the Microsoft data mining algorithms, as well as examinations of how each algorithm performs its particular brand of magic. You learned about the SQL Server Data Mining architecture and how you (as a developer or IT pro) can manage the server, write data mining applications, and extend the data mining capability of SQL Server Analysis Services. You also learned how to integrate with other Business Intelligence (BI) components, including on-line analytical processing (OLAP), SQL Server Integration Services (SSIS), and Reporting Services.

Data Mining in SQL Server 2008 is an evolutionary change based on the revolutionary advancement in data mining from SQL Server 2005 over SQL Server 2000. With the advanced data mining functionality, tools, and APIs packaged with a popular database at a low price point, SQL Server 2008 will continue the paradigm shift in the data mining industry that really accelerated with the 2005 release. Since 2005, many application vendors who previously would never have dreamed of adding predictive functionality to their applications are now doing so because of the ubiquitous availability of data mining technology. New data mining consultancies have sprung up around the SQL Server Data Mining platform, and existing consultancies have added SQL Server to their repertoire and/or completely converted their customers from competing products to SQL Server.

The following sections review the highlights of SQL Server 2008 data mining features.

State-of-the-Art Algorithms

SQL Server Data Mining contains nine world-class data mining algorithms covering the following areas:

- **Microsoft Naïve Bayes** (Chapter 6) — Naïve Bayes is a simple and efficient algorithm for classification. It analyzes pairwise relationships between each of the input attributes and each predictable target. It's an excellent choice for getting started with data exploration, and also for performing classification when there are many inputs — particularly in text mining scenarios.

- **Microsoft Decision Trees** (Chapter 7) — Microsoft's state-of-the art Decision Trees algorithm performs classification and regression, and can build multiple trees in a single model to perform association analysis.

- **Microsoft Linear Regression** (Chapter 7) — This algorithm is for those who want to do simple linear regression analysis. Internally, it uses the same regression algorithm as Microsoft Decision Trees.

- **Microsoft Time Series** (Chapter 8) — The Time Series algorithm underwent a major reworking in SQL Server 2008 to include both an auto-regressive tree with cross-prediction (ARTxp) for short-term accuracy and Auto-Regressive Integrated Moving Averages (ARIMA) for long-term predictive stability. Also, SQL Server 2008 introduces the capability to provide time series data for forecasting to enable what-if and product substitution scenarios.

- **Microsoft Clustering** (Chapter 9) — Clustering performs both probabilistic (Expectation Maximum, or EM) and distance-based (K-means) segmentation. Because of its generalization and application to the DMX framework, the Microsoft implementation allows for interesting application scenarios such as anomaly detection.

- **Microsoft Sequence Clustering** (Chapter 10) — This algorithm takes probabilistic clustering techniques and adds sequential analysis. This allows you to analyze both descriptive attributes and behavioral attributes in a single model.

- **Microsoft Association Rules** (Chapter 11) — Association Rules has proven to be one of the most popular algorithms since it originally shipped in SQL Server 2005. It provides a powerful and scalable correlation counting engine, which is applied to derive insight from transactional data. It is typically used for efficient market basket analysis.

- **Microsoft Neural Network** (Chapter 12) — This algorithm was designed to mimic natural neural patterns. Although it's slower than other algorithms for classification and regression, it performs deeper analysis to find complicated nonlinear patterns.

- **Microsoft Logistic Regression** (Chapter 12) — Logistic regression is often used to perform regression analysis when there are discrete inputs, or even discrete outputs. The Microsoft implementation uses the same core as the Microsoft Neural Network algorithm.

- **Text mining** (Chapter 14) — Although not a data mining algorithm per se, text mining can be performed with SQL Server 2008 by using the SSIS term extraction and term lookup transforms to convert unstructured data to structured data. This enables classification, clustering, association, and other techniques to be applied to text documents with data mining algorithms.

If your needs require you to go beyond the standard capabilities, SQL Server Data Mining is fully extensible through .NET stored procedures and plug-in algorithms that embed seamlessly to take advantage of all the platform capabilities and integration.

Easy-to-Use Tools

SQL Server 2008 provides different sets of tools for different sets of users. For non–data miners, the Table Analysis Tools for Excel 2007 provide one-click analysis of their Excel data — creating meaningful and actionable results without requiring any understanding of the data mining technologies underneath. Data Mining Client for Office 2007 allows novice and professional data miners to exploit the familiarity of Excel, and still have access to the majority of the data mining functionality of SQL Server Analysis Services.

For developers and advanced users, Business Intelligence Development Studio (BI Dev Studio) provides a complete set of tools to create, analyze, and manage data mining objects inside the Visual Studio interface. The Data Mining Wizard is a handy and powerful tool to help you build data mining structures and models from any data source, including OLAP cubes. With a few mouse clicks, you can build a very sophisticated mining model. The Data Mining Designer allows you to add models, set parameters, filter data, and otherwise customize your models as necessary for your business problems. Accuracy tools are also provided, including the new cross-validation feature, so you can compare and contrast the quality of your models before you commit to deployment.

Simple-Yet-Powerful API

When it comes to the integration of models into real-world applications, SQL Server opened a new chapter in data mining. The creation of DMX provides a rich SQL language familiar to the throngs of developers and database administrators (DBAs) who are already close to their data. Performing complex predictions against data mining algorithms no longer requires investments in learning proprietary scripting interfaces. Instead, it is reduced to a JOIN in a familiar SQL query. For the first time, those responsible for creating applications and handling data are empowered to leverage data mining technology using tools they already understand.

Integration with Sibling BI Technologies

Rarely can a data mining problem be solved with only a data mining tool. SQL Server Data Mining sits among a family of BI technologies that can be leveraged together to enhance and develop this new breed of intelligent applications. Following are some examples:

- **Office integration** — Integration with Excel and Visio provides the power of data mining to the decision makers of the organization, and allows you to share results using Excel Services or Visio's Save to Web feature.

- **SSIS integration** — Integration with SSIS injects the power of data mining into your operational data flows and data pipelines.

- **OLAP integration** — Integration with OLAP allows you to mine against complex multidimensional calculations and use the results to create self-organizing cubes. Mining models integrated with OLAP cubes are accessible through any OLAP client, such as Excel Pivot Tables and the ProClarity decomposition trees.

- **Reporting Services integration** — Integration with Reporting Services provides a user-friendly presentation layer to display and distribute interactive reports driven by your data mining models.

Exploring New Data Mining Frontiers and Opportunities

Data mining continues to be the fastest growing segment in the BI community, with SQL Server Data Mining's share of the market growing faster than the rest. Traditionally, data mining, predictive analytics, machine learning, and so on have been limited to an audience of analysts who hold advanced degrees in statistics. The typical usage scenario was that the IT department would build a data warehouse or data mart, and data miners would extract sample sets to analyze. After the model was built, data miners would publish reports that included the findings to their business managers. This process typically took a few months. As a result, data mining was previously considered a reserved area for power analysts.

Since SQL Server 2005, and continuing in SQL Server 2008, this perception has changed. SQL Server Data Mining is designed to be accessible to not only the traditional data mining audience, but to diverse populations of information workers and developers as well. SQL Server Data Mining has the following goals:

- **Make end users smarter** — By providing immediate predictive results in familiar Office applications, all information workers may extract more information from their data, thus enabling them to make better decisions.

- **Make developers smarter** — Developers are empowered with easy-to-use and powerful analysis tools. This enables them to dig inside their own databases and discover the gold mine of previously hidden data patterns and relationships.

- **Make applications smarter** — Data mining is not just for decision support systems — it can also be integrated with line of business applications for daily operations. Data mining can be completely embedded into applications where the consumers don't even know they are receiving predictive results. For example, an online DVD retail site can automatically give you suggestions based on your profile or your shopping basket. If you enter a new customer into the customer relationship management (CRM) system, the application will tell you in real time the personalized products or services you can provide to this customer. In an enterprise resource planning (ERP) application, the system will give you the forecast number of products for future production. If you browse a cube, the tools will show you the anomalies in the cube with a single click. With the simple APIs of SQL Server Data Mining, embedding data mining is possible with just a few lines of code.

Further Reference

To learn more about data mining, you can use some of the resources listed here.

Microsoft Data Mining

Following are some resources for more information on Microsoft data mining:

- SQL Server Books Online is the official document of the product. It contains details about concepts, references, samples, and tutorials.

- `SQLServerDataMining.com` is the most thorough online reference outside of Books Online. It is an unofficial website maintained by the product team members, including Bogdan Crivat and Jamie MacLennan, co-authors of this book. The site hosts a running instance SQL Server Analysis Services and several thin-client data mining application demos. There are many resources, such as links to all relevant sites, tips and tricks, source code downloads, white papers, and case studies.

- The SQL Server website (`microsoft.com/sql/technologies/dm`) contains useful information and case studies of different components of SQL Server, including data mining and other BI features.

- Blogs from the two of the authors, Jamie MacLennan and Bogdan Crivat are available at `blogs.msdn.com/jamiemac/` and `bogdancrivat.net/dm/`, respectively.

- The official forum site for SQL Server Data Mining is `forums.microsoft.com/MSDN/ShowForum.aspx?ForumID = 81`. This is by far the best place for you to reach Microsoft data mining product team members.

General Data Mining

The following is a list of recommended data mining books for your further reading:

- *Data Mining: Concepts and Techniques, Second Edition* by Jiawei Han and Micheline Kamber (San Francisco: Morgan Kaufmann Publishers, 2005).

- *Principles of Data Mining (Adaptive Computation and Machine Learning)* by David J. Hand, Heikki Mannila, and Padhraic Smyth (Cambridge, MA: MIT Press, 2001).

- *The Elements of Statistical Learning* by Trevor Hastie, Robert Tibshirani, and Jerome H. Friedman (New York: Springer Verlag, 2003).

- *Data Mining Techniques: For Marketing, Sales, and Customer Relationship Management, 2nd Edition* by Michael J. A. Berry and Gordon S. Linoff (Indianapolis: John Wiley & Sons, 2004).

Data Sets

This appendix describes the data sets used throughout the book. All data sets are provided as SQL backup files. The data sets are generally available in each of the chapter-specific downloads on the companion website (www.wiley .com/go/data_mining_SQL_2008) as well as in the Appendix A downloads.

MovieClick Data Set

The MovieClick data set consists of almost 3200 results from a survey taken by Microsoft employees in November 2002. Questions were asked about their movie watching behavior, demographics, and favorite hobbies, movies, actors, and directors. Table A-1 shows the questions that were asked in the survey. The results of the survey were used to test and exercise the data mining capabilities of SQL Server 2005 while in development.

The survey resulted in eight tables: one for the main survey responses, and one each for questions 8, 9, 13, 14, 15, 26, and 27. The main table results in the case table for data mining analysis, and the additional tables become nested tables. Figure A-1 shows a data source view (DSV) representing the relationships between these tables.

> **NOTE** Some flaws in the survey methodology were discovered when the results were examined. Favorite movies, actors, and directors were selected from an alphabetical list. This resulted in an unexpected number of selections starting with the letter *A*, which is evident in the resulting mining models.

Table A-1 Movie Survey Questions

1. What is your preferred format for pre-recorded movies?

2. How often do you watch pre-recorded movies?

3. How often do you rent pre-recorded movies?

4. How often do you watch Pay-Per-View events or movies?

5. How often do you purchase pre-recorded movies?

6. How often do you watch movies in theaters?

7. How often do you watch movies on a movie network (television)?

8. Which criteria are most important in choosing a particular movie?

9. Which movie channels do you watch most frequently?

10. How do you watch broadcast television?

11. How many televisions do you have in your home?

12. Who generally picks the movies you watch?

13. Enter your favorite movies:

14. Enter your favorite actors and actresses:

15. Enter your favorite directors:

16. Age:

17. Gender:

18. Marital Status:

19. Number of children:

20. What level of education have you completed?

21. Do you currently own or rent your home?

22. How many bedrooms do you have in your home?

23. How many bathrooms do you have in your house?

24. How many cars do you own?

25. How do you connect to the internet from home?

26. Which of the following technologies do you own?

27. What are your favorite hobbies/areas of interest?

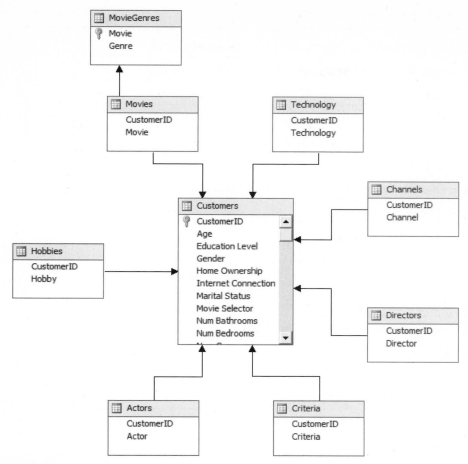

Figure A-1 Movies DSV

Voting Records Data Set

The Voting Records data set contains selected issues presented for voting in the House of Representatives in 2002. In addition to the results for each vote — Y, N, or abstain (null) — each row contains the name and party affiliation of each representative.

Table A-2 lists the issues that are captured in this data set.

Wine Sales

The Wine Sales data set contains 15 years of monthly wine sales in Australia for the following categories: Red, Rose, Fortified, Dry White, Sweet White, and Sparkling. The data was pulled from the Time Series Data Library (www-personal.buseco.monash.edu.au/~hyndman/TSDL/index.htm) on February 24, 2008.

Table A-2 Voting Issues

Bankruptcy Abuse Prevention and Consumer Protection Act
To reduce preexisting PAYGO balances
Homeland Security Act
Help America Vote Act
To Authorize the Use of United States Armed Forces Against Iraq
Child Abduction Prevention Act
Help Efficient, Accessible, Low Cost, Timely Healthcare Act of 2002
Abortion Non-Discrimination Act
Consumer Rental Purchase Agreement Act
Consumer Rental Purchase Agreement Act
Improving Access to Long-Term Care Act
National Aviation Capacity Expansion Act
Fed Up Higher Education Technical Amendments of 2002
Cyber Security Enhancement Act
Arming Pilots Against Terrorism Act
Inland Flood Forecasting and Warning System Act
Social Security Program Protection Act
Permanent Death Tax Repeal Act
Investing in America's Future Act
Customs Border Security Act
Afghanistan Freedom Support Act
Highway Funding Restoration Act
Farm Security Act
Child Custody Protection Act
Pension Security Act
Class Action Fairness Act
Higher Education Act Amendments

Foodmart

The Foodmart data set is the sample data set included with many versions of SQL Server and Microsoft Access. The version of the Foodmart project used in this book has an additional attribute for building time series on OLAP cubes.

College Plans Data Set

The College Plans data set comprises real data from a Midwest college concerning high school students intent to attend college based on a number of factors. These factors are parental encouragement, parental income, IQ, and gender. The original data set contained all columns as discrete variables, with the income and IQ variables bucketed into ranges. In the supplied data set, continuous values for income and IQ have been imputed from the original ranges. You can see artifacts from this imputation by analyzing the data.

Supported Functions

This appendix lists (as a reference) all the functions supported by DMX. The first section covers the native DMX language functions. The next two sections list the Visual Basic for Applications (VBA) and Excel functions that can be called as stored procedures from the DMX language. The last section of this appendix describes supplemental stored procedures for creating and deleting data set objects.

DMX Language Functions

These functions are natively supported by the DMX language. Each individual function may or may not be supported by any particular algorithm. Table B-1 lists the functions that operate on scalar columns and Table B-2 lists functions that operate on table columns.

VBA Functions

Table B-3 lists the supported VBA functions.

Excel Functions

Table B-4 lists the supported Excel functions.

Table B-1 Prediction Functions on Scalar Columns

FUNCTION	RETURN VALUE	DESCRIPTION
`Cluster()`	Cluster identifier	Cluster identifier that the input case belongs to with the highest probability. It also can be used as a `<cluster column reference>` for a `PredictHistogram` function.
`ClusterDistance ([Cluster Identifier])`	Continuous value	Distance from the center of the cluster that is identified by `Cluster Identifier` or the highest probability cluster. Typically this value is `1-ClusterProbability()`.
`ClusterProbability ([Cluster Identifier])`	Probability (0-1) of cluster membership	Probability that the input case belongs to the cluster that is identified by `Cluster Identifier` or the highest probability cluster.

`IsDescendant`
 	
`(<node id>)`
	Boolean	Returns `true` if the current node is a descendant of the specified node. This function is used only in content queries.

`IsInNode`
 	
`(<node id>)`
	Boolean	Returns `true` if the current case belongs to the specified node. This function is used only in queries on model cases.

`IsTestCase()`	Boolean	Returns `true` if the current case is part of the holdout set for the model or structure. This function is used only in queries on model or structure cases.
`IsTrainingCase()`	Boolean	Returns `true` if the current case is part of the training set for the model or structure. This function is used only in queries on model or structure cases.

(continued)

Table B-1 (*continued*)

FUNCTION	RETURN VALUE	DESCRIPTION
`Lag()`	Integer	Returns the time slice between the date of the current case and the last date of the training set. This function is used only in queries on model cases for time series models.
`Predict`	Scalar value based on the specified column type	Returns the non-`Missing` value with the highest probability for the specified scalar column. Specifying `INCLUDE_NULL` will consider the `Missing` state as well.
`(<column reference>` `[, (EXCLUDE_NULL |` `INCLUDE_NULL)]` `[, INCLUDE_NODE_ID])`		
`PredictAdjusted` `Probability`	Adjusted probability (0-1) of the prediction	An adjusted likelihood (as calculated by the mining model) of the most probable non-`Missing` state or the target state if specified. The adjusted likelihood is calculated to promote less popular results and penalize states that are highly popular. Specifying `INCLUDE_NULL` will consider the `Missing` state as well.
`(<column reference>` `[ INCLUDE_NULL |` `<target state>])`		
`PredictCase` `Likelihood`	Likelihood of a case	Returns the likelihood as calculated by a cluster model. Normalized (default) results are in the 0−1 range, but are not a probability.
`( [ NORMALIZED |` `NONNORMALIZED ] )`		

(*continued*)

Table B-1 (*continued*)

FUNCTION	RETURN VALUE	DESCRIPTION
PredictHistogram	Table	Returns a histogram containing statistics of all possible states of the specified column. When a continuous column is specified, the histogram contains a row for the Missing state and a row with statistics about the predicted value.
(<column reference >|<cluster column reference>)		
PredictProbability	Probability (0-1) of the prediction	Likelihood (as calculated by the mining model) of the most probable non-Missing state or the target state if specified. Specifying INCLUDE_NULL will consider the Missing state as well.
(<column reference> [INCLUDE_NULL | <target state>])		
PredictStdev	Standard deviation of target	Standard deviation (the square root of the variance) describing the distribution for continuous predictions.
(<column reference >)		
PredictSupport	Predicted support	Count of cases in support of the most probable non-Missing state or the target state if specified. Specifying INCLUDE_NULL will consider the Missing state as well.
(<column reference> [INCLUDE_NULL | <target state>])		

(*continued*)

Table B-1 (*continued*)

FUNCTION	RETURN VALUE	DESCRIPTION
`PredictTimeSeries` `(<column reference>`	Table containing forecasted results	Forecasts the next $n1$ data points (with a default of 1) or from time slices $n1$ to $n2$ if $n2$ is specified. EXTEND_MODEL_CASES and REPLACE_MODEL_CASES specify how to treat data indicated in the PREDICTION JOIN clause, if any.

`[, <n1>]`
`[, (<n2> |`
`EXTEND_MODEL_CASES |`
`REPLACE_MODEL_CASES])`		

`PredictVariance`
 	
`(<column reference>)`
	Variance of the target	Variance describing the distribution for continuous predictions.

`RangeMax`
 	
`(<column reference>)`
	Continuous value based on the column type	Gives the upper end of the predicted bucket for a discretized column, or the overall maximum for continuous columns.

`RangeMid`
 	
`(<column reference>)`
	Continuous value based on the column type	Gives the midpoint of the predicted bucket for a discretized column, or the overall mean for continuous columns.

(continued)

Table B-1 (*continued*)

FUNCTION	RETURN VALUE	DESCRIPTION

`RangeMin`
 	
`(<column`
`reference>)`
	Continuous value based on the column type	Gives the low end of the predicted bucket for a discretized column, or the overall minimum for continuous columns.

`StructureColumn`
 	
`('structure column`
`name')`
	Value from the structure column	Returns the value of the structure column that matches the specified string for the current case. This function is used only in queries on model cases.

Table B-2 Prediction Function on Table Columns

FUNCTION	RETURN VALUE	DESCRIPTION

`Predict`
 	
`(<column reference>`
`[ <options>] )`
	Table	`Predict` is polymorphic to the other table-predicting functions. The available options are determined by what the `Predict` function resolves, based on whether the specified table column is a simple table, or if it contains time series or sequences).

`TopCount`(`<table expr>`, `<rank expression >`, `<count>`)	Table	Return the specified number of items in a decreasing order based on the rank expression.
`TopSum`(`<table expr>`, `<rank expression >`, `<sum>`)	Table	Returns the first *n* rows in decreasing order by the rank expression such that the sum of the rank expression is at least the specified sum.

(*continued*)

Table B-2 (*continued*)

FUNCTION	RETURN VALUE	DESCRIPTION
TopPercent(<table expr>, <rank expression >, <sum>)	Table	Returns the first *n* rows in a decreasing order of the rank expression such that the sum of the ranked values is at least the given percentage of the total sum of ranked values.
PredictTimeSeries (<column reference> [, <n1>] [, (<n2> || EXTEND_MODEL_CASES || REPLACE_MODEL_CASES])	Table	Forecasts, for each series in the specified table, the next *n1* data points (with a default of 1), or from time slices *n1* to *n2* if *n2* is specified. EXTEND_MODEL_CASES and REPLACE_MODEL_CASES specify how to treat data indicated in the PREDICTION JOIN clause, if any.
PredictSequence (<column reference> [, <n1>] [, <n2>])	Table	Returns the sequence of states of the next *n1* steps in a table, or the states from *n1* to *n2*.
PredictAssociation (<column reference>	Table	Returns the associated items based on the input case in order of descending probability or adjusted probability. If a count is specified, PredictAssociation returns only the top count number of items.

(continued)

Table B-2 (*continued*)

FUNCTION	RETURN VALUE	DESCRIPTION
[, $AdjustedProbability]		
[, EXCLUDE_NULL || INCLUDE_NULL		
[, INCLUSIVE || EXCLUSIVE || INPUT_ONLY]		
[, INCLUDE_STATISTICS		
[, INCLUDE_NODE_ID		
[, <count>])		

Table B-3 Supported VBA Functions

aBS	cVErr	isDate	nPER	sqr
array	date	isEmpty	nPV	str
aSC	dATE$	iSERROR	oct	str$
aSCB	dATEADD	isNull	oct$	strComp
aSCW	dateDiff	isNumeric	partition	strConv
aTN	datePart	isObject	pMT	string
cBOOL	dATESERIAL	lCase	pPMT	string$
cBYTE	dATEVALUE	lCase$	pV	switch
cCUR	day	lEFT	qBColor	sYD
cDATE	dDB	lEFT$	rATE	tAN
cDBL	error	lEFTB	rGB	tIME
choose	error$	lEFTB$	rIGHT	tIME$
cHR	eXP	lEN	rIGHT$	timer
cHR$	fix	lENB	rIGHTB	timeSerial
cHRB	format	lOG	rIGHTB$	tIMEVALUE
cHRB$	fv	lTrim	rnd	tRIM

(*continued*)

Table B-3 (continued)

cHRW	hex	lTrim$	round	tRIM$
cHRW$	hex$	mID	rTrim	typeName
cINT	hOUR	mID$	rTrim$	uCase
cLNG	iIF	mIDB$	sECOND	uCase$
cOS	iMEStatus	mINUTE	sgn	val
cSNG	inStr	mIRR	sIN	varType
cSTR	iNT	mONTH	sLN	wEEKDAY
cVAR	iPMT	nOW	space	yEAR
cvDate	iRR			

Table B-4 Supported Excel Functions

Acos	Acosh	And	*Application
Asc	Asin	Asinh	Atan2
Atanh	AveDev	Average	BetaDist
BetaInv	BinomDist	Ceiling	ChiDist
ChiInv	ChiTest	Choose	Clean
Combin	Confidence	Correl	Cosh
Count	CountA	*CountBlank	*CountIf
Covar	*Creator	CritBinom	*DAverage
Days360	Db	Dbcs	*DCount
*DCountA	Ddb	Degrees	DevSq
*DGet	*DMax	*DMin	Dollar
*DProduct	*DStDev	*DStDevP	*DSum
*DVar	*DVarP	Even	ExponDist
Fact	FDist	Find	FindB
FInv	Fisher	FisherInv	Fixed
Floor	Forecast	*Frequency	FTest
Fv	GammaDist	GammaInv	GammaLn

(continued)

Table B-4 (*continued*)

GeoMean	*Growth	HarMean	*HLookup
HypGeomDist	*Index	Intercept	Ipmt
Irr	IsErr	IsError	IsLogical
IsNA	IsNonText	IsNumber	Ispmt
IsText	Kurt	Large	*LinEst
Ln	Log	Log10	*LogEst
LogInv	LogNormDist	*Lookup	Match
Max	*MDeterm	Median	Min
*MInverse	MIrr	*MMult	Mode
NegBinomDist	NormDist	NormInv	NormSDist
Or	*Parent	Pearson	Percentile
PercentRank	Permut	Pi	Pmt
Poisson	Power	Ppmt	Prob
Product	Proper	Pv	Quartile
Radians	*Rank	Rate	Replace
ReplaceB	Rept	Roman	Round
RoundDown	RoundUp	RSq	Search
SearchB	Sinh	Skew	Sln
Slope	Small	Standardize	StDev
StDevP	StEyx	Substitute	*Subtotal
Sum	*SumIf	SumProduct	SumSq
SumX2MY2	SumX2PY2	SumXMY2	Syd
Tanh	TDist	Text	TInv
Transpose	*Trend	Trim	TrimMean
TTest	USDollar	Var	VarP
Vdb	*VLookup	Weekday	Weibull
ZTest			

ASSprocs Stored Procedures

The ASSprocs assembly and source code are available for download on this book's companion website (www.wiley.com/go/data_mining_SQL_2008). This assembly contains functions to create and delete data source objects. To add the assembly to your server, find the Assemblies folder (typically located directly under the Object Explorer server icon in SQL Server Management Studio). Right-click the folder and select New Assembly. In the New Assembly dialog box, browse to the location where you have built or downloaded the ASSprocs assembly.

> **NOTE** Important: Because the ASSproc functions use Analysis Management Objects (AMO), you need to select Unrestricted in the Permissions section of the dialog box. Without the unrestricted permission, the ASSproc functions will fail to execute. If you did not properly set the permissions when installing the assembly, you can change them by right-clicking the assembly in the Object Explorer and selecting Properties.

The ASSprocs assembly contains two functions: CreateDataSource and DropDataSource. The CreateDataSource function is called like this:

```
CALL ASSprocs.CreateDataSource('<datasource name>',
                    '<connection string>',
                    '<impersonation mode>',
                    '<account name>',
                    '<password>')
```

The parameters for CreateDataSource are the following strings:

- datasource name — This string is used for the name and ID of the new data source. The specified string must represent a valid Analysis Services identifier but must not already be in use by an existing data source.

- connection string — This is the complete connection string to the source database. Consult your database documentation for details on how to construct an appropriate connection string. CreateDataSource will accept any string as a connection string. Errors will be raised for invalid strings only when the data source is used in a query. Note that if the connection string contains embedded single quotes ('), they must be doubled (' ') before sending in a function call.

- impersonation mode — This identifies the Impersonation mode for the data source. CreateDataSource accepts the following strings as valid values for Impersonation mode:

  - Default

  - ImpersonateServiceAccount

- `ImpersonateAnonymous`
- `ImpersonateCurrentUser`
- `ImpersonateAccount`

If `ImpersonateAccount` is specified, the account name and password parameters must also be specified.

- `account name` — This is the account name to be used when the Impersonation mode is `ImpersonateAccount`. Leave this as an empty string (`' '`) for other Impersonation modes.
- `password` — This is the account name to be used when the Impersonation mode is `ImpersonateAccount`. Leave this as an empty string (`' '`) for other Impersonation modes.

The `DropDataSource` function has the following signature:

```
CALL ASSprocs.DropDataSource('<datasource name>')
```

Unlike the `CreateDataSource` function, `DropDataSource` does not fail on an invalid data source name. In DMX scripts, you should attempt to drop a data source prior to creating a data source in order to avoid errors if the data source already exists.

Index